The Religious Roles of the Papacy:
Ideals and Realities, 1150-1300

Edited by Christopher Ryan

No one doubts that the papacy played a crucial role in the development of medieval christendom. However, it is less widely recognized that the papacy itself was the subject of development during the medieval period, which was, as modern studies are increasingly bringing to light, a time of rich diversity, marked by vast changes both intellectual and institutional.

The studies in this volume explore important aspects of the papacy during a particularly formative period of its history, stretching from the years following the Gregorian reform to those immediately preceding the exile in Avignon. They concentrate on a central feature of the papacy which the abundance of studies on the relationship between papacy and politics can tend to obscure, namely, that the papacy is in the first place a religious entity, claiming leadership in a community whose *raison d'être* is the life of faith, hope and charity. Within that religious perspective these studies attempt to catch images and ideas which fed the minds of people engaged in significantly different areas of the Church's life: the academic community, the local church in its liturgy and administration, and the popes themselves together with the papal curia. Special emphasis has been given to a comparatively neglected aspect of studies of the medieval papacy, that of the theology of the papacy, which evinced remarkable change in the course of the period discussed here. Two studies of the attitude of the Church in the East add to the diversity of viewpoints from which the papacy is presented.

Original sources have been quoted abundantly, normally with a translation or paraphrase supplied.

PAPERS IN MEDIAEVAL STUDIES

8

THE RELIGIOUS ROLES OF THE PAPACY: IDEALS AND REALITIES 1150-1300

edited by

Christopher Ryan

PONTIFICAL INSTITUTE OF MEDIAEVAL STUDIES

CANADIAN CATALOGUING IN PUBLICATION DATA

Main entry under title:
  The Religious roles of the papacy

(Papers in mediaeval studies, ISSN 0228-8605 ; 8)
"Based on papers delivered at a conference hosted by the Pontifical Institute of
Mediaeval Studies, Toronto, from May 13th to 16th, 1985."
Includes bibliographical references and index.
ISBN 0-88844-808-2

1. Papacy - History - To 1300 - Congresses.   2. Popes - Primacy - Congresses.
3. Church history - 12th century - Congresses.   4. Church history - 13th century
- Congresses.   I. Ryan, Christopher, 1943- .   II. Pontifical Institute of
Mediaeval Studies.   III. Series.

BX1805.R45 1988   262'.13   C88-094862-0

© 1989 by

Pontifical Institute of Mediaeval Studies
59 Queen's Park Crescent East
Toronto, Ontario, Canada M5S 2C4

PRINTED BY UNIVERSA, WETTEREN, BELGIUM

Distributed outside North America by
E. J. Brill, Postbus 9000,
2300 PA Leiden, The Netherlands
Brill ISBN 90 04 08945 4

Contents

PART THREE: PAPAL SOURCES

Abbreviations

DTC	*Dictionnaire de théologie catholique*
MedS	*Mediaeval Studies*
PG	*Patrologia Graeca*
PL	*Patrologia Latina*
RHE	*Revue d'histoire ecclésiastique*
RS	Rolls Series
RTAM	*Recherches de théologie ancienne et médiévale*

Introduction

Students of the middle ages need no reminding that the papacy was one of the dominant influences on the life and culture of that period. Interest in the medieval papacy, however, is by no means confined to professional medievalists; the papacy itself has long been of interest to many people and the importance of the medieval period in shaping the development of that institution is increasingly being recognized. A new book on the medieval papacy, then, seems in no need of an apology, at least as regards its subject matter.

The studies in this volume are based on papers delivered at a conference hosted by the Pontifical Institute of Mediaeval Studies, Toronto, from May 13th to 16th, 1985 under the same title as that of this volume; all have been expanded from their original form, some extensively. The conference had its origin in the observation that, while generations of medievalists have accorded the papacy the accolade of their scholarly labours, the lion's share of work has gone to consideration of the relationship between Church and State, or, less grandly, to questions of papacy and politics. Clearly, this is an important and often fascinating focus of interest. No one could claim, however, that it tells the whole story, and indeed concentration on the more political aspects of the papacy can obscure the fact that by nature the papacy is primarily a religious entity: from the earliest times it has been seen, and has understood itself, as called to exercise leadership *within* the christian community, a body defined in the first place by its commitment to follow Christ by a life of faith, hope and charity. Everything flows from that radical claim to religious leadership. The conference was conceived as a contribution towards drawing more attention to the specifically religious dimensions of the medieval papacy, as the title suggests. The central questions addressed in different ways in the various papers were: what roles in the nurturing of the community's religious life were ascribed ideally to the papacy? what roles did the papacy in fact play in fostering, or hindering, this life?

Any attempt to give a comprehensive reply to these questions would require combing sources of the utmost diversity. A topic to which allusion has already been made, the relationship of the papacy to politics, may furnish a ready example. The dividing line between religion and politics has always been notoriously difficult to specify, and seldom more so than when this problem is raised with regard to the middle ages: the notion that there was one *societas christiana*, a single entity embracing both civic and religious life, was then still alive, and, in some quarters, extremely well. Sources which deal with political questions often, therefore, have much to say about the religious roles of the papacy. Practicality, however, dictated some narrowing of range in the sources to be examined for the conference and volume, and, in line with the genesis of the conference, sources dealing with directly political topics or with questions falling in the general area of Church-State relations were by and large excluded. The sources studied here are, then, for the most part religious in the strict sense. It would be a happy outcome of the conference if scholars who feel that the views put forward here need to be complemented or challenged were stimulated into presenting further studies on the medieval papacy.

Within the confines set by religious sources, the conference called on the expertise of scholars working in a variety of disciplines. It was felt that unity and comprehensiveness of a kind would best be served by examining three broad groups of sources: those of theology in the more strictly technical sense; those belonging to local churches; and those of the papacy itself. Within each of these the net was cast fairly wide. In the first group this volume contains essays on the tradition of biblical exegesis (Froehlich), on theological works written between 1150 and 1250 both within and without the academic milieu (Principe), and on the most influential theologian of the latter half of the thirteenth century, Thomas Aquinas (Ryan). Medieval theology of the papacy in the strict sense is perhaps one of the most neglected areas of scholarship dealing with the papacy, and it is hoped that the extended treatment of the studies in this group will map the theological terrain more clearly and challenge some common assumptions. In the second group there is a study of the liturgical sources which investigates the degree of influence of the papacy on local liturgies (Gy), and essays on the view of the papacy which emerges from sermons of continental and of English provenance (Bougerol and Roberts) and from the registers of a busy and harassed Archbishop of Canterbury, John Pecham (Sheehan). These studies all deal with western Europe, and they are complemented by an essay in each section on aspects of the Byzantine church: one considers eastern theology in the relatively pacific twelfth century, before the barbarities of the fourth crusade (Spiteris); the other examines in the following century the widespread attitudes of hostility and revulsion among the Greeks which doomed the union purportedly effected by their leaders at Lyons (Nicol). The section employing sources from the papal court begins and ends with studies of what is revealed by such different artefacts as law (Silano) and the visual arts (Gardner). In between come an essay on the relationship of the papacy to the most important academic centre of the period, the university of Paris (Lewry), and a study of arguably one of the most important but least examined papal topics of the period, its attitude to non-christians (Synan), while any tendency to equate papal sources with personal papal pronouncements is obviated by a study of the cardinals' view of the papacy (Zacour).

In the nature of the case these essays are presented largely by way of *sondages*. Many of the subjects treated would merit a book-length study; many important topics are not discussed. Two absences in particular deserve comment. It regrettably proved impossible to include studies based on vernacular literature, a neglected and difficult, but potentially rewarding, area of investigation for our theme, which might reveal as much by eloquent silence as by positive testimony. There is only one study here based principally on legal sources; this reflects not a lack, but an *embarras de richesse*: much light has already been thrown on the religious dimension of the papacy by historians of canon law, and it was felt that it would be more profitable to concentrate on other areas which have not been so well served.

The period selected suggested itself as a relatively homogeneous one, lying between the years following the Gregorian reform and those immediately preceding the transfer of the papacy to Avignon. It was certainly the conclusion of the participants at the conference that momentous changes occurred in the exercise and perception of the papacy in the period studied, more than sufficient to mark it as a century and a half of crucial importance in the development of the papacy, and as a period meriting greater attention than it has hitherto received from those interested in the papacy as a religious entity. This volume offers to a wider audience evidence from which this conclusion might be drawn.

A word should be said on the method of quoting sources. While these studies address medievalists in that they are intended to carry knowledge of the medieval papacy beyond the present boundaries, it is hoped that they will also be of service to a wider audience. It is scarcely to be expected, however, that all non-medievalists will have a ready command of medieval Latin. For the most part, therefore, sources have been quoted here in translation in the body of the text, with the Latin original appearing in the footnotes. Authors of these studies were encouraged to quote liberally from their sources, in the hope that it would help specialists and non-specialists alike to have many of the key texts on the medieval papacy available for consultation in a single volume.

It remains for me to perform the pleasant task of offering thanks. My personal thanks go to the other members of the organizing committee of the conference, all then colleagues on the Fellowship of the Pontifical Institute: Ambrose Raftis, Michael Sheehan, and Leonard Boyle, whose place was taken, when he was appointed Prefect of the Vatican Library, by Osmund Lewry, whose recent untimely death deprived the world of scholarship of a distinguished and humane presence. My thanks go, too, to the President and Fellows of the Pontifical Institute, whose generosity in granting me sabbatical leave in my last year as a Fellow eased the final stages of editorial work on this volume. On behalf of the organizing committee I should like to thank all those who accepted the committee's invitation to deliver papers at the conference, especially since many agreed to shift the focus of their current research to accomodate the committee's requests. We should also like to thank the Council of the Institute, and the Social Sciences and Humanities Research Council of Canada, whose financial assistance made the conference and the publication of this volume possible. I should like, finally, to thank the secretary of the Institute, Teresa Kowalska, whose patience during the preparation of the conference and of this book was sorely tried, but never, remarkably, beyond endurance.

Cambridge   CJR

Part One

Theological Sources

1

Saint Peter, Papal Primacy,
and the Exegetical Tradition, 1150-1300

Karlfried Froehlich

1.

Three biblical texts have traditionally been cited as the religious foundation of papal primacy: Matt. 16:18-19; Luke 22:32; and John 21:15-17. All three come from the gospels; all three reflect a picture of Peter which attributes to this apostle a special role in the genesis of the church and its development after Christ's resurrection. The combination of the three passages in support of the primatial argument reaches far back in the history of the Roman papacy. Leo I and Gelasius I seem to have been the first to use it.[1] To a medieval pope such as Innocent III (1198-1216), the triad appears to be thoroughly traditional. In his writings, Innocent even likes to present the three texts in a logical order by means of a sophisticated scholastic distinction: it was on three occasions, he suggests, that Christ committed the primacy over the whole church to Peter, *ante passionem* (Matt. 16), *circa passionem* (Luke 22), and *post passionem* (John 21).[2] Despite this impres-

---

[1] Leo I, *Tractatus* 83.1-3 (CCL 138A, ed. A. Chavasse, 1973, pp. 520f., ll. 20-63); cf. *Sermo* 82:3 (*PL* 54: 424f.); Gelasius I, *Epist.* 14 "Tractatus" (*PL* 59: 89BC); see also Gregory I, *Epist.* VII.37, ll. 10-15 (CCL 140, ed. D. Norberg, 1983, p. 501).

[2] Innocent III, *PL* 215: 28AB, 1344A; 217: 658D-659A, 778B-D; a similar distinction appears in a letter of Leo IX (*PL* 143: 756AB).

The Religious Roles of the Papacy: Ideals and Realities, 1150-1300, ed. Christopher Ryan, Papers in Mediaeval Studies 8 (Toronto: Pontifical Institute of Mediaeval Studies, 1989), pp. 3-44. © P.I.M.S., 1989.

sive pedigree, however, it would be a mistake to assume that the papal interpretation was the standard exegesis everywhere. It is the thesis of this paper that, quite on the contrary, the understanding of these Petrine texts by biblical exegetes in the mainstream of the tradition was universally non-primatial before Innocent III, and that it was the innovative exegetical argumentation of this imposing pope which began to change the picture.

Recent scholarship on Innocent III has stressed not only the political achievement of the pope's pontificate but his thorough familiarity both with the theological and canonical literature of his time as it is reflected in his writings.[3] For our purposes, his treatise, *De missarum mysteriis*, written during his early years and perhaps revised after 1198, contains a very instructive chapter "De primatu Romani pontificis" which opens with a systematic reference to the three Petrine texts.[4] The chapter itself presents in a concise form the entire biblical argument for Petrine primacy and its application to the pope which Innocent would use throughout his later pontificate. A quick glance at this text will give us a good starting point for our deliberations.

Innocent's purpose is the description and exposition of the papal mass of his day. Chapters 1-7 describe the six clerical orders from cantors to bishops which surround the celebrating pontiff; the discussion abounds with references to the appropriate Old Testament types. The point of chapter eight and its title is the contrast between the one and the many; the text emphasizes the uniqueness of the pontiff in the image of the one Peter as well as his superior hierarchical rank. There is only one Peter, and Peter always is first: "Omnibus autem apostolis Christus unum praeposuit, videlicet Petrum, cui totius ecclesiae principatum et ante passionem et circa passionem et post passionem commisit." In commenting on Matt. 16:18, the pope readily admits the rival tradition of an authority to bind and to loose given to all bishops. He refers to John 20:23 (cf. Matt. 18:18) but returns immediately to the exclusiveness of Matt. 16:19: Peter alone can bind the others but cannot be bound by them. When Innocent comes to Luke 22:32, he first notes the plural: "Satan has desired you (plural)" but then insists on the singular in the continuation of the verse: "I have prayed for you (singular)

---

[3] See especially the fine study by Wilhelm Imkamp, *Das Kirchenbild Innocenz' III (1198-1216)*, Päpste und Papsttum, vol. 22 (Stuttgart, 1983), pp. 6-7 and 10-46.

[4] Innocent III, *De sacro altaris mysterio* I.8 (*PL* 217: 778B-779C). For the necessary correction of the traditional title see Michele Maccarone, *Studi su Innocenzo III*, Italia Sacra: Studi e Documenti di Storia Ecclesiastica, 17 (Padova, 1972), pp. 344f.; David F. Wright, "A Medieval Commentary on the Mass: Particulae 2-3 and 5-6 of the *De Missarum Mysteriis* (ca. 1195) of Cardinal Lothar of Segni (Pope Innocent III)," Ph.D. Thesis, Notre Dame University, 1977, pp. 45-56; Imkamp, *Kirchenbild*, pp. 46-53.

that your faith may not fail." His subsequent statements concerning the firmness of Peter's faith, couched in the hallowed language of papal self-predication, reveal at every point the biblical matrix out of which they have grown. As we shall see, the pope's remark that Peter's faith did not fail in any temptation presupposes a specific interpretation of Peter's denial (Matt. 26:69-75 and parallels). The statement that the faith of the apostolic see, "founded on the firm rock in stable solidity, could never be stained by the filth of errors," echoes Ecclus. 26:24 ("fundamenta aeterna supra petram solidam") as well as Jesus' parable in Matt. 7:25. The assumption that the papal see has remained "without spot or wrinkle" uses the words of Eph. 5:27; the *Decretum Gelasianum* had already narrowed the referent of the church mentioned in this verse to the Roman church.[5]

Innocent's explanation of John 21 concentrates on Jesus' final command to Peter, "Follow me!" (v. 19). Beyond the implication for Peter's martyrdom and its particular form, the pope connects the phrase with the uniqueness of Peter's teaching office ("non solum genere martyrii sed et in ordine magisterii") and links it with John 1:42 where, at the beginning of the gospel, the name of Cephas is announced. Innocent is well aware that Cephas is the equivalent of Petros. Nevertheless, he also uses the widespread popular spiritual etymology, inaugurated in the fifth century by Optatus of Mileve, which associated the name with the Greek *kephalê*, head. Many exegetes before him had done so.[6] In our text, it is precisely this idea of Peter as the "head" and the apostles as "members" that prefaces one of Innocent's characteristic phrases: "caeteri sacerdotes vocati sunt in partem sollicitudinis, sed summus pontifex assumptus est in plenitudinem potestatis." The distinction between *plenitudo potestatis* and *pars sollicitudinis* appears to have been first employed in a letter of Leo I which Gratian's *Decretum* cites at C.3 q.6 c.8.[7] Perhaps it echoed the term *plena potestas* in the language of Roman law, as Walter Ullmann has suggested; but it is also connected to a rich background of biblical allusions, certainly in the mind of Innocent: "*sollicitudo*" recalls Pauline texts such as Rom. 12:8; II Cor. 7:12 and 11:28, or I

---

[5] Denzinger-Schoenmetzer, *Enchiridion Symbolorum*, 36th ed. (1976), no. 351.

[6] Optatus of Mileve, *Contra Parmenianum* II.2 (CSEL 26, ed. C. Ziwsa, 1893, p. 36, ll. 12-15): "igitur negare non potes scire te in urbe Roma Petro primo cathedram episcopalem esse conlatam, in qua sederit omnium apostolorum caput Petrus, unde et Cephas est appellatus"; see Yves Congar, "Cephas - Cephalê - Caput," *Revue du moyen-âge latin* 8 (1952) 5-42. Late medieval theologians also cite Pseudo-Dionysius, *De divinis nominibus* III.2 (*PG* 3: 681c/d).

[7] Leo I, *Epist.* 14.2 (*PL* 54: 671b): "Vices enim nostra ita tuae credidimus charitati, ut in partem sis vocatus sollicitudinis, non in plenitudinem potestatis." On this text, see Ernst Caspar, *Geschichte des Papsttums von den Anfängen bis zur Höhe der Weltherrschaft*, 1 (Tübingen, 1930), p. 455.

Peter 5:7 where "pastors" are addressed in clear distinction from Christ, the "princeps pastorum" (v. 4). Innocent's wording which speaks of the high priest being "assumed" into the plenitude of power may well echo Heb. 5:1 ("omnis namque pontifex ex hominibus assumptus ..."). Even more intriguing is the possibility that his understanding of the term, *plenitudo potestatis*, might reflect, on the one hand, Christ's own words: "data est mihi omnis potestas in caelo et in terra" (Matt. 28:18) or the "plenitudo Christi" texts in Ephesians and Colossians (e.g. Eph. 1:23, 4:13; Col. 1:19, 2:9), and, on the other hand, passages such as John 1:16 ("de plenitudine eius nos omnes accepimus") and Ps. 132:22 ("sicut unguentum in capite quod descendit in barbam, barbam Aaron") which suggest the notion of participation and hierarchical transmission. We will return to these bold appropriations of christological texts later. Here too Innocent's point is the uniqueness of the one among and above the many, Peter among the apostles, the pope among the bishops.

The remainder of the chapter demonstrates the reality of Petrine primacy again and again in a calculated crescendo of exegetical observations tracing the "mysteries" of the Petrine pattern in the New Testament. Christ asked all apostles about his identity, but Peter alone answered for all, "quasi primus et potior" (Matt. 16:15f.). All the apostles were sitting in the boat, terrified; Peter alone stepped out, fearless (Matt. 14:25-29). Many disciples left Jesus; Peter alone answered: "Lord, where shall we go?" (John 6:67-70). Jesus looked at all the disciples but only Peter was addressed with the word about forgiveness (Matt. 18:15ff. and 21f.). All the disciples fled; Peter alone drew the sword (John 18:10). And when, after the Resurrection, other apostles approached the Lord in their boat, it was Peter who threw himself into the water to walk toward him (John 21:7f.). The string of scriptural passages closes with a reference to the first appearance of the risen Lord: "prius se Petro quam caeteris ostendit apostolis" (I Cor. 15:5-6; cf. Luke 24:34). For Innocent, scripture clearly made a point through the mysterious pattern of these texts: Peter was the first and must remain first. As modern readers, we cannot but admire this comprehensive vision of the biblical Peter foreshadowing the reality of the high medieval papal office. The Petrine texts and their primatial interpretation nourished the vision, and the reality of papal authority nourished the search for an appropriate biblical interpretation.

Innocent obviously was convinced of the compelling truth of this biblical vision and made a coherent case for it in his rhetoric. He may have deepened as well as broadened the biblical argument at points. His use of the main Petrine texts in support of Roman primacy, however, followed a tradition of long standing which can be traced in the pronouncements of his predecessors ever since the tentative efforts of Stephen I, the biblical rhetoric of Leo I, and its systematic elaboration by Gelasius I. But the primatial interpretation was by no means the only, or even the primary one in the early and medieval history of exegesis. Many interpretations were possible. We should not be surprised that, in the medieval exegetical tradition, even Matt. 16:18f., Luke 22:32, and John 21:15-17 were not necessarily "Primatworte."[8]

The medieval interpretation of scripture had an intriguing history of its own.[9] As the work of Arthur Maria Landgraf and others has demonstrated, it moved into a new stage of independent theologizing with the emergence of exegetical *quaestiones* in the schools of the eleventh and twelfth centuries. At the risk of oversimplifying a complex phenomenon, we may characterize the exegetical school tradition of our period, expressed in the scriptural commentaries from Lâon, St. Victor, and the young universities, by pointing to four factors:

1. There was a strong dependence on the patristic tradition, especially Augustine and other Western Fathers, with only slowly growing knowledge of Eastern exegetes, but also a lively interest in recent commentaries.

2. While attention was increasingly given to the literal sense, a vivid interest in symbolic and spiritual interpretation remained dominant, with the tropological sense being favored.

3. Careful attention to textual details, parallels, and cross connections by word association formed the backbone of exegetical work, at the expense of contextual considerations.

4. The context of biblical passages became more important with the emergence of the scholastic method, especially its technique of *distinctiones* which began to dominate the *quaestiones* often found as integral parts of the commentaries.

If we keep these general presuppositions in mind, we will not be surprised at the often bewildering and unfamiliar panorama of the interpretation of Petrine texts that unfolds when we look at the medieval exegetical tradition.

---

[8] It is a major flaw of the otherwise meritorious book by Joseph Ludwig, *Die Primatworte Matth. 16,18.19 in der altkirchlichen Exegese*, Neutestamentliche Abhandlungen, 19.4 (Münster, 1952), that the author simply assumes the Roman primatial interpretation of Matt. 16:18f. to have been the "normal" meaning of these verses from the very beginning. Ludwig presupposes what would need to be proved. His presupposition leads to the circular argument that the use of Matt. 16:18f. must be assumed behind every expression of a Roman primatial consciousness in the early church. For a detailed criticism of Ludwig see my *Formen der Auslegung von Matth. 16,13-18 im lateinischen Mittelalter* (Th.D. dissertation, Basel, 1961; Teildruck Tübingen, 1963).

[9] A comprehensive history of medieval exegesis has not been written. My observations are supported by the available standard literature which includes the works of Beryl Smalley, Henri de Lubac, Ceslas Spicq, among others.

2.

Perhaps the most instructive case is that of Matt. 16:18-19.[10] It is quite clear to modern exegetes that all three parts of the passage, the name-giving, its interpretation by Jesus' word about the founding of the church on the rock, and the promise of the keys, speak about the person of Peter, even if the nature of his prerogative and the application to any successors is set aside. The medieval interpretation shows a very different picture. The name-giving (v. 18a) was generally regarded as Jesus' answer to Peter's confession which, as the context suggested to medieval exegetes, Peter had uttered *pro omnibus*.[11] Following Origen, Chrysostom, and Jerome, exegetes widely assumed that in Peter the reward for the correct confession of Christ, the son of God, was given to all true believers; all Christians deserved to be called *petrae*.[12] Even Augustine's formulation, informed by a traditional North African concern for the unity of the church, that in Peter *unus pro omnibus* had answered and received the reward, did not suggest more than a figurative reading of Peter as an image of the true church.[13] In light of Peter's subsequent fall and denial, the name itself was regularly declared to be derived from Christ, the true rock. Augustine, who followed Origen in this assumption, was fascinated by the dialectic of the "blessed" Peter (Matt.

---

[10] For the following, I am drawing on my Basel thesis, *Formen der Auslegung von Matth. 16,13-18* (see above, note 8). As a control of my generalizations I am reproducing in the appendix to the present article the section on Matt. 16:18f. from the *Commentarius in Matthaeum* by Petrus de Scala (Scaliger) of Bergamo OP (d. 1295), one of the manuscript commentaries used in that study. Cf. Friedrich Stegmüller, *Repertorium Biblicum Medii Aevi*, vol. 4 (Madrid, 1954), p. 395, no. 6847.

[11] Jerome, *Commentarius in Evangelium Matthaei* III, ad 16:18 (*PL* 26: 121C): "Quia tu mihi dixisti: 'Tu es Christus Filius Dei vivi,' et ego dico tibi, non sermone casso et nullum habente opus, sed dico tibi, quia meum dixisse fecisse est: Quia tu es Petrus, et super hanc petram aedificabo Ecclesiam meam." The *Glossa interlinearis* remarks on v. 16: "Sciunt et apostoli, sed Petrus respondet unus pro omnibus," and on v. 18: "In Petro omnibus respondet," *Bibliorum Sacrorum Tomus V cum Glossa ordinaria et Nicolai Lyrani expositionibus...* (Lugduni, 1745), f. 52ʳ; cf. Petrus de Scala, *In Matthaeum* (ll. 1-3).

[12] Origen, Fragment 345.II on Matt. 16:18 (GCS *Origines* 12, ed. E. Klostermann, 1941, p. 149); Chrysostom, *In Matthaeum Hom.* 54 (*PG* 58: 534B); Ambrose, *Expositio Evangelii secundum Lucan* VI.98f. (CSEL 32: 4, ed. C. Schenkl, 1902, p. 275). In the early Middle Ages, Jonas of Orleans (d. 843) declared (*De cultu imaginum* III; *PL* 106: 376A): "Multi namque et penes omnes petram super quam aedificatur Ecclesia fidem intelligunt beati Petri quae communis est totius Ecclesiae, videlicet eam quae paulo ante promissionem hanc praecesserat."

[13] Augustine, *Tractatus in Ioannem* 118.4, ll. 21-26 (CCL 36, ed. Willems, 1954, pp. 656f.): "... solus Petrus respondit: Tu es Christus Filius Dei uiui; et ei dicitur: Tibi dabo claues regni caelorum, tamquam ligandi et soluendi solus acceperit potestatem; cum et illud unus pro omnibus dixerit, et hoc cum omnibus tamquam personam gerens ipsius unitatis acceperit; ideo unus pro omnibus quia unitas est in omnibus"; cf. 124.5 (ibid., p. 684f.).

16:17) being addressed as "Satan" a few verses later (v. 23). In Peter, weak in himself and strong only in his connection with Christ, the church could see the image of its own total dependence on God's grace.[14]

In harmony with his ecclesiology, but against the meaning of the text, Augustine rigorously separated the name-giving from its explanation: Christ did not say to Peter: "your are the rock," but "you are Peter." The church is not built upon Peter but upon the only true rock, Christ.[15] Augustine and the medieval exegetes after him found the warrant for this interpretation in I Cor. 10:4 ("petra autem erat Christus"). The allegorical key of this verse had already been applied to numerous biblical rock passages in the earlier African *testimonia* tradition. Matt. 16:18 was no exception. If the metaphor of the rock did not refer to a negative category of "hard" rocks, it had to be read christologically.

The same result was obtained when exegetes focused on the image of the "building of the church." The rock metaphor in Matt. 16:18 stressed the firmness of the church's foundation. But the foundation image itself, *funda-mentum ecclesiae*, was clearly explained in another key passage of the New Testament: "Another foundation can no one lay except the one that is laid, which is Christ Jesus" (I Cor. 3:11).[16] The same interpretation of the "firm foundation" being Christ seemed inevitable when exegetes associated Matt. 16:18 with Jesus' parable of Matt. 7:24 which spoke of the building of a house on firm ground. The exegetical tradition since Origen and the *Opus imperfectum in Matthaeum* identified the house with the church so that the

---

[14] On the various aspects of Augustine's interpretation of Matt. 16:18f. see Anne-Marie La Bonnardière, "Tu es Petrus. La péricope Matthieu 16,13-19 dans l'œuvre de St. Augustin," *Irénikon* 34 (1961) 451-499.

[15] Augustine, *Retractationes* I.20.2 (CSEL 36, ed. Knöll, 1902, pp. 97, l. 15 - 98, l. 13): "scio me postea saepissime sic exposuisse, quod a domino dictum est: tu es Petrus, et super hanc petram aedificabo ecclesiam meam, ut super hunc intelligeretur, quem confessus est Petrus dicens: filius Dei uiui, ac si Petrus ab hac petra appellata personam ecclesiae figuraret, quae super hanc petram aedificatur et accepit claues regni caelorum. non enim dictum illi est: Tu es petra, sed Petrus; petra autem erat Christus." The combination with I Cor. 10:4 appears frequently; cf. *Enarr. in ps.* 60:3 (*PL* 36: 726): "Recolamus Evangelium: super hanc petram aedificabo ecclesiam meam; ergo illa clamat a finibus terrae, quam voluit aedificari super petram. Ut autem aedificaretur ecclesia super petram, quis factus est petra? Paulum audi dicentem: petra autem erat Christus"; *Sermo* 295.1-4 (*PL* 38: 1348D-1350D); *Tractatus in Ioannem* 124.5 (CCL 36, ed. Willems, 1954, pp. 684f., ll. 47-79).

[16] See, e.g., Hrabanus Maurus, *Commentaria in Matthaeum* II.c.7 (*PL* 107: 852AB): "Fundamentum quod apostolus Paulus architectus posuit unum est: Dominus noster Jesus Christus. Super hoc fundamentum stabile et firmum et per se robusta mole fundatum aedificatur Christi ecclesia." Bruno of Segni, *Expositio in Psalmos*, ad ps. 86.1 (*PL* 164: 1032B): "Fundamentum aliud, ait Apostolus, nemo potest ponere praeter id quod positum est, quod est Christus Jesus. De quo et beato Petro Dominus ait: Tu es Petrus, etc."; cf. also Petrus de Scala, *In Matthaeum* (ll. 30-31).

wise master builder had to be Christ who builds the church upon the firm rock, himself.[17] Even in a secondary moral interpretation which explained the master builder as the virtuous Christian, the image of the strong foundation was invariably christologized, often with direct reference to I Cor. 3:11 and 10:4, or even Matt. 16:18. A good Christian must build the house of his life on Christ.[18] Applied to the imagery of Matt. 16:18, the final scope of Jesus' parable again reinforced a christological reading: the house of the wise master builder, Jesus taught, stands firm against all assaults of wind, flood, and weather. The parallel to Matt. 16:18c was very obvious to the interpreter: if the *portae inferi* cannot prevail against it, the church must indeed be built on the one rock that cannot be moved, Christ.

The logic of these parallel texts must have seemed inevitable to medieval exegetes. In none of the biblical building and foundation passages which were understood as referring to the church was Matt. 16:18 used as a hermeneutical key that would suggest Peter as the foundation. On the contrary, the clear Petrine meaning of the verse was silenced by the weight of the christological parallels. In medieval exegesis, these keys governed not only all references to the building of the church in the New Testament but also its Old Testament prefigurations: Christ was the foundation of the church prefigured in Solomon's temple (I Kings 5ff.), in the house which Wisdom built for herself (Prov. 9), and in the cosmological foundation images of the Psalms (Ps. 79:69; 86:1; 101:26; 103:5 etc.).[19]

The exegetical consequences of this situation were astonishing. Even an instance such as Eph. 2:20, where the church of the saints is said to be built on "the foundation of the apostles and prophets," was pressed into the

---

[17] Origen, Fragment 153 on Matt. 7:24-27 (GCS *Origines* 12, ed. E. Klostermann, 1941, p. 76); *Opus imperfectum in Matthaeum* (Ps.-Chrysostom): Hom. 20 (*PG* 56: 744A-745A). In the Middle Ages, see, e.g., Anselm of Lâon, *Enarrationes in Matthaeum*, ad 7:24 (*PL* 162: 1317D): "In primis Christus ille homo sapiens, qui aedificavit ecclesiam suam super petram, id est super semetipsum, et tunc omnia genera tentationum impulerunt eam nec tamen cecidit"; also Petrus de Scala, *In Matthaeum* (ll. 22-26).

[18] Origen, Fragment 152 on Matt. 7:24-27 (GCS *Origines* 12, ed. E. Klostermann, 1941, pp. 75f.); *Opus imperfectum in Matthaeum* (Ps.-Chrysostom): Hom. 20 (*PG* 56: 745D-746C): "Huic ergo viro sapienti Christo similis est Christianus omnis, qui aedificat se super petram, id est Christum. Qui enim audit verba Christi et facit ea, ipse est qui aedificat se super petram Christum..."; cf. again Anselm of Lâon, *Enarrationes in Matthaeum*, ad 7:24 (*PL* 162: 1318A): "Huic potest comparari, ut diximus, qui audit verba Dei et facit ea, quia domum suam, id est collectionem virtutum aedificavit supra petram, id est Christum." The combination is succinctly expressed in the *Glossa ordinaria* (*PL* 114: 112A): "Qui aedificavit: Ille aedificat in Christum qui quod audit ab illo facit. Super petram: A qua Petrus nomen accepit pro firmitate fidei, id est, super seipsum aedificavit Ecclesiam."

[19] See my *Formen der Auslegung*, pp. 28f. A model interpretation of Solomon's temple during the Middle Ages was Bede's treatise, *De templo Salomonis* (*PL* 91: 737-868), with its important first chapter.

christological mold by an attributive reading of the genitive: "built on the foundation, upon which apostles and prophets rest also — Christ."[20] The apparent warrant was provided by the designation of Christ as *summus angularis lapis* in the same verse; based on Isa. 28:16 and Ps. 117:22, the image of the cornerstone had been appropriated as a messianic prediction in the earliest Christian tradition already (Rom. 9:33; Mark 12:10; Acts 4:11; I Peter 2:4-7). Still, the verse in Ephesians, together with other texts such as Rev. 21:14 where the twelve apostles are called the foundations of the new Jerusalem, did suggest the language of the apostles as "secondary" foundations after Christ.[21] In this connection, medieval exegetes sometimes could speak of Peter as the "second" foundation of the church because among the apostolic *fundamenta* he was closest to the cornerstone; in the metaphorical language of Matt. 16:18: Peter alone derived his name directly from Christ's strength.[22] From the middle of the thirteenth century on, exegetes occasionally suggested two foundations for the church: "Are Christ and Peter foundations? We have to answer that Christ is it of himself, Peter insofar as

[20] Pelagius, *Commentarius in epistolas Pauli* (ed. A. Souter, *Texts and Studies* IX.2, 1929, p. 356): "Fundamentum apostolorum et prophetarum Christus est"; Haymo of Auxerre (Ps.-Haymo of Halberstadt), *Expositio in Epistolas Pauli,* ad Eph. 2:20 (*PL* 181: 1229c): "Fundamentum apostolorum et prophetarum omniumque fidelium Christus est, quia in fide illius sunt fundati et stabiliti, sicut ipse dixit: Super hanc petram, id est super me, aedificabo ecclesiam meam, quae constat ex angelis et hominibus iustis. Omnis enim qui fidem Christi habet, super ipsum est fundatus, ipso summo angulari lapide Christo Jesu. Quomodo est Christus et fundamentum et summus lapis? Per hoc quod ab illo perficitur atque completur ipsa fides ideoque omnes electi in ipso sunt fundati"; Hervaeus Burgidolensis, *Commentaria in epistolas D. Pauli,* ad Eph. 2:20 (*PL* 181: 1229c): "... super fidem Christi, super quam primo fundati sunt apostoli et prophetae. Christus enim fundamentum est totius divini templi vel divinae civitatis ... et ipse totum spiritale portat aedificium. Ipse ergo est fundamentum apostolorum et prophetarum, quia super illum incumbunt et firmi permanent apostoli et prophetae, qui totam deinde fabricam sancti aedificii portant."

[21] See the formulation in Bruno of Segni, *Expositio in Psalmos,* ad ps. 86:1: "Fundamentum igitur fundamentorum Christus est, siquidem et apostoli et prophetae fundamenta sunt." Psalm 86(87):1 ("Fundamenta eius in montibus sanctis") was one of the instances where the plural, *fundamenta,* encouraged a distinction between apostles as a foundation and Christ, the *fundamentum.* Rev. 21:14 was another; cf. Rupert of Deutz, *In Apocalypsin* lib. XII, ad 21:14 (*PL* 169: 1197c): "Idem apostoli qui portae ipsi civitatis huius et fundamenta sunt. Nam super fidem illorum fundata est ecclesia Dei; verumtamen ita, ut fundamentum ipsorum Christus sit. Denique ab hoc fundamento unico ipsi fundamenta sic dicuntur, quomodo unus idemque primus eorum a petra qui sine dubio Christus est, dictus est Petrus."

[22] See, e.g., Gerhoh of Reichersberg, *Commentarium in ps.* 14:4 (*PL* 193: 828D and 829A): "Juravit, id est firmissime promisit proximo suo Petro Apostolo, qui ipsi angulari lapidi est in fundamento ecclesiae proximus..."; "quia specialiter prae ceteris apostolis ipse fuit petrae proximus, a qua dictus est Petrus." Similarly Radulph Ardens, *Homilia* 23 (*PL* 155: 1391A); Rupert of Deutz, *Commentarius in Ioannem* at 1:46 (*PL* 169: 268c-269A); Peter of Blois, *Sermo* 28 *de ss. Petro et Paulo* (*PL* 207: 644B).

he has the confession of Christ, insofar as he is his vicar;"[23] or: "The entire firmness of this church flows principally from the solidity of the one rock (*petra*) and the one Peter (*Petrus*) who is the vicar of the rock."[24]

How then could a papal interpretation make use of Matt. 16:18 at all? Here we have to remember that, before Augustine, the natural reading of the verse assumed the clear identity of name and function: You are Peter, and upon you, the rock, I will build my church.[25] Whatever precise content was given to the meaning of "rock," even the early Western tradition from Tertullian and Cyprian to Marius Victorinus and Hilary read: "super te." But within the scope of this early equation of *petra* = *Petrus*, two different exegetical accents emerged: most of the Eastern exegetes, especially after the doctrinal controversies of the fourth century, read v. 18 as the culmination of vv. 16-17: "upon this rock" meant "upon the orthodox faith which you have just confessed."[26] Introduced in the West by Ambrose and the translation of Antiochene exegetes, this *petra* = *fides* equation maintained an important place alongside the christological alternative, or as its more precise explanation: the rock of the church was Christ who was the content of Peter's confession.[27] The North African catechetical tradition, on the other hand,

---

[23] Thomas Aquinas, *Super Matthaeum*, on Matt. 16:18 (ed. R. Cai, 5th ed., Torino, 1951, p. 211, nos. 1383-1384): "Alia expositio: super hanc petram, id est super te petram, qui a me petra trahes tu quod sis petra; ita super te petram aedificabo ecclesiam meam. Sed quid est? Estne Christus et Petrus fundamentum? Dicendum quod Christus secundum se, sed Petrus inquantum habet confessionem Christi, inquantum vicarius eius. Ad Eph. II.20...; Apoc. XXI.4." Cf. Nicholas of Lyra, *Postilla super totam Bibliam*, vol. 4 (Strassburg, 1492; repr. Frankfurt, 1971) at Luke 22:32: "... ecclesia Romana quae a Petro post Christum fundata est."

[24] Bonaventure, *De perfectione evangelica* q.4 a.3 in concl. (*Opera Omnia*, Quaracchi, Tom. 5, 1891, p. 195a): "Tota firmitas ipsius ecclesiae principaliter manat a soliditate unius petrae et unius Petri qui est vicarius petrae; in cuius rei signum dictum est Petro: Et super hanc petram aedificabo ecclesiam meam."

[25] The patristic material for this section is discussed by Ludwig, *Die Primatworte*. For needed corrections, see my *Formen der Auslegung*, pp. 93-117 and 126-133.

[26] E.g., Gregory of Nyssa, *Encomium in S. Stephanum protomartyrem* II (*PG* 46: 733): "According to the gift bestowed on him by the Lord, (Peter) is the inconcussible, utterly firm rock upon which the Redeemer built the Church.... Our praise does not refer to the fisherman, but to his firm faith and the firmity of the whole Church." Ludwig, *Die Primatworte*, pp. 48ff., discusses further authors of the fourth century. For Chrysostom see especially his *Homilia* 54.1-3 *in Matthaeum* (*PG* 58: 531-536), and *Homilia* 2 *in principium Actorum* (*PG* 51: 86).

[27] Ambrose, *Expositio evangelii secundum Lucan* VI.98 (CSEL 32.4, p. 275): "Enitere ergo ut et tu petra sis. Itaque non extra te, sed intra te petram require. Petra tua actus est, petra tua mens est. Super hanc petram aedificatur domus tua, ut nullus possit nequitiae spiritalis uerberari procellis. Petra tua fides est, fundamentum est fides ecclesiae. Si petra fueris, in ecclesia eris quia ecclesia super petram est"; or, with a polemical twist: *De incarnationis dominicae sacramento* IV.32 (*PL* 16: 826): "hic, inquam, ubi audiuit: 'Uos autem quid me dicitis?', statim loci non immemor sui primatum egit, primatum confessionis utique, non honoris, primatum fidei, non ordinis." For a medieval echo, see Petrus de Scala, *In Matthaeum* (ll. 17-33) with its frequent reference to Peter's faith and confession.

understood the word about Peter, the rock of the church, as the preface to v. 19: Peter was the rock, because he received the keys of the kingdom, which signified the church's exercise of penitential discipline. Tertullian, nevertheless, regarded the Peter of Matt. 16:18-19 as the representative of the entire church or at least its "spiritual" members. Cyprian understood him as symbolizing the unity of all bishops, the privileged officers of penance.[28] It was as a specialization of this view of Peter, the bearer of special authority, that the papal interpretation of Matt. 16:18 emerged. Beginning with Stephen I and Damasus I, the Cyprianic terminology of *solus Petrus, una cathedra, super unum* in the exegesis of the passage was applied to Rome alone as the see of the privileged Peter of Matt. 16:18f.[29] Leo I gave this interpretation its characteristic form: following the old equation *petra* = *Petrus*, and ignoring the typology of *unus pro omnibus*, he emphasized two points: first, the character of the scene was a bestowal of authority; for Leo, even the traditional derivation of Peter's name from Christ, the rock, could serve this purpose — its meaning was participation in Christ's authority and power. The second point was the argument for a living Peter on the basis of the dynamics of the Matthaean verses; a strong foundation must mean perpetuity of both Peter's faith and Peter's authority.[30] It is likely that, as

---

[28] Tertullian, *De pudicitia* xxi.9-10 (CCL 2, 1954, pp. 1327f.); cf. *De praescriptione haereticorum* xxii.4 (CCL 1, 1954, p. 203); *Scorpiace* x.8 (CCL 2, 1954, p. 1088). Cyprian frequently used the phrase, "Petrus super quem aedificavit ecclesiam"; for him, the one Peter, the first to receive the penitential keys which all other bishops also exercise, was the biblical type of the one episcopate, which in turn guaranteed the unity of the church. The one Peter equalled the one body of bishops: *Epistola* 73.7 (CSEL 3.2, ed. W. Hartel, 1868, p. 783, ll. 13-17): "Manifestum est autem ubi et per quos remissa peccatorum dari possit quae in baptismo scilicet datur. Nam Petro primum Dominus super quem aedificauit ecclesiam et unde unitatis originem instituit et ostendit, potestatem istam dedit, ut id solueretur quod ille soluisset..."; *Epistola* 70.3 (ibid., p. 769, ll. 19-20): "... una ecclesia a Christo domino nostro super Petrum origine unitatis et ratione fundata." The famous chapter 4 of *De unitate ecclesiae* in its short version (CSEL 3.1, ed. W. Hartel, 1868, pp. 212, l. 5 - 213, l. 13) contains the same argument.

[29] For Pope Stephen's exegesis we have the indirect witness of Firmilian of Caesarea (Cyprian, *Epistola* 75 [CSEL 3.2, pp. 810-827], esp. c.17 [pp. 821, l. 14 - 822, l. 6]). Pope Damasus' position may be reflected in materials incorporated into the *Decretum Gelasianum* (Denzinger-Schoenmetzer, *Enchiridion Symbolorum*), nos. 350-351. On the arguments of both popes, cf. Caspar, *Geschichte des Papsttums*, 1: 79-83 and 196-256.

[30] The most important texts are Leo's *Sermones 3-5 in cathedra Petri* (CCL 138, pp. 10-25). For the first point above, see *Sermo* 4.2 (ibid., p. 19, ll. 68-73): "Quia tu es Petrus: Id est, cum ego sim inviolabilis petra, ego lapis angularis, qui facio utraque unum, ego fundamentum praeter quod nemo potest aliud ponere, tamen tu quoque petra es, quia mea virtute solidaris, ut quae mihi potestate sunt propria, sint tibi mecum participatione communia"; for the second point, see *Sermo* 3.3 (ibid., p. 12, ll. 58-60): "Manet ergo dispositio veritatis, et beatus Petrus in accepta fortitudine petrae perseverans suscepta ecclesiae gubernacula non reliquit." On Leo's argument, see also Caspar, *Geschichte des Papsttums*, 1: 426-431 and 527-531.

Walter Ullmann has claimed, Leo saw the idea of the living Peter on the papal throne more in terms of legal heredity than in terms of mystical identification, and understood his role as *vicarius Petri* primarily in this legal sense.[31] But his interpretation of the biblical text was not purely legal. He also understood the need for a living Peter in terms of the alternative option of exegeting Matt. 16:18 under the old equation, as the need for the continuing presence of the voice of orthodox faith against heresy: "You are the Christ, the Son of the living God."[32]

A basic lack of the primatial context also characterizes the exegetical tradition about the "keys of the kingdom of heaven" (Matt. 16:19). Again, the major reason may have to be sought in the influence of biblical parallels. In the patristic commentaries, the keys were understood as penitential authority, primarily the priestly power of excommunication and reconciliation. This understanding was nourished by the parallel passages of Matt. 18:18 ("Amen dico vobis, quaecumque alligaveritis super terram, etc.") and especially John 20:23, where binding and loosing seemed to be explained as the retaining and forgiving of sins.[33] Both texts, however, extended this power beyond the one Peter to all apostles. Thus, exegetes were faced with the fact that "what was bestowed on Peter, was also given to all apostles."[34]

[31] See Walter Ullmann, "Leo ɪ and the Theme of Papal Primacy," *Journal of Theological Studies*, N.S. 11 (1960) 25-51.

[32] Cf., e.g., *Sermo* 3.2 (CCL 138, p. 12, ll. 44-47): "Soliditas enim illius fidei quae in apostolorum principe est laudata, perpetua est. Et sicut permanet quod in Christo Petrus credidit, ita permanet quod in Petro Christus instituit."

[33] The combination of Matt. 16 and 18 with John 20:23, and the explanation of the power of the keys through the latter passage is not warranted by the biblical text itself. In the early medieval tradition it was developed by Bede in his *Homilia* 16 on the feast of Peter and Paul (*PL* 94: 222ᴅ-223ᴀ). There is patristic precedent, especially in the North African tradition, even though Matt. 18:18 does not seem to have been quoted there before Tyconius (*Beati in Apocalypsin Libri* xɪɪ; ed. H. A. Sanders, Rome, 1930, p. 86): Cyprian, *Epistola* 75.16 (Firmilian of Caesarea; CSEL 3.2, pp. 820, l. 26 - 821, l. 6); *De unitate ecclesiae*, chapter 4 (long version). Peter Abaelard again attempted to distinguish the ecclesiastical power to excommunicate, given to all apostles and bishops (Matt. 16:19 and 18:18), from a new gift of the Spirit and of forgiveness, bestowed after the Resurrection on worthy apostles and prelates only (*Peter Abelard's Ethics*, ed. D. E. Luscombe, Oxford, 1971, pp. 124, l. 30 - 126, l. 17).

[34] Augustine, *Sermo* 149.6 (*PL* 38: 802ᴅ): "Petrus enim in multis locis Scripturarum apparet quod personam gestet ecclesiae maxime illo in loco ubi dictum est: Tibi dabo, etc. (Matt. 16:19). Numquid istas claves Petrus accepit et Paulus non accepit? Petrus accepit et Johannes et Jacobus non accepit? Aut non sunt istae in Ecclesia claves, ubi peccata quotidie dimittuntur? Sed quoniam in significatione personam Petrus gestabat Ecclesiae, quod illi uni datum est, ecclesiae datum est." A good medieval example is Rupert of Deutz, *De Trinitate et operibus eius*: *In IV evangelia XXV De primatu Petri* (CCCM 23, ed. Hrabanus Haacke, 1972, p. 1813, ll. 1258-1277): "Et tibi dabo claues regni caelorum. Pars iuris caelestis et senatoriae dignitatis, quae subiecta est his verbis: Et quodcumque ligaveris super terram, erit ligatum et in caelis etc. (Matt. 16:19). Ceteris quoque apostolis communiter contradita est. Dixit enim

Almost invariably, they discussed the verse in the context of lengthy considerations of penance and of the priestly powers, declarative or effective, in relation to this sacrament. Ludwig Hödl has traced the complicated development through the early scholastic Sentences and the exegetical *quaestiones* literature; he pointed to the erosion of the priestly power of the keys with the change from public to private penance and from the accent on the *forum externum* to effective contrition and the *forum internum*.[35]

Since Bede, the plural "keys" were understood as a *clavis scientiae* and a *clavis potestatis* — the designation of the first one echoing Luke 11:52 ("Vae vobis legisperitis, qui tulistis clavem scientiae"); the second perhaps derived from the "key of David" (Isa. 22:22; Rev. 3:7).[36] The first, more problematic key was identified as the *discretio* exercised by the priest who, as Jerome had explained, discerns and pronounces authoritatively about the presence or absence of leprosy, i.e., sin (Luke 17:14; Lev. 14:2f.).[37] Medieval theologians saw difficulties with this concept. They tried to distinguish the *clavis scientiae* clearly from the main key which had to be at least the authority to excommunicate, if not to impose and remit penances. But can *scientia* really be a key? Can and must every priest be assumed to have discretionary knowledge? And with regard to the power to admit or to exclude from the kingdom: is it simply given with the priestly *ordo*? Does one not have to add the concept of proper jurisdiction to its exercise? The commentaries on Matt. 16:19 do reflect some of these discussions which led to ever more elaborate revisions

---

alibi: Amen dico uobis, quaecumque alligaueritis super terram, erunt ligata in caelo etc. (Matt. 18:18). Itemque et alibi: Quorum remiseritis peccata, remittuntur eis, et quorum retinueritis, retenta sunt (Io. 20:23). Itaque potestas quidem communis est omnium, sed unum et singulare unius est Petri priuilegium, cui prius et singulariter dictum est: Tibi dabo claues regni caelorum"; cf. his *Commentary on John*, XIV, at 20:23 (*PL* 169: 812A).

[35] Ludwig Hödl, *Die Geschichte der scholastischen Literatur und der Theologie der Schlüsselgewalt*. I. Teil. *Die scholastische Literatur und die Theologie der Schlüsselgewalt von ihren Anfängen an bis zur Summa Aurea des Wilhelm von Auxerre*, BGPTMA, Band XXXVIII, Heft 4 (Münster, 1960), esp. pp. 376-391 ("Rückblick").

[36] Bede, *Homilia* XVI (*PL* 94: 222): "... absque ea confessione et fide regnum coelorum nullus posset intrare. Claves autem regni coelorum ipsam discernendi scientiam potentiamque nominat, qua dignos recipere in regnum, indignos secludere deberet a regno."

[37] Jerome, *Commentarius in Evangelium Matthaei*, III, on Matt. 16:19 (*PL* 26: 122AB): "Istum locum episcopi et presbyteri non intelligentes aliquid sibi de Pharisaeorum assumunt supersticio, ut vel damnent innocentes, vel solvere se noxios arbitrentur: cum apud Deum non sententia sacerdotum, sed reorum vita quaeratur. Legimus in Levitico de leprosis, ubi jubentur ut ostendant se sacerdotibus, et si lepram habuerint, tunc a sacerdote immundi fiant (Lev. 14:2-4); non quo sacerdotes leprosos faciant et immundos, sed quo habeant notitiam leprosi et non leprosi, et possint discernere qui mundus, qui immundus sit." While, in the Middle Ages, Jerome's *sententia* could be used to stress the necessity of oral confession, it also pointed to the limits of the priestly powers and provided the warrant for the strong tradition of a merely declarative understanding of absolution.

of the traditional concept of the keys, including their reduction to a single key.[38] What they show even more clearly is that the weight of the biblical and traditional authorities was still stronger than any pressure for theological accommodation. Exegetes could not leave it at one key only when they discussed Matt. 16:19.[39] On the other hand, the christological accent of v. 18 could make itself felt even in the interpretation of v. 19. To some exegetes, it seemed noteworthy that Christ reserved the key of death and hell to himself (Rev. 1:8); others emphasized that all priestly forgiveness is derived from the one who alone absolves and binds, Christ. In this connection, the reference of Gregory I to John 11:44 was often repeated: Christ alone raised Lazarus; the disciples were only ordered to untie him.[40]

For a long time, the parallel passages of Matt. 18:18 and John 20:23 prevented any discussion of Matt. 16:19 from focusing on Peter and his special privileges. Occasionally, the commentaries expanded the address of the word: "Dixit Dominus Petro et omnibus sequacibus eius."[41] In other interpretations, the *pro omnibus* of v. 16 is repeated: "I will give you — not only for yourself, but also for others: for just as Peter's confession was the confession of others, so this power given to Peter is understood to be given to others." Surprisingly, the commentator of the early fourteenth century adds: "... though to Peter more principally inasmuch as he was the chief of the others."[42]

The mention of a special prerogative for Peter in connection with Matt. 16:19 seems to have become more prominent from the middle of the thirteenth century on: the power, exegetes explained, was common to all, certainly to all apostles, but it was first given to Peter and was channelled through him. For an explanation of this trend one could point to the possibility that increased attention paid to the literal sense and the plain

---

[38] Hödl, *Schüsselgewalt*, pp. 380f., cites a number of earlier theologians and canonists for this latter position; from the school of Peter the Chanter he mentions Robert of Courson and an anonymous *quaestio* in an Erlangen MS (Bibl. univ., Cod. lat. 260). In most instances, the biblical plural is explained as the two *usus* of the one key of priestly *auctoritas*.

[39] The section from Petrus de Scala's commentary, *In Matthaeum* (ll. 44-55) demonstrates not only the general impact of these discussions on an exegete of the late thirteenth century but also the attempt to maintain two keys while actually arguing for one only.

[40] Gregory I, *Homilia* 26 (*PL* 76: 1200). The interpretation goes back to Augustine, *Tractatus in Ioannem* 49.24 (CCL 36, p. 431, ll. 22-25); cf. 22.6 (ibid., p. 227, ll. 35-38); *Enarrationes in psalmos*, CI, *sermo* 2.3 (CCL 40, p. 1440, ll. 7-20).

[41] Peter of Poitiers, *Sententiae* III.xvi (*PL* 211: 1075C).

[42] Nicholas of Lyra, *Postilla*, vol. 4 (Strassburg, 1492), on Matth. 16:19: "Et tibi dabo, non solum pro te set etiam pro aliis. sicut enim confessio Petri erat confessio aliorum, ita potestas haec data Petro intelligitur dari aliis, licet Petro principalius quantum erat aliorum capitaneus."

meaning of the biblical text since the rise of the Victorine School allowed exegetes to perceive more clearly the Petrine accent of the verse, even against the common reading which was dominated by the parallels. Even more likely, it may have been the exegesis of the popes, especially the biblical rhetoric of Innocent III, that forced a different reading upon the minds, a reading which tended to reverse the previous logic of the three parallel texts. If Peter received the keys first, it was through him, even from him, that all prelates must have them. Such an understanding was not directly warranted by the biblical text. But it seemed to be supported by other "apostolic" traditions: the Pseudo-Dionysian corpus which enjoyed a new vogue during our period, and the Pseudo-Clementine *Epistola ad Iacobum* which held a prominent place in the False Decretals and seemed to say exactly what the Bible did not say: that Peter handed on his power of binding and loosing to Clement, and through him to all prelates of the church.[43]

One can observe this new accent in Bonaventure's commentary on the Lucan parallel (Luke 9:21). The Cyprianic-Augustinian theme of the church's unity and the symbolic Peter, speaking and acting as *unus pro omnibus* is still dominant, but Peter's exemplary faith and confession are supplemented by his *universalis praelatio*. The one Peter answered for all apostles *tamquam unus praelatus universalis Ecclesiae*.[44] Albert the Great, in his Commentary on Matthew, drew on the Innocentian language of *plenitudo potestatis* and *participatio sollicitudinis* in explaining the special Petrine meaning of Matt. 16:19: of course, the church is built on the rock of Peter's firm confession, and Peter was not the only one to receive what was given, as John 20:23 makes clear; but within the unity of the church's ministerial

---

[43] The text of the *Epistola ad Jacobum* may be found in GCS, *Die Pseudoklementinen*, I, ed. B. Rehm, 1953, pp. 5-9 (1.1-4.4). For an interpretation, see Walter Ullmann, "The Significance of the Epistola Clementis in the Pseudo-Clementines," *Journal of Theological Studies*, N.S. 11 (1960) 295-317. Hödl points to the great importance of the *sententia Clementis* for the medieval idea of the transmission of the keys (*Schlüsselgewalt*, pp. 42f., 388f.). One of his texts, from a set of anonymous *sententiae de clavibus* of the twelfth century, reads: "Sane claves istae a Christo sumpserunt exordium dicente ad Petrum: quodcumque ligaveris etc. A Petro autem ad Clementem Christo largiente pervenerunt, cum diceret: trado tibi a Domino mihi traditam potestatem ligandi atque solvendi, ut de omnibus de quibuscunque decreveris super terram, hoc decretum sit in caelis. Ubi vero Clementi hoc dixit, in Clemente successoribus Clementis hoc dixit, sicut in Decretis dictum est, beatus Petrus perennem meritorem dotem cum hereditate innocentiae transmisit ad posteros. A Romanis ergo pontificibus vicariis Petri claves et curam pastoralem habent quicunque habent, primi vero ad quos derivata est, pontifices sunt, a pontificibus ad sacerdotes usque descendit" (pp. 20, l. 7 - 21, l. 16).

[44] Bonaventure, *Commentarius in Evangelium S. Lucae* IX.33, on Luke 9:20f. (*Opera Omnia*, Quaracchi, Tom. 7, 1895, p. 226).

orders, the one successor of Peter receives in fulness the power in which others only participate.[45]

Thomas Aquinas seems to have combined both tendencies, the exegetical interest in the plain sense and the use of Innocentian language.[46] Even his short *divisio* of Matt. 16:18-19 stresses the obvious Petrine accent: the two verses speak of the two gifts the earthly Jesus gave to Peter in response to Peter's confession — the name and the power. The name signified the founding of the church; for v. 18b Thomas seriously considered the *altera interpretatio* that the church was built on Peter, of course in strict dependence upon Christ, the true rock. The power comes with the keys of forgiveness, linked to Peter's role as *vicarius Christi.* Aquinas noted the future tense, *dabo*, in v. 19. The keys to open the lock of our sins were forged in Christ's passion and could only be given after the Resurrection (John 21:15-17). With this interpretation, Thomas opened the meaning of the passage toward the church of his own time. In doing this, however, he not only incorporated Innocentian language into his commentary but also drew the exegetical consequence: Peter alone received the keys directly; all others have them from him. Here the Petrine accent of Matt. 16:19 finally triumphs over the meaning of the parallel, and not vice versa. Innocent could not have formulated the contemporary application of the verse more concisely: "In this fashion, the pope who occupies the place of Saint Peter has plenary power, but others have their power from him." [47] As yet, I have not found an equally bold and ingenious reinterpretation of the exegetical tradition in any other commentary of the period. Aquinas' voice may have remained relatively isolated at that point. In the mainstream of exegetical literature, the traditional parallels

---

[45] Albert, *In Evangelium Matthaei*, on 16:19 (*Opera Omnia*, ed. Borgnet, Tom. 20, 1893, p. 642): "Ergo 'dabo tibi' singulariter; non quod singulariter accepit Petrus, sed quia in unitate ordinis Ecclesiae unus est qui accipit in plenitudine potestatis, qui est successor Petri, et Petrus in potestate. Alii autem in eadem unitate accipiunt in parte potestatis, eo quod vocantur in partem sollicitudinis. Et ideo Ioan. xx.22 et 23 dicitur pluraliter: Accipite spiritum sanctum...." Another instance of the appropriation of Innocentian language occurs in Albert's interpretation of Matt. 14:29 (ibid., p. 603): "... instructio fuit mundi gubernatoris, qui non in una navicula veniret, sed totum mundum gubernans vicarius Christi perfectus esse probaretur. Eccle. 8:4: Sermo illius potestate plenus est.... (Et descendens): Et multa fecit et dixit talia. Hoc autem competit vertici apostolorum, vicario Domini, qui mundi debuit suscipere gubernacula sicut diximus."

[46] Thomas Aquinas, *Super Matthaeum*, nos. 1383-1386 (ed. A. Cai, pp. 211f.).

[47] Ibid., no. 1393 (p. 212): "Sed est alia quaestio, quia alibi habetur, Io. xx.23: Quorum remiseritis peccata, remittentur eis; hic vero solum hoc dicit Petro. Dicendum quod immediate dedit Petro, alii vero a Petro recipiunt; ideo ne credantur ista solum dici Petro, dicit: Quorum remiseritis, etc. Et hac ratione Papa, qui est in loco Sancti Petri, habet plenariam potestatem, alii vero ab ipso." Cf. also the differentiation between *potestas universalis* and *in aliquo loco* in Thomas' comment on Matt. 18:18 (ibid., no. 1524 [p. 233]).

of John 20:23 and Matt. 18:18 continued to dominate the interpretation of Matt. 16:19. To endorse the primatial potential of the text was still the exception.

3.

We find the same distance from themes of Petrine primacy in the exegetical tradition about Luke 22:31-32. Modern theologians have issues of indefectibility and infallibility on their minds when they consider these verses: "Simon, Simon, ecce Satanas expetivit vos ut cribraret sicut triticum; ego autem rogavi pro te, ut non deficiat fides tua; et tu aliquando conversus confirma fratres tuos." Medieval exegetes found very different contexts for the interpretation of these words. They took their clue from the patristic tradition.

Luke 22:32 marks a climax in the passion story. The following verse reports the prediction of Peter's denial. For the Peter image in the New Testament itself, and even more so for later interpreters, this denial posed serious problems, especially when it was compared with other texts concerning Peter. Matt. 16:16-19 depicted Peter as the bold confessor of his Lord who was royally rewarded. What then was the meaning of the same Peter's fall and denial a few chapters later? In the patristic period, attempts had already been made to reduce the seriousness of the denial and to mitigate Peter's fall. Gerhoh of Reichersberg referred to "magni patres ante nos" to support his interpretation that Peter, "caught in bad company for a moment, denied Christ with his mouth but remained his friend in his heart." [48] The distinction he draws between heart and mouth comes from Rom. 10:8-10; in the exegetical literature, Rom. 10:10 ("corde enim creditur ad iustitiam, ore autem confessio fit ad salutem") was often associated with the story of Peter's denial.[49] Some exegetes used the phrase, "ore solummodo non corde," in order to excuse Peter.[50] Gerhoh's reference would apply especially to Ambrose among the Fathers who, in his commentary on Luke, suggested that the denial applied to Peter's promise to die with Jesus only; Peter's

[48] Gerhoh of Reichersberg, *Commentarium in psalmos*, on Ps. 7:1 (*PL* 193: 721D-722A): "Sicut enim ille Chusi exterius adhaesit Absaloni et visus est abnegare David cuius tamen in corde amicus intimus fuit [II Reg. 15-17]; sic apostolus Petrus malorum societati ad horam conjunctus Christum verum David negavit ore, cuius tamen amicus permansit in corde, quemadmodum a magnis patribus ante nos dictum est."

[49] Peter Lombard, *Collectanea in Epistolas Pauli*, on Rom. 10:10 (*PL* 191: 1476A); with a direct reference to Luke 22:32: Rupert of Deutz, *Commentaria in Evangelium Sancti Iohannis* XI (CCCM 9, ed. R. Haacke, 1969, p. 695, ll. 968-970): "Hoc enim est unde rogaui pro te, Petre, ut dum uoce negas, saltem in corde fides tua non deficiat."

[50] Abaelard, *Sermo* 27 (*PL* 178: 549B); cf. *Sermo* 23 (ibid., 525A); William of St. Thierry, *Liber de natura et dignitate amoris* VI (*PL* 184: 390).

answers in the courtyard, particularly the one to the maid ("I do not know the man" Luke 22:57), could be read as orthodox, anti-Arian confessions of the divinity of the Son.[51]

Such apologetics, however, did not find much favor. In the Middle Ages, Jerome's sharp reaction against this "frivolous" interpretation was often quoted.[52] The exegetical mainstream followed him and Augustine. As we noted in connection with Matt. 16, the Bishop of Hippo was fascinated by the stark contrast between beatitude and curse, strength and weakness, fall and exaltation on the part of a Peter in whom he saw the *figura* of the church as well as of every believer. Peter had already been given first place; now he fell back behind even the weakest martyr who had stood up for Christ. There would have been no return for him had the Lord not intervened with his forgiveness and his prayer.[53] Following Augustine, medieval exegetes rarely tried to soften the denial but explained it as part of God's providential pedagogy. The psychological need of a special lesson for the all too impulsive Peter had been emphasized by Eastern fathers, especially Chrysostom whose interpretation became quite popular in the West in the later Middle Ages.[54] Ambrose found in the incident a more general admonition to strengthen ascetic awareness among all prelates, while constantly stressing Peter's tears as the proper fruit of his divinely endorsed trial: "Beware of pride! Beware of the world!"[55] The most common extension of Augustine's figurative

[51] Ambrose, *Expositio Evangelii secundum Lucan* x.78-87 (CSEL 32.3, ed. Schenkl, pp. 485-488).

[52] Jerome, *Commentarius in Matthaeum* IV, on Matt. 26:72 (*PL* 26: 211AB): "Scio quosdam pii affectus erga apostolum Petrum locum hunc ita interpretatos ut dicerent Petrum non Deum negasse sed hominem; et esse sensum: Nescio hominem quia scio Deum. Hoc quam frivole sit, prudens lector intelligit; sic defendunt apostolum, ut Deum mendacii reum faciant..."; cf. Rabanus, *Commentarius in Matthaeum* VIII, at 26:72 (*PL* 107: 1123D); Paschasius Radbertus, *Expositio in Matthaeo* XII (CCCM 56B, ed. B. Paulus, 1983, p. 1340, ll. 2392-2399).

[53] Augustine, *Enarrationes in psalmos* XLI.43, on Ps. 41:8 (CCL 38, ed. Dekkers-Fraipont, 1956, pp. 470f., ll. 40-43): "quanta profunditas infirmitatis latebat in Petro, quando quid in se ageretur intus nesciebat et se moriturum cum Domino temere promittebat! Quanta abyssus erat!" See also *Sermo* 285.6 (*PL* 38: 1292CD); *Sermo* 286.2-3 (ibid., 1298); *Tractatus in Ioannem* 113.2 (CCL 26, pp. 636f., ll. 15-45).

[54] Chrysostom, *In Matthaeum*, Homilia 82(83):2 (*PG* 58: 741B-D); sections of this text appeared in Aquinas' *Catena Aurea* (ed. A. Guarienti, Torino, vol. 2, 1953, p. 289b) as well as Hugh of St. Cher's *Postilla*, Tomus sextus: *In Evangelia* (Venice, 1732), f. 261ᵃ.

[55] Ambrose, *Expositio Evangelii secundum Lucan* x.50 (CSEL 32.3, ed. Schenkl, p. 475, ll. 5-7): "Caue ergo iactantiam, caue saeculum; ille enim confirmare iubetur fratres suos qui dixit: Omnia reliquimus et secuti sumus te"; cf. his *In ps. XLIII enarratio*, no. 40 (*PL* 14: 1162C-1163B); similarly Haymo of Halberstadt, *Homilia* 70 *de tempore* (*PL* 118: 454C): "... providentissima dispensatione Domini hoc factum est, ut quem cunctae Ecclesiae praeferre disposuerat, semetipsum negare permitteret, ut ex sua fragilitate disceret aliis peccantibus qualiter misereri debuisset."

understanding, however, was the most general one: the fallen Peter became the type of the *lapsus* and of the *poenitens*, the outstanding example of human infirmity even among Christians, of the Christian's total dependence on God's grace, and of his need for proper penance.[56] Peter's tears as well as his threefold "confession" in John 21 held a firm place in the medieval discussions of the penitential process and the restoration of the sinner.

Medieval exegetes read Luke 22:31f. in this context. Jesus' prayer for Peter, as Bede noted (with Chrysostom), did not ask that Peter be spared temptation but that he might return to his pristine condition by doing penance. Temptations are useful for the saints; they teach them humility and render them stronger. Thus, "strengthening the brothers" meant that a saint ought to lift up and comfort the weaker Christians by his or her penance so that they would not despair of their salvation.[57] This very broad application could be focused, as we saw, on the prelates of the church; thus, the verse could address the theme of the "humble prelate" who, like Peter, should remember his human weakness and be prepared to strengthen others, just as he himself was dependent on receiving strength from above. In this connection, the commentators also reflected on the appropriateness of such a lesson precisely for Peter whom the Lord intended to place above the others. But this did not necessarily lend a primatial accent to the verse. On the contrary. Chrysostom, after raising the question why Jesus mentioned only Peter in his prayer, had already given the classical answer which Hugh of St. Cher condensed into a single poignant phrase: "(Jesus) shows that Peter's fall was all the more serious, being that of a prelate."[58]

Peter's faith was not central for this line of argument since the attention focused on the second part of the verse: "et tu aliquando conversus confirma fratres tuos." The theme of faith did become central, however, when the parallel to Matt. 16:16-17 was considered. Augustine saw the depth of Peter's fall in most vivid relief when he described it as the denial of the very faith the Apostle himself had confessed at Caesarea Philippi. The contrast could not be more disturbing. In this context, Luke 22:32 lent support to the

---

[56] Gerhoh of Reichersberg interpreted the entire Psalm 24 (25) as spoken by Peter, the representative of the *ecclesia poenitens* (*PL* 193: 1115-1118).

[57] Cf. Bede, *In Lucam* VI, at 22:31f. (CCL 120, p. 382f., ll. 783-810); also *In Samuelem prophetam allegorica expositio* I.12 (*PL* 91: 542BC): "Et oravit Dominus Patrem pro fidelibus suis, ut non deficeret fides eorum (Luke 22:32)." Both the *Glossa ordinaria* and *interlinearis* draw all their material from Bede: *Bibliorum Sacrorum* (Lugduni, 1745), f. 177ᵛ.

[58] Hugh of St. Cher, *Postilla*, Tomus Sextus (Venice, 1732), f. 261ʳᵃ: "Pro omnibus petiit. Joh. 17:11: 'Pater sancte, serva eos in nomine tuo.' Sed quare hic de solo Petro? Solutio: Ostendens quod difficilior est casus eius, id est praelati."Cf. Chrysostom, *In Matthaeum*, Hom. 82:3 (*PG* 58: 741C).

only understanding of faith which seemed to reckon with both sides of the
biblical evidence, and which the later Augustine and his friends fervently
defended in the Pelagian controversy: faith, they held, was a gift which always
remains dependent on the giver. Even Peter's confession of Matt. 16:16 was
"revealed" to him by the Father. To claim faith as one's own possession
would deny its very nature. Thus, Luke 22:32 proved that Peter's perseverance in faith was in no way his own achievement; Christ had to pray for him
that his faith might not fail.[59]

In Matt. 16:16, Augustine had laid the stress on the confessing Peter as
figura ecclesiae, speaking *pro omnibus*. The same interpretation applied to
Luke 22:32 in much of the exegetical tradition. Already before Augustine,
the Ambrosiaster refused to change the accent on the disciples in v. 31 to an
accent on Peter alone in v. 32: "Clearly, in Peter all are contained; praying
for Peter, (Jesus) is understood to have prayed for all. It is always the people
who are rebuked or praised in a leader. This is why he also says elsewhere:
'I pray for those whom you have given me' (John 17:9)."[60] Augustine was
equally clear about this point.[61] For medieval exegetes, various verses from
John 17 continued to provide biblical warrant for the extension of Jesus'
prayer in Luke 22:32 far beyond Peter. All Christians, they concluded, are
warned here how easily their faith can fail, but they also receive encouragement by the assurance of Christ's intercession for them.[62] In the general
stream of normative exegesis, the Peter who was upheld by Christ's prayer
and whose faith was tempted yet did not finally succumb clearly remained

[59] Augustine, *Tractatus in Ioannem* 53.8 (CCL 36, p. 456, ll. 14-18): "Audiamus Dominum dicentem: Rogaui pro te, Petre, ne deficiat fides tua; nec sic estimemus fidem nostram
esse in libero arbitrio, ut diuino non egeat adiutorio"; cf. *De correptione et gratia* VIII.17 (*PL*
44: 926A-C); VI.9 (ibid., 921D-922A); XII.38 (ibid., 946AB); Prosper of Aquitaine, *De vocatione
omnium gentium* I.24 and II.28 (*PL* 51: 685A and 713BC); *Contra collatorem* XV.3 (*PL* 51:
257C-258A).

[60] Ambrosiaster (Ps.-Augustine), *Quaestiones in Novum Testamentum*, no. 75 (*PL* 35:
2273A): "Quid ambigitur? Pro Petro rogabat et pro Jacobo et Johanne non rogabat, ut de
caeteris taceam? Manifestum est in Petro omnes contineri; rogans enim pro Petro pro
omnibus rogasse cognoscitur. Semper enim in praeposito populus aut corripitur aut laudatur.
Quia et alio loco dicit: 'Ego pro his rogo quos mihi dedisti' (Ioa. 17:9)."

[61] E.g., *Enarrationes in psalmos* CVIII.5, on Ps. 108(109):5 (CCL 40, p. 1587, ll. 8-10):
"quamquam bene intelligatur etiam pro discipulis suis orasse, quod etiam ante passionem suam
dixit, ne deficeret fides eorum..."; CXVIII. *Sermo* 13.3, on Ps. 118(119):43 (ibid., p. 1706,
ll. 11f.): "non omnimodo ex ore Petri, in quo erat typus ecclesiae, uerbum ueritatis ablatum
est."

[62] See John Cassian, *Collationes* III.16 (CSEL 13.2, ed. M. Petschenig, 1886, pp. 88, l. 16
- 89, l. 8); Rupert of Deutz, *Commentaria in Evangelium Sancti Iohannis* XII at 17:15 (CCCM
9, p. 703, ll. 1607-1616).

figura ecclesiae; for most exegetes, this meant in the first instance: type of
the universal church and of every individual believer.[63]

The identity of the church which was addressed in the Peter of Luke
22:31f. was, however, open for a Roman specialization also. Occasionally we
find comments which identify it with the *ecclesia Petri* in a narrower sense:
"I have prayed for you etc. (Luke 22:32): (Christ) did not say this spiritually
of the faith in Peter's own mind, but of the faith of the church which he
wanted to be governed by Peter." [64] This particular quotation belonged in the
context of twelfth century anti-Waldensian polemics. It shows that a bridge
did exist, certainly in the context of anti-heretical arguments, to the positive
assertion of the indefectibility of Peter's faith which may be traced in the
papal use of Luke 22:32 since Leo I and Pelagius II (578-590), and is found
most prominently in the correspondence of Rome with the East since the
Photian schism. While Leo I, in his references to Luke 22:32, seems to have
reflected less on Peter's unshakeable faith than on the future function of
"strengthening the brothers," he did use the term "indeficiens" in connection
with his doctrine of the living Peter.[65] Pelagius II, on the other hand, in a
doctrinal dispute with the Istrian bishops, not only opened his quotation of
all three Petrine texts with Luke 22:32, but interpreted the verse by stating
laconically that "the truth cannot lie, and Peter's faith will not be shaken or
altered in eternity." [66] Leo IX's first Epistle to Patriarch Michael Cerularius
of Constantinople, authored by Humbert of Silva Candida in 1053, echoed
this language at a time when the West had become convinced that Eastern
christendom, especially the See of Constantinople, was the crib and cradle
of heresy: "To this day the faith of the Roman church which is built upon the

---

[63] Gerhoh of Reichersberg, *Commentarius in psalmos* II, on Ps. 27:2 (*PL* 193: 1215c),
where Christ is the speaker: "Ego autem nunc orans et extollens in cruce manus meas ad
templum sanctum tuum rogo non solum pro Petro, ut non deficiat fides eius, sed etiam pro
tota Ecclesia et pro unoquoque fideli in Ecclesia, ut fides eius non deficeret." Cf. also his
commentary on Ps. 24:7 (ibid., 1117b).

[64] Ekbert of Schönau (d. 1184), *Sermo* 10 *contra Catharos* (*PL* 195: 73): "Ego rogavi etc.
Quod utique non dicebat spiritualiter pro illa fide quae in mente Petri erat, sed de fide ecclesiae
quam voluit gubernari a Petro." Cf. *Sermo* 3 (ibid., 21d-22a).

[65] Leo I, *Sermo* v.4 (CCL 138, p. 24, ll. 78-80): "... [Petri] qui sedi suae praeesse non
desinit et indeficiens obtinet cum aeterno sacerdote consortium." The *Thesaurus Linguae
Latinae* suggests a possible link to a formulation in the Ambrosiaster's commentary on II Tim.
1:1-2 (CSEL 81.3, ed. H. J. Vogels, 1969, p. 295, ll. 17-19): "ut [Timotheus] per traducem
indeficiens sit idoneus doctor per quem adserta ueritas multos adquirat ad uitam promissam."

[66] Pelagius II, *Epistola* I.5-6 *ad episcopos Histriae* (ACO IV.2, ed. E. Schwartz, 1914, p. 105,
ll. 20-29): "nostis enim in euangelio Dominum proclamantem: Simon, Simon, etc. (Luke
22:31f.). considerate carissimi, quia ueritas mentiri non potuit nec fides Petri in aeternum
quassari poterit uel mutari. nam cum omnes discipulos diabolus ad cribrandum poposcerit, pro
solo Petro se Dominus rogasse testatur et ab eo ceteros uoluit confirmari."

rock through Peter has not failed, nor will it fail in ages to come, because the Lord Christ prayed for it (Luke 22:32)." [67]

Parallel to this development, the papal claim that the faith had always been preserved intact in the Roman church had been expressed for a long time by the quotation of Eph. 5:27 ("ut exhiberet sibi gloriosam ecclesiam non habentem maculam aut rugam aut aliquid huiusmodi") in a specified application to the Roman church.[68] The combination of Eph. 5:27 and Luke 22:32 provided the biblical warrant for the famous *sententia* 22 of Gregory VII's *Dictatus papae*: "Quod Romana ecclesia numquam erravit nec in perpetuum scriptura testante errabit." There may be more behind this sentence, however. As did Leo IX before him, Gregory VII read the assurance of the inerrant faith of the *ecclesia Romana* also in Matt. 16:18c. Following a tradition going back to Origen and Jerome, these popes understood the *portae inferi* in terms of the tongues of heretics which, according to Jesus' promise, would never prevail against the rock of Peter's faith. It is no surprise that Gregory VII, convinced of his own calling to organize the apocalyptic fight for the divine truth, took Luke 22:32 as a direct prediction of the papacy's teaching mission to the world of his day, particularly in relation to the situation in the East.[69] We should note, however, that even in the

---

[67] Leo IX (Humbert), *Epistola* 1 *ad Michaelem Constant. patriarcham* (*Acta et Scripta*, ed. C. Will, Leipzig, 1861, p. 81b): "Nam Romanae ecclesiae fides per Petrum super petram aedificata nec hactenus deficit, nec deficiet in saecula Christo eius domino rogante pro ea, ceu testatur sub ipsa passione sua: Ego rogavi pro te, Petre, etc. (Luke 22:32). Quo dicto demonstravit fidem fratrum vario defectu periclitandum, sed inconcussa et indeficiente fide Petri velut firmae anchorae subsidio fingendam et in fundamento universalis ecclesiae confirmandam." The other important text is the following (ibid., p. 68): "Taliter sancta Ecclesia super petram, id est Christum, et super Petrum vel Cepham filium Ioannis qui prius Simon dicebatur, aedificata, quia inferi portis, disputationibus scilicet haereticorum, quae vanos ad interitum introducunt, nullatenus foret superanda. Sic pollicetur ipsa veritas, per quam sunt vera, quaecumque sunt vera: Portae inferi non praevalebunt adversus eam (Matt. 16:18). Cuius promissionis effectum se precibus impetrasse a patre idem Filius protestatur, dicendo ad Petrum: Simon, ecce Satanas etc. (Luke 22:31f.) ... erit ergo quisquam tantae dementiae qui orationem illius, cuius velle est posse, audeat in aliquo vacuam putare? Nonne a sede principis apostolorum, Romana videlicet ecclesia, tam per eundem Petrum quam per successores suos, reprobata et convicta atque expugnata sunt omnium haereticorum commenta [conventa?], et fratrum corda in fide Petri, quae hactenus nec deficit nec usque in finem deficiet, sunt confirmata."

[68] See above, note 5. The references to Eph. 5:27 by Siricius (*PL* 13: 1156A) and Leo I (Tractatus 65, CCL 138A, p. 395, l. 10) do not yet show this specialization.

[69] Gregory VII, *Registrum* VII.II.31 *ad Henricum regem* (MGH *Epistolae selectae* II.2, ed. E. Caspar, 1923, p. 167, ll. 4-9): "Armenii etiam fere omnes a catholica fide oberrant, et pene universi orientales praestolantur, quid fides apostoli Petri inter diversas opiniones eorum decernat. Instat enim nostro tempore ut impleatur, quod pius Redemptor speciali gratia dignatus est apostolorum principi indicare ac praecipere dicens: Ego pro te rogavi, Petre etc. (Luke 22:32)." For Gregory's interpretation of Matt. 16:18c, see *Registrum* I.64 (ibid., p. 93)

formulation of the *Dictatus papae* the church for whose faith Christ prayed in the person of Peter remained a collective *ecclesia Romana*, not the person or the office of Peter's successor himself.

The personal accent came out more strongly when popes focused on the second part of the verse, the task of "strengthening the brothers." Combined with Matt. 16:18f. and John 21:15-17, this text could then reenforce the idea of a universal primacy exercised by the pope himself as Peter's successor. Leo I already employed the combination in order to suggest this application which became standard practice thereafter.[70] Leo also found other biblical expressions for the Petrine task of "strengthening the brothers." The Pauline *sollicitudo omnium ecclesiarum* of II Cor. 11:28 was one of them;[71] its constant repetition by later popes helped to emphasize the universal accent of Luke 22:32 as well: to strengthen the brothers meant the universal supervision of all bishops.

One can say that Innocent III fused both lines of papal interpretation, reading the task of "strengthening" specifically as part of the pope's universal teaching ministry.[72] At this point, he followed in the footsteps of Gregory VII. As Wilhelm Imkamp has shown, however, Innocent went one step further. He applied Luke 22:32 to himself personally — not as an expression of boundless self-confidence, but as a divine challenge and an awesome responsibility.[73] Nourished in the exegetical tradition, he read the verse in the context of Peter's denial and the theme of the "humble prelate." Innocent was aware of the canonical possibility of an erring pope (c.6 Dist.40 *Decreti Gratiani*). Nevertheless, Jesus' prayer rendered such a case unlikely in his opinion: God would hardly allow a pope to fall into doctrinal error when he prayed for his

---

and III.18 (ibid., p. 284). His prophetic consciousness and its biblical basis are convincingly discussed by Christian Schneider, *Prophetisches Sacerdotium und heilsgeschichtliches Regnum im Dialog 1073-1077*, Münsterische Mittelalterschriften, 9 (München, 1972).

[70] Leo I, *Sermo* 4.2f. (CCL 138, pp. 19f., ll. 68-104) with Matt. 16:18f. and Luke 22:32; 4.4 (ibid., p. 21, ll. 110-115) with Luke 22:32 and John 21:15-17; 83.2f. (CCL 138A, pp. 520f., ll. 26-63) with all three texts.

[71] The papal use of II Cor. 11:28 seems to begin with Siricius (384-399), *Epistola ad Himerium episc. Tarragonensem* (*PL* 13: 1138A); *Epistola 5 ad episcopos Africae* (*PL* 13: 1156A). On the development of the papal use of the term *sollicitudo* see Charles Pietri, *Roma Christiana*, vol. 2, Bibliothèque de l'École Française d'Athènes et de Rome, 224 (Rome, 1976), pp. 1518-1523.

[72] Innocent III, *Epistola 209 ad patriarcham Constant.* (*PL* 214: 760AB): "... ex hoc innuens manifeste quod successores ipsius a fide catholica nullo umquam tempore deviarent, sed revocarent magis alios et confirmarent, etiam hesitantes"; *De sacro altaris mysterio* I.8 (*PL* 217: 778CD): "Ad Petrum enim tamquam ad magistrum pertinet caeteros confirmare cuius fides in nulla tentatione defecit. Fides enim apostolicae sedis super firmam petram stabili soliditate firmata, nullis umquam errorum sordibus potuit inquinari; sed absque ruga manens et macula pro necessitate temporum a caeteris maculas detersit errorum."

[73] Imkamp, *Kirchenbild*, pp. 318-320.

faith spiritually in the person of Peter.[74] Here, it seems to me, the extension of the biblical text is finally focused on the successor of Peter himself.[75]

Another observation seems important to me. Innocent III enhanced his interpretation by introducing Heb. 5:7 ("exauditus est pro sua reverentia") into the exegesis of Luke 22:32: Christ prayed for the indefectibility of Peter's faith, and his prayers were always heard.[76] I have not found this combination in the earlier exegetical tradition. It may have been suggested by earlier commentaries on *III Sent.* dist. XVII c. 3, where the issue was discussed, "whether Christ's every prayer or wish was fulfilled," and where Luke 22:32 was quoted by Peter Lombard in a patristic argument about Matt. 26:39 taken from Hilary; another possibility might be *IV Sent.* dist. XX c. 3-4, where later commentators cited Luke 22:32 and Heb. 5:7 together in an argument about the validity of indulgences. It is also possible, of course, that Innocent added the Hebrews quotation himself. At any rate, I find it interesting that the combination began to appear in exegetical writings soon after him. Albertus Magnus used it in his commentary on Luke 22:32 where other traces of the papal interpretation can be found as well, including the new Innocentian accent on the person of the pope: why was Peter alone addressed? Because he was *principalis*, and from him Christ's consolation was to descend to others in proper order. To whom does the promise of a finally indefectible faith apply? To the See of Peter and to his successor.[77] The

---

[74] *Sermo 3 in consecratione pontificis* (*PL* 217: 665A): "Propter causam vero fornicationis Ecclesia Romana posset dimittere Romanum pontificem. Fornicationem non dico carnalem, sed spiritualem, quia non est carnale sed spirituale coniugium, id est propter infidelitatis errorem. ... Ego tamen facile non crediderim, ut Deus permitteret Romanum pontificem contra fidem errare, pro quo spiritualiter oravit in Petro: Ego, inquit, pro te rogavi, Petre, etc. (Luke 22:32)." Cf. ibid., col. 656D, 670B.

[75] This does not mean that Innocent regarded himself as "infallible" either as a person or as an office-holder. In an article published in 1976, Brian Tierney investigated the interpretation by the canonists of Innocent's Decretal "Majores" (*Liber Extra* III.42.3; Friedberg 2: 644), where Matt. 16:16 and Luke 22:32 are cited in support of the pope's right to judge all major cases in the church, especially those touching the faith: "A Scriptural Text in the Decretales and in St. Thomas: Canonistic Exegesis of Luke 22:32," *Studia Gratiana* 20 (1976) 363-377. Tierney concluded that such an interpretation cannot be found there. Rather, while the pope's binding jurisdiction in matters of faith was upheld, the concept of indefectibility and inerrancy in faith as derived from Luke 22:32 remained strictly confined to the church: "Ecclesia universalis non potest errare."

[76] *Sermo 2 in consecratione pontificis* (*PL* 217: 656C); *Sermo 3* (ibid., 662A).

[77] Albertus Magnus, *In Evangelium Lucae*, at 22:32 (*Opera Omnia*, ed. Borgnet, Tom. 23, p. 685a): "De primo dicit: Ait autem Dominus: Simon. Qui ipse principalis fuit: et ideo sibi dicitur, ut per ipsum haec confortatio ad alios ordinate derivetur. Ps. 132:2: Sicut unguentum etc. Ego autem: Quem pater in omnibus exaudit, Ad Heb. 5:7: Exauditus est pro sua reverentia; Ioan. 11:42: Ego sciebam quia semper me audis. Ut non finaliter deficiat fides tua. Hoc argumentum efficax est pro sede Petri et successore ipsius, quod fides eius non finaliter deficiat."

word "finaliter" is important here. Like the additional quotation of Nahum 1:15 ("non adjiciet ultra, ut pertranseat in Belial; universus interiit"), it reminds the reader that this faith still encounters temptation, testing, even possible denial on the part of Peter and his successor, but it will ultimately not be overcome. "Peter's fall was not final." [78] Consistent with this understanding, Albert did apply Luke 22:32 to the faith of the universal church elsewhere, and his interpretation of "strengthening the brothers" stressed in very traditional terms the personal lesson of Peter's denial for the apostle and all Christians, and the need for penance and humility. [79]

Bonaventure was equally aware of the combination of Luke 22:32 with Heb. 5:7, as his Commentary on the Sentences shows. [80] He did not use it, however, in his Commentary on Luke, although we find other elements of the papal interpretation echoed there: Peter was specially addressed in Luke 22:31f., because, as the first foundation stone, he had to be strong in the imminent trial as an example for all to ponder. Christ's prayer, therefore, meant first of all Peter himself as he faced his fall; but it could also refer to the *ecclesia Petri*. Bonaventure cited John 17:20 for this extension ("non pro eis autem rogo tantum"). He did not take up the accent on the person of the pope himself, although, similar to Albert, he introduced the notion of hierarchical order: Christ's prayer strengthens the church's principal members and through them the weak ones. [81]

Thomas Aquinas did not leave a full exposition of Luke 22:32 as part of his exegetical writings. Again, his *Scriptum super Sententiis* proves that he

---

[78] Ibid., p. 686b: "... non finalis fuit Petri casus." The term "finaliter" entered the exegetical tradition with Chrysostom's *Homily* 82.3 on Matt. 26 (*PG* 58: 741D; cf. above n. 54): "He did not say: that you may not deny, but that your faith may not fail, *hôste mê teleon apolesthai*." While Aquinas' quotation of this text in the *Catena Aurea* breaks off before the last clause, Hugh of St. Cher includes it: "Non dixit Dominus ut neges, sed ut non deficiat fides tua, ut non finaliter periret." *Postilla*, Tomus Sextus (Venice, 1732), f. 177vb. The term also appears in Lyra's *Postilla*, ad loc.: "Ego autem pro te rogavi ut non deficiat fides tua, scilicet finaliter."

[79] Ibid., p. 685b-686a. On the universal church: *IV Sent.* d.20 a.17 arg.4 (*Opera Omnia*, ed. Borgnet, Tom. 29, p. 850): "Ego rogavi etc. (Luke 22:32). hoc autem Petro dictum est in persona Ecclesiae: ergo Ecclesia universalis non errat...."

[80] Bonaventure, *IV Sent.*, d.20 p.2 a.1 q.2 (Quaracchi, 4: 532): "ita dictum est Petro (Luke 22:32): Ego pro te rogavi, etc.; constat quod hoc dictum est Petro in persona ecclesiae; sed Christus exauditus est in omnibus pro sua reverentia (Heb. 5:7), ergo et in isto. Et si hoc, ecclesia universalis non decipitur nec errat."

[81] Bonaventure, *Commentarius in Evangelium S. Lucae* XXII.42f. (Quaracchi, 7: 552): "... vel potest illud referri ad Ecclesiam Petri pro cuius fide rogavit Dominus secundum illud (John 17:20): Non pro eis rogo, etc. ... Ideo addit: Et tu aliquando conversus, confirma fratres tuos. ... Ex quo apparet quod Christus ipse orando et interpellando confirmat principalia membra.... Sed per principalia confirmat infirma." Cf. ibid., 9.34, p. 227: "Hinc est quod Petrus est vocatus et ei concessum est, ut de Ecclesia eius numquam deficiat vera fides, infra (Luke 22:32)."

knew of the Innocentian addition of Heb. 5:7 to the interpretation of the verse.[82] Other scattered instances make clear that he was certainly open for the papal accents in his exegesis. In a curious passage of his Commentary on Matthew at 16:18c, which is strongly reminiscent of Leo IX and Gregory VII, he first interpreted the *portae inferi* as "heretics, tyrants, demons" and then went on to extol the unstained faith of the *ecclesia Romana*, the true *ecclesia Petri*, in contrast to the heretical depravity of the East: "In Constantinople, there were heretics, and the labor of the apostles was lost. Only Peter's church remained intact. Therefore, (Jesus) said: I have prayed for you, Peter, that your faith may not fail (Luke 22:32). This applies not only to the church of Peter but to Peter's faith and the entire Western church. Hence, I believe that Western Christians owe greater reverence to Peter than to other apostles."[83] The unusual polemic may well reflect Thomas' use of materials on the primacy of Rome which Nicholas of Durazzo had forged and compiled for the second part of his *Libellus de fide Trinitatis* as a weapon against the Greeks, and which had come to Thomas' attention in 1263. In fact, Thomas included in his *Catena Aurea* at Matt. 16:18 a section of this "source" under the name of Cyril of Alexandria which closely resembles our text, including the reference to Luke 22:32.[84] It is well known, of course, that Thomas made use of Innocent's appropriation of the Lucan verse in the Decretal "Majores" when he came to the response of a. 10 of his *Summa Theologiae* II-II, q. 1;[85] his reference to the pope as the proper

[82] Aquinas, *Scriptum super Sententiis* IV dist.20 a.3, s.c. (ed. M. F. Moos, Paris, 1947, p. 1024, no. 70).

[83] Aquinas, *Super Matthaeum*, no. 1385 (ed. A. Cai, p. 212): "Et qui sunt portae inferi? Haeretici: quia sicut per portam intratur in domum, sic per istos intratur in infernum. Item tyranni, daemones, peccata. Et quamvis aliae Ecclesiae vituperari possint per haereticos, Ecclesia tamen Romana non fuit ab haereticis depravata, quia supra petram erat fundata. Unde in Constantinopoli fuerunt haeretici, et labor Apostolorum amissus erat; sola Petri Ecclesia inviolata permansit. Unde Luc. XXII.32: Ego rogavi pro te, Petre, ut non deficiat fides tua. Et hoc non solum refertur ad Ecclesiam Petri, sed ad fidem Petri, et ad totam occidentalem Ecclesiam. Unde credo, quod occidentales maiorem reverentiam debent Petro quam aliis Apostolis." With Eschmann (*MedS* 18 [1956] 232-240), and Shooner (*Bulletin Thomiste* 10 [1957-1959] 153-157), I would argue for a late dating of the Matthew lectures.

[84] Aquinas, *Catena Aurea* I (ed. A. Guarienti, p. 252): "Cyrillus in Lib. thesauri. Secundum autem hanc Domini promissionem [Luke 22:32] Ecclesia Apostolica Petri ab omni seductione haereticaque circumventione manet immaculata, super omnes praepositos et Episcopos, et super omnes primates Ecclesiarum et populorum in suis Pontificibus, in fide plenissima et auctoritate Petri. Et cum aliae Ecclesiae quorumdam errore sint verecundatae, stabilita inquassabiliter ipsa sola regnat, silentium imponens et omnium obturans ora haereticorum...." See the modern printing of the *Liber de Fide* in vol. 40 of the Leonine edition of Thomas' works (Rome, 1969), no. 98, ll. 33-41, p. A 145ᵇ. According to the Preface (p. A 16), a source for this piece has not been found.

[85] The reference to Luke 22:32 in connection with a canonical authority strongly suggests that Thomas had Innocent's Decretal "Majores" in mind, even though his textual allusion

authority for drawing up new symbols *ad vitandum insurgentes errores* may indicate that Thomas' mind was on the East here also. Even in this particular text, however, there is no clear indication that Thomas endorsed Innocent's special application of Luke 22:32 to the pope personally. In the very next article of the same question, quoting the verse again, he was already returning to the traditional framework of the test and trial of Peter's faith in the prelates of the church and the application of the notion of inerrancy to the church universal.[86] Even beyond his alignment with the common exegetical tradition at this point, however, Thomas was undoubtedly at ease with the different scope of the older tradition. The texts from Bede, Theophylactus, Cyril, Chrysostom, and Ambrose which he assembled in his *Catena Aurea* at Luke 22:32 clearly ensured the perpetuation of a strongly tropological reading of the verse in the exegetical literature of the future, even though at least some consideration could now be given to the accents of a special papal understanding as well.[87]

4.

Again, the situation seems not much different when we come to John 21:15-17. Modern exegetes regard these verses as part of an appendix to the Fourth Gospel. Whatever the source, they recognize, however, that these words envisage for Peter a leadership role in the early Christian community which was at least open toward the concept of a functional Petrine primacy.[88] It is surprising to discover that, while the primatial accent was not totally absent, the medieval exegetical tradition normally discussed the passage with other contexts in mind.

---

seems to be to Gratian's Dist. XVII c.5 (Friedberg, p. 52). See Tierney, "A Scriptural Text," p. 364. For a cautious interpretation of article 10, see Yves Congar, "Saint Thomas Aquinas and the Infallibility of the Papal Magisterium: Summa Theologiae II-II q.1 a.10," *The Thomist* 38 (1974) 81-105.

[86] II-II q.2 a.6 ad 3: "... humana cognitio non fit regula fidei, sed veritas divina. A qua si aliqui majorum deficiant, non praejudicat fidei simplicium qui eos rectam fidem habere credunt, nisi pertinaciter eorum erroribus in particulari adhaereant contra universalis ecclesiae fidem, quae non potest deficere, Domino dicente: Ego pro te rogavi, Petre, ut non deficiat fides tua (Luke 22:32)."

[87] Nicholas of Lyra's comment on the verse (*Postilla*, vol. 4, Strassburg, 1492, ad loc.) illustrates the new balance: "ut non deficiat fides tua, scilicet finaliter. Non enim rogavit quod Petrus non caderet, sed ut in casu non remaneret. Ideo sequitur: Et tu aliquando conversus, scilicet de peccato ad gratiam, confirma fratres tuos. Hoc dicitur ei quia ecclesia erat sibi committenda ut habetur Io. ultimo (21:15-17).... Ex hoc etiam patet fidem non deficere usque ad finem mundi, potissime in ecclesia Romana quae a Petro post Christum fundata est."

[88] See *Peter in the New Testament: A Collaborative Assessment by Protestant and Roman Catholic Scholars*, ed. Raymond E. Brown et al. (Minneapolis and New York, 1973), pp. 195-212.

Two authors clearly dominated the scene: Augustine and Bede. Augustine's *Tractatus* 123 *in Iohannem*, together with several of his sermons (253, 295, 296, and 299), seems to have provided the main model of interpretation; it was frequently copied or excerpted. An important early medieval commentary which circulated under the name of Bede, for example, simply reproduced *Tractatus* 123 sentence by sentence at John 21:15-17.[89] Bede's authentic *Homilia* 15 *in ss. Petrum et Paulum* supplied the second key text. In Carolingian times, Alcuin's Commentary followed Bede to the letter; sermon collections such as Raban's Homiliary and Smaragdus' Commentary on the *Liber Comitis* incorporated sizeable sections together with excerpts from Augustine, when they dealt with our text.[90] The *Glossa ordinaria* still followed this trend and restricted its material to these two sources. Thomas Aquinas' selection for his *Catena Aurea* added a third key text, the Latin translation of John Chrysostom's Homily 88 on the Gospel of John, which was also cited by Hugh of St. Cher and Bonaventure. Moreover, Thomas used three paragraphs from Theophylactus; his "Alcuin" quotation came from Bede.[91]

Both Augustine and Bede interpreted John 21:15-17 in a moral, tropological vein as the text itself seemed to demand: the Lord certainly knew in advance the answer to his questions. He did not ask even for Peter's sake but for the benefit of others. Thus, the short exchange was meant to teach the apostles and us the requirements of true discipleship. Augustine emphasized the connection with Peter's denial: "To the threefold denial corresponds the threefold confession, lest the tongue serve love less than fear."[92] We note again Augustine's fascination with the contrast between Peter the denier and Peter the lover, Peter's fear and love, weakness and strength. These contrasts, however, are no longer paradoxical; rather, they reflect a "before" and an "after," the turning point being Christ's death and resurrection. In this connection, Augustine returned time and again to Peter's promise before the

---

[89] Augustine, *Tractatus in Iohannem* 123.4-5 (CCL 36, pp. 677-679); the sermons are printed in *PL* 38. For the Ps.-Bede text, see *PL* 92: 929f.

[90] Bede, *Homilia* 15 *in ss. Petrum et Paulum* (*PL* 94: 214D-219B); Alcuin, *Commentarius in Iohannem* VIII, c. 44-45 (*PL* 100: 1000D-1002D); Rabanus, *Homilia* 108 (*PL* 110: 348f.); Smaragdus, *Collectiones* (*PL* 102: 387-389).

[91] Thomas Aquinas, *Catena Aurea* II (ed. A. Guarienti, pp. 590-591). The Chrysostom homily is printed in *PG* 59: 477D-480.

[92] *Tractatus in Iohannem* 123.5 (CCL 36, p. 678, ll. 4-7): "Redditur negationi trinae trina confessio, ne minus amori lingua serviat quam timori." Cf. *Sermo* 253.1 (*PL* 38: 1180A): "impleatur numerus dilectionis, ut deleat numerum negationis"; or, with a reference to Matt. 16:19, *Sermo* 295.4 (*PL* 38: 1350C): "Ter vincat in amore confessio, quia ter victa est in timore praesumptio. Solvendum est ter quod ligaveras ter"; also *Sermo* 299.7 (*PL* 38: 1372D): "Ter amor confessus est, ter timor damnatus est."

passion: "animam meam pro te ponam" (John 13:37). Here Peter, ignorant, presumptious, fearful, and self-centered, had the divine order backward: he promised what he could not deliver. The master had to die for the servant before the servant could die for him.[93] Peter tried to prevent Jesus from dying because he was himself still afraid of death, and out of this fear denied his Lord. But now that Christ had died and was alive again, Peter could die also, in order to follow Christ and inherit life.[94] One can see that Augustine understood John 21:15-17 primarily from the vantage point of v. 18, the prediction of Peter's martyrdom. "Feed my sheep" meant first of all loving the flock to the point of giving one's life for it. The imperative was a challenge to Peter to prove his love: "Feed my sheep! I commend to you my sheep. Which sheep? Those whom I bought with my blood. I died for them. You love me? Die for them!"[95] Thus, the central lesson of John 21:15-17 concerned the requirement of love, ultimate love, as the proof of true discipleship, Peter being the outstanding example. All that was asked was love, all that was answered was love, and loving Christ meant suffering for him. This, of course, was a message for all Christians. Augustine's sermons for the feast of Peter and Paul made this point emphatically: the martyrs' love of the apostles is an example and an encouragement for us all.[96]

Bede recognized the same message, although he switched the center of interpretation away from v. 18. What we are being taught in John 21:15-17, is the lesson of perfect love. Through his threefold question the Lord teaches us to love God with all our heart, mind, and strength (Matt. 22:37; cf. Deut. 6:5); through his command to feed the sheep and his prediction of Peter's passion he adds the love of neighbor as its true test.[97] Bede's interpretation included some details which made their way into numerous later commentaries. One was the insistence on a deeper sense behind the name used here for Peter: "Simon Iohannis." Jerome's and Isidore's etymologizing opened

[93] *Sermo* 296.1 (*PL* 38: 1353AB): "Plus promiserat quam poterat. ... Animam meam, inquit, pro te ponam (John 13:37). Hoc pro servo Dominus erat facturus, non servus pro Domino"; cf. *Tractatus in Iohannem* 123.4 (CCL 36, p. 677, ll. 17-27); *Sermo* 299.7 (*PL* 38: 1372D).

[94] *Tractatus in Iohannem* 123.4 (CCL 36, p. 677, ll. 27-37); *Sermo* 253.3 (*PL* 38: 1180CD); *Sermo* 296.2 (*PL* 38: 1333B-D); *Sermo* 297.1 (*PL* 38: 1359C).

[95] *Sermo* 296.3 (*PL* 38: 1334C): "Pasce oves meas, commendo tibi oves meas. Quas oves? Quas emi sanguine meo. Mortuus sum pro eis. Amas me? Morere pro eis!"; cf. *Tractatus in Iohannem* 123.5 (CCL 36, p. 679, ll. 65-69); *Sermo* 253.2 (*PL* 38: 1180AB).

[96] *Sermo* 296.2 (*PL* 38: 1334AB): "Non aliud quam Amas interrogatur; non aliud quam Amo respondetur"; cf. *Sermo* 299.7 (*PL* 38: 1372D-1373A): "Et quia amabat, indicatur ei passio eius. Hoc enim erat amare, usque ad passionem per Christi amorem pervenire." Cf. *Sermo* 295.8 (*PL* 38: 1352C).

[97] Bede, *Homilia* 15 (*PL* 94: 214D); cf. *In Canticum Canticorum expositio* IV.5 (*PL* 91: 1156C).

its meaning: "Simon oboediens, Iohannes dicitur Dei gratia"; our true love of God is a gift of grace (Rom. 5:5).[98] Bede also continued Augustine's psychological interest in the details of the passage. "Do you love me more than these?" Mindful of his former experience with self-confidence, Peter did not dare to answer this question, leaving the judgment to God: "Lord, you know." Bede found here a special lesson of Christian humility: We all should be less sure of ourselves and less judgmental of the motives of others.[99]

On the whole, medieval exegetes enriched, but did not alter the interpretive thrust of Augustine's and Bede's tropology. Rabanus could correct Augustine by maintaining that *diligis* and *amas* differed in meaning. Bernard of Clairvaux could specify the threefold love more precisely as loving "dulciter, prudenter, fortiter."[100] But the majority was content with repeating or paraphrasing those main sources when they discussed the general lesson of love in our passage.

The theme of "feeding the sheep," however, led the interpreter into yet another context. The patristic tradition, including Augustine and Bede, saw the Peter of John 21:15-17 also as *figura* of all shepherds and pastors, i.e., all prelates in the church. Numerous biblical associations came to mind with the mention of "flock," "feeding," and "sheep": the prophetic words against the false shepherds of Israel (Ezek. 34); the good shepherd of John 10:1-18; elders and bishops as shepherds of their flock (Acts 20:28); and especially I Peter 5:1-4, the classical New Testament admonition to church leaders to feed the flock. Augustine saw the context for John 21:15-17 not only in vv. 18-21, but also in the earlier part of the chapter. His *Sermons* 248-252 *de duabus piscationibus* compared John 21:1-14 with Luke 5:1-11 under the aspect of the apostolic mission: "fishing" meant the preaching of the servants of the word. Thus, in *Sermo* 296 Augustine emphasized that the command to feed the sheep is given "to all of us who minister to you with word and sacrament." All the apostles heard what Peter heard and followed the

---

[98] *Homilia* 15 (*PL* 94: 215ʙ). The source of this etymology is Jerome (e.g., *PL* 26: 121) and Isidore, *Etymologiae* vii.9 (*PL* 82: 287).

[99] *Homilia* 15 (*PL* 94: 215c): "Scio quidem quia ipse te, ut tu melius nosti, integro corde diligo; quantum vero te alii diligant, mihi quidem ignotum, sed tibi omnia sunt nota. Cujus cautela responsionis nostrae profecto est institutio locutionis simul et cogitationis, ut videlicet eius exemplo discamus minus de nostrae conscientiae puritate praesumere, minus temere de fraternae conscientiae occultis judicare, in dubiis maxime rebus, et quae qua intentione vel necessitate gerantur. inspicere nequimus...." The psychological aspects of the passage were also a main concern of the Chrysostom text introduced later.

[100] See Bernard of Clairvaux, *Sermo* 29 *de triplici dilectione Dei* (*PL* 183: 620); Rabanus, *Homilia* 108 (*PL* 110: 349): "dilectio" is superior to "amor". This is the reason why Peter was saddened; Jesus used "amor," not "dilectio," in his third question. The same text appears in Smaragdus (*PL* 102: 389).

example of his sacrificial love, handing on the challenge to all prelates.[101] Augustine drew heavily on I Peter 5:1-4 at this point. In *Tractatus* 123 he insisted on the pronoun: "Feed my sheep" — not yours! False shepherds seek their own gain (II Tim. 3:1-5); true pastors love Christ's flock to the end.[102] When one asks the question: Was Peter, as a prelate today, fit to receive the care of the sheep? The answer is: Christ "looks for the fitness of the servant in his martyrdom." [103]

In the second part of his Homily, Bede took up the same themes. One of his first concerns was the close connection between John 21:15-17 and Luke 22:32: "To feed the sheep of Christ means to strengthen the faithful lest they fall away from the faith; it means to strive constantly that they may advance in their faith." [104] In a long section on "feed my sheep" Bede echoed Augustine. Nevertheless, he spelled out three modes of feeding: prelates owe their subjects the example of virtue, the proclamation of the word, and material support in their earthly needs.[105] Later authors sometimes modified this "triplex edulium"; one fairly common list specified *vita, doctrina, oratio* as its elements.[106] Another clarification in which medieval exegetes were interested concerned the different designations for the flock: *agnos-agnos-oves*. A frequent explanation in the thirteenth century spoke of "beginners," "advanced," and "perfect" Christians.[107] But in the twelfth century, Rupert of

---

[101] Augustine, *Sermo* 296.1 (*PL* 38: 1353A): "Admonuit nos omnes, qui vobis verbum et sacramentum Domini ministramus, pascere oves suas"; cf. ibid. 5 and 11 (*PL* 38: 1354D and 1358C); *Tractatus in Iohannem* 123.5 (CCL 36, p. 679, ll. 62-64).

[102] *Tractatus in Iohannem* 123.5 (CCL 36, pp. 678f., ll. 8-62); cf. *Sermo* 295.5 (*PL* 38: 1350Df.).

[103] The argument about Peter's "fitness" occurs in *Sermo* 296.4 (*PL* 38: 1354BC): "Commendat oves idoneo an minus idoneo? ... idoneitatem servi in passione sanguinis quaerit."

[104] Bede, *Homilia* 15 (*PL* 94: 216D-217A): "Pascere ergo oves Christi est credentes Christo, ne a fide deficiant, confirmare, et ut in fide magis magisque proficiant instanter operam dare." Paschasius Radbertus, in the hermeneutical preface to his *Commentary on Matthew*, argued that Luke 22:32 and John 21:15-17 had the same *sensus*, even though the *superficies litterae* appears to be so different: *Praefatio* (CCCM 56, p. 8, ll. 216-221).

[105] *Homilia* 15 (*PL* 94: 277A): "Nam et terrena subsidia necesse est, ut subditis rector ne desint diligenter praevideat, et exempla virtutis simul cum verbo praedicationis eisdem sollicitus impendat." The same triad appears, e.g., in the *Glossa ordinaria* and in Bonaventure's *Commentary*. Thomas Aquinas and Nicholas of Lyra have *doctrinae* (Lyra: *veritatis*) *verbum, vitae exemplum, temporale subsidium*.

[106] Cf. a passage in a commentary on Stephen of Muret's *Sentences* from the eleventh century (CCCM 8, *Scriptores ordinis Grandimontensis*, ed. Io. Becquet, 1968, p. 471, ll. 265-270): "... quasi diceret: Pasce uita, pasce doctrina, pasce oratione sancta; id est exemplo, documento, orationisque adiumento." Hugh of St. Cher specified "exemplum, verbum, orationis suffragium."

[107] E.g., Thomas Aquinas, *Lectura super Iohannem*, no. 2625 (ed. A. Cai, p. 483a): "in Ecclesia sunt tria genera hominum, scilicet incipientium, proficientium, et perfectorum." Nicholas of Lyra repeated this explanation.

Deutz had distinguished little and more mature lambs from the sheep "who can rule the flock of lambs," illustrating the numerical relation of these groups by referring to the mystery of the 153 fish in John 21:12: 100 + 50 + 3; many subjects; far fewer, but worthier prelates.[108] Rupert borrowed the basic idea from a well-known homily of Gregory I which had as its text, not John 21:15-17, but the preceding pericope. Gregory already suggested the parallel between the "actions" of John 21:1-14 and the "words" of vv. 15-17: what was later explained in words, was signified in the prior action of the great catch of fish.[109] Both scenes concerned the prelates of the church.

With all of this wide-ranging tropology, little room was left, it seems, for the consideration of Peter's special leadership according to the mandate of John 21:15-17. Augustine pointed primarily to Peter's leadership in martyr-dom; Peter would be Christ's foremost follower in the manner of his death, and the apostles would follow him as disciples follow a teacher. Bede's Homily shows traces of a widespread general formula which one can find in all kinds of medieval texts and which speaks of Peter being "entrusted with the care of the whole church." [110] In the framework of an exegetical treat-ment, Gregory I's above-mentioned homily expressed it succinctly: "Ipsi quippe sancta ecclesia est commissa, ipsi specialiter dicitur: Simon Iohannis, diligis me? Pasce oves meas." Reinterpreting the Augustinian contrast between "before" and "after," Gregory distinguished here and elsewhere the time before the bestowal of the Holy Spirit from the time after. A weak Peter denied Christ because "the Spirit was not yet given" (John 7:39); the Peter who, with all the apostles, had received the Spirit, was ready not only to die

---

[108] Rupert of Deutz, *Commentaria in Iohannis Evangelium* XIV (CCCM 9, 1969, p. 785, ll. 1192-1215): "Nam sicut tracto reti in terram centum quinquaginta tres pisces distincte numerati sunt, ita et nunc in pastorali curae distinctione primo centum agnos, deinde quinquaginta agnos, tandemque, cum dicit: 'Pasce oves meas', tres subaudire operae pretium est, ut ita sint in pascuis Simonis Petri agni pariter et oues centum quinquaginta tres sicut in reti quod ille traxit in terram totidem fuere pisces."

[109] Gregory I, *Homiliae in Evangelia* II.24 (*PL* 76: 1185D-1186A): "Jam credo quod vestra charitas advertat quid est quod Petrus rete ad terram trahit? Ipsi quippe sancta Ecclesia est commissa, ipsi specialiter dicitur: Simon Johannis, amas me? Pasce oves meas (John 21:16 f.). Quod ergo postmodum aperitur in voce, hoc nunc signatur in opere." This text is frequently quoted, especially the sentence on Peter's special commission: cf. Rabanus, *Homilia* 10 (*PL* 110: 115); Alcuin, *Commentary on John*, at 21:11 (*PL* 100: 996 f.); Haymo of Halberstadt, *Homilia* 76 (*PL* 118: 477B); Rupert of Deutz, *Liber de divinis officiis* VIII.9 (CCCM 7, ed. R. Haacke, 1967, p. 284, ll. 989-997).

[110] *Tractatus in Iohannem* 124.1 (ll. 19-22): "Cur enim dicitur Petro: Sequere me, nec dicitur ceteris qui simul aderant? Et profecto eum sicut magistrum discipuli sequebantur. Sed si ad passionem intelligendum est, numquid solus pro Christiana ueritate passus est Petrus?" Bede, *Homilia* 15 (*PL* 94: 216D): "Provida dispensatione tertio confitenti amorem, tertio aeque pascendas suas oves commendat, quia decebat ut quoties in pastoris fide titubaverat, toties cum renovata fide pastoris membra quoque ejusdem pastoris jubeatur curare."

but also to exercise the authority of the leader and shepherd which was announced to him in Matt. 16:18f.[111] This "historical" vision of Peter, "restored to the leadership of his prior dignity," [112] or, in Gregorian terms, revived by the grace of the Spirit and specially charged with the care of the church after Easter, stands behind many allusions to John 21:15-17 in medieval sources. Sometimes we barely notice it, sometimes it is developed into a full vision of the divinely intended order of the church.[113] In the exegetical literature, such a vision might have led to a primatial reading of the passage. In reality, this step was rarely taken.[114] Commentators would at best mention the *cura totius gregis* as a personal prerogative of Peter but would immediately extend the application to all prelates of the church.[115]

[111] Cf. *Moralia in Job* (*PL* 76: 33 f.); Ps.-Gregory, *In primum Regum expositiones* v.30 (*PL* 79: 466D-467A).

[112] Alcuin, *Epistola* 36 *ad Arnonem* (*PL* 100: 195CD): "(Petrus) quem Christus post resurrectionem pietatis intuitu trina dilectionis suae professione ad pristinae dignitatis principatum revocavit...."

[113] Bede himself offers a statement of this kind in his *Commentary* on I Peter 5:2 (*PL* 93: 64D): "Sicut Dominus beato Petro totius gregis eius, id est ecclesiae, curam habere iussit, ita ipse Petrus sequentibus ecclesiae pastoribus iure mandat ut eum quisque qui secutus est gregem Dei sollicita gubernatione tutetur." A particularly full statement, not from an exegetical source, is the following from Rupert of Deutz' *De operibus Spiritus Sancti* II.28 (CCCM 24, ed. R. Haacke, 1972, p. 1901, ll. 1533-1550): "Princeps quippe apostolorum Petrus destinatus fuerat, et huic specialiter magna post Christum danda potestas uel iam data erat, dicente Christo Filio Dei uiui, quem confessus fuerat: Beatus es, etc. (Matt. 16:17-19). Item: Simon Iohannis, diligis me plus his? Pasce agnos meos. Pasce oues meas. Tali et tanta praeeunte evangelicae veritatis auctoritate christianissimi imperatores post multa tempora, omnesque ecclesiarum principes hoc censuerunt et lege perpetua firmauerunt, ut sicut imperatori omnes praefecti uel iudices, sic beato Petro et secundum dignitatem eius excellenti Romano pontifici ceteri subiecti sint ecclesiarum pontifices. Magnus honor, grandis celsitudo."

[114] I found one such text, again not from an exegetical source, in Hugo of Rouen's (d. 1164) *Tractatus de memoria* II.5 (*PL* 192: 1310AB): "Ibi Petrus petra factus supereinituit, sed in passione Domini negando fractus corruit; mox vero, respiciente Domino, poenituit et Petrus fieri iterum reformatus lacrymando promeruit, et in Spiritu Sancto surrexit; qui ter negaverat, tertio est interrogatus Domino dicente: Petre, amas me? Domine, inquit, tu scis quia amo te, et amoris merito qui est ex Spiritu Sancto dixit ei cujus sunt omnia: Pasce agnos meos, pasce oves meas. Ecce iterum Petrus Ecclesiae Christi praeficitur. In uno Petro praesens Ecclesia tota colligitur. Ea propter Petri successores Romani Pontifices potestate praeeminenti ex virtute Christi in unitate Spiritus Sancti Catholicam tenent Ecclesiam, docent et ordinant...." A quotation of Luke 22:32 concludes the paragraph.

[115] Bruno of Segni's *Commentary on the Gospel of John* may serve as an example (*PL* 165: 600A-D). Bruno interpreted the lambs and sheep as subordinates and prelates over whom Peter has the pastoral oversight, but he did not draw the connection to the papal office: "Prius agnos, deinde oves ei commisit; quia non solum pastorem, sed pastorum pastorem eum constituit. Pascit ergo Petrus agnos, pascit et oves; pascit filios, pascit et matres; regit et subditos et praelatos. Omnium igitur pastor est quia praeter agnos et oves in ecclesia nihil est. Nihil, inquam, quod suis pastoribus Dominus commiserit...." In his *Commentary on Matthew*, at 10:10 (*PL* 165: 159), Bruno explained the apostles' mission "without a staff" as reflecting the pre-Easter situation: the Spirit was not yet given; their real mission started with Matt. 28:18-20 and John 21:15-17.

This reluctance is doubly surprising as the Augustinian tradition itself contained some hints in the direction of a special Petrine primacy. In *Sermo* 295.4, Augustine qualified the statement that in Peter all apostles were addressed by noting: "When Christ speaks to one only, he commends unity; to Peter in the first place, since Peter is first among the apostles." [116] The remark certainly invited a primatial reading. Close inspection reveals that it paraphrased the Cyprianic language of *De Unitate* c. 4. Cyprian, of course, understood the biblical Peter as representative of the unified episcopate, not of the bishop of Rome. But the potential of applying his formulations to the See of Rome exclusively was present, as we saw in the discussion of Matt. 16:18f. Augustine's *Tractatus* 123 contained another hint with primatial potential. Christ, Augustine maintained, expects a valiant fight for truth against sin especially from the pastors to whom he committed his sheep "to be fed, that is, to be taught and ruled." [117] Bede included this clause in his Homily 15 but applied it to Peter alone: "After having committed his sheep to Peter to be fed, that is, to be taught and ruled, Christ said...." [118] In this form, it often appeared when Bede was quoted.

The clues were not picked up. This time, even the thirteenth century brought no change. Albertus Magnus' extensive treatment of our passage in the Commentary on the Gospel of John[119] described Peter as "now firm like a rock, not squirming at the voice of a maid" (p. 711b), and understood the scene clearly as a conferral of the *officium curae pastoralis* which involved a *collatio potestatis* (p. 710a). But the application remained strictly confined to the prelates of the church in general. Albert did not pursue the primatial potential of the passage at any point; he simply organized his exposition around the issues discussed in the tradition. Bonaventure's *Commentary on the Fourth Gospel* presents a similar picture.[120] In Bonaventure's exegetical comments properly speaking there is no mention of any prerogative of Peter; the influence of Augustine's spiritual agenda seems all-pervasive. For Bona-

---

[116] Augustine, *Sermo* 295.4 (*PL* 38: 1550c): "Merito etiam post resurrectionem Dominus ipsi Petro oves suas commendavit pascendas. Non enim inter discipulos solus meruit pascere dominicas oves; sed quando Christus ad unum loquitur, unitas commendatur; et Petro primitus quia in Apostolis Petrus est primus."

[117] *Tractatus in Iohannem* 123.5 (cccl 36, p. 680, ll. 98-101): "... quanto magis debent usque ad mortem pro ueritate certare et usque ad sanguinem aduersus peccatum, quibus oues ipsas pascendas, hoc est, docendas regendasque, committit."

[118] Bede, *Homilia* 15 (*PL* 94: 217d): "Unde nunc ipse postquam pascendas oves suas Petro, hoc est, plebes docendas gubernandasque commisit, subsequenter addidit...."

[119] Albertus Magnus, *Enarrationes in Ioannem* (*Opera omnia*, ed. Borgnet, Tom. 24; Paris, 1890, pp. 710a-712b).

[120] Bonaventure, *Commentarius in Ioannem* xxi.30-37 (*Opera*, Quaracchi; vol. 6 [1893], pp. 524b-526b); cf. also his *Collationes in Ioannem* (ibid., pp. 624a-625b).

venture, love was the theme of the section: first, the confirmation of Peter's love (vv. 15-17), and then, the announcement of its ultimate test (vv. 18-19) (p. 524b). Like Augustine, Bonaventure paid special attention to the psychological elements of the exchange. He also added a number of *quaestiones*. Most of them raised traditional issues and received traditional answers: why did the Lord ask about the love of others when Peter could not know? Why was the same question asked three times? Why the difference between lambs and sheep? The first *quaestio* would have presented an opportunity to affirm the Petrine primacy and move on to the pope: Why was Peter alone asked about his love? (p. 526a). Bonaventure had two replies. The first pointed clearly to Peter's privilege: "To him among the others was the care of the flock to be specially committed." Bonaventure added Chrysostom's description of the personal privilege of Peter which we will find quoted elsewhere in the thirteenth century: "Eximius apostolorum erat Petrus, et os apostolorum, et vertex collegii." [121] But any possible extension to the papal office was passed over in favor a second answer: Peter needed the personal address more than others because his denial made him feel inferior and less worthy than they.

Thomas Aquinas recognized that, exegetically, John 21:15-17 must be interpreted as a scene about Peter. In his *Lectura super Iohannem* he distinguished the preceding section (vv. 1-14) with its focus on all apostles, from two special sections, one about Peter (vv. 15-19), and one about John (vv. 20-23).[122] He also used Chrysostom's phrase in a side remark about the congruity of Christ commending the flock to Peter, not to someone else (no. 2623). But throughout the exposition the Peter of our verses was *figura praelatorum* in general for Thomas, not the model of a pope. Again, the list of issues to be discussed was provided by Augustine and Bede, though Thomas could raise the question of the difference between "diligo" and "amo" (no. 2622) and draw on other traditions. Aristotle's *Politics*, for example, suggested the argument about "diligis me plus his?" A leader must be "more excellent" than his subjects, according to the Philosopher. But in

---

[121] Ibid., p. 526a: "Responsio una est, quia sibi erat cura gregis specialiter committenda inter alios, ideo ab eo specialiter de dilectione quaeritur. Unde Chrysostomus: Eximius Apostolorum erat Petrus, et os discipulorum, et vertex collegii; propterea, alios praeteriens et transcurrens huic de talibus loquitur." Both answers in a similar form are also found in Hugh of St. Cher's *Postilla, Tomus Sextus* (Venice, 1732), fol. 398[vb]: "Et nota quod specialiter loquitur Petro soli, alios praeteriens. Cur hoc? Respondemus: Eximius apostolorum erat Petrus, et os discipulorum, et vertex collegii. Ideo et Paulus ascendit videre Petrum prae aliis (Gal. 1:18 f.). Item in hoc primo eum alloquitur et interrogat, dat ei fiduciam de negatione dimissa, et ostendit quoniam oportet eum audire de reliquo."

[122] Thomas Aquinas, *Lectura super Iohannem*, Lectio III.1-4, on John 21 (ed. R. Cai; Torino, 1952, pp. 481a-483b), nos. 2614-2627.

the light of the Lord's question and its difficulty, it is sufficient in the election of a prelate to use one's best human judgment to determine the fitness of a candidate (no. 2619f.). What is missing in Thomas' elaborate exegesis is any bridge to a primatial or papal interpretation. That this omission was not universal, may be demonstrated by a glance at Nicholas of Lyra.[123] In his exposition of John 21:15-17, Nicholas followed Aquinas in many details, including the argument about "diligis me plus his?" for which he now cited appropriate texts from canon law. He also divided the passage in the same manner as Thomas: vv. 15-19 contain the Lord's special message to Peter, vv. 20-23 the message to John. In the *argumentum* of the Peter section, however, Nicholas did allude to the papal interpretation: "primo committitur Petro super ecclesiam universalem regiminis officium," although the accent shifted immediately to the requirements for the *pastorale officium* of all prelates.[124]

Where, then, did the specialization of John 21:15-17 for the primatial argument have its place? Undoubtedly, it had a long history in the writings of popes and curial theologians. The letter of the Roman clergy to Carthage after the martyrdom of Pope Fabian in 250 cited John 21:15-17 together with Ezek. 34:3f. and John 10:11f. as biblical warrant for the task of their shared leadership in the Roman Church, "keeping the flock in the place of the pastors." [125] But the passage may have been quoted among the "cetera uel superba uel ad rem non pertinentia" with which Pope Stephen I, in his lost letter of 256 to the African bishops, justified his special primatial claims, according to Cyprian and Firmilian of Caesarea.[126] Leo I definitely included John 21:15-17 in his biblical argument for Petrine primacy and its extension to the living Peter in the See of Rome. We saw that he was the first to use the triad of Matt. 16:18f., Luke 22:32, and John 21:15-17 as primatial texts. He also could pair John 21 individually with Matt. 16 to argue that the gift of the keys and the care of the sheepfold placed Peter above the other apostles, or with Luke 22 to argue that, acting in and through the pope and strengthening the latter with his words and prayers, Peter was carrying out both the mandate of the passion night and the commission of John

---

[123] Nicholas of Lyra, *Postilla*, vol. 4 (Strassburg, 1492), ad loc.

[124] Ibid.: "Circa primum sciendum quod Christus committendo Petro pastorale officium ipsum ter examinavit de dilectione, qua pastores ecclesiae debent Deum prae ceteris hominibus diligere...."

[125] Cyprian, *Epistola* 8.1 (CSEL 3.2, p. 486, ll. 5-19): "... et cum incumbat nobis, qui uidemur praepositi esse et uice pastorum custodire gregem...."

[126] Cf. Cyprian, *Epistola* 74.1 (CSEL 3.2, p. 799, ll. 13-14) and 75.16 (ibid., pp. 820, l. 24 - 821, l. 13).

21:15-17.[127] Leo's appropriation of the passage became a model for his successors. Although Gregory I influenced the exegesis more decisively through his spiritual understanding of the entire chapter, he could give the text a strictly papal interpretation in his correspondence.[128] An excerpt from Benedict VI (d. 973) may sum up the elements of this interpretation for the early Middle Ages: "... of these (apostles) and of the whole church (Christ) established Peter as the prince to whom he entrusted the flock of the church when he said to him the third time: Feed my sheep!, and to whom he also handed on the power to bind and to loose saying: I will give you the keys of the kingdom of heaven, etc. And such power was not only bestowed on Peter, but the same power to bind and to loose was handed over to his successors who hold his place in the church." [129] The centuries saw little change in this rhetoric. The *cura totius gregis* as a task and privilege of the pope remained an important argument in Gregory VII's controversy with the German king. When Christ said to Peter: whatever you bind, etc. (Matt. 16:19), "are kings excepted, or are they not of the sheep whom the Son of God entrusted to blessed Peter?" [130] This papal use of John 21:15-17 and its rhetorical expression were certainly known to the exegetes and theologians. On the other hand, popes often were aware of the theological tradition and could apply the lesson of the passage to fellow bishops and other prelates.[131]

---

[127] See above, note 1. The argument from Matt. 16:19 and John 21 is found in *Tractatus* 73.2 (CCL 138A, p. 451, ll. 31-34): "Magna sunt reuelata mysteria .... In his per insufflationem Domini infunditur apostolis omnibus Spiritus Sanctus, et beato Petro apostolo supra ceteros post regni claues ouilis dominici cura mandatur"; the argument combining Luke 22:32 and John 21 occurs in *Sermo* 4.4 (CCL 138, p. 21, ll. 113-128): "... quod tantam potentiam dedit ei quem totius Ecclesiae principem fecit, ut si quid etiam nostris temporibus recte per nos agitur, recteque disponitur, illius sit gubernaculis deputandum, cui dictum est: Et tu conuersus confirma fratres tuos, et cui post resurrectionem suam Dominus ad trinam aeterni amoris professionem mystica insinuatione ter dixit: Pasce oues meas. Quod nunc quoque proculdubio facit et mandatum Domini pius pastor exsequitur, confirmans nos cohortationibus suis et pro nobis orare non cessans, ut nulla temptatione superemur...."

[128] See, e.g., *Registrum* V.37 *ad Mauritium Augustum* (CCL 120, ed. D. Norberg, 1982, p. 309, ll. 38-41); VII.37 *ad Gregorium Eulogium episc. Alex.* (ibid., p. 50, ll. 13-15).

[129] Benedict VI (d. 973), *Epistola 1 ad Fredericum Salisburgensem episcopum* (PL 135: 1082AB): "... duodecim elegit apostolos, quos ad seminandum verbum Dei in corda fidelium in universum transmisit orbem; quorum atque totius Ecclesiae sanctum Petrum constituit principem, cui gregem commisit ecclesiasticum, tertio ei dicens: Pasce oves meas (John 21:15-17); cui etiam ligandi atque solvendi tradidit potestatem dicens: Et tibi dabo, etc. (Matt. 16:19). Et non solum sancto Petro potentia, sed etiam suis successoribus, ejus vicem in Ecclesia tenentibus, eadem ligandi atque solvendi a Deo tradita est potestas."

[130] *Registrum* VIII.21 to Hermann of Metz (*Das Register Gregors VII.*, ed. E. Caspar; MGH *Epistolae Selectae* II.2, 1923, p. 548, ll. 10-18); cf. I.15 (ibid., II.1, 1920, p. 24, ll. 34-36).

[131] E.g., Leo I, *Tractatus* 63.6 (CCL 138, p. 386, ll. 106-112); Gregory I, *Regula Pastoralis* I.5 (PL 77: 745); *Epistola* V.20 (PL 77: 745); VII.40 (PL 77: 899); Silvester II, *Sermo de episcopis* (PL 139: 171).

The fact remains that, while it was well established through papal usage, the primatial interpretation of the passage was not at the core, perhaps not even at the fringe of the earlier exegetical tradition and throughout the thirteenth century.

5.

Innocent III was well aware both of the exegetical tradition and the primatial argumentation of his predecessors. It is no surprise to find that his sermon on John 21:15-17 tried to combine the two.[132] Unexpectedly, however, Innocent discusses the prerogatives of Peter only in the first few lines of his exposition, where he skilfully combines Matt. 16:17-19 ("from faith to keys") with John 21 ("from love to the care of the flock"). After this excursion, he leaves the primatial theme, never to return to it again. The bulk of the sermon exegetes the passage as an exhortation about the virtues of a good prelate, addressed to his fellow bishops. It is clear that Innocent is simply following the tradition. Still, while the traces of Augustine and Bede are clearly visible, Innocent also made his own contributions. He interpreted the three orders of lambs and sheep in terms of the Ezekielian triad (Ezek. 14:14) as "virgines, continentes, et conjugati," which then allowed him to give an appropriate explanation of Peter's sadness over the Lord's third inquiry (546CD). He also modified the traditional formula for the threefold command to read: "pasce exemplo, pasce documento, pasce sacramento divinae communionis." (546B). I suspect that for this particular change he was indebted to Peter Comestor.[133] In any event, the sermon is certainly evidence that Innocent was fully equipped and able to argue as a professional exegete himself.

Yet, while he honored and used the tradition of exegesis, he blended the professional effort with the application of a spiritual hermeneutic which read the biblical texts in light of his deep personal conviction that the Bible proclaims "mysteriously" the reality of thirteenth century papal primacy. Ernst Kantorowicz has called this rhetorical phenomenon "monopolizing by exclusion." [134] The papal office claimed for itself that which was applied to

---

[132] Innocent III: *Sermo* XX *de sanctis* (*PL* 217: 543C-548C).

[133] See Peter Comestor: *Sermo* 44 (*PL* 198: 1825D): "Propter hunc triplicem panem dictum est ter Petro: Pasce oves meas, ac si diceret ei Dominus: Pasce Eucharistia, pasce doctrina, pasce bona vita. Quod autem dictum est Petro, et apostolis omnibus est dictum, et vobis eorum vicariis et successoribus. Ergo pascite pane angelico, pascite verbo, pascite exemplo!"

[134] Ernst Kantorowicz, "Deus per naturam, deus per gratiam," *Harvard Theological Review* 45 (1952-1953) 271 f.: "This monopolizing by exclusion was indeed a very mediaeval method; the office claimed what was valid for man at large." Among other topics, Kantorowicz

a wider group. Innocent was a master of this method. He was, however, not its inventor. We discussed its early traces in the primatial exegesis of Stephen I and Leo I. Later popes not only continued this tradition but expanded it. It would be interesting to investigate a document such as Gregory VII's *Dictatus Papae* against the background of the specialized papal exegesis of particular biblical passages reflected in its statements.[135] Moreover, popes before Innocent III had already monopolized unusual biblical texts such as Jer. 1:10 ("Ecce constitui te super gentes et super regna") which was applied to Christ or to a wider group of leaders earlier.[136]

It seems that Innocent added considerably to the store of monopolized passages. He chose mostly texts with an earlier history of christological interpretation: Prov. 8:15 ("per me reges regnant"); Ps. 110:4 ("Tu es sacerdos in eternum secundum ordinem Melchisedek"); Acts 10:42 ("iudex vivorum et mortuorum"); Rev. 19:6 ("rex regum et dominus dominantium").[137] In his study of Innocent's rhetoric, Imkamp found that the "head" metaphor by which Innocent frequently expressed the papal plenitude of power, was "strongly marked by christological terminology and probably also content"; in this connection, he speaks of a "christological detour" in the primatial argument.[138] The phenomenon is indeed striking. It is related to the new papal self-consciousness which expressed itself in the title, "Vicarius Christi." Michele Maccarone has traced the earlier history of this title and has shed light on Innocent's central role in filling the term with new content.[139] The title, "Vicar of Christ," opens a list of papal epithets in Innocent's inaugural oration: "Profecto vicarius Jesu Christi, successor Petri, Christus Domini, Deus Pharaonis, inter Deum et hominem constitutus." The term, "Deus Pharaonis," was borrowed from Exodus 7:1 and appeared among the string of images for the papal office which Bernard of Clairvaux

---

discusses the papal appropriation of Ps. 81(82):6 ("dii estis") and I Cor. 2:15 ("spiritualis [homo] iudicat omnia").

[135] Such a project would supplement K. Hofmann's important study on the canonistic background: *Der Dictatus Papae Gregors VII. Eine rechtsgeschichtliche Erklärung* (Paderborn, 1933). Some attention has been given more recently to the biblical background of DP 23 (Walter Ullmann, "Romanus Pontifex indubitanter efficitur sanctus: Dictatus Papae 23 in retrospect and prospect," *Studi Gregoriani* 6 [1959-1961] 229-264) and DP 11 (Christian Schneider, *Prophetisches Sacerdotium*, esp. pp. 110-118).

[136] The history of this passage has been traced masterfully by Yves Congar, "'Ecce constitui te super gentes et regna (Jer. 1:10)' in Geschichte und Gegenwart," in *Theologie in Geschichte und Gegenwart. Michael Schmaus zum 60. Geburtstag*, ed. J. Auer and H. Volk (München, 1957), pp. 671-696.

[137] See, e.g., *Sermo 3 de diversis* (*PL* 217: 665B); Imkamp, *Kirchenbild*, pp. 297-299.

[138] Imkamp, *Kirchenbild*, pp. 285 f.

[139] Michele Maccarone, *Vicarius Christi: Storia del titolo papale*, Lateranum, N.S. 18.1-4 (Rome, 1952), esp. pp. 109-118.

had incorporated into his treatise, *De consideratione*.[140] Bernard's list featured all but one of Innocent's terms above. The context for his statement was a critical, reformist assessment of the papacy. Apparently, Innocent responded sympathetically to this fervent plea for a biblical ideal of the pope as *figura ecclesiae* and as exemplar of the true Christian life in the imitation of Christ.[141] He carried the office as an awesome personal responsibility, upheld by the conviction that, although unworthy, he like Peter stood in the place of Christ. Exegetically, his "christological detour" may not have been a detour at all. Innocent could fully absorb and digest the exegetical tradition and yet see no difficulty in moving from Christ to Peter, to the Pope, and on to all bishops and priests. They all are located on a continuum, because the rights and responsibilities, while shared in different measure, are the same for all the shepherds of the flock. Innocent's interpretation of I Cor. 3:10-11 may illustrate the point: Christ, of course, remains the *fundamentum fundamentorum*, as the tradition holds; but Peter is the *fundamentum secundarium*, fully sharing with Christ his name of "rock," his power and authority, and passing on this role to all prelates *in partem sollicitudinis*.[142]

We can now summarize our findings. The earlier exegetical history of Matt. 16:18-19, Luke 22:32, and John 21:15-17 was largely out of step with the primatial interpretation of these passages which had itself a long history among papal writers since the fifth, perhaps even the third century. The mainstream of exegesis followed an agenda set by patristic precedent, especially Augustine, but also other Western fathers. In the case of Matt. 16:18-19, the tradition was dominated by the christological interpretation of the "rock" of the church, nourished by powerful biblical parallels such as I Cor. 10:4, Matt. 7:24-25, and I Cor. 3:11. For Luke 22:32, the tradition focused on the context of Jesus' passion and Peter's denial, applying the verse in a tropological way to the theme of the "humble prelate." In the case of John 21:15-17, the traditional interpretation drew on the biblical imagery of flock and shepherds as a metaphor of the *cura pastoralis* in the church and saw in the text a lesson about the qualities of the "good prelate." From the middle of the thirteenth century on, we found evidence that the specialized papal interpretation of Petrine passages made its way into the exegetical literature. It certainly did not replace the traditional agendas but sometimes

---

[140] Bernard, *De consideratione* II.8.15 (*Opera*, vol. 3; ed. J. Leclercq and H. M. Rochais; Rome, 1963, p. 423). On Bernard's view of the papacy in *De consideratione* see Bernard Jacqueline, *Épiscopat et papauté chez S. Bernard de Clairvaux* (Saint-Lo, 1975), pp. 195-220.

[141] On Bernard's influence on Innocent III, see Jacqueline, *Épiscopat*, pp. 304 f.

[142] *Sermo 21 de sanctis* (*PL* 217: 552BC); cf. *Sermo 1 in communi sanctorum* (*PL* 217: 602A); *Sermo 2* (*PL* 217: 603A).

supplemented them. It seems significant to me that, in a striking way, this new accent in interpretation followed the imaginative fusion of exegesis and papal ideology which characterized the work of Innocent III. Its reception was stronger where Innocent's initiative was stronger, as in the case of Matt. 16:18-19 and Luke 22:32; it was less pronounced where Innocent's exegesis followed the traditional agenda, as in the case of John 21:15-17. Is it an exaggeration to suggest that the work of Innocent III, much admired in the thirteenth century by theologians and canonists, must have played a considerable role in bringing about the change?

Appendix

PETRUS DE SCALA (d. 1295), Commentary on Matthew 16:16-19, Paris, BN, lat. 15596, ff. 194r-195r.

Respondens autem petrus: Unus pro omnibus, ut dicit interlinearis. Ecce secundum, scilicet confessio dominice incarnationis. Chrysostomus: quando plebis consilium interrogat, alii dixerunt quod interrogatum est; quando autem mentem eorum, petrus os apostolorum et vertex prosiluit et ait: *Tu*;
5 discretive, quia unigenitus Dei, Ioa. 1. *Es*: substantive, sine principio et fine, exod. III° Ego sum qui sum etc. *Christus*: (reference to Ambrose) ... exprimit etiam dignitatemn regiam et sacerdotalem et gratiae plenitudinem... .
Respondens autem Jhesus dixit ei. Et commendatur ipsa confessio primo ex veritatis simplicitate, cum dicit: *Beatus es symon*; interlinearis: tam alte
10 fidei confessione, Rom. X°: ore autem confessio fit ad salutem. Et significanter dicit symon, quia, ut dicit beatus Cesarius, sicut ignis non est sine calore, ita nec vera obedientia sine caritate. *bariona*: In hoc ostenditur esse dei filius per gratiam, quia confessus est christum filium dei per naturam; nam bariona interpretatur filius columbe siriace: et ut dicit Jeronimus, quidam
15 volunt, quod hoc nomen bariona sit scriptorum vicio depravatum, ut pro Bariohanna, id est filio iohannis, sit scriptum una sillaba subtracta bariona.

Secundo commendatur ipsa confessio ex divina revelatione, unde subdit: quia *caro et sanguis non revelavit tibi*, id est, carnalis sensus nec humana sapientia, eccles. xvii°: quid nequius quam quod excogitavit caro et sanguis.

20 *Sed pater meus qui est in celis*: non quod ubique non sit, sed in celis dicitur esse, quia ibi relucet nobilior eius actus, phil. iii, si quid aliter sapitis, et hoc deus revelavit vobis. *Et ego etc.*: hic quarto subditur divini muneris promissio; promittit autem stabilimentum ecclesie sibi commisse quantum ad tria. primo quantum ad fidem veritatis; secundo ad gratiam in amore bonitatis: *et porte*;

25 tertio quantum ad eminenciam collate potestatis: *et tibi dabo*. dicit ergo: *et ego dico tibi*, scilicet qui confessus es me filium Dei; *quia tu es petrus*, ob fortitudinem fidei et confessionis constanciam; augustinus in libro retract. xx: non petro dictum est: tu es petra, sed petrus; petra autem erat christus, i cor. x° quem confessus Petrus a petra nomen hoc accepit.

30 *Et super hanc petram*: quam confessus est, 1. Cor. iii: fundamentum aliud nemo potest ponere praeter illud quod positum est quod est christus ihesus. Vel *super hanc petram*: id est super fidei firmitatem secundum Jeronimum, ii Thim. ii°: fundamentum fidei stat. *Edificabo ecclesiam meam*: Jere. xxxi: In caritate perpetua attraxi te miserans et edificaberis in eodem. Ecce dies

35 veniunt, dicit dominus, et edificabitur civitas domino. *et porte*, id est peccata in me, blandimenta, hereses, secundum Jeronimum et Bedam, et dicuntur porte inferi, quia ad infernum ducunt. Unde Jeronimus: prava infidelium opera ineptaque colloquia porte sunt inferi, in quantum suis vel actoribus vel sequacibus iter perditionis ostendunt; tren. ii. defixe sunt in terra porte eius

40 etc.

Non prevalebunt adversus eam, scilicet quod de ecclesia defficiat vera fides, luc. xxii°: ego pro te rogavi, petre, ut non defficiat fides tua; vel defficiat amor divine bonitatis de ecclesia, Rom. viii°: Quis nos separabit a caritate christi etc. *Et enim dabo*: hic tertio ponitur ecclesie stabilimentum, quantum ad

45 eminentiam potestatis, ubi primo tangit potestatis collationem, secundo eius executionem, ibi: *et quodcumque etc.*; dicit ergo, quantum ad primum: *Et tibi dabo claves regni celorum*. Jeronimus et Rabanus: claves sunt scientia discernendi et potentia, qua dignos recipere et indignos excludere deberet a regno; clavis enim hic dicitur potestas iudicandi in foro animarum, non

50 corporum; potestas autem iudicandi integratur ex duobus: ex potestate discernendi in cause examinatione, et diffiniendi in cause determinatione per sententiam condempnatoriam vel absolutoriam. prima potestas appellatur hic scientia, secunda potentia; et sicut in sole una est potentia liquefaciendi et indurandi in sua radice, sed due in effectibus, ita est una clavis in radice sed

55 due in effectibus, propter quod pluraliter dicit: *Claves.*

2

The School Theologians' Views
of the Papacy, 1150-1250

Walter H. Principe C.S.B.

1. Introduction: Theological Background Before 1150

    1.1. Pseudo-Dionysius the Areopagite (ca. 500)
    1.2. The *Summa Sententiarum* (before 1141, perhaps 1138)
    1.3. Peter Abelard (1079-1142)
    1.4. Hugh of St. Victor († 1142)

2. School Theologians of the Latter Half of the Twelfth Century

    2.1. Introduction
    2.2. Peter Lombard (ca. 1100-1160)
    2.3. The Power of the Keys
    2.4. Authoritative Papal Teaching About Faith

3. The First Half of the Thirteenth Century

    3.1. The Power of the Keys
    3.2. The Sacrament of Order and the Papacy
    3.3. Authoritative Papal Teaching About Faith
    3.4. The Question-Literature
    3.5. The *Summa Fratris Alexandri* (ca. 1240-1245)
    3.6. Albert the Great (ca. 1200-1280)

4. Conclusion

The Religious Roles of the Papacy: Ideals and Realities, 1150-1300, ed. Christopher Ryan, Papers in Mediaeval Studies 8 (Toronto: Pontifical Institute of Mediaeval Studies, 1989), pp. 45-116. © P.I.M.S., 1989.

Some understanding of the religious ideal of the papacy can be gathered from theological views concerning the Church and the pope's role within the Church and in relation to secular authorities. Another essay will examine the theology of the papacy presented by a number of monastic or episcopal authors and by writers defending the Church against heterodox opinions in the period from 1150 to 1250. This essay will restrict itself to the works of the school theologians in order to see what they had to say about the papacy. With a very few exceptions, the works of canonists are left aside, although the influence of their texts will be frequently mentioned; indeed, they will be seen to be an important component of the developments found in the theologians. Also, although the time period of the study begins at 1150, it will be necessary to recall the teachings of a few earlier theologians whose ideas stand behind the discussions to be examined here.

1. INTRODUCTION: THEOLOGICAL BACKGROUND BEFORE 1150

1.1. Pseudo-Dionysius the Areopagite (ca. 500).

The doctrine of Pseudo-Dionysius about hierarchies influenced a number of twelfth- and thirteenth-century theologians. According to him, the angelic hierarchies consist of three triads of angels, each with three grades within it. Although his work on the Church was called "The Ecclesiastical Hierarchy" in some manuscripts of the work, his text, which speaks only of "our" hierarchy by contrast with the angelic hierarchies, gives no foundation for this title.[1] As will be seen in the following essay, Bernard of Clairvaux made a general comparison between hierarchy in the Church and the heavenly hierarchies. It was only in the thirteenth-century, however, that some theologians worked out a complete parallel between the Pseudo-Dionysius' nine angelic grades and nine grades they saw within the sacrament of Order in the Church. With respect to the papacy, this parallelism led them to ask whether the papacy constituted a distinct grade or degree within this sacrament.[2] For the Pseudo-Dionysius himself, only the first of the three triads, that of the Seraphim, Cherubim, and Thrones, has a corresponding parallel of gradations within the Church's sacrament of Order. The second ecclesial triad of the Pseudo-Dionysius, comprising the initiated as distinguished from the ordained initiators or administrators of the sacraments, is made up of lay persons. The third triad in the Church consists for him of three sacraments,

---

[1] See Paul Rorem, *Biblical and Liturgical Symbols Within the Pseudo-Dionysian Synthesis,* Studies and Texts 71 (Toronto: Pontifical Institute of Mediaeval Studies, 1984), p. 28.

[2] See below, section 3.2.

Baptism, Synaxis (or Eucharist or Communion), and Myron (or Anointing). Therefore the parallel between nine grades or degrees within the sacrament of Order and nine degrees of angelic hierarchies is not really the doctrine of this influential eastern author.[3]

1.2. The *Summa Sententiarum* (before 1141, perhaps 1138).

This work, by Bishop Odo of Lucca, influenced many authors, the most important of whom was Peter Lombard.[4] Of interest for our topic because of their influence are Odo's remarks about the powers of the keys possessed by priests.[5] Here the text of Matthew 16:19 ("I will give you the keys of the kingdom of heaven" etc.) is not reserved to Peter and to the popes viewed as his successors but is understood to apply to all priests. This was to be the most usual practice of the future with respect to the power of the keys, whereas the related text of Matthew 18:18 ("Whatever you bind [in the plural: *alligaveritis*] on earth shall be bound in heaven, and whatever you loose [*solveritis*] on earth shall be loosed in heaven"), which Matthew presents as addressed to all the apostles, is rarely used in such discussions.

Odo's concern here, to be sure, is not about a distinction between the pope on the one hand and bishops or priests on the other, but rather with the keys as belonging to ordained ministers and not to unordained persons, no matter what their ability to exercise one element of the powers of the keys, discernment or judgment (*discretio*). After citing the text of Matthew, Odo says that the keys it speaks of are discernment and power (*potestas*): the former is needed to judge which persons are to be "bound" and which "loosed" by the use of the latter. Both keys, he insists, are given only to priests when the bishops ordains them.[6]

Further on in the same discussion Odo quotes Origen saying that this power was given to Peter *alone* and to those who "imitate" Peter or who

---

[3] See Rorem, p. 29. For a detailed exposition of the three triads see ibid., pp. 29-46.

[4] Unless noted otherwise, this and the following study will rely for authorship, dating, manuscripts, influence, etc., on A. M. Landgraf, *Introduction à l'histoire de la littérature théologique de la scolastique naissante*, ed. A.-M. Henry, trans. L.-B. Geiger (Montréal: Institut d'Études Médiévales; Paris: Vrin, 1973). In quoting texts from the *PL* we shall frequently alter the punctuation and sometimes the spelling in order to clarify the meaning of the texts. All translations are our own.

On the *Summa sententiarum* and its influence see Landgraf, pp. 98-102.

[5] See ch. 14; *PL* 176: 152A-153B.

[6] Ibid.; *PL* 176: 152A: "In hoc loco dicendum videtur de clavibus quas habent sacerdotes. Dictum est Petro et in Petro aliis: *Tibi dabo claves regni caelorum.* Videndum quid sint et quando dentur et qui habeant. Istae claves sunt discretio et potestas. Prius enim est discernere qui sunt ligandi, qui solvendi, et post utendum est potestate. In consecratione per ministerium episcopi dantur hae claves solis sacerdotibus."

"follow in the footsteps" of Peter.[7] It is clear from the context that Odo includes priests among the "imitators of Peter" even though the Matthean text shows Christ speaking to Peter alone. What is significant here is the extension of the Petrine powers of the keys to all priests by reason of their ordination. Here and in later authors there is no consciousness of a sharp distinction between the successor of Peter and bishops or priests when there is question of the fundamental power of the keys. This is because these powers were seen to derive from priestly ordination rather than from some other special power, position, or privilege.

1.3. Peter Abelard (1079-1142).

A third earlier theologian whose influence is to be looked for in our period is Peter Abelard. Without going into his doctrine on the papacy, we simply note that in his *Sic et non* he gathered a number of patristic texts concerning Peter that could have influenced later thinking on the papacy.

In chapter 93 Abelard presents texts concerning the question, "That Peter or Paul and the other apostles are equal, and are not equal." Many of the texts argue that Paul, at least, is the equal of Peter; some indicate that a few or all of the other apostles are likewise equal to Peter.[8] Even more significant is chapter 95, which is entitled: "That Christ alone is the foundation of the Church, and against this." Although a number of texts, especially those from Cyprian, Jerome, and Leo, speak of Peter as somehow a foundation of the Church, other texts identify the rock that is the foundation of the Church with Christ (thus Augustine, a text of Jerome, Pseudo-Jerome), with the Trinity or with faith in the Trinity (Jerome), with the apostles (Jerome), or with bishops (Origen).[9]

Abelard does not give his own opinion: the *Sic et non* was meant to present problems found in authoritative texts because of the apparent or real conflicts seen when they were juxtaposed, conflicts needing resolution by use of the principles Abelard lays out in his prologue.[10] But these chapters show at least that in the period we shall study there could be no uniform interpretation of the Matthean text about the Church's rock foundation.

---

[7] Ibid.; 152c: "Haec potestas soli Petro concessa est et imitatoribus Petri. Nam quicumque vestigia Petri imitantur recte habent ligandi et solvendi potestatem."

[8] See *Sic et Non: A Critical Edition*, eds. Blanche B. Boyer and Richard McKeon (Chicago-London: The University of Chicago Press, 1966-67), pp. 316-318; the title reads: "Quod Petrus vel Paulus et ceteri apostoli sint aequales et non."

[9] See ibid., pp. 319-322; the title reads: "Quod solus Christus fundamentum sit Ecclesiae et contra."

[10] See ibid., pp. 89-104.

1.4. Hugh of St. Victor († 1142).

It is rare to find among medieval theologians of the twelfth or thirteenth century an organized treatment of the Church.[11] Hugh of St. Victor's *On the Sacraments of the Christian Faith* (*De sacramentis christianae fidei*), which was written between 1136 and 1141 and was a constant influence in the succeeding century, is such a rarity. Its book 2 begins with an examination of the Incarnation and the union of Christ's members with him and with the Father. The next part of this book begins with a discussion of the grace flowing from Christ the Head to the members and then at once gives eight chapters on the Church; these lead quite naturally into a third part on ecclesiastical orders. Both the second and third parts contain various statements about the pope.[12] Before examining these texts, however, we should note that this systematic section, so easily accessible, is not Hugh's total view of the Church. This section must be seen in the full context of the *De sacramentis* itself and, even more, against the rich but less systematically organized doctrine in Hugh's liturgical, scriptural, and spiritual works.[13]

In the *De sacramentis* Hugh first gives a definition of the Church that is more strongly theological than canonical: "Holy Church is the body of Christ given life, united by one faith, and made holy by one Spirit." [14] Emphasis on membership in Christ and the gift of the Spirit to the Church continues throughout this chapter.[15] Then, after speaking of clerics and laity as two walls (*parietes*) or two sides (*latera*) of the Church,[16] Hugh contrasts two lives, one earthly, another heavenly, one bodily and the other spiritual. To maintain justice in each life, he says, various powers are established.[17]

---

[11] See Johannes Beumer, "Zur Ekklesiologie der Frühscholastik," *Scholastik* 26 (1951) 364-389, and "Ekklesiologische Probleme der Frühscholastik," ibid. 27 (1952) 183-209, and Yves Congar, *L'Église: De saint Augustin à l'époque moderne*, Tome 3, fasc. 3 of *Histoire des Dogmes* (Paris: Cerf, 1970), chs. 7-8, for studies of the ecclesiology of this period.

[12] Book 2, part 1, is found in *PL* 176: 371c-416b; part 2 of book 2 is found ibid., 415a-422b, and part 3 ibid., 421b-434b.

[13] On this point and for a study of this richer theology see Jean Châtillon, "Une ecclésiologie médiévale: L'idée de l'Église dans la théologie de Saint-Victor au XIIᵉ siècle," *Irénikon* 22 (1949) 115-138, 394-411, and Congar, p. 159. For Congar's summary of Hugh's doctrine see ibid., pp. 159-160.

Such a corrective is needed to balance studies of Hugh such as that by Walter Ullmann, *The Growth of Papal Government in the Middle Ages*, 3rd ed. (London, 1970), pp. 437-442, which concentrates on "the hierocratic theme" of ecclesial and especially papal government.

[14] II, 2, 2; 416b-c: "Ecclesia sancta corpus est Christi uno Spiritu vivificata et unita fide una et sanctificata."

[15] See ibid.; 416c-417a.

[16] See ibid., ch. 3; 417a-d. For the situation of these metaphors in the ecclesiology of the period see Congar, pp. 179-180.

[17] Ibid., ch. 4; 417d-418b: "Duae quippe vitae sunt: una terrena, altera coelestis; altera corporea, altera spiritualis .... Deinde alii qui ea potestate officii [officit *PL*] commissi

The king has power over earthly things, the supreme pontiff power over spiritual goods, and all things are subjected to spiritual life. To the extent, then, that spiritual life is nobler than earthly life and spirit nobler than body, to that extent spiritual power precedes earthly or secular power in honour and dignity.[18] Hugh goes further. The spiritual power has the role of establishing the existence of earthly power and of judging it if it is not good. Why is this? Because spiritual power was the first to be instituted by God, and it can be judged only by God and not by others, as 1st Corinthians says: *The spiritual man judges all things, but is himself to be judged by no one*.[19]

Although here Hugh is thinking primarily of relations between the spiritual and the temporal in terms that undoubtedly reflect the investiture discussions, it could be asked whether he would also apply the same principle to conclude that the pope cannot be judged by a council or by others in the Church. In any case, the relations among the various ecclesiastical prelates is his concern in the following chapter, where he gives certain principles that were to be important for later discussions of the papacy among theologians.

In this next chapter, then, after stating that all ecclesiastical administration consists in orders, sacraments, and precepts,[20] Hugh begins by examining orders. Although priest and deacon differ in sacramental grade or degree (*gradus*), he says, others, such as deacon and archdeacon, are in the same

---

secundum aequitatem dispensent, ut nemo fratrem suum in negotio supergrediatur sed justitia inviolata conservetur. Propterea in utroque populo secundum utramque vitam distributo potestates sunt constitutae."

[18] Ibid.; 418B-C: "Ad potestatem regis pertinent quae terrena sunt et ad terrenam vitam facta omnia. Ad potestatem summi pontificis pertinent quae spiritualia sunt, et vitae spirituali attributa universa. Quanto autem vita spiritualis dignior est quam terrena et spiritus quam corpus, tanto spiritualis potestas terrenam sive saecularem potestatem honore ac dignitate praecedit."

[19] Ibid.; 418C: "Nam spiritualis potestas terrenam potestatem et instituere habet ut sit, et judicare habet si bona non fuerit. Ipsa vero a Deo primum instituta est et, cum deviat, a solo Deo judicari potest, sicut scriptum est: *Spiritualis dijudicat omnia et ipse a nemine judicatur*." The scriptural text is 1 Cor 2:15; English from *RSV*.

Ullmann (cited above, n. 13), pp. 438-446, provides a good summary and commentary on the background of this important statement and on the text itself. The metaphors of the head and body, and especially of the soul giving life to and directing the body, provide the framework for this doctrine. "The point we wish to make," he says, "is that the teleological principle [the objects and ends of the *universitas christianorum* assigning its functions] was transposed onto the plane of allegory," that is, by "the comparison of the Christian body corporate and politic with the human body," each body being "considered organic entities" (p. 442).

[20] For Hugh the sacrament of Order refers to the persons of prelates, whereas sacraments refer to their ministry and precepts to the way of life of those subject to them; ibid., ch. 5; 418D-419A: "Ordines consideramus in personis praelatorum, sacramenta in ministerio eorum, praecepta in conversatione subjectorum."

gradus sacramentally by reason of their "excelling power" of ministering to the priest in the Eucharist; yet they differ in their ministerial power since the archdeacon has added duties towards the Church under or in place of the bishop.[21]

The same distinction, important for later differentiation between pope or bishop and ordinary priests, is now applied to priests and bishops; here bishops are given the title "pontiff or high(est) priest" (*pontifex sive summus sacerdos*). Priests and bishops constitute the same degree (*gradus*) in the sacrament since in a certain way they share the unique dignity of consecrating the body and blood of Christ and of baptizing, catechizing, preaching, binding and loosing.[22] But to bishops is given a unique or special power not possessed by priests: bishops can dedicate churches, ordain, impose hands, consecrate chrism, and give a general blessing to all.[23] This special power has already been indicated by Hugh to be a special ministerial power (*potestas in ministerio*), and in his conclusion to this discussion he also calls it a difference in dignities: "And so in this way the difference of degrees in sacred orders is one thing and the difference of dignities in the same degree is another."[24]

In the third part of book 2, entitled *On ecclesiastical orders*, Hugh examines each of the seven grades or degrees within the one sacrament of Order: each differs in that "through spiritual power it continually rises higher to deal with sacred things." These seven degrees are doorkeepers, lectors, exorcists, acolytes, subdeacons, deacons, and priests.[25] After priests comes a higher degree, that of the "princes among priests" (*principes sacerdotum*), the bishops. Next in higher degree come archbishops, then primates, then

[21] Ibid.; 419A: "De ordinibus hoc primum attend<end>um est quod alii sunt secundum gradum differentem, sicut est diaconus et sacerdos, alii in eodem gradu secundum potestatem excellentem, sicut diaconus et archidiaconus unus gradus est in sacramento, non tamen una potestas in ministerio: diaconus enim sacerdoti ministrat in sacramento corporis et sanguinis Christi. Archidiaconus autem hoc plus habet quod, praeter ministerium altaris, sub episcopo et vice episcopi curam habet ecclesiarum et causas ecclesiasticas examinat et ministeria dispensat."

[22] Ibid.; 419A-B: "Similiter sacerdos et pontifex sive summus sacerdos unus gradus est [et *PL*] in sacramento (diversa tamen potestas in ministerio) quia cum utrisque corporis et sanguinis Christi consecrandi, baptizandi, catechizandi, praedicandi, ligandi, solvendi una quodammodo sit dignitas ...."

[23] Ibid.; 419B: "... pontificibus tamen ecclesias dedicandi, ordines faciendi, manus imponendi, sacri chrismatis consecrandi, communem super populum benedictionem faciendi singularis data est potestas."

[24] Ibid.: "Sic itaque alia est differentia graduum in sacris ordinibus, alia est in eodem gradu differentia dignitatum."

[25] Ch. 5; 423A-B: "Sequuntur deinde septem graduum promotiones, in quibus per spiritualem potestatem altius semper ad sacra tractanda conscendit: primus gradus est ostiariorum; secundus lectorum; ... septimus sacerdotum."

patriarchs (although, he adds, some would equate primates and patriarchs).[26]
Finally and highest of all there is the pope:

> After all these comes the supreme pontiff, for whom church custom has
> established the name "pope," that is, "the father of fathers." He is the chief
> and greatest successor of the apostolic see in the Roman Church: hence Holy
> Church has the custom of calling him "apostolic" in a special way. Every
> ecclesiastical order must obey him, for he presides in the place of Peter, the
> prince of the apostles, and he alone by a preeminent dignity has the keys of
> binding and loosing all on earth.[27]

This strong statement of papal dignity and prerogatives, owing much to Ivo
of Chartres and Gratian's *Decretum*,[28] alludes to the Petrine text about the
power of the keys and in this instance distinguishes a special dignity in the
pope of binding and loosing. Yet for Hugh, if he is consistent with what he
has already said, as a special dignity it would constitute a special ministerial
power but not a difference in power by reason of the sacrament of Order.
Later theologians will develop this distinction made by Hugh between papal
power and the power of others to bind and loose in certain circumstances
or cases.[29]

Before leaving Hugh, we should mention that although he has a commentary on the *Celestial Hierarchy* of the Pseudo-Dionysius and although he
justifies the use of corresponding names for the earthly and heavenly
hierarchies, he does not make the detailed link between angelic hierarchies

---

[26] Ibid.; 423B: "Hic gradus dispares in eodem ordine habet dignitates, nam post sacerdotes
altiores sunt principes sacerdotum, id est, episcopi, supra quos iterum sunt archiepiscopi, et
supra illos qui dicuntur primates, supra quos quidam patriarchas constituere volunt, alii
eosdem primates et patriarchas dicunt."

[27] Ibid.; 423B-C: "Post hos omnes sequitur summus pontifex, quem papam, id est, patrum
patrem consuetudo ecclesiastica nominare instituit. Hic est principalis et maximus sedis
apostolicae in Ecclesia Romana successor, unde et ipsum specialiter apostolicum Sancta
Ecclesia nominare consuevit. Cui, vice Petri principis apostolorum praesidenti, omnis ecclesiasticus ordo obtemperare debet, qui solus praerogativa dignitatis claves habet ligandi omnia
et solvendi super terram."

Throughout this and the following study many titles of the pope will be met. On these titles
see, among many studies, Yves Congar, "Titres donnés au pape," *Concilium: Revue internatio-
nale de théologie*, no. 108 (Tours, 1975) 55-64 (rpt. in his *Droit ancien et structures ecclésiales*
[London: Variorum Reprints, 1982] no. VI), and the references there. Two studies of the title
Vicarius are those by Michele Maccarrone, *Vicarius Christi: Storia del titolo papale* (Rome:
Lateran University, 1952), and G. Corti, *Il Papa Vicario di Pietro: Contributo alla storia
dell'Idea papale* (Brescia, 1966): Corti's study was unavailable to me.

[28] See Joseph De Ghellinck, "Le traité de Pierre Lombard sur les sept ordres ecclésiastiques: Ses sources, ses copistes," *RHE* 10 (1909) 290-302, 720-728, 11 (1910) 29-46; on
Hugh see p. 720.

[29] See below, sections 2.3 and 3.1.

and degrees in the sacrament of Order that later theologians will develop.[30] He may, however, have contributed to this development by this general justification of such parallelism.

2. SCHOOL THEOLOGIANS OF THE LATTER HALF OF THE TWELFTH CENTURY

2.1. Introduction.

By contrast with the monastic and episcopal theologians whose views are to be surveyed in the parallel essay, the schoolmen of the last half of the twelfth century have very little to say about the papacy. One reason is that their treatises lack a section directly concerned with the Church. It should be realized, however, that when the Church is viewed, as it should be, as more than a juridical institution, these authors do present a considerable theology of the Church when they deal with Christ, the Holy Spirit, the virtues, and especially the sacraments, all so crucial to the full realization of the Church.

Neither should the scriptural commentaries of these school theologians be forgotten. To take an outstanding example, Peter Lombard has little about Christ as Head of the Church in his *Sententiae*, but his Pauline commentaries, which circulated widely as the *Magna glosatura* and became an authoritative text, present rich texts on this theme.[31] Under the influence of Lombard's *Glosatura* and stimulated by texts of Hugh of St. Victor, Bernard of Clairvaux, and others, theologians of this period introduced the theme of Christ as Head of the Church, his Body, into their *summae* and glosses on Lombard's *Sententiae*; this theme was constantly amplified in the thirteenth century.[32] But neither in the latter twelfth century nor often in the first half of the thirteenth century is a link made between the pope as head of the Church and Christ as Head.

Theologians in this period tended to leave many of the institutional and juridical questions about the Church, and even discussions of some sacra-

[30] See his *Expositio in hierarchiam coelestem S. Dionysii Areopagitae* IX, 12; *PL* 175: 1107B-1112A. For later theologians see below, section 3.2.

[31] The only texts on Christ as Head that I have found are in 3 *Sent.*, d. 13, no. 2; eds. PP. Collegii S. Bonaventurae (i.e., Ignatius Brady), *Magistri Petri Lombardi Sententiae in IV libris distinctae*, vol. 2, 3rd ed. (Grottaferrata [Roma], 1981), p. 84; and 4 *Sent.*, d. 24, c. 1, no. 2 (ibid., pp. 393-394).

For his Pauline epistles see his *Collectanea in omnes D. Pauli Apostoli epistolas*; *PL* 191: 1297A-1696C; *PL* 192: 9A-520A.

[32] See, for example, W. Principe, "*Quaestiones* concerning Christ from the First Half of the Thirteenth Century: IV. *Quaestiones* from Douai MS 434: Christ as Head of the Church; The Unity of the Mystical Body," *MedS* 44 (1982) 1-82, including the bibliography in note 1, pp. 1-2.

mental problems, to the canonists. Thus the author of the Pseudo-Poitiers *Gloss* on the *Sententiae* of Lombard remarks about the validity of ordinations by heretics that the question is "more ... a matter for decretals than theological,"[33] and the author of the Vatican *Summa* "Ne transgrediaris" leaves the whole discussion of the sacrament of Order to what has been treated "beyond what is sufficient" by the decretists. He adds that for this reason the topic is rarely or never solemnly disputed by those who are theologians exclusively.[34]

2.2. Peter Lombard (ca. 1100-1160).

By contrast with this attitude of theologians, Peter Lombard was important for bringing into theology many texts on the Church previously collected by canonists. So well did he order this data that it became useful not only for theologians but also for many canonists who used his work: thus Gabriel Le Bras salutes Lombard as the "prince du droit canon."[35] We shall see in the next section that this material was sometimes important for the developing theology of the papacy in the early thirteenth century as Lombard's *Sententiae* became the object of university commentaries.

In all this material in Lombard, however, there is little on the papacy. His main texts concerning the pope occur within his discussion of ecclesiastical orders in distinction 24 of book 4. In this distinction he draws primarily on Hugh of St. Victor and Gratian, and through Hugh on Isidore of Seville and Yvo of Chartres.[36] For Lombard the "greater pontiffs" are vicars of the twelve apostles, whereas priests are vicars in the Church of the seventy-two other disciples chosen by Christ. He continues: "One stands out among the apostles as their chief, Peter, whose vicar and successor is the supreme pontiff: hence he is called 'apostolic'; he is also called 'pope', that is, the father of the fathers."[37]

---

[33] Quoted in L. Hödl, "Die kirchlichen Ämter, Dienste und Gewalten im Verständnis der scholastische Theologie (Der scholastische Traktat *De ordinibus* in historischer und systematischer Sicht)," *Franziskanische Studien* 43 (1961) 1-21, on p. 12: "magis ... decretalis quam theologica."

[34] Ms Vat. lat. 10754, fol. 43va, quoted ibid., p. 12: "Sexto loco videndum est de sacramento ordinis, quod est Ecclesiae vɪᵐ sacramentum. Sed ut reverentia decretistis, qui de eo ultra quam satis est in prima Decretorum parte pertractant, deferatur, et quia exinde a puris [pueris *Hödl*] theologis raro vel numquam sollemniter disputatur, hunc tractatum cum silentio praeterimus."

[35] See his "Pierre Lombard, Prince du droit canon," in *Miscellanea Lombardiana* (Novara: Istituto Geografico de Agostini, 1957), pp. 245-252.

[36] See the article by De Ghellinck cited above, n. 28, and the note in Lombard, 4 *Sent.*, d. 24; ed. Brady, p. 393.

[37] 4 *Sent.*, d. 24, c. 11, no. 4; ed. Brady, p. 404: "Christus quoque *duodecim elegit discipulos prius, quos et apostolos vocavit* (Luke 6:13): quorum vicem gerunt in Ecclesia maiores pontifices; deinde *alios septuaginta et duos discipulos designavit* (Luke 10:1): quorum

Like Hugh, the Lombard holds that ranks or levels above the priesthood, such as the episcopacy, are not distinct new orders but rather dignities or offices or both: "There are certain other names not of orders but of dignities or of offices .... 'Bishop' is a name for a dignity and at the same time of an office."[38] This holds also for the pope, who is (again, following the *Decretum*) the "prince of priests" and the "high priest" who "makes priests and levites and disposes all ecclesiastical orders."[39] When Peter Lombard examines the power of the keys, he quotes a text of Bede (which he gives as Jerome's) to show that if all priests have the power of binding and loosing, Peter received this power in a special way; therefore, he adds, whoever is separated from unity in faith and from the society of the Church cannot be loosed from sin or enter heaven.[40] This text, which will appear in later theologians, relates the papal office to unity of faith and ecclesial communion, at least as a sign of these.

Peter Lombard's *Sententiae* contain nothing further that is directly about the pope. Thus the summaries of his work or glosses on it written in the last half of the twelfth century were not invited to any serious reflection about the pope. His scriptural commentary does, however, transmit a revised version of a text from Augustine on Christ as the rock on which the Church is founded and on the naming of Peter as rock "from the rock which you have confessed, the rock you have recognized by saying: *You are the Christ, the Son of God.*"[41] In the slightly revised and augmented text of Augustine, Lombard's commentary pictures Christ as saying to Peter:

---

vicem in Ecclesia tenent presbyteri. Unus autem inter Apostolos princeps exstitit, Petrus, cuius vicarius et successor est Pontifex Summus: unde dicitur Apostolicus; qui etiam Papa vocatur, scilicet Pater Patrum."

[38] Ibid., cc. 14-15; Brady, pp. 405-406: "Sunt et alia quaedam, non ordinum, sed dignitatum vel officiorum nomina. ... Dignitatis simul et officii nomen est episcopus."

[39] Ibid., c. 16; Brady, p. 406: "Pontifex princeps sacerdotum est, quasi via sequentium, ipse et summus sacerdos nuncupatur: ipse enim sacerdotes et levitas efficit, ipse omnes ecclesiasticos ordines disposuit." This is all a quotation from Isidore, *Etymologiae* 7, 12, 13; *PL* 82: 291c (as is noted in the edition of Lombard here).

[40] 4 *Sent.*, d. 19, c. 1, no. 9; Brady, p. 367: "Quod vero hanc potestatem habeant omnes sacerdotes, Hieronymus testatur super illum locum Evangelii, ubi Dominus dixit Petro: *Tibi dabo claves regni caelorum* etc.: 'Habent', inquit, 'eandem iudiciariam potestatem alii Apostoli, habet et omnis Ecclesia in episcopis et presbyteris; sed ideo Petrus eam specialiter accepit ut omnes intelligant quod quicumque ab unitate fidei et societate Ecclesiae se separaverit, nec peccatis solvi nec caelum potest ingredi'." (Punctuation slightly changed.)

[41] *Collectanea in 1* Cor. *1:13 (Divisus est Christus?)*; *PL* 191: 1538A-B: "... Fundamenta diversa ponere praesumebant, cum unum sit fundamentum Ecclesiae quod nemo mutare potest, scilicet Christus Jesus. Ipse enim solus est petra, supra quam fundata est Ecclesia, a qua nominatus est Petrus, Domino ad illum dicente: *Tu es Petrus* etc. (*Matth.*, xvi). Simon enim antea vocabatur. Hoc autem nomen, scilicet Petrus, a Domino ei impositum est. Et dicitur Petrus in figura Christiani populi, a petra Christo. Quia enim petra Christus dicitur,

"*On this rock*, that is, on myself, the Son of God, and not on you, *I will build my Church.* I will build you and others on me, not myself on you." For [the commentary continues] they are not said to be Peter's but Christ's; they are not called "Petrines" from Peter but "Christians" from Christ, lest hope should be put in humans.[42]

This text will appear frequently in later theologians; it is important for interpretation of the Matthean text in relation to the pope, especially as it stands over against a maximizing interpretation of the papacy which would see the Church as built on Peter, the rock, and on his successors.

2.3. The Power of the Keys.

Although there is little direct reflection on the papacy among theologians in this period, there are some points to be noticed. These occur especially with reference to the power of the keys and the use of this power in the Church for the sacrament of Penance, for excommunications, and for indulgences and dispensations. Within the extensive studies of the sacrament of Penance by Paul Anciaux and of the power of the keys by Ludwig Hödl, the bulk of the material deals with ordinary priests and only occasionally, indeed rather rarely, with the pope.[43] The text of Matthew 16:19 is quite

---

et Petrus dicitur populus Christianus. Ita ergo Petrus a petra, non petra a Petro dicitur, quomodo non a Christiano Christus, sed a Christo Christianus vocatur. Tu es ergo, inquit, Petrus dictus a petra, quam confessus es, quam cognovisti, dicens: *Tu es Christus, Filius Dei*."

Cf. Augustine, *Tractatus in Iohannem*, tract. 124, 5 (Joan. 21, 19-23); CCL 36: 684-685: "... Sed quando dictum est: *Tibi dabo claues ... solutum est in caelis*, uniuersam significabat ecclesiam, quae in hoc saeculo diuersis tentationibus uelut imbribus, fluminibus, tempestatibus quatitur et non cadit, quoniam fundata est super petram unde Petrus nomen accepit: non enim a Petro petra, sed Petrus a petra; sicut non Christus a christiano, sed christianus a Christo uocatur. Ideo quippe ait Dominus: *Super hanc petram aedificabo ecclesiam meam*, quia dixerat Petrus: *Tu es Christus Filius Dei uiui*. Super hanc ergo, inquit, petram quam confessus es, aedificabo ecclesiam meam." (Punctuation slightly altered.)

[42] Ibid., *PL* 191: 1538B-C: "... *Super hanc petram*, id est, super meipsum Filium Dei, non super te *aedificabo Ecclesiam meam*, super me aedificabo te et alios, non me super te. Non enim dicuntur esse Petri, sed Christi, non a Petro Petrini sed a Christo Christiani, ne esset spes in homine."

This part of the text is an interpretation and expansion of Augustine's passage (ibid., CCL 36: 685): "Super hanc ergo, inquit, petram quam confessus es, aedificabo ecclesiam meam. Petra enim erat Christus; super quod fundamentum etiam ipse aedificatus est Petrus. Fundamentum quippe aliud nemo potest ponere praeter id quod positum est, quod est Christus Iesus."

It is uncertain whether this part of the text is from Lombard himself or from an author standing between Augustine and him; Bede and Rhabanus Maurus do not give such a text: cf. Bede, *In S. Joannis Evangelistam expositio*, c. 21 (*PL* 92: 934A-C), where the Augustinian passage is repeated at length.

[43] See Paul Anciaux, *La Théologie du Sacrement de Pénitence au XIIᵉ siècle* (Louvain: Nauwelaerts; Gembloux: Duculot, 1949), and Ludwig Hödl, *Die Geschichte der scholastischen*

regularly broadened from Peter to include all priests. Anciaux gives texts from Bandinus, Peter Manducator, Gandulph of Bologna, Peter Cantor, Peter of Capua, and Stephen Langton that do this without remarking it in any way.[44] In a few cases authors do mention that the keys or the power of binding and loosing were first given to Peter or given to him in a special way and then to others. Thus Udo says: "Where are those keys, which the Lord handed over to Peter and his successors, saying: *I will give you the keys* etc.?"[45] Odo of Ourscamp speaks of Peter's passing on the powers to his successor personally, and Peter of Capua remarks that the text about binding and loosing was said "to Peter and his followers."[46]

In a homily Radulphus Ardens, quoting Matthew 16:19, first shows the relation of Peter (and all the apostles) to Christ as pastor and foundation of the Church: although Christ alone is pastor and alone the real foundation of the Church (*substantialiter ... fundamentum*), Peter is called pastor by denomination from Christ, and Peter and the other apostles are called the foundations of the Church (undoubtedly denominatively from Christ as well); so, too, he continues, although only Christ is the rock, yet Peter is called rock by denomination from him.[47] This is really an adaptation of the

---

Literatur und der Theologie der Schlüsselgewalt, 1. Teil: *Die scholastische Literatur und die Theologie der Schlüsselgewalt von ihren Anfängen an bis zur Summa Aurea des Wilhelm von Auxerre,* Beiträge zur Geschichte der Philosophie und Theologie des Mittelalters 38/4 (Münster Westfalen: Aschendorff, 1960).

[44] See pp. 493, n. 2 (Bandinus), 495-496, n. 5 (Peter Manducator), 479-480, nn. 2-3 (Gandulph), 504 (Peter Cantor), 515-516 (Peter of Capua), 518 (Langton). Praepositinus, however, speaking of the powers of a bishop concerning indulgences, which he calls *absolutiones,* affirms the bishops' power to grant them "quia Dominus dicit, *quodcumque solveritis super terram erit solutum et in celis.* Sed hanc absolutionem facit episcopus iuste et sine errore. Ergo iste dans absolutus est." Text from his *Summa* IV: *De satisfactione,* ed. Daniel Edward Pilarczyk, *Praepositini Cancellarii de Sacramentis et de Novissimis [Summae Theologicae Pars Quarta]: A Critical Text and Introduction* (Rome: Editiones Urbanianae, 1964) p. 73. In this case the text addressed to all the apostles supports the authority of the bishop as successor of the apostles.

[45] "Ubi sunt claues ille, quas Dominus tradidit Petro et successoribus eius dicens, Tibi dabo claues etc.?" Quoted in Anciaux, p. 492. Cf. the statement of the Vatican *Summa* "Ne transgrediaris" (MS Vat. lat. 10754): "De potestate vero sacerdotum dicens Petro, et in eo omnibus sacerdotibus ait (Mt. 16:19): *Quodcumque ligaveris ....*" Quoted in Hödl, p. 299.

[46] Odo says: "Hanc potestatem Petrus Clementi commisit, dicente auctoritate: potestatem mihi a Domino Jesu traditam tibi trado ligandi et solvendi" (quoted by Anciaux, p. 495, n. 1). Peter of Capua remarks: "Item, dictum est Petro et sequacibus suis: Quodcumque ligaveris super terram, etc." (quoted ibid., p. 519).

[47] "*... Et super hanc petram aedificabo ecclesiam meam.* Sicut enim, quamvis solus Christus sit pastor, tamen ab eo denominative Petrus dicitur pastor, et quamvis solus Christus sit substantialiter ecclesiae fundamentum, tamen Petrus ceterique apostoli ecclesiae fundamenta dicuntur: ita quamvis solus Christus sit petra, tamen denominative ab eo Petrus dicitur petra." Quoted by Hödl, p. 295, n. 11; from *Homil.* 23, *in festo Petri apostoli* (*PL* 155: 1391).

text of Augustine seen in the Lombard. Radulphus continues by saying that
although all the apostles received the keys equally, Peter was addressed alone
to show that anyone who rejects unity with the church is deprived of the
powers of binding and loosing.[48]

Magister Martinus reports an argument saying that the authority of prelates
is as much their own as the pope's authority is his. He replies that the
authority of prelates is a lesser one constituted under the other and greater
authority of the pope.[49] This is one argument in a whole series about the keys
and excommunication, but in both question and reply it is taken for granted
that the pope has a greater power. This is usually the case in such discussions;
it may explain why there is a lack of extensive examination of the papacy's
power or roles in many questions.

Excommunication and obedience are related by Peter Cantor to the power
of the keys. Comparing the powers of primates and metropolitans with that
of the pope, he says: "As for the supreme pontiff, it is certain that he has the
fullness of power."[50] As for obedience, he gives the case of a command by
the pope. Some people, he says, think they would not be guilty of disobedience if they were to refuse to obey a written mandate of the pope in cases
where the mandate did not command expressly in virtue of obedience. Peter
finds this hard to believe ("mirum est").[51] He comments that in both the Old
and New Testaments commands were given without such a formula and yet
those receiving them were bound to obey. He gives as one example the case
of Saul's receiving a simple command and being punished by God for not
obeying it.[52] Another practical case discussed by Peter Cantor is whether a

---

[48] "Porro duae claves omnibus aequaliter apostolis dantur. Unde et post resurrectionem
suam Dominus eis inspirans ait: *Accipite spiritum sanctum.* ... Hic tamen ad solum Petrum
sermo dirigitur ut ostendatur quia qui unitatem ecclesiae non sequitur, a clavibus ligandi atque
solvendi privatur." Quoted ibid.

[49] "Item, papa in sacris oraculis suis auctoritate apostolica interdicit aliquid. Quam
auctoritatem habuit Petrus in ecclesia, habet omnis praelatus vel apostolicus. Ergo auctoritate
sua ligat vel solvit praelatus. Responsio: Quandam auctoritatem minorem habet praelatus, quia
ligat vel solvit; et illa minor auctoritas constituta est sub quadam alia maiore auctoritate."
Quoted in Hödl, p. 249.

[50] *Summa de sacramentis et animae consiliis,* IIa pars, no. 154, ed. Jean-Albert Dugauquier, Analecta Mediaevalia Namurcensia 7 (Louvain: Nauwelaerts; Lille: Giard, 1957),
p. 379: "De summo pontifice certum est quod habeat plenitudinem potestatis."

[51] Ibid., no. 155; pp. 380-381: "Officio clauium annexa est obedientia .... Item, *melior est
obedientia quam uictima* [1 Sam. 15:22; Eccl. 4:17]: Sed mirum est cum scribit summus
pontifex ita: 'Mandamus ut hoc facias,' si non obeditur tali mandato, ut dicunt quidam, non
incurrunt ex hoc reatum inobedientie, nec ex aliquo mandato nisi sic scribatur: 'Mandamus
et mandando precipimus in uirtute obedientie'."

[52] Ibid., p. 381: "Hec enim forma precipiendi non inuenitur in ueteri testamento, et tamen
ligabat. Vnde quia Saul pepercit Agag regi pinguissimo non parcitum est ei a Samuele quin
mordaciter argueret eum, sed nec a Domino. Simplicem tamen preceptionem accepit Saul.
Simile preceptum habes in actibus [*sic*] et in aliis locis." Vide Act 10:13 et 15:28.

deacon or subdeacon delegated by the pope has the power of the keys. Peter maintains that such a delegate has "the mandate of the lord pope in this matter and the use of the keys of the lord pope for a time, and so he can bind by the authority of the lord pope."[53] Thus even without the order of priesthood such a person could for a time have the use of the power of the keys by reason of papal delegation.

With respect to indulgences, it is remarkable that Peter Lombard's *Sententiae* have no discussion of them. Indeed, this subject began to interest theologians seriously only towards the end of the twelfth century. Before that, one meets passing references to them in Simon of Tournai and Radulphus Ardens, who use the terms *absolvere* and *remissio*.[54] Peter of Poitiers is one of the first to use the term that was to become common for a long time, *relaxationes*.[55] In a few texts the pope's authority in the matter of indulgences is indicated. Thus Peter Cantor, faced with opposed opinions about the time one is freed by such a *relaxatio*, says: "Which of the opinions is true, consult the lord pope or the bishop who gives such a relaxation. It is not for me to raise my mouth to heaven."[56] It is to be noted here that bishops are also seen to have the power to grant indulgences. This point, and the pope's greater authority, are brought out in MS Erlangen 260 when it lists conditions for indulgences, among them "the devotion of the general church that emits them, namely that of the lord pope or of the bishop in his diocese."[57] Here the pope is linked with the *ecclesia generalis* and his powers of granting indulgences is extended to this realm.

---

[53] Ibid., De excommunicatione, no. 7; Dugauquier, p. 440: "Item. Queritur utrum diaconus aut subdiaconus qui habet curam animarum possit ligare et soluere. ... Dicendum quod non. Possunt tamen aliis precipere ut hoc faciant. Sed nunquid idem dicendum de iudice diacono uel subdiacono a domino papa delegato? Forte non, cum habeat mandatum domini pape super hoc et ipse habet ad tempus usum clauium domini pape, et ita potest ligare auctoritate domini pape."

[54] See Hödl, p. 230 (for Simon of Tournai) and pp. 245-246 (for Randulphus), as well as pp. 258-259, where a list of questions on the topic is given. See also Nikolaus Paulus, "Die Ablasslehre der Frühscholastik," *Zeitschrift für katholische Theologie* 34 (1910) 433-472, especially, for the late 12th century, pp. 435-449 (Peter Cantor, Alan of Lille, the canonist Alanus, Praepositinus, and Girardus of Cambrai).

[55] 3 *Sent.*, c. 16; *PL* 211: 1076A (quoted by Hödl, p. 258): "Cum autem dictum sit quod sacerdos solvit aliquem iniungendo ei satisfactionem vel aliquid relaxando de poena ...."

[56] *Summa de sacramentis*, IIa pars, no. 110; ed. Dugauquier, pp. 195-196: "Utra opinionum vera sit, consule dominum papam uel episcopum qui talem dat relaxationem. Non est meum ponere os meum in caelum." Quoted by Hödl, pp. 286, 319.

[57] "In relaxationibus quinque ad minus sunt attendenda, scilicet ... devotio ecclesiae generalis mittentis scilicet domini papae vel episcopi in sua diocesi ...." Quoted by Hödl, p. 333.

We have already seen a text from Praepositinus maintaining a bishop's right to grant indulgences; see above, n. 44. In the same section Praepositinus gives an argument, with which he seems to agree, that the giving of indulgences is a "generalis ... consuetudo ecclesiae contra quam disputare non licet. Ergo talis absolutio valet" (quoted by Pilarczyk, p. 73).

Towards the end of the twelfth century or in the first years of the thirteenth century questions began to be raised about the power of the pope to grant a common indulgence to those who had different obligations regarding works of satisfactory penance; another case was that of persons who had not confessed their sins and so would not know what penance they were bound to do: could the pope grant them a common indulgence?[58] In a similar vein questions were raised about the pope's power to dispense from tithes or from the law. One questioner notes that the pope had dispensed the Cistercians from tithes and had done the same for the Hospitalers and Templars, and these were laymen. Could he, then, dispense all lay people from this obligation of tithes?[59] The author replies that it is not in his competence, and indeed it is impossible, to define what the pope can do. He cites the case, astonishing to theologians of that time, of Alexander III's allowing a wife who had not had relations with her husband to enter religion.[60] One explanation for this dispensation is that the pope would not have said it was possible

---

[58] Paris, BN, MS lat. 14526, fol. 141vb: "Item, sicut summus pontifex non potest iniungere communem satisfactionem ambobus peregrinis ad eum venientibus, cum quidam magis sunt rei quam alii, et indiscrete iniungere parem satisfactionem dispariter reis, quia contra illud esset: *facite dignos fructus poenitentiae*, nec etiam minimo eorum potest iniungere satisfactionem nisi cognito peccato per confessionem, multominus potest facere communem relaxationem dispariter ligatorum nec etiam aliquos relaxare a modico nisi peccato per confessionem agnito et quanta ligatus sit satisfactione." Quoted by Hödl, pp. 340-341. Scriptural text: Luke 3:8.

[59] Paris, BN, MS lat. 14556, fol. 243va: "Item, quaeritur quantum dominus <papa> possit dispensare circa solutionem decimarum vel circa ius. Constat quod dispensavit cum ordine Cisterciensi ita quod solvere non tenetur, licet quidam solvant. Dispensavit etiam cum Hospitaliariis et Templariis, qui laici sunt. Sed constat quod in Lege decimae Levitis dabantur et solvebantur, quorum vicem clerici nunc [tunc MS] gerunt: ergo et istis solvi debebantur decimae. Cum ergo dominus papa quibusdam laicis dispensavit, scilicet Templariis, quaeritur utrum possit omnibus laicis dispensare ita quod non teneantur eas solvere." (Quoted by Hödl, p. 344, but corrected here from the manuscript.)

[60] Ibid.: "Dicimus quod non est nostrum nec possibile definire quantum dominus papa possit. Nam quis auderet <dicere> ante tempus Alexandri quod uxor incognita a viro possit se transferre ad religionem, et quis ante non negaret dominum papam posse circa hoc dispensare, cum videret in Evangelio ...: *Quod ergo Deus coniunxit, homo non separet* [Mark 10:9, Matt. 19:6.]"

Discussing a definition of matrimony, Praepositinus adverts to the decision of Alexander, which he accepts quite easily by suggesting that the original marriage intention included the possibility of common consent allowing such a separation for entry into religion. See his *Summa: De matrimonio et primo de causis*; ed. Pilarczyk (see above, n. 44) p. 101: "Item queritur ad quid ponatur in descriptione, *individuam vite consuetudinem retinens. ...* Eadem est obiectio [as concerning the marriage of infidels] inter sponsum et sponsam de matrimonio quod est, etc. Nam et illud potest dissolvi si alter transeat ad religionem sicut dicit Alexander tertius. Dicimus ergo quod in his verbis notatur propositum numquam divertendi nisi de pari consensu." Praepositinus also quotes Pope Hadrian as an "authority" concerning the validity of marriage between slaves even when the master is opposed, see ibid.; p. 105. Pilarczyk identifies the canonical source as *Comp.* Ia, c. 1, 1 IV. tit. 9 (ibid., n. to 37-41).

unless it had been revealed to him. The author seems to imply that likewise in the case of tithes only a revelation could allow the pope to dispense the laity since this would be against the gospel. But, he adds disarmingly, if the pope acts differently, I will admit I was deceived.[61]

2.4. Authoritative Papal Teaching About Faith.

The attitude expressed by the theologian in the text just quoted invites another inquiry about the pope. We shall see in the following essay that the episcopal and monastic authors made important statements about the role of the pope with regard to teaching, especially in matters of faith. Did the schoolmen speak about this, and so strongly? It would seem not. Artur Landgraf's prodigious reading of printed and manuscript material of the twelfth and early thirteenth centuries uncovered only a very few texts, and these quite hesitant ones, about the pope's power to decide matters of faith by himself.[62] Peter Cantor, finding some difficulties with Pope Alexander III's decision about a returning pilgrim's marital problems, asks how the Holy Spirit taught the decision to the pope. He seems to accept the decision reluctantly, simply quoting texts from scripture to indicate that the Holy Spirit would not permit the pope to be in error or ignorance.[63] Here again,

---

[61] Paris BN, MS lat. 14556, fol. 243va: "Praeterea tamen decretalis fuit data. Dicit [Dicunt MS] quisque dominum papam posse dispensare qui prius negabat sic fuisse, et credibile est quod dominus papa numquam hoc dixisset nisi esset ei revelatum. Modo similiter dicimus quod papa non posset dispensare cum his qui penitus laici sunt ne solvant, id est, decimas nummicas, cum in Evangelio sit expressum, et hoc confirmet nova decretalis quae de illis solvendis occurrit, ne praeceptum evangelicum de illis videatur commutatum vel commutandum. Si vero aliter a papa fiat, dicam me fuisse deceptum."

[62] See his "Scattered Remarks on the Development of Dogma and on Papal Infallibility in Early Scholastic Writings," *Theological Studies* 7 (1946) 577-582, reprinted with the addition of a few texts as "Sporadische Bemerkungen im Schriftum der Frühscholastik über Dogmenentwicklung und päpstliche Unfehlbarkeit," in his *Dogmengeschichte der Frühscholastik* 1/1 (Regensburg, 1952) pp. 30-36.

[63] The case was that of a man returning from a pilgrimage to Jerusalem and finding his wife married to another and with two children by her second partner. Alexander prescribed that he should neither take back his wife nor marry another. Peter Cantor comments (*In 1 Joan.* 2; Paris BN, MS lat. 176, fol. 282, quoted by Landgraf, pp. 578-579 and 31-32): "Et constat quod matrimonium fuit inter illum et illam vel non. Si non: quare aliam non potuit ducere? Si vero matrimonium fuit inter eos, quare non est ei reddita? Quomodo Spiritus Sanctus docuit hoc dominum papam? Videtur autem quod si Spiritus Sanctus fuerit in aliquo, non permitteret eum errare vel ignorare. Unde: *Paraclitus Spiritus Sanctus docebit vos omnem veritatem* [cf. Joan. 16:13]. Item, *si quid petieritis in nomine meo, fiet vobis* [cf. Joan. 15:16]. Cum ergo iste in quo est Spiritus Sanctus petat in nomine Christi ut ei matrimonium reveletur, an hoc sit an non, numquid ei revelabit Spiritus Sanctus? Et item: *qui manet in me non ambulat in tenebris* [cf. Joan. 8:12]. Et habet *Glossa*: 'Nec in tenebris peccatorum nec in tenebris ignorantiae'." (Punctuation slightly changed.)

Peter Cantor speaks of another limitation of papal power and of possible papal error while discussing dispensation from vows: "... Nisi causa in natura sui sit sufficiens ad rumpendum

as in the text seen at the end of the previous sub-section, there is question of a revelation to the pope to help him make a decision. In this case, however, the matter is one of fact, although a doctrine about matrimony is implied.

The clearest case in the twelfth century of a papal directive about a doctrine of faith was Alexander III's anathema pronounced against those who held that "Christ according as he is man is not something (*aliquid*)," a condemnation he issued on his own in letters addressed to certain French bishops.[64] Some theologians were surprised and disturbed over this action because it was taken by the pope without his invoking a council or synod.[65] Peter of Capua reflects this atmosphere when he says that before Alexander's decree it was not, according to some theologians, an article of faith to say that Christ as man is *aliquid*. From the whole context of his discussion it can be seen that he judged them to be in factual error about the doctrine before the decree without their being at fault at that time. But if this teaching is said to have become an article of faith after the decree, the question then is whether indeed the pope can establish such an article by himself.[66] Peter's own

---

uotum uel iuramentum, non potest dominus papa rumpere illud uel mutare uel etiam dispensare, sed solum iudicare de causa an sit uel non sit sufficiens ad rumpendum uel pocius non obseruandum uotum uel iuramentum, quia rumpi proprie non dicitur sed non obseruari, cum subsit causa efficiens non obseruandi. Ab initio enim tenet si fuerit licitum. Si uero illicitum, ipso iure irritum est ab initio. Sepe tamen dominus papa dispenset in huiusmodi ubi dispensandum non esset quia fallitur propter obscuritatem cause, et approbat factum illius ecclesia, sed non Deus." *Summa de sacramentis*, Appendix V, 18; ed. Dugauquier, III, 2b (Louvain-Lille, 1967) p. 732.

[64] See Walter Principe, *The Theology of the Hypostatic Union in the Early Thirteenth Century*, vol. 1: *William of Auxerre's Theology of the Hypostatic Union*, Studies and Texts 7 (Toronto: Pontifical Institute of Mediaeval Studies, 1963), pp. 67-68 and p. 201, n. 52.

[65] See A. Landgraf, "Diritto canonico e teologia nel secolo XII" in *Studia Gratiana* 1, eds. J. Forchielli and A. M. Stickler (Bologna, 1953) pp. 394-395, and "Scattered Remarks," p. 580, where he gives a text of the Vatican *Summa* "Ne transgrediaris" (MS Vat. lat. 10754) in which, referring to Pope Alexander's anathematizing of the *non-est-aliquid* doctrine concerning Christ, the author asks "an summus pontifex aliquem possit de novo articulum instituere." An argument quotes the pope's decision as proof that this is possible, but the author replies that the pope's authority is not enough unless he has the authority and consent of a "common (general?) council": "Solutio: Ad quod respondemus quod bene potest cum auctoritate et consensu communis concilii, et quilibet prudens et discretus debeat ei acquiescere nec sine periculo possit contra recalcitrare" (fol. 5v).

As N. Haring notes in his "The Case of Gilbert de la Porrée Bishop of Poitiers (1142-1154)," *MedS* 13 (1951) 37, there was indeed a (local) conciliar debate about the question at Tours in 1163 in the presence of Pope Alexander III, but no decision was made at the time.

[66] For the whole context see MS Vat. lat. 4304, fol. 39vb. Two questions are examined, the one at hand about Christ and another about whether it is an article of faith that Paternity is the Father or God. Peter first speaks of this: "Respondeo: Paternitatem esse Patrem vel Deum non est articulus fidei, et ideo utraque pars potest teneri sine periculo quia invincibilis

position is that the pope has such a power and that if someone knowingly and seriously denies the article, he sins mortally at least by disobedience.[67]

Despite these doubts, Alexander's text came to be considered definitive and authoritative; it was constantly quoted as an authority in the christological debates of the late twelfth and the thirteenth centuries. Of course, like all authoritative texts, it was constantly subject to interpretation and was read in different ways by different authors.[68]

Here it can be helpful to go outside the texts of theologians to recall the opinions of the canonist, Huguccio, who so strongly influenced theologians of this period. Landgraf gives a text from him in which he maintains that in some cases (provided there is no evil in the decision) the pope can prescribe that his opinion be held even against that of a council, and he can require obedience in such cases.[69] Yet in other texts Huguccio says that one must determine whether the pope is speaking as pope or only as a master giving his opinion; in the latter case he could err. Moreover, even if the pope should err, the Roman Church never errs as a totality: the Roman Church for him is either the whole Catholic Church, or the pope and the cardinals, and

---

ignorantia omnino hic excusat, nec peccat aliquo modo vel qui hoc negat vel qui asserit. Si tamen alterutrum esset peccatum, maius peccatum esset hoc negare quam asserere. Si quis etiam de hoc dubitaret, potius deberet adhaerere parti affirmativae quia postea inveniuntur locutiones in scripturis ut nihil est in Deo quod non sit Deus et huiusmodi. Etiam quod Christus sit aliquid secundum quod homo est articulus. Sed quidam hoc negabant ante datum decretum. Ergo errabant. Quod si dicatur quod tunc non erat hic articulus sed tantum post datum decretum, quaeritur ergo utrum papa possit facere aliquem articulum."

[67] Ibid.: "Respondeo: Hoc concedo (concedere MS) quod 'Christus non sit aliquid secundum quod homo' ante datum decretum tunc non erat articulus. Sed nunc est articulus, id est, peccat mortaliter qui hoc scienter negat quia saltem est inobediens. Et ubi talis est quaestio quod utraque pars habet auctoritates et rationes, potest papa instituere ut tantum alterum teneatur et de cetero erit illa pars articulus, id est, mortaliter peccat qui <eam> scienter et serio negat."

[68] For the subsequent history of interpretation of the decree see Principe, *Hypostatic Union*, 1: 68, 71-74, and 201-206.

[69] See Landgraf "Diritto canonico," p. 395, n. 130: "In illa synodo colligitur, quod papa potest quoslibet iudicare etiam invitis episcopis suis, et quod absque sinodo [*sic*] sive concilio potest novos canones condere et quod contra voluntatem concilii potest sententiare. Sed ecce, congregatum est concilium de toto orbe. Oritur dubitatio. Fertur una sententia a solo papa, alia ab omnibus aliis. Que ergo cui est preponenda? Dicunt hic, quod sententia pape. Distinguo tamen et dico: si altera continet iniquitatem, illi preiudicatur. Si vero neutra videtur continere iniquitatem et dubium est, que veritatem continet, pares debent esse et ambe teneri et hec vel illa pro voluntate potest eligi, quia paris sunt auctoritatis, cum hinc sit maior auctoritas, inde maior numerus .... Si tamen papa precipiat, ut sua sententia teneatur et non teneatur sententia concilii, obediendum est ei et sua[m] sententia[m] tenenda[m] et non illa[m] ..." (final corrections by Landgraf). This text is also given by Landgraf in his "Sporadische Bemerkungen," p. 33, n. 8; it is from *Summa Decreti*, c. 9, q. 4 (Bamberg MS Can. 40, fol. 130).

neither the whole Church nor all the cardinals will err.[70] Here we find an opinion that will also be seen in Gerhoh of Reichersberg, who likewise distinguished between the pope as a private person and the Roman Church, the true possessor of indefectibility in faith.[71] On these grounds, as Landgraf notes, Huguccio rejected certain decisions of Alexander III.[72] But when it came to the authoritative decision about Christ's being *aliquid* as man, Huguccio is firmer in maintaining the pope's authority and goes further than Peter of Capua: he says that those who oppose the pope's decision are guilty of heresy and are excommunicated.[73] Even in this strong text, however,

[70] Text from Landgraf, "Sporadische Bemerkungen," p. 34, n. 13: "Sed dico quod Romana Ecclesia dicitur tota Catholica Ecclesia, que numquam in totum erravit, vel Romana Ecclesia dicitur papa, card<inales>, et licet ille erravit, non tamen cardinales, vel saltem non omnes" (from dist. 19; fol. 14).
A similar idea occurs later when the case of Pope Anastasius is presented as a difficulty about the inerrancy of the pope: 'A recta-apostolico', id est apostolicorum 'numquam errasse'. Obicitur de Anastasio. Sed forte processit. Vel forte melius quod est, loquitur universali Ecclesie, que numquam desinet, licet forte possit deficere. Licet enim papa Romanus aliquando erraverit, non ideo Romana Ecclesia, quae non solus papa intelligitur, sed universi fideles. Nam Ecclesia est congregatio fidelium, ut di. 1 Ecclesia, que etsi Rome non sit, est tamen in partibus gallicanis potissime vel ubicumque fideles existunt. Et ecclesia quid[em] potest desinere esse, sed numquam contigit. Nam Petro et universe ecclesie in prima Petri dictum est: *Non deficit fides tua* ... [cf. Luke 22:32]" (quoted by Landgraf, "Scattered Remarks," p. 581, and "Sporadische Bemerkungen," p. 35).
[71] See the following essay, "Monastic, Episcopal, and Apologetic Theology of the Papacy, 1150-1250," sect. 1.2.b.
[72] See "Sporadische," p. 34. On the other hand, Master Simon of Tournai, whose *quaestiones* come from the last part of the twelfth century, entertains the possibility that the Church could err in canonizations; see J. Warichez, introd. and ed., *Les "Disputationes" de Simon de Tournai: Texte inédit*, disp. 92, q. 4 (Louvain, 1932) p. 267: "Item queritur, utrum omnibus canonizatis debeamus sollemnizare. Videtur quod non. Multi enim damnati errore Ecclesie sunt canonizati; quibus non est sollemnizandum. Redditur. Esse potest quod multi sunt canonizati, tamen parendum est Ecclesie que precepit eis sollemnizari, dum eos canonizavit." Simon's *quaestiones*, which range over many varied theological problems, have practically nothing on the Church and nothing at all on the pope. There is a brief discussion of the two swords in terms of *princeps* and *pontifex* (disp. 82, q. 4; p. 239), but this does not refer specifically to the pope: "Redditur: Materialem gladium causam habere a spirituali. Coniuncti enim sunt isti duo gladii, ut alter non possit esse sine alio. Unde Dominus: *Ecce gladii duo hic* [Luke 22:38], quasi simul coniuncti. Sed materialis a spirituali est. ... In omni enim ritu coniuncta sunt ista duo: regnum et sacerdotium." Peter is mentioned once (disp. 82, q. 1, p. 238), when it is asked if he did not unjustly excommunicate Saphira and Anania; cf. Acts 5:3-4. Simon says: "Redditur. Quod pretore auctore fit, iuste fieri interpretamur, ait lex romana. A simili ergo, quod Deo auctore et Spiritu Sancto instigante Petrus fecit, iuste fecit. ... Eo ipso aliquid iustum est, quia a Domino iussum est." Whether Simon would extend this to popes is problematic. This lack of interest in the pope seems typical of the period; the same is true of other authors we have been able to examine, e.g., the influential Praepositinus.
[73] See Landgraf, "Sporadische Bemerkungen," p. 33, n. 10: "Ergo cum Alexander sententialiter dixit quod Christus est aliquid secundum quod homo, in extra 'Cum Christus', et hoc non contineat iniquitatem nec pendeat ex arbitrio aliorum, ita credendum est et pec<c>at qui dissentit et macula excommunicationis et heresis notatur ...."

Huguccio indicates that one must make a judgment whether or not a decision of the pope "contains iniquity"; it may have been this qualification that allowed Huguccio to reject some decisions of the pope by seeing them as coming from him as from a fallible human person.

*
* *

Judging from the rather occasional texts that have been seen in this section as well as from the silence of most *sententiae* and *summae*, we may conclude that the school theologians of the twelfth century displayed relatively little interest in the papacy. Perhaps, as secular masters, they were more attuned to their particular or local churches and prelates, more concerned about issues closer to home. Judging from the reaction to the intervention of Alexander III, we might conclude that they expected and were used to a more synodal (today we would say collegial) manner of settling questions. Again, they may have been less interested in concrete practical pastoral matters, where questions about the pope did arise occasionally and were to do so increasingly in the thirteenth century, to which we now turn.

3. The First Half of the Thirteenth Century

3.1. The Power of the Keys.

In the late twelfth century, we have seen, questions about the power of the keys led to passing remarks about the pope. This was also true in the first half of the thirteenth century. And as commentaries on Lombard's *Sententiae* became part of the university curriculum, his distinctions concerning Penance in book 4 occasioned comments about the pope. Also, his distinctions on marriage impediments or on dispensations from vows gave rise to references to the pope. Within these areas in Lombard new discussions of dispensations and indulgences again led to some references to the pope's powers.

The Petrine text of Matthew 16:18 found no uniform interpretation among theologians of the early thirteenth century. Both Stephen Langton and Godfrey of Poitiers quote earlier interpretations referring the *petra* of the text to Christ and seeing Peter receiving his name from Christ, the rock (*petra*).[74] Each, however, prefers to view *Petrus* and *petra* as referring to constant, firm

---

[74] "Ad sequentes dicimus quod illud Matthei: *Tu es Petrus et super hanc petram*, id est, super meipsum petram, cuius nominis tu es particeps quia a me petra diceris Petrus, *edificabo Ecclesiam meam.*" Quoted by Anciaux (see above, n. 45), p. 520. For a similar text from Godfrey see ibid., p. 581. Cf. also the citation of this text in Lombard's scriptural commentary; see above, pp. 55-56.

faith: the promise to Peter is that he will receive help lest he err, a helpful gift he received, however, only at Pentecost.[75]

Within this context one finds statements about the pope having the highest power of absolving from sin. Stephen Langton sees the power of the keys as more and more extensive, beginning with monks without prelacy, and moving up to parish priests, bishops, and the pope.[76] Godfrey of Poitiers again seems to depend on Langton for a similar statement.[77] For both authors the possession of the keys comes from ordination, but their use depends on another authority: these authors are moving towards the distinction between order and jurisdiction that will become clearer in the near future.[78]

Robert Courson calls this added element of authority a *licentia* coming to an ordained person from his abbot or bishop or the pope. In ordination the person receives a key that gives him authority to bind and loose; the license from the superior authority gives him the key habitually, which passes into act when he actually binds or looses.[79] A more difficult case is faced by Courson: What of the power of excommunication in someone delegated by the pope? If the delegate is an ordained priest, there is no problem. But what, it is asked, if such a delegate is not an ordained priest, e.g., a subdeacon or acolyte? Robert Courson replies that such a delegate's mandate does not include the use of the keys since he does not have the keys if he is not an ordained priest. His delegation gives him "the use and the office of a spiritual

---

[75] "Alio modo sic exponitur: *super hanc petram*, id est, super firmitatem fidei *tue edificabo Ecclesiam meam*. Et ad hanc expositionem pertinet predicta auctoritas, in qua debet fieri uis in hoc quod dicitur: *edificabo*. Edificium enim firmitatem et constantiam notat. Vnde bene concedimus quod si illa glosa, scilicet *edificabo ... regni celorum*, statim dedisset, non inueniret error postea in eo locum, sed illud, super firmitatem fidei tue *edificabo Ecclesiam meam*, non est ei datum usque quando indutus est uirtute ex alto, scilicet in Pentecoste. Vnde remotio erroris non est referenda tantum ad clauium collationem, sed potius ad confirmationem per uerbum edificandi notatam." Quoted in Anciaux, p. 520; cf. Godfrey, quoted ibid., pp. 581-582.

[76] "Quidam sacerdotes, ut simplices monachi, qui non habent praelationem, habent claves sine executione sive sine usu. Quidam vero, ut parrochiales, habent minorem executionem, episcopi maiorem, summus pontifex maximam." Quoted in Hödl (see above, n. 43) p. 352, n. 16.

[77] "Dicimus quod quidam habent claues, sed non executionem clauium, ut simplices monachi. Alii habent paruam executionem ut simplices sacerdotes. Alii magnam ut episcopi. Dominus papa maximam." Quoted in Anciaux, p. 580.

[78] See below, pp. 83-87.

[79] "Solutio. Sicut dicimus in secularibus litteris quod aliud est habere naturaliter, aliud in habitu, aliud in usu ..., ita est de fatuo uel claustrali ordinato in sacerdotem, qui in receptione ordinis recipit clauem et ita recipit sacramentaliter auctoritatem ligandi et soluendi. Cum uero fatuus discretior efficitur et claustralis licentiam habet a suo abbate uel episcopo uel domino papa clauem habet in habitu, quia promptus est ad ligandum et soluendum. Cum uero actualiter ligat uel soluit iam habet actum siue usum ligandi et soluendi." Quoted in Anciaux, p. 570.

privilege that derives from the general use of the keys, which the pope extends to all." This last phrase is suggestive of the pope's universal power. Courson continues: "By this privilege he can interdict land, suspend others, forbid entry to the church or reception of the sacraments to some. But he must not absolve penitents or impose penances himself but only through his chaplain," who would be ordained.[80]

Godfrey of Poitiers repeats this teaching, saying that the delegates "have from the authority of the lord pope a certain sub-authority by which they can excommunicate ...." [81]

In a question *de relaxationibus* Godfrey of Poitiers summarizes two arguments that begin with the pope's fullness of power in the matter of absolution, especially in the matter of indulgences freeing a person from the penalty owing to sin. Quoting the Petrine promise, the argument says that the pope, like Peter, has the fullness of power and so can absolve a person from all sin.[82] So too, a text from Paul shows that "if the pope condones a penalty, his condonation is of as great value as if Christ were to condone it."[83] Another detailed argument again refers to the pope's power of granting indulgences.[84]

Although in his solution and responses Godfrey does not seem to reply directly to these arguments, he does indicate that the *relaxatio* or indulgence granted by the pope must be related only to sins that have been confessed; this is clearly his view because he says the indulgence does not apply to sins

[80] "De legato (Delegato *ed.*) misso a domino papa dicimus quod si non est sacerdos, sicut non habet claues, ita non recipit de mandato delegationis usum clauium. Sed recipit ex auctoritate legationis et legantis usum et officium spiritualis priuilegii deriuati a generali usu clauium, quem extendit dominus papa ad omnes. Et de illo priuilegio potest terram interdicere, istos suspendere, illos ab ingressu ecclesie et perceptione sacramentorum arcere. Sed non debet, cum non habeat claues, penitentes absoluere uel penitentias iniungere per se sed potius per suum capellanum." Quoted ibid., p. 573.

[81] "Dicimus quod ab auctoritate domini pape habent quamdam subauctoritatem, qua possunt facere excommunicare et qua possunt interdicere ingressum ecclesiae et suspendere." Quoted ibid., p. 583.

[82] "Item, *quaecumque solveris super terram erunt soluta* etc. Sicut habuit Petrus plenitudinem potestatis, ita et papa habet. Ergo si papa absolvit me ab omni peccato, absolutus sum." Quoted in Hödl, p. 356.

[83] "Item: Ad Corinthios Apostolus (2 Cor 2:10): *Cui vos donatis et ego, cui autem donavi propter vos feci in persona Christi*, et subiungit glossa, ac si Christus donaret. Sed constat, quod loquitur de condonatione poenae. Ergo si papa condonat de poena, tantum valet, quantum si Christus condonaret." Quoted ibid. The text goes on to say that a text of the *Glossa* supports this position about the pope: "Pro Domino papa facit glossa in Marco super illum locum (6. 28): *caput Johannis datum est puellae*, dicit ibi glossa: caput Johannis etc. puellae de gentibus id est Romanae ecclesiae. Romanae ergo ecclesiae datum est caput gratiae Dei, quia Johannes interpretatur gratia Dei." Quoted ibid.

[84] "Cum ergo dicit Dominus papa, quod quicumque obtulerit huic ecclesiae etc. non dicit qui obtulerit nummum vel obulum sed qui obtulerit!" Quoted ibid., p. 358.

that have been forgotten (and not confessed).[85] Further on, Godfrey indicates the power of the pope to relate the merits of any person to the burden or obligation of any other person, as well as his power to associate the merits of evil persons with the merits of the Church: the point of this is that if the merits of the church do not help to save the evil, at least they lessen the penalties they receive.[86]

As questions about indulgences grew more complicated during the succeeding decades of the thirteenth century, theologians began to recognize certain limits to the pope's power of granting indulgences. The total remission of all sins and immediate entry into heaven promised by preachers to those who took the cross on the crusades was one subject of controversy. William of Auxerre gives arguments opposed to these promises and then a counter-argument saying that "the lord pope has the fullness of power; therefore he can make so great a relaxation."[87] In his own solution William says that the pope's fullness of power extends to the crusaders' sharing all the suffrages of the Church, but it does not empower the pope to grant that a person owing a penalty should go to heaven at once without paying the penalty: the person must bring forth fruits of penance, which can be done either by himself or by the Church for him. William gives the example of a usurer: the pope cannot make his pilgrimage useful if the usurer fails to make restitution.[88]

Alexander of Hales, in his *Gloss on the Sententiae* of Peter Lombard, introduces a brief discussion of *relaxationes*. He shows the same concern for

---

[85] "Item pono, quod papa faciat sic relaxationem sicut dictum est: aut intelligit rectam relaxationem pro peccatis quae confessus est aut supra rectam pro istis vel pro illis; si tantum rectam, ergo non valet relaxatio ad peccata oblita; si supra rectam, non videtur quod debito modo fiat, immo quia sic intelligit, ut de illis remittatur, cum ea confessus fuerit secundum partem oblationis quae facta est pro illis." Quoted ibid.

[86] "Unde mihi videtur quod cum omnia beneficia ecclesiae referantur ad portandum peccata huius ab illo qui potest referre, videtur, inquam, quod statim liberatus, si decedit evolat. Cuiuslibet enim merita refert papa ad portandum cuiuslibet onera, et merita malorum, quae per se non prosunt ad salutem, sociata meritis ecclesiae multum valent ad delendum poenas malorum ...." Quoted ibid., p. 360.

[87] *Summa aurea* IV, tr. 14, c. 3; ed. Jean Ribaillier, Spicilegium Bonaventurianum, 19 (Grottaferrata: Collegium S. Bonaventurae ad Claras Aquas, 1985), p. 358: "Sed contra. Dominus papa habet plenitudinem potestatis; ergo facere potest tantam relaxationem."

[88] Ibid., p. 359: "Ad illud ergo quod obicitur, quod dominus papa habet plenitudinem potestatis, dicimus quod habet hanc potestatem, ut faciat cruce signatos participes omnium suffragiorum ecclesie; sed non habet hanc potestatem, ut istum qui est debitor pene faciat evolare sine solutione, immo necesse est quod suscipiat de manu Domini duplicia et quod faciat dignos fructus penitentie. Sed intelligitur facere penitentiam, si vel ipse vel ecclesia faciat pro eo, sicut dominus papa non potest facere quin usurarius cruce signatus restituat quod habet de usura, ad hoc ut peregrinatio sit ei utilis."

For more on William of Auxerre's teaching on indulgences see N. Paulus, "Die Ablasslehre" (cited above, n. 54).

interior dispositions as William of Auxerre. To an argument saying that the Church does not lie in promising a full condonation of due penance, and to another argument pointing to the promise of indulgences made by prelates or "the lord pope," Alexander replies by insisting on the need for faith, for a correct judgment of the work substituted for the penalty, and for charity and contrition.[89] It should be noted here that Alexander's *Gloss* is remarkable for its introduction of a great deal of canonical material in its fourth book. By comparison with works to this time, his *Gloss* is a veritable mine of canonical quotations, and shows the opening of theologians to many problems either not discussed before or examined with little reference to the canonical materials that had often helped shape practice and theory.[90]

[89] See his *Glossa in quatuor libros Sententiarum* IV, d. 20, n. 14, I.f; eds. PP. Collegii S. Bonaventurae, 4 (Quaracchi, 1957) pp. 357-358: "Praeterea, Ecclesia universalis non peccat: quod patet, quia Dominus oravit pro ea, Luc. 22, 32, quod non deficeret fides eius in persona Petri; et in omnibus *exauditus est pro sua reverentia*, ut ad Hebr. 5, 7. Ergo Ecclesia non mentitur promittendo huiusmodi indulgentiam."

The second argument is found ibid., IV.n; ed. cit., 4: 359: "Praeterea, cum fiunt relaxationes a praelatis vel a domino Papa, quod 'quicumque contulerit [unum denarium] fabricae huius ecclesiae, remittimus ei tertiam partem iniunctae poenitentiae', et ille conferat: remittiturne ei tota poenitentia, si tres denarios conferat? Si non, tunc videtur Ecclesia deludere conferentes."

Hugh of Saint-Cher presents a similar argument about the Church's not deceiving: "Sit ergo quod sacerdos discretus iniungat alicui poenitentiam minorem condignam et ille faciat eam prout debet. Quaeritur an illa sit absolutus et videtur quod sic, quia facit quidquid iniunxit ei Ecclesia et per hoc credit absolvi. Ergo vel absolvitur vel Ecclesia decipit eum, quia si iniunxisset ei Ecclesia maiorem, libenter fecisset eam. Sed constat quod Ecclesia non decipit. Ergo ille est absolutus" (MS Vat. lat. 1098, fol. 165ra-va).

Alexander's answers are as follows: "Ad hoc autem quod relaxatio per quam in alio satisfacit recte fiat, exigitur fides vel intentio dantis: oportet enim ut credat ab Ecclesia posse fieri huiusmodi relaxationem; recta aestimatio: non enim pro obolo vel quantolibet fit quantacumque relaxatio. Facienda autem est huiusmodi aestimatio: quantum vellet dedisse ut absolveretur a tertia parte poenitentiae. Et si tantum dederit, exsistens in caritate aliisque convenientibus, tunc fit relaxatio; alioquin esset iniustitia, cum omni peccato poena propria debeatur" (*Glossa in Sent.* IV, 20, 14, IV, p; ed. cit., 4: 359). On the need for contrition he says: "Ad illud vero quod quaeritur, utrum possit fieri relaxatio sine aliqua poena illius cui fit, dicimus quod non. Oportet enim ad minus quod contritionem habeat, et praeter hoc, aliquam poenam sensibilem" (ibid. IV, 20, 14, IV, s: ed. cit., 4: 361).

Hugh of Saint-Cher's solution to the problem posed to him is as follows: "Dicimus igitur quod illa completa poenitentia minori condigna, tertio modo sumendi condigna, absolutus est quoad forum Ecclesiae militantis, sed non quoad forum Dei. Unde si decedat, sic residuum solvet" (MS cit., fol. 165va). The text goes on to explain that the person would have to pay the rest of his debt in purgatory.

[90] Whereas the first three books, according to the excellent indexes of the Quaracchi editors, contain less than ten references to the decretals or Gratian's *Decretum*, book 4 has several hundred such references. See "Index II: Auctores," ed. cit., 4: 602-603. In the late twelfth century Peter Cantor had already begun this process of including more canonical material, since he deals with many practical cases in his *Summa de sacramentis et animae consiliis*; see above, nn. 50-53, 56. Praepositinus quotes a fair number of texts from Gratian, but nowhere near the number given by Alexander; see the edition of Pilarczyk (cited above, n. 44).

In his *quaestiones* Alexander goes into greater detail about the power of the keys and about indulgences and here he includes a number of remarks about the pope. The final sub-section of his discussion of the keys is entitled: "How far does the pope's power of the keys extend?"[91] This is the clearest and most direct examination of papal power found thus far in any school theologian, and even though it is fairly brief, it marks an important turning point in theology. The first query met in the discussion is similar to that faced by William of Auxerre: since the pope has the fullness of power (*plenitudo potestatis*) can he not relax all penalty?[92] Alexander's reply again focuses on interior dispositions. God's justice requires a penalty for sin, so that the penitent must undergo some penalty, at least that of contrition: the will to undergo a penalty for sin that is part of contrition is itself already penal. Without this there can be no remission of the penalty due to the sin.[93]

The question then becomes more concrete. Cannot the pope bring it to pass that someone who has been given the penance of fasting should not have to fast? Alexander's reply is worth quoting in full:

> In so far as it pertains to the power of the Church, it is necessary that that penalty or a greater one be fulfilled by the Church. Therefore the pope cannot bring it about that neither that person nor anyone else should not perform that penance. However, he can bring it about that the person [who is the penitent] should not do it and that another should do it for him. This is the plenitude that belongs to him, because my penalty helps you and yours helps me if we are in charity.[94]

Alexander adds other causes that reflect the history of the times:

> There can be another cause [for relaxing penalties], namely, the need of the Church or the spread of heresies or the gaining of the Holy Land. This, joined

---

[91] See his *Quaestiones disputatae "Antequam esset frater"* 3: *Quaestiones* 60-68, q. 61, membrum 4, nos. 67-68; eds. PP. Collegii S. Bonaventurae (Quaracchi, 1960), pp. 1231-1232. The title, on p. 1231, reads: "Quousque extenduntur claves Papae."

[92] Ibid., no. 67; p. 1231: "Item quaeritur: cum Papa habeat plenitudinum potestatis, numquid potest relaxare omnem poenam?"

[93] Ibid.: "Respondeo: De iustitia Dei est quod poena sequatur peccatum; unde oportet quod poenitens aliquam poenam sustineat, ad minus contritionis. Unde dicitur in relaxationibus: 'qui vere contriti sint'; voluntas enim sustinendi poenam pro peccato, quae est in contritione, valde poenalis est. Haec autem est pars poenitentiae iniunctae, et sine hac non potest fieri remissio poenae."

[94] Ibid., no. 68: p. 1231: "Sed potestne facere Papa ne iste ieiunet, cui iniunctum est ieiunium? – Respondeo: Quantum est de potestate Ecclesiae, oportet quod ab Ecclesia expleatur illa poena vel maior. Non ergo potest facere Papa quod iste non faciat illam poenitentiam nec aliquis alius; potest tamen facere quod iste non faciat, et alius pro eo faciat – et haec est plenitudo quae residet apud ipsum – quia poena mea adiuvat te, et tua me, si sumus in caritate."

with [the pope's] fullness of power, produces the effect. Or it can happen as well from the merits of the co-members of the Church. And when it happens from such a cause together with [the pope's] power, then it comes from the power of God's mercy, which by reason of such a cause, joined to the fullness of power given to the pope, produces a relaxation of this kind.[95]

This reply is a remarkable instance of both assertion of full papal power and reminder of the greater role of God and of the communion of charity and merits of the members of the Church; throughout runs an awareness of limitations on the papal power.

The questioner then asks who is to do satisfaction for a person whose penalty has been relaxed by the pope. This seems to refer to the performance of the lesser penal or penitential work (almsgiving, prayer, etc.) that replaces the actual penalty.[96] Alexander replies that the one whose penalty has been relaxed should be the one who makes satisfaction. If the person cannot do it, then "he who has power has the duty to make satisfaction together with the co-members in the Church." Although the pope takes on himself the penalty of the one whose penalty is relaxed, the penitent must make satisfaction if he can; otherwise "the Church and he who has power are obliged to make satisfaction."[97] From the way the question is posed, it seems clear that Alexander means that the pope himself is obliged to satisfaction if the penitent cannot make it. The pope would have to do it either personally or through the merits of the Church.

A final important point about the papacy comes within a discussion of whether indulgences can be given through priests who are not bishops. Alexander maintains that their powers are not on the same level as that of

---

[95] Ibid.; pp. 1231-1232: "Potest iterum esse alia causa, scilicet necessitas Ecclesiae, pullulatio haeresum, vel acquisitio Terrae Sanctae. Haec, coniuncta cum potestatis plenitudine, facit sequi effectum; vel etiam ex meritis commembrorum Ecclesiae. Et quando fit ex causa, cum potestate, tunc venit ex virtute misericordiae Dei, quae ratione talis causae, cum potestate cuius plenitudo data est Papae, facit huiusmodi relaxationem."

[96] Ibid., q. 62, no. 24; p. 1241: "Ponamus ergo quod Papa relaxet isti poenam iniunctam sibi. Numquid ipse tenetur satisfacere pro illo, vel commembra Ecclesiae pro illo commembro suo, vel Papa cum membris, vel membrum cui fit relaxatio cum commembris suis et capite, scilicet Papa?"

[97] Ibid.: "Respondeo: Membri cui fit relaxatio est satisfacere dum potest; sed si non potest, tunc habentis potestatem cum commembris est satisfacere. Unde, licet Papa in se suscipit poenam illius cui fit relaxatio, tamen tenetur poenitens satisfacere dum potest; si vero non possit, obligatur Ecclesia et ille qui potestatem habet ad satisfaciendum."

The change in greater concentration on the pope in Alexander and those after him is illustrated by a similar discussion in Praepositinus, writing some twenty or thirty years earlier. His discussion is entirely about a bishop and the pope is not mentioned. See his *Summa* IV: *De satisfactione*; ed. Pilarczyk (see above, n. 44) p. 73: "Solutio. Credimus valere talem absolutionem. Nam in tali casu episcopus pro talibus satisfacere debet quia si in nullo fecerit potius ei imputabitur quam illi."

the pope or bishops, "for the pope has power over all members of the Church, the bishop over all the members of the Church committed to him since he is called to a portion of solicitude (*in partem sollicitudinis*) ...."[98] Ordinary priests and bishops can impose a penance and remit part of the penalty that is due while enjoining the rest upon the penitent. But the pope's power is greater:

> There is another relaxation which derives from the discretion found in him who has power over the universal Church since it belongs to him to consider the need of this or that Church. Therefore this power resides in him who has the greater dignity in the Church because it concerns a necessity arising within the Church. Hence a relaxation of the entire penalty belongs only to him who has the fullness of power.[99]

Bishops, he says, have an analogous power of relaxation towards those into whose "portion of solicitude" they are called. Alexander concludes with another important statement: "... Although the pope confers [part] of his power on those he has called to a portion of solicitude, power is nevertheless not lessened in him; on the contrary, the fullness of power abides in him."[100]

In all this we find the most explicit treatment of papal powers seen thus far among the school theologians. It is a doctrine that continues the views we shall see in Bernard and other non-school theologians but that now applies them to new issues entering the school debates more and more.

In a question *De relaxationibus* Philip the Chancellor, according to his reporter, made a comparison among ministers of the Church similar to that made by Alexander of Hales. After saying that simple priests have a lesser power of the keys and so cannot commute the entire temporal penance to

---

[98] Ibid., no. 27; p. 1242: "Respondeo: Aliter est in sacerdotibus maioris dignitatis et minoris. Papa enim habet potestatem super omnia membra Ecclesiae; episcopus super omnia membra Ecclesiae quae sibi commissa sunt, quia vocatur in partem sollicitudinis ...."

[99] Ibid.; p. 1234: "Est iterum alia relaxatio, quae est a discretione residente penes eum qui habet potestatem super universalem Ecclesiam, quia eius est considerare necessitatem huius ecclesiae et illius. Haec ergo potestas residet penes illum qui habet maiorem dignitatem in Ecclesia, quia est circa necessitatem emergentem in Ecclesia. Unde relaxatio quae est totius poenae solum illius est, qui habet plenitudinem potestatis."

[100] Ibid.: "Potestas autem relaxandi residet etiam aliquo modo penes illos qui in partem sollicitudinis sunt vocati: penes enim illos residet portio potestatis, sicut ille penes quem residet plenitudo eis determinavit. Et notandum quod, licet Papa contulit de potestate eis quos vocavit in partem sollicitudinis, non tamen diminuitur in ipso potestas; immo permanet in eo plenitudo potestatis."

For a more complete study of Alexander of Hales (and of the *Summa Fratris Alexandri*) on indulgences, see Karl Frings, "Der Ablass nach der Lehre des Alexander von Hales und der Summa Halensis," in *Miscellanea Martin Grabmann: Gedenkblatt zum 10. Todestag*, Mitteilungen des Grabmann-Instituts der Universität München, Heft 3, ed. M. Schmaus (Munich: Max Hueber, 1959) pp. 31-54.

something else, Philip distinguishes between *ordo* and *potestas* in ministers: the former is equal in all, the latter is not. Indeed, he continues,

> power is greater in the lord pope than in the patriarchs, and it is greater in them than in archbishops, while in the latter it is greater than in bishops, and so on with the rest: for just as in the heavenly hierarchy some are superior and nobler — those who see more things and more secret things in the mirror of eternity — and others are lesser and inferior, so in the human hierarchy it is similar.[101]

Here again we have a clear statement of gradation, not in order (of which we shall see more in the next section), but in power. It is interesting to note the link Philip sees between the human and the heavenly hierarchy, a theme adumbrated by Bernard and Hugh of St. Victor but greatly developed in the thirteenth century.

One of the most interesting discussions of papal power in relation to indulgences is found in the question *De relaxatione* of Guerric of St. Quentin. He meets two problems. Will the pope's granting indulgences without exacting equivalent recompense not exhaust the spiritual goods of the Church? And can the pope grant an indulgence to himself for all the temporal penance he should do? Guerric's initial statement, which was challenged, had been that "the pope has the goods of the Church in his hand and therefore without any injury he can distribute them to whom he wills."[102]

As for the first question, after considerable debate Guerric solves the problem by pointing to the infinite merits of Christ. Since the pope is "the vicar of the Church" (*vicarius Ecclesiae*, an interesting title we have not found before), he can distribute the merits of Christ — in so far as he is guided by his anointing — and so he can give indulgences even to an infinite

---

[101] Douai, Ville MS 434, I, 79vb: "Hunc actum gratiae plenioris non habet clavis in simplici sacerdoti, et ideo non potest commutare totam temporalem in aliam temporalem, tamen aliquid de poenitentia ex causa commutare potest. Unde nota quod duo sunt in ministeriis, ordo et potestas quae ordinem comitatur. Ordo aequaliter est in omnibus ministris Christi sacerdotibus, sed non potestas; immo, maior est potestas in domino papa quam in patriarchis, et in eis quam in archiepiscopis, in illis autem maior quam in episcopis et sic de aliis: sicut enim in caelesti hierarchi quidam sunt superiores nobiliores — qui plura et secretiora vident in speculo aeternitatis — alii minores et inferiores, similiter est in humana hierarchia."

[102] Todi, Biblioteca communale MS 71, fol. 44vb: "Postea quaeritur utrum possint fieri relaxationes, quod non videtur: per relaxationes enim fit subtractio de bonis communibus ecclesiae et nulla fit ei recompensatio. Ergo iniuriatur ei. Sed non est iniurandum Ecclesiae; ergo etc. — Dicebat quod papa habet bona Ecclesiae in sua manu et ideo absque omni iniuria potest distribuere cui vult. — Contra: Papa minister est Ecclesiae et dispensator. Ergo sicut minister bona domini sui non potest distribuere nisi ad eius utilitatem, ita nec papa bona Ecclesiae nisi ad utilitatem Ecclesiae. Non est autem utilitas Ecclesiae quod fiat bonorum spiritualium subtractio et nulla recompensatio .... Ex hoc etiam videtur quod posset thesaurus Ecclesiae exhauriri cum semper fiat subtractio et nulla fiat recompensatio sive restauratio."

number of persons without thereby diminishing the infinite treasury of the Church.[103]

Another argument elicits further remarks about the pope in which Guerric resorts to Innocent III's marriage imagery. Since the pope is the "bridegroom of the Church, and especially of the universal Church, he should succeed to Christ himself in all the goods pertaining to the education of the children of the Church. Now this is especially the accumulated merit of Christ."[104] Guerric further justifies this by glossing the text of Matthew 16:18, laying stress on the word *quodcumque*: this "whatever," he says, indicates "universality and a type of certitude" belonging to the pope's power of the keys.[105]

As for the second question about the pope's power to grant himself a full indulgence, Guerric holds that the pope can indeed grant himself a full indulgence but only if, as is the case with others, he fulfils all the conditions required for such an indulgence to be valid.[106]

An anonymous commentary on book 4 of the *Sentences* formerly but incorrectly attributed to Odo Rigaldus gives, in its distinction 20, a teaching similar to that of Guerric's, although it is not so fully developed as his.[107]

---

[103] Ibid., fol. 45va: "... Ideo Christus ... totum thesaurum exposuit, meritum scilicet vitae suae et passionis suae, et ideo vicarius Ecclesiae, scilicet papa, prout unctio docet eum, potest distribuere, et ideo infinitis personis posset dare indulgentias: cum enim meritum Christi sit infinitum, et quantumcumque sumitur de infinito non potest minui quia semper remanet infinitum, ideo quantascumque indulgentias faciat papa, etsi personis infinitis, semper remanet thesaurus infinitus nec potest minui."

[104] Ibid., fol. 45vb: "Quod autem quaeritur unde habetur quod meritum Christi sit de thesauro Ecclesiae, respondeo: Ex hoc quod sponsus Ecclesiae et maxime Ecclesiae universalis, scilicet papa, debet succedere ipsi Christo in omnibus bonis quae ad educationem Ecclesiae filiorum pertinent. Hoc autem maxime est meritum Christi accumulatum." For Innocent III see the following essay, "Monastic, Episcopal, and Apologetic Theology, 1150-1250," sect. 1.4.

[105] Ibid.: "Hoc etiam habetur, Matt. 16, ubi dicitur: *Quaecumque solveritis super terram* etc., et exponitur dupliciter, scilicet de solutione a culpa, et sic *solveritis*, id est, solutum ostenderitis, vel de solutione a poena, et sic *solveritis* poenam, scilicet relaxando. Per hoc quod dicitur *quodcumque*, in quo notatur universalitas et quaedam certitudo, patet quod non intelligitur de relaxatione quae fit ex vi clavium quae non est universalis nec certa, unde intelligitur dare quae fit ex thesauro, et quia merita Ecclesiae non sufficerent personis infinitis, ut ostensum est, cum sint finita absque merita Christi, verum est quod cum dicit *quodcumque solveritis* etc., quod suum meritum dedit eis dispensandum: aliter enim non *quodcumque* solveritis esset solutum cum sine merito Christi merita Ecclesiae infinitis personis non sufficerent."

[106] Ibid.: "Quod quaeritur utrum papa sibi possit assumere relaxationes, respondeo sic: alioquin peioris conditionis esset. Quod dicitur necesse est ipsum evolare etc., respondeo: non oportet: plures enim sunt conditiones quae requiruntur ad hoc quod indulgentiae valeant, quae sicut in aliis requiruntur, ita et in papa ad hoc quod accipiat indulgentias. Si igitur ⟨sunt⟩ omnes circumstantiae quae ad hoc requiruntur, potest esse quod evolet."

[107] On this commentary, written about 1250 and showing dependence on Guerric's *Quaestiones de sacramentis*, see Kilian F. Lynch, "The Alleged Fourth Book on the Sentences of Odo Rigaud and Related Documents," *Franciscan Studies* 9 (1949) 87-145; Ermenegildo

Among the requirements for an indulgence (the author uses both terms, *relaxatio* and *indulgentia*) is the authority of the one giving it and also "a just necessity on the part of the universal Church or of a particular Church." [108] Although the pope is not mentioned specifically, the authority mentioned would be his in relation to the need of the universal Church.

The treasury of the blood of Christ is possessed by the Church, says this commentator, and the Church can distribute this to whom it pleases. [109] In addition to this treasury, the authority of the Church also has control of the merits of all the members of the Church, and so "the lord pope" can distribute them as he sees it needed for the Church. The author compares this activity to the digestive function of the stomach, which distributes nourishment to the various members of the body according to their need. [110]

Another type of indulgence, or rather dispensation, conferred by the popes caused difficulty for the prolific Parisian theologian, William of Auvergne, who became bishop of Paris in 1228. Although he has two considerable treatises on the sacrament of Penance, he does not speak of the pope in them. [111] But in a treatise on benefices in which he strongly argues that clerics should have only one and not several benefices, he meets the objection that the pope sometimes dispenses in this matter by allowing more than one benefice to a cleric. William replies that these papal dispensations are "above us": [112] it is not clear whether he means that they are exceptional because

---

Lio, "Nuove fonti domenicane nei Commentarii dello Pseudo-Oddone Rigaldi al IV° libro delle Sentenze," *Franziskanische Studien* 33 (1951) 385-420; and Kilian F. Lynch, "Edition of Distinctions XXVI and XXVII of *Anonymous Brussels: Bibliothèque Royale 1542*," *Franciscan Studies* 15 (1955) 283-311, 384-415, especially pp. 283-284. We shall refer to the author as Pseudo-Odo since it is linked with Odo Rigaldi's authentic 3 books in the Brussels manuscript and was formerly thought to be Odo's work.

[108] Brussels, Bibl. Royale MS 1542 (11614), fol. 213va *in marg.*: "Respondeo: Potest dici quod relaxatio iuste facta efficaciam habet, et sic intelligitur haec auctoritas: *Quodcumque ligaveris* etc. Ad hoc autem quod iuste fiat etc. exiguuntur sex, duo a parte illius qui facit et duo a parte illius cui facit et duo a parte utriusque. A parte illius qui facit exigitur auctoritas sicut est in episcopis. Item, iusta necessitas, scilicet Ecclesiae universalis aut particularis."

[109] Ibid.: "Hunc thesaurum habet ⟨Ecclesia⟩ in sua manu; ideo pro necessitate Ecclesiae potest distribuere cui vult."

[110] Ibid.; fol. 213va-vb *in marg.*: "Alia causa est quia merita omnium membrorum Ecclesiae regit auctoritate sibi data a Domino, et ideo, sicut venter dividit secundum proportionem alimentum diversimode diversis membris secundum magis et minus, sic dominus papa pro necessitate distribuere potest suffragia membrorum Ecclesiae ubi pro necessitate Ecclesiae viderit expedire."

[111] The treatises are *De sacramento poenitentiae* and *Tractatus novus de poenitentia*; they are edited in *Guilelmi Alverni opera omnia Parisiis 1674*, 2 vols. (rpt., Frankfurt am Main: Minerva, 1963) 1: 451b-512b for *De sacramento* and 1: 570b-592b for *Tractatus novus.*

[112] *Tractatus de collatione et singularitate beneficiorum*, c. 6; *Opera omnia* 2: *Supplementum*, p. 260b: "Quod si abjecerit nobis de dispensationibus apostolicis, respondimus quod illa supra nos." Punctuation is slightly changed here and in the following texts.

coming from the pope and therefore beyond the ordinary order of things, or
that they are beyond his ability to explain. Yet, he continues, "if they are
considered more carefully, they are invalid, and we hold the same opinion
about every dispensation that has been made [in the matter of plural
benefices] nor do we presume to interpret."[113] William apparently wishes to
maintain his theological principles and conclusions about benefices and
therefore he wants to condemn any plurality of benefices, even if a dispensation for such plurality comes from the pope; yet he is cautious about
making such a conclusion.

He further softens his implicit criticism of such dispensations by adding
that however extensive the grace of papal dispensations, the pope does not
dispense the avarice, greed, or ambition of the persons receiving them.
Playing on the word "indulgence", he says that the pope "by his indulgences
does not indulge these and other vices, for he does not intend to feed or
nourish the plagues of vices from the temporal goods of the Church: these
he knows very well are established and given over to the Lord in order to
sustain the servants of God in his service."[114]

Here we see a struggle within William similar to one we shall see in Robert
Grosseteste over the pope's appointment of his nephew to a benefice that
Robert thought him unworthy to hold.[115] Something of the same struggle will
be seen in Albert the Great, and another essay in this symposium examines
an analogous struggle in Archbishop John Pecham.[116] In each case theologians or theologian-bishops found their theological principles and reforming
zeal countered if not actually betrayed by actions of the pope, and their
struggle to come to terms with their loyalty to the pope and still maintain
their principles makes poignant reading.

The last theologian to be examined in this section is the Dominican
theologian, Richard Fishacre, whose *Commentary on the Sentences*, the first
of its kind at the University of Oxford, was written between 1240 and 1245.
This author, together with Alexander of Hales, the *Summa Fratris Alexandri*,
and Albert the Great, is exceptional in this period for the great use he makes

---

[113] Ibid.: "... diligentius consideratae, irritae sunt, et de omni dispensatione facta idem
sentimus, nec interpretari praesumimus."

[114] Ibid.: "Econtrario tamen indubitanter sciendum est quod Romanus Pontifex, quantumcumque largam dispensationis gratiam videatur facere in beneficiis cum aliquibus personis,
tamen non dispensat cum avaritia, cupiditate, vel ambitione earum, nec indulget eis indulgentiis suis et his vel aliis vitiis: non enim intendit pascere vel nutrire pestes vitiorum de bonis
temporalibus ecclesiasticis quae plene novit ad sustentationem servorum Dei in ejus servitio
certificata esse Domino et ablata."

[115] See the following essay, "Monastic, Episcopal ...," section 2.2.

[116] For Albert see below, pp. 110-111, and, for Archbishop Pecham, Michael M. Sheehan,
"Archbishop John Pecham's Perception of the Papacy," below, pp. 299-320."

of canonical materials within his theological discussions of the sacraments. Many of his questions take on a very practical bent. This might be a matter of practical English temperament (Alexander of Hales was also English); it might also have come from his awareness that his students needed to be well instructed in pastoral matters, especially as his Dominican confreres were very active in the apostolate of confessing as well as preaching.[117]

Several times within the distinctions concerning Penance or Order Fishacre mentions the pope's supreme power. In distinction 18, dealing with the keys, he suggests that the power of discernment and the power of executing a sentence, while often found conjoined in ecclesiastical judges, "are sometimes found divided, as when the lord pope asks something of some bishop and provides others as executors: for the power of discerning between God and the penitent is one key and the power of demanding a decree of execution is another."[118]

Speaking of the variety of peoples, altars, and prelates in the Church, he adds the phrase, "although the Roman bishop is over all."[119] The pope's higher power of absolving is mentioned several times, e.g., when someone is erroneously excommunicated: "these the pope usually absolves for the sake of being sure";[120] in some cases of irregularity: "he should send him to the bishop so that, if he can, he may dispense him; if he cannot, let him send him with letters to the pope";[121] in a number of excommunications whose

---

[117] On Fishacre see W. Principe, "Richard Fishacre's Use of Averroes with Respect to Motion and the Human Soul of Christ," *MedS* 40 (1978) 350, n. 2 (bibliography), and T. Käppeli, *Scriptores Ordinis Praedicatorum medii aevi*, 3 vols. to date (Rome: S. Sabina, 1970-) 3 (1980) 303-306.

[118] Text edited from Oxford, Balliol College, MS 57 (=B), fols. 283vb-284ra, and Oxford, Oriel College, MS 43 (=O), fol. 105a-b: "Iste ergo constitutus arbiter et iudex inter Deum et homines habet duplicem potestatem vel unam habentem actum duplicem: una est potestas discernendi et alia — vel eiusdem alius actus — potestas demandandi sententiam executioni, et forte sunt duae potestates, quia sicut frequenter inveniuntur coniunctae, ut in iudicibus subdelegatis, tamen aliquando inveniuntur divisae, sicut cum dominus papa demandat alicui episcopo aliquid et dat alios executores: una ergo clavis est potestas discernendi inter Deum et poenitentem, et alia est potestas demandandi decretum executioni."

[119] B, fol. 287ra; O, fol. 153a: "... sed quia Ecclesiae per orbem terrarum dilatatae multus est populus, ideo et nunc multa sunt templa, multa altaria, multi earum praelati, licet Romanus super omnes, et ideo placuit Ecclesiae ut non quilibet sacerdos in quemlibet sed potius in sibi subditos habeat potestatem et usum potestatis, et qui subiectos non habent, licet habeant potestatem, non tamen habent usum eius."

[120] B, fol. 285va; O, fol. 109b: "In his casibus ad probationem eorum, etiam si absolutionem non petant, debent admitti donec ipsis constiterit in aliis evitari, quamvis tales papa consueverit ad cautelam absolvere."

[121] B, fol. 287va; O, fol. 153b: "Sequitur attendere de quibus absolutio est petenda, et sunt casus in quibus proprius sacerdos non potest absolvere. ... Tertius, ubicumque invenerit irregularitatem contractam: propter illam enim debet mittere eum ad episcopum ut, si potest, dispenset; si non potest, cum litteris eum mittat ad papam."

absolution the pope alone can give: "one who is excommunicated can be absolved by his bishop or proper priest from every excommunication whether grave or lesser when it is an excommunication laid down by the law unless the founder of the canons has reserved it to himself; now the pope has reserved absolution to himself in six cases." [122]

The root of all this papal power is indicated most clearly when Fishacre glosses words of Lombard in distinction 24:

> "Apostolic", that is, successor of the Apostle; "the pope, namely the Father of Fathers," has the beginning (*principium*) of jurisdiction and not an end (or limit: *finem*) because the beginning (*principium*) of authority over ordinary humans ought to be in him without end (or limit); or from "papa," which is a sign of admiration, for he ought to be admirable and excelling in matters of law. [123]

For Fishacre, then, the authority of the pope seems to have no limits. An emphasis on the pope's role in matters of law is seen in his second interpretation of "pope" based on a different etymology. Earlier, we have seen, he spoke of the pope as the "founder of canons" (*conditor canonum*).

Richard Fishacre also mentions a number of cases of dispensations which only the pope can give. Only the pope can dispense those twice married or the illegitimate so that they can be ordained. [124] Only the pope can dispense a priest who has committed certain crimes so that he can then be restored to his order or promoted. [125] When it comes to times for ordaining, others are limited to the ember days and two other Saturdays, whereas "only the

---

[122] B, fol. 287va; O, fol. 154a: "De absolutione in foro Ecclesiae videndum quis potest absolvere et de modo absolvendi. De primo, regulariter tene quod ab omni excommunicatione, sive maiore sive minore, lata a iure potest absolvi a suo episcopo vel proprio sacerdote nisi conditor canonum (canonis *B*) sibi reservavit. Reservavit autem sibi papa absolutionem in sex casibus."

[123] B, fol. 297ra; O, fol. 186b: "*Apostolicus*, id est apostoli successor; *papa, scilicet pater patrum*, habet principium dictionis, non finem, quia principium auctoritatis in puris hominibus in ipso debet esse sine fine; vel a 'papae', quod est admirationis signum: debet enim esse admirabilis et excellens in iura ...." The second derivation comes from the interjection *papae!*, derived from the Greek, meaning "wonderful!"

[124] Ibid., d. 25: B, fol. 299vb; O, fol. 193b: "et in hoc casu et in praecedente solus papa dispensat" (cases of illegitimacy); ibid.: B, fol. 299vb; O, fol. 193b-194a: "vel e converso pater duxit aliam, qua mortua duxit istam, et dico legitimum ad omnes actus scilicet excepto episcopatu, ad quem non potuit promoveri sine dispensatione papae" (again, a case of illegitimacy).

Concerning the ordination to the *subdiaconate* of those twice married, Fishacre says that, according to some, this can be done by the bishop, "sed nunc certius tenetur quod nonnisi a papa, quia ius expressum prohibet" (ibid., d. 24: B, fol. 298va; O, fol. 190b).

[125] Ibid.: B, fol. 303vb; O, fol. 202b: "Et nota hic tres regulas: Prima est qui peccavit mortaliter post baptismum non potest promoveri .... Contra: Has tres regulas potest papa dispensare in omni casu cum in multis non dispensat. Sed non sic episcopi ...."

pope can confer the subdiaconate on Sundays and other important feasts; but any bishop can confer other minor orders on Sundays and on important feasts." [126] Frequently Fishacre appeals to canonical texts to support his various opinions; it is likely these that are the source of his strong assertion of papal power and prerogatives.

We shall see that this strong doctrine of the papacy is found as well in the two important authors to be examined in the last section. It is clear that by the fourth and fifth decades of the thirteenth century the school theologians were developing the theology of the papacy in ways that emphasized papal power as very widespread and only relatively limited.

3.2. The Sacrament of Order and the Papacy.

The most properly theological debate about the papacy emerged in the schools within an examination of the number of orders within the sacrament of Order. The doctrine of seven orders had been traditionally related to Christ's life and to the seven gifts of the Holy Spirit; now it faced a challenge based on the general doctrine of the Pseudo-Dionysius. Guy of Orchelles, writing between 1215 and 1220, is the first scholastic theologian known to propose nine orders and to speak of the pope relative to this new enumeration. [127]

Guy first appeals to the Dionysian doctrine (as he reads it), and since this becomes a standard argument in the debate, his interpretation should be seen. Guy maintains that the church's hierarchy "is disposed so as to be like the heavenly hierarchy. Therefore since in the heavenly hierarchy there are nine orders of angels, so in the ecclesiastical hierarchy there should be nine orders of ministers." [128] Guy supports this with a text of Exodus 25:40 in which God says to Moses that he should make a tabernacle entirely like the

---

[126] Ibid.: B, fol. 304vb; O, fol. 205a: "... tamen solus papa potest conferre subdiaconum in dominicis et aliis festis praecipuis; quilibet vero episcopus potest conferre alios minores ordines in dominicis et aliis praecipuis festis."

[127] See Augustine McDevitt, "The Episcopate as an Order and Sacrament on the Eve of the High Scholastic Period," *Franciscan Studies* 20 (1960) 96-148 (p. 98 for Guy's role in proposing nine orders). On the history of the episcopacy as an order see also A. M. Landgraf, "Die Lehre vom Episkopat als Ordo," in his *Dogmengeschichte der Frühscholastik* 3/2 (Regensburg, 1955) pp. 277-302. See also L. Hödl, "Die kirchlichen Ämter," cited above, n. 33.

[128] *Tractatus de Sacramentis Ex Eius Summa De Sacramentis Et Officiis Ecclesiae*, eds. Damian et Odulph Van den Eynde, Franciscan Institute Publications, Text Series 4 (St. Bonaventure, N.Y.: The Franciscan Institute, 1953) no. 185; p. 175 (all references will be to this edition): "... Ut dicit beatus Dionysius in *Hierarchia* sua, ecclesiastica hierarchia disposita est ad similitudinem hierarchiae caelestis. Ergo dum in hierarchia caelesti sint novem ordines angelorum, et in ecclesiastica hierarchia novem ordines debent esse ministrorum."

one shown him on the mountain; Guy argues that this points to a likeness between the Church militant and triumphant and therefore to nine orders of ministers corresponding to nine orders of angels.[129]

After focusing the debate on whether episcopacy is a distinct order, Guy in his main reply accepts nine orders of ministers corresponding to the nine orders of angels. For him the ninth order consists of archbishops and patriarchs.[130] Among the five patriarchal sees the Roman Church, "which is the mother and mistress of all Churches," is first. The others do indeed "maintain their own dignity in such a way, that is, that after their bishops [that is, those over the other four patriarchal sees] have received the pallium from the Roman pontiff, this being the ensign of the fullness of episcopal dignity, and after they have made an oath of fidelity and obedience to him, they may then legitimately confer the pallium on their own suffragans." [131]

After indicating that archbishops and patriarchs form only one order differing in more or less power, Guy adds significantly:

> The pope is not in an order but is above all the orders of ministers in that he is the vicar of him to whom *all power in heaven and on earth was given*: for he is the successor of Peter and the vicar of Jesus Christ.[132]

Thus the discussion of the number of orders within the sacrament of Order leads Guy to important statements about the primacy of the pope and his greater power in relation to all others, including patriarchs. The pope for Guy is not only Peter's successor and vicar but also vicar of Jesus Christ.

As for Guy's influential interpretation of the Pseudo-Dionysius, it is, we have seen, incorrect in that the latter does not give a detailed comparison of nine orders of ministers to nine orders of angels; the only correspondence

---

[129] Ibid.; p. 176: "Item, dicit Dominus ad Moysen: *Fac mihi tabernaculum iuxta omnem similitudinem eius quod ostensum est tibi in monte.* 'Iuxta omnem' dicit; ergo in omnibus debet esse similitudo inter Ecclesiam militantem et triumphantem. Ergo sicut in Ecclesia triumphante sunt novem ordines angelorum, sic et in Ecclesia militante debent esse novem ordines ministrorum."

[130] Ibid.: "Dicimus ergo, sine praeiudicio melioris sententiae, quod sunt novem ordines ministrorum Ecclesiae, respondentes in numero novem angelorum ordinibus, videlicet septem praesignati, et episcopatus octavus, archiepiscopatus nonus vel patriarchatus."

[131] Ibid.; pp. 176-177: "Sunt autem quinque patriarchalium ecclesiarum sedes, quarum prima, Deo disponente, est Romana ecclesia, quae omnium ecclesiarum mater est et magistra, ... servata tamen cuilibet propria dignitate, ita videlicet quod, postquam earum antistites a Romano Pontifice receperint pallium, quod est plenitudinis dignitatis episcopalis insigne, praestito sibi fidelitatis et oboedientiae iuramento, licenter et ipsis suffraganeis pallium largiuntur."

[132] Ibid.; p. 177: "Sic ergo archiepiscopus et patriarcha maiori et minori tantum differunt potestate, unde pro uno accipiuntur ordine. Papa autem non est in ordine, sed est super cunctos ordines ministrorum, utpote vicarius illius cui *data est in caelo et in terra omnis potestas*: est enim successor Petri et vicarius Iesu Christi."

is between the first three angelic orders and hierarchs, priests, and deacons.[133] Bernard of Clairvaux and Hugh of St. Victor made general comparisons of the two hierarchies but without the details Guy introduces; nevertheless, his interpretation came to figure regularly in subsequent debates about orders, including questions about the pope.[134]

William of Auxerre follows Guy in accepting nine orders. For him bishops are the eighth order, archbishops the ninth. Unlike Guy, William locates the pope within and not above the ninth order. He relates the nine orders to the angelic hierarchy, basing his choice of the archbishopric as ninth order on a text of Hebrews saying that the lesser is blessed by the greater and on the fact that bishops are blessed and consecrated officially by archbishops.[135]

Thus far William has not mentioned the pope, but a counterargument brings up the case of bishops who consecrate archbishops and of the cardinal bishop of Ostia who consecrates the pope even though he is not of greater power than the pope.[136] In reply William distinguishes dignity of office from "dispensative necessity." Normally the more dignified in office consecrates the less dignified. But in cases of necessity a bishop can consecrate an archbishop, and since the pope has no superior or equal, it is necessary that he be consecrated by an inferior.[137]

Although Alexander of Hales seems finally to decide that there are only seven orders, he presents the opinion about nine orders quite favourably, with long analyses of the Pseudo-Dionysius' hierarchies and the relation of the nine ecclesial orders to the nine angelic orders with their functions of purging, illumining, and perfecting.[138] His conclusion is that perfect charity,

---

[133] See above, section 1.1; pp. 46-47.

[134] For Hugh see above, section 1.4. For Bernard see the following essay, "Monastic, Episcopal, ..." section 1.1.a; p. 128.

[135] *Summa aurea* IV, tr. 16, c. 2; ed Ribaillier (cited above, n. 87), p. 373: "Quod autem archiepiscopatus et episcopatus sunt duo ordines preter alios septem, ut sint novem ordines in humana hierarchia sicut in celesti, probatur per auctoritatem Apostoli qui dicit ad Hebreos, VII: *Sine ulla contradictione, quod minor a maiore benedicitur.* Ergo maior est qui benedicit quam qui benedicitur. Sed archiepiscopus de officio suo benedicit et consecrat episcopum; ergo maiorem dignitatem habet quam episcopus; et ita maiorem ordinem." William gives another argument (ibid.) saying that Moses was the greater priest because he consecrated Aaron.

[136] Ibid.; p. 374: "Sed contra hoc obicitur, quia episcopus consecrat archiepiscopum, et Hostiensis consecrat papam, non tamen est maioris potestatis."

[137] Ibid.: "Ad hoc dicimus sine preiudicio melioris sententie quod aliud est quod ex dispensativa necessitate fit, aliud quod ex dignitate officii. Archiepiscopus enim consecrat episcopum ex dignitate officii sui, et secundum hoc maioris dignitatis est .... Quando vero episcopus consecrat archiepiscopum, dispensativa necessitas est, sicut cum ad sacerdotem proprie pertinet baptizare, in articulo necessitatis tamen licite alius baptizat quam sacerdos. Similiter cum dominus papa non habet superiorem vel parem, de necessitate inferior consecrat eum."

[138] See his *Glossa* (cited above, n. 89) IV, d. 24, 3a-h; 4: 401-407.

being the mark of the highest triad, should be found perfectly in priests, more perfectly in bishops, and most perfectly in the pope, "the father of fathers," the one who holds "the fullness of power which he has as vicar of Peter, prince of the apostles."[139]

Although Alexander presents this position so positively, he appears finally to reject it and to maintain only seven orders or degrees within the sacrament of Order because he relates this sacrament (and its degrees) to the Eucharist. The episcopal dignity adds nothing to priestly power for the Eucharist and so is not an eighth order within the sacrament of Order; it adds certain other powers but no new character.[140] As for bishops consecrating archbishops, this is done by a power granted from the pope, which Alexander designates as an archiepiscopal power. The pope is consecrated by the bishop of Ostia as one pontiff by another, but the pope receives the fullness of power not from the consecrating bishop but by the grant of this power once made to Peter, whose vicar he is. The execution of his power consists in the agreement of all to obey him, and this arises from the cardinals agreeing to elect him.[141]

---

[139] Ibid., 3g; 4: 405-406: "Secundum autem opus consummationis triplex distinguitur Ordo. Est enim perfecta caritas quae accendit ad amorem Dei et superioris. Haec in sacerdotes extendi debet; similiter gratia prima potestatis, sicut et potestas respectu Baptismi et Poenitentiae. Perfectior autem debet esse in episcopis: unde 'superintendentes' dicuntur, quibus est plenior gratia potestatis distributa, ut benedicendi abbates, consecrandi virgines, dedicandi ecclesias et confirmandi. Est perfectissima, quae debet esse in Papa, scilicet 'pater patrum'. Huic est collata plenitudo potestatis: hanc enim vice Petri, principis Apostolorum, obtinet. Secundum hunc modum configuratur ecclesiastica hierarchia in numero Ordinum angelicae hierarchiae." The long analysis and the concluding phrase seem to indicate that Alexander hesitates between the two opinions and seeks to show how each has its value; we shall see this compromise solution in subsequent authors.

[140] Ibid., 2k; 4: 401: "Ad hoc ergo sacramentum ordinari convenit omnem potestatem spiritualem, quae fundatur in fide Trinitatis. In hac autem fide Trinitatis datur character spiritualis, a quo est signaculum in quibusdam sacramentis. Ex quo perpenditur: cum potestas Ordinis sacramentalis sit ad sacramentum Communionis, et hoc pertineat ad Ordinem sacerdotalem, in eo debet stare omnis Ordo. Dignitas vero episcopalis, quae superadditur, est ratione causarum, et quia ibi suppletur potestas Domini in conferendo Ordinem sacerdotalem. Sicut Moyses, licet non esset summus sacerdos simpliciter, tamen erat summus sacerdos quoad hoc, quod consecravit Aaron." Earlier, speaking of the character conferred in Order and its distinction from the characters of Baptism and Confirmation (ibid., 2e; 4: 400), Alexander adds (2f; ibid.): "Si vero obicitur de episcopatu, solvendum est per hoc quod dicitur 'signaculum'. Non enim novus character imprimitur, sed gratia confertur ad quamdam spiritualem potestatem, praeexistenti charactere sacerdotali." Cf. ibid., 3m; 4: 410.

[141] Ibid., 9t; 4: 426: "Si vero de episcopo obicitur qui consecrat archiepiscopum, vel de Ostiensi qui consecrat Papam, respondemus quod episcopus consecrat eum non in quantum est archiepiscopus, sed potestatem archiepiscopalem habet a Papa. Consecratur autem Papa in quantum pontifex ab alio pontifice, sed plenitudinem potestatis tantum recipit ex collatione facta Petro, cuius est vicarius. Consensus autem ad obediendum, in quo est exsecutio potestatis, est in concordi electione cardinalium."

Hugh of St. Cher also accepts nine orders; he counts the episcopacy as the eighth but hesitates about the ninth, being unclear as to whether it is the archiepiscopacy or clerical tonsure.[142] If the bishop of Ostia consecrates the pope, he has this power from the pope — a statement that repeats William of Auxerre's but adds that the power comes from the pope.[143]

The link of the sacratem of Order (and so of its degrees or ranks) with the Eucharist, indicated by William of Auxerre in an argument against his position and affirmed more strongly by Alexander of Hales, became decisive for other leading theologians of the first half of the thirteenth century. Although Roland of Cremona's *Summa* seems to have had little influence in the schools, his strong statement is worth noting: the highest power of the priestly order is consecration of the body and blood of Christ; hence there can be no order above it. Paul therefore called bishops "priests," and in antiquity the Supreme Pontiff was usually called "presbyter of Rome" (*presbyter Romanus*) and sometimes "bishop of Rome" (*episcopus Romanus*).[144]

Roland is quite sarcastic about those holding the other opinion. The added powers of bishops and archbishops, he says, are "only names of diverse administrations" and therefore "since these sorts of things are only certain accidentals above the priestly order, it is a wonder of human stupidity and inconsistency that a bishop should disdain to be called 'priest', and that an archbishop or patriarch or pope should also disdain (this name), and that they should wish to be denominated by accidentals." His conclusion is

---

[142] See McDevitt (cited above, n. 127) pp. 111-113, and for the texts from Hugh, pp. 130-132. Hugh repeats Guy's listing of the five patriarchates and the first place given to the "[patriarcha] Romanus, qui successit Petro, qui fuit princeps Apostolorum," and their reception of the pallium from the Pope (ibid., p. 131). William of Auxerre had mentioned, but not accepted, the idea that tonsure could be the ninth order (*Summa aurea* IV, tr. 16, c. 1; ed. Ribaillier [above, n. 87], p. 371): for him tonsure "est signum materiale ad preparandum ad suscipiendos ordines, propter quod non est sacramentum, set sacramentale, sicut presignatio in baptismo."

Hugh does not repeat Guy's statement about the pope being above all orders; he seems to include him in the same rank with other patriarchs, although first among them.

[143] See McDevitt, p. 132: "Similiter papa, cum non habeat superiorem, dat potestatem Ostiensi ut eum consecret; hanc eandem potestatem dat cuilibet alio episcopo."

[144] Text in McDevitt, p. 134: "Quidam dicunt quod non sunt nisi septem ordines, sicut supra diximus, et dicimus iterum. Et in hac opinione sumus nos. Et ultimus et summus est ordo sacerdotalis, et alii ordines redeunt ad ipsum. Et illud summum quod potest facere ille ordo est consecratio Corporis et Sanguinis Christi, et haec est eius virtus summa, secundum quod loquitur Aristoteles de virtute in *Libro Coeli et Mundi*, quod ipsa est ultimum de potentia. Unde supra ordinem sacerdotalem nullus est ordo. Unde et Apostolus ad Timotheum vocat episcopos 'presbyteros'. Et antiquitus solebat dici de summo pontifice 'presbyter Romanus', et aliquando 'episcopus Romanus'." McDevitt refers to book 1, ch. 11 of the *De caelo et mundo*; the scriptural reference is to 1 Tim. 3:2 and 4:14,22.

strongly judgmental: "It is clear that those who rejoice in those dignities and not rather in their being priests are arrogant and, as Gregory says, 'have lapsed into the crime of apostasy.'" [145]

With less invective but similar firmness William of Auvergne, Philip the Chancellor, Guerric of St. Quentin, Richard Fishacre, and Albert the Great reject nine orders. The link with the Eucharist is their main argument, although some also stress the character conferred only at the level of priesthood (e.g., Philip the Chancellor) or the priest as transmitter of grace to others (Guerric); none leaves anything special for bishops, archbishops, or the pope in the matter of Order even though these are said to have special powers by reason of their dignity or office. This discussion, it can be seen, helped to clarify the distinction between the sacrament of Order and the power of jurisdiction, a distinction to which the canonists were also coming at this time. [146]

---

[145] Ibid.; p. 135: "Nec ideo archiepiscopus apponit ordinem, nec episcopus vel archidiaconus, et sic de aliis; sed augent illa quae secundum ordinem presbyteratus sunt .... Patet ergo, quod non sunt illa nisi nomina diversarum administrationum .... Sed cum huiusmodi non sint nisi quaedam accidentalia supra ordinem sacerdotalem, mirum est de humana stultitia et contingentia, quod episcopus dedignatur vocari 'presbyter', et archiepiscopus et patriarcha et papa dedignarentur, et velint denominari ab accidentibus. Patet quod illi qui gaudent in illis dignitatibus, et non magis quod sunt sacerdotes, quod arrogantes sunt, et 'ad crimen apostasiae', secundum quod dicit Gregorius, 'delapsi'. Item patet quod sunt adventitiae naturae hospitales, quia accidens est adventivae naturae, ut dicit Philosophus, et ita illi sunt hospites et advenae Testamentorum, et non sunt 'cives et domestici Dei'." McDevitt gives the references as follows: Gregory, *XL Homiliarum in Evang. Libri Duo*, I, Hom. 17 (*PL* 76: 1303); Aristotle, *Metaphisicorum Liber*, III, cap. 4; ed. Firmin-Didot, vol. 2, p. 506, ll. 7sqq.; Eph., 2, 19.

[146] For these authors (except for Albert, to be seen later) see McDevitt, pp. 115-129, 136-148. McDevitt summarizes William of Auvergne's teaching on the episcopacy but does not give William's remarks about the pope. Those who hold that the episcopacy is an order distinct from "a lesser priest," William says, will have to say that archiepiscopacy, patriarchates, and finally the papacy, are orders. But the pope, he adds, is no greater than Peter: he is only his successor as to power and dignity and in his letters he calls himself only bishop, and in granting privileges he calls himself "bishop of the Catholic Church." Christ wished to be named only bishop, priest, and pontiff and nothing more. Hence there is no order beyond the episcopacy (understood by William as not distinct from priesthood as to Order but only as to greater excellence and as having special powers; see McDevitt, pp. 109-111).

The text is found in his *De sacramento ordinis*, c. 13, in *Opera omnia* (cited above, n. 111) 1: 553b: "Si quis autem dicere voluerit episcopatum esse ordinem aliud a sacerdotio minori, non opponimus nos, nec contradicimus; verum non effugiet facile quin oporteat eum dicere archiepiscopatum ordinem esse et deinde primatum, postea patriarchatum et novissime papatum. Manifestum autem est quod ipse non est major quam Petrus: non est enim nisi successor ipsius quantum ad potestatem et dignitatem, nec ipse vocat se nisi episcopum: in litteris suis scribit se 'episcopum' et in privilegiis nominat se 'episcopum catholicae ecclesiae'. In historiis legitur ubique: 'Silvester, episcopus urbis Romae', 'Bonifacius, episcopus urbis Romae'. ... Amplius, ipse Dominus Jesus Christus non plus quam episcopus est in dignitatibus ecclesiasticis secundum quod homo, in cujus gratiam nec archiepiscopus nec primas nec patriarcha nominari voluit, sed episcopus et sacerdos tantum et pontifex. Manifestum ergo est

Within this discussion, the most interesting for our subject of the papacy is that found in book 4 of the commentary incorrectly associated with Odo Rigaldus. The question is put specifically: "Whether the papacy is an order," and it is argued that the papacy is a distinct order because the pope has an excellency of power over bishops and all others and because he has the power of the keys in fullness.[147]

The Pseudo-Odo summarizes the two positions. Those who distinguish orders in relation to the members of the Church count nine orders; those who relate them to the power of consecrating and receiving the Eucharist count seven, the most powerful and noblest being the priesthood. The first group says that episcopacy and papacy are two distinct orders because they have special powers over the members of the Church which differentiate them from other orders and from each other: the pope's power is *plena*, the bishop's is not.[148]

Among those who hold for nine orders, however, some reject the papacy as one of the nine. When someone is elected to the papacy, they argue, nothing is done to him: he is not blessed and nothing else is done. The pope receives fullness of power from the very canonical election. Hence the nine orders for them are the usual seven, plus episcopacy and the clerical state (an opinion seen in Hugh of Saint-Cher).[149]

---

ultra episcopatum nullum esse ordinem." (Punctuation altered.) William adds that bishops are the "apostolorum successores."

For the canonists at this time see R. P. Stenger, "The Episcopacy as an Ordo according to the Medieval Canonists," *MedS* 29 (1967) 67-112; he cites Martinien Van de Kerckhove, *La notion de juridiction dans la doctrine des décrétistes* (Assisi, 1937).

[147] The discussion about the papacy as an order begins in dist. 24 on fol. 217va-vb *in marg. inf.* of Brussels, Bibl. Royale, MS 1542 (11614): "Item, quaeritur utrum papatus sit ordo, et videtur quod sic quia ibi datur excellentia (217vb) potestatis super episcopos et omnes. Quare videtur quod sit ordo. Item, quia habet potestatem clavium in plenitudine."

[148] Ibid.; fols. 217vb-218ra *in marg. inf.*: "Respondeo: Quoniam ordines possunt dupliciter distingui: Ordo enim proprie dicitur signaculum potestatis spiritualis. Potestas autem ista potest attendi vel comparatione ad membra Ecclesiae vel comparatione ad sacramentum [sacramenta MS] Communionis. Secundum ultimum modum distinguuntur septem ordines, quorum potissimus et nobilissimus est ordo sacerdotis, et sumitur numerus hoc modo quia potestas spiritualis respectu sacramenti Communionis vel est ordinata ad consecrationem vel ad ipsius corporis sumptionem .... (fol. 218ra) Et sic pontificatus non est ordo quia non determinavit aliquam potestatem respectu consecrationis dominici Corporis, immo habet tantam simplex sacerdos quantam episcopus.

"Alio modo potest considerari ut dicit potestatem comparatam ad diversa officia respectu membrorum Ecclesiae, et, sicut quidam dicunt, sunt novem ordines quia episcopatus et papatus, quia alia est potestas secundum speciem quae est potestas episcopi supra membra Ecclesiae, alia quae est papae quia papae est potestas plena, episcopi vero non plena. Unde dicunt quod papatus est ordo."

[149] Ibid.; fol. 218ra-rb *in marg. inf.*: "Alii dicunt quod papatus non est ordo, et hoc est quia cum aliquis eligitur in papatum, nihil circa illum (218rb) fit, nec benedictio nec aliud,

The author seems content to accept either seven or nine orders, depending on which aspect one examines. Only when he is queried about deans and archdeacons does he clarify his ideas about the special powers of the pope. In the sacrament of Order, he says, a spiritual power ordered to a spiritual act of grace is given. But such a grace is not given to deans or archdeacons: they are given only a power of jurisdiction to the extent that they take the bishop's place.[150] The same is true, he continues, of the papacy. If we speak of judiciary power, the pope's power differs from that of others because he excels above all members of the Church. But with respect to the spiritual act (deriving from the power of Order), the pope's power is not different from that of a bishop: to consecrate bishops belongs to bishops (by reason of the sacrament of Order); thus bishops consecrate the pope and archbishops, so that there is no difference in Order. The difference comes in the execution of power and this execution is related to their dignity. Hence archiepiscopacy and papacy are names of dignities, not of orders. Nevertheless, he adds, some say the opposite.[151]

Here the distinction between jurisdiction and Order is greatly clarified; papal power is a power of jurisdiction and does not derive from an order. The author builds on this to make some interesting remarks about the power of the pope in relation to that of archbishops and bishops. Their power, he says, is not diversified according to substance or species; it differs in them only by extension. This is seen in that "the lord pope is consecrated by bishops in so far as he is a bishop and not in so far as he is pope, but he receives the fullness of power in his canonical election."[152] This is similar to

---

sed ex ipsa electione canonica consequitur illa plenitudine potestatis. Unde dicunt quod non est ordo, sed tamen sunt novem, scilicet ipsi septem et clericatus et episcopatus."

[150] Ibid.; fol. 218rb *in marg. inf.*: "Quod quaeritur de decanatu et archidiaconatu, dicendum quod non sunt ordines sed dignitates adminiculatores ad Ordinem, nec in istis confertur signaculum, id est, character. Item, potestas quae confertur in Ordine est potestas spiritualis, id est, ad actum spiritualem gratiae, sed in decanatu et archidiaconatu datur potestas iurisdictionis tantum et non ad aliquem actum spiritualis gratiae in quantum, scilicet, gerunt vicem episcopi."

[151] Ibid.: "Similiter dicendum est de papatu, quod loquendo de potestate iudiciaria, alia est potestas papae et aliorum, quia superexcellit omnia [superexcellentia MS] membra Ecclesiae; loquendo autem de potestate ut est ad spiritualem actum, non est alia quia episcopos consecrare [*add.* non MS] est episcoporum sive episcopalis ordinis, nam episcopi consecrant papam et archiepiscopos, sed potestatis executio respicit dignitatem. Unde archiepiscopatus et papatus sunt nomina dignitatum, non ordinum. Tamen alii dicunt oppositum." For the corrections of the MS see below, n. 155.

[152] Ibid.; fol. 218rb-va *in marg. inf.*: "Quod obicitur quod 'maior a minore non benedicitur', dicendum quod quamvis sit maior (218va) potestas papae quam episcopi, tamen non diversificatur secundum substantiam vel secundum speciem, sed tantum alia et alia est, id est, magis vel minus extensa: dominus enim papa consecratur ab episcopis in quantum episcopus, non in quantum papa, sed plenitudinem potestatis sortitur in electione canonica."

the position of Alexander of Hales. Another conclusion follows regarding archbishops, who have greater power than bishops in so far as they are vicars in their province of the "lord pope." Hence they cannot consecrate a bishop until they have the pallium from the pope, nor can they cite someone who is subject to a bishop except by appellation: for, he says, the lord pope has power in fullness by reason of his canonical election by the cardinals and therefore the order of bishop, archbishop, and papacy do not differ; each is a dignity because it is dignities that are distinguished according to greater and lesser.[153]

This is the fullest treatment of the papacy in relation to the sacrament of Order and the now clearly distinguished notion of jurisdiction that we have found in the *summae* or commentaries of this period. A possible rival to this treatment might seem to have been found in an anonymous *quaestio* found in Prague, Universitní Knihovna, MS 667 (IV.D.13), fols. 34va-35rb, entitled "Quaestio de sacramento ordinis," in which a sub-question asks "utrum papatus sit ordo."[154] But comparison of this *quaestio* with the text of the commentary just seen reveals an extremely close and often identical text concerning the nature of the sacrament of Order, the various opinions about whether there are seven or nine orders, and all the statements about the pope that have been seen in the commentary. This includes the clear distinction between the power of Order and the power of jurisdiction and the relations between the pope and the bishops as vicars in their provinces of the pope.[155]

---

[153] Ibid.; fol. 218va *in marg. inf.*: "Archiepiscopátus vero, quod sit maioris potestatis, hoc non nisi in quantum vicem gerit domini papae in provincia. Unde non potest consecrare episcopum donec habet pallium a papa, nec potest citare subditum episcopi nisi per appellationem: dominus enim papa potestatem habet in plenitudine ex electione canonica cardinalium, et ideo non est alius ordo episcopatus, archiepiscopatus, papatus, sed sunt dignitates, quia dignitates distinguuntur secundum maius et minus."

[154] The *quaestio* is described by Bertrand-G. Guyot, "Quaestiones Guerrici, Alexandri et aliorum magistrorum Parisiensium (Praha, Univ. IV.D.13)," *Archivum Fratrum Praedicatorum* 32 (1962) p. 19: it is a part of his no. 21.I, fols. 34va-35rb, and is interspersed in the discussion of orders on these folios.

[155] To show the closeness of the two texts (and to justify the corrections of the Brussels MS made in n. 151), we give the text of the *Quaestio* on these last two points from fol. 35ra: "Quod obicitur de decanatu et archidiaconatu, dicendum quod non sunt ordines, sed sunt dignitates quae adminiculatores ad ordines, nec in illis confertur signaculum, id est, character. Item, potestas quae confertur in Ordine est potestas spiritualis ad actum spiritualem gratiae, sed in decanatu et archidiaconatu datur potestas iurisdictionis tantum et non ad aliquem actum spiritualis gratiae, scilicet, in quantum gerit vicem episcopi (cf. n. 150). Similiter dicendum est de papatu, quod loquendo de potestate iudiciaria, alia est potestas papae et aliorum, quia SUPEREXCELLIT OMNIA membra Ecclesiae; loquendo autem de potestate ut est ad spiritualem actum gratiae, non est alia quia episcopos consecrare EST episcoporum sive episcopalis ordinis, nam episcopi consecrant papam et archiepiscopum, sed potestatis executio respicit dignitatem. Unde archiepiscopatus et papatus sunt nomina dignitatis, non ordinum. Tamen aliqui dicunt oppositum." The practical identity of the texts is evident; the emphasized words are those which help to correct the text given in note 151 so that they make sense.

Whether the two texts come from the same author or which one has copied the other is a matter that can be left aside here. It suffices to note that this is the only example found thus far of a disputed question dealing expressly with the papacy as an order in the period before 1250.

This brief survey of the new theological development about the papacy in relation to the sacrament of Order shows that these theologians in a certain way came full circle back to the positions of Hugh of St. Victor seen at the beginning of our study. But they do so within a more sophisticated problematic and with new applications to the relations between the pope and others. We shall see their strong centralizing tendencies developed in other ways in the two theologians to be studied in our last two sub-sections.

3.3. Authoritative Papal Teaching About Faith.

Although the late twelfth-century authors had something to say about the authority of the pope in teaching matters of faith,[156] this topic does not seem to have attracted the interest of the thirteenth-century theologians before Albert the Great, whose position will be seen below.[157] Places more likely to contain such a discussion have been examined in William of Auxerre, Alexander of Hales, Hugh of St. Cher, Roland of Cremona, Odo Rigaldus, and Richard Fishacre, but nothing has been found: these places include those where the *Filioque* and its addition to the creed is examined, and studies of faith, especially the articles of faith.[158]

In this period, however, as canonical materials were used extensively by authors such as Alexander of Hales, Richard Fishacre, and Albert the Great, texts of various popes were prominent among the authorities quoted. They were always handled with reverence and accepted as convincing unless they were being used to begin a theological debate or needed clarification, to say nothing of benign interpretations.[159] There was a kind of tacit acceptance of papal authority when past papal statements or interventions were noticed but little or no advertence to the pope's role in the present.

One important evidence of papal authority in matters of faith, however, was the role and influence of the pope in university affairs. It is quite remarkable to look through the *Chartularium* of the University of Paris and

---

[156] See above, section 2.4.

[157] See section 3.6.b.

[158] Commentaries on the *Filioque* usually occur in relation to 1 *Sent.*, d. 11, and on the articles of faith in 3 *Sent.*, dd. 23-25.

[159] The classic study of such interpretation is that of M.-D. Chenu, "Authentica et Magistralia," ch. 16 of his *La théologie au douzième siècle*, Études de philosophie médiévale 45 (Paris: Vrin, 1957).

see the constant preoccupation of the popes with matters there. That these were not only administrative concerns is clear from interventions in matters of doctrine, e.g., the pope's legate, Robert Courson, approving restrictions at Paris on lectures concerning Aristotle's metaphysics and natural philosophy as well as on commentaries on these works.[160] Again, in 1231 Pope Gregory IX renewed these prohibitions and established a commission to purify these books of error so as to allow their use.[161] That such prohibitions needed renewal perhaps shows, however, that if papal authority was acknowledged, it was not always followed wholeheartedly, but that is nothing new in history.

3.4. The Question-Literature.

One of the best gauges of theological interest in this period is the list of titles and subdivisions of *quaestiones* that were debated at this time. It is significant that for the first half of the thirteenth century, the lists and indexes compiled by various researchers give, within larger questions, only three brief sub-questions directly concerned with the pope. One we have seen in Alexander of Hales;[162] another asks about the question we have just seen, that is, whether the papacy is a distinct order within the sacrament of Order;[163] the third, by Guerric of St. Quentin, is a short discussion of why Peter was chosen to be leader of the Church rather than John the Baptist and, among the apostles, in preference to James and John.

In this last question an argument is made that John the Baptist, having made a clearer confession of Jesus than did Peter, deserved to be chosen as head or leader of the Church.[164] Guerric replies that John's role was to go

---

[160] See H. Denifle, ed., *Chartularium universitatis Parisiensis*, vol. 1 (Paris, 1889; rpt. Brussels, 1964), no. 20; pp. 78-79. Papal interest was, to be sure, not only normal but even necessary for the masters at Paris to become a corporation or *universitas*: see Gaines Post, "Parisian Masters as a Corporation," in his *Studies in Medieval Legal Thought: Public Law and the State, 1100-1322* (Princeton, N.J.: Princeton University Press, 1964), pp. 27-60, for the history of this incorporation and the role of the pope. (The essay was originally published in *Speculum* 9 [1934] 421-445.) Nevertheless, the meticulous care of the pope not only in matters of doctrine but even in such details as fixing fees shows a striking concern on the part of the supreme pontiffs for this important educational venture sponsored by the Church: see Gaines Post, "Masters' Salaries and Student Fees in the Medieval Universities," *Speculum* 7 (1932) 181-198. See as well the essay in this collection by P. Osmund Lewry, "Papal Ideals and the University of Paris, 1170-1303," pp. 363-388.

[161] See *Chartularium*, no. 87; pp. 143-144.

[162] See above, pp. 70-71.

[163] See above, pp. 87-88.

[164] Guerric of Saint-Quentin, *Quodlibetum* 3, a. 4; text edited from Prague, Universitni Knihovna, MS 667 (IV.D.13), fol. 153rb *in marg. sup.*, and MS Vat. lat. 4245, fol. 65va: "Quarta quaeritur quare Petrus accepit principatum Ecclesiae potius quam alius. Si propter hoc quia

ahead of Christ as his precursor rather than to follow him as his successor: this latter role is that which belongs to the head of the Church.[165] Moreover, Guerric adds, Christ's successor should be specially instructed in matters of faith and morals and so should be one of the apostles, and among these it should be either Peter or James or John, who were the best instructed and who were special to Christ. Which of these three was most suited? Peter, he replies, for prelates should be compassionate as well as zealous and well-instructed. But Peter, who fell (by his denial of Christ) and rose again (by his repentance and Jesus' forgiveness) had a special occasion for compassion and greater reason for being compassionate than James or John, and this is why he was chosen to be head of the Church.[166]

This inquiry, coming as one among many diverse topics in a quodlibetal question, shows by its relative insignificance that at this period the theology of the papacy, with the exceptions seen in the previous sub-sections, did not evoke the curiosity and interest it was to have later on in the century and in the fourteenth century.

3.5. The *Summa Fratris Alexandri* (ca. 1241-1245).

The Franciscan *summa* attached to the name of Alexander of Hales, and the Dominican theologian, Albert the Great, each made significant contributions to the theology of the papacy in this period; therefore they will be studied in sections separate from the others seen thus far.

---

confessus est Christum esse Filium Dei et ideo meruit ut sibi daretur potestas Ecclesiae: sed clarior fuit confessio Joannis Baptistae, Joan. 1 [29], dicentis: *Ecce Agnus Dei.* Ergo Joannes potius debuit habere primatum Ecclesiae quam Petrus."

A second redaction of the question is found in Paris, BN, MS Nouv. Acq. 1470, fol. 153vb: here it adds the text of John 1:30: *Qui post me venit* etc.

[165] "Responsio: Joannes praecursor fuit Christi nascendo, praedicando, et moriendo. Ergo non potuit nec debuit esse successor; ergo nec primas Ecclesiae cum primas Ecclesiae sit successor Christi." The second redaction is practically the same, except that it speaks of *princeps* rather than *primas.*

[166] "Item, successor Christi debet esse constitutus a Christo et habere specialem instructionem in ecclesiasticis et alios excedere. Unde debet esse de choro apostolorum. Sed quia debuit habere principatum, debuit habere specialem instructionem a Christo et distinctionem, et ideo debuit esse de tribus qui speciales fuerunt Christo, scilicet Petrus, Joannes, et Jacobus. Sed praeter hoc, in praelato requiruntur tria (sive ad praelationem) etiam praeter instructionem, scilicet zelus et ratio compassionis et gratia. Propter hoc, quia Petrus lapsus est, habuit maiorem occasionem compatiendi, unde inter tres habuit rationem maiorem compatiendi. De choro ergo apostolorum debuit esse, et de specialioribus specialius iste praeeligendus erat in praelatum."

The second redaction excludes Paul because Christ's successor should be chosen by Christ "et ideo, cum vivente Christo non esset Paulus conversus, non fuit princeps Ecclesiae." Whereas the first redaction lists four requirements, namely, *instructio, zelus, ratio compassionis,* and *gratia,* the second redaction lists only three: *scientia, dilectio,* and *compassio.* Of Peter it says: "quia ... cecidit et resurrexit, compati aliis didicit."

Although Alexander of Hales greatly influenced the early Franciscan school of theology through his teaching and through his authentic works, the *Gloss on the Sentences* and numerous theological *quaestiones*, he was not the author in the strict sense of the *Summa Fratris Alexandri*. He may indeed have instigated and guided the progress of the work, composed between 1241 and 1245, but the redaction of books 1 and 3 is now known to have been the work of his Franciscan confrère, John of La Rochelle, whereas book 2 was put together by an anonymous friar who has been nicknamed "Frater Considerans" because he uses the term *considerans* so frequently when introducing his materials. Since book 4 was composed only in 1268, fifteen years after Alexander's death, by William of Middleton, it falls outside the time limits of our study and therefore will not be considered here.[167]

Book 3 of the *Summa* contains sections on the commandments and on the role of judges. Here there occur questions about the pope that had not, to the best of our knowledge, been raised before in the first half of the thirteenth century. These questions seem to have been stimulated by the regular use in this work of canonical texts, especially those of Gratian. Hugh of St. Victor appears, together with references to incidents in the life of the apostle Peter that are applied to the relations of the pope with others.

Are those who have spiritual power prohibited from putting anyone to death, it is asked? Arguments claim that they do sometimes have this power. Did not Chrysostom and Gregory indicate that Peter killed Ananias and Saphira or at least handed them over to death? Did not Pope Leo IV and Pope Gregory the Great muster forces to defend Rome against invading Saracens and Longobards? Does not the emperor receive his authority for his office, and so for killing evildoers, from the pope, so that the pope is implicated by the use of this authority deriving from him?[168]

After quoting several texts from Gratian, including Bernard's admonition to Pope Eugene not to take the sword, the *Summa* states that ministers of the New Testament are prohibited from killing even for the sake of justice. There are two reasons for this:

---

[167] On the *Summa Fratris Alexandri*, Victorin Doucet's *Prolegomena*, a mine of information for all early thirteenth-century theology, is the basic reference; see *Alexandri de Hales ... Summa theologica seu sic ab origine dicta "Summa Fratris Alexandri"*, 4: *Liber tertius (Prolegomena)* (Quaracchi, 1948). For John of La Rochelle's role see pp. 360-369. For the redactor of book 2 see F.-M. Henquinet, "Fr. Considerans, l'un des auteurs jumeaux de la Summa Fratris Alexandri primitive," *RTAM* 15 (1948) 76-96. All references will be to the Quaracchi edition, using its numbers for each article rather than the cumbersome internal divisions of the work itself; all our texts are from book 3 (volume 4), so that only page references will be given after the article reference.

[168] No. 360, args. 3, 4, 8, 9, 10; pp. 535-536.

... Ministers of the New Law must be ministers of meekness and love in order
to draw men to the good .... Ministers of the New Law are ministers of the
sacrament of union: for the sacrament of the altar represents the union of
Christ and the Church, which is signified by the union of body and soul ....
Hence whoever dissolves the union of body and soul cannot show forth in
himself the union of this sacrament ....[169]

All ministers of the altar in any degree must avoid division, it concludes,
for this is opposed to unity; therefore they may not kill, shed blood, or
mutilate a member.[170]

As for Peter's supposedly having killed Ananias and Saphira, the *Summa*
says he did not kill them; he only predicted their death and made it clear that
the reason for it was their guilt. He did not hand them over to others to be
killed, but excommunicated them so that they were handed over to the death
inflicted by the devil.[171]

Although Leo and Gregory mustered armed forces, this means not that it
is licit for a priest or pope to take up arms, but that they can persuade the
secular prince, to whom the material sword is committed, to take up arms
against evildoers.[172]

Finally, with respect to the emperor's implicating the pope in his killings
because he receives authority from the pope, the reply says "it is true that he
receives power from the pope to punish evildoers, but he receives the exercise
of the power from the law. It is from God, therefore, through the pope, that
he receives the authority to be a minister of the law and of divine justice,

---

[169] Ibid., solutio; p. 536b: "... ministri Novae Legis debent esse ministri mansuetudinis et
amoris ad alliciendum homines ad bonum. ... Ministri Novae Legis sunt ministri sacramenti
unionis. Sacramentum enim Altaris repraesentat unionem Christi et Ecclesiae, quam significat
unio animae et corpus .... Unde qui dissolvit unionem corporis et animae, sacramenti illius
unionem in se non potest demonstrare ...."

[170] Ibid.: "... Cum alii Ordines Ecclesiae ad sacramentum Altaris referantur, quia omnes
ordinati aut conficiunt sacramentum aut deserviunt conficienti, debent carere divisione, quae
opponitur sacramento unitatis; et ideo non licebit ministris Ecclesiae interficere, sanguinem
effundere, membrum mutilare."

[171] Ibid., ad 3 et ad 4; p. 537a: "Ad illud Chrysostomi dicendum quod improprie dicitur
Petrus homicidium fecisse. Hic enim dicitur res fieri illo tropo quo in Scriptura fieri dicitur,
cum praedicitur vel innotescit. Petrus ergo dicitur Ananiam et Saphiram interfecisse, quia
eorum mortem, quam diabolus efficere debebat, praedixit et causam, scilicet culpam, patefecit.
... [Ad 4] Tradere ... morti est pluribus modis .... Alio modo tradere morti inferendae a
daemone, et istud tradere est excommunicare; et hoc modo tradidit Paulus et etiam Petrus
Satanae, sed non intentione occisionis, sed intentione punitionis ad correctionem aliorum,
sicut Petrus ...."

[172] Ibid., ad 8-9; p. 537b: "Ad illud Leonis et Gregorii dicendum quod hoc non dicitur
propter hoc quod liceat sacerdoti vel Papae arma arripere, sed quia possunt saeculari principi,
cui materialis gladius commissus est, armorum sumptionem contra maleficos suadere, sicut illi
qui habent et minoribus et maioribus divinas leges exponere et praedicare, in quibus
praecipitur saecularibus potestatibus: *Maleficos non patieris vivere*, Exod. 23 [22:28]."

whereas it is from the law itself that he receives the authority to use the ministry of justice."[173] As for the implication of the pope, the *Summa* distinguishes between the authority of ordering (*iubendi*) and the authority of intimating (*innuendi*). "In the authority of ordering it does follow that 'he does what is done by his authority,' but it does not follow in the authority of intimating," and it is this latter authority that is found in the pope and in priests. "Now this intimating is really the preaching of the divine law and an urging that princes obey the divine law."[174] A quotation from Bernard's *De consideratione* on the material and spiritual sword shows that the *Summa* is drawing on the abbot's doctrine for these replies.

This discussion is important not only for its doctrine about the limitations of the pope's power in such matters but also for what it says about the relations between the pope and secular authorities. It is also another example of the entry into theological discussion of matters often left to canonists.

In a section on judicial precepts the relations between different ranks of persons enters the picture. Can an inferior pass judgment on a superior? Here again the examples of Peter and other popes enter the discussion.[175] The position of the *Summa* is between the extremes of the two sets of arguments, one denying any such power of judgment, the other affirming it. Judging in the strict sense, the *solutio* says, involves a superior authority to examine, accuse, and punish, but this belongs only to superiors with respect to inferiors and not vice versa. Judgment, however, may be taken in a broader sense to include accusing (*arguere*), reproving (*corripere*), and warning (*monere*). Only a superior may accuse; equals may reprove or reproach; inferiors may warn or advise their superiors, as Bernard said he was doing to Pope Eugene. "But to judge out of charity (extending the meaning of the word to include warning) belongs to good subjects with respect to bad prelates."[176]

---

[173] Ibid., ad 10; p. 538a: "Ad illud quod obicit de Imperatore quod ordinatur a Papa, dicendum quod verum est quod recipit potestatem a Papa ad puniendum maleficos, executionem autem potestatis accipit a lege. A Deo ergo per Papam recipit auctoritatem, ut sit minister legis et iustitiae divinae, sed ab ipsa lege auctoritatem usus ministerii iustitiae."

[174] Ibid., ad 11; p. 538a-b: "Si autem obiciatur quod 'ille facit cuius auctoritate fit; unde Papa et episcopi, qui habent praepositos iudices sanguinis, videntur occidere', dicendum quod est auctoritas iubendi et est auctoritas innuendi. In auctoritate iubendi sequitur: 'ille facit cuius auctoritate fit': in auctoritate vero innuendi non sequitur. Est autem auctoritas iubendi occidere maleficos penes Imperatorem, auctoritas vero innuendi penes Papam et sacerdotes. Est autem ista innuitio divinae legis, ut dictum est, praedicatio, et ut principes legi divinae obediant exhortatio."

[175] See no. 412, arg. 1 and 6; p. 602a.

[176] Ibid.; 602b: "Solutio: Iudicare dicitur proprie et improprie. Secundum quod dicitur iudicis iudicare proprie, et iudex proprie dicitur ex auctoritate superiori in examinandis factis, arguendis et puniendis. Hoc modo iudicare superiorum est respectu inferiorum, non e converso .... Alio modo iudicare dicitur communiter, extenso vocabulo ad arguere, corripere,

One argument had quoted Peter Lombard's saying in his *Gloss* that "the king has no one who judges his deeds." The *Summa's* reply to this invokes Hugh of St. Victor's teaching:

> In the order of secular powers no one is greater than the king or emperor, just as in the order of spiritual powers no one is greater than the pope; yet, comparing the spiritual power to the temporal, the spiritual power is above the secular as the spirit is above the body. Hence also Jeremiah 1:10 says: *Behold, I have constituted you over nations and kingdoms ....*[177]

When Paul reprehended Peter, the *Summa* says in reply to another argument, it was because Peter had led the Gentiles away from the truth of the gospel. Prelates who fall away in faith or lead others away by word or example should be reprehended. But Paul reprehended Peter in that he was his equal in purity of life and knowledge of the truth, but he was not his equal in the office of ecclesiastical dignity, "for as to the dignity of prelacy Peter had no equal among the apostles."[178] And when Peter replied to those who disapproved of his going to Cornelius and other Gentiles, he did not invoke the power of his office by which he could have said that the sheep do not reprehend their pastor; instead, he invoked the authority of divine power by which the Gentiles had received the Holy Spirit.[179] In both cases, then, the

---

monere. Et arguere proprie est superiorum respectu inferiorum .... Corripere est respectu parium .... Monere vero est inferiorum respectu superiorum; Bernardus *Ad Eugenium*: Moneo te, non arguo. ... Iudicare ex caritate, extenso vocabulo in monendo, bonorum subditorum est respectu malorum praelatorum."

[177] Ibid., ad *a*; p. 603a: "... In ordine potestatum saecularium nullus est maior rege vel imperatore, quemadmodum in ordine potestatum spiritualium nullus maior est Papa; tamen, collatione facta potestatis spiritualis ad saecularem, potestas spiritualis est super saecularem, sicut spiritus est supra corpus. Unde et Ierem. 1, 10 dicitur: *Ecce constitui te super gentes et regna ....*" For Hugh of St. Victor on this point see above, section 1.4.

[178] Ibid., ad *e*; p. 603b: "Ad illud quod obicitur quod Paulus Petrum reprehendit, dicitur quod Petrus, sicut dicitur ad Gal. [2:14], 'cogebat *gentes iudaizare* et suo exemplo a veritate Evangelii recedere. Pari autem modo reprehendendus est qui in se a fide exorbitat et qui alios exemplo vel verbo deviat. Hoc ergo exemplo non probantur praelati non arguendi a subditis, si a fide exorbitaverint vel alios exorbitare' fecerint. − Et quod obicitur quod 'Petrum Paulus non reprehenderet nisi se non imparem sciret', est intelligendum non de paritate quae est in officio ecclesiasticae dignitatis, sed de paritate quae erat in puritate vitae et notitia veritatis. Nam quantum ad dignitatem praelationis Petrus inter Apostolos non habebat parem." The long quotation is from Gratian, *Decretum*, C. 2, q. 7, c. 39, #4; ed. Aem. Friedberg, *Corpus iuris canonici* 1 (Leipzig, 1879) 495-496: cited by the Quaracchi editors, p. 603, n. 9.

[179] Ibid., ad 6; p. 604b: "Ad illud quod obicitur quod 'arguebant Iudaei Petrum, quia intraverat ad Cornelium', dicendum, secundum B. Gregorium: 'Petrus potestatem regendi acceperat, et tamen idem Apostolorum primus querimoniae contra eum a fidelibus factae cur ad gentes intrasset, non ex potestate officii, qua posset dici "oves pastorem suum non reprehendant" sed auctoritate divinae virtutis, qua gentiles acceperant Spiritum Sanctum, respondit'." The quotation from Gregory is from his *Epistulae*, xi, ep. 45 (*PL* 77: 1160), found in Gratian, *Decretum*, C. 2, q. 7, c. 40 (Friedberg 1: 496): cited by the Quaracchi editors, p. 604, n. 7.

Summa preserves the position of Peter (and by implication of the pope) as being above judgment by inferiors even if there are sometimes grounds for reprehension − if, for example, the pope were to err in faith or lead others to do so.

The *Summa Fratris Alexandri* returns to this issue in a chapter dealing with differences among judges, asking at one particular point "whether the supreme spiritual power, which belongs to the supreme pontiff, can have any human power that may judge it?" [180] The author recalls the texts we have already seen and then quotes a canon in the *Decretum* that leads him to conclude that "the supreme pontiff is the ordinary judge of individuals, and there is no one who judges him except God." [181] With respect to Paul's reprehending Peter, this time the author quotes Lombard's gloss on Galatians 2:14, which says that Paul used the liberty of charity and Peter accepted his rebuke by the piety of humility, thereby leaving an example that later persons of greater dignity should not disdain to be corrected by those of lesser dignity. [182]

In the same chapter, returning to the relations of the secular and spiritual powers, the *Summa* repeats much of Hugh of St. Victor's teaching, and when speaking of priestly power says that "the supreme pontiff is the vicar of Peter, to whom is committed the fullness of powers in the keys, Matthew 16:18: *You are Peter* etc., and *I will give you the keys*, as well as the universal care of the flock, John 21:17: *If you love me, Simon, feed my sheep.*" [183] In

---

[180] No. 415, V: p. 609b: "Item, quaeritur utrum suprema potestas spiritualis, quae est Summi Pontificis, possit habere aliquam humanam quae ipsam diiudicet."

[181] Ibid. V, solutio; p. 612a: "Ad illud quod quaeritur 'utrum possit esse aliqua humana potestas, quae habeat diiudicare Summum Pontificem', dicendum quod, sicut ostendebatur, Summus Pontifex non potest ab alio quam a Deo iudicari, sicut dicit *Canon, Causa* IX, quaest. 3: 'Facta subditorum a nobis iudicantur, nostra vero a Domino iudicantur'. Ex quo accipitur quod Summus Pontifex iudex est ordinarius singulorum, et nullus est qui eum iudicat nisi Deus."

The editors refer to Can. 15; Friedberg 1: 610.

[182] Ibid. V, ad 1-4; p. 612b: "Ad illud ... quod obicitur de Petro, qui sustinuit reprehensionem Pauli, dicendum quod illud dicitur factum ad exemplum humilitatis, non ex necessitate iuris. Unde ad Gal. 2, 14, super illud: *Dixi Cephae coram omnibus*, dicit *Glossa*: 'Ipse Petrus, quod a Paulo fiebat utiliter libertate caritatis, pietate humilitatis accipit, atque ita exemplum posteris tribuit quod non dedignarentur maiores, ubi forte recti tramitem reliquissent, a posterioribus corrigi. Laus itaque iustae libertatis in Paulo et sanctae humilitatis in Petro emicuit'."

The editors refer to the *Glossa Lombardi* on Gal. 2:14 (*PL* 192: 109), and identify its source as Augustine, *Epist.* 82, c. 2, n. 22 (*PL* 33: 285sq.).

[183] Ibid., Solutio I-II; p. 610a-b for the whole text; the quotation is from 610b: "... Summus Pontifex vicarius Petri, cui committitur plenitudo potestatis in clavibus, Matth. 16, 18: *Tu es Petrus* etc. *et tibi dabo claves*; et universalis cura gregis, Ioan. ultimo, 17: *Si diligis me, Simon, pasce oves meas.*"

relations with the secular power, the spiritual power, as Hugh of St. Victor says, institutes the secular power and has the right to judge it if it is not good.[184] Its judgment is carried out because it is vicar of God; its power extends to spiritual but not bodily punishment, the power of the keys giving it the ability to exclude those excommunicated or to reconcile the penitent.[185] The *Summa* also repeats Hugh's statements about the spiritual power directing and judging the earthly power as well as his remarks about ecclesiastical possessions.[186]

The *Summa Fratris Alexandri*, it can be seen, is a strong exponent of papal authority, including the pope's judicial authority and his strong rights in relation to secular power. It introduces into its far-reaching theological synthesis problems and responses that had formerly been treated mainly if not exclusively by the canonists.

3.6. Albert the Great (ca. 1200-1280).

Although Albert the Great has important things to say about the papacy in his scriptural commentaries and in his *De mysterio sacrificii Missae*, these works were written after 1250 and so fall outside our time period. Our study will therefore limit itself to his *Commentary on the Sentences*, whose composition was completed shortly before 1250.[187] This should suffice since,

---

[184] See ibid., Solutio IV; p. 611a. For Hugh, see above, section 1.4.

[185] Ibid., ad 1; p. 611a-b: "Spiritualis ... potestas non iudicat secundum hominem vel secundum humanam legem, sed in quantum residet vice Dei, sicut dicitur Apostolis, Matth. 10 [Potius Luc. 10, 16 *eds.*]: *Qui vos audit, me audit*, et sicut dicit Apostolus, II ad Cor. 5, 20: *Pro Christo legatione fungimur*; et secundum potestatem ad vindictam spiritualem, non corporalem. '... Iudex terrenus ... portat gladium *ad vindictam malefactorum, laudem vero bonorum* [1 Pet. 2:14]; isti [sacerdotes] claves habent ad exclusionem excommunicandorum et reconciliationem poenitentium'."

The quotation is from Gratian, *Decretum*, C. 2, q. 7, c. 41, nos. 3, 5, 6 (Friedberg 1: 497): cited by the editors in n. 4.

[186] See ibid., Solutio IV, ad 2; p. 611b. Hugh's statements about the directing and judging power have been seen above, pp. 49-50. His remarks about church possessions are taken by the *Summa Fratris Alexandri* from *De sacramentis* II 2, 4 (*PL* 35: 1636).

[187] On the dating of these works see James A. Weisheipl, "Albert der Grosse: Leben und Werke," in Manfred Entrich, ed., *Albertus Magnus: Sein Leben und seine Bedeutung* (Graz: Styria, 1982) pp. 9-60, especially pp. 42-44 (scriptural commentaries: after 1262; revised versions of commentaries on the synoptic gospels, 1270-1275), p. 44 (*De mysterio*: late work, perhaps his last writing), p. 19 (*Sentences*: final redaction of book 4 after 25 March 1249, but not long afterwards).

The study by Wilhem Scherer, *Des seligen Albertus Magnus Lehre von der Kirche*, Freiburger theologischen Studien 32 (Freiburg im Breisgau: Herder, 1928) examines the primacy of Peter and his successors according to Albert in ch. 4 and the infallibility in teaching of the Church and of the pope in ch. 5, but, as Yves Congar remarks in *L'Église* (cited above, n. 11) p. 230, n. 1: "le sujet serait à réétudier avec les ressources d'une méthode historique." Although Scherer assembles much valuable information, he fails to consider chronology of the

more than any other work in this period, his *Commentary* gives a well developed theology of the papacy. Like Richard Fishacre and the *Summa Fratris Alexandri*, Albert frequently introduces canonical materials, especially in book 4 where he discusses many practical matters of sacramental theology. From its beginnings the Order of Preachers had a distinctly pastoral bent, and every Dominican house of any size was geared to study related to pastoral care. Besides the *Decretum* and the *Decretals*, the *Summa de casibus* of Raymund of Pennafort was widely used by Dominicans even though, for Albert, Raymund by comparison with Augustine and Gregory is a *novitius* as an "authority" when it comes to defining penance.[188] Albert frequently refers to these canonical works and examines many practical cases such as the obligation of restitution, although at one point he rather wearily remarks: "These and like matters should better be considered by those skilled in law than by theologians, and so I will say without prejudice what seems reasonable."[189]

Although Albert often comments on the papacy within discussions of other questions, he sometimes examines the papacy itself quite explicitly. He looks at the powers of the pope within the Church; he studies the role of pope in relation to the teaching of faith; he speaks frequently about the pope's power in cases of absolution, indulgences, and dispensations. Our presentation will be divided according to these three topics.

3.6.a. *Papal Power Within the Church.*

Albert uses the title *vicarius Christi* of the pope and in one text says that "in place of Christ on earth there is only one pope."[190] In this latter text he

---

works and development in Albert's thought; he summarizes doctrine but gives few texts; his problematic reflects the apologetic theology of his time. His work is also less useful for our period because he draws much more on Albert's later works than on his *Sententiae*.

A different approach to the Church in Albert's theology is found in Antonio Piolanti, *Il Corpo Mistico e le sue relazioni con l'Eucaristia in S. Alberto Magno*, 2nd ed., Studi di Teologia Medievale della Pontificia Università Lateranense 1 (Rome, 1969); on its merits and limitations see the review by W. Principe, *The Thomist* 35 (1971) 182-183.

[188] On Dominican studies and the books used see Leonard E. Boyle, *The Setting of the "Summa theologiae" of Saint Thomas*, The Etienne Gilson Series 5 (Toronto: Pontifical Institute of Mediaeval Studies, 1982) pp. 3-4, 15. The comparison of Raymund with Augustine and Gregory occurs in 4 *Sent.*, d. 16, a. 10; eds. Augustus and Aemilius Borgnet, *B. Alberti Magni opera omnia*, vol. 29 (Paris, 1894) p. 575b. All future references will be to this edition of the *opera omnia* by volume and page number. Unless otherwise noted, all references will be to Albert's commentary on book 4 of the *Sentences*.

[189] D. 15, a. 44, sol.; 29: 534a: "Haec et hujusmodi magis considerari habent a Jurisperitis quam a Theologis: et ideo sine praejudicio dico quod rationale videtur."

[190] For *vicarius Christi* see d. 17, a. 30, resp. (29: 699b); d. 27, a. 22 ad 4 (30 [Paris, 1894], 184b). For the other text see d. 19, a. 10 ad 3 (29: 812b): "... loco Christi in terris non est nisi unus papa."

speaks about the pope's relationship with bishops: taking the place of Christ, the pope can act in all things, whereas others with jurisdiction are called *in partem sollicitudinis* and cannot extend their jurisdiction beyond that which is permitted them.[191] Asking how it is that the Church can establish a particular mode of solemnizing vows, Albert answers that the care of all the Churches and persons falls upon the pope, that he has all the power of ordering whatever in the Church will exclude heresies, schisms, and scandals, and so he can establish detailed modes of life lest schisms and heresies arise.[192] Elsewhere he speaks of the pope as the "universal governor of the Church" (*universalis gubernator Ecclesiae*) and compares him to the head of the Mystical Body.[193]

The basis for this kind of relationship Albert sees in the gospel texts establishing Peter over all the Twelve and over the seventy-two disciples chosen by Christ. The familiar texts of Matthew and Luke recur.[194] Since, he concludes, this order of jurisdiction was first instituted by Christ the Lord, the Lord placed Peter over others "so that according to him [Peter] he might confer the execution of the office which he gave when he breathed upon them and said: *Receive the Holy Spirit* etc."[195] This is an important statement because Albert, while admitting that all the apostles received the power of forgiving sins directly from Christ, sees the role of Peter (and so of the pope) as required to confer the practical exercise of this power.

An argument seeking to prove that there can be only one proper priest for a penitent describes the Church as a kind of pyramid leading to the unitary pope at the peak; although Albert refuses the conclusion, he does not reject the image.[196] But the most explicit text about the relationship of the pope to

---

[191] Ibid.: "... non est nisi unus Papa: et ille potest facere in omnibus: sed alii in partem sollicitudinis vocati sunt, et ideo non licet eis extendere jurisdictionem ultra quam permissum est eis."

[192] D. 38, a. 13; 30: 414a: "Dicendum quod sollicitudo omnium Ecclesiarum et personarum incumbit summo Pontifici, et omnis potestas ordinandi in Ecclesia illa quae excludunt haereses et schismata et scandala; et ideo statuit modos vivendi certos ...."

[193] D. 20, a. 17, sc 3; 29, 850a: "Universalis gubernator Ecclesiae, praecipue in his quae tota Ecclesia recipit et approbat, non est credendus fallere velle aliquem ...."
For the comparison to the head, see the texts below, nn. 239 and 240.

[194] D. 17, a. 40 ad auct. 1; 29, 724b: "... Dominus praesupposuit ordinem in discipulis quem ante fecerat, scilicet Petrum super omnes esse et super omnes alios. Matthaei enim, x, 1 et seq., elegit duodecim et sub illis designavit alios septuaginta duos [cf. Luke 10:1]. Petrum omnibus praeposuit, Matth. xvi, 19, ubi dixit: *Tibi dabo claves regni coelorum.* Et Luc. xi [= xxii], 32, ubi dixit: *Et tu aliquando conversus confirma fratres tuos.*"

[195] Ibid.: "Cum igitur hic ordo jurisdictionis a Domino prius institutus fuerit, praeposuit illum ut secundum illum conferret exsecutionem officii quod dedit, quando insufflavit et dixit: *Accipite Spiritum sanctum* etc."

[196] D. 17, a. 41, 7m; 726b: "Sic se habet populus ad sacerdotem ut sacerdos ad Episcopum et Episcopus ad Archiepiscopum et ille ad Primatum, id est, Papam ...."
Albert gives no reply to this argument and seems to accept the imagery and doctrine.

other prelates occurs in an article in which it is asked whether a superior is always to be obeyed. Albert distinguishes two ways in which a superior power and inferior power can be related. In some cases the entire inferior (*tota inferior*) comes from the superior: he gives the example of a proconsul's power coming from the power of the emperor and of a bishop's power coming totally from the pope. In such cases, the superior's power remains "ordinary and immediate to all the inferior subjects." The other relation is that in which both superior and inferior come from one universal, which subjects the inferior to the superior only in some matters and not in others. In this case, the inferior can issue prescriptions that cannot be retracted by the superior: this is the case, he says, with the power of a bishop and archbishop in their relations with the pope.[197]

In the first case, Albert looks at the relations of the pope and bishops: here the bishop is the inferior with respect to the pope, and they are ordered to each other in such a way that the bishop has everything from the pope, the pope's superior power remaining ordinary and immediate to all the bishops. The second case is that of a bishop in relation to an archbishop: both powers come forth from one universal power, the pope. The pope submits the inferior (the bishop) to the superior (the archbishop) in some things but not in others. In these latter matters the bishop can then prescribe things that the archbishop cannot retract: the pope's limitation of the archbishop's power in some cases is an empowering of his inferior, the bishop, in certain areas. Albert's final remark, "thus the power of the bishop and of the archbishop are related in comparison to the pope," makes it clear that for Albert it is the pope who regulates their relationship of power; he suggests once again that all their power comes from the pope, whose power is immediate and total with respect to his inferiors, the archbishops and bishops.

An example of the superior power of the pope in relation to the inferior power of a bishop is given by Albert when he replies to the question whether bishops can grant indulgences. An argument holds that since only the pope, "who is constituted over all," has power over the treasures of the Church,

---

[197] In 2 *Sent.*, d. 44, a. 6, sol.; ed. cit. 27 (Paris, 1894) p. 693b: "Solutio. Dicendum quod superior et inferior habent se duobus modis, scilicet ut in ordine ad se invicem ita quod tota inferior exeat a superiori, sicut potestas Proconsulis a potestate Imperatoris et Episcoporum a Papa: et tunc superior potestas remanet ordinaria et immediata omnibus subditis inferioribus .... Quandoque autem sic se habent ut ambae sint exeuntes ab una universali quae subdit inferiorem superiori in quibus vult, et in quibus non [*om. Borgnet*] vult non subdit: et tunc inferior potest aliquid praecipere quod superior non potest retractare: et sic se habent potestas Episcopi et Archiepiscopi in comparatione ad Papam."

The text has been corrected by comparison with Krakow, Bibl. Jagiellonska MS 1181, fol. 207vb.

only he can grant indulgences.[198] An argument favoring the other side of the question gives Albert's basis for his solution: whoever has both the power of the keys and jurisdiction has the power of giving indulgences.[199] In his main reply Albert maintains that the bishop can give indulgences in his own diocese and that they can be as great as he wishes them to be unless the "lord pope" limits this power specifically as has been done, he reports, by the pope's limiting indulgences to forty days.[200] In reply to the argument about who has power over the treasury of the Church, Albert states that the bishop has such power over the treasures of his diocese as well as over the treasures of the passion of Christ, "although not so fully as does he who has the universality of power."[201] Albert thus asserts the basic power and rights of the bishop but at the same time indicates the universal power of the pope and his right to intervene in details of the exercise of episcopal power.

On at least one occasion Albert uses the marriage image that was so dear to Innocent III, but he applies it equally to the relations between all prelates and their Churches. The sacrament of Order, he says, makes a man both bride and bridegroom, for the whole Church is espoused to God in the prelate and God is joined to the people in the prelate, so that he is a median between God and the people and has the place of each. As bride, he wears the ring of faith and charity, signifying lack of division of the Church in heart and body and its union with God. The image used in the special way Pope Innocent III applied it does not appear to have found application in Albert.[202]

---

[198] D. 20, a. 21; 29: 857b: "Ipse [Episcopus] non habet potestatem in thesauris Ecclesiae, sed solus Papa, qui super totum est constitutus: et indulgentiae vim trahunt a thesauris Ecclesiae, sicut jam ostensum est: ergo Episcopus dispensare non potest."

[199] Ibid.: "In contrarium hujus est quod qui habet jurisdictionem et claves habet potestatem dandi indulgentias quia claves cum jurisdictione comitatur potestas dandi indulgentias: ergo videtur quod habeat potestatem."

[200] Ibid.; 29: 857b-858a: "Episcopus in sua dioecesi potest dare indulgentiam, et quantum vult, nisi a constitutione Domini Papae distincte sit limitata: sicut modo est ad quadraginta dies."

[201] Ibid., ad 1; 29: 858a: "Ad primum ergo dicendum quod ipse habet in potestate thesauros suae diocesis et passionis Christi, licet non adeo plene sicut ille qui habet universalitatem potestatis: et ideo non adeo magnam et plenam potest conferre indulgentiam. Unde prima non est vera."

[202] D. 1, a. 10, ad quaest.; 29: 23b-24a. The question that Albert answers is why a (canonical) irregularity impedes one from the sacrament of Order but not from other sacraments. Albert replies: "... Ordo collocat hominem in duplici statu, scilicet sponsi et sponsae: desponsatur enim tota Ecclesia in Praelato Deo, et Deus in Praelato conjungitur populo: et ideo medius est inter Deum et populum, et habet locum utriusque, et ideo in quantum est sponsa habet annulum fidei et charitatis, et significatur quod non sit divisus, sicut et Ecclesia indivisa in corde et corpore significavit, et jungitur Deo: et quoad hoc inidoneitatem et irregularitatem inducit bigamia. Quia vero ipse communionem totius populi facit in loco Dei qui communem facit populum, ideo irregularitatem inducit communio in excommunicatione."

For Innocent III see the following essay, "Monastic, Episcopal ...," section 1.4.

Is the pope's jurisdiction over ecclesiastical goods so sweeping that the pope can receive such goods from churchmen without committing simony? This is an argument Albert has to meet.[203] Simony, he replies, gets its name from the contract that Simon wanted to make with Peter, who was the "pope of the apostles" (*papa apostolorum*); if there was a possibility of simony for Peter, so much the more can someone commit simony with other popes.[204] As for the pope's universal jurisdiction over the goods of the Church, Albert says (in a very strong statement) that "no one has rights in the Churches except through him [the pope]," but he adds: "I do not think this derives from the fact that they belong to him or that he confers them as belonging to himself, but rather because the guardianship of defending them was conferred upon him."[205] Within this limitation of papal right should be noted, however, the strong statement that rights in the Church come to persons only through the pope.

The pope's power of jurisdiction is asserted very strongly by Albert when he examines the question whether the papacy is an order within the sacrament of Order. Actually, he does not ask this question directly but lays the groundwork for his view by stating that priesthood "has one principal act, namely to confect the Body and Blood of the Lord; it has another secondary act, given for preparing the people to communicate worthily in the Body and Blood of Christ, and this is the act of binding and loosing. But all other orders subminister to the priesthood in either of those acts."[206]

On this basis he accepts only seven divisions within the sacrament of Order. His chief reason is the eucharistic relationship and not, for example, the earlier idea that the seven degrees or orders within Order are related to the seven gifts of the Holy Spirit. One argument says this link is incorrect since those receiving even the first order should already possess all seven gifts.[207] Although Albert tries to "save" the authority of Lombard, who makes

---

[203] D. 25, a. 4, 2m; 30: 91a: "Nulla persona habet jus in bonis ecclesiasticis nisi per jurisdictionem Domini Papae: ergo sicut ipsa persona accipit, ita Papa potest accipere."

[204] Ibid., sc 1; 30: 91a: "Simonia dicta est simonia a contractu quem voluit facere Simon cum Petro qui erat Papa Apostolorum: ergo multo magis cum aliis Papis potest committi simonia."

[205] Ibid., ad 2; 30: 91b: "... Verum est quod nullus habet jus in Ecclesia nisi per ipsum: sed tamen non puto hoc esse ex eo quod sua sint et conferat ut sua, sed quia collatum est ei patrocinium defensionis ...."

[206] D. 24, a. 5, resp.; 30: 36a: "... presbyteratus ... unum habet actum principalem, scilicet conficere corpus et sanguinem Domini: et alium secundarium, qui est datus ad praeparandum populum ut idonee communicet corpori et sanguini Christi, et hic actus est ligare et solvere. Omnes autem alii ordines sunt subministrantibus illi in altero actuum istorum."

[207] D. 24, a. 6, 2m; 30: 37b: "Donis Spiritus sancti habitis, tunc primum accipiendus est primus ordo: ergo omnia dona praeexiguntur ante ordinis susceptionem. Non ergo secundum numerum donorum accipitur numerus ordinum."

such a link, and although he briefly describes how it is done, he concludes that such an exposition is tortured (*extorta*); he prefers to reject the whole idea, although he adds that if anyone is inclined to accept such a link, his exposition of it could be used.[208]

Peter Lombard had said that the order of bishops is fourfold. Commenting on this statement within distinction 24, Albert denies that the episcopacy is an order:

> All this is clear from what has been said because, since there can be no more excellent act than confecting the Body of Christ, there can be no order beyond priesthood. But what [Lombard] enumerates as distinct things are really offices of jurisdiction over the Mystical Body: its care belongs to those who have these offices, and when they receive these offices, they receive grace not for the purpose of an order but for the execution of jurisdiction in the Church provided they are worthy.[209]

Only when Albert replies to the question how and in what way these offices are conferred does he mention the pope explicitly. How can bishops, who are of lesser rank, bless archbishops, it is asked? And how is it that the bishop of Ostia, the pope's inferior, blesses the pope? Do these not imply a consecration and conferring of jurisdiction?[210] Albert maintains first of all that an archbishop is not consecrated by a bishop; the archiepiscopal right (*ius*) is conferred on him by the pope.[211] So too, he adds, "the supreme pontiff is not consecrated by the bishop of Ostia in so far as he [the pope] is supreme but only in so far as he is a pontiff; but the jurisdiction of universal power descends upon him from the Lord in that he succeeds Peter."[212]

---

[208] Ibid., sol.; 30: 37b: "Videtur enim hoc esse falsum. ... Quod hic puto esse concedendum. Sed quod dicit [Lombardus], intendit tantum propter idoneitatem accipientis: tamen quidam sunt qui dicunt quod ostiariis attribuitur timor, qui principium est sapientiae sive ostium; exorcistis autem scientia .... Sed tamen quia extorta est expositio, primum plus placet. Sed si quis ita dicere vult, poterit respondere quod adaptantur modo praedicto."

[209] D. 24, a. 39, resp.; 30: 81a: "Totum istud patet per antedicta: cum enim nullus possit esse actus excellentior quam conficere corpus Christi, nullus potest esse ordo post sacerdotium. Sed jurisdictionum officia sunt quae enumerat distincta super corpus mysticum, cui intendunt taliter officiati, et quando consequuntur, accipiunt gratiam non ad ordinem sed ad exsecutionem jurisdictionis in Ecclesia si sunt digni."

[210] D. 24, a. 40, 1m et 2m; 30: 81b: "1. Dicit enim Apostolus ad Hebr. vii, 7, quod *sine ulla contradictione, quod minus est a meliore benedicitur.* Ergo Archiepiscopus non benedicitur ab Episcopo: ergo nec consecratur: ergo nec confertur ei jurisdictio aliqua: sed secundum omnem usum Ecclesiae Archiepiscopus benedicitur ab Episcopo: ergo etc. 2. Eadem est objectio de Domino Papa, quem benedicit Ostiensis episcopus."

[211] Ibid., ad 1; 30: 81b: "... Archiepiscopus non consecratur ab Episcopo sed potius Episcopus ab eo: sed jus Archiepiscopale confertur ei a Papa cum pallio: unde cum major est Episcopus, non benedicitur ab Episcopo."

[212] Ibid., ad 2; 30: 81b: "... Etiam summus Pontifex non consecratur ab Ostiensi episcopo

Papacy, then, for Albert clearly belongs exclusively to the realm of jurisdiction and of duties and powers in relation to the Mystical Body; it is not of the sacramental order. It does not come to the pope through any ecclesiastical agency or ministry but directly from God because the pope is the successor of Peter. Although Albert does not mention canonical election as others did, he would likely see this as the moment of reception of jurisdiction, unless he would choose the moment of blessing by the bishop of Ostia. But in either case, it is an office coming to the pope from God and it gives him the power to confer rights, powers, and offices on all others in the Church, including archbishops.

Further examples of the pope's powers, and also of limitations of them, will be seen in sub-section 3.6.c. Before coming to them, however, the pope's powers in relation to the teaching of faith will be examined.

3.6.b. *Papal Power in Relation to the Teaching of Faith.*

Although Albert speaks more frequently of the *Church's* role in preserving faith than he does of the *pope's* office, at the same time he sees the pope as the one through whom the Church's role is exercized concretely.[213] Speaking about an alternate form of Baptism that was allowed for a time in the Church, he holds that this was tolerated temporarily lest there be scandal and that this decision was "from the command of the Holy Spirit inspiring the Church." Yet, he adds, the pope had some doubt about the matter and in practice acted differently in a case that came to his attention.[214]

Defending the Church's prescriptions about the degrees of consanguinity in marriage, Albert says that the Church instituted these under the inspiration of the Holy Spirit (*Spiritu sancto inspirata*) and he gives reasons for it.[215] In another case of marriage impediments he defends certain concessions by

---

in quantum est summus sed in quantum est pontifex tantum: sed jurisdictio universitatis [*sic*] potestatis descendit in ipsum a Domino, ex hoc quod Petro succedit."

The word *universitatis*, where one might expect *universalis*, is found in Borgnet and in Yale Univ., MS Beineke 20, fol. 197rb, and Groningen, Bibl. der Rijksuniversiteit, MS 13, 1-2, fol. 156vb.

[213] See, for example, d. 23, a. 21, resp.; 30: 29rb: "Si tamen ab aliquo patre sancto vel a Domino Papa aliter in hac quaestione determinari invenitur, magis judicarem illius sententiae standum quam meae ...."

[214] D. 3, a. 2, ad 8; 29: 66a: "... Cum dicitur: Baptizetur servus Christi etc., praeintelligitur expressio vel intellectus verbi primae personae, et quoad hoc tolerari potuit ad tempus propter scandalum et ex imperio Spiritus sancti inspirante Ecclesiam. Tamen Papa in hoc dubius fuit: quia de illis qui sunt in Dalmatio primo respondit quod rebaptizarentur, et postea permisit et ut caveretur in posterum praecepit: quosdam autem fratres in ordine nostro existentes, tres ad minus in urbe Roma rebaptizari praecepit."

[215] D. 40, a. 8, sol.; 30: 452b: "Ad hoc dicendum quod Ecclesia fecit hoc Spiritu sancto inspirata ...."

saying that God conceded many things to "the inspired Church" for a time, things he did not promulgate because the state of the primitive Church could not endure certain prescriptions.[216] Discussing the words in the eucharistic consecration that are not found in the scriptures, Albert maintains that these added words came "from the Lord's handing them over" (*ex traditione Domini*) and quotes Pope Innocent III saying that "the Roman Church has always preserved with integral faith what it received from the apostles themselves," including the rites of worship.[217] As for confessing to a priest, Albert says that this is prescribed by the Church and that "the Church prescribes only what is just."[218] Defending the practice of indulgences, he holds that Christ's prayer for Peter's faith not to fail was said to Peter "in the person of the Church" (*in persona Ecclesiae*) and therefore when it grants indulgences, "the universal Church does not err."[219] On the other hand, Albert does admit that the Church can err in an individual case of excommunication.[220] In all this can be seen Albert's sensitivity to the developing traditions within the Church. He sees the role of the pope as that of a guide directing the Church correctly in accepting such developments.

Most of the preceding cases involve practice directly and faith only indirectly. In another text Albert distinguishes between open or explicit heresy and implicit heresy. The latter, he says, is an assertion from which heresy follows, such as a command by the Church to do something which at the present time is not prescribed. Should the Church do this, one is

---

[216] D. 42, a. 14, ad 1m; 30: 486a: "... Deus multa Ecclesiae inspiratae concessit pro tempore promulganda quae ipse non promulgavit quia status primitivae Ecclesiae talia pati non potuit eo quod tunc personae erant secundum diversus ritus conjunctae, et voluit Deus omnes in unam Ecclesiam congregari et nulli facere ad fidem accessum difficilem."
Cf. d. 35, a. 16, ad 1 (30: 366a), in which, discussing a marriage question, Albert says: "... Dominus ideo dedit Ecclesiae claves et inspirationem Spiritus Sancti ut in talibus ordinet expedientia ...."

[217] D. 8, a. 7 resp.; 29: 195a: "... ex traditione Domini habetur .... Dicit enim Apostolus, I ad Corinth. xi, 23: *Ego enim accepi a Domino quod et tradidi vobis.* Quod autem Ecclesia ab Apostolis traditum acceperit, dicit Innocentius III sic: 'Romana Ecclesia istud integra semper fide servavit quod ab ipsis Apostolis, qui eam praesentialiter sacris instituere doctrinis et Ecclesiastici ritus regulam docuerunt, accepit'."

[218] D. 17, a. 3, sc 1; 29: 663b: "Ecclesia nihil statuit nisi justum ...."

[219] D. 20, a. 17, sc 4; 29: 850a: "... Ecclesia universalis non errat; ergo videtur quod indulgentia valeant." Although this is a *sed contra* argument, it seems to be Albert's opinion. Another *sed contra* argument (d. 24, a. 8; 30: 42a) defends the ordination of ignorant priests by saying: "... Vidimus in multis terris sacerdotes omnino ignaros ... et tamen non condemnantur sed sustinentur ab Ecclesia: cum igitur Ecclesia non erret, videtur quod sacerdotes non teneantur ad habendum scientiam." Albert in a sense agrees when he sets lower limits than theological science as a prerequisite (ibid., resp.; 30: 42a-b).

[220] D. 17, a. 63, sol.; 29: 758a: "... Licet erret Ecclesia, tamen Deus approbat quod iste se gerat pro excommunicato et alii vitent eum."

obliged to obey the order; if one refuses, it is a heresy of disobedience to the power and ordering of the keys.[221] This recalls statements seen earlier from authors of the late twelfth century.[222]

As for the pope himself (and not the Church more generally), it should be noted how frequently Albert quotes papal texts as authorities, even though he will sometimes discuss their correct interpretation. Two arguments, whose premises he does not dispute, hold that since Berengarius' confession of faith about the Eucharist was received by the pope and several bishops, it is rash to think differently about it;[223] moreover, what is published throughout the world by the Apostolic See as faithful is to be held by faith, and this was the case with Berengarius' confession.[224] It is the principles invoked here more than the particular case that are noteworthy.

In a text already seen Albert maintains that the care of all Churches and all persons falls upon the pope; and that he has all power of ordering in the Church whatever will exclude heresies, schisms, and scandals.[225] At one place he speaks about the pope's receiving power from the influx of the Holy Spirit.[226] Elsewhere he teaches that the pope, like the apostles, could not change the form of Baptism "except through a revelation of the Holy Spirit and for a great need on the part of the Church."[227] And in a discussion about repetition of Anointing of the Sick, he gives his own opinion but defers to any possible determination of the question coming from one of the fathers or the lord pope, who represent for him the "inspiration of the Church."[228]

---

[221] D. 17, a. 33; 29: 705b: "Implicita autem haeresis est assertio ex qua sequitur haeresis, sicut est ista: quia licet modo non teneamur confiteri Episcopis tribus vel duobus, si tamen praecipiatur ab Ecclesia, tunc tenemur. Unde si ego dico non esse confitendum Episcopis illis, ex hoc sequitur quod non sit obediendum potestati et ordinationi clavium: et ideo haeresis est."

[222] See above, section 2.4.

[223] D. 13, a. 7, 1m; 29: 342b: "Si enim haec confessio fuit recepta a Papa Nicolao et pluribus Episcopis, tunc videtur temerarium esse si aliquis aliter sentiat ...."

[224] Ibid., 2m; 29: 342b: "Item, quidquid per sedem Apostolicam in diversis partibus mundi publicari praecipitur ut fidele, illud pro fide tenendum est: sed confessio ista imperio Nicolae Papae publicata est: sic ergo pro fide tenenda est."

[225] See above, n. 192.

[226] D. 20, a. 20, ad 2; 29: 857a: "... tali Papae influit Spiritus sanctus ea quae sunt potestatis."

[227] D. 3, a. 2, ad q. 7; 29: 67a: "Ad aliud dicendum quod Papa non potest, sicut nec Apostoli potuerunt, nisi per revelationem Spiritus sancti et magnam Ecclesiae necessitatem."

[228] D. 33, a. 21, resp.; 30: 29b: "Si tamen ab aliquo patre sancto vel a Domino Papa aliter in hac quaestione determinari invenitur, magis judicarem illius sententiae standum quam meae: quia magis in hac parte credendum est inspirationi Ecclesiae quam rationi conjecturanti ex incertis."

See a similar statement in d. 19, a. 7, ad 1m; 29: 809b: "Et hoc mihi videtur nisi auctoritas superioris aliud forte judicaverit: quia in talibus puto standum esse Pontificum et superiorum judicio ...."

In this text we see once again the link Albert makes between the pope and the inspiration of the Church.

Albert's most important text on the pope's role in relation to faith comes when he is analyzing the articles of faith. Comparing the Apostles' Creed with the *Symbolum Patrum* (the Nicene-Constantinople Creed), Albert asks whether new creeds could be produced or new articles of faith expressed if there were the same need for them as formerly for the other creeds.[229] Albert replies as follows:

> ... If necessity should require it, the pope, after convoking a council of skilled persons and invoking the Holy Spirit, could still make plain and put among the explicit articles something that is implicitly contained in the Apostles' Creed because this would not be inventing some new article but rather making explicit an article that was always present. This is what Anselm says in his book, *De processione Spiritus Sancti.*[230]

As has been mentioned earlier, this strong, clear statement is the only one we have found on this topic after probing likely places in other authors of the thirteenth century.[231] It is to be noted that Albert indicates the need of a council of experts and also a limit: only what is implicit in the creed may be made explicit in such new formulations.

3.6.c. *The Power of the Pope in Particular Cases.*

The examples given earlier already indicate papal power in certain cases. Here we shall examine Albert's discussion of the power of the keys, dispensations, and indulgences. Like his predecessors, Albert applies the Petrine text of Matthew 16:19 ("Whatever you bind") to all priests and not only to the pope when the power of the keys is involved.[232] He distinguishes in the power of the keys what derives from the sacrament of Order and what is a matter of jurisdiction. Jurisdiction descends from the supreme pontiff, Albert says, and it is the pope who determines the matter over which this delegated jurisdiction extends: hence heretics, although they have the power of the keys if they are validly ordained, lack the execution of this power since

---

[229] In 3 *Sent.*, d. 24, a. 7, 7m; ed. cit. 28 (Paris, 1894), 463: "Septimo quaeritur utrum adhuc plura possint fieri symbola et articuli exprimi si fuerit eadem causa quae prius fuit?"

[230] Ibid., ad 7; 28: 464b: "Ad aliud dicendum quod si urgeret necessitas, adhuc posset Papa, convocato concilio peritorum et invocato Spiritu Sancto, aliquid quod implicite continetur in symbolo Apostolorum explanare et ponere inter articulos explicitos quia hoc non esset novum articulum invenire sed eum qui semper erat explicare: et hoc dicit Anselmus in libro *De processione Spiritus Sancti.*" Cf. Anselm, *De processione Spiritus Sancti*, c. 12, in F. S. Schmitt, ed., *Opera omnia* 2 (Rome, 1940) p. 211.

[231] See above, section 3.3.

[232] See d. 18, a. 1, sc 1 and resp. (29: 764a) and d. 18, a. 15 resp. (29: 791b).

they no longer have jurisdiction coming from the pope.[233] It comes as no surprise, then, when Albert lists not only the bishop or legate but also the pope among those "who in the keys have greater jurisdiction."[234]

A case that probably reflects the situations Dominicans sometimes found themselves in, with relation to the rights of the parish priest to hear his parishioners' confessions, is that of priests who have the privilege of confessing "those whom some [priests] move by the words of their preaching." Albert maintains that "it is most firmly to be believed that the supreme pontiff gave this [privilege] because of the very great negligence of priests," and he elaborates this remark from his personal experience and with considerable vehemence.[235] This text suggests a significant point: was Albert's (and other Mendicants') strong papalist doctrine an outgrowth of the support they were receiving from the pope in the face of opposition from parish priests, bishops, and, in the universities, from the secular masters?

Can the key of jurisdiction be used on those who are not one's subjects, Albert asks? The question pertains to bishops concerning those not of their diocese or to papal legates. Albert says that no one can exceed his jurisdiction so as to excommunicate or absolve those not subject to this jurisdiction. If, however, the pope wishes to punish a crime, he can issue a constitution placing someone under another forum for the sake of punishing him. This is by reason of the pope's authority. Indeed, the pope may also allow legates of the Apostolic See to intervene in dioceses outside Rome; thus he may allow his legates to give the benefit of absolution to persons who have been condemned, and this in order that the people may be more devout in showing the honour and reverence that is always owed to a papal legate. But this is not allowed to bishops or others. Only the pope takes the place of Christ on earth, Albert continues, and therefore only he can exercise power

---

[233] D. 18, a. 6, resp.; 29: 773a: "Responsio. Dicendum in ista quaestione quod est potestas clavis ex ordine et est potestas ex jurisdictione: sicut enim supra patuit, omnis actus quaerit materiam circa quam sit, et illi in clavibus sunt subditi qui non nisi per jurisdictionem a summo Pontifice descendentem haberi possunt. Dicendum ergo quod haereticus [haeresis Borgnet] in forma Ecclesiae habens ordines habet claves secundum quod potestas sumitur ex ordine, sed non habet ex jurisdictione et ideo exsequi nihil omnino potest ...."

[234] D. 18, a. 11, resp.; 29: 784b: "... Ille qui habet in clavibus majorem jurisdictionem sicut Episcopus, Legatus, et Papa ...."

[235] D. 17, a. 44, resp.; 29: 736a: "Respondeo sine praejudicio quod si privilegium audiendi confessiones per modum supra dictum daretur alicui, sicut datum est privilegium audiendi eos quos movent aliqui verbo suae praedicationis: firmissime credendum est quod propter nimiam sacerdotum negligentiam hoc summus Pontifex dedit: quia peccatis nostris crescentibus in hoc fine saeculi, etiam perpauci inveniuntur sacerdotes qui veri sint pastores, sed potius vicarii conducti pretio vili ...." His strong remarks continue onto 736b.

over all; others only share in his pastoral care and therefore have a limited jurisdiction they cannot exceed.[236]

Finally with respect to the keys, Albert wonders whether women such as abbesses have the power of the keys since they do govern monasteries and do receive vows of obedience. Albert's answer is that they lack the keys both of Penance and of power in ecclesiastical cases, but that they do have some power of governing, which is conceded to them either by their religious order, the abbot, or the pope. This concession is only "for use" (*ad usum*: that is, it is not granted permanently or habitually) and to maintain propriety in convents.[237] As for the promise of obedience, it is not made to the abbess as to a superior or as to one having care of souls; it is promised through her to the abbot, bishop, or pope.[238]

When Albert examines the power of dispensation, he is most formal about the special powers of the pope. Albert is one of the few theologians in the period studied here to use the analogy of the pope as head of the Mystical Body, in this case to vindicate the pope's power to dispense in ways others cannot. The head, he says, retains to itself certain powers in the natural body that it does not give to others. Again, the power that rules life is reason, which is seated only in the head; the same should be true of the power of

---

[236] D. 19, a. 10, resp.; 29: 812b: "Dicendum quod nullus potest jurisdictionem suam ultra quam sibi a suo superiori permissum est ad alienum subditum extendere excommunicando vel absolvendo, vel etiam in penitentia absolvendo nisi eo modo quo supra dictum est." To the first argument (812a) that since a bishop can excommunicate and absolve those who are not his subjects, so can a priest, Albert replies (812b): "Ad primum dicimus quod ratione delicti ex constitutione Papali efficitur quis alterius fori: et hoc factum est in poenam: unde in aliis casibus non potest fieri." When an argument points to the action of legates in order to come to the same conclusion, Albert says (ad 2m; 812b): "Ad aliud dicimus quod non est simile de Legatis et aliis: Legatus enim Apostolicae sedis debet habere reverentiam: et ideo patitur Papa ut his per quos transit beneficium impendat ut devotiores sint ad honorem sibi exhibendum: secus autem est in aliis Episcopis et plebanis: et ideo talia facere non possunt." When Christ's healing of a non-Israelite and the parable of the good Samaritan are adduced as new proofs that those with the power of the keys may act beyond their jurisdiction (3m; 812a), Albert says: "Ad aliud dicendum quod loco Christi in terris non est nisi unus Papa: et ille potest facere in omnibus: sed alii in partem sollicitudinis vocati sunt et ideo non licet eis extendere jurisdictionem ultra quam permissum est."

[237] D. 19, a. 7, resp.; 29: 809a: "Dicendum quod mulier nullam habet clavem nec in foro poenitentiae nec in foro causarum: sed commissam sibi quoad usum tantum aliquem potest gubernare potestatem. Dico autem potestatem commissam, ab ordine vel abbate vel a papa concessam: quia mulier non est proprium subjectum potestatis, sed subjectionis in spiritualibus. Sed tamen ratione periculi, quia periculosum est viros gubernare foeminas continua communicatione et cohabitatione cum ipsis, ideo committitur ipsis regimen potestatis ...."

[238] Ibid., ad 1; 29: 809b: "... Obedientia non promittitur abbatissae ut superiori vel habenti curam animarum: sed per ipsam promittitur abbati vel Episcopo vel Papae: et propter periculum cohabitationis permissum est abbatissae recipere." The rest of this text is given above, n. 228 (2nd text).

dispensing: it should be chiefly (*praecipue*) the pope's.[239] These *sed contra* arguments he accepts as his own, and then says:

> It should be said without any doubt that all the power of dispensing fully (*plenarie*) exists in the head of the Church, as these last reasons prove, and is found in other prelates only to the extent it is granted to them; therefore they can dispense in those things in which they are not expressly prohibited by law.[240]

In the article preceding this one Albert disagrees with jurists who, admitting that the pope can dispense a person from being a religious, deny that he can dispense a religious in such a way that the religious may have property. If he can do the greater, Albert argues, he can certainly do this lesser thing.[241]

Can someone twice married be dispensed so as to be able to take sacred orders? Albert holds that bishops can dispense from this impediment and ordain him to minor orders but that in the case of major orders only the pope can dispense.[242] The replies to some of the arguments interpret certain

---

[239] D. 37, a. 17, sc 1 & 2; 30: 418a-b: "1. In corpore humano quaedam officia ita retinet caput in corpore naturali quod non ea committit aliis membris: ergo in corpore mystico ita debet esse: sed hoc praecipue videtur debere esse in dispensationibus: ergo potestas dispensandi debet esse penes caput, id est, Papam tantum. 2. Item, vis regitiva vitae ratio est, et non habet sedem nisi in capite: ergo similiter debet esse in corpore mystico: cum ergo principalius sit in regimine dispensandi potestas, videtur quod non sit nisi penes Papam."

[240] Ibid., resp.; 30: 418b: "Responsio. Dicendum quod absque dubio omnis potestas plenarie dispensandi est in capite Ecclesiae, sicut probant ultimae rationes, et in aliis praelatis tantum quantum eis conceditur: et ideo in his dispensare possunt in quibus expresso jure non prohibentur." Concrete examples follow: bishops are prohibited from dispensing from a vow to go to the Holy Land and, he thinks, from perpetual vows; they may dispense from temporary vows.

Albert continues to use this metaphor of headship when he meets an argument saying prelates need dispensing power for the good of their neighbour (ibid., 2m; 30: 418a). "Regimen est duplex, scilicet universale et particulare: et ideo in magnis non committitur potestas dispensandi habenti regimen particulare quia ex hoc contingeret quod quandoque surgeret deformitas membrorum contra caput: oportet enim in membris ordinem servare ad caput: et ideo statuitur in jure quod in aliquibus omnium membrorum recursus sit ad caput Ecclesiae sicut omnium membrorum quantum ad vim motivam et sensitivam recursus est ad caput in corpore organico physico" (ibid., ad 2; 30: 418b; text corrected in last line).

[241] D. 38, a. 16, resp.; 30: 417a: "Nec approbo solutionem illam Jurisperitorum qui dicunt quod non potest dispensari quod religiosus possit habere proprium, sed potius dispensatur ut non sit religiosus et tunc licet ei habere proprium. Quia non sunt nisi verba: qui enim potest quod est majus potest et id quod est minus; sed magis est religiosum fieri non religiosum quam religiosum habere proprium: ergo si Papa potest primum, potest et secundum."

[242] D. 27, a. 22, quaestio et resp.; 30: 183b and 184a-b: "Sed tunc ulterius quaeritur per quem posset dispensari [bigamia], utrum per Episcopum suum vel tantum per Dominum Papam? ... Responsio. Dicendum quod cum bigamo poterit dispensari: et sine praejudicio dico quod per Episcopum potest dispensari ad minores ordines si necesse fuerit, hoc est, usque ad subdiaconatum, et quod ministret in susceptis .... Si autem in saeculo maneat, ad majores [minores *Borgnet*] ordines suscipiendos dispensare non potest nisi solus Papa." Albert adds

authoritative texts as indicating that only the pope can dispense in this latter case.[243]

Finally, a discussion of indulgences elicits from Albert several remarks about the pope. Against those denying the efficacy of indulgences Albert quotes a gloss on a Pauline text saying that Paul forgave as if Christ himself had condoned the fault. Albert adds that the pope has as much power to condone as Paul had; bishops, on the other hand, have their power of condoning from the pope.[244] He adds:

> It should not be believed that the universal ruler of the Church would wish to deceive anyone, especially in those things which the whole Church receives and approves. Now it is clear that the pope preaches and causes it to be preached that indulgences have value. Therefore, it seems, they simply have the value they are preached as having.[245]

Two texts of scripture are also adduced to prove that the Church, succeeding to Peter, receives the power to grant indulgences.[246] The main response indicates that this power comes from the jurisdictional authority possessed by the pope, the bishop, or the pope's legate and others.[247]

The granting of indulgences, Albert argues, does not depend on the personal worth of the pope. He devotes a whole article to the question whether a pope in mortal sin can grant indulgences.[248] The negative position maintains that this is a dead work that cannot give life; the pope is a channel through which the Holy Spirit flows and if he is in mortal sin, the Holy Spirit

---

(184a) that if such a person enters religious life, a bishop can also dispense him so that he can receive major orders.

[243] See ibid., ad 1m, ad 4m; 30: 184b.

[244] D. 20, a. 17, sc 1; 29: 849b: "II ad Corinth. ii, 10: *Nam et ego quod donavi, si quid donavi, propter vos in persona Christi.* Glossa, 'Ac si Christus condonasset': sed constat quod hoc quod Christus condonat condonatum est: ergo et quod Apostolus condonavit: sed tantae potentiae est Papa quantae Paulus: ergo et quod Papa condonat condonatum est: ergo et quod illi condonant qui ut condonare possint habent a Papa: ergo tantum valent indulgentiae quantum ab his qui eas dant valere dicuntur." Although this is a *sed contra* argument, he makes no comment on it and it is in accord with his main position.

[245] Ibid., sc 3; 29: 850a: "Universalis gubernator Ecclesiae, praecipue in his quae tota Ecclesia recipit et approbat, non est credendus fallere velle aliquem: constat autem quod ipse indulgentias valere praedicat et praedicare facit: ergo, ut videtur, simpliciter valent sicut valere praedicantur."

[246] Ibid., sc 4 & sc 5; 29: 850a: the texts are those of Luke 22:32 (Christ's prayer that Peter's faith should not fail) and Matth. 18:22 (Christ tells Peter to forgive seventy times seven times).

[247] Ibid., resp.; 29: 850b: "Duae autem [conditiones] sunt ex parte dantis, quarum prima est dantis auctoritas ex jurisdictione quam habet, sicut Papa, Episcopus, Legatus, et hujusmodi. Alia est pia causa dantem movens, non privata sed publica."

[248] It is d. 20, a. 20; 29: 856b-857a.

pours nothing in or through him; as the ray of the sun is intercepted by a cloud, so the grace of the Holy Spirit is intercepted by sin with the result that an indulgence which flows or should flow from such a pope is a grace intercepted by sin and therefore does not come to us, and therefore an indulgence is not valid.[249]

The opposing argument uses the example of prophecy, likening it to a "grace and divine ray"; scripture shows that both Caiphas and Balaam (presumably sinners) were channels of prophecy. Hence, Albert says, indicating his own view, indulgences are of equal value, whether given by a good or bad pope.[250] He completes his own position in his replies to the arguments. To give indulgences is a charismatic gift (*gratia gratis data*) and this kind of gift or grace works its effect from a power given the person and not (as with *gratia gratum faciens*, a grace making someone pleasing to God) from a person's goodness of life.[251] Again, the pope is, as was argued, a channel for the gifts of the Holy Spirit. If the pope is in mortal sin, the Holy Spirit nevertheless pours into him those things belonging to his power regardless of the quality of his life.[252] Finally, with respect to the sun and ray example, sin interrupts only the ray of *gratia gratum faciens*, not the ray of power: this is a *gratia gratis data* of the same sort as prophecy; so too with the case in point, the giving of indulgences.[253]

Although this article may seem at first sight somewhat esoteric, it is of practical importance to see how a theologian like Albert viewed the papal power and its exercise as independent of the pope's life, whether good or evil. This was indeed practical, given the vagaries of history and the lives of individual medieval popes; it was also important in view of the frequent attacks by those rejecting as invalid the ministries of evil prelates.

It has been necessary and indeed fruitful to devote so much attention to Albert since in him we see the culmination of a century of developing thought

---

[249] See ibid., 1m, 2m, & 3m; 29: 856b-857a.

[250] Ibid., sc.; 29: 857a: "... Prophetia est gratia et radius divinus: et tamen fluxit per Caipham eo quod esset pontifex anni illius, ut dicit Evangelista Joannes, xi, 51. Idem habetur per hoc quod legitur, Numer. xxii, xxiii et xxiv, quia praeclarissima prophetia per iniquissimum fluxit Balaam toti Synagogae et Ecclesiae. Propter hoc dicimus quod indulgentiae aequaliter valent, sive a malo sive a bono dentur."

[251] Ibid., ad 1; 29: 857a: "Ad primum ergo quod contra objicitur dicendum quod dare indulgentias est gratia gratis data, quae potestatis est, non bonitatis vitae: et omnes tales gratiae aequaliter fiunt per bonos et malos."

[252] Ibid., ad 2; 29: 857a: "Ad aliud dicendum quod prima <Papa est rivus cui fons ... est Spiritus Sanctus> est vera: secunda <Spiritus Sanctus nihil influit> est falsa quia tali Papae <in mortali peccato> influit Spiritus Sanctus ea quae sunt potestatis."

[253] Ibid., ad 3; 29: 857a: "Ad aliud dicendum quod peccatum non intercipit radium nisi gratiae gratum facientis. Jam autem dictum est quod iste radius est potestatis et gratiae gratis datae sicut et prophetia."

among theologians. For this reason, and because his teachings are so extensive and scattered, we shall recall them in a brief summary.

For Albert, the pope as successor of Peter has universal jurisdiction ("jurisdiction of universal power," he calls it once). This comes to him from the Lord. He is vicar of Christ, is the only one to take the place of Christ, and is over all as universal governor of the Church. He is earthly head of the Mystical Body or Church. His universal jurisdiction is unique — there is only one pope; other prelates have jurisdiction "coming down from the Supreme Pontiff" over only a part of the Church. The pope's power is ordinary and immediate to all the Church; hence he can intervene everywhere, for example, by defining the relations between his subordinates such as bishops and archbishops, leaving to bishops certain powers that cannot be interfered with by archbishops but that, it would seem, the pope himself could control or limit. These statements indicate that for Albert bishops have no authority or jurisdiction independently of the pope but rather derive all from him. As part of his universal authority and governance the pope wields power against all heresies, schisms, and scandals. The pope has jurisdiction over all ecclesiastical goods, but only as steward and not as owner. The papacy and episcopacy are not orders within the sacrament of Order but rather offices with power: although Albert does not say so explicitly, it could be inferred that for him the priestly functions of the bishops would derive not from the pope but from God in their ordination as priests.

In questions of faith, Albert says several times that the Holy Spirit inspires the Church; it has always guarded the faith, and it never orders anything that is unjust. The Church does not err (yet Albert does recognize that the Church can err in a particular case such as excommunication of someone who does not deserve it). If the Church issues a new command, it is implicit heresy to disobey it. In practice, for Albert these statements about the Church really refer to the pope, the head of the Church. In doubtful matters of theological investigation or of Church practice, Albert says several times that he is ready to accept whatever the pope decides. For him the pope has the power and the duty to eliminate all heresies. If there is need and the pope consults experts, he can even introduce a new article into the creed. We may ask if this is not already a full-blown teaching of infallibility of papal teaching. It seems to be at least a teaching of inerrancy of the Church and likely of the pope. Nor does Albert seem anywhere to have made a distinction seen in earlier authors between the pope, who might err personally, and the Church of Rome (whether the diocese or the universal Roman Church), which never errs: this might indicate that he sees inerrancy as something more personal than did his predecessors.

Finally, the pope's extensive jurisdictional power means that, according to Albert, he can intervene throughout the Church in particular cases. We have already mentioned his power to limit bishops in their granting of indulgences. According to Albert, the pope can also take action in individual dioceses in other matters related to the sacrament of Penance, as well as in excommunications, or in imposing penalties or absolving from them: these actions he can undertake either directly or through his legate. Vows of religious women are made to him through the abbess; he can dispense religious from their vows and remove impediments to ordination to major orders. The pope can grant full or plenary indulgences. Even mortal sin in a pope does not invalidate the exercise of his powers.

This doctrine, extensive both in quantity and in degree, reveals in Albert, rather more than in earlier theologians, the strong papal theology that will be seen in the monastic and episcopal reformers in the following essay. Through Albert especially their views entered the mainstream of theological speculation in the schools and, in certain respects, receive even greater intensification.

4. Conclusion

For school theologians between 1150 and 1250, one of the most influential sources for the theology of the Church and of the papacy within the Church was the *De sacramentis* of Hugh of St. Victor. His doctrine of the Headship of Christ supplied for a lack in Peter Lombard's *Sentences* (although Lombard's commentaries on Paul also filled this lack). Hugh's strong assertion of the primacy of the spiritual over the temporal and secular was also echoed in later authors. His distinction between sacramental grade (shared equally by priests and higher prelates by reason of priestly ordination) and dignity (giving special powers to bishops and higher prelates, including the pope) is at the root of later distinctions between the sacrament of Order and the power of jurisdiction. When discussing the various dignities, Hugh transmits teachings about the pope as supreme pontiff, successor of the apostolic see, "apostolic," and successor to Peter with special power of the keys.

Between 1150 and 1200 school theologians tended to leave many matters, even of sacramental theology, to the canonists. Hence many areas where one would expect examination of the pope's role were not touched upon in their works. Their discussions about the power of the keys centred almost exclusively on the role and power of keys in all priests and prelates, and even of unordained delegates; the place of the pope's keys was mentioned often only in passing or peripherally. At this period, however, the spread of a theology of Penance stressing satisfaction by penal works (itself undoubtedly reenforced by Anselm's satisfaction-theory of Christ's redeeming work), as well as the taking up of the cross on the Crusades, led to an increased practice of indulgences. Discussion of the power to give indulgences, attributed to bishops as well as to the pope, began to focus theologians' attention on certain issues: the universal and greater power of the pope to grant indulgences; limitations on his power; the possibility of universal or plenary indulgences. Papal interventions in matters of faith, especially Alexander III's pronouncements concerning the humanity of Christ, sparked some fragmentary but important theological investigations concerning the pope's role individually, in relation to the Church of Rome, and with respect to councils and synods. Some theologians spoke of the pope as being led or inspired in decisions by the Holy Spirit or by a special revelation. In the schools, however, a distinction was sometimes made between the pope as a person, even as a private theologian, and the Church of the see of Rome as the true depository of certitude and inerrancy in matters of faith: the pope, some said, could err even in faith, but the Roman Church as a whole would not.

In the thirteenth century, discussion of the power of the keys and especially of indulgences and dispensations increased in length and sophistication. Limits to papal powers were indicated, but there was also affirmed the pope's disposition of the treasury of the infinite merits of Christ together with those of the universal Church. In this discussion we have met for the first time the interesting title given the pope by Guerric of St. Quentin: "vicar of the Church" (*vicarius Ecclesiae*).

The thirteenth century saw the introduction of the most original theological discussion about the papacy, that is, whether the papacy constituted a distinct order within the sacrament of Order. Although this question was first discussed by secular masters, it was by and large theologians among the Mendicant Friars who most influenced the development of theology of the papacy. Owing, it seems, to the pastoral interests and zeal of these new religious communities, their theologians introduced a good deal of canonical material into their works; this allowed them to discuss many practical matters that would be important to their confreres in their apostolate, matters that seemed to be of less concern to the secular masters of theology. Most important for the extensive use of canonical materials were Alexander of Hales in his own *Gloss on the Sentences of Peter Lombard*, Richard Fishacre, the *Summa Fratris Alexandri*, and Albert the Great; most of this canonical material was brought into discussions of sacramental theology in commentaries on book 4 of the *Sentences*. The Franciscan and Dominican theologians increasingly stressed the prerogatives of the pope in discussions about the power of the keys in relation to confessions (one of their important pastoral works), dispensations, indulgences, and the granting of delegated jurisdiction (another matter that touched their apostolic concerns). Undoubtedly the role of theologians from the Mendicant Orders in reenforcing the authority and position of the pope was consonant with their own special status, granted by the pope, in relation to the particular or local Churches in which they exercised their apostolate, including university teaching. Indeed, in practice the influence of the Mendicants in this area seems to have been decisive for the development of the strongly papalist theology that was to prevail: a hermeneutics of suspicion would incline one to see much self-interest in their strong espousal of papal prerogatives and authority.[254]

Although little question-literature directly concerned with the papacy appeared in the first half of the thirteenth century, the debate, already mentioned, about the sacrament of Order helped clarify the distinction between Order and the power of jurisdiction. Although a few theologians viewed the papacy as a distinct ninth order analogous to one of the nine heavenly hierarchies of the Pseudo-Dionysius, most theologians held it to be a special office with powers that came to be identified as jurisdictional rather than sacramental: on the level of sacrament, priests, bishops, archbishops, patriarchs, and pope were all considered equal because of the sacramental power of confecting the Eucharist, considered the highest and most distinctive element of the sacrament of Order.

Finally, special mention should be made of the distinctive contributions of the *Summa Fratris Alexandri*, composed by and for the Franciscan school of this period and afterwards, as well as those of the Dominican master, Albert the Great. The *Summa*, using, as has been said, considerable canonical material, introduced into theological debate matters pertaining to the relations between the pope and his subjects, including secular rulers (Hugh of St. Victor's influence also returned here). Albert the Great, whose contributions have already been summarized, presents the most thoroughgoing discussion of the papacy met in this period, including important

---

[254] On the role of the controversies about the Mendicant Orders in the development of teaching concerning the universal papal primacy see Josef Ratzinger, "Der Einfluss des Bettelordensstreites auf die Entwicklung der Lehre vom päpstlich Universalprimat, unter besonderer Berücksichtigung des heiligen Bonaventura," in *Theologie in Geschichte und Gegenwart* [Festgabe Michael Schmaus], eds. Johann Auer and Hermann Volk (Munich: Karl Zink, 1957) pp. 697-724, especially 697-711; Yves Congar, "Aspects ecclésiologiques de la querelle entre mendiants et séculiers dans le seconde moitié du XIIIᵉ siècle et le début du XIVᵉ siècle," *Archives d'histoire doctrinale et littéraire du moyen âge* 28 (1961) 35-151; and, in the present volume, Christopher Ryan, "The Theology of Papal Primacy in Thomas Aquinas," pp. 193-225.

statements about the pope as the source, apparently, of all episcopal right and power, and as the inspired guardian of the faith possessing the right even to introduce new articles into the creed when there is a need in the Church to make explicit what was implicit in earlier creeds. Whether at this stage of his teaching Albert holds for a doctrine of infallibility of papal teaching is not perfectly clear, but he certainly holds for the inerrancy of the Church and, apparently, for the general inerrancy of the pope as inspired representative of the Church. He does, however, admit the possibility of papal error in individual cases of excommunication.

As for the source of episcopal authority, when this is touched upon directly or indirectly, the authority of ordinary bishops, although less than that of the pope and although subject to him in its exercise, was viewed as coming not from the pope but from God. Only at the very end of our period do we find in Albert the idea that bishops other than the pope receive their power, jurisdiction, and authority from the pope as his delegates.

The religious ideal of the papacy was influenced, however, not only, and perhaps not even principally, by the work of the school theologians. In addition to the work of these theologians, important theological contributions came as well from certain bishops and monastic leaders. The following essay will examine some of the most important contributions from these sources.

3

Monastic, Episcopal, and Apologetic Theology of the Papacy, 1150-1250

Walter H. Principe C.S.B.

The Religious Roles of the Papacy: Ideals and Realities, 1150-1300, ed. Christopher Ryan, Papers in Mediaeval Studies 8 (Toronto: Pontifical Institute of Mediaeval Studies, 1989), pp. 117-170. © P.I.M.S., 1989.

2. The First Half of the Thirteenth Century

    2.1. Apologetic Works Against the Heterodox
        2.1.a. Ermengaud of Beziers (fl. early 13th C.)
        2.1.b. Durandus of Huesca (fl. 1222-1224)
        2.1.c. Moneta of Cremona († 1260)

    2.2. A Theologian Become Bishop: Robert Grosseteste (ca. 1175-1253; Bishop
    of Lincoln, 1235)

3. Summary and Conclusion

Whereas the previous essay restricted itself to the works of the school theologians in order to gain some understanding of their religious ideal of the papacy, this essay will examine the theology of the papacy found in a number of authors from outside the schools. These include monastic authors, bishops, and writers defending the Church against attacks on the Church made by heterodox groups in the period from 1150 to 1250.

1. The Latter Half of the Twelfth Century

1.1. Two Monastic Authors: Bernard of Clairvaux and Peter the Venerable.

1.1.a. *Bernard of Clairvaux (1090-1153).*

Bernard of Clairvaux's theology of the papacy can be fully understood only within the background of his entire theology of the Church as it is found in all his works, whether homiletic, epistolary, or more consciously theological. Yves Congar's study of Bernard's ecclesiology shows that the Cistercian abbot had an extremely spiritual image of the Church, in which the theme of the Church as Spouse of Christ predominated with respect to others such as the Mystical Body of Christ or the People of God. Yet, Congar adds, Bernard also sees the Church as a City whose King is Christ: Bernard is aware of the concrete existence of the Church in time, with both its lofty calling and its only too evident failures.[1] Bernard Jacqueline has examined the historical and institutional contexts of Bernard's views on the papacy. If Bernard was influenced by the Gregorian Reform, Jacqueline says, he must

---

[1] See Congar, "L'ecclésiologie de S. Bernard," in *Saint Bernard théologien,* in *Analecta Sancti Ordinis Cisterciensis* 9 (1953) 136-190; rpt. in Y. Congar, *Études d'ecclésiologie médiévale* (London: Variorum Reprints, 1983) no. VII; English version: "The Ecclesiology of St. Bernard," *Cistercian Studies* 1 (1961) 81-141. See also Jean Leclercq, "St. Bernard on the Church," *Downside Review* 85 (1967) 274-294.

nevertheless be seen within the spirit of the canons regular with their emphasis on the "apostolic life" (*vita apostolica*) and, even more, within the Benedictine tradition as interpreted by the Cistercians reacting against the centralizing power and authority of Cluniac abbots.[2] We shall see that Bernard's concern for episcopal authority is an important counterbalance to his exalted views of the papal authority and ministry.

A recent interesting thesis by Richard V. Ver Bust has especially studied this aspect of the papacy as a ministry. Ver Bust examines the role of the pope as seen by Bernard in its relation to the rest of the Church, as well as his views on the nature of papal authority and papal ministry.[3] Our survey can touch only a few points in Bernard's important and much-studied views of the papacy.

Bernard clearly and strongly supports papal primacy and authority. In a well-known passage of the *De consideratione*, a passage written after July 1148,[4] Bernard first reminds the former Cistercian monk, now become Pope Eugene III, about his human condition as mortal man although possessing reason; he then speaks about the dignity and powers of the pope. He begins as follows:

> Come, let us investigate even more diligently who you are; that is, what part you play in the Church of God at this time. Who are you? The high priest,

[2] See Jacqueline, *Épiscopat et Papauté chez saint Bernard de Clairvaux* (Saint-Lô, 1975); its ch. 12 appeared in an earlier shorter form in *Studia Gratiana* 14 (1967) 219-239. See also his earlier work, *Papauté et épiscopat selon saint Bernard de Clairvaux* (Saint-Lô, 1963).

[3] "A Theology of Papal Ministry As Proposed by Bernard of Clairvaux," Thesis, Marquette University, 1980 (Ann Arbor, Mich.: University Microfilms International, 1981). Bibliography is given on pp. 223-229. An earlier survey of writing on the *De consideratione* is given by Elizabeth Kennan, "The *De consideratione* of St. Bernard of Clairvaux and the Papacy in the Mid-Twelfth Century: A Review of Scholarship," *Traditio* 23 (1967) 73-115.

See also John Sommerfeldt, "Charismatic and Gregorian Leadership in the Thought of Bernard of Clairvaux," in *Bernard of Clairvaux: Studies Presented to Dom Jean Leclercq*, ed. Basil M. Pennington, Cistercian Studies 23 (Washington, D.C., 1973) pp. 73-90, and Elizabeth Kennan, "Antithesis and Argument in the *De consideratione*," ibid., pp. 91-109.

These studies, together with those of Congar and Jacqueline, help to overcome the rather one-sided views in the otherwise excellent section on Bernard in Walter Ullmann's study, *The Growth of Papal Government in the Middle Ages*, 3rd ed. (London, 1970) pp. 426-437.

[4] *De consideratione ad Eugenium Papam*, eds. J. Leclercq and H. M. Rochais, in *Sancti Bernardi Opera*, vol. 3: *Tractatus et opuscula* (Rome, 1963) pp. 379-493. Page references for the Latin text will be to this edition; page references in parentheses will be (except where we note our own translation) to the English translation by John D. Anderson and Elizabeth T. Kennan, *Five Books on Consideration*, vol. 13 of *The Works of Bernard of Clairvaux*, The Cistercian Fathers Series, 17 (Kalamazoo, Michigan, 1976). On the dates of individual books of the work, which was composed between 1148 and 1153, see Jacqueline, *Épiscopat*, p. 196.

Except for this translation and that of Grosseteste by Pantin (see below, section 2.2), all translations in this essay are my own.

the Supreme Pontiff. You are the prince of the bishops, you are the heir of the Apostles; in primacy you are Abel, in governing you are Noah, in patriarchate you are Abraham, in orders you are Melchisedech, in dignity you are Aaron, in authority you are Moses, in judgment you are Samuel, in power you are Peter, by anointing you are Christ. You are the one to whom the keys have been given, to whom the sheep have been entrusted.[5]

After extolling the pope with such lofty titles, Bernard compares the pope to other bishops. Although he recognizes that they as shepherds have true authority over their individual flocks, for him the pope is shepherd not only of all the sheep but also of these bishops who are shepherds:

It is true that there are other doorkeepers of heaven and shepherds of flocks; but you are more glorious than all of these, to the degree that you have inherited a name more excellent than theirs. They have flocks assigned to them, one flock to each; to you all are assigned, a single flock to a single shepherd. You are the one shepherd not only of all the sheep, but of all the shepherds.[6]

To prove this position, Bernard invokes the text of John 21:17 about Peter's feeding the sheep:

Do you ask how I can prove this? From the word of the Lord. For to whom, and I include not only bishops but also Apostles, were all the sheep entrusted so absolutely and completely? "If you love me, Peter, feed my sheep." What sheep? The people of this or that city or region, or even of this or that kingdom? "My sheep," he said. To whom is it not clear that he did not exclude any, but assigned them all? There is no exception where there is no distinction.[7]

Bernard gives a philosophical justification for such a disposition by Christ: unity brings perfection, a perfection lacking in numbers higher than one

[5] II, 8, 15; 423 (66): "Age, indagemus adhuc diligentius quis sis, quam geras videlicet pro tempore personam in Ecclesia Dei. Quis es? Sacerdos magnus, summus Pontifex. Tu princeps episcoporum, tu heres Apostolorum, tu primatu Abel, gubernatu Noe, patriarchatu Abraham, ordine Melchisedech, dignitate Aaron, auctoritate Moyses, iudicatu Samuel, potestate Petrus, unctione Christus. Tu es cui claves traditae, cui oves creditae sunt."
[6] Ibid.; 423 (66-67): "Sunt quidem et alii caeli ianitores et gregum pastores; sed tu, tanto gloriosius quanto et differentius, utrumque prae ceteris nomen hereditasti. Habent illi sibi assignatos greges, singuli singulos; tibi universi crediti, uni unus. Nec modo ovium, sed et pastorum tu unus omnium pastor."
[7] Ibid.; 423 (67): "Unde id probem quaeris? Ex verbo Domini. Cui enim, non dico episcoporum, sed etiam Apostolorum sic absolute et indiscrete totae commissae sunt oves? *Si me amas, Petre, pasce oves meas.* Quas? Illius vel illius populos civitatis, aut regionis, aut certe regni? *Oves meas,* inquit. Cui non planum, non dedignasse aliquas, sed assignasse omnes? Nihil excipitur, ubi distinguitur nihil." For the scriptural text cf. John 21:17.

because these introduce division. Therefore, although the other apostles each received a single church community to shepherd, they recognized the need for the unity achieved through Peter for the universal Church:

> And perhaps the rest of the disciples were present when the Lord, entrusting all to one man, commended unity to all in one flock with one shepherd according to the statement, "One is my dove, my beauty, my perfect one." Where unity is, there is perfection. Other numbers do not possess perfection but division, as they depart from unity. Thus it is that each of the other apostles received a single community, for they understood this mystery. James, who appeared as a pillar of the Church, was content with only Jerusalem, leaving to Peter the universal Church.[8]

Evoking two frequently-used phrases, Bernard says that "according to your own canons, others are called to *share* concern for the Church (*in partem sollicitudinis*), but you are called to the fullness of power (*in plenitudinem potestatis*)."[9] He expands these remarks by comparing the limited power of other bishops and the apparently sweeping powers of the pope:

> The power of the others is bound by definite limits; yours extends even over those who have received power over others. If cause exists, can you not close heaven to a bishop, depose him from the episcopacy, and even give him over to Satan? Your privilege is affirmed, therefore, both in the keys given to you and in the sheep entrusted to you.[10]

Bernard adds a rather far-fetched argument for his views, based on the scriptural account that Peter swam alone to meet the risen Lord: this, he says, shows "Peter's unique pontificate" (*singularis pontificii Petri*). "What does this mean?" he asks. "It is," he replies, "assuredly a sign of the unique pontificate of Peter through which he received not just a single ship to govern, as each of the others, but the whole world. For the sea is the world;

---

[8] Ibid.; 423-24 (67): "Et forte praesentes ceteri condiscipuli erant, cum, committens uni, unitatem omnibus commendaret in uno grege et uno pastore, secundum illud: *Una est columba mea, formosa mea, perfecta mea.* Ubi unitas, ibi perfectio. Reliqui numeri perfectionem non habent, sed divisionem, recedentes ab unitate. Inde est quod alii singuli singulas sortiti sunt plebes, scientes sacramentum. Denique Iacobus, qui videbatur columna Ecclesiae, una contentus est Ierosolyma, Petro universitatem cedens." Scriptural text: cf. Cant. 6:8.

[9] Ibid. II, 8, 16; p. 424 (68): "Ergo, iuxta canones tuos, alii in partem sollicitudinis, tu in plenitudinem potestatis vocatus es." Translation slightly altered.

[10] Ibid.; p. 424 (68): "Aliorum potestas certis artatur limitibus; tua extenditur et in ipsos, qui potestatem super alios acceperunt. Nonne, si causa exstiterit, tu episcopo caelum claudere, tu ipsum ab episcopatu deponere, etiam et tradere Satanae potes? Stat ergo inconcussum privilegium tuum tibi, tam in datis clavibus quam in ovibus commendatis."

the ships are the churches."[11] Continuing this nautical image, he draws a
similar conclusion about Peter's walking on the waters "like the Lord."
Ignoring the fact that Peter sank into the waters and was chided by Christ
for his lack of faith, Bernard concludes that this incident shows Peter to be
the unique vicar (*unicum ... vicarium*) of Christ. Peter is to preside over all
the many waters or individual ships, that is, over all peoples and individual
churches:

> Thus it is that, at another time, Peter walking on the waters like the Lord,
> showed himself to be the unique vicar of Christ who was to preside not over
> a single people but over all, since "many waters" signifies "many peoples."
> Thus, although each of the others has his own ship, to you is entrusted the
> greatest of all, made from all the others, the universal Church which is spread
> throughout the whole world.[12]

Another list of papal titles and prerogatives, but one mingled with duties,
occurs at the end of book 4 before Bernard turns to consideration of God
and the role that prayer to God must play in the life of the pope. In this
concluding passage Bernard says:

> For the rest, consider that you ought to be a model of justice, a mirror of
> holiness, an exemplar of piety, a preacher of truth, a defender of the faith, the
> teacher of the nations, the leader of Christians, a friend of the Bridegroom,
> an attendant of the bride, the director of the clergy, the shepherd of the
> people, the instructor of the foolish, the refuge of the oppressed, the advocate
> of the poor, the hope of the unfortunate, the protector of orphans, the judge
> of widows, the eye of the blind, the tongue of the mute, the support of the
> aged, the avenger of crimes, the terror of evil men, the glory of the good, the
> staff of the powerful, the hammer of tyrants, the father of kings, the moderator
> of laws, the dispenser of canons, the salt of the earth, the light of the world,
> the priest of the Most High, the vicar of Christ, the anointed of the Lord, and,
> finally, the god of Pharaoh.[13]

---

[11] Ibid.: "'Quid istud'? Nempe signum singularis pontificii Petri, per quod non navem
unam, ut ceteri quique suam, sed saeculum ipsum susceperit gubernandum. Mare enim
saeculum est; naves, Ecclesiae."

[12] Ibid.: "Inde est quod altera vice instar Domini gradiens super aquas, unicum se Christi
vicarium designavit, qui non uni populo, sed cunctis praeesse deberet: siquidem aquae multae,
populi multi. Ita, cum quisque ceterorum habeat suam, tibi una commissa est grandissima
navis, facta ex omnibus ipsa universalis Ecclesia, toto orbe diffusa."

In a letter to Pope Eugene, Bernard refers to him as the "bishop of the world"; *Epistola*
240, 1; eds. J. Leclercq and H. M. Rochais, in *Sancti Bernardi Opera*, vol. 8 (Rome, 1977),
p. 123: "Haec atque huiusmodi digna sunt vestro apostolatu, summam Sedem nobilitant,
decent plane orbis Episcopum."

[13] *De consideratione* IV, 7, 23; p. 466 (137): "De cetero oportere te esse considera formam
iustitiae, sanctimoniae speculum, pietatis exemplar, assertorem veritatis, fidei defensorem,
doctorem gentium, christianorum ducem, amicum sponsi, sponsae paranymphum, cleri

Among these many titles should be noted that of *amicus sponsi*, a title for the pope that will play an important role in Innocent III's theology of the papacy.[14] Imposing as are many of these titles, almost all of them imply an onerous duty for the pope, and both Bernard's exaltation of the pope and his stress on papal duties are better understood if one examines the context of the passage. It comes at the end of two books in which Bernard has described at great length the evils afflicting the Church in Europe and particularly in Rome, and in which he has offered advice on how things are to be improved in personnel and in procedures. The passage, then, is a call to Eugene III to be strong in exercising his role not only as ruler and administrator but also as prophet. Thus he concludes this list of titles with an exhortation to the pope to be strong against evil-doers, to act in a super-human way, to let evil-doers see his anger, fear his prayers, be led to a fear of God's anger and judgment in the pope's reproaches.[15]

Another contextual element that helps understand these exalted titles is the introduction to the passage, in which Bernard reminds the pope that his powers are to be exercised maternally and fraternally, and in conjunction with other bishops rather than in a lordly way over particular churches and their pastors:

> Before everything else, you should consider that the Holy Roman Church, over which God has established you as head, is the mother of churches, not the mistress; furthermore, that you are not the lord of bishops, but one of them, and the brother of those who love God and the companion of those who fear him.[16]

We shall see more of this aspect of Bernard's view of the papacy, but first he should be heard speaking about the teaching office of the pope. A text just

---

ordinatorem, pastorem plebium, magistrum insipientium, refugium oppressorum, pauperum advocatum, miserorum spem, tutorem pupillorum, iudicem viduarum, oculum caecorum, linguam mutorum, baculum senum, ultorem scelerum, malorum metum, bonorum gloriam, virgam potentium, malleum tyrannorum, regum patrem, legum moderatorem, canonum dispensatorem, sal terrae, orbis lumen, sacerdotem Altissimi, vicarium Christi, christum Domini, postremo deum Pharaonis."

[14] See below, section 1.4.

[15] *De consideratione* IV, 7, 23; p. 466 (138): "Intellige quae dico: dabit tibi Dominus intellectum. Ubi malitiae iuncta potentia est, aliquid tibi supra hominem praesumendum. Vultus tuus super facientes mala. Timeat spiritum irae tuae, qui hominem non veretur, gladium non formidat. Timeat orationem, qui admonitionem contempsit. Cui irasceris tu, Deum sibi iratum, non hominem putet. Qui te non audierit, auditurum Deum, et contra se, paveat. Quod reliquum est, de his quae supra te sunt, incumbit iam disputatio, quam uno libro, Deo adiuvante, solvere spero, et me pariter absolvere promissione mea."

[16] Ibid.; pp. 465-466 (137): "Consideres ante omnia sanctam Romanam ecclesiam, cui Deo auctore praees, ecclesiarum matrem esse, non dominam; te vero non dominum episcoporum, sed unum ex ipsis, porro fratrem diligentium Deum et participem timentium eum."

quoted speaks of the pope as a preacher of truth, a defender of the faith, teacher of the nations, instructor of the foolish, and light of the world, and invites him to correct abuses.[17] Elsewhere Bernard tells the pope that, like one of the prophets, he must root up and destroy errors by his teaching but also, like them, act humbly and not as a ruler when doing this. Prophecy, he says, is a ministry, not a dominion; one should root up with a hoe, not with a sceptre.[18]

In at least two of his letters Bernard is forceful and clear in recalling the pope's role as arbiter and guide in matters touching on faith. His letter on Abelard's errors, written to Pope Innocent II, speaks of the indefectibility of the Roman See:

> It is necessary that your apostolic person should receive reports about certain dangers and scandals appearing in the kingdom of God, especially those touching on faith. For I consider it most especially proper that damages to faith should be mended in the very place where faith can undergo no falling away. This surely is the prerogative of your See. For to whom else was it ever said: "I have prayed for you," Peter, "that your faith should not fail"?[19]

Bernard then uses the rest of the Lucan text (22:32) to remind the pope of his duty to act as vicar of Peter by strengthening those weak in faith and eliminating enemies of faith:

> Therefore, what the rest of the text says is demanded of the successor of Peter: "And you," it says, "when once you have turned, strengthen your brothers." Surely that is now necessary. The time has come, most beloved Father, for you to recognize your primacy, to prove your zeal, to honour your ministry. In doing so you will clearly fulfil your role as vicar of Peter, whose See you also hold, if by your warnings you strengthen the hearts of those fluctuating in faith and if by your authority you destroy those who corrupt the faith.[20]

---

[17] See above, p. 122.

[18] *De consideratione* II, 6, 9; pp. 416-417 (56-57): "Puta te velut aliquem de Prophetis. An non satis ad te? Et nimium. Sed gratia Dei es id quod es. Quid? Esto quod Propheta; numquid plus quam Propheta? Si sapis, eris contentus mensura, quam tibi mensus est Deus. Nam quod amplius est, a malo est. Disce exemplo prophetico praesidere non tam ad imperitandum quam ad factitandum quod tempus requirit. Disce sarculo tibi opus esse, non sceptro, ut opus facias Prophetae. Et quidem ille non regnaturus ascendit, sed exstirpaturus. Putasne et tu invenias aliquid elaborandum in agro Domini tui? Et plurimum."

[19] *Epistola* 190 *ad Innocentium II*, prologus; ed. cit. 8 (Rome, 1977), p. 17: "Oportet ad vestrum referri apostolatum pericula quaeque et scandala emergentia in regno Dei, ea praesertim quae de fide contingunt. Dignum namque arbitror ibi potissimum resarciri damna fidei, ubi non possit fides sentire defectum. Haec quippe huius praerogativa Sedis. Cui enim alteri aliquando dictum est: *Ego pro te rogavi*, Petre, *ut non deficiat fides tua*?" Scriptural text: Luke 22:32.

[20] Ibid.: "Ergo quod sequitur a Petri successore exigitur: *Et tu aliquando*, inquit, *conversus, confirma fratres tuos*. Id quidem modo necessarium. Tempus est ut vestrum agnoscatis, Pater

Although it would be an exaggeration to see in these texts the doctrine of papal infallibility that was to develop later, Bernard's attitude does indicate a decisive role for the pope in determining matters of faith.[21]

When Bernard speaks about the relation of the pope to the Church and to bishops and others in the Church, he rejects, as has been seen, a dominating or domineering role for the pope.[22] In a number of texts Bernard repeats this theme. Despite the pope's high dignity and prerogatives, he is not a lord exercising dominion (which in Bernard's day often implied ownership); he is rather a steward or servant exercising a ministry or a service. Thus when Bernard asks the reason why the pope has been put above (*superior*) others, he replies:

> We cannot ignore the fact that you have been elected to the supreme position, but, indeed, it must earnestly be asked, "for what purpose?" Not, in my opinion, to dominate (*ad dominandum*). ... And, therefore, we will understand ourselves better if we realize that a ministry (*ministerium*) has been imposed upon us rather than a dominion (*dominium*) bestowed.[23]

Again, after insisting that concern for the Churches does not mean dominion like that of kings over nations and after declaring that by Christ's teaching "dominion is forbidden to Apostles,"[24] Bernard quotes Christ's words

---

amantissime, principatum, probetis zelum, ministerium honoretis. In eo plane Petri impletis vicem, cuius tenetis et Sedem, si vestra admonitione corda in fide fluctuantia confirmatis, si vestra auctoritate conteritis fidei corruptores."

Writing to the canons of the church of Lyons in opposition to their establishing the feast of the Immaculate Conception, Bernard first gives his arguments that only Jesus was conceived of the Holy Spirit and without sin and that such a feast would be a novelty, something bold and even superstitious, and then adds that "consulenda erat prius Apostolicae Sedis auctoritas et non ita praecipitanter atque inconsulte paucorum sequenda simplicitas imperitorum." He adds, however, that he is ready to yield to a sounder wise person and that he reserves all this and like matters to the authority and scrutiny of the Roman Church: "Quae autem dixi, absque praeiudicio sane dicta sint sanius sapientis. Romanae praesertim ecclesiae auctoritati atque examini totum hoc, sicut et cetera quae huiusmodi sunt, universa reservo, ipsius, si quid aliter sapio, paratus iudicio emendare": *Epistola* 174, 9; ed. cit., vol. 7 (Rome, 1974), p. 392.

[21] On this see Congar, *L'ecclésiologie* (cited above, n. 1) p. 160.

[22] See the text quoted above, p. 123.

[23] *De consideratione* II, 6, 9; p. 416 (56): "Factum superiorem dissimulare nequimus; sed enim ad quid, omnimodis attendendum. Non enim ad dominandum opinor. ... Et nos igitur, ut multum sentiamus de nobis, impositum senserimus ministerium, non dominium datum." Further on (ibid., 10; p. 417) he continues in the same vein: "Blanditur cathedra? Specula est. Inde denique superintendis, sonans tibi episcopi nomine non dominium, sed officium."

[24] See ibid. II, 6, 10; p. 418 (58-59): "Quod habuit [Apostolus], hoc dedit: sollicitudinem, ut dixi, super ecclesias. Numquid dominationem? Audi ipsum: *Non dominantes*, ait, *in clero, sed forma facti gregis.* ... Vox Domini est in Evangelio: *Reges gentium dominantur eorum, et qui potestatem habent super eos benefici vocantur.* Et infert: *Vos autem non sic.* Planum est: Apostolis interdicitur dominatus." The scriptural texts are 1 Pet. 5:3 and Luke 22:25.

advising those who are in superior rank to become like servants, and then concludes: "This is the apostolic way of life: dominion is forbidden; ministry is required ...."[25]

In another passage Bernard twice likens the pope's role to that of a steward of property not belonging to the steward. If the pope has inherited the ruling office of the apostles, it is not as if he possessed the world; he is to serve like a steward:

> Their rule was greatly strengthened; they were made rulers over all the earth. You have succeeded them in this inheritance. And so you are the heir and your inheritance is the earth. But we must weigh with serious consideration to what extent this portion belongs to you or belonged to them. I do not think it is unconditionally yours but <it> is subject to limitations. It seems to me that you have been entrusted with stewardship over the world, not given possession of it.[26]

You are like a steward who is not lord of an estate, Bernard admonishes the pope; you are not the lord; you must preside in order to provide, and you must counsel, administer, and serve.[27]

Bernard has a similar line of argument when he speaks to pope Eugene about his relations with bishops. We have already seen a text in which he tells the pope that he is "not the lord of the bishops, but one of them," and their brother.[28] In another passage Bernard maintains that bishops receive their powers not from the pope but from God. Writing to Henry, bishop of Sens, he says: "... You have received the keys of the kingdom of heaven, which have been given over to you with God as their author ...."[29] And in an extended

---

[25] See ibid., II, 6, 11; p. 418 (59): "At si interdictum tenemus, audiamus edictum: *Qui maior est vestrum,* ait, *fiat sicut iunior, et qui praecessor est, sicut qui ministrat.* Forma apostolica haec est: dominatio interdicitur, indicitur ministratio ...." For the scriptural text cf. Luke 22:26.

[26] Ibid. III, 1, 1; p. 431 (80): "Nimis confortatus est principatus eorum: constituti sunt principes super omnem terram. Eis tu successisti in haereditatem. Ita tu heres, et orbis hereditas. At quatenus haec portio te contingit, aut contigerit illos, id sobria consideratione pensandum. Non enim per omne reor modum, sed sane quodamtenus, ut mihi videtur, dispensatio tibi super illum credita est, non data possessio." The sentence "Ita ... hereditas" is not translated by Anderson and Kennan but has been given in our text.

[27] Ibid. III, 1, 2; p. 432 (80-81): "'Quid?' inquis. 'Non negas praeesse, et dominari vetas?' Plane sic. Quasi non bene praesit, qui praeest in sollicitudine. Numquid non et villa villico, et parvulus dominus subiectus est paedagogo? Nec tamen villae ille, nec is sui domini dominus est. Ita et tu praesis ut provideas, ut consulas, ut procures, ut serves. Praesis ut prosis; praesis ut fidelis servus et prudens, quem constituit Dominus super familiam suam."

[28] See the text quoted above, p. 123.

[29] *Epistola* 42 *ad Henricum Senonensis archiepiscopum* (sometimes entitled *De moribus et officio episcoporum*) 1, 1; ed. cit. vol. 7 (Rome, 1974), p. 101: "Igitur ex quo regni coelorum claves, Deo auctore, vobis traditas suscepistis ...."

passage of book 3 of the *De consideratione*, in which he calls attention to the many abuses arising from what he sees as the pope's excessive readiness to grant exemptions and dispensations, he forcefully recalls to the pope the "intermediate" authority and power of others, prerogatives that are from God and that are distinct from his:

> Can you be of the opinion that it is lawful for you to cut off the churches from their members, to confuse the order of things, to disturb the boundaries which your predecessors have set? If the role of justice is to preserve for each what is his, how can it befit a just man to take from each what belongs to him? You are wrong if you think your apostolic power, which is supreme, is the only power instituted by God. If you think this, you disagree with him who says, "There is no power except from God." Equally, what follows, "Who resists the power, resists the ordinance of God." Even though this is principally on your behalf, it is not solely on your behalf. The same one also says, "Let every soul be subjected to higher powers." He does not say "to a higher power" as if in one person, but "to higher powers" as if in many. Therefore, yours is not the only power from God; there are intermediate and lesser ones.[30]

Appealing to the image of the Church as Body of Christ, he continues by saying that the pope would be creating a monster if by his interventions he upset the order established by God. Bernard is quite clearly thinking of dispensations or exemptions making abbots equal to or independent of bishops, whose authority is from God:

> And just as those whom God has joined together must not be separated, so those whom God has made subordinate must not be made equal. You create a monster if you remove a finger from a hand and make it hang from a head, above the hand and on a level with the arm. So it is in the body of Christ if you put members in places other than where he arranged them.[31]

---

[30] *De consideratione* III, 4, 17; p. 444 (101): "Tunc denique tibi licitum censeas, suis ecclesias mutilare membris, confundere ordinem, perturbare terminos, quos posuerunt patres tui? Si iustitiae est ius cuique servare suum, auferre cuiquam sua iusto quomodo poterit convenire? Erras si, ut summam, ita et solam institutam a Deo vestram apostolicam potestatem existimas. Si hoc sentis, dissentis ab eo qui ait: *Non est potestas nisi a Deo.* Proinde quod sequitur: *Qui potestati resistit, Dei ordinationi resistit,* etsi principaliter pro te facit, non tamen singulariter. Denique idem ait: *Omnis anima potestatibus sublimioribus subdita sit.* Non ait: 'sublimiori', tamquam in uno, sed *sublimioribus,* tamquam in multis. Non tua ergo sola potestas a Domino; sunt et mediocres, sunt et inferiores." The scriptural texts are from Rom. 13:1-2.

[31] Ibid.; p. 444 (101-102): "Et quomodo quos Deus coniunxit non sunt separandi, sic nec quos subiunxit comparandi. Monstrum facis si, manui submovens, digitum facis pendere de capite, superiorem manui, brachio collateralem. Tale est si in Christi corpore membra aliter locas quam disposuit ipse."

To bolster his view of God's established order of authority in the Church, Bernard makes a comparison found in the Pseudo-Dionysius, although we are not sure whether he took it from him or not. The order of authority and power have "an exemplar in heaven," he says, and this was seen by the Son.[32] As in heaven there is a ranking among angelic orders, so on earth God has arranged an order — under the pope — of prelates, priests, and abbots.[33] Bernard concludes by emphasizing that this order is from God:

> It must not be thought insignificant that this order has God as its author, and derives its origins from heaven. But if a bishop should say, "I do not want to be under the archbishop," or an abbot, "I do not want to obey the bishop," this is not from heaven. Unless perhaps you have heard any of the angels saying, "I do not want to be under the archangels," or someone from one of the lesser ranks saying that he refused to be subject to anyone but God.[34]

It is interesting that Bernard should make this comparison, which will reappear in thirteenth-century theologians.[35] His text may have set theologians to thinking about the link between the nine choirs of angels and the various degrees or grades in the sacrament of Order.

We cannot go into Bernard's well-known doctrine of the two swords, spiritual and material, used as a basis for recourse to civil power to aid the Church. It is well, however, to take account of Congar's remark that this doctrine has often been badly presented or misinterpreted.[36]

In conclusion, it may be said that if Bernard stresses the great dignity and many prerogatives of the pope both in the order of rule or jurisdiction and in the order of teaching, he still insists that the papacy is a ministry of service rather than a dominating power. The papal ministry must in its practice respect the legitimate authority of bishops and others in the Church and must correct abuses in a prophetic spirit. The final book of the *De consideratione*

---

[32] Ibid., 4, 17; p. 445 (102-103): "Nec vilem reputes formam hanc, quia in terris est: exemplar habet e caelo. Neque enim Filius potest facere quidquam, nisi quae viderit Patrem facientem, praesertim cum ei sub Moysi nomine dictum sit: *Vide omnia facias secundum exemplar, quod tibi in monte monstratum est.*" Scriptural text: Exod. 25:40.

[33] Ibid., 4, 18; p. 445: "... sicut illic Seraphim et Cherubim, ac ceteri quique usque ad angelos et archangelos, ordinantur sub uno capite Deo, ita hic quoque sub uno summo Pontifice primates vel patriarchae, archiepiscopi, episcopi, presbyteri vel abbates, et reliqui in hunc modum."

[34] Ibid.: "Non est parvi pendendum quod et Deum habet auctorem, et de caelo ducit originem. Quod si dicat episcopus: 'Nolo esse sub archiepiscopo', aut abbas: 'Nolo oboedire episcopo', hoc de caelo non est. Nisi tu forte angelorum quempiam dicentem audisti: 'Nolo sub archangelis esse', aut ex alio quolibet inferiorum ordinum aliquem non ferentem subesse cuiquam, nisi Deo."

[35] See the preceding article, "The School Theologians' Views of the Papacy, 1150-1250," section 3.2.a.

[36] See his *L'Église* ... (cited ibid., n. 11) pp. 142-145.

stresses the need for the pope to be a person of prayer and for him and the curia to give an example of good life and unity that is modelled on and reflects the unity and holiness of the Trinity and of the blessed in heaven, to the consideration of which Bernard directs the pope's attention and which he describes at some length. In this way Bernard presented to the pope, and to succeeding generations so much influenced by his writings, a very lofty religious ideal of the papacy that went far beyond a mere discussion of canonical powers and privileges while not neglecting some of the fundamental issues in these.

1.1.b. *Peter the Venerable, Abbot of Cluny (ca. 1092-1156).*

Another important monastic author outside the school tradition is the Abbot of Cluny, Peter the Venerable, whose influence, although less than Bernard's, was still considerable. His thought on the papacy has been ably presented by Jean-Pierre Torrell, who rightly situates it within his study of the larger topic of Peter's entire ecclesiology. Our presentation depends almost entirely on Torrell's fine exposition.[37]

Since one of Peter's important themes is that of the Church as a believing community, but one threatened by the heresies of his day, he emphasizes the traditional great teachers of the Church. First among these are the apostles, and first among them as teacher is, for the abbot, not Peter but Paul, who is several times named "the highest teacher of the Church, after Christ."[38] Although the Abbot of Cluny strongly insists on tradition, he recognizes that diverse usages and practices have developed during the Church's long history, for example, in matters of fasting, about the date of Easter, or concerning the use of leavened or unleavened bread. Hence he urges Pope Eugene III to practice moderation before such diversity so long as unity in faith and charity is preserved.[39]

The titles used of the pope by Peter the Venerable are divided by Torrell into three groups.[40] One group of titles relates the pope to both Christ and the Church: for example, the pope is "the chief pastor of the sheep of Christ"

---

[37] See his "L'Église dans l'œuvre et la vie de Pierre le Vénérable," *Revue thomiste* 77 (1977) 357-392, 558-591, and also the study by Glauco M. Cantarella, "Un problema del XII secolo: l'ecclesiologia di Pietro il Venerabile," *Studi Medievali*, serie terza, 19 (1978) 159-209. More general studies include Jean Leclercq, *Pierre le Vénérable* (Saint-Wandrille, 1946), and *Petrus Venerabilis, 1156-1956: Studies and Texts Commemorating the Eighth Centenary of His Death*, eds. Giles Constable and James Kritzeck, Studia Anselmiana 40 (Rome, 1956).

[38] "Summus post Christum ecclesiae magister": see Torrell, p. 558, who cites four texts using this title of Paul.

[39] See ibid., pp. 560-562.

[40] See ibid., pp. 572-574.

or "after, Christ, the head of the members of Christ on earth." [41] A second group of titles relates the pope to the apostles. In one text the abbot calls the pope the vicar of the Apostle of the Gentiles, that is, of Paul, but most often he relates the pope to Peter or even identifies him with Peter: the pope holds "the seat of Peter" and is "the successor of the blessed apostle Peter," and once the phrase about Paul as highest teacher is restated with reference to Peter: "Peter, the highest teacher of the Church, after Christ." [42] The third group of titles relates the pope to the Church as pontiff or high priest. The terms most frequently used are "supreme pontiff" (*summus pontifex*) and "Roman pontiff" (*romanus pontifex*), but the terms "universal pontiff" (*universalis pontifex*) and "general pontiff" (*universus pontifex*) also occur. [43] To be located in this same third group are names such as "pastor," "father," "rector" or "ruler" (*rector*), and "universal pope." [44] Of special interest are titles setting forth the pope as teacher: besides those already mentioned one finds "highest teacher of the Church of God" and "highest teacher of Christians." [45]

Although Peter cites a case where certain local judges resisted the pope's right to intervene in disputes, he himself criticizes these judges and recognizes the pope's office of superior judgment. Moreover, Peter clearly recognizes that the pope is above all the bishops. [46] Yet, like Bernard speaking to Pope Eugene, Peter could adopt an attitude of counsellor and advisor to popes, especially towards Innocent II. He does the same even with the Cistercian pope, Eugene III. Although he applies to this pope the famous text of Jeremiah 1:10: "See, I have set you this day over nations and over kingdoms, to pluck up and to break down, to destroy and to overthrow, to build and to plant," he adds that since Eugene is neither God nor the prophet Jeremiah (to whom the words were addressed), he can be mistaken or be deceived by those who are not of Jesus Christ. [47] In another text Peter

---

[41] See ibid., p. 572: "praecipuus ouium Christi pastor"; "caput ... membrorum Christi post Christum in terris." References in Torrell; they are scattered through Peter's many works, but most of those given by Torrell come from various letters.

[42] See ibid., pp. 572 and 573: The titles are: "vices illius qui apostolus gentium a Deo factus est"; "sedes Petri"; "beati apostoli Petri successor"; "summus post Christum magister ecclesiae Petrus."

[43] Quoted, with references, by Torrell, p. 573.

[44] Ibid.: "pastor"; "summus pater" (and "universalis pater"); "summus ecclesiae Dei rector"; "universalis papa."

[45] Ibid.: "summus ecclesiae Dei magister"; "summus Christianorum magister."

[46] See ibid., p. 574, including n. 36.

[47] *Letter* 158; ed. and introd. Giles Constable, *The Letters of Peter the Venerable*, 2 vols., Harvard Historical Series, 78 (Cambridge, Mass.: Harvard University Press, 1967) 1: 377: "Est autem uestrum, totius aecclesiae dei *in* hac *ualle lacrimarum* [Ps. 83(84):7] peregrinantis causas audire, auditas discutere, discussas iudicio apostolico diffinire. Et licet persona uestra

recognizes indirectly that the Church's power to intervene in some ways in secular affairs rests finally with the pope, but only in so far as he is a servant of the Church.[48]

As for other scriptural texts that were quoted about the pope, Peter uses Matthew 16:18-19 to exalt Christ rather than Peter or the pope. In one case, however, he uses it, together with Luke 22:32 ("When you have turned again, strengthen your brethren") to justify Cluniac exemption from bishops: the pope, he argues against Bernard, is the bishop whom Cluniacs obey and by whom they can be punished. As Torrell notes, this is a rather circumstantial statement about the pope's authority: elsewhere Peter appeals to the catholicity of the Church in order to justify Cluniac exemption. Peter seems less interested in papal authority in matters of faith or regarding bishops than in justifying Cluniac independence of bishops in the areas of his monasteries. Yet the text has some importance for his thought on the papacy.[49]

The scriptural text that Peter prefers as expressing the pope's role is Paul's text (2 Corinthians 11:28) about his daily "solicitude for all the Churches" (*sollicitudo omnium Ecclesiarum*), a concern that for Peter is supremely the pope's and yet is shared with other pastors.[50] Paul's use of the plural, "Churches," in this text is significant for Peter since he likens even the monastery to a Church and compares the abbot's authority over his monks to that of the pope over the universal Church. According to Torrell, Peter the Venerable seems to have viewed the differences of powers found in popes, bishops, and abbots as differences of degree and not of kind.[51] By way of summary and conclusion concerning Peter the Venerable, Torrell's judgment serves best:

> Une chose du moins est claire: la prééminence reconnue au pape, son pouvoir dans l'Église, son devoir d'enseigner, de reprendre, de corriger, de juger de façon ultime, bref l'ensemble des fonctions que Pierre lui reconnaît incontestablement, ne font pas de lui un être d'exception et la charge du souverain pontificat n'est en rien comparable à ce qu'elle deviendra bientôt. ... Il faut

---

constituta sit super gentes et regna, ut euellat et destruat, et disperdat et dissipet, et aedificet et plantet, tamen, quia nec deus, nec Hieremias propheta, cui hoc dictum est, estis, potestis falli, potestis ab his, qui ea quae non Ihesu Christi, sed *quae sua sunt* quaerunt [cf. 1 Cor. 13:5], decipi." This is numbered as *Epistola* 12 in *PL* 189, 411D-412A. Text quoted in Torrell, p. 575, n. 45; in n. 46 Torrell refers to an article by Yves Congar on the scriptural text: "'Ecce constitui te super gentes et super regna' (Jer. 1, 10)" in *Theologie in Geschichte und Gegenwart: Michael Schmaus zur sechzigsten Geburtstag* (Munich, 1957) pp. 671-696.

[48] See Torrell, pp. 575-576.
[49] See ibid., pp. 576-577.
[50] See ibid., p. 577.
[51] See ibid.

reconnaître que Pierre le Vénérable ... prolonge sur ce point la tradition
ancienne plus qu'il ne préfigure l'évolution à venir.[52]

1.2. Two episcopal authors: Anselm of Havelberg and Gerhoh of Reichers-
berg.

1.2.a. *Anselm of Havelberg († 1158).*

A bishop who develops theology on the papacy in this period is the former
Premonstratensian canon regular, Anselm, bishop of Havelberg. His work,
called *Dialogues*, was addressed to Pope Eugene III in the middle of the
twelfth century, and it contains one of the most thorough discussions of the
papacy at this time.[53] Anselm presents books 2 and 3 of the work as accounts
of talks and debates he had held in 1236 with Greek theologians, especially
Nicetas of Nikomedia, on questions dividing the eastern and western
Churches; among these was the Roman primacy. A valuable study by
Hermann-Josef Sieben examines the debated question whether these dialogues report an actual discussion or are a work composed by Anselm, perhaps
based on such a discussion but elaborated later.[54] If, as Sieben thinks, the
latter alternative is more likely, it may mean that Anselm balances his
strongly papalist position by putting into Nicetas' mouth arguments not only

---

[52] See ibid., p. 578.

[53] On Anselm's life and works see L. Ott, "Anselm von Havelberg," *Lexikon für Theologie
und Kirche*, 2nd ed., 1 (1957) 594-595, and especially Raymond E. Bierlein, "Anselm of
Havelberg: His Life and Works," Thesis, Western Michigan University, 1971 (Ann Arbor,
Mich.: University Microfilms International, s.d.). The *Dialogi* are found in *PL* 188:
1139A-1284B. A new edition of book 1 has been edited by Gaston Salet: *Anselme de
Havelberg, Dialogues, Livre I: "Renouveau dans l'Église"*, Sources chrétiennes 118 (Paris,
1966). The *Dialogues* are dated variously: 1149-1150 (Ott, col. 595), 1149-1152 (Bierlein,
p. 34), 1149 (Salet, p. 9, and cf. p. 28, n. 1 concerning the date given in a manuscript: Salet
says: "cette date est contestable").

[54] "Die eine Kirche, der Papst und die Konzilien in den Dialogen des Anselm von
Havelberg (†1158)," *Theologie und Philosophie* 54 (1979) 219-251; see also the same
author's *Die Konzilsidee des lateinischen Mittelalters (847-1378)* (Paderborn-Munich, etc.:
Ferdinand Schöningh, 1984), ch. 4, which is entitled: "Anselm von Havelberg (†1158) oder
gregorianische Konzilsidee versus griechische." Other studies include K. Fina, "Anselm von
Havelberg: Untersuchungen zur Kirchen- und Geistesgeschichte des 12 Jahrhunderts," *Ana-
lecta Praemonstratensia* 32 (1956) 69-101, 193-227; 33 (1957) 5-39, 268-301; 34 (1958)
13-41; Walter J. Edyvean, *Anselm of Havelberg and the Theology of History* (Rome: Officium
Libri Catholici, 1972); Jannis Spiteris, *La critica bizantina del Primato Romano nel secolo XII*
(Rome: Pont. Inst. Orientalium Studiorum, 1978), ch. 2, sect. 2 (pp. 85-108); N. Russel,
"Anselm of Havelberg and the Union of the Churches," *Sobornost* 1 (1979) 19-41, 2 (1980)
29-41. See also the essay by Jannis Spiteris in this volume, "Attitudes fondamentales de la
théologie byzantine, en face du rôle religieux de la papauté au XIIᵉ siècle."

of eastern theologians but also of westerners favouring a more conciliarist or synodalist view of the Church over a papal monarchial outlook.[55]

In any case, the prologue written to Eugene III presents a statement that could already be said to anticipate the Bull, *Unam sanctam*, of Pope Boniface VIII: "And so I have done what the apostolic authority has ordered, that authority which must always be complied with not only for the sake of devout humility but also as necessary for eternal salvation."[56]

When Anselm discusses the differences between the eastern and western Churches, he asks why the easterners, if they make so much of past authority, refuse to accept the statutes of the Holy Roman Church, "which through God and from God and in the next place after God has obtained the primacy in the universal Church spread throughout the whole world."[57]

Anselm quotes a text that he thinks belongs to the Council of Nicea — a text declaring the primacy of the Holy Roman Church — and then appeals to Matthew 16:18-19 in support of this.[58] He adds that the Roman Church has been consecrated not only by the blood of Peter but also by that of Paul, who died on the same day as Peter in Rome.[59] Anselm recognizes that there were other patriarchal sees, Alexandria and Antioch, but first mentions their relation to Peter historically in order to conclude: "The Holy Roman Church was chosen before others by the Lord and was granted a special privilege and was blessed by him, and is preeminent over all Churches as by a certain prerogative, and precedes them by divine right."[60]

---

[55] See Sieben, "Die eine Kirche," pp. 225-228, especially p. 227.

[56] *Dialogi*, Prologus; ed. Salet, *Dialogues*, pp. 28, 30: "Feci itaque quod jussit apostolica auctoritas, cui semper obtemperandum est non tantum devota humilitate, verum etiam aeternae salutis necessitate."

[57] Ibid. II, 5; *PL* 188 (here and henceforth), 1213D: "Quod si eorum qui hic praefuerunt auctoritas tanta est apud vos ut eorum qualiacunque statuta inviolabilia existimetis, et attenditis tantum eorum qui illa statuerunt nudam auctoritatem et non potius eorum quae statuta sunt veritatem, quare non potius suscipitis statuta sacrosanctae Romanae Ecclesiae, quae per Deum et a Deo et post Deum proximo loco auctoritatis primatum obtinuit in universa quae per totum mundum sparsa est Ecclesia?"

[58] Ibid.; 1213D-1214A: "Ita enim de illa in Nicaeno Concilio primo a trecentis decem et octo patribus statutum legitur: 'Sciendum sane est et nulli catholico ignorandum quoniam sancta Romana Ecclesia nullis synodicis decretis praelata est, sed evangelica voce Domini ac Salvatoris nostri primatum obtinuit, ubi dixit beato Petro apostolo: *Tu es Petrus, et super hanc petram aedificabo Ecclesiam meam ... erunt soluta et in coelis*' (Matth. xvi, 18, 19)." This text is called the *praefatio Nicaeni Concilii*, but it is from an early western source and not from the Council of Nicea; see Sieben, "Die eine Kirche," pp. 223-224, 235.

[59] Ibid.; 1214A-B.

[60] Ibid.; 1214C: "Ad hoc etiam sancta Romana Ecclesia prae caeteris a Domino praeelecta, speciali privilegio ab ipso donata est et beatificata, et quasi quadam praerogativa omnibus Ecclesiis praeeminet et jure divino antecellit."

Where other Churches have fallen into error, Anselm continues, the Roman Church was founded on a rock by the Lord so as never to be weakened in faith. The text of Luke 22:32 about Peter's not failing in faith and confirming his brothers means, Anselm says, that the Roman Church is always to remain immovable and constant in the faith and is to correct others like a provider and doctor and father and teacher having care and concern for all. This privilege of prelacy belongs rightly to this Church since it has this privilege from the Lord of preserving integrity of faith.[61] After listing the heresies that had arisen in the east,[62] Anselm repeats the Lucan text and concludes:

> Therefore, because the Holy Roman Church has, by the Lord's aid, preserved the purity of right faith, it has merited to be the mother of all Churches, and all who wish to be called and to be sons of God and of the Church rightly imitate it with due humility in all the ecclesiastical sacraments. Although there may be different practices and ecclesiastical customs by reason of the diversity of each people, all of whom can scarcely conform to the Roman Church, yet, as I have said, in ecclesiastical sacraments there must never be any discord from the most holy mother of all, the Roman Church.[63]

It is worthwhile noting that for Anselm the primacy and preeminence of the Roman Church, expressed several times through the image of the Roman Church as mother of all Churches, is explicitly linked with the role he sees for it in guarding purity of faith rather than with exercise of jurisdiction: in correcting and strengthening others in faith, the Roman Church is to act as *omnium provisor* and *doctor* and *pater* and *magister*. Anselm recognizes a role for the daughter Churches and sees the need for diversity of practices and customs so long as there is unity of faith, which is to be assured by the primacy and eminence of the mother Church.

---

[61] Ibid.; 1214D-1215A: "Unde et Dominus sciens alias Ecclesias haeretica impulsione nimium vexandas, et Romanam Ecclesiam, quam ipse supra petram fundaverat, nunquam in fide debilitandam, dixit Petro: *Ego pro te rogavi, Petre, ut non deficiat fides tua, et tu aliquando conversus confirma fratres tuos*; ac si aperte ei dicat: 'Tu qui hanc gratiam accepisti ut, aliis in fide naufragantibus, semper in fide immobilis et constans permaneas, alios vacillantes confirma et corrige, et tanquam omnium provisor et doctor et pater et magister omnium curam et sollicitudinem gere'. Merito ita privilegium praelationis super omnes accepit qui in conservanda integritate fidei prae omnibus privilegium a Domino susceperat."

[62] Ibid. II, 6; 1215A-1216D.

[63] Ibid.; 1217A-B: "Quia ergo sacrosancta Romana Ecclesia conservata virginitate rectae fidei, opitulante Domino, Ecclesiarum omnium mater esse meruit, merito omnes qui filii Dei et Ecclesiae dici et esse volunt, illam in omnibus ecclesiasticis sacramentis debita humilitate imitantur; et licet pro diversitate cujusque gentis diversi mores et ecclesiasticae consuetudines habeantur, et in his minime conformari possint omnes Romanae Ecclesiae, tamen in ecclesiasticis, sicut dixi, sacramentis nulla unquam debet esse discordia a sacratissima matre omnium Romana Ecclesia."

How does Nicetas (in the *Dialogues*) react to this? He does not deny a certain primacy to Rome: it can be called the first see (*prima sedes*) and can be a court of appeal in ecclesiastical disputes. But the bishop of Rome should not be called the "prince of priests" or the "highest priest" or anything of this kind but only, he says, the "bishop of the first see." [64] In past times, Nicetas continues, agreement was reached by consultation among the sister Churches. The primacy of Rome was a primacy only of honour, not of independent action standing in judgment of all other Churches in a spirit that is hardly fraternal and not even paternal. Notice, he concludes, that none of the creeds requires us to confess belief in the Roman Church but rather in the one, holy, Catholic, and apostolic Church.[65]

Scriptural texts are now presented by each debater. Nicetas argues that all the apostles received the power to forgive sins, as is clear both from John 20:22-23, where Jesus is described as breathing on the apostles to confer the Holy Spirit and give them the power to forgive or retain sins, and from the text of Matthew, in which the power of binding and losing on earth is given to all the apostles. Moreover, he goes on, the Holy Spirit came upon all the apostles at Pentecost.[66]

Anselm agrees that the apostles shared all this, but he insists that these powers were given to Peter in a special way. Peter was constituted the gate-keeper of heaven (*janitor coeli*: Matthew 16:19) and was specially told to feed the sheep (John 20:23).[67] After alluding to several actions described in the Gospels and Acts that for him show the preeminence given to Peter, Anselm concludes with a firm affirmation of the pope's exalted position:

> Hence it befits none of the faithful to doubt in any way or to question, but rather to hold most firmly that Peter was constituted by the Lord as the prince of the apostles. Now just as only the Roman pontiff, as vicar of Peter, is vicar of Christ, so clearly other bishops are vicars of the apostles under Christ, and vicars of Christ under Peter, and vicars of Peter under the Roman pontiff who is his vicar. In this there is nothing derogatory to any of the apostles if each humbly accepts the office he is charged with.[68]

---

[64] Ibid. II, 7; 1217D-1218A: "... Roma eminentissima sedes imperii primatum obtinuit, ita ut prima sedes appellaretur et ad eam de dubiis causis ecclesiasticis a caeteris omnibus appellatio fieret, et ejus judicio ea quae sub certis regulis non comprehenduntur dijudicanda subjacerent. Ipse tamen Romanus pontifex nec princeps sacerdotum nec summus sacerdos aut aliquid hujusmodi sed tantum primae sedis episcopus vocaretur."

[65] Ibid. II, 7-8; 1218A-1220A.

[66] Ibid. II, 9; 1221B-D.

[67] Ibid. II, 10; 1222A-B.

[68] Ibid.; 1223A: "Quocirca nulli fidelium convenit aliquatenus dubitare seu in quaestionem ponere sed firmissime tenere quod Petrus a Domino princeps apostolorum sit constitutus. Quemadmodum autem solus Romanus pontifex vice Petri vicem gerit Christi, ita sane caeteri

This strong statement views the pope as the only immediate vicar of Christ because only he is the vicar immediately of Peter. The other bishops are vicars of the other apostles immediately, but they are vicars of Christ only through the Roman pontiff as vicar of Peter, the vicar of Christ immediately.

Although Nicetas (again, as reported in the *Dialogues*) is willing to agree that most heresies were found in the east, he argues that these heresies were in fact eliminated by eastern councils.[69] To this Anselm first replies by appealing to the analogy of Christ as Head and then by insisting that historically the popes had always intervened to eliminate the heresies that had arisen in the east and elsewhere. To admit that the eastern councils and sees had settled these matters independently of the pope would mean for him the despicable idea that the Church has two or more heads. Therefore, applying Pauline texts about Christ as Head of the Church, he says:

> ... Christ, the Head of the Church, ascending on high, committed his position on earth to Peter, the prince of the apostles. Peter, following Christ's footsteps to martyrdom, chose Clement to replace him as vicar, and thus the Roman pontiffs were substituted as vicars of Christ one after the other in order, and are head of the Church on earth, that Church whose Head in heaven is Christ. And so do not make one or several heads in the one body of the Church — in any body that is terribly indecent, indecorous, monstrous, contrary to perfection, and close to disintegration.[70]

Anselm thus gives a strongly papalist doctrine with respect to the basic authority and special prerogatives of the pope. At the same time, through his reporting and editing he makes the pope aware of the sensitivities of eastern Churches and their claims in the name of tradition. By recognizing diverse practices and customs owing to the diversities of peoples, diversities that are to be in concord with the Roman Church, Anselm asserts the importance of catholicity, understood as allowing diversity within unity of faith. Among the duties of the pope for the whole Church, his preserving unity of faith against

---

episcopi vicem gerunt apostolorum sub Christo, et vice Christi sub Petro, et vice Petri sub pontifice Romano ejus vicario, nec in hoc aliquatenus derogatur alicui apostolorum si unicuique humiliter suum attribuitur officium."

[69] Ibid. II, 11; 1223B-1224D.

[70] Ibid. II, 12; 1225A-B: "Apostolus dicit: *Caput Ecclesiae Christus* [Eph. 5:23], *caput autem Christi Deus* [1 Cor 11:3]. Sed caput Ecclesiae Christus, ascendens in altum, vicem suam in terris Petro apostolorum principi commisit. Petrus ad martyrium vestigia Christi sequens, Clementem sibi vicarium subrogavit, et sic Romani pontifices per ordinem consequenter vice Christi substitui, caput Ecclesiae sunt in terris, cujus Ecclesiae caput Christus est in caelis. Noli itaque in uno corpore Ecclesiae duo vel plurima capita facere quia valde est indecens in quolibet corpore et indecorum et monstruosum et perfectioni contrarium et corruptioni proximum."

error seems to be for Anselm the principal function of the pope, the one that most validates his primacy.

1.2.b. *Gerhoh of Reichersberg (1093-1169).*

In the early 1950s, at one of the monthly "Journées sacerdotales" held at the Couvent Saint-Jacques in Paris, Yves Congar once spoke of the congenital need of some of his French compatriots to go to Rome to get their countrymen condemned (he may have been alluding to his own experiences at this period): this phrase is fairly well suited to Gerhoh of Reichersberg. The German bishop was undoubtedly a sincere person zealously concerned over only too evident abuses, and he did much in his own diocese to correct them. But he felt frequently urged to go to his cardinal friends or to the pope in Rome in order to urge them to intervene against local bishops and priests misusing church funds or living immorally; above all, he sought their intervention to have certain theological opinions condemned.[71]

To this end he exalts the authority of the Apostolic See. For Gerhoh the pope is "the vicar of Peter" or the "successor of Peter."[72] Rome is the "seat of justice, in which after Peter the apostle, the chief pastor of the sheep, up to our own times justice has flourished and pastoral care has been watchful ...."[73] When duly elected and consecrated, the pope "rightly takes the place of Peter in what pertains to the chair of pontifical office even if he is not his equal in merit or faith."[74] Hence Gerhoh several times uses the term "apostolic" or variants of it to signify the pope's relation to the apostle Peter.[75]

---

[71] On Gerhoh see Damien van den Eynde, *L'œuvre littéraire de Géroch de Reichersberg* (Rome, 1957); Peter Classen, "Gerhoh de Reichersberg," *Dictionnaire de Spiritualité* 6 (1967) cols. 303-308; Erich Meuthen, "Gerhoh von Reichersberg (1092/93-1169)," *Theologische Realenzyklopädie* 12 (1984) 457-459. References to his writings will be to various works in his *Opera Inedita*, eds. Damianus and Odulphus Van den Eynde and Angelinus Rijmersdael, Spicilegium Pontificii Athenaei Antoniani 8-10, 2 vols. in 3 (Rome, 1955-1956), and to his *Liber de novitatibus huius temporis* (henceforth = *De novit.*), ed. Nikolaus M. Haring in *Letter to Pope Hadrian about the Novelties of the Day*, Studies and Texts 24 (Toronto: Pontifical Institute of Mediaeval Studies, 1974).

[72] For *vicarius Petri* see *De ordine donorum* (henceforth = *De ord.*) (*Opera Inedita*, p. 66); for *successor Petri* see ibid. (p. 254: twice), *De novit.*, Prologus, 6 (Haring, p. 24); 2, 1 (p. 25); 2, 6 (p. 26).

[73] *De laude fidei* (henceforth = *De laude*); *Opera Inedita*, p. 210: "... sedem iustitiae, in qua post Petrum apostolum, praecipuum pastorem ovium, usque ad haec nostra tempora viguit iustitia et vigilavit pastoralis cura ...."

[74] *Opusculum ad cardinales: Opera Inedita*, p. 313: "... iure obtinet locum Petri, quantum attinet ad cathedram pontificalis officii, etiamsi forte non sit aequalis meriti seu fidei."

[75] These occur in *De novit.* (ed. Haring) as follows: *apostolatus tui* (Prologus, 1; p. 23); *congruentem sancto apostolatui tuo* (41, 9; p. 106: in this text Bernard's *De consideratione* is

A long and at first enigmatic section of his work, *On the Novelties of These Days* (*De novitatibus huius temporis*), compares the patriarch Jacob with Peter in order to draw out lessons about the pope and in order to invite him to act. When scripture promises that Christ "will rule in the house of Jacob forever," Gerhoh says, "the house of Jacob is correctly understood as holy Church, which has been entrusted to blessed Peter as to another Jacob."[76] As in the Old Testament Jacob was the only person whose name was changed completely, so in the New Testament only Peter's name was completely changed from Simon to Cephas or Peter. That is why, Gerhoh continues, it is right for the successors of Peter to have new names given them when they are enthroned in his chair.[77] Again, Jacob was strong against the angel, so strong that he was told he would prevail against men; Peter, strengthened in faith, heard the Lord say to him: "You are Peter, and on this rock I will build my Church and the gates of hell will not prevail against it."[78] Several other comparisons finally enable us to see where Gerhoh is taking his argument. As Jacob pronounced a curse even while blessing his sons, so Peter cursed Simon Magus, and every successor of Peter has with just zeal cursed the successors of the same Simon Magus.[79] Gerhoh now comes to the point: "Would that you, Adrian, successor of Peter the apostle, would be inflamed with the zeal you should have against the successors of Simon Magus who do business in the house of the Lord."[80] A long approach to seeking a condemnation of simony, but one that reenforces Gerhoh's views of the relation between the pope and Peter!

For Gerhoh the authority of the apostolic see is so great that the Roman pontiff is subject to no one's judgment, that is, no human person's judgment.[81] He once mentions the pope's role as one of *sollicitudo*, undoubtedly referring to the Pauline text seen in Peter the Venerable and Anselm (2 Cor

---

used); *in cathedra potestatis apostolice* (4, 9; p. 32). In *De laude* (*Opera Inedita*, p. 213) we find *sedis apostolicae auctoritas* and *apostolica edicta*.

On these terms see Congar, "Titres donnés au pape" (cited in the preceding essay, n. 27) pp. 57-59.

[76] *De novit.* 1, 3; Haring, p. 25: "Ergo iuxta uerbum ipsius Christus *regnabit in domo Iacob in eternum et regni eius non erit finis* [Luke 1:32-33]. Domus uero Iacob recte intelligitur sancta ecclesia, beato Petro uelut alteri Iacob credita ...."

[77] Ibid. 1, 3-2, 1; Haring, p. 25.

[78] Ibid. 2, 1-2; Haring, p. 25.

[79] Ibid. 2, 5; Haring, p. 26.

[80] Ibid. 2, 6; Haring, p. 26: "Atque utinam tu, Adriane, successor Petri apostoli, zelo debito accendaris contra successores Symonis magi negociantes in domo domini."

[81] *Opusculum ad cardinales*; *Opera Inedita*, p. 315: "... Romanus pontifex nullius hominum iudicio subiaceat." Cf. ibid.; p. 324: "Marcellinus papa, cum tamquam summus pontifex a nemine iudicaretur, sed sibimetipsi relinqueretur iudicandus, ore damnavit proprio factum suum; quod nisi damnasset, ipse utique damnatus in damnatione permansisset."

11:28).[82] In one text we have found Gerhoh speaking about the authority of the pope with respect to bishops, but it is to lament their disobedience. After commending Bernard's *De consideratione* to Adrian as "befitting your holy apostolicity," he adds that Adrian is a man like Eugene, but a man established by divine power and exercised by regular discipline. "You have bishops under you," Gerhoh reminds him, "and it is a miserable thing that you should say to one, 'Go', and he does not go, and to another, 'Come', and he does not come."[83]

Although Gerhoh is concerned about simony, immorality in clerical life, and misuse of church funds for military and other secular purposes, one of his main concerns is unsound doctrine. Hence in his frequent laments about what he considers false teachings by his contemporaries, he expounds a forceful doctrine of papal authority in teaching and defending the true faith. In the *Libellus de ordine donorum* he professes that he never wants to dissent from the doctrine and faith of the holy apostolic see.[84] He declares that the Roman pontiffs have cast out heretics and schismatics who had invaded the inheritance of Christ and have defended truth against heretics as well as the unity of the Church against schismastics.[85] When divergent opinions are encountered among the Fathers, he says, it is useful to set forth these opinions so that a decision can be made about them by "that Holy See which is, before others, the rule of justice."[86]

The *Book on Praise of the Faith (Liber de laude fidei)* gives one of his most vigorous statements about the pope. Discussing a question about matrimony that had recently been settled by Popes Innocent II and Eugene III, Gerhoh relates that in past times some ancient and catholic doctors had held an opinion different from that of these popes. Gerhoh follows his remark with a comment showing that for him to disagree with the Church of Rome means being a heretic:

---

[82] *De laude; Opera Inedita*, p. 210: "... apostolicae sollicitudinis oculi ...."

[83] *De novit.* 41, 9; Haring, pp. 105-106: "... talia multa his similia per te consideranda relinquimus atque, ut id competentius possis, libellum *De consideratione* ab abbate Clareuallensi predecessori tuo, sancte recordationis Eug(enio) pape dictatum, sic legens considerare curato quasi optime congruentem sancto apostolatui tuo. Nam et tu sicut ille homo es, sub potestate diuina constitutus et regularibus disciplinis exercitatus, habens sub te pontifices et hoc est miserabile quod dicis huic: Vade, et non uadit; et alteri: ueni, et non uenit."

[84] *Opera Inedita*, p. 66: "Stat quippe mihi hoc propositum, in nullo umquam dissentire a sanctae apostolicae sedis doctrina et fide ...."

[85] Ibid.; p. 73: "... Pontifices Romani, annitentibus aliis orthodoxis, haereticos ac schismaticos ab hereditate pervasa eiecerunt, contra haereticos veritatem, contra schismaticos Ecclesiae unitatem fortissime defendendo ...."

[86] Ibid.; pp. 157-158: "In quorum exspectatione sanctorum patrum opiniones adeo variantur ut non sit inutile diversorum diversas opiniones ponere, determinandas in illa sancta sede quae prae ceteris est regula iustitiae."

> If they were living today and had heard about the censure coming from the apostolic see, without doubt they would not have dissented from it but would have corrected their statements lest, by disagreeing with the Roman Church, they should become heretics since, as has been said before us, "He who is in discord with the Holy Roman Church is a heretic." [87]

Gerhoh seems to have some people in Rome, perhaps in the papal curia, in mind when making the previous remarks, for he adds:

> Far be it that among the members of the Holy Roman Church there should be numbered members who, even if they are in the city of Rome, which is metaphorically called Babylon, presume to contradict the most sound doctrine of the aforesaid Roman pontiffs ....[88]

Later in the same work Gerhoh says that "among all the gates lifted up, the ones lifted highest are the successors of Peter. No one is to be heard contrary to them in the doctrine of faith: this has never failed in Peter or in the see of Peter and will never fail." [89] Although in a number of the texts that have been quoted Gerhoh seems to be thinking primarily if not exclusively of the pope himself, several of them speak more directly of the Roman Church. In one text Gerhoh makes a clear and important distinction between the person of a pope and the see of Peter or the Roman Church. Speaking about Pope Liberius, who in the fourth century signed an Arian formulary, he admits that the pope failed in the faith of Peter, but that the Roman Church kept the faith through the priest, Eusebius: "... Even when the faith of Peter seemed to have failed in Pope Liberius, nevertheless that faith continued to thrive in the see of Peter, which is the Roman Church, whose noblest member was the priest, Eusebius, who until his death fought against the aforesaid Pope Liberius and the Emperor Constantius, who were promoters of the Arians." Since he preserved the honour of the Roman Church by confessing his faith unto death, it is he, Gerhoh remarks, who should be considered a successor of Peter: "... He underwent a glorious death and honoured the see of blessed Peter by his suffering and confession, or

---

[87] Ibid.; p. 214: "... quamquam de hoc aliter videantur sentire quidam doctores antiqui et catholici. Qui si hodie viverent, audita censura sedis apostolicae, absque dubio non ab ea dissentirent, sed sua dicta corrigerent ne ab Ecclesia Romana discordantes haeretici fierent, quia ut ante nos dictum est 'haereticum esse constat qui a sancta Romana Ecclesia discordat'." The editors say that the origin of the last statement is uncertain.

[88] Ibid.; pp. 214-215: "Absit autem ut inter sanctae Romanae Ecclesiae membra censeantur qui, etsi sunt in urbe Roma, quae tropice dicitur Babylonia, praesumunt contradicere sanissimae praedictorum pontificum Romanorum doctrinae ...."

[89] Ibid.; p. 254: "Inter omnes enim portas elevatas altissime sunt elevati successores Petri, contra quos nullus audiendus est in doctrina fidei, quae in Petro Petrique sede numquam defecit nec umquam deficiet ...."

rather he preserved it in its ancient honour. Hence, in my opinion, when those eternal gates have been raised up, that outstanding son of the Roman Church should be numbered among the chosen successors of Peter." [90]

This remarkable text continues a tradition, known in this time, that an individual pope might fall into heresy but that the Roman Church itself would survive such a pope and maintain integrity of faith. It is an important qualification of theory and, if popularized, would have affected the religious ideal of the papacy so far as the person of an individual pope was concerned. The distinction was undoubtedly forced upon interpreters to explain this or other embarrassing cases of apparent personal defection in faith.

One of Gerhoh's strongest statements about the pope's teaching role (and here he seems again to be speaking of the individual pope) is found in the prologue of the *De novitatibus*. The whole work is, of course, an appeal to the pope to intervene against various novelties, including novelties in the doctrine of faith. Citing the text of Isaiah 55:2 about the word coming forth from God's mouth and not returning empty, Gerhoh adds a significant phrase: "Therefore ... 'the word that has proceeded from the mouth of God' *through the successors of Peter* 'will not return to him empty but will do whatever it wishes and will prosper in those to whom it is sent ...'." [91] This is surely a forceful statement in that it identifies the teachings of the pope with the very word coming from the mouth of God.

The pope's role in dealing with dangerous doctrines is emphasized by Gerhoh when he appeals to the pope to pronounce anathemas:

> By saying, "If anyone should say this or that which is discovered to be opposed to sound doctrine, let him be anathema," you will gain glory for yourself and victory against the enemies. For because God loves mercy and

---

[90] Ibid.: "... etiam quando in papa Liberio visa est Petri fides deficisse, tamen viguit in Petri sede, quae est Ecclesia Romana, cuius membrum nobilissimum presbyter Eusebius erat, qui usque ad mortem contra iam dictum papam Liberium et imperatorem Constantium, fautores Arianorum, certans, gloriosa morte occubuit, sedemque beati Petri sua passione atque confessione honestavit, immo in antiqua honestate conservavit. Unde istum Ecclesiae Romanae filium egregium inter electos Petri successores portis elevatis, portis aeternalibus, annumerandum censemus."

[91] *De novit.*, Prologus, 6; Haring, p. 24: "Quia ergo *uerbum de ore dei* per Petri successores *egressum non reuertetur ad eum uacuum sed faciet quaecumque uoluit et prosperabitur in his ad que missum est* ...." Towards the end of this work, after a detailed discussion of what he sees as the errors of Gilbert of Poitiers, Gerhoh looks to the pope to see what is right since the pope receives secret inspiration from the heavenly Father: "Et ideo illum deum recentem, cui eternitas asseritur non esse substantialis, recipere differimus donec audiamus quid inde censeat successor Petri, cui non caro et sanguis per argumenta philosophica sed pater celestis occulta inspiratione reuelauit quid inter aduersa uel diuersa sentientes approbat uel improbet" (43, 19; Haring, p. 111).

truth, the Lord will give grace and glory to those who maintain mercy and defend the truth.[92]

Gerhoh ends the *De novitatibus* on an element of pathos, leaving it to the pope to do what he can no longer do because of bodily weakness:

> ... Whenever I hear something contrary between the teachings of the Church and that of the schoolmen, I put more faith in churchmen than in schoolmen. And because I am now weak in body and no longer able to act by myself, I am taking care, at least by letter, to indicate certain things to the one to whom belongs the office of confirming the brethren and of weakening the enemies so that the gates of hell may not prevail in our day against the Church committed to Peter, founded on the rock, and strengthened by the faith of Peter.[93]

It is appropriate to end a survey of Gerhoh's views with his reference to the Petrine text of Matthew since Gerhoh is such a fervent supporter of papal authority. On the other hand, he seems to have had little to say about the pope's relations with bishops, except for his remark that the pope can give orders to bishops that they should obey. In matters of doctrine, his statements about the role of the see of Peter, which he clearly distinguishes at times from the person of the pope, and his ideas about its role of teaching, deciding, and anathematizing are the strongest we have found thus far. For Gerhoh the faith of the Roman See cannot fail. Its teachings, if rejected, make one a heretic. Peter's successors have the duty to root out all novelties and errors in matters of faith.[94]

Like Bernard and Peter the Venerable, Gerhoh's exaltation of the papal office and his appeals to the pope and Roman curia are motivated by concern

---

[92] Ibid. 47, 3; Haring, pp. 116-117: "... dicendo: Si quis hoc uel hoc dixerit quod sane doctrine aduersari deprehensum fuerit, anathema sit, conparabis gloriam tibi, contra hostes uictoriam. Quia enim misericordiam et ueritatem diligit deus, gratiam et gloriam dabit dominus misericordiam tenentibus et ueritatem defendentibus."

[93] Ibid. 49, 2; Haring, p. 118: "Vnde quotiens inter ecclesiastica et scolastica documenta contrarietatem audio, ego magis ecclesiasticis quam scolasticis fidem habeo. Et quia debilis iam corpore non ualeo per me ipsum, saltem per literas inde quedam insinuare curo illi ad cuius pertinet officium confirmare fratres et infirmare hostes ut porte inferi non preualeant in diebus nostris aduersus ecclesiam Petro commissam, in petra fundatam, Petri fide roboratam."

[94] A study of Gerhoh's concept of heresy has been made by Peter Classen, "Der Häresie-Begriff bei Gerhoh von Reichersberg und in seiner Umkreis," in *The Concept of Heresy in the Middle Ages (11th-13th C.): Proceedings of the International Conference, Louvain, May 13-16, 1973*, eds. W. Lourdaux and D. Verhelst, Mediaevalia Lovaniensia Series 1, Studia IV (Leuven and The Hague: Martinus Nijhoff, 1976), pp. 27-41. The study has been reprinted in *Ausgewählte Aufsatze von Peter Classen*, in Konstanzer Arbeitskreis für mittelalterliche Geschichte, Vortrage und Forschungen 28 (Sigmaringen: Thorbeke, 1983), 460-473. The International Conference volume also has an essay by O. Hagender, "Der Häresiebegriff bei den Juristen des 12. und 13. Jahrhunderts," pp. 42-103.

for reform and correction of abuses that were seen by him as difficult, if not impossible, to eradicate at the local level. These same abuses not only troubled sincere zealous persons such as Gerhoh; they also provoked reaction and criticism of the Church, especially her prelates, on the part of various groups of people who were soon judged to have slipped into heterodoxy. In the following section we shall examine some of the issues involved in these criticisms.

1.3. Apologetic Works against the Heterodox.

Although it has not been possible to examine here the works of heterodox thinkers and the movements they represented in order to see their attitude towards the papacy,[95] some indication of their views can be seen from the outlook and teaching of Catholic apologists responding to their tenets. At the same time one might expect to find positive statements about the papacy from these apologists. In fact, however, within the wide-ranging debates extending to many areas of doctrine, discussions about ecclesiastical authority centered more on bishops and priests than on the pope. With the exception of the first author examined here, the works dealt with in this section date from the last quarter of the twelfth century.

1.3.a. *Hugh of Rouen, Bishop of Amiens († 1164).*

Hugh of Rouen's *Contra haereticos* was written around 1147. In one section of its three books Hugh deals at length with the clergy but alludes to the pope only in passing. Hugh exalts the office of bishops: for him they take the place of Christ and are chief builders of the house of God; they are successors of the apostles; they are preeminent by reason of their singular excellence since they have the special and unique power of giving the Holy Spirit through the imposition of hands.[96]

---

[95] On these movements see the many publications of Christine Thouzellier, in particular her *Hérésies et hérétiques: Vaudois, Cathares, Patarins, Albigeois*, Storia e Letteratura 116 (Rome: Edizioni di Storia e Letteratura, 1969), and her *Catharisme et Valdéisme en Languedoc à la fin du XII⁰ et au début du XIII⁰ siècle*, 2nd ed. (Paris-Louvain: Nauwelaerts, 1969; rpt. Marseille: Lafitte, 1982). Also René Nelli, *Dictionnaire des Hérésies méridionales et des mouvements hétérodoxes ou indépendants apparus dans le midi de la France depuis l'établissement du Christianisme* (Toulouse: Édouard Privat, 1968); *Heresies of the High Middle Ages*, trans. and annotated by Walter L. Wakefield and Austin P. Evans (New York-London: Columbia Univ. Press, 1969), pp. 122-351 (documents and texts); R. Manselli, *Il secolo XII. Religione popolare ed eresia*, 3rd ed., Storia 12 (Rome: Jouvence, 1983).

A bibliographical study covering twenty years of publications has been produced by Carl T. Berkhout and Jeffrey B. Russell, *Medieval Heresies: A Bibliography 1960-1979*, Subsidia Mediaevalia 11 (Toronto: Pontifical Institute of Mediaeval Studies, 1981).

[96] *Contra haereticos* II, 1; *PL* 192, 1273C-D: "Episcopi toto terrarum orbe dispositi funguntur vice Christi, et principaliter aedificant domum Dei. Sicut enim summus pontifex et universalis episcopus noster Jesus Christus ex omnibus discipulis suis elegit duodecim quos

The source of pontifical authority and episcopal dignity is, for Hugh, the grace of the Holy Spirit poured out by Christ, the pontiff and bishop according to the order of Melchisedech. The Petrine text of Matthew he refers to all bishops, so that each bishop is seen as foundation of the Church since through the bishop the Church has the Holy Spirit.[97]

When Hugh enumerates the successors of the apostles, he names them "apostolic men, pontiffs and bishops" and says that "by heavenly power they continually build the house of Christ."[98] The bishops hold up this house, he adds, by seven columns, which are the seven degrees or grades within the sacrament of Order: priesthood, diaconate, subdiaconate, etc., each of whose members is delegated by the bishop for his duties.[99] In all this one sees a strong emphasis on bishops as successors of the apostles. It is unclear whether Hugh is thinking of the pope when he uses the title "apostolic man" or "pontiff" together with "bishop" in the same list. He makes no explicit statement about the pope; his main concern against heresies is to stress the legitimacy of all the ordained as well as the primary role of bishops.

1.3.b. *Vacarius († post 1198).*

Later in the century Vacarius' *Book against Many Various Errors* (*Liber contra multiplices et varios errores*) seeks to reply to the position of Ugo Speroni that no one can be a priest or a Christian without purity and holiness of life.[100] Vacarius says he does indeed wish all were spiritual, pure, and

---

caeteris praeferens apostolos nominavit, quos etsi puros homines sui tamen officii fecit esse consortes et divinae magnificentiae compotes, ita quoque ipsorum in episcopali gratia successores praesules sive pontifices excellentia singulari praeeminere fecit ut more apostolico Sanctum donent Spiritum his quibus rite manus imponunt." (Punctuation has been changed here and in the following texts of Hugh.)

[97] Ibid.; 1275A-B: "*Ubi* autem *venit plenitudo temporis,* in qua *misit Deus Filium suum* pontificem et episcopum secundum ordinem Melchisedech in aeternum, effusa est a sede majestatis superabundans et largiflua septiformis gratia Spiritus Sancti, ex quo pontificalis auctoritas et episcopalis dignitas plenius excrevit (Gal. 4:4). Hinc Petro ait: *Tu es Petrus, et super hanc Petrum* (sic) *aedificabo Ecclesiam meam* (Matt. 16:19). Est enim et Petrus in ea et ipsa in Petro, episcopus in Ecclesia et Ecclesia in episcopo. Est Episcopus Ecclesiae fundamentum quia per episcopum habet Ecclesia Spiritum Sanctum."

[98] Ibid.; 1275D: "Post apostolos enim secuti sunt viri apostolici, pontifices et episcopi, qui virtute coelesti semper aedificant domum Christi ...."

[99] Ibid.: " ... semper aedificant domum Christi quam sustentant septem columnis: septem enim sunt gradus illi perutiles et necessarii ad sustentandum et conservandum domum Dei manu pontificis perornati gratia septiformi. Hi sunt secundi ordinis viri, scilicet presbyteri, et post eos Levitae seu diaconi; exinde subdiaconi, acolythi, exorcistae, lectores, ostiarii, pro officiis ab episcopo sibi delegatis."

[100] Vacarius' treatise is edited by Ilarino da Milano, *L'eresia di Ugo Speroni nella confutazione del Maestro Vacario: Testo inedito del secolo XII con studio storico e dottrinale,* Studi e testi 115 (Vatican City, 1945). It is dated as of "the late seventies or the early eighties"

perfect, but he insists that the "office of administration" differs from the "merit of religion and charity," the former being "in matters of here and now" (*in rebus istis*) and the latter "in the mind of a person" (*in mente ipsius hominis*). One can exist without the other: "... Just as many have charity without the priestly office, so many can and do have the priesthood without charity."[101]

The apostle Peter, he says, was blessed not because of his office but because of his faith. Nor does it follow from this that everyone chosen by Christ for some office is blessed since, as he says candidly, "many, indeed an innumerable number of persons, were promoted through God who were wretched, as many indeed now are." Although God is free and good, all his ministers are not necessarily like him.[102]

This is the only reference in the work that could have some application to the papacy. It shows once again, however, the application of the Petrine text to all priests; its use for the pope would be the same as for all other priests — office does not ensure or require holiness, desirable as that might be.

1.3.c. *Bernard of Fontcaude († ca. 1192).*

Bernard, abbot of Fontcaude (*Fons Calidus*), wrote his *Tract against the Waldensian Sect* some time after 1181.[103] Bernard begins by describing a debate between Waldensians and Catholics before a judge chosen by both sides in which the judge declared the Waldensians to be in heresy. He then declares his intention to give the arguments presented on each side and after that to present the scriptural witnesses needed to bolster Catholic faith. His

---

by Nicholas M. Haring, "The 'Tractatus de Assumpto Homine' by Magister Vacarius," *MedS* 21 (1959) 149. Both authors supply other information about Vacarius' life and writings.

[101] *Liber*, 25, ɪ and 1; p. 550: (ɪ) "Ideoque spirituales esse debent eius sacerdotes et mundi et perfecti. (1) Et utinam sic esset, sicut esse debet ad honorem Dei et nominis christiane religionis. Si vero hoc debitum ad necessitatem etiam officii trahatur, sicut laboras ostendere, in vanum est hoc et falsum .... Quid enim commune habet officium amministracionis, que est in rebus ipsis, ad meritum religionis et caritatis, que est in mente ipsius hominis? Constat enim quod alterum sine altero et est et esse potest. Quia sicut multi caritatem habent sine officio sacerdotali, ita multi habere possunt et habent sacerdocium sine caritate."

[102] Ibid., 25, ɪɪɪ, 3; p. 551: "... Nec Petrus dictus est beatus per officium, sed per fidem, qua dixit: *Tu es Filius Dei.* Neque ex hoc sequitur quod omnis ille sit beatus, qui per Christum Ihesum, qui est hostium, ad aliquod intrat officium, cum ad innumera officia multi et innumerabiles promoti sunt per Deum, qui fuerunt miseri; et nunc etiam sunt. Neque enim sequitur, si Dominus est et liber et bonus, quod omnes eius ministri in hoc seculo tales sint."

[103] On Bernard see B. Heurtebize, "Bernard ... de Fontcaude," *Dictionnaire d'histoire et de géographie ecclésiastiques* 8 (1935) cols. 662-663, and J. Daoust, "Bernard of Fontcaude," *New Catholic Encyclopedia* 2 (1967) 340. His work is found in *PL* 204:·793-840. It can be dated after 1181 since it begins with a reference to Pope Lucius ɪɪɪ as "presiding over the Holy Roman Church": Lucius ɪɪɪ began his papacy in 1181.

first chapter, he says, is against those who say that we ought not to obey the Supreme Pontiff or other prelates.[104]

Bernard first accuses the Waldensians of disobedience against the "Roman Church," which has the fullness of power for binding and loosing; it also has the dignity whereby it grants dispensations to other Churches.[105] (In this text the contrast between the Roman Church and other Churches indicates that when Bernard says "Roman Church," he is thinking not of the universal Church but of the particular Church of Rome.) Moreover, Bernard continues, they lack obedience to bishops and priests even though Pope Gregory maintains that bishops take the place of Christ's disciples and in receiving ruling power have the authority to bind and loose.[106]

By this authority, Bernard maintains, the Roman Church and other bishops to whom Christ gave the power of binding and loosing bind these disobedient heretics with excommunication, following the example of Paul in punishing every disobedience.[107] Further on he reaches his conclusion: "Since therefore Christ and the apostles prescribed that bishops and priests are to be obeyed, whoever does not obey them becomes as a consequence disobedient to Christ and to his apostles."[108]

In Bernard we find the first clear mention of the papacy in this kind of apologetic work, and here, it should be noted, it is not the person of the pope but rather the Roman Church that is said to be the subject of fullness of power and to have the dignity of dispensing other Churches.

1.3.d. *Alan of Lille († 1203).*

Among Alan of Lille's many writings is a substantial work of apologetics in four books, his *On the Catholic Faith, or Against the Heretics, Waldensians, Jews, and Pagans,* in whose second book he tries to convince the Walden-

---

[104] *Tractatus adversus Waldensium sectam,* c. 1; *PL* 204: 795D.

[105] *Tractatus* 1, 1; 795D: "In primis igitur arguuntur de inobedientia quia scilicet non obediunt Ecclesiae Romanae, quae plenitudinem habet potestatis ligandi et solvendi, et dignitatem caeteras Ecclesias dispensandi."

[106] Ibid. 1, 2; 795D: "Praeterea nec episcopis nec sacerdotibus obtemperant cum, teste beato Gregorio, locum discipulorum Christi habeant episcopi, et auctoritatem ligandi et solvendi qui locum regiminis sortiuntur."

[107] Ibid.; 795D-796A: "Hac ergo auctoritate Romana Ecclesia caeterique episcopi, utpote quibus dictum est: *Quodcumque alligaveritis super terram erit ligatum et in coelo, et quodcumque solveritis super terram erit solutum et in coelis* (Matth. 16), praefatos haereticos excommunicationis vinculo innodarunt, *in promptu habentes* cum Apostolo *ulcisci omnem inobedientiam* (2 Cor. 10)."

[108] Ibid., 1, 4; 796C: "Cum igitur Christus et apostoli praecipiant obediendum esse episcopis et presbyteris, quicunque eis non obediunt consequenter Christo et ejus apostolis inobedientes existunt."

sians that other human beings, especially prelates, should be obeyed.[109] He first cites several scriptural authorities urging such obedience and then recalls the doctrine of the Pseudo-Dionysius about lesser angels obeying higher angels; armed with these authorities, he next speaks of ordered powers within the Church and in secular society, in both of which obedience is required.[110]

After distinguishing cases of grave and less grave disobedience, Alan comes to the situation where a lay person is commanded by a prelate not to preach because of that person's lack of knowledge:

> It is not licit for a lay person to preach, and it is dangerous for him to do so because he neither understands what he is saying nor does he understand the scriptures which he presumes to expound. Therefore if a prelate enjoins silence upon him, he is bound to be silent and if he does not, he sins mortally.[111]

A penalty of excommunication could be invoked against them if they refused to cease preaching. That, in fact, is why the Waldensians, who continued to preach despite its being against the precept of "the Lord Pope" and indeed against the whole Church, were excommunicated by the Lateran Council. Hence, Alan adds, we should not communicate with them since they are cut off from the Church.[112]

They are excommunicated, Alan adds, because they usurp an office against faith, an office that is not theirs; their actions are derogatory to the Church they preach about in words, and they are detractors of the Roman Curia "since it amounts to a sacrilege to dispute about what the Supreme Pontiff has done."[113]

Thus Alan sees at least a disciplinary role for the pope in a matter that touches on faith ("they usurp an office that is not theirs, contrary to the faith"); it is sacrilegious to oppose the pope. Noteworthy as well is Alan's link between the pope and the Roman curia; the text gives the impression that for Alan there is no distinction between the two.

---

[109] See his *De fide catholica sive Quadripartita magistri Alani editio contra haereticos, Valdenses, Iudaeos et paganos*; *PL* 210: 303-430. For book 2 see ibid., 377-400.

[110] See II, ch. 4; *PL* 210: 381D-382B.

[111] Ibid.; 382B-C: "Praedicare autem laico non licet, et ei periculosum est quia non intelligit quod dicit, nec Scripturas intelligit quas exponere praesumit. Ergo si praelatus ei injungat ut taceat, tenetur tacere et si non tacet, mortaliter peccat."

[112] Ibid.; 382C: "Unde si sub poena excommunicationis prohibet ei praedicare, si praedicet, sententiae excommunicationis subjacet. Quare isti Waldenses, qui contra praeceptum domini papae praedicant immo contra totam Ecclesiam, huic sententiae subjacent. In Concilio etiam Lateranensi in eos sententia excommunicationis lata est. Unde eis etiam communicandum non est cum sententia apostolica ab Ecclesia praecisi sint."

[113] Ibid.; 382C-D: "Ideo autem excommunicati sunt quia officium non suum usurpant contra fidem et quidem verbis Ecclesiam praedicant cui factis derogant et os in coelum ponunt, Romanae curiae detrahentes, cum instar sacrilegii sit de facto summi pontificis disputare."

1.3.e. *Bonacursus (fl. 1190?).*

The final section of the work attached to the name of this person, that is, the *Life of the Heretics* or the *Brochure against the Cathars*, contains a section that may well have been added by a second editor to the original work.[114] The date of composition is difficult to establish; 1190 has been suggested, but with little foundation. The short section against the Arnaldists gives the author's reply to their contention "that on account of the malice of clerics the sacraments of the Church ... are to be avoided."[115] Bonacursus, or his editor, distinguishes between the "power of office" (*potestas officii*) and the person to whom this ecclesiastical office is committed, and argues from both scripture and the fathers that if the recipient receives the sacrament worthily, the unworthiness of the minister fails to impede its good effect.[116] But here and throughout the work there is no mention of the pope, nor indeed of bishops or of their authority.

1.3.f. The "Summa contra haereticos" (ca. 1200+).

This work, dated by its editors as from the end of the twelfth or the first decades of the thirteenth century, was formerly attributed to Praepositinus of Cremona; now, however, this attribution is generally questioned or rejected.[117] In chapter 11 the author gives considerable details about the Pasagini, who, he says, reject ecclesiastical offices, "saying they are superfluous." He then replies to their arguments with his own, based on scriptural texts, in defence of prelates and the duty of obedience to them. But in all this discussion there is no special mention of the pope.[118]

To the extent that one can judge the mentality of the times from the description of those considered heretics and the response to them, it would

---

[114] The work is contained in *PL* 204: 775A-792D. For the date and the possibly added section see F. Vernet, "Bonacursus," *DTC* 2/1 (1923) 953-954. The section against the Arnaldistae is found on cols. 791A-792D.

[115] *Vita haereticorum: Adversus Arnaldistas*; 791A: "Quod pro malitia clericorum sacramenta Ecclesiae dicunt esse vitanda."

[116] Ibid.; 791B: "Quod si malis, dum tolerantur vel ignorantur, officium ecclesiasticum commissum fuerit, aut forte bonus post acceptum beneficium malus esse incipit, tu quis es qui alienum servum judices? Suo domino stat aut cadit: potestatem etenim officii quam accepit non amittit quandiu Ecclesiae judicio a praelato non [suo *PL*] damnatus fuerit. Sacramenta itaque ecclesiastica ab eo si tu digne acceperis, quamvis indigne ministraverit, tibi non sibi profutura accipe." The witnesses of scripture and the Fathers follow ibid., 791B-792A.

[117] It was edited by Joseph Garvin and James Corbett (Notre Dame, Ind.: Univ. of Notre Dame Press, 1958). For the date see p. xiv; on the authorship see p. xv and the note by A.-M. Henry in Landgraf (cited in the preceding essay, n. 4) p. 155.

[118] For the chapter see ibid., pp. 158-159; the quotation is from p. 158.

appear that the pope was less present to the thought and imagination of people in the latter half of the twelfth century than were the bishops and priests exercising ecclesiastical office. These works suggest the interest for our topic of contributions from other disciplines concerning communication methods and results in this period as well as artistic and literary representations of the pope and other ecclesiastical authorities.

1.4. Innocent III (1160-1216; Pope 1198).

Although Lotario de' Conti di Segni's major influence on the theory and practice of the papacy came in the thirteenth century, our study will limit itself to his theological thought in the very last years of the twelfth century, leaving to other studies in this symposium the task of examining his thought and practice during his years as pope in the first decades of the thirteenth century. This means that his theological thought will be examined as it was expressed either just before and/or within the first year of his pontificate. The two works of this period are his *On the fourfold kinds of marriage* (*De quadripartita specie nuptiarum*), written either before or during his first year as pope, and the sermon *On the four species of espousals* (*De quatuor speciebus desponsationum*), preached in 1199 on the first anniversary of his consecration. The first of these will be referred to as his "treatise," the second as his "sermon." [119]

The treatise applies the allegorical method of exegesis to psalm 44 (45): "My heart has uttered a good word" and to other texts of scripture. In heavy dependence on the Victorines and Bernard, it develops the ecclesial image of the Church as the Bride of Christ. Speaking of the three goods traditionally seen in marriage: fidelity (*fides*), children (*proles*) and sacrament (*sacramentum*), he relates fidelity to chastity, children to fecundity, and

---

[119] The texts will be cited from Connie Mae Munk, "A Study of Pope Innocent III's Treatise: *De quadripartita specie nuptiarum*," 2 vols., Thesis, University of Kansas, 1975 (Ann Arbor, Michigan 48106: Xerox University Microfilms, 1976), which contains a Latin edition (with translation) of both the treatise indicated in the title and the sermon *De quatuor speciebus*. Pagination begins anew for each edition and each translation.

Besides Munk's introductory study see also W. Ullmann, "Pope Innocent III," *New Catholic Encyclopedia* 7 (1967) 521-524; M. Maccarrone, "Innocenzo III prima del pontificato," *Archivo storico italiano* 66 (1943) 59-134; James Powell, *Innocent III: Vicar of Christ or Lord of the World?* (Boston: Heath, 1963); W. Imkamp, *Das Kirchenbild Innocenz' III (1198-1216)* (Stuttgart: Hiersemann, 1983); idem, *"Pastor et sponsus.* Elemente einer Theologie des bischöflichen Amtes bei Innocenz III," in *Aus Kirche und Reich: Studien zu Theologie, Politik und Recht im Mittelalter: Festschrift für Friedrich Kempf ...*, ed. H. Mordeck (Sigmaringen: Thorbeke, 1983) pp. 285-294 (unavailable to me). There is another translation of the treatise on marriage by E. J. Crook, with an introduction, in *Spiritualität heute und gestern: Internazionales Kongress vom 4. bis 7. August 1982* (Salzburg, 1982) pp. 1-95 (unavailable to me).

sacrament to stability.[120] Speaking of the inseparable sacrament between Christ and the Church, he mentions Christ's question put to the apostles whether they would go away, Peter's reply "on behalf of the whole Church," and Christ's promise to be with the Church for all time.[121]

Peter is also mentioned, together with Paul and the other apostles, as fulfilling the levirate function of begetting children on behalf of Christ: as in the Hebrew practice the children were named from the dead brother and not from the substitute father, so those begotten by the apostles "are not called Petrines from Peter or Paulines from Paul, but Christians from Christ ...." [122] Here the text transmitted from Augustine by Lombard has been slightly expanded to include Paul and has been set within the continuing marriage metaphor of Lotario di Segni. He adds that the apostolic order that has received ruling authority in the Church is not the bridegroom but the friend of the bridegroom (*amicus sponsi*).[123] Here Bernard's imagery reenforces his own thought.

These are the main texts in the treatise that have some bearing on the papacy. In the sermon, however, Innocent, now celebrating his first anniversary as pope, stresses the pope's role and powers, working out his ideas through constant application of the marriage metaphor to the pope and bishops and their relations. Within the sermon there also occur several allusions to canonical questions that had been or were being debated.[124]

A scriptural text quoted at the outset establishes the metaphorical pattern: "He who has the bride is the bridegroom; the friend of the bridegroom, who stands and hears him, rejoices greatly at the bridegroom's voice" (John 3:29). Innocent uses this text, repeating the "friend of the bridegroom" (*amicus sponsi*) theme from Bernard, to say: "It is I, brothers, who am the friend of the bridegroom, to whom the bridegroom says in a friendly way:

---

[120] For a summary and analysis of these points see Munk 1: 14-22.

[121] *De quadripartita* 2, 39; Munk 2: 28: "Sacramentum autem inter Christum et Ecclesiam inseparabile perseverat. ... Christus quoque cum dixisset Apostolis: *Numquid et vos vultis abire?*, Petrus pro tota respondit Ecclesia: *Domine, verba vitae aeternae habes et ad quem ibimus?* Ad hoc inseparabile sacramentum pertinere dignoscitur quod Christus loquens apostolis catholicae promittit ecclesiae: *Ecce ego vobiscum sum omnibus diebus usque ad consummationem saeculi.*" Texts quoted are John 6:68-69 and Matt. 28:20 respectively. (Punctuation and capitalization have been slightly altered here and in subsequent texts.)

[122] Ibid. 3, 14; Munk 2: 87: "... quos Apostoli non in suo sed tuo genuerunt honore, quia non a Petro petrini vel a Paulo paulini, sed a Christo christiani dicuntur ...."

[123] Ibid.: "Sed suscitat ei semen frater qui <accipit> uxorem ipsius: id est, apostolicus ordo, qui sponsam Christi, scilicet sanctam Ecclesiam, regendam suscepit, qui non sponsus sed amicus sponsi est ...."

[124] See *De quatuor speciebus*; Munk 2: 4-8 (of the edition), where the canonical references are included in the notes.

Friend, go up higher (Luke 14:10) ...."[125] The reason, he says, is that he has become the successor of Peter, who professed his love for Christ three times.[126]

Innocent will go further than this, however. He prepares the way by asking what is the source of his joy, that joy spoken of in the opening text. Is it because of Christ's voice promising him the keys or setting him over peoples and kingdoms? This, he replies, would be a source of fear rather than joy, especially if we recall the warnings of scripture and the injunction that the greater should be servants of all.[127] No, he continues, his joy is because of Christ's promise to be with him always to the end of the world and his special prayer for Peter to protect him from Satan.[128] If the Lord promised a struggle, Innocent continues, he also promised victory through Peter's unfailing faith. At the same time he gave him the duty of strengthening his brothers, promising prayers to help him.[129]

Having evoked these texts, Innocent repeats his opening texts and then asks the assembled bishops: "Am I not the bridegroom and each of you the friend of the bridegroom?"[130] Here he has changed the application of the metaphor: he, the pope, is now bridegroom, and the friend of the bridegroom is each of the bishops. The pope, he says, is indeed bridegroom, for he has as his spouse the Roman Church with all her noble attributes: "with this Church (bride) is my sacramental marriage, with it is my nuptial exchange."[131]

After contrasting the moment when the pope's spiritual marriage is ratified (that is, at his election) with that of bishops (that is, when they are confirmed and consecrated), Innocent repeats the teaching of his treatise about the three conjugal goods, fidelity, children, and sacrament, and applies it to make

[125] Ibid.; Munk 2: 2-3: "Ego sum, fratres, amicus sponsi cui sponsus amicabiliter ait: *Amice, ascende superius* ...." Text from Luke 14:10.

[126] Ibid.; Munk 2: 3: "... illius successor effectus qui terna responsione dixit ad sponsum: *Domine, tu scis quia amo te.*" Text from John 21:17.

[127] See ibid.

[128] Ibid.; Munk 2: 3-4: "Propter quam autem uocem mihi gaudendum est? Super illam utique quam Dominus ait apostolos: *Uobiscum ergo omnibus diebus usque ad consummationem seculi.* Et specialiter Petro: *Symon, Sathanas expetiuit uos ut cribraret quasi triticum, sed ego pro te rogaui* etc. Hec est illa uox sponsi propter quam gaudeo ...." Texts from Matt. 28:20 and Luke 22:31.

[129] Ibid.; Munk 2: 4: "... quia sicut predixit Symoni pugnam, quod promittit uictoriam, sic iniungit officium, quod inpendit auxilium. Pugnam predicit cum ait: *Satanas expetiuit uos.* ... Uictoriam uero promittit cum addit: *non deficiat fides tua.* Nam *hec est uictoria que uincit mundum, fides nostra.* Officium iniungit cum ait: *Confirma fratres tuos.* Auxilium autem inpendit cum ait: *Ego pro te rogaui, Petre.*" Texts from Luke 22:32 and 1 John 5:4.

[130] Ibid.: "An non ego sum sponsus et quilibet uestrum amicus sponsi?"

[131] Ibid.: "Cum hac mihi sacramentale coniugium, cum hac mihi commercium nuptiale."

important conclusions about the role of the pope. The pope and the Roman Church, he says, have always been so faithful to each other that they have never fallen into heresy. The Roman Church does not follow heretics and schismatics; rather, it acts strongly against them and hears only the catholic and apostolic voice; it gives and receives the conjugal debt, receiving from the pope the debt of providence and rendering to him the debt of reverence.[132]

Pursuing this imagery, Innocent holds that the Roman Church pays a debt of reverence to no one except the Roman pontiff because it has, after God, no other superior (some manuscripts say that it is the pope who has no other superior).[133] How is it an exchange of debts, Innocent asks, if the pope has the debt or duty of care or providence not only for the Roman Church but for all Churches? To answer the implied charge of polygamy or infidelity, Innocent uses the allegory of Sarah and Hagar in a way that may or may not have pleased the assembled bishops. Sarah was Abraham's wife, Hagar the slave girl introduced to Abraham to bear him children. In the same way the Roman pontiff has the Roman Church as his bride, whereas the other Churches are subject to it and are brought into the pope to receive the debt of care from him.[134] In his allegorizing interpretations Innocent has outlined a whole position on the supremacy of the pope and the Roman Church and the subjection of the other Churches to him and to it.

When it comes to allegorizing the conjugal good of *sacramentum*, however, Innocent introduces a qualification that we have seen in other authors. This good, we recall, points to the stability and permanence of the marriage alliance between the pope and his bride, the Roman Church. This is so firm,

---

[132] Ibid.; Munk 2: 6-7: "Fides ad castitatem, proles ad fecunditatem, sacramentum ad stabilitatem refertur. Tantam enim fidem Romanus pontifex et Ecclesia Romana sibi semper ad inuicem seruauerunt ut eis congrue ualeat adaptari quod Ueritas inquit in euangelio: *Cognosco oues meas* etc.; *alienum non sequuntur sed fugiunt quia non nouerunt uocem alienorum*. Alieni sunt heretici et schismatici, quos Ecclesia Romana non sequitur, sed persequitur et fugit et fugat. Suum autem cognoscit et audit, non apostaticum sed apostolicum, non catharum sed catholicum; recipiens et reddens debitum coniugale, recipiens ab eo debitum prouidentie et reddens debitum reuerentie." Texts from John 10:14, 5.

[133] Ibid.; Munk 2: 7: "... Porro ... Ecclesia Romana debitum reuerentie nulli prorsus inpendat nisi Romano pontifici, quia post Deum alium superiorem non habet ...." For *quia* some manuscripts read *qui* (ibid., note to line 159).

[134] Ibid.: "... Quid est hoc quod Romanus pontifex debitum providentie non utique Romane tantum Ecclesie sed omnibus omnino uidetur Ecclesiis exhibere? ... Quid ergo? Iudicabitur ad inparia? ut secundum quod legitur in ueteri testamento, unus possit habere plures sed una non possit habere plures. Nonne legistis quod Abraham habuit Saram uxorem, que tamen Agar famulam suam introduxit ad illum: nec commisit propter hoc adulterium sed officium adimpleuit. Sic et Romanus pontifex sponsam habet Romanam Ecclesiam, que tamen Ecclesias sibi subiectas introducit ad ipsum ut ab eo recipiant debitum providentie: quod quanto plus redditur, tanto magis debetur. Sed nunc fit in spiritu quod tunc in carne fiebat ...."

he says, that it can be broken only by death.[135] But spiritual fornication, that is, an error in faith on the part of the pope, gives the Roman Church cause to dismiss the pope: this is an error of infidelity (he plays on the word "faith" rooted in "infidelity"). As John says, "he who does not believe is already judged."[136] The last phrase may recall the common teaching that the pope has no one but God to judge him; in the case of infidelity in faith, the pope is already judged and can be dismissed.

Having said this, Innocent recalls the Lord's promise of future prayer that Peter's faith will not fail. Therefore, he says, he would not easily believe that the Lord would permit the pope to err against faith.[137] Perhaps reassured by this recollection, Innocent then repeats that he is the bridegroom and that his bride has given him a most precious dowry — the fullness of spiritual things, the breadth of temporal things, and greatness and abundance of both of these. Bishops, on the other hand, have only a partial care of the Church; only Peter has the "fullness of power" (*plenitudo potestatis*). The mitre signifies the pope's authority in spiritual matters, his crown the role he has in temporal affairs since he is constituted vicar of Christ, the king of kings and lord of those who rule as well as his being the eternal priest according to the order of Melchisedech.[138]

An interesting question to be put to this text is who exactly is the bride who gives Innocent this dowry of such extensive power in spiritual and temporal matters. Since, according to the allegory, he is the bridegrom of the Roman Church, it would seem to be this Church that, by electing him, has conferred this power on him. Innocent seems to mean that the power attached to the office itself, and ultimately derived not from the Roman Church but from God, becomes his dowry when he is elected pope. The

---

[135] Ibid.; Munk 2: 8-9: "Sacramentum ... inter Romanum pontificem et Romanam Ecclesiam tam firmum et stabile perseuerat, ut nisi per mortem nunquam ab inuicem separentur ...."

[136] Ibid.; Munk 2: 9: "Propter causam uero fornicationis Ecclesia Romana posset dimittere Romanum pontificem: fornicationem dico non carnalem, sed spiritualem, quia non est carnale sed spirituale coniugium, id est, propter infidelitatis errorem, quoniam *qui non credit iam iudicatus est* ...." Scriptural text from John 3:18.

[137] Ibid.: "Ego tamen non facile crediderim ut Deus permitteret Romanum pontificem contra fidem errare, pro quo specialiter orauit in Petro ...."

[138] Ibid.; Munk 2: 9-10: "Hec autem non nupsit uacua, sed dotem mihi tradidit absque precio preciosam, spiritualium uidelicet plenitudinem et latitudinem temporalium, magnitudinem et <multitudinem> utrorumque. Nam ceteri uocati sunt in partem sollicitudinis, solus autem Petrus assumptus est in plenitudinem potestatis. In signum spiritualium contulit mihi mitram, in signum temporalium dedit mihi coronam; mitram pro sacerdotio, coronam pro regno, illius me constituens uicarium, qui habet in uestimento et in femore suo scriptum *Rex regum et Dominus dominantium: sacerdos in eternum secundum ordinem Melchisedech.*" Scriptural texts from Apoc. 19:16 and Ps 109 (110):4.

context seems to indicate this, since he goes on to discuss the question of consent to episcopal election and to allude again to the need for bishops to have their elections to the episcopacy confirmed, presumably by the pope.[139]

Innocent concludes his sermon by again calling the attendant bishops "friends of the bridegroom" (*amici sponsi*), implying anew that he himself is the bridegroom (*sponsus*). He asks for their prayers for him so that he may render his conjugal debt to the Church in such a way that he may be ready to meet that other and first bridegroom, Christ, when he comes.[140]

In summary, for Innocent III the pope is the friend of Christ, bridegroom of the Church, because he succeeds Peter, who showed himself to be Christ's friend by professing his love for him three times. The source of Innocent's joy in this office is less the power of the keys given him (it is interesting that the Matthean text occurs only in passing in the sermon) and more Christ's promise to remain with the Church and Christ's prayer for Peter's perseverance in faith. Like Peter, the pope is to confirm his brothers. Besides being the friend of Christ, the bridegroom of the Church, the pope himself is bridegroom of the Roman Church whereas the bishops are friends of the pope as bridegroom. The pope and the Roman Church have full power (*plenitudo potestatis*) and the care of all the Churches, which are subject to them and owe them reverence. The pope and the Roman Church are also the unshakeable guardians of faith against heresy and schism. Although it is unlikely, given Christ's prayer for him, the pope could fall into error in faith; such infidelity or spiritual fornication would be cause for his dismissal by the Roman Church.

This entire use of marriage imagery constitutes an extension of metaphorical and allegorical language, originally used to describe the relations of Christ and the Church, now to fit a particular area, the theology of the papacy. This was an extension of imagery that produced in Innocent's mind many canonical and other practical consequences. Such wholesale and uncontrolled use of metaphor in theology is surely deficient in method, but it may well be that Innocent already had definite opinions about the papacy and the Church and, as has happened in other times and other debates, simply used such imagery and allegory as a tool that he hoped would make his views more acceptable. One wonders what remarks the bishops made to each other as they left, especially as they recalled their being compared to Hagar, the slave girl brought in to satisfy Abraham's desire for children!

---

[139] See ibid.; Munk 2: 10-11.

[140] Ibid.; Munk 2: 11: "Uos autem fratres et filii, qui estis amici sponsi, gaudio gaudetis propter uocem sponsi, puras manus sine disceptacione leuetis ad Deum, ... in oracione petentes ut ita reddam Ecclesie debitum coniugale quod veniente sponso cum uirginibus sapientibus merear accensis lampadibus ad nuptias introire, ipso prestante."

2. First Half of the Thirteenth Century

2.1. Apologetic Works Against the Heterodox.

As in a previous section, this study will examine works written in answer to those attacking the Catholic Church; from these it may be possible to see, indirectly, how important the papacy was as an object of their attack and, directly, what Catholic authors had to say about the papacy in reply. Three works of this period will be examined.

2.1.a. *Ermengaud of Béziers (fl. early 13th C.).*

The Ermengaud of Béziers who is author of an *Opuscule against the Heretics (Opusculum contra haereticos)* was formerly thought to be an abbot of Saint-Gilles de Nîmes (1175-1195), but recent research has shown him to be a thirteenth-century converted Cathar who belonged to a group of "Poor Catholics" led by Durandus de Huesca, whose teaching will be examined shortly.[141] His *Opuscule*, in fact, is hardly original since it is by and large a summary of a work by Durandus, the *Anti-Heresy Book (Liber anti-heresis)*, which exists in manuscripts.[142] The defence of Catholic doctrine includes, among many other things, a defence of oral confession and the imposition of satisfaction by a duly ordained and appointed priest.[143] The power of binding and loosing, he says, was given by the Lord to men, as John 20:23 testifies.[144] God alone forgives sin, but he does so through his minister. Or, if men are said to forgive sin, it is not of themselves that they do it. It is God who forgives through their ministry. God forgives sin through himself when he wishes; men do so not of themselves but from God's grace which is in them and works through them. It is in this sense that it is true that only God forgives sin.[145]

---

[141] On Ermengaud see É. Delaruelle, "Ermengaud de Béziers," *Dictionnaire d'histoire et de géographie ecclésiastiques* 5 (1963) cols. 754-757; this article summarizes the research of Antoine Dondaine, "Durand de Huesca et la polémique anti-cathare," *Archivum Fratrum Praedicatorum* 29 (1959) 268-276, and Ch. Thouzellier, "Le 'Liber anti-heresis' de Durand de Huesca et le 'Contra hereticos' d'Ermengaud de Béziers," *RHE* 55 (1960) 130-141, which is reproduced as ch. 3 of her *Hérésies et hérétiques* (cited above, n. 95) pp. 39-49.

[142] See Dondaine, pp. 250-260, and Thouzellier, "Le 'Liber ...'." Ermengaud's chapter 13 is chapter 17 in Durandus' work, and his chapter 14 is chapter 16 in Durandus. Ermengaud's work is examined ahead of Durandus' *Liber contra Manichaeos* since the latter was written after Ermengaud's summary of Durandus' earlier work.

[143] Ermengaud's work is contained in *PL* 204: 1235A-1272B. For his defence of oral confession and imposition of satisfaction see ch. 13; 1259B-1260C.

[144] Ibid.; 1260C: "Et haec est potestas quam Dominus dedit hominibus, scilicet potestas ligandi et solvendi. Dicit namque ipsa Veritas: 'Quorum remiseritis peccata, remittuntur eis, et quorum retinueritis, retenta sunt."

[145] Ibid.; 1260D: "... nunc pro officio suo sacerdos, cum audierit peccatorum varietates, sciat quis ligandus sit vel quis solvendus .... Et ita Deus dimittit peccata per ministrum. Cum

In the following chapter Ermengaud describes in some detail the ceremony of *consolamentum* practised by the sect; this was a laying on of hands by members of the sect, who were not ordained.[146] Ermengaud rejects this: it is judged by the Roman Apostolic Church as very evil and as a mortal error because it is done by unqualified persons. Moreover, this practice was not established by Christ or by the apostles. After his resurrection, Christ gave the power of baptizing and imposing hands in the Lord's name only to ordained apostles and to those ordained by them.[147]

After quoting several scriptural texts to support his position, Ermengaud asserts that after Christ's ascension his apostles, whom he had chosen during his life, established in all the Churches bishops, priests, and deacons to enact the divine mysteries. The apostles, when ordaining them, gave them the same power and "tradition" as they themselves had received from Christ. To go against this apostolic tradition is to be in grave error and to work death for oneself.[148]

The apostles imposed hands only on those they wished to ordain as preachers, priests, or deacons. When the unordained are seen in scripture to have preached and baptized, they used the form given them by Christ and not some *consolamentum*.[149]

This is all Ermengaud has to say about ecclesiastical order and powers. Although he strongly maintains the apostolic succession and tradition, he

---

enim Deus dimittat peccata et homo dimittat, aliter (tamen) Deus et aliter homo: Deus ex semetipso quia per semetipsum, quando vult, peccata dimittit; homines non ex se sed ex gratia in eis et per eos operante. Et ita verum est quod Deus solus peccata dimittit ...."

[146] See ch. 14; 1262B-1264B.

[147] Ibid.; 1263A-B: "Romana vero apostolica Ecclesia omnia ista praefata quae ab haereticis conficiuntur pessimos et mortales errores esse multis auctoritatibus judicat quia non sunt a talibus personis facta a quibus fieri debent, neque a Jesu Christo institutum est neque ab apostolis, neque in tempore eorum factum est. ... Sed post resurrectionem potestatem baptismi et manus imponendi in nomine Domini tantum apostolis ordinatis dedit et concessit ut qui ab eis ordinati fuerint eamdem potestatem baptizandi et manus imponendi habebant, videlicet quos Deus elegerit et ipsi dignos judicaverint."

[148] Ibid.; 1263C-D: "Et postquam Dominus noster Jesus Christus apostolos elegit, et post ejus ascensionem apostoli per universas Ecclesias episcopos et presbyteros et etiam diaconos ad peragenda omnia divina mysteria constituerunt et eamdem potestatem et traditionem quam ipsi a Christo acceperant illis a se ordinatis concedebant, quisquis contra hanc apostolicam traditionem facit et credit multum errat et mortem sibi operatur."

[149] Ibid.; 1264A-B: "Item, apostoli, quos ordinare volebant praedicatores, presbyteros, vel diaconos super populum, manus tantum imponebant. De aliis non invenimus in sacra scriptura nisi quod praedicabant et baptizabant eos cum invocatione Spiritus Sancti ut Dominus noster Jesus Christus eos docuerat et eis mandaverat .... Sed formam et modum dedit eis, qui usque hodie in Ecclesia assidue retinetur. Unde valde assidue mirandum est a quo talis 'consolamenti' consuetudo haereticorum habuerit initium vel sumpsit exordium quia neque a prophetis neque a Christo neque ab apostolis neque ab apostolicis viris, apostolorum successoribus, initium habere videtur ...."

makes no special mention of the pope. Bishops, priests, and deacons are the ones whose special powers he is concerned to defend against the heterodox.

2.1.b. *Durandus de Huesca (fl. 1222-1224).*

Some time between 1222 and 1224 Durandus de Huesca completed a *summa* written in opposition to the Cathari, *A Book against the Manichees* (*Liber contra Manichaeos*). In it he summarizes their teaching, gives the scriptural texts they used, and then seeks to refute their accusations against the Church.[150]

One teaching of those whom Durandus calls "Manichees" is that the world is evil and in fact was created by the devil. A text they quoted, Durandus says, was 1 John 5:19: "The whole world is in the power of the evil one": this world they understood to be the Roman bishop and all his subjects.[151] At this point Durandus deals with the more general question about the goodness of the world as created by God and not with this particular view. Later on, however, he identifies the "kingdom of this world" with the earth given to humans to govern, and further on with the Roman Church as the "kingdom of God."[152] The heretics, he says, claim that the kingdom of the world that is the Roman Church is not the kingdom of God because in it there are many who are corrupt and who are fixed in their evil works. Durandus turns this argument against them: if corruption destroys the kingdom of God, their own corruptions mean that their church is not the kingdom of God. Durandus points out that they are known to have corruption within them and to be divided and to be engaged in condemning each other.[153]

Although the Roman Church has evil and unjust workers in it, Durandus continues, it has good and just workers as well; more importantly, all are

---

[150] See *Une somme anti-cathare: Le "Liber contra Manicheos" de Durand de Huesca*, ed. Christine Thouzellier, Spicilegium Sacrum Lovaniense: Études et Documents 32 (Louvain, 1964). All references are to this edition. For the dating see pp. 35-38.

[151] Ibid. c. 4; pp. 116 and 118: "De compilatione Manicheorum. De presenti mundo nequam et malo et toto posito *in maligno* Iacobus ait in epistola sua. ... Si *mundus positus est in maligno* et si non est diligendus, neque ea que in eo sunt. Ergo non est credendum quod sint propria Christi, quia non sunt ex Patre. Et si non sunt ex Patre, ergo non sunt Christi. ... Responsio: ... Hunc *mundum positum in maligno* intelligunt esse romanum episcopum cum omnibus suis subiectis."

[152] Ibid., c. 5; p. 138: "Unde patet quod regnum huius mundi, id est terra, sua est, ex quo dat eam cui vult." This follows quotations of texts in which God is said to have given these kingdoms to earthly kings. For the identification with the Roman Church see the following note.

[153] Ibid.: "Item, si regnum mundi, id est ecclesia romana, non est regnum Dei, quia plures sunt in ea corrupti et pravis operibus inoliti, ergo regnum eorum, id est *ecclesia* que *malignantium* dicitur, non est regnum Christi. Nam multas scimus habuisse corruptiones et etiam divisi sunt in tres partes et unaqueque pars iudicat aliam et condempnat." Scriptural text: Ps. 25:5.

united in one faith and one baptism and do not condemn each other in judgment, but rather confess one true all-powerful Lord.[154] In these texts, the "Roman Church" likely has the same meaning as in the earlier text in which the heretics, according to Durandus, identified the evil world (and so its kingdom) with "the Roman bishop together with all his subjects." The pope does not seem to have been singled out for special recrimination by the heretics except in so far as he is considered with the whole Church and as its head.

A few other texts refer either to the "Church" (*ecclesia*) or to the "Holy Church" (*ecclesia sancta*), and in each case these are identified with the "Roman Church" (*Romana ecclesia*), which seems to mean the entire Church and not only the pope together with the Church of the diocese of Rome. Those who confess the faith of Christ professed by the Roman Church are not heretics, Durandus says in one place,[155] and in another he speaks of what "the holy Church truly confesses"; almost at once he adds that the Roman Church is firmly rooted in orthodox faith and does not depart from that faith which it confessed at Baptism.[156]

These are the only references that have been found to the Church and the pope. We see that while Durandus strongly defends the Church as the true Church of Christ and indeed as the kingdom of God and of Christ on this earth, he finds it unnecessary to say anything in particular in defence of the papacy. It would seem that at this date, as in the twelfth century, the focus of heretical criticism was more on corrupt clergy in general or in particular localities than on the papacy.

2.1.c. *Moneta of Cremona († 1260).*

Moneta of Cremona joined the Dominicans around the year 1219 or 1220 and was frequently occupied with the heretical movements of his time. He has been praised as giving a very balanced and knowledgeable account of the different movements in his *Five Books against the Cathars and Waldensians*, written in 1244.[157] After ranging over most doctrines of the heretics and

---

[154] Ibid.; p. 139: "Romana vero ecclesia, licet multos habeat pravos operarios et iniustos, nonnullos tamen habet bonos et iustos et omnes *una fide, uno baptismo,* non sese iudicando dampnantes, *unum* verum omnipotentem *Dominum* confitentur." Scriptural text: Eph. 4:5.

[155] Ibid., c. 10; p. 181: "Et hoc notate quod quicumque fidem Christi credunt quam romana ecclesia confitetur non ex hereticis surrexerunt neque ab eis exierunt ...."

[156] Ibid., c. 14; p. 237: "... quod et sancta ecclesia veraciter confitetur. ... Nam romana ecclesia, cum membris suis inconvulsis radicibus in fide permanens orthodoxa quam Christus tradidit suis fidelibus, non discedit a fide quam in baptismate suscipit confitendo."

[157] On Moneta and the dates see M.-M. Gorce, "Moneta de Crémone ou Simoneta," *DTC* 10/2 (1929) cols. 2211-2215; for appreciation of his account see ibid., cols. 2212-2213.

invoking the Church's teaching against them, he turns in the fifth book to their tenets about the Church and their criticisms of the "Roman Church," the title Moneta constantly uses for it. At the start of book 5 Moneta settles the question of what he means by the Church. It is, he says, the congregation of the faithful and is equivalent to the Roman Church.[158]

The first chapter of book 5 deals with the charge — the first time we have seen it in this literature — that the Roman Church is to be identified with the beast of chapter 17 of the Apocalypse (verse 3), and that the woman seated on the beast signifies the pope, the head of the Roman Church: the latter identification is made by the heretics because they say that the woman drunk with the blood of the saints signifies the Roman Church, which orders the killing of saints (whom they identify with themselves, Moneta adds).[159] This statement undoubtedly reflects the events of the crusades against the heretical sects or the acts of the Inquisition.

Moneta spends the whole of this first chapter as well as the next refuting this identification; he does so by using many texts of the Apocalypse and other scriptural passages. He begins by pointing out that the scriptural text distinguishes between the beast and the woman, and here he opposes the identity they make between them.[160] This shows that, as the text just seen indicates, for Moneta the heretics tended to identify the pope and the Roman Church in some ways.

In seeking to prove that the "poor of Lyons" are not the Church of God, Moneta argues from the intermediary role of Peter in the forgiveness of Cornelius' sins (Acts 10); if Peter was an intermediary in that case, the pope

---

[158] *Venerabilis patris Monetae Cremonensis, Ordinis Praedicatorum ... Adversus Catharos et Valdenses libri quinque*, ed. Thomas Augustinus Ricchinius (Ricchini) (Rome, 1743; rpt. Ridgewood, N.J.: Gregg Press, 1964) V, 1; pp. 389b-390a: "... Solet ... quaerere haereticus quae sit Dei Ecclesia. Ad quod dicendum quoniam haereticus primo debuisset quaerere quid sit Ecclesia. Quam quaestionem determinans (determinantes *ed.*) dico quod Ecclesia est congregatio fidelium: haec autem est illa Ecclesia quae dicitur Ecclesia Romana, quidquid eius aemuli fabulentur." Punctuation and spelling slightly altered. All references will be to book 5 of this edition according to chapter, section, and pagination of the edition.

[159] 1, 1; 397b: "... per bestiam enim Ecclesiam Romanam intelligunt, et per mulierem; ibi enim, capite 17, v. 3, legitur bestia fuisse coccinea, ibidem etiam legitur, v. 4, quod mulier induta sit *coccino, et purpura, et inaurata auro, et lapide pretioso, et margaritis, habens poculum aureum in manu*, et haec dicunt convenire domino papae, qui est caput Romanae Ecclesiae. Eodem etiam capite dicitur mulier ebria de sanguine sanctorum, quod Ecclesiae Romanae adscribunt propter hoc quia occidi eos iubet: se enim sanctos credunt." Scriptural text: Apoc. 17:4.

[160] See ibid., cc. 1-2; 397a-401a, for this long argumentation, which begins (397a): "Solutio ad ista facilis est si discutiatur littera Apocalypsis. Dico ergo quod haereticus infelix primo in hoc erravit quod idem intellexit per bestiam et mulierem: hoc enim esse non potest: primo, quia dicitur quod mulier sedebat super bestiam; ergo aliud est mulier quam bestia."

must be intermediary for the remission of the sins of their leader, Valdes. This, he concludes, shows that the pope is the heir of the primitive Church.[161]

Was it licit for Valdes to leave the Roman Church in order to restore the Church that in his opinion was destroyed at the time of Pope Silvester? If this were so, Moneta replies, others could do the same, and where would be the unity of the Church?[162] Perhaps there would be one Church in general, they suggest, but several particular Churches.[163] Moneta replies that in that case Valdes and the others would be supreme pontiff of the Church, and then in the one Church there would be many supreme pontiffs, which would be evidently unfitting.[164]

One whole section of book 5, chapter 2, is concerned with the beginning of the Church from Christ through Peter and its continuance through the successors of Peter. The Cathars, Moneta says, deny this beginning and succession, holding among other things that the Church began with Constantine or Silvester, and that Peter was never in Rome.[165] To the first of these arguments Moneta replies that although Silvester received certain powers from Constantine, his spiritual power of binding and loosing came to him from elsewhere.[166] As for the charge that Peter was not in Rome, Moneta appeals to the first letter of Peter, which speaks of his being in Babylon, which signifies Rome.[167]

---

[161] 1, 4; 402b: "Item, Act. 10 habetur quod Cornelio dimissa sunt peccata a Deo, sed per interpretem personam, scilicet Petrum quo, loquente verba Dei in domo Cornelii, cecidit Spiritus Sanctus super omnes qui audiebant verbum. Igitur, si remissa sunt peccata Valdesio a Deo, per aliquem ministrum sunt ei remissa, sed per quem nisi per papam non est ostendere. Ergo papa cum suis haeres est primitivae Ecclesiae."

[162] 1, 5; 408a: "Item, si licitum fuit Valdesio exire de Romana Ecclesia ut restitueret Ecclesiam secundum suam falsam opinionem in Silvestro destructam, quare non alii in alia provincia tunc temporis? Et iterum, quare non tertio adhuc in tertia provincia vel regno; quare etiam non aliis pluribus? Sic autem tot possunt esse Ecclesiae designari quot regna vel provinciae. Quomodo autem stabit illud Canticorum 6, v. 8: *Una est columba mea?*"

[163] Ibid.: "Forte dicet quod una esset columba, id est, Ecclesia in genere, licet plures particulares."

[164] Ibid.: "Contra: Nonne etiam Valdesius fuit Summus Pontifex secundum eos: utique loco Silvestri? Sed eadem ratione quilibet aliorum restituentium Ecclesiam, ex dictis, esset summus pontifex. Sic igitur in una Ecclesia essent multi pontifices summi, quod inconveniens esse patet, quia nec in Veteri Testamento tale quid invenitur; inde etiam plura inconvenientia sequerentur."

[165] For the first argument see 2, 1 (409b); for the second see 2, 1 (411a).

[166] 2, 1; 410a: "Solutio: Dico quod Silvester potestatem spiritualem, ligandi scilicet et solvendi, non habuit a Constantino nec illa potestate pontificali successit ei, licet illa quae tu dixisti ab illo habuerit, et imperii saecularis honorificentiam in Italia et occidentalium regionum provinciis, ut habetur in privilegio Ecclesiae in Decretis ...."

[167] 2, 1; 411a: "Praeterea, mirum est quod auses es dicere Petrum non fuisse Romae cum dicat Petrus in fine primae [tertiae *ed.*] epistolae, v. 13 (5:13): *Salutat vos Ecclesia quae est in Babylone collecta* [coelecta *Vulg.*]. Per Babylonem Romam significari videtur. Numquid non dicitur de hac Babylone, Apoc. 17, v. 18: *Quod* [quae *Vulg.*] *habet regnum super reges terrae*: non est autem dubium quod Romae tunc conveniebat potius."

Finally, Moneta cites the text of Matthew 16:18 in at least two different places. In the first it is used by the heretics to oppose Moneta's assertion that the Church began from Abel. In the text, they argue, Jesus says that he *will* build his Church, so that "if it was to be built, therefore it did not yet exist."[168] Moneta replies that the Church was to be built on Peter's confession or on his faith that Christ was the Son of the living God, but it was already built before Christ's becoming man on the confession that Christ was to be and was to be born of the Virgin.[169]

It should be noted that Moneta interprets the rock not of Peter but of the confession of faith about Christ. When the text recurs later, Moneta stresses the added part, "and the gates of hell shall not prevail against it," since he is arguing here that the Church of Christ, once established, will never fail. In the same context he quotes another Petrine text, Luke 22:32, and concludes: "... therefore neither his faith nor the Church fails."[170]

From Moneta's very thorough examination of the positions of the Cathars and Waldensians it can be seen that toward the middle of the thirteenth century, at least, the pope and the Petrine succession of the pope were issues of controversy. This may have been the case earlier, although we have found little evidence of it. If it was not an issue earlier, we may ask other disciplines why the pope became a more central focus of attention only towards the middle decades of the thirteenth century. We have already seen that among the school theologians a similar pattern of greatly increased interest in the papacy emerged at roughly the same time.[171] The other disciplines may help to understand this parallel development.

2.2. A Theologian Become Bishop: Robert Grosseteste (ca. 1175-1253; Bishop of Lincoln, 1235).

Robert Grosseteste, the former master of theology become bishop of Lincoln, has been described by William Abel Pantin as "probably the most

---

[168] 2, 1: 409a: "Ad idem etiam inducunt illud Matt. 16, v. 18, ubi Christus ait Petro: *Super hanc petram aedificabo Ecclesiam meam.* Si aedificanda erat, ergo nondum erat."

[169] Ibid.: "Solutio: Aedificanda erat supra hanc confessionem sive fidem huius: *Tu es Christus filius Dei vivi* [Matt. 16:16]; aedificata [aedificat *ed.*] tamen erat, priusquam Christus homo esset factus de Virgine, super confessionem istam quod Christus esset futurus et nasciturus de Virgine."

[170] 2, 3; 415a: "Item, Matt. 16, v. 18, dicitur quod Christus ait Petro: *Super hanc petram aedificabo Ecclesiam meam, et portae inferi non praevalebunt adversus eam*; quod non esset si defecisset." The second text is found ibid.; 415b: "Item, Luc. 22, v. 32, dicit Christus Petro: *Ego autem rogavi pro te, ut non deficiat fides tua.* Ergo fides eius non defecit; ergo nec Ecclesia ...."

[171] See the preceding essay, "The School Theologians' Views of the Papacy, 1150-1250," especially section 3.

fervent and thoroughgoing papalist among medieval English writers." [172] That this statement is not exaggerated — and indeed that it might be extended beyond English writers — is evident from three long texts quoted by Pantin, one from 1236 shortly after Grosseteste had become bishop of Lincoln, one from 1239, and a third written to Pope Innocent IV at Lyons in 1250.

Echoing his scientific vision of the physical universe and his interest in the Pseudo-Dionysian hierarchies with their functions of purging, illuminating, and perfecting inferiors, Grosseteste speaks of the pope as the centre and source of all spiritual life in the universe. The sun purges darkness, he says: it lights up the world, and regulates other bodily movements. He then compares the pope to the sun as follows:

> ... So in the universe of the Church the supreme pontiff takes the place of the sun, by the excellent light of his teaching and good works purging the world from the darkness of error, and by a singular prerogative illuminating it unto the knowledge of truth, and by his disposition ordering, regulating and governing all the movements of actions in the universal Church. [173]

Further on in the same letter he leads into the theme of obedience to the Holy Roman Church by another reference to the pope as sun and, this time, to the cardinals as hinges of the Church:

> ... After the world's Creator and Redeemer and the heavenly court of the blessed spirits of angels and saints, the state, the beauty and order of the universal Church are due to its sun and its hinges, that is, to the supreme pontiff and his assistants, the cardinals. And so to the Holy Roman Church is due from all sons of the Church the most devout obedience, the most honoured reverence, the most fervent love, the most subject fear. [174]

---

[172] See his essay, "Grosseteste's Relations with the Papacy and the Crown," in *Robert Grosseteste: Scholar and Bishop*, ed. D. A. Callus (Oxford: Clarendon, 1955) pp. 178-215, and the whole volume for many aspects of Grosseteste's life and thought. The quoted statement is on p. 183.

[173] *Epist.* 36 (to Cardinal Gil [Egidius] de Torres); ed. H. R. Luard, *Roberti Grosseteste ... epistolae*, Rerum Britannicarum medii aevi scriptores 25 (London, 1861) p. 126: "... Sicut in mundo visibili sol iste conspicuus suo praeeminente lumine mundi tenebras purgat, singulariterque mundum illustrat, motuque suo ordinatissimo, ut opinantur mundi sapientes, caeteros motus corporales naturales ordinat et regulat; sic in orbe ecclesiae summus pontifex vicem solis obtinet praecellenti luce doctrinae et eximiorum operum, mundum purgans errorum tenebris, ad veritatis cognitionem singulari praerogativa eundem illuminans, omnes etiam motus actionum in universali ecclesia sua dispositione ordinans, regulans, et gubernans." The English translations are from Pantin, but with some changes in punctuation; this text is in Pantin, p. 184.

[174] Luard, ibid.: "... Post mundi Conditorem et Redemptorem, curiamque caelestem ex spiritibus beatis angelorum et sanctorum adunatam; status, decor, et ordo universalis ecclesiae debet se suo soli, suis cardinibus; hoc est, summo pontifici sibique assistentibus cardinalibus; ideoque sanctae Romanae ecclesiae debetur ab universis ecclesiae filiis devotissima obedientia,

As the lower orders in the heavenly hierarchy receive from the higher, he continues, so in the ecclesiastical hierarchy those who rank below the pope receive "from the supreme pontiff and the cardinals closely attending him the light of the teaching of the faith and the guidance (*moderamen*) by which they ought to live in the house of God ...."[175]

This letter, addressed to a cardinal, is interesting for the link it makes between the high prerogatives of the pope and the body of cardinals in the Roman Church as sources of such direction and guidance. Something of this has been seen in twelfth century authors, who saw in the whole Church of Rome and not only in the person of the individual pope the repository of the promises made to Peter.

In the second letter, which is really a long treatise written by Grosseteste to establish his authority and rights more firmly in relation to the dean and chapter of Lincoln, he again exalts the pope, this time to associate the bishop with him:

> ... The Lord Pope ... has the fullness of power *over the nations and over kingdoms, to root up and to pull down, and to waste and to destroy, and to build and plant.* ... But because, for the multitude of his subjects, he cannot by himself do in act what he nevertheless can do in power, namely bear the burden of all and sundry, there are chosen to share in his solicitude the prelates of churches, namely the bishops, so that drawing on the fullness of his power, they may help him to bear his burden ....[176]

Using a philosophical principle about influencing and being influenced, Grosseteste clearly delineates the difference between episcopal and papal power. There are reserved to the pope

honoratissima reverentia, ferventissimus amor, subjectissimus timor ...." Translation from Pantin, p. 184, slightly altered.

[175] Luard, p. 127: "... sic et in hierarchia ecclesiastica, qui sacri principatus ordinem et universalis ecclesiae unitatem non deserunt, quo sublimiores sunt in dignitatis ecclesiasticae gradibus, eo a summo Pontifice sibique conjunctissime assistentibus cardinalibus lumen doctrinae fidei et moderamen, quo oportet et decet in domo Dei conversari, suscipientes ...." Translation from Pantin, p. 185. Grosseteste's remarks about the role of the cardinals may be compared with the findings of Norman Zacour in his study in the present volume, "The Cardinals' View of the Papacy, 1150-1300," pp. 413-438.

[176] *Epist.* 127 (to the Dean and Chapter of Lincoln); Luard, p. 364: "... Dominus Papa ... plenitudinem habet potestatis *super gentes et super regna; ut evellat et destruat et disperdat et dissipet et aedificet et plantet.* ... Sed quia prae multitudine subditorum solus non potest per actum, quod tamen potest per potestatem, onus universorum et singulorum sustinere, assumpti sunt in parte suae sollicitudinis ecclesiarum praelati, videlicet, episcopi, ut participantes de suae potestatis plenitudine secum sustentent onus suum ...." The scriptural text is Jer. 1:10. Translation from Pantin, p. 185.

For the kind of opposition Grosseteste was encountering, see Frank A. C. Mantello, "Bishop Robert Grosseteste and His Cathedral Chapter: An Edition of the Chapter's Objections to Episcopal Visitation," *MedS* 47 (1985) 367-378.

certain greater things, which he alone can do, and which no bishop can by
the episcopal power derived from the apostolic power. For the order of reason
and nature demands that the influencing power (*virtus influens*) should be
able to do more than the recipient of influence (*recipiens de influentia*) and
that which has power only by reason of what it receives from influence.[177]

Grosseteste concludes this remark by again comparing the pope to the sun
and other bishops to the moon and stars. "... The lord pope shows his
presence, in respect of whom all other prelates are like the moon and stars,
receiving from him whatever power they have for the illumination and
nourishment of the Church."[178]

What is remarkable in all these texts is that Grosseteste sees all episcopal
power as deriving from papal power and having its existence and rights only
by participation in that power. His reliance on the hierarchical model and on
his example of the physical universe leads him to neglect aspects of the gospel
teaching about the role of the Twelve or about the historical development of
patriarchal sees that would lead others to a less monolithic view of episcopal
authority.

In his written memorandum presented to Pope Innocent IV and several
cardinals at Lyons on 13 May 1250, Grosseteste again uses the imagery of
the sun and its roles of illumining, giving life, etc., and concludes: "... So this
most Holy See ought to have all these things, spiritually understood, within
itself causally, and ought to cause all these things to flow unceasingly into that
whole spiritual world of which it is the spiritual sun, and so save that spiritual
world."[179]

---

[177] Ibid.: "... reservatis sibi [papae] quibusdam majoribus, quae potest ipse solus, et quae
de potestate episcopali derivata a potestate apostolica nullus potest episcopus. Hoc enim exigit
ordo rationis et naturae, ut virtus influens plus possit quam recipiens de influentia et potens
solum ex eo quod ab influentia recepit ...." Translation from Pantin, p. 185.

[178] Ibid.; Luard, p. 390: "Ita dominus Papa, respectu cujus omnes alii praelati sunt sicut
luna et stellae, suscipientes ab ipso quicquid habent potestatis ad illuminationem et vegetationem ecclesiae, suam exhibet praesentiam." Translation from Pantin, p. 186, slightly altered.

[179] *Memorandum*; ed. Servus Gieben on pp. 350-369 of his "Robert Grosseteste at the
Papal Curia, Lyons 1250, Edition of the Documents," *Collectanea franciscana* 41 (1971)
340-393. This text is from no. 25 of the edition (pp. 361-362): "Haec sedes sacratissima
tronus Dei est et sicut sol mundi totius in conspectu eius. Unde sicut causaliter est in sole tota
huius mundi illuminatio, vegetatio et vitae sensibilis nutritio, augmentatio, consummatio,
conservatio, pulchritudo, decor et venustas, et ipse haec omnia in hunc mundum sensibilem
semper influit et sic efficit et conservat hunc mundum sensibilem perfectum, sic oportet hanc
sedem sacratissimam haec omnia spiritualiter intellecta in se causaliter habere et in mundum
spiritualem universum, cuius est sol spiritualis, eadem omnia incessanter influere et sic
mundum spiritualem salvare."

On this memorandum see Pantin, pp. 209-215, Gieben, pp. 340-343, and R. W. Southern,
Robert Grosseteste: The Growth of an English Mind in Medieval Europe (Oxford: Clarendon,

While exalting the pope with lofty titles, Grosseteste gently but firmly, in the manner of Bernard, admonishes the pope that his high position makes demands on him:

> ... But the names of immaterial things by which, in all expressions of praise, your eminence is signified most plainly and fully, are "angel" and "god." ... You are the angel of angels and the god of gods; you cannot be named in a more excellent way. Lest therefore your naming be empty and in vain, you among all mortals must needs be most highly assimilated and conformed to the angels and to God, so that there may not appear to be or actually be anything in you except what is angelic and divine, and that you may be the light and sun of the world, shining most clearly without any darkness or remission of light or of vital heat, nourishing and giving life to the world ....[180]

In the document given to the pope and cardinals at Lyons the bishop of Lincoln deduces an important conclusion from the lofty position he assigns to the pope:

> Those who preside in this Holy See are most principally among mortals clothed with the person of Christ, and therefore it is necessary that in them especially the works of Christ should exist and should shine and that there should be nothing contrary to Christ's work in them. And for the same reason, just as the Lord Jesus Christ must be obeyed in all things, so also those who preside in this Holy See, in so far as they are clothed with Christ and as such are truly presiding, must be obeyed in all things. But if any of them (which God forbid) should put on in addition the clothing of kinship and the flesh or of the world or of anything else except that of Christ, and for love

---

1986), ch. 11 (pp. 272-295), who discusses the document in the whole context of Grosseteste's relations with the pope and curia.

A much earlier and uncritical edition of the text is called a *sermo* (which it was not) by its editor, Edward Brown, *Sermo Roberti Lincolniensis Episcopi, propositus coram Papa et Cardinalibus in Consilio Lugdunensi, cum quadam Epistola,* edited in his *Appendix ad Fasciculum rerum expetendarum et fugiendarum, ab Orthuino Gratio editum Coloniae A.D. MDXXV sive tomus secundus* (London, 1690) 2: 250-257; this text is from 2: 254. The translation, from Pantin, p. 188, is based on the text of Brown but needs no alteration in view of the new edition.

[180] Text edited from London, Br. Museum MS 7.E.II (= L), fol. 393va, and Oxford, Exeter College MS 21 (= E), fol. 132B: "... Immaterialium vero nomina quibus planissime et plenissime significatur vestra in omnibus laudibus eminentia sunt 'angelus' et 'deus'. ... Vos estis angelus angelorum et deus deorum; excellentius nominari non potestis. Ne ergo inanis et vacua sit vestra nominatio, necesse est quod summe inter mortales assimilemini et conformemini angelis et Deo, ut non videatur vel sit in vobis quicquam praeter angelicum et divinum, et sic sitis lux et sol mundi, clarissime lucens absque aliqua tenebrositate aut lucis remissione et calore vitali [*add.* irremissio L] mundum vegetans et vivificans ...." E has many obvious faults which have not been noted. The translation, based on Pantin (p. 187), has been altered in places.

of such things should command anything contrary to Christ's precepts and
will, anyone who obeys him in such things manifestly separates himself from
Christ and from His body which is the Church, and from the one presiding
in this see in so far as he is clothed with the person of Christ and to that extent
truly presiding.[181]

This, indeed, is the basis on which the bishop of Lincoln, who had so exalted
the papacy, finally came to reject Pope Innocent's "provision" or appointment of his own nephew to a canonry in Lincoln in 1253.[182] Here Grosseteste-
te's great zeal for the pastoral care of his flock comes to the fore:

... This would be evidently a falling off and corruption and abuse of its [the
Apostolic See's] most holy and plenary power .... No faithful subject of this
same See ... can admit to mandates, precepts or other demonstrations of this
kind coming from any quarter, no, not even if they came from the highest
order of angels. He must needs repudiate them and rebel against them with
all his strength.[183]

Grosseteste appeals to his need to obey in a higher way and so to disobey
in the present situation:

Because of the obedience by which I am bound to the Holy See, as to my
parents, and out of love of my union with the Holy See in the body of Christ,
... as an obedient son I disobey, I contradict, I rebel. ... The Apostolic See in
its holiness cannot destroy, it can only build. This is what the plenitude of
power means; it can do all things to edification. But these so called provisions
do not build up, they destroy. They cannot be the work of the Blessed
Apostolic See ....[184]

---

[181] *Memorandum*, 26; ed. Gieben, pp. 362-363: "Praesidentes huic sacrae sedi principa-
lissime inter mortales personam Christi induuntur et ideo oportet, quod in eis maxime sint
et relucent Christi opera et nulla sint in eis Christi operibus contraria; et propter idem, sicut
Domino Iesu Christo in omnibus est oboediendum, sic et praesidentibus huic sacrae sedi, in
quantum indutis Christum et in tantum vere praesidentibus, in omnibus est obtemperandum.
Si autem quis eorum − quod absit − superinduat amictum cognationis et carnis aut mundi aut
alicuius alterius praeterquam Christi et ex huiusmodi amore quicquam praecipiat Christi
praeceptis et voluntati contrarium, obtemperans ei in huiusmodi manifeste se separat a Christo
et a corpore ipsius, quod est Ecclesia, et a praesidente huic sedi in quantum induto personam
Christi et in tantum vere praesidente."
Pantin's translation (p. 189), based on Brown's edition, has been altered in several places.
[182] *Epist.* 128; Luard, pp. 432-437. On the letter and its teachings see Pantin, pp. 189-192.
[183] Luard, p. 436: "Hoc enim esset evidenter suae sanctissimae potestatis et plenissimae
vel defectio vel corruptio vel abusio .... Nec potest quis ... eidem sedi subditus et fidelis ...
hujusmodi mandatis vel praeceptis vel quibuscunque aliis conaminibus undecunque emananti-
bus, etiamsi a supremo Angelorum ordine eveniret, obtemperare; sed necesse habet totis
viribus totum contradicere et rebellare." Pantin's translation (pp. 189-190) has been slightly
changed to be a more literal rendering.
[184] Luard, pp. 436-437: "Propter hoc, reverendi domini, ego ex debito obedientiae et
fidelitatis, quo teneor, ut utrique parenti, Apostolicae sanctissimae sedi, et ex amore unionis

One can sense the bishop's hurt and pain throughout the whole letter. He who had so exalted the papacy finds that the person holding the office betrays the lofty role that is his; therefore, although reluctantly, he must refuse obedience to the pope. Obedience to the light and sun of the spiritual world was not required, indeed was to be refused, if that light and sun did not appear angelic and divine. In Grosseteste's reaction we see an application once again of the distinction between the person of the pope and the Church of Rome or the Apostolic See, a distinction maintained by several twelfth-century authors: error or defection is possible in the person of the pope, so that discernment is needed in obeying or not obeying his commands.[185]

3. SUMMARY AND CONCLUSION

Except for the influential writings of Hugh, the eminent theologian of the school of St. Victor, the theology of the papacy was most developed in the latter half of the twelfth century not by schoolmen but by monastic and episcopal authors; among the latter we have counted Pope Innocent III in the period just before and during the first year of his pontificate.

The monastic authors, Bernard of Clairvaux and Peter the Venerable, and the episcopal authors, Anselm of Havelberg and Gerhoh of Reichersberg, were primarily interested in reform of the Church, often at the local level, and they looked to the pope for aid where local authorities were at fault or were inadequate to meet the situation. Their theology often reflects the development of papal authority gained during the investiture struggles, including (especially for Bernard) the authority of the pope in relation to secular matters. Views of the Eastern Church about the papacy were reflected in the writings of Anselm of Havelberg based on his contacts with Orthodox theologians of the east.

---

in corpore Christi cum ea, ... filialiter et obedienter non obedio, contradico, et rebello. ... Apostolicae sedis sanctitas non potest nisi quae in aedificationem sunt, et non in destructionem; haec enim est potestatis plenitudo, omnia posse in aedificationem. Hae autem quas vocant provisiones, non sunt in aedificationem sed in manifestissimam destructionem; non igitur eas potest beata sedes Apostolica ...." Translation from Pantin, p. 190.

[185] Brian Tierney, in his article, "Grosseteste and the Theory of Papal Sovereignty," *Journal of Ecclesiastical History* 6 (1955) 1-17, examines the teaching of canonists on justified disobedience to papal commands. He shows that Grosseteste's position was in accord with this teaching, including that of the very pope he was resisting, for in his *Commentaria* Innocent IV held that one would sin by obeying an unjust command that would be strongly presumed to disturb the status of the Church (see p. 15). Grosseteste seems also to have applied a *theology* of legitimate disobedience to a command "contrary to Christ's precepts and will" (see the text in n. 181).

While reminding Pope Eugene III of his exalted state and imposing titles, Bernard urges him to use his authority in a religious, even prayerful way, as a ministry for the reform of the Church. The pope's lofty prerogatives are not for his own personal aggrandisement but impose upon him duties of prophetic challenge and witness to the whole Church, including bishops subject to his authority. Yet, for Bernard, the pope must be a steward rather than a lord, a brother to other bishops whose authority, he insists, comes not from the pope but from God. One of Bernard's most important concerns was purity of faith, and he stresses the pope's role as guardian of faith and arbiter of disputes in matters of doctrine.

Peter the Venerable presents the pope's role in relation to Christ and the Church, to the apostles (especially Peter, but also to Paul as teacher), and to the universal Church over which he presides as supreme or universal. The abbot asserts the pope's universal authority in order to claim him, against critics like Bernard, as bishop for the otherwise exempt Cluniac communities. At the same time, like Bernard, he admonishes the pope to exercise a ministry of solicitude for all the Churches, respecting diversities that are not inimical to the one faith.

While asserting the primacy of the pope in conversation with his Orthodox interlocutor, Anselm of Havelberg gives some account of the complaints of the Orthodox about the style in which the papacy was exercised and about what seemed to them exaggerated claims. Anselm does not dwell on the question of jurisdiction but rather insists on the role of the pope in guarding purity and unity of faith.

Gerhoh of Reichersberg presents a very lofty ideal of the papal prerogatives and duties because he is so concerned with seeking papal help to solve such problems as simony, abuse of clerical office, and above all matters of incorrect and even (in his view) heretical teachings. Yet he distinguishes between the person of the pope and the see of Peter, the former of which can err whereas the latter never will. This distinction is found in a number of authors in this period.

One who admits this possibility of papal error and even infidelity, although with evident reluctance, is Pope Innocent III as he began his years of papal rule. Christ's promise always to remain with the Church and his prayer that Peter's faith should not fail reassure him that this eventuality is rather unlikely, and strengthens Innocent's otherwise strong assertions of his role not only as friend of Christ, the bridegroom of the Church, but even as himself the bridegroom of the Church of Rome and also one charged with care for all the Churches; their bishops are subject to the pope and the Roman Church, which have the fullness of power. All this doctrine Innocent III expresses in an elaborate extension of the metaphor of Christ's marriage with his Church, pressing the metaphor for doctrinal applications that are hardly warranted by the metaphor itself.

Although the apologetic works of the twelfth century that have been examined show little evidence of need to defend the pope in particular (rather than prelates in general) against criticisms and attacks from heterodox groups, by the time in the thirteenth century that Moneta of Cremona wrote his thorough analysis of the heterodox movements he knew as inquisitor, the papacy had become a point of contention between members of these movements and Catholics. Moneta finds it necessary to reply to their identification of the pope with the scarlet woman of the *Apocalypse* and to their historical views about the development of the papacy, which for them invalidated the claims for the papacy made by the Catholic Church. This he does not so much by appeals to patristic or later tradition, but by arguments drawn from those scriptures relied upon by his opponents.

While the other authors surveyed in this study generally had an increasingly lofty idea of the pope's titles, authority, powers, and privileges, none of them, not even Innocent III, goes to the extremes that Robert Grosseteste does by applying his scientific analogies and Pseudo-Dionysian hierarchical categories to the relations of the pope with bishops and the rest of the Church. In his exaggerated view the bishops and all others with authority in the Church are in place simply to supply in practice for the universal and detailed exercise of power that belongs to the pope and that derives from him to them because he cannot in fact do everything. So lofty was Grosseteste's theological and religious ideal of the pope that he was inevitably disappointed with the reality he encountered and was forced into the position of refusing obedience to the pope actually existing, in the name of obedience to a mythically uncompromised and unsullied pope.

*
* *

The period from 1150 to 1250 saw a fairly constant assertion on the part of this type of author of the primacy and preeminent authority of pope, including his role as guardian of the faith and corrector of error. Except for Robert Grosseteste, those who speak about the relations of the pope with other bishops still assign an independent source of authority for bishops even if bishops are subordinate in the exercise of this authority to that of the pope. What is open to critical reflection in several of them is the dubious theological method they used in applying to the theology of the papacy their personal, idiosyncratic allegorical interpretations of scripture (e.g., Bernard about Peter walking on the water; Gerhoh about Jacob and Peter) or unwarranted detailed conclusions from metaphors (e.g., Innocent's deductions from the marriage metaphor or Grosseteste's elaborations of his scientific models). Undoubtedly they had their own ideas — and likely their personal, not always completely uninterested reasons — firmly in place for their conclusions about the papacy, and may have used these allegories and metaphorical details as rhetorical devices to persuade their readers or hearers of what they already held, but such allegories and metaphors have their force and influence in history (one thinks of another of Bernard's, the two swords), and can have the effect, as they seem to have had here, of bolstering theories in ways that are not always well balanced or complete.

The results of this and the previous study call for comparison with the contributions of other studies in this symposium as well as with the results of research in still other disciplines. The theologians, whether of the schools or of other backgrounds, never operated in a vacuum, so that much is to be learned from their various contexts even while the influence of their own theology is being assessed in relation to the religious ideal of the papacy.

4

Attitudes fondamentales de la théologie byzantine, en face du rôle religieux de la papauté au XIIème siècle

Jannis Spiteris

INTRODUCTION

Le XIIème siècle est celui qui, plus que tout autre, peut nous aider à comprendre les attitudes fondamentales de la théologie byzantine en face du rôle religieux de la papauté. En effet, après le sac de Constantinople par les Latins de la IVème croisade—1204—et les incroyables horreurs par eux commises, l'attitude des Grecs en face des Latins et de la papauté qui les représente, devient pathologiquement hostile.

Innocent III lui-même, écrivant à son légat Pietro di San Marcello, s'exprime ainsi:

> Comment peut-on faire pour ramener l'Église à l'unité et comment attendre d'elle qu'elle soit dévouée au Siège Apostolique après qu'il l'ait affligée et persécutée? Elle n'a vu dans les Latins que des exemples de malveillance et d'œuvres ténébreuses; à cause de cela, elle est en droit de les détester comme des chiens.[1]

Le XIIIème siècle donc, mais plus encore à cause de la tentative d'union du Concile de Lyon (7 Mai–17 Juillet 1274), est chargé de tensions et de

---

[1] *Epist.* VIII: *PL* 214: 126.

The Religious Roles of the Papacy: Ideals and Realities, 1150-1300, ed. Christopher Ryan, Papers in Mediaeval Studies 8 (Toronto: Pontifical Institute of Mediaeval Studies, 1989), pp. 171-192. © P.I.M.S., 1989.

ressentiments qui empêchent les Byzantins d'affronter le problème de la papauté avec plus de sérénité. Ce n'est pas par simple hasard qu'apparaissent au XIIIème siècle les pamphlets anti-latins et anti-papauté les plus féroces.[2] On dit tout bonnement dans un opuscule anti-Latin du XIIIème siècle que le Pape "non seulement n'est pas un pasteur, mais encore est une simple brebis et une brebis galeuse qui a besoin de soin, puisqu'il est pire que toutes les autres têtes du troupeau, et il faut que les autres s'éloignent de lui pour ne pas être infectés."[3]

ÉLÉMENTS HISTORIQUES DÉTERMINANTS

Des faits historiques contingents, des intérêts politiques inspirés d'idéologies dans lesquelles les frontières entre politique et religion se confondent, ont contribué, en cette période, à faire prendre conscience aux Byzantins des exigences du primat romain et, par conséquent, à les laisser déterminer leurs attitudes. Voyons brièvement ces éléments déterminants.

Durant le XIIème siècle, et plus précisément dans la seconde moitié, les idées réformatrices de Grégoire VII trouvent leur application maximale. Il suffit de penser au *Décret* de Gratien promulgué vers 1140, dans lequel les idées centralisatrices et hiérocratiques de Grégoire trouvent leur apothéose.

Le représentant le plus éminent de ces idées est Innocent III, qui, dans son échange de lettres avec le Patriarche Jean Camateros dans les années 1199-1200, aura l'occasion de les bien faire connaître aux Grecs.[4]

Ce développement de l'ecclésiologie romaine centralisée à l'extrême, sera porté à la connaissance des Byzantins par divers facteurs, avant tout par les croisades, qui laisseront une très mauvaise impression aux Byzantins.[5] Elles représenteront toutefois une occasion déterminante pour mettre en contact les deux peuples et les amener à une connaissance mutuelle. Ainsi les Grecs connaîtront en théorie et en pratique l'ecclésiologie latine avec la place que la papauté y occupe.[6]

---

[2] Cf. V. Laurent - J. Darrouzès, *Dossier grec de l'union de Lyon* (Paris, 1976), pp. 45-52.

[3] Texte de K. Diobouniotis, Ἐπετηρὶς Ἑταιρίας Βυζαντινῶν Σπουδῶν 15 (1939) 43. Cet opuscule a été pendant longtemps faussement attribué au patriarche Michel d'Anchialos, mort vers 1179. Il s'agit en réalité d'un texte du XIIIème siècle, en forme de dialogue. Cf. J. Darrouzès, "Les documents byzantins du XIIe siècle sur la primauté romaine," *Revue des Études Byzantines* 23 (1965) 79-82.

[4] Cf. J. Spiteris, *La critica bizantina del Primato Romano nel secolo XII* (Rome, 1979), pp. 255-261.

[5] Voir, par exemple, les impressions de Théophilacte de Bulgarie: *Ep.* XI: *PG* 126: 324, et d'Anne Comnène, *Alexiade*, X, 5: ed. B. Leib, *Anne Comnène: Alexiade, Règne de l'empereur Alexis I Comnène 1081-1118*, 3 vols (Paris, 1937-1945), 2: 232-233.

[6] Cf. L. Lamma, *Comeni e Staufer: Ricerche fra Bisanzio e l'Occidente nel secolo XII* (Rome, 1955), 1: 19-30; A. Beyer, "Cultural Relations between East and West in the Twelfth

Les ambassades fréquentes qui viennent de l'Occident, presque toujours composées de prélats ecclésiastiques, pour traiter d'alliances politiques entre les empereurs d'Orient et les empereurs germaniques, seront aussi l'occasion prochaine de discussions autour du problème de la réunification des deux Églises. En ces circonstances, les ambassadeurs-théologiens latins ne manqueront pas de faire connaître à leurs partenaires grecs le développement de l'ecclésiologie traditionnelle latine.

Un autre fait historique qui détermine l'attitude des Byzantins vis-à-vis de la papauté, est la politique des Comnène. Ceux-ci s'employèrent par tous les moyens à restaurer l'antique empire de Justinien, comprenant tant l'Orient que l'Occident sous l'unique couronne du Basileus de Constantinople. Les Comnène, spécialement Emmanuel, comprennent que pour réaliser ce rêve d'hégémonie ils ont besoin du pape.[7] Ce rêve hégémonique des Comnène fait se déchaîner d'une façon nouvelle et plus aiguë la polémique des deux empires. Dans la conscience des Byzantins est toujours vive la persuasion que l'empire est unique et que le véritable héritier est le basileus. L'empereur germanique non seulement est un usurpateur, mais encore attente à l'unité de l'Église. Le Pape, créateur et soutien de cette "scission" de l'empire, se trouve, par là même, disqualifié sur le plan religieux aux yeux des Byzantins.[8] De fait, pendant cette période, l'idéologie politique dicte dans une large mesure le comportement religieux des Byzantins. Nous sommes en plein dans l'atmosphère typiquement médiévale de la "société chrétienne" ou de la "chrétienté," dans laquelle réalité politique et réalité religieuse se présentent comme deux faces d'une même médaille.[9]

Critères idéologiques des deux Églises pour mesurer le rôle religieux de la papauté

Il n'est pas possible de parler du rôle religieux de la papauté si on ne détermine d'abord les critères idéologiques et théologiques qui inspirent les

---

Century," dans *Relations Between East and West in the Middle Ages*, par les soins de D. Baker (Edinburgh, 1973), pp. 77-94.

[7] Pour une vision d'ensemble sur la politique occidentale de Manuel Comnène, voir H. von Kap-Herr, *Die abendländische Politik Kaiser Manuels mit besonderer Rucksicht auf Deutschland* (Strassburg, 1881); F. Chalandon, *Les Comnène: Études sur l'Empire byzantin au XIᵉ et au XIIᵉ siècle* (Paris, 1912; New York, 1960), 2: 556-653.

[8] Voir p.ex., le chapitre VII du livre V de l'*Epitome* de l'historien byzantin Jean Cinname, ed. A. Meineke (Bonn, 1836), 218-220.

[9] Voir à ce sujet L. Prosdomici, "Per la storia della cristianità medioevale," dans *Le istituzioni ecclesiastiche della "Societas Christiana" nei secoli XI-XII. Papato, Cardinalato, Episcopato*, Atti della Settimana internazionale di Studio, Mendola 26-31 maggio 1971 (Milano, 1974), pp. 13-18.

deux traditions pendant cette période et sur la base desquels on juge et mesure ce rôle. Nous avons un exemple typique, révélateur de ces deux mentalités, dans les "Dialogues" d'Anselme, archevêque d'Havelberg, avec l'archevêque grec Nicétas de Nicomédie, qui eurent lieu à Constantinople en 1136. Ces Dialogues, qui nous ont été transmis en latin par Anselme lui-même, ont été composés en 1148.[10]

Anselme est un des meilleurs représentants des réformateurs de son époque. De son côté, Nicétas appartenait à cette élite de Constantinople, qui reflétait les idées et les sentiments officiels. De fait, il était le premier des professeurs de droit à l'université de la capitale. La différence avec laquelle on conçoit le rôle religieux de la papauté dépend de la vision ecclésiologique différente des deux traditions et de la place différente accordée à l'autorité impériale par les deux peuples.

Les idées d'Anselme

A. Anselme conçoit le rapport Église grecque - Église romaine en termes de pure obéissance. Il répète avec une insistance obstinée que l'Église grecque doit *obéir* à l'Église romaine, doit accepter les usages romains parce que l'Église de Rome

> a obtenu pour Dieu et de Dieu et en premier lieu après Dieu, le primat d'autorité sur l'Église entière qui est répandue dans l'univers.[11]

Et ceci, non à cause des décisions conciliaires, mais à cause de Pierre vivant dans ses successeurs.[12]

B. L'ordre hiérarchique dans l'Église est conçu par Anselme comme une monarchie stricte et absolue. Ce qui se décide dans le Concile, dit-il, c'est l'œuvre du Pape et non des pères conciliaires avec le Pape. Il ne faut pas attribuer aux membres ce qui appartient à la tête.[13].

De fait la tête de l'Église, comme Vicaire du Christ, c'est le Pape. Ici se manifeste l'ecclésiologie typique basée sur la thèse, devenue commune au XIIème siècle, du "Christo capite" (du Christ tête) et de la "gratia capitis" (de la grâce de la tête), comme principe et raison de la vie surnaturelle des membres. La carence de pneumatologie de la théologie occidentale empêche de saisir la fonction de l'Esprit comme principe et trame de l'unité ecclésiale entre la tête et les membres, fonction attribuée par contre à la "gratia capitis"

---

[10] Cf. *PL* 188: 1210-1245.

[11] *PL* 188: 1213D; cf. aussi 1211D et 1217B.

[12] Le "principe de Pierre" du primat est affirmé sur la base d'un texte du Pseudo-Isidore. Voir *PL* 188: 1213D-1215AB.

[13] *PL* 188: 1226B.

comme grâce de l'humanité du Christ à la place de la promotion de la part de l'Esprit.[14]

Nous assistons ici à un processus de réduction typique des réformateurs. Tout, dans l'ordre de la grâce, arrive aux membres à partir du Christ. Son Vicaire sur terre est le Pape; donc tout dans l'Église, dans l'ordre juridique, dérive de lui. Comme sommet de l'Église, la tête concentre en elle tout le corps, l'Église catholique s'identifie avec l'Église romaine, et celle-ci avec le Pape.[15]

C. La conséquence la plus immédiate de cette ecclésiologie à forte concentration christologique, est que Pierre et le pape, son successeur, sont élevés au-dessus, et donc en-dehors du collège apostolique et du collège épiscopal.[16]

D. La signification religieuse de la papauté est présentée ainsi aux Grecs par les réformateurs romains en termes de pure "puissance," de "juridiction." C'est l'exaltation de la puissance de Pierre (et du Pape) posée comme absolue, et équivalente, en quelque sorte, à la puissance divine même.[17] C'est, au fond, la signification de la formule "vicarius Christi" référée au Pape, et qu'Anselme emploie souvent dans sa discussion avec Nicétas de Nicomédie. Il faut remarquer que, pour les Grecs, le "Vicarius Christi" était l'empereur seul.[18]

E. Le critère de l'unité pour Anselme ne sera pas la vérité révélée en elle-même, mais en tant qu'enseignée par l'Église romaine. De là dérive la nécessité absolue d'obéir à cette Église, de la part de tous ceux "qui ... désirent être sauvés." En effet, "celui qui est en désaccord avec l'Église romaine manifeste sans aucun doute qu'il est hérétique."[19]

---

[14] Cf. Y. Congar, *L'Église de Saint Augustin à l'époque moderne* (Paris, 1970), pp. 161-164.

[15] Sur ce sujet cf. G. B. Ladner, "The concepts of 'ecclesia' and 'christianitas' and their relation to the idea of papal 'plenitudo potestatis' from Gregory VII to Boniface VIII," dans *Sacerdozio e regno da Gregorio VII a Bonifacio VIII*, Miscellanea Historiae Pontificiae, 18 (Roma, 1954), pp. 42-77.

[16] Ainsi s'exprime Anselme: "Quocirca nulli fidelium convenit aliquatenus dubitare, seu in questione ponere, sed firmissime tenere, quod Petrus a Domino princeps apostolorum sit constitutus. Quemadmodum autem solus Romanus pontifex vice Petri vicem gerit Christi, ita sane caeteri episcopi vicem gerunt apostolorum sub Christo, et vice Christi sub Petro et vice Petri sub pontifice Romano et ejus Vicario": *Dial.*, Lib. III, chap. x: *PL* 188: 1223A.

[17] M. Maccarone, "La teologia del primato romano del secolo XI," dans *Le istituzioni ecclesiastiche della "Societas Christiana" dei secoli XI-XII*, p. 45.

[18] Sur le développement de ce titre et sur ses implications voir M. Maccarone, *Vicarius Christi: Storia del titolo papale* (Rome, 1952).

[19] *PL* 188: 1226A.

Tels étaient, dans leurs grandes lignes, les principes d'interprétation de la signification religieuse de la papauté chez les Latins, imposés aux Grecs sans que ceux-ci eussent derrière eux le développement des siècles d'élaboration théologique sur lesquels se fondaient les réformateurs romains. Ces mêmes concepts, et même plus radicalisés, seront présentés au patriarche Jean Camateros par le pape Innocent III en 1199-1200.[20]

Il est évident qu'une telle vision religieuse de la papauté posait d'énormes difficultés pour être acceptée par les Grecs, dont les présupposés ecclésiologiques étaient absolument contraires.

Les idées de Nicétas

A. Pour Nicétas, en effet, il existe une incompatibilité absolue entre le mode romain de concevoir le primat et la possibilité de sauver l'autonomie des évêques et du concile—en terminologie moderne—une incompatibilité entre la papauté et la collégialité. Les Grecs voient dans la papauté une institution qui absorbe en elle-même tous les autres évêques avec leur mission d'enseigner, de prêcher et de guider le troupeau confié à eux; si ce qu'affirme Anselme était vrai,

> Seul le pape serait évêque, lui seul serait maître, lui seul serait précepteur, seul, comme l'unique bon pasteur, il répondrait uniquement devant Dieu des brebis qui seraient confiées à lui seul.[21]

Cette hypertrophie de la signification religieuse de la Papauté est contraire, selon Nicétas, soit à l'ecclésiologie byzantine, soit à l'orgueilleuse conscience éthique et intellectuelle que les Grecs avaient d'eux-mêmes. Si le pape décide par lui seul et impose ses décisions aussi à l'Église orientale, affirme l'évêque de Nicomédie:

> Alors on pourra sûrement affirmer que nous sommes esclaves et non fils de l'Église et nous le serions en effet. S'il était nécessaire d'agir ainsi et d'imposer sur nos épaules un tel poids, la conclusion serait que seule l'Église romaine serait libre, et que seule elle établirait des lois valides pour toutes les autres

---

[20] Cf. J. Spiteris, pp. 255-261.

[21] *PL* 188: 1219. Nicétas n'avait pas tort de voir dans le pape le péril d'un sur-évêque. De fait, saint Bernard voyait dans l'évêque de Rome l'"Orbis episcopus," cf. *Ep.* 240: *PL* 182: 432B. Il faut noter ici, cependant, qu'en réalité la réforme n'avait pas l'intention de mortifier la fonction épiscopale, mais visait plutôt à une "restauration" ecclésiologique pivotant sur le rétablissement de l'immunité épiscopale. Voir à ce sujet O. Capitani, *Immunità vescovili ed ecclesiologia in età "pregregoriana" e "gregoriana": L'avvio alla "restaurazione"* (Spoleto, 1966). Grégoire VII, même, considérait les évêques comme "vicaires du Christ" et ses "frères" avec lesquels il voulait réformer l'Église. Voir I. Melemberg, *Der Primat der römischen Kirchen und Handeln Gregors VII* (S. Gravenhage, 1965), pp. 53-79.

Églises, pendant qu'elle-même serait sans loi. En ce cas elle semblerait, et serait en réalité, non une mère aimante pour ses fils, mais une maîtresse d'esclaves, dure et impérieuse. Alors à quoi nous servirait notre science des Écritures; à quoi servirait la formation doctrinale de nos maîtres, à quoi serviraient les nobles génies et les sages grecs?[22]

B. Nicétas, comme du reste tous les autres personnages de cette période, est disposé à reconnaître dans la papauté un aspect religieux. On reconnaît à Rome un droit d'appel de la part des autres Églises:

> Je ne nie pas la primauté de l'Église romaine [affirme Nicétas]. En effet, parmi les sièges patriarcaux Rome, le plus éminent des sièges de l'empire, obtient la primauté; et on faisait appel à lui pour les causes douteuses et pour les autres causes. On se soumettait à son jugement pour tous les cas non-prévus par des lois certaines.[23]

Mais il s'agit ici d'une primauté "à la grecque":

> Nous ne nions pas la primauté de l'Église romaine dans un système d'Églises-sœurs, et nous la reconnaissons comme première en l'honneur à l'occasion des conciles œcuméniques où elle préside.[24]

Par ce texte nous pouvons comprendre la nature de cette primauté que les Grecs étaient disposés à concéder à Rome. Il s'agit d'une primauté d'honneur dans le contexte d'"Églises-sœurs," donc entre Églises égales en tout et unies entre elles par des liens de communion et non de dépendance. De là le refus de reconnaître au pape des titres comme ceux de "Princeps sacerdotum," "Summus sacerdos."[25]

Cependant (et ici se trouve la plus grande différence entre les deux Églises pour l'interprétation exacte du rôle de la papauté), Nicétas ne nourrit pas le moindre doute que cette primauté a une origine impériale. C'est l'empereur Phocas qui décréta que le siège de Rome est la tête de toutes les Églises.[26] Le principe politique a supplanté celui de Pierre dans la conscience des Byzantins. C'est pour ce motif que la primauté ne peut être stable, mais est sujette aux déplacements de la capitale impériale et à la fidélité de l'Église romaine à l'empire. Nicétas annonce avec force le principe de la "translatio imperii" et en tire les conséquences:

> Après que, par volonté divine, l'empire ait été transféré en cette cité impériale, à cause de la dignité de l'empire, Constantinople est devenue tête de l'Orient

---

[22] *PL* 188: 1218.
[23] *PL* 188: 1217D.
[24] Ibid.
[25] *PL* 188: 1218A.
[26] *PL* 188: 1217A.

et Nouvelle Rome; en conséquence elle peut traiter des raisons ecclésiastiques et les résoudre de sa propre autorité.[27]

Rome, du reste, a perdu toute trace même de sa primauté d'honneur à cause de son infidélité à l'empire,

> quand, sortant de sa compétence, elle attaqua la monarchie, en divisant l'empire (avec la concession de la dignité impériale à Charles) et a séparé les évêques et l'Église occidentale de l'Église orientale.[28]

Les Églises sont divisées parce que l'Empire est divisé; et la responsabilité est entièrement celle du pape, qui a trahi en couronnant Charlemagne.[29] Ici Nicétas touche un des problèmes les plus caractéristiques de l'idéologie médiévale byzantine: le problème de l'unité et de l'universalité de l'empire et de l'empereur, représentant unique du Dieu unique. À Byzance, bien que le principe de l'apostolicité ne soit pas inconnu (au concile de Lyon les unionistes n'ont aucune difficulté à le reconnaître), c'est un fait établi que l'idéologie officielle ne connaît qu'une seule source de l'autorité juridique: l'impériale. En conséquence l'Église, pour ce qui regarde son organisation et son activité juridictionnelle, dépendra du pouvoir absolu de l'empereur.[30]

Anselme comprend qu'une telle conception de l'empire détruit à la base la signification religieuse de la papauté comme elle était conçue par les réformateurs, c'est-à-dire comme "Fons et Origo" du droit, directement pour l'Église et indirectement pour la légitimation de l'empire. La réaction est immédiate et violente. Admettre un autre chef dans l'unique corps du peuple chrétien, constitué d'une manière indivisible de l'Église et de la société civile, signifie créer un monstre à deux têtes: l'empereur et le pape. Cela signifie tomber dans un dualisme manichéen. Cela signifie que le successeur de Pierre n'est plus le pape, mais l'empereur.[31] En somme, aux yeux des Latins, le plus grand péril pour la signification religieuse de la papauté est constitué par les prétentions universalistes des basileus de Byzance.

Comme conclusion de cette première partie à caractère général, nous pouvons dire que l'attitude fondamentale des Grecs du XIIème siècle, en ce qui

---

[27] *PL* 188: 1219A.

[28] Ibid.

[29] *PL* 188: 1231A.

[30] Voir, pour les siècles précédents, les conclusions de l'étude de M. Magi, *La sede romana nella corrispondenza degli imperatori e patriarchi bizantini* (Rome-Louvain, 1972), pp. 282-286. Voir aussi Y. Congar, *L'Ecclésiologie du haut Moyen Âge: De Saint Grégoire le Grand à la désunion entre Byzance et Rome* (Paris, 1968), pp. 344-357. Pour une vue générale de ce problème, cf. A. Michel, "Der Kampf um das politische oder petrinische Princip der Kirchenführung," dans *Das Konzil von Chalkedon; Geschichte und Gegenwart*, par les soins d'A. Grillmeier et H. Bacht, 3 vols (Würzburg, 1951-1954), 2: 491-562.

[31] *PL* 188: 1225D.

concerne la papauté, n'est que le résultat de l'évolution naturelle des principes politico-ecclésiastiques existant depuis le commencement de la "Chrétienté" byzantine. Le principe de la collégialité et celui de l'empire, en se développant, en pénétrant dans la conscience byzantine parallèlement au développement ecclésiologique romain de la "monarchia Petri," ne pouvaient avoir comme résultat que le rejet presque complet de la papauté, rejet commencé le jour où Rome cessa d'être capitale de l'empire. Le "Filioque" n'est qu'un prétexte théologique construit "a posteriori." Examinons donc de manière plus organique les comportements des Byzantins à l'égard de la papauté et les principes qui les inspirent.

LES BYZANTINS VOIENT DANS LE PAPE SURTOUT UN PASTEUR

Si les Byzantins ne sont pas disposés à voir dans le pape la source du "jus," parce que cela caractérise le basileus, toutefois, comme pasteur, ils nourissent pour lui un certain respect. Basile d'Archide, archevêque de Thessalonique, vers la fin de 1155, écrivait au Pape Adrien IV en réponse à une lettre envoyée par ce dernier:

> Nous avons reçu ta lettre, très saint pape, et de celle-ci nous avons compris la hauteur de ton génie, la profondeur de ton humilité, la largeur de ton affection et de ta charité selon Dieu, par laquelle ton cœur apostolique, ou plutôt tes entrailles s'élargissent pour recevoir et accueillir toutes les Églises dans le Christ. ... Nous avons écouté ta voix qui parlait comme père, comme pasteur, mais aussi comme tête des pasteurs.[32]

Ce texte nous montre que, vers la moitié du XIIème siècle, nous trouvons encore des Grecs de la valeur et de l'autorité de Basile de Thessalonique, pour qui l'évêque de Rome possède une signification, et peut jouer un rôle, au sein de l'Église universelle. Certes, on peut dire que beaucoup de ces expressions sont dues à la courtoisie épistolaire, mais il serait injuste de les vider complètement de leur sens en tant que témoignage positif en faveur de la papauté. Michel d'Anchialos, patriarche de Constantinople (mort vers 1173), en réponse à une lettre envoyée par le pape Alexandre III,[33] lui écrit en se félicitant de tous ceux qui œuvrent pour l'unité de l'Église. S'adressant directement au pape, il dit:

> Nous pensons aussi la même chose de ta perfection sacerdotale. Tu as, en effet, tout considéré comme choses sans importance. Tu as plutôt renoncé à

---

[32] *PG* 119: 927c et 929c.
[33] Cf. G. Hofmann, "Papst und Patriarch unter Kaiser Manuel I Komnenes. Ein Briefwechsel," Έπετηρὶς Έταιρίας Βυζαντινῶν Σπουδῶν 23 (1953) 74-82.

tout et as adhéré à Dieu exclusivement. Selon les principes de Dieu et avec sa grâce, tu cherches à te considérer et à être un avec tous ceux qui sont proches de Dieu et s'honorent d'avoir été appelés par lui. En toi, ton cœur tout entier brûle de vouloir être un disciple authentique de notre Seigneur Jésus-Christ; et tu as en toi le signe évident de cette disposition à l'amour et à la paix qui opère l'unité de tous, qui s'oppose à toutes les formes de division. C'est ainsi que faisait précisément le Coryphée des apôtres inspirés et bénis, notre grand maître Pierre, qui s'est efforcé de ramener tous les hommes à l'unité sur la base de l'unicité de la foi.[34]

Le Patriarche n'a donc aucune difficulté à voir un autre élément spiritual dans le pape: son zèle pour l'unité, et ceci en conformité avec Pierre, coryphée des apôtres. Ce thème du pape comme défenseur d'unité, nous le retrouvons en d'autres documents. Démétrius Tornikès, sorte de ministre des affaires étrangères de l'empereur Isaac II Ange, rédigeait en 1193 deux lettres au nom de l'empereur, adressées au pape Célestin III.[35] La seconde lettre porte comme entête: "Isaac Ange ... à Célestin très saint pape de Rome, honneur lui appartient en tant que père spirituel." Et la missive conclut:

> Voici donc ce que ma souveraineté fait savoir à ta sainteté, afin que, conformément à la révérence et à la piété qui te conviennent, sonne ta flûte et que s'étende ton bâton pastoral pour réunir tous les chrétiens en un seul bercail et enseigner à tous le zèle nécessaire pour n'avoir d'autre inimitié que contre le serpent, c'est-à-dire contre Satan et les infidèles.[36]

L'estime du pape comme défenseur d'unité, nous la trouvons encore dans une lettre du patriarche Jean Camateros adressée, en 1199, au pape Innocent III:

> J'ai pris connaissance de ta lettre, et après l'avoir étudiée attentivement, je n'ai pu faire moins que de louer dignement ta sainteté pour le zèle divin et pour l'ardente disposition qu'elle montre au sujet de notre union dans la foi. Par là, tu montres en effet à mon humilité le contenu de ta vertu et la digne diligence de ton pontificat.[37]

Si, d'une part, les Byzantins sont disposés à louer la figure pastorale et sacerdotale du pape, spécialement son zèle pour l'unité, bien plus, s'ils l'encouragent en cette voie parce qu'elle ne présuppose pas l'exercice de la juridiction, d'autre part, ils sont profondément déçus et scandalisés quand le

---

[34] G. Hofmann, pp. 78-79.
[35] Cf. *Georges et Démétrios Tornikes. Lettres et Discours*, ed. J. Darrouzès (Paris, 1970), p. 315.
[36] Ed. Darrouzès, p. 315.
[37] Cf. J. Spiteris, p. 262.

pape, à leur yeux, dégrade son image sacerdotale par des comportements typiquement "impériaux." Pour eux est inconciliable et complètement étrange la figure du pape qui s'était développée en Occident, justement en cette période, comme "dux et sacerdos." [38] Cette *Weltpolitik* des papes faussera l'idéal spirituel et pastoral que les Byzantins étaient disposés à reconnaître dans l'évêque de Rome. Anne Comnène, l'intelligente et cultivée fille aînée de l'empereur Alexis Comnène, dans l'*Alexiade*, composée en 1148,[39] en parlant des papes, ne réussit à les voir que sous leur profil politique. Par exemple, Grégoire VII: elle le présente comme ambigu et cruel,[40] comme dangereux rival du basileus, parce que, allié avec l'ennemi le plus mortel des Byzantins, le normand Robert Guiscard, il combat contre l'empereur d'Allemagne Henri IV, ami du basileus.[41] Et c'est pour cela qu'Anne refuse au pape des titres comme "souverain pontife," "premier de toute l'œcuménicité." Elle raconte le conflit entre l'empereur d'Allemagne et le pape Grégoire VII, et s'arrête avec horreur sur les outrages que les légats de l'empereur ont dû subir à la curie romaine:

> La pudeur qui convient à une femme, et surtout à une princesse de sang royal, m'empêche de révéler ces sévices. ... Voici à quel point de barbarie peut arriver un pontife, même un "souverain pontife," que l'Occident considère comme le premier de toute l'*oikouméné*, comme disent et pensent les Latins. Mais c'est de l'arrogance de leur part.[42]

En 1137 l'empereur Jean Comnène envoie une délégation pour rencontrer le pape Innocent II, lequel conduisait personnellement sa milice contre l'empereur d'Allemagne Lothaire III (1125-1137). Comme de coutume, avec les arguments de nature politique, on trouve l'occasion de discuter aussi d'arguments religieux. Le moine Pierre le Diacre, bibliothécaire du monastère du Mont-Cassin, affronte un philosophe grec, non autrement identifié, de la délégation grecque. Celui-ci manifeste l'impression la plus mauvaise qu'ont eue les Grecs de voir le pape vêtu en guerrier, guider ses troupes à cheval:

> Vos pontifes, comme votre pape Innocent, se lancent à la guerre, soudoient des soldats, se pavannent avec des vêtements de pourpre (propres à l'empereur).[43]

---

[38] Cf. W. Ullmann, *The Growth of Papal Government in the Middle Ages* (London, 1970), pp. 306-309.

[39] Éd. avec trad. française: B. Leib, *Anne Comnène: Alexiade*, 3 vols (Paris, 1937-1945).

[40] *Alexiade*, I, 13: éd. Leib, 1: 48.

[41] *Alexiade*, I, 13: éd. Leib, 1: 47-51.

[42] *Alexiade*, V, 3, 7: éd. Leib, 2: 13-24.

[43] Pierre le Diacre, *Chronicon Casinense*, IV: *PL* 173: 957c.

Si les Grecs n'ont pas de difficulté à respecter le pape quand il se présente comme pasteur et sincère promoteur de l'unité de l'Église, ils sont contraires à l'idée d'un pape à prétentions juridiques universelles. Les arguments opposés à cette prétention, qui proviennent de leur ecclésiologie, mais surtout de leur mode de concevoir le pouvoir impérial, peuvent se réduire schématiquement aux suivants:

(A) *Le Christ, seule tête de l'Église*

Aux affirmations des Latins, selon lesquels le pape, comme "Vicarius Christi," est la tête de l'Église ou, comme on dit le plus souvent, l'Église romaine est "caput omnium ecclesiarum," les polémistes byzantins de cette période opposent avec insistance que seul le Christ est tête de l'Église universelle.

> L'Église de Dieu est unique, écrit Démétrius Tornikès (1193), soumise à un unique pasteur: le Christ. ... Pour moi, en effet, il n'existe qu'un seul Maître, une seule Tête, et non Paul, Apollos ou Céphas. Seul le Christ, en effet, est le Rédempteur. Donc, du moment que le Maître unique est le Christ et que l'unique Esprit-Saint est celui qui régit toutes choses, quelle supériorité ou infériorité pourrait-il y avoir entre les diverses Églises?[44]

La structure ecclésiologique de l'Église Orientale, de soi, n'exclut pas que, à côté de la tête, du fondement, du maître principal de l'Église, c'est-à-dire du Christ, il y ait une tête secondaire et dépendante de lui. Balsamon, le grand canoniste de l'Église byzantine, un des plus enflammés adversaires de la primauté de Rome (mort après 1195), n'hésite pas à assigner le titre de "vicaire de Dieu et du Christ" aux cinq patriarches.[45] Il justifie théologiquement ce titre et les conséquences qui en découlent, en recourant à son principe préféré, "le principe de l'onction":

> Nous croyons que, en vertu de l'onction, ceux-ci (les cinq patriarches) sont rendus parfaits dans la sainteté. Pour cela, nous les appelons "Oints" (Christs) du Seigneur et très saints, et nous les rangeons parmi les saints et théophores de notre Père. En adhérant à eux, nous sommes certains que les portes du royaume du ciel sont ouvertes et closes par eux, et que par leur propre bouche Dieu annonce les choses futures comme si elles venaient de sa propre bouche.[46]

---

[44] J. Darrouzès, *Georges et Démétrios Tornikes*, pp. 346 ss. passim.
[45] Théodore Balsamon, *Meditatio sive responsa de patriarcharum privilegiis*: *PG* 138: 1021B.
[46] *PG* 138: 1021A.

Du reste, la tradition unanime de l'Église orientale, comme celle de l'Église occidentale, considère l'évêque comme vicaire du Christ dans son Église locale.[47]

S'il en est ainsi, pourquoi alors, quand il s'agit de l'évêque de Rome, les Byzantins insistent-ils tellement sur l'unicité de la seigneurie du Christ, comme s'il était impossible qu'une seule personne en assume le rôle pour l'Église universelle? "Christ unique tête de l'Église" contre le pape "vicarius Christi" ne s'inspire pas tant de motifs ecclésiologiques que de motifs politico-religieux. En effet, du point de vue ecclésiologique, les Byzantins admettent les cinq patriarches comme tête de l'Église à la place du Christ (il s'agit donc, non d'une personne, mais d'un groupe). Ils admettent l'évêque comme tête et représentant du Christ au sein de son Église locale. (Il s'agit alors, non de l'Église dans sa totalité, mais d'une église particulière.) Pour eux, comme personne singulière, et dans la totalité de la "société chrétienne," la place du Christ, c'est le basileus qui la tient.[48] Le pape comme "Vicarius Christi" représente un concurrent dangereux du basileus; pour cela, il est éliminé par l'argument "le Christ tête unique de l'Église." En effet, beaucoup de pouvoirs qu'ils ne sont pas disposés à concéder au pape, ils les concèdent volontiers à l'empereur. Balsamon, en commentant le canon XVI du synode de Carthage, rapporte la pensée des autres canonistes et la complète par la sienne, au sujet de la "juridiction" ecclésiastique de l'empereur:

> L'empereur n'est assujetti ni aux canons ni aux lois; il a la faculté d'ériger les sièges épiscopaux. ... Il peut encore dispenser des canons non seulement les séculiers, mais aussi les moines. En effet, si cela est concédé aux évêques, à plus forte raison cela est-il concédé aussi à l'empereur, qui n'est pas obligé de suivre les canons.[49]

Balsamon n'a pas de difficulté à affirmer que "le pouvoir impérial peut tout faire," [50] même dans le domaine ecclésiastique, puisque ce pouvoir lui a été concédé d'En-Haut.[51] Donc, par volonté divine, l'empereur "peut créer de nouveaux épiscopats ou transformer ceux-ci en métropoles selon ce que bon lui semble." [52] L'ultime cour d'appel n'est pas le patriarche, et encore moins le pape, mais l'empereur. En effet, ce dernier peut reprendre un procès

---

[47] Jean Chrysostome, *In 2 Tim., Hom.* 2, 4: *PG* 62: 204-205.

[48] Cf. M. Maccarone, "Il sovrano vicarius Dei nell'alto medioevo," dans *The Sacral Kingship - La regalità sacra. Contributi al tema dell'VIII Congresso Internazionale di Storia delle Religioni*, Roma, aprile 1955 (Leiden, 1959), pp. 581-594.

[49] *In Can. XVI Conc. Carteg.*: *PG* 138: 93.

[50] *PG* 138: 73D.

[51] Cf. G. A. Rhalles et N. Potles, Σύνταγμα τῶν θείων καί ίερῶν κανόνων (Athènes, 1953), 2: 247-248; voir aussi 3: 542.

[52] Rhalles-Potles, 2: 392-393.

ecclésiastique et en faire une révision. Bien plus, le patriarche lui-même peut être jugé par lui.[53] En somme, tout ce que les canonistes rapportent au pape, "Vicarius Christi," les canonistes byzantins l'appliquent à leur "Vicaire du Christ": l'empereur.

(B) *La Pentarchie contre la "monarchie de Pierre"*

Dans le temps où les relations entre les deux Églises étaient plus ou moins normales, la pentarchie, c'est-à-dire la direction collégiale de l'Église par les cinq patriarches, n'avait pas de fonction anti-romaine; tout au plus tempérait-elle d'une certaine façon les prétentions monarchiques de Rome.[54] À partir du XIIème siècle et par la suite, la pentarchie est utilisée en un sens nettement anti-romain, pour s'opposer à la "monarchia Petri."

Selon Nicétas de Nicomédie et Jean Camateros, l'évêque de Rome pourrait posséder encore une légère prééminence d'honneur parmi les sièges patriarcaux, mais seulement à l'intérieur d'une ecclésiologie d'Églises égales, d'Églises-sœurs. Le patriarche Camateros écrit à Innocent III:

> Tu affirmes que l'Église romaine est la mère de toutes les Églises. Mais ceci n'a pas le témoignage de l'Écriture, ni n'a été décidé par un Concile. Ce n'est certes pas parce que Pierre a prêché l'Évangile à Rome, car il a prêché aussi en d'autres cités. Et ce n'est pas non plus parce qu'il est mort à Rome, car cela fut un pur hasard. Il n'est donc pas possible que Rome soit la mère de toutes les Églises, puisqu'elles sont cinq, les grandes Églises qui possèdent la dignité patriarcale, et Rome se recrute la première parmi les Églises-sœurs du même rang....[55]

Camateros donne la vraie raison pour laquelle Rome est le premier siège "inter pares":

> Ces honneurs furent concédés à votre Église à cause de l'empire et du sénat; si à présent cette raison (historique) ne subsiste plus, eh bien! je préfère ne pas en parler.[56]

Les Byzantins, même quand ils sont gentils, comme le patriarche Jean Camateros, ce qu'ils concèdent à Rome d'une main, ils le reprennent de l'autre. Par la dernière phrase Camateros voudrait dire: avec la translation de l'empire et du sénat à la Nouvelle Rome, l'Église des Romains a perdu la première place dans l'ordre des patriarcats en faveur de l'Église de Constantinople.

---

[53] Cf. *PG* 137: 1312A. Sur toute cette question, voir A. Michel, *Die Kaisermacht in der Ostkirche (843-1204)* (Darmstadt, 1959).

[54] J. Spiteris, pp. 10-11.

[55] Pour les textes et le commentaire, voir J. Spiteris, pp. 269-272.

[56] Texte dans Spiteris, p. 276.

Mais cette conclusion, les autres écrivains byzantins l'avaient déjà tirée, ainsi Nicétas Seides (mort après 1117),[57] Nil Doxapatrès,[58] et surtout le canoniste Théodore Balsamon qui, plus que tous, a contribué à l'enracinement idéologique du schisme. Ceux-ci concèdent aux patriarches beaucoup de ces privilèges typiquement papaux, comme la fonction de direction pour toute l'Église.[59]

Théoriquement Rome est partie intégrante de ce corps patriarcal. Mais, hélas, fait remarquer le canoniste, l'évêque de Rome s'est séparé du corps des cinq patriarches. Et il ne peut que manifester sa peine pour le schisme du pape et prier, attendre la conversion.[60] Ce schisme papal est politique: le pape est "coupé de la source" impériale de ses privilèges (il use de la parole forte "ἐϰϰοπή").[61] Il s'agit d'un refus total non seulement de la papauté mais aussi des Latins:

> Depuis de nombreuses années, l'Église Occidentale, c'est-à-dire Rome, s'est séparée de la communion spirituelle avec les autres patriarches, et s'est séparée des coutumes et des dogmes de l'Église catholique, elle est devenue étrangère aux orthodoxes. Pour cette raison le pape n'est pas mentionné dans les dyptiques en communion avec les autres patriarches. Ainsi aucun Latin ne devrait recevoir la communion de divins et saints mystères par une main sacerdotale, à moins qu'il ne récuse d'abord les dogmes et coutumes latines et ne se conforme aux canons des orthodoxes.[62]

Désormais, à l'intérieur de la "taxis" de la pentarchie, la première place est due au patriarche de Constantinople, parce qu'il hérite des privilèges de l'Antique Rome sur la base de la "donatio Constantini."[63] Ces auteurs donc, soucieux d'ôter de son piédestal l'évêque de l'Ancienne Rome, pour le remplacer par celui de la Nouvelle Rome, n'hésitent pas à "politiser" l'antique principe ecclésiologique de la pentarchie. Malgré leurs affirmations sur la nécessité de la pentarchie pour l'intégrité du corps de l'Église (les cinq sens), et sur leur origine divine, en pratique ils la détruisent en la remplaçant par une tétrarchie. L'évêque de Rome est exclu par son "hérésie" politique. Les autres différences dogmatiques dont on accuse l'Église de Rome sont plutôt des prétextes.

---

[57] Cf. R. Gahbauer, *Gegen den Primat des Papstes. Studien zu Nikitas Seides: Edition, Einführung, Kommentar* (München, 1975), pp. 72-75.

[58] Spiteris, pp. 137-153.

[59] Cf. *PG* 138: 1016c.

[60] Cf. *PG* 138: 1020d.

[61] *PG* 138: 1016.

[62] *PG* 138: 968b; voir aussi Zonaras: *PG* 137: 488d.

[63] *PG* 137: 485d-488b.

(C) *Critique du principe de l'apostolicité de Pierre*

Il n'y a pas de rencontre, il n'existe pas de correspondance entre Grecs et Latins dans laquelle, comme dit Théophilacte de Bulgarie, les représentants de Rome "n'avancent pas en premier lieu la confession de Pierre," ne "brandissent pas," ne déploient pas comme un étendard de bataille "les clés de Pierre." [64] Les Grecs comprennent qu'à la base des affirmations primatiales des Latins, il y a "le principe de l'apostolicité de Pierre": Pierre a reçu du Seigneur une primauté qui passe à son successeur, l'évêque de Rome.

Les Grecs, même en cette période, n'ont pas de difficulté à considérer Pierre comme "le Coryphée des Apôtres," le "Clavigère" des Cieux. À la fin du siècle, le patriarche Jean Camateros, interprétant la pensée de ses contemporains, écrit au pape Innocent III:

> Nous considérons Pierre comme celui qui fut honoré comme le premier parmi les disciples du Christ, et comme celui qui précède les autres dans l'honneur, et qui fut célébré pour sa prééminence. [65]

Ces allusions à la primauté de Pierre ont cependant, pour les auteurs grecs, une signification complètement différente de celle donnée par les auteurs latins. Pour les Grecs, Pierre est le premier des apôtres parce qu'il a confessé le premier la foi en la divinité de Jésus-Christ, et il reste pour toujours la pierre de l'Église, parce que cette dernière est fondée sur la foi de Pierre, c'est-à-dire sur la divinité du Christ. [66]

Théophilacte considérait encore Pierre comme détenteur d'un privilège personnel qui, bien que dans la suite il ait été étendu à tous les autres apôtres, fut néanmoins communiqué à lui seul d'abord. Et c'est "à lui seul et non pas à un autre apôtre que le Seigneur a conféré la présidence de tous les agneaux de l'univers." [67] Après lui, en revanche, on part du principe que tout ce que le Seigneur a conféré à Pierre s'étend automatiquement à tous les apôtres. C'est le principe que nous pouvons appeler: "principe d'intercommunicabilité des privilèges entre tous les apôtres." Nicétas de Nicomédie énonce ainsi ce principe:

> Ce n'est donc pas au seul Pierre, mais à tous avec Pierre, et avec tous à Pierre, qu'est confié ce qui a été dit sans distinction par le Seigneur.

Ainsi, comme le Saint-Esprit, au jour de la Pentecôte est descendu de façon égale sur tous les Apôtres, "ainsi donc nous reconnaissons à Pierre la

---

[64] Cf. *PG* 126: 241BC.
[65] Texte dans Spiteris, p. 276.
[66] Cf. N. Afanassieff, N. Kuolomzine, J. Meyendorff, A. Schmemann, *La primauté de Pierre dans l'Église orthodoxe* (Paris-Neuchâtel, 1960), pp. 91-115.
[67] *In Johan. Comment.*: *PG* 124: 309A.

puissance reçue du Seigneur, de sorte que nous ne puissions pas la croire diminuée par l'autorité des autres apôtres... ." Ainsi Nicétas peut-il conclure:

> Ce n'est donc pas au seul Pierre qu'il semble qu'on doive attribuer un privilège qui, par le don du Seigneur, est commun à tous.[68]

Ce principe sera développé ensuite par Jean Camateros. Celui-ci cependant le situe au-dedans d'un autre principe cher aux polémistes byzantins: "Pierre, Docteur universel." Le pape ne peut se considérer comme le successeur de Pierre pour le simple motif que les apôtres ne sont pas considérés "évêques d'une cité," c'est-à-dire liés à une cité, mais maîtres de l'*oikouméné*. Pour les Byzantins, faire de Pierre l'évêque de Rome, signifie réduire sa portée universelle, l'humilier. Nous trouvons déjà cet argument dans Andronic Camateros, dans un dialogue rapporté par lui entre l'empereur Manuel Comnène et quelques cardinaux:

> Vous dites [affirme l'empereur] que Pierre, bien qu'il soit maître de l'*oikouméné* est devenu maître de la seule Rome par le fait que, après avoir commencé sa prédication en Judée, il a terminé sa vie apostolique à Rome. Avec cela, les promesses faites par le Sauveur à Pierre, et qui, selon l'interprétation des Saints Pères, ont une signification générale concernant tous les croyants, sont par vous réduites dans leur portée, sont restreintes à la seule Rome.[69]

Jean Camateros insiste sur ce point: pour lui ce serait "limiter à la seule Rome l'honneur dû à Pierre, alors qu'au contraire, il fut envoyé pour enseigner à tous les Juifs circoncis dans toute l'*oikouméné*." À ce sujet, il ne fait donc que rapporter la très ancienne tradition selon laquelle l'apôtre ne peut être lié à aucun lieu, mais est mandaté pour l'entière *oikouméné*.[70]

Jean Camateros insiste à diverses reprises et de façons différentes sur le concept de l'universalité de l'apostolat en général, et en particulier celui de Pierre. Pour lui une "monopolisation" de Pierre par la seule Rome est inadmissible. C'est pourquoi il demande au pape:

> Si le premier des Apôtres a enseigné à Rome comme aussi bien en d'autres cités, pour quel motif Rome fait-elle exclusivement sien, ce qui appartient aussi aux autres cités?[71]

---

[68] *Dial.* III, 9: *PL* 188: 1221cd.

[69] Voir le texte d'Andronic Camateros dans son *Arsenal* (Ἱερά Ὁπλοθήκη) traduit et publié par nous dans Spiteris, p. 187.

[70] Cf. J. Colson, "Le ministère apostolique dans la littérature chrétienne primitive: apôtres et épiscopes sanctificateurs des nations," dans *L'Épiscopat et l'Église universelle*, publ. sous la direction d'Y. Congar et B.-D. Dupuis (Paris, 1962), pp. 134-169; J. Rammers, "La succession apostolique de l'Église entière," *Concilium* 34 (1968) 34-47.

[71] Pour les textes rapportés et autres semblables, voir les deux lettres de Jean Camateros publiées par nous dans Spiteris, pp. 324-331.

Ces argumentations seront reprises de façon beaucoup plus claire par Nicolas Mesarites, en 1206, dans un dialogue avec quelques Latins:

> Il est vrai que Pierre, le coryphée des apôtres, est allé à Rome, mais cela n'a rien de grand et de glorieux. En effet, il est venu à Rome pour affronter Simon le Magicien, comme il était aussi allé pour la première fois à Antioche, non comme évêque mais comme docteur. C'est Lin, en effet, qui est le premier évêque de Rome, élu par toute la sainte et divine assemblée des apôtres, ensuite Sixte, le troisième Clément le saint martyr, placé à la place de Pierre sur le trône pontifical. Il est donc faux que Pierre fut évêque de Rome. Ce dont les Italiens croient faire honneur à Pierre, en réalité le déshonore, parce qu'ils font du docteur de l'Univers, l'évêque d'une seule cité. Ils se font gloire à eux-mêmes, en se faisant successeurs de Pierre.[72]

(D) *Le Principe politique remplace celui de l'apostolicité*

Dans le présent essai nous avons fait allusion, plusieurs fois, au principe politique qui, pour les Grecs, est à la base de toute primauté dans l'Église. Étant donnée l'importance unique de cet argument nous le reprenons ici d'une façon systématique. Les Byzantins n'ont pas de difficulté à admettre que Rome soit "trône apostolique."[73] Nil Doxapatrès considère l'Église romaine comme "Église apostolique."[74] Ils n'ont pas de difficulté à admettre l'apostolicité d'un siège, étant donné que les sièges orientaux les plus importants sont d'origine apostolique. On cherche à donner une origine apostolique aussi au siège de Constantinople, en recourant à la légende de Saint André.[75] L'apostolicité d'un siège n'a cependant aucun effet primatial:

> Il ne faut pas (note Démétrius Tornikes) faire dépendre de la sépulture d'un apôtre la suprématie donnée à l'Église, mais plutôt à l'empire.[76]

Presque tous les polémistes anti-latins du XIIème siècle, avec une insistance excessive, font dépendre la primauté de l'empereur. En tenant présent à l'esprit l'insistance, la quantité, l'importance données par les autres Grecs au soi-disant *Reichskirchenrecht*, nous pouvons affirmer que ce n'est pas la

---

[72] Éd. par A. Heisenberg, *Neue Quellen zur Geschichte des lateinischen Kaisertums und der Kirchenunion*, Sitzungsberichte der Bayer. Akademie der Wissenschaften, Philosophisch-philologische und historische Klasse, Jahrgang 1923, 2 (München, 1923), 1: 22.

[73] Voir Jean II de Kiev (fin du XIème siècle) dans S. A. Pavlov, *Essai critique sur l'histoire de l'ancienne polémique gréco-russe contre les Latins* [en russe] (Saint-Pétersbourg, 1878), pp. 169-186.

[74] N. Doxapatrès, Τάξις τῶν πατριαρχικῶν Θρόνων: éd. G. F. Parthey, *Hieroclis Synecdemus et Notitiae graecae episcoporum* (Berlin, 1866), p. 268.

[75] Doxapatrès, Τάξις: éd. Parthey, pp. 296 et 297.

[76] Éd. Darrouzès, p. 346.

pentarchie, le Christ tête unique de l'Église, mais le principe politique de l'empire qui inspire le plus l'attitude polémique des Grecs par rapport à la papauté. Au principe de la "monarchia Petri," nos auteurs opposent le principe de la "monarchia imperii." Voici une synthèse des idées qui composent ce principe dans ses conséquences logiques et systématiques:

(a) *L'empereur est l'unique autorité naturelle, après Dieu, tant pour nous que pour vous.*

Ce principe est énoncé par le patriarche Michel d'Anchialos dans une lettre adressée au pape Alexandre III.[77] Dans l'unique empire œcuménique il ne peut y avoir deux autorités universelles; Byzance doit sacrifier l'autorité universelle du pape pour sauver l'autorité universelle du basileus. La conséquence de cette prémisse est:

(b) *Dans les limites de l'empire œcuménique, expression géographique de l'Église œcuménique, il n'existe aucun primat ecclésiastique à caractère universel qui ne soit l'émanation du basileus.*

Georges Tornikes énonce ainsi ce principe:

les trônes d'aujourd'hui et les dignités ont été distribuées entre les Églises selon les principautés.[78]

L'application la plus immédiate de ce présupposé est:

(c) *L'Église de Rome a reçu la primauté sur les autres Églises, non à cause de Pierre, mais à cause de la dignité de l'Empire.*

Andronic Camateros résume ainsi cette pensée des Byzantins dans son "Arsenal Sacré":

Ce n'est pas pour le motif que vous croyez [c'est-à-dire Pierre], mais à cause de l'honneur inhérent à l'empire et à la monarchie dont l'Ancienne Rome était honorée, même avant la prédication des apôtres, et qui lui confère l'hégémonie sur toute l'*oikouméné*, qu'elle possède la primauté sur toutes les autres Églises.[79]

Pour l'historien byzantin Jean Kinnamos dans son *Epitome*, composée entre 1180 et 1183, l'honneur (la primauté) dû au pape n'est pas autre chose qu'une émanation du trône impérial "par lequel le pape participe au trône."[80]

---

[77] Éd. Hoffmann, pp. 80 ss.
[78] Éd. Darrouzès, p. 331.
[79] Voir le texte édité par nous dans Spiteris, pp. 323-324, et pour la trad., p. 188.
[80] Voir le texte: J. Cinname, *Epitome*, éd. A. Meineke (Bonn, 1836), pp. 218-220.

Pour un Byzantin, admettre que l'Église possède une primauté qui ne soit pas due à l'empereur mais à Pierre, serait à la vérité une folie. Nil Doxapatrès, en se référant au XXVIIIème canon du concile de Chalcédoine, écrivait:

> Comme tu peux constater par ce canon, sont évidemment dans l'erreur tous ceux qui, *délirant*, disent que Rome a été préférée à cause de saint Pierre. Voici au contraire que ce canon du saint concile dit de façon claire que Rome avait été préférée, parce qu'elle commandait.[81]

De là, l'autre conclusion de nos polémistes:

(d) *Avec la translation de l'empire par Constantin, l'Ancienne Rome a perdu tous ses privilèges en faveur de la Nouvelle Rome (Constantinople).*

La première conséquence du transfert de l'empire de l'Ancienne Rome à la Nouvelle Rome se rapporte à la supériorité éthique des Byzantins:

> peut-être ignorez-vous [demande Nicétas Seidès aux cardinaux, ses interlocuteurs] que vous êtes plutôt nos sujets et nos tributaires, du moment que l'empire a été transféré ici.[82]

Cette dépendance politique de l'Occident par rapport à l'Orient, même si elle n'est plus réelle dans la période dont nous nous occupons, porte comme conséquence que, même du point de vue religieux, les Latins dépendent des héritiers de l'empire. Même l'Église de Rome dépend de l'Église de Constantinople. Anne Comnène considère simplement comme "arrogance" de parler encore du pape comme "souverain pontife" ou "premier de tous" et elle en donne la raison:

> Mais cela est arrogance de leur part, puisque, alors que la Seigneurie du monde fut transférée de l'Ancienne Rome dans notre cité impériale, et avec elle le Sénat et toute la structure hiérarchique, fut transférée aussi la primauté hiérarchique des trônes. La primauté ecclésiastique fut accordée par l'empereur au siège de Constantinople par sa fondation, mais surtout par le synode de Chalcédoine, lequel fait monter Byzance au premier rang, et à elle furent soumises les Églises de l'*oikouméné* entière.[83]

Même les auteurs qui, comme nous l'avons vu, sont disposés à reconnaître à Rome une primauté d'honneur, la font dépendre, directement ou indirectement, de la fidélité de Rome à l'empire.

---

[81] N. Doxapatrès, *Τάξις*: éd. Parthey, p. 289.
[82] Cf. Spiteris, p. 73.
[83] Anne Comnène, *Alexiade*: éd. Leib, 1: 48.

CONCLUSION

L'attitude fondamentale des Byzantins par rapport à la papauté est, au fond, inspirée par deux principes: le principe de la collégialité sous la forme réduite de la "pentarchie," et le principe politique. Sont-ils deux principes indépendants ou l'un dépend-il de l'autre?

Après l'examen de tous les documents de l'époque en notre possession, nous pouvons conclure que la pentarchie utilisée au sens antipapal n'est pas inspirée avant tout de présupposés d'ordre biblico-théologique, mais découle comme une conséquence nécessaire de la conception théologico-philosophique de l'état chez les Byzantins.

Par conséquent, le refus de la papauté n'est pas dû, dans sa racine, à des exigences d'ordre ecclésiologique, mais à une nécessité d'ordre politique. En d'autres termes: l'unique alternative ecclésiologique à l'intérieur du système politique dans lequel s'incarne l'Église byzantine ne pouvait être que le principe de la pentarchie. L'admission du "principe de Pierre," et donc d'un principe monarchique, comme critère de la primauté sur une Église universelle, dans une société médiévale, dans laquelle n'existe aucune distinction nette entre la société civile et la société religieuse, entre Église et État, aurait détruit à la base même le système étatiste byzantin.

Seule la pentarchie (donc un groupe moral et non *une personne singulière*) pouvait exister à côté du basileus, avec les fonctions directives universelles. C'est seulement ainsi que l'on pouvait sauver la conception typiquement médiévale d'une seule tête dans l'unique corps social de la société chrétienne. Par là, on ne veut pas affirmer que la structure collégiale de l'Église n'ait point en soi une origine biblique et qu'elle soit un pur produit de l'empire romano-byzantin. Nous affirmons seulement que la collégialité dans sa phase de "conscientisation" dans l'Église de culture gréco-byzantine représente un processus causé par la réalité politique, à l'intérieur duquel cette Église est structurée. Mais cette même réalité politique a empêché les Byzantins de découvrir l'autre dimension de la structure de l'Église, également enracinée, comme la collégialité, dans la Bible: le service de Pierre. Cet aspect religieux de la papauté, bien qu'il ne soit pas ignoré du monde byzantin, subit toutefois dialectiquement une formidable pression de la part du principe politique dominant, jusqu'à ce qu'il soit exclus positivement et totalement par les polémistes byzantins du XIIème siècle. Durant le concile de Lyon, le courant grec des unionistes cherchera à discuter à la lumière "du principe de Pierre," mais sans succès. Désormais, le principe politique règne souverainement dans les milieux officiels.

Pour se rendre compte ultérieurement que la critique antiromaine des Byzantins n'est pas inspirée du tout par des motifs de nature biblico-théologique, mais du fait que l'Église grecque était incarnée dans la structure impériale, il est intéressant de confronter cette critique à celle des autres Églises orientales en dehors de l'orbite, des influences et des structures de l'empire byzantin. Ces Églises orientales, composées de peuples qui ne se sentent pas héritiers de l'empire romain, acceptent en général le principe de l'apostolicité de Pierre comme norme pour la primauté de l'Église. Si elles refusent la primauté romaine, elles le font sur la base d'autres principes, différents de ceux que nous rencontrons chez les polémistes byzantins. Du reste, les Églises de Perse, d'Égypte, d'Arménie, de Syrie, embrassent la doctrine de Nestorius ou celle d'Eutychès, principalement poussées par le désir de l'indépendance par rapport au joug impérial byzantin.[84]

Plusieurs raisons théologiques contre la primauté romaine utilisées en cette période par les polémistes byzantins sont même aujourd'hui répétées par les orthodoxes, en oubliant qu'elles sont inspirées d'une idéologie politique précise, totalement dépassée aujourd'hui. Congar se demandait déjà: "Où est aujourd'hui le pouvoir du basileus?"[85]

[84] Il est symptomatique que "nestorien" voulait dire "persan" alors qu'au contraire "éphésien," dit avec mépris, voulait dire "byzantin," c'est-à-dire ennemi des persans. De même "jacobite" voulait dire "syrien," alors que par contre "melchite" voulait dire "impérialiste," c'est-à-dire fidèle à l'empire grec. Leur critique antipapale, donc, ne pouvait être inspirée de quelque principe politique qu'eux-mêmes refusaient. Sur toute cette question voir le travail de W. de Vries, *Der Kirchenbegriff der von Rom getrennten Syren* (Rome, 1955).

[85] Voir son introduction au volume de W. de Vries, *Orient et Occident: Les structures ecclésiales vues dans l'histoire des sept premiers conciles œcuméniques* (Paris, 1974), p. 6.

The Theology of Papal Primacy
in Thomas Aquinas

Christopher Ryan

My concern in this essay will be to determine Aquinas' theology of the relationship between the pope and the bishops, and specifically of their relationship in the exercise of authority in the church. It might be claimed that this goal, however desirable, is impossible to achieve, since there is no lengthy treatment of the topic in Aquinas and much of what he has to say is *obiter dictum*. These limitations must be acknowledged, but the degree of constraint they impose is exaggerated in such an objection. It will be the argument of this essay that Aquinas speaks at sufficient length and with sufficient clarity for us to be able to discern a definite and consistent view of the nature of the primacy of papal authority with respect to the bishops. In the nature of the case there must be an element of interpretation; were this not so, there would scarcely be call for the present attempt to clarify what has become a contentious issue.

Granted the relatively fragmentary nature of the evidence, and the consequent heightened dangers attendant on imprecise language, there is much to be gained by stating clearly at the outset the case that will to be argued here. Aquinas' view of the relationship between popes and bishops can best be characterized by the phrase "a universal derivational theory of spiritual power." By this I mean that for Aquinas the entire spiritual power of the bishops derives from that of the pope. It is particularly important to be clear about what is intended here by the term spiritual power. Both the term and its content I take from Aquinas himself. Aquinas puts forward his understand-

The Religious Roles of the Papacy: Ideals and Realities, 1150-1300, ed. Christopher Ryan, Papers in Mediaeval Studies 8 (Toronto: Pontifical Institute of Mediaeval Studies, 1989), pp. 193-225. © P.I.M.S., 1989.

ing of "potestas spiritualis" when he addresses the question in the *Summa theologiae* of whether or not a schismatic has any power. He writes: "It must be said in reply that spiritual power is of two kinds, one of which is sacramental and the other jurisdictional. Sacramental power on the one hand is that power which is conferred by some form of consecration. ... Jurisdictional power on the other hand is that which is conferred by a simple command on someone's part." [1] After discussing the problem in hand, he concludes with regard to schismatics: "When, therefore, it is said that such people do not have spiritual power, this is to be understood either of the second [jurisdictional] power, or, if it refers to the first power, this is not to be taken as referring to the very essence of the power, but to its legitimate use." [2] It is the second, more restricted meaning of spiritual power, found in the concluding words of the passage just quoted, that I adopt in this essay: spiritual power consists of the power of jurisdiction and the right to exercise a sacramental power already possessed. So when I characterize Aquinas' view of the relationship between the role of the pope and the bishops as "a universal derivational theory of spiritual power" I mean that for him all valid possession of purely or intrinsically jurisdictional power in the church, and all right to the exercise of purely sacramental power, derive from the pope to the bishops. Put otherwise, a bishop's entire power to exercise the *cura animarum* validly or legitimately derives from the pope.

Two further clarifications are called for. First, in explaining the meaning of my description of Aquinas' view I have spoken of 'the purely or intrinsically jurisdictional power.' The need to add 'or intrinsically' arises from the peculiar nature of the sacrament of penance. According to the sacramental theology of the middle ages, penance, unlike the other sacraments, requires for its *valid* exercise not only the priestly character conferred by orders but also jurisdiction in the internal forum. While, for instance, the power of orders is all that is required for a priest to celebrate the Eucharist validly, in the case of the sacrament of penance when a priest lacks proper jurisdiction

---

[1] *S. T.* II-II, q. 39, a. 3: "Respondeo dicendum quod duplex est spiritualis potestas: una quidem sacramentalis; alia iurisdictionalis. Sacramentalis quidem potestas est quae per aliquam consecrationem confertur. ... Potestas autem iurisdictionalis est quae ex simplici iniunctione hominis confertur." Where possible the Leonine edition of Aquinas' works has been used, with the exception of the *Summa contra Gentiles*, for which the Leonine edition as emended by L. R. Carcedo and A. R. Sierra (Madrid, 1967) has been used. For each work of which no Leonine edition has yet been published the edition used has been indicated after the first quotation. To facilitate reference, the paragraph and line numbers which feature in the recent works of the Leonine edition have been given. Translations throughout are my own.

[2] Ibid.: "Cum ergo dicitur tales non habere potestatem spiritualem, intelligendum est vel de potestate secunda: vel, si referatur ad primam potestatem, non est referendum ad ipsam essentiam potestatis, sed ad legitimum usum eius."

no valid sacramental act takes place. Second, I confine myself to addressing directly the question of the relationship between the pope and the bishops. No one disputes that for Aquinas any spiritual power held by a cleric lower than a bishop derives from that of a bishop; the only point at issue is the accuracy of my contention that for him a similar derivational theory of spiritual power obtains between the bishops and the pope. It was, of course, a common doctrine in the middle ages, and one accepted by Aquinas, that no lay person simply as such had any spiritual power vis-à-vis other members of the church.

I shall discuss Aquinas's texts, and argue my case, principally by examining the view of Aquinas put forward by Yves Congar in a seminal essay written over 20 years ago: "Aspects ecclésiologiques de la querelle entre mendiants et séculiers dans la seconde moitié du XIIIᵉ siècle et le début du XIVᵉ siècle." [3] No one has done more than Congar to illuminate the ecclesiology of the middle ages in general, and of Aquinas in particular. [4] The essay referred to, running to a small book of some 120 pages, was a pioneering work and has proved to be of enduring interest. Brian Tierney, scarcely an historical bedfellow of Congar, pays it this handsome tribute in his controversial *Origins of Papal Infallibility 1150-1350*: "On the theological repercussions of the [secular-mendicant] dispute the outstanding work is Y. Congar 'Aspects ecclésiologiques....' ... This magisterial article ... provides an indispensable starting point for all subsequent work in this field." [5] I shall, in addition, sharpen the question vis-à-vis papal primacy and bring out my own interpretation more clearly by differentiating my position from that expressed in the vigorous criticism of Congar made by a former pupil of Tierney, Charles Zuckerman, in an article entitled "Aquinas' conception of the papal primacy in ecclesiastical government." [6] I shall conclude by making some

---

[3] *Archives d'histoire doctrinale et littéraire du moyen âge* 28 (1961) 35-151 (cited hereafter as Congar).

[4] See especially, in addition to the article cited in the previous note, *L'Ecclésiologie du haut moyen âge, de saint Grégoire à la désunion entre Byzance et Rome* (Paris, 1968), *L'Église de s. Augustin à l'époque moderne* (Paris, 1970), and the essays now contained in three collections: *Droit ancien et structures ecclésiales* (London, 1982), *Études d'ecclésiologie médiévale* (London, 1983) and *Thomas d'Aquin: sa vision de théologie et de l'Église* (London, 1984). Despite its somewhat Trollopean title, an important essay dealing with matters relating to our theme which is not included in these collections is "S. Thomas et les Archidiacres," *Revue Thomiste* 57 (1957) 657-671.

[5] *Origins of Papal Infallibility 1150-1350* (Leiden, 1972), p. 59, n. 1.

[6] *Archives d'histoire doctrinale et littéraire du moyen âge* 40 (1973) 97-134 (hereafter cited as Zuckerman). In this article Zuckerman draws on his unpublished Ph.D. thesis: "Dominican Theories of the Papal Primacy 1250-1320" (Cornell Univ., 1971; Ann Arbor, Michigan: University Microfilms International, 1984), esp. pp. 26-92. More recently Zuckerman has argued that the view he ascribed earlier to Aquinas is to be found in Bernard of Auvergne

brief remarks on where I think Aquinas is, so to speak, to be located on the theological map of the late thirteenth-century theology of the papacy.

The seminal article referred to above is marred by a notable obscurity in its treatment of Aquinas. In part this arises from the fact that Congar's language is occasionally opaque at significant moments. More importantly, however, the obscurity is due to his ascribing at various times to Aquinas two points of view which are incompatible.

On the one hand Congar begins by attributing to Aquinas a view which is essentially identical to the interpretation proposed in this essay. He first describes Aquinas as maintaining that the bishops hold their jurisdiction from the pope: "... quant au problème du rapport entre juridiction des évêques et autorité du pape, il ... devrait être réexaminé à partir d'une analyse très précise des textes et du contenu exact des expressions employées. Ce point est souverainement important lorsqu'il s'agit de savoir si les évêques tiennent, ou non, leur juridiction du pape. Pour les Mendiants, pour Thomas d'Aquin comme pour Bonaventure, la réponse affirmative ne fait pas de doute...." He goes on immediately to ask: "mais qu'entendent-ils exactement par là?" [7] Shortly thereafter, introducing his discussion of what Aquinas means, he uses terms which imply that by the term jurisdiction he understands both jurisdiction in the strict legal sense and the right to exercise the priestly sacramental power. He cites the canonists to explain what Aquinas means by jurisdiction and how he envisages the bishops' holding their jurisdiction from the pope: "... la 'juridiction' conférait moins un pouvoir, une faculté, qu'une possibilité ou une légitimité d'action: l'*usus* de la *potestas* afférante à l'*officium* sacerdotal." [8]

However, there is another major theme in Congar's article which I believe is not compatible with the one he espouses in the passages which I have quoted. Before beginning his review of what he considers to be the main

---

"probably ... in the first decade of the thirteenth century": "Some Texts of Bernard of Auvergne on Papal Power," *Recherches de théologie ancienne et médiévale* 49 (1982) 174-204 (quotation at p. 175). In this later article Zuckerman writes somehwat curiously: "At the beginning of the secular-mendicant disputes in the mid-thirteenth century, several friars out of eagerness to buttress their conception of papal authority did juxtapose certain scriptural passages in a way that implied the papacy to be the source of sacramental as well as jurisdictional authority (ZUCKERMAN ['Aquinas' conception ...'] 121-127). However this implication was almost certainly unintentional, and no later mendicant writer repeated the interpretation in question." The only friar to whom this view is ascribed in the article referred to is Aquinas, and there Zuckerman treats the juxtaposition as intentional.

[7] Congar, pp. 88-89.

[8] Ibid., p. 90. In referring to the canonists Congar has in mind principally the idea of distribution or allocation of prelacies in particular locations: see ibid., pp. 90-93 and 150. On the interpretation of Aquinas' use of canonistic language see below p. 201, esp. n. 31.

Thomistic texts *ad rem*, he writes: "Quand donc on voit dans le pape l'origine de la *jurisdictio* ou de la *potestas* des prélats, de quoi s'agit-il au juste? Est-ce d'une véritable communication de *pouvoir*? Alors, la *plenitudo potestatis* du pape représenterait la plénitude qualitative de *la* source, aucun pouvoir n'existerait dans l'Église sinon par participation à cette source. Nous croyons que telle est la position de S. Bonaventure. Mais il peut s'agir d'autre chose." [9] By *pouvoir* here, it may be remarked, Congar is certainly referring to some power other than the sacramental power of orders as such, for shortly before in the same paragraph he notes that no contemporary writer believed that the sacramental power or priestly character derived from the pope: "Il n'est pas un seul théologien ou canoniste qui fasse dériver du pape le pouvoir sacerdotal comme pouvoir sacramental." He cannot, then, be understood to mean that where Bonaventure thought the essential sacramental power or character of orders was communicated by the pope this was not so for Aquinas; like all their contemporaries, they were at one in holding that the sacramental power of orders as such did not derive from the pope but from the rite of ordination. Granted this, Congar's words inevitably suggest that Aquinas, unlike Bonaventure, maintained that some power touching either jurisdiction or the right to exercise the sacrament of orders was held by the bishops independently of the pope, and was not possessed by way of derivation from him.

Likewise after his review of the texts, in summarizing "les idées qui s'en dégagent," Congar rejects the idea that Aquinas held that the pope is the source of all power, though here he does so with an obscurely phrased tentativeness: "Ses textes ne nous paraissent pas imposer l'idée que [la *plenitudo potestatis*] serait pour lui *la* source unique dont toute *potestas* dériverait dans l'Église, à la manière dont toute grâce vient du Christ, Chef du Corps mystique." [10] It is difficult to regard as a significant clarification of Aquinas' thought Congar's disclaimer of a parallel in Aquinas between the pope's plenitude of power and Christ's being the source of all grace, for clearly any strict comparison would have put Aquinas outside the bounds of orthodoxy.[11] More pertinently, perhaps, since for Congar the derivation of

---

[9] Ibid., p. 91. Throughout this essay italics occurring in quotations from secondary sources are in the original.

[10] Ibid., p. 95.

[11] Aquinas does, of course, hold that in a certain manner the pope acts in the place of Christ. Indeed he endorses strongly and frequently the notion of the pope as the vicar of Christ: see especially his words quoted at n. 92 below. Maccarone writes: "Particolare sviluppo della dottrina contenuta nel titolo *vicarius Christi* troviamo nel massimo teologo del secolo XIII, San Tommaso d'Aquino," *Vicarius Christi: Storia del titolo papale* (Rome, 1952), p. 136. Maccarone argues this point at ibid., pp. 136-140.

the essential sacramental power from the pope is not in question, his assertion that Aquinas in ascribing plenitude of power to the pope did not mean that all power in the Church derives from the pope as the unique source once more suggests that there is some power other than the sacramental power of orders as such which belongs to the bishops independently of the pope. In concluding the paragraph from which the last quotation was taken, Congar writes in a similar vein and with like obscurity: "*Plenitudo potestatis* nous semble signifier, chez S. Thomas, non pas nécessairement 'fons et origo', mais le pouvoir du chef de toute la communauté qui, comme tel, possède la totalité des pouvoirs ecclésiastiques, en compréhension comme en extension." [12]

A similar point may be made with regard to what Congar says in the concluding section of his essay.[13] What emerges in the concluding summary is the importance he attaches to a theologian's view regarding the derivation of spiritual power for characterising his theology of the papacy. Speaking of the subject of this concluding section, Congar writes: "Les conclusions les plus importantes pour nous concernent l'histoire des doctrines ecclésiologiques. C'est sur ce terrain principalement que se situait notre recherche." [14] His second and final subject in this section is the relationship between the power of the pope and that of the bishops. He notes that all theologians of the time accepted that the pope possessed the totality of ecclesiastical power, but distinguishes between significantly different ways of understanding this held by two groups. A first group is comprised of the secular masters, and of some mendicants, among whom, Congar says, is "probablement S. Thomas d'Aquin." [15] This first group holds that "les clefs ont été promis à Pierre pour l'Église; elles appartiennent donc à l'Église. Les évêques les reçoivent immédiatement de Dieu"; there is implied here a "multiplication du pouvoir ecclésiastique dans les évêques." [16] This first group is distinguished from a second (which includes notably Bonaventure) largely because of the latter's holding the view that "[le] pape est la source de toute hiérarchie, c'est-à-dire de tout pouvoir; il est le principe du pouvoir des évêques, comme ceux-ci sont le principe du pouvoir des curés." [17]

In two claims regarding particular points of Aquinas' theology of papal primacy and the episcopacy we may also discern Congar's advocacy of the view that the bishops hold some spiritual power independently of the pope.

---

[12] Congar, p. 95.
[13] Ibid., pp. 145-151.
[14] Ibid., p. 147.
[15] Ibid., p. 150.
[16] Ibid., p. 150.
[17] Ibid., p. 151.

Regarding the bishops he writes: "... chaque évêque a une juridiction immédiate dans son diocèse: lui seul est proprement prélat...." [18] With respect to the pope he intimates that there is a specificity or limitation to his plenitude of power: "Chaque fois, *plenitudo potestatis* désigne une *potestas* ... supérieure à celle des simples évêques, mais rendant compte de facultés et d'actes précis." [19]

It will, I trust, by now be apparent that it is a feature of Congar's treatment of Aquinas that he tends to minimize the extent of Aquinas's claims on behalf of the papacy with respect to the spiritual power of the bishops. This feature will become more evident when we come shortly to review his analyses of the individual major texts of Aquinas on our theme.

To turn now briefly to Charles Zuckerman's article. While I fail to be persuaded by the arguments which Zuckerman brings forward in support of the two fundamental theses presented in the first part of his article,[20] that for Aquinas jurisdiction is simply the power of government in the church and is non-sacramental in origin,[21] I am indebted to him for a number of points he makes in the second part regarding the derivation of power in the church from the pope.[22] Here I shall examine only his view that Aquinas implies that the very power of orders itself derives from the pope to the bishops (and all clergy).[23] Having discussed a passage from the *Commentary on the Sentences* in which Aquinas asserts that Christ gave the power of orders to the apostles, but that of jurisdiction to Peter, Zuckerman judges the view expressed there to be eccentric in Aquinas' writings, in that (according to Zuckerman) it contradicts a view repeatedly implied by Aquinas elsewhere.[24] He asks: "How then, it may well be asked, could Aquinas have repeatedly written of Peter as the source of the other apostles' authority, not only without specifying that this derivation referred to jurisdiction alone, but in ways which implied that the authority derived from Peter to the other apostles had included orders as well?" [25] Shortly thereafter, with respect to the application of the biblical texts to the subsequent life of the church, Zuckerman concludes: "In this context, one can understand how an early pro-papal theologian [i.e., Aquinas] could adopt a line of argument which would imply that the papacy was the source of orders as well as of jurisdiction." [26]

[18] Ibid., p. 95.
[19] Ibid., p. 95.
[20] Zuckerman, pp. 99-115.
[21] See especially ibid., pp. 99, 104-108 and 111-115.
[22] See especially ibid., pp. 116-122.
[23] Ibid., pp. 123-128.
[24] Ibid., pp. 123-124.
[25] Ibid., p. 124.
[26] Ibid., p. 126.

From the point of view of this paper, the problem poses itself: how can such radically different interpretations of Aquinas' thought arise? Congar, having asserted or implied the universal derivation of jurisdiction from the pope, in effect neutralizes this interpretation by radical qualification; Zuckerman, by contrast, extends the principle of universal derivation to cover the essential power of the sacrament of orders too.

The heart of Congar's argument vis-à-vis Aquinas[27] is to be found where he quotes and comments on what he judges to be the principal texts touching the question: "Comment S. Thomas parle-t-il de la subordination du pouvoir des évêques par rapport à celui du pape?"[28] I can do no better, in putting forward what I understand to be Aquinas' position on the relationship of episcopal to papal power and specifying how my interpretation differs from that of Congar, than follow Congar's chronological review of the texts, and examine his comments on them; I shall, in addition, bring into the discussion along the way a number of important texts not considered by Congar.

Congar begins by quoting the following passage on obedience from *In II Sent.*, d. 44:

> It must be said in reply that a superior and an inferior power can be related in two ways. Either such that the inferior power totally originates from the superior, so that the whole force of the inferior is founded on the force of the superior; in this case one is simply and in all cases more bound to obey the superior than the inferior, just as in the events of nature the first cause has a greater influence on what is caused by the second cause than has the second cause itself, as is stated at the beginning of the *Book of Causes*. It is in this way that the power of God is related to every created power; in this way, too, the power of the emperor is related to the power of the proconsul; in this way also the power of the pope is related to all spiritual power in the church: for by the pope himself the various grades of dignities in the church are both disposed and ordered; so his power is a kind of foundation of the church, as is clear from Matthew 16....[29]

---

[27] Congar, pp. 93-95.

[28] Ibid., p. 93.

[29] *In II Sent.*, d. 44, *expos. textus*: "Respondeo dicendum quod potestas superior et inferior dupliciter possunt se habere. Aut ita quod inferior potestas ex toto oriatur a superiori, et tunc tota virtus inferioris fundatur supra virtutem superioris, et tunc simpliciter et in omnibus est magis obediendum potestati superiori quam inferiori; sicut etiam in naturalibus causa prima plus influit supra causatum causae secundae quam etiam ipsa causa secunda, ut in lib. *De causis*, in princ., dicitur, et sic se habet potestas Dei ad omnem potestatem creatam; sic etiam se habet potestas imperatoris ad potestatem proconsulis; sic etiam se habet potestas papae ad omnem spiritualem potestatem in Ecclesia: quia ab ipso papa gradus dignitatum diversi in Ecclesia et disponuntur et ordinantur; unde ejus potestas est quoddam Ecclesiae fundamentum, ut patet Matth., xvi" (ed. P. Mandonnet, Paris, 1929). The similarities between Aquinas' analysis here and the earlier discussion of obedience to a superior by Albert the Great are notable: see above, p. 99.

On this Congar comments: "Il s'agit évidemment ici d'un rapport de dépendance selon la causalité...." This scarcely very clear phrase he shortly thereafter expands: "Notons cependant la raison de dépendance que précise S. Thomas: 'quia ab ipso papa gradus dignitatum diversi in Ecclesia et disponuntur et ordinantur'. Le pape distribue et institue les divers postes de prélature. Il semble que nous soyions dans la ligne des textes canoniques cités plus haut." [30] The circumlocution in Congar's opening comment is understandable since, as we have seen, he does not wish to ascribe to Aquinas the view that all spiritual power in the church derives from the pope. Yet such a view gives the most natural interpretation of the passage quoted: "... the inferior power totally originates (*oriatur*) from the superior, so that the whole force of the inferior is founded on the force of the superior ... in this way also the power of the pope is related to all spiritual power in the church." Again in drawing attention to the canonistic language of disposing and ordering Congar is highlighting language that is of itself softer than that of origination or derivation.[31] It can readily be understood why Aquinas would make use of such language: it was rooted in church tradition and familiar in the schools of his day. But what any author means by such language must be gathered from an analysis of the context in which he uses such terms. In the case in hand, this means in the first place reading such language in the light of the preceding *oriatur* and the accompanying comparison with the First Cause and with the emperor, both of which clearly indicate derivation of the lower power from the higher. Thus it appears that when Aquinas makes use of the canonistic language he does so in order to draw from it the highest imaginable superiority that such language will bear: the softer tone, so to speak, and the simply implicit notion of derivation contained in the language of distribution become firm and explicit in Aquinas' interpretation, where he speaks of the originating of all spiritual power in the pope.

The sequel to this passage is not cited by Congar. It deals with the second way in which a higher and lower power can be related, and confirms the interpretation just given. There, too, the strong language of papal power as a source of the bishops' power is found: "Again a superior power and an inferior power can be related to each other in such a way that both originate from some single supreme power, which subjects one to the other as it

---

[30] Congar, p. 93.

[31] I prescind entirely from the question of how accurate Congar is in ascribing to the canonists this view of jurisdiction and of its derivation from the pope to the bishops. It is impossible here to enter into the complex question of the diverse views of the canonists on the relation of the pope to the bishops; see, for instance, the recent study by K. Pennington: *Popes and Bishops: The Papal Monarchy in the Twelfth and Thirteenth Centuries* (Philadelphia, 1984), esp. pp. 1-2 and 190-195.

wishes: and then one is not superior to the other except in matters in which one is placed under the other by the supreme authority; it is only with respect to those matters that one is more bound to obey the superior than the inferior, and this is how the powers of a bishop and an archbishop are related to each other, being powers which descend from the power of the pope." [32]

The second text quoted by Congar is a brief excerpt from *In IV Sent.* d. 20: "In reply to the third question it must be said that the pope has the fulness of pontifical power, like a king in a kingdom. But bishops are assigned particular charges (*assumuntur 'in partem sollicitudinis'*), like judges set over individual cities." [33] Congar comments: "Ces derniers mots rappellent l'idée exprimée par le Pseudo-Lucius ... et reprise par les canonistes. ... Nous croyons que l'on reste ici dans la perspective selon laquelle le pape distribue les charges ou les prélatures comme Pierre était censé avoir envoyé les autres Apôtres prêcher et avoir institué des primats, archevêques et évêques." [34] I have already noted that the language of distribution, which is here implied in the traditional "assumuntur in partem sollicitudinis," must be interpreted according to its particular context. We may observe here that the other imagery used by Aquinas points to more than the specification of an area for the exercise of an independently possessed power: the relationship of king to judges set over cities is plainly that of the source of power to those holding delegated power.

Before going on to consider the third text quoted by Congar, four other early passages not discussed by him should be examined; in these, too, the relationship of the bishops' power to that of the pope is described explicitly or implicitly in terms of the former's deriving from the latter. Three occur in Book Four of the *Commentary on the Sentences*; one is found in the *Contra impugnantes Dei cultum* written in reply to William of St. Amour in 1256, shortly after the completion of the *Commentary on the Sentences*.

In *In IV Sent.* d. 18, discussing the question of whether or not any priest can excommunicate, Aquinas gives the following as the first argument in favour of a positive answer (which he will argue against): "For excommunication is an act of the keys. But every priest has the keys. Therefore every priest

---

[32] *In II Sent.*, loc. cit.: "Possunt iterum potestas superior et inferior ita se habere, quod ambae oriantur ex una quadam suprema potestate, quae unam alteri subdit secundum quod vult; et tunc una non est superior altera nisi in his quibus una supponitur alii a suprema potestate; et in illis tantum est magis obediendum superiori quam inferiori; et hoc modo se habent potestates et episcopi et archiepiscopi, descendentes a papae potestate."

[33] *In IV Sent.*, d. 20, a. 4, q. 3: "Ad tertiam quaestionem dicendum quod Papa habet plenitudinem pontificalis potestatis, quasi Rex in regno. Sed Episcopi assumuntur 'in partem sollicitudinis,' quasi judices singulis civitatibus praepositi...." (ed. P. M. F. Moos, Paris, 1947).

[34] Congar, pp. 93-94.

can excommunicate." [35] Aquinas' reply must be quoted in full for the import of its final sentence to be grasped:

> In reply to the first argument it must be said that excommunication is not an act of the keys directly, but rather with respect to an exterior judgment. But a sentence of excommunication, though it is promulgated in an exterior judgment, nonetheless pertains to entry to the Kingdom, in that the church militant is the way to the church triumphant, and therefore that jurisdiction whereby a man can excommunicate may be called a key. Granted this, some people make a distinction between the key of orders, which all priests have; and the key of jurisdiction in the judicial forum, which only judges of the external forum have. God, however, gave both to Peter, Matthew 16:19; and it descends from him to others who have both. [36]

Aquinas' language is obscure at several points in this passage. One important point, however, touching the relationship between pope and bishops, seems clear beyond serious doubt. In the body of the *quaestiuncula* he gives it as the more reasonable opinion that only bishops and major prelates have the power to excommunicate by their own authority (*propria auctoritate*). In this they are distinguished from simple parochial priests. When, then, Aquinas in this reply refers to those who have both keys, he is referring to bishops and major prelates. His view, therefore, seems to be the following: bishops and major prelates have both keys by their own authority when considered in relation to simple priests; but viewed in the perspective of the universal church they hold these keys from the pope. Since Aquinas cannot be saying that they hold from the pope the key considered as the sacramental power of orders, he must be taken as referring to the exercise of this key as requiring jurisdiction from him. What makes Aquinas' statement regarding the derivation of the keys from the pope more striking is that it is not demanded by the argument; he unexpectedly widens the perspective. It is almost as if the statement about the descent of both keys from Peter is meant to correct a possible misunderstanding of his assertion that the power of excommunication is held *propria auctoritate* by bishops and major prelates.

---

[35] *In IV Sent.*, d. 18, q. 2, a. 2, q.ᵃ 1, arg. 1: "Excommunicatio enim est actus clavium. Sed quilibet sacerdos habet claves. Ergo quilibet potest excommunicare."

[36] Ibid.: "Ad primum ergo dicendum quod excommunicatio non est actus clavis directe, sed magis respectu exterioris judicii. Sed sententia excommunicationis, quamvis in exteriori judicio promulgetur, quia tamen aliquo modo pertinet ad aditum Regni, secundum quod Ecclesia militans est via ad triumphantem, ideo etiam talis jurisdictio per quam homo excommunicare potest, clavis dici potest. Et secundum hoc a quibusdam distinguitur quod est clavis ordinis, quam omnes sacerdotes habent; et clavis jurisdictionis in foro judiciali, quam habent soli judices exterioris fori. Utramque tamen Deus Petro contulit, Mat., xvi, 19; et ab ipso in alios descendit qui utramque habent."

For Aquinas, then, anyone who holds dual jurisdiction does so in virtue of holding this ultimately from the pope.

A further, and this time relatively lengthy, statement about the relation between papal and episcopal power occurs in distinction 19 of the same book. The subject with which we are concerned again arises in the context of a question regarding jurisdiction and the key. Aquinas states: "It seems that a priest may use the key he has with respect to anyone." [37] The first argument in favour of this position (a position which Aquinas rejects) is based on John 20:22: "The power of the keys descends to priests in virtue of the authoritative word of the Lord, John 20:22, in which he says: 'Receive the Holy Spirit. Whose sins you shall retain shall be retained.' But he said that indeterminately concerning all people. Therefore whoever has the key indeterminately can use it with respect to anyone." [38] Aquinas replies:

> In reply to the first argument it must be said that for absolution from sin two powers are needed, namely, the power of orders and the power of jurisdiction. The first power is equal in all priests, but not the second. And so where the Lord, at John 20:22, gave to all the apostles in common the power of remitting sins, this is understood as referring to the power attaching to orders. That is why those words are addressed to priests, too, when they are ordained. But to Peter individually he gave the power of remitting sins, at Matthew 16:19, so that it might be understood that Peter himself has precedence in the power of jurisdiction. The powers of orders, however, considered in itself, extends to all those requiring absolution. And so the Lord said indeterminately 'whose sins you shall forgive', understanding, however, that the use of that power ought to take place according to the disposition of Peter, granted the power given to him.[39]

---

[37] *In IV Sent.*, d. 19, q. 1, a. 3, q.ª 1: "Videtur quod sacerdos possit uti clave quam habet in quemlibet hominem."

[38] Ibid., arg. 1: "Potestas enim clavium in sacerdotes descendit ex illa Domini auctoritate qua dixit (Joan., xx, 22): 'Accipite Spiritum Sanctum. Quorum remiseritis peccata, remittentur eis.' Sed illud indeterminate dixit de omnibus. Ergo habens clavem indeterminate potest ea uti in quoslibet."

[39] Ibid.: "Ad primum ergo dicendum quod ad absolutionem a peccato requiritur duplex potestas: scilicet potestas ordinis, et potestas jurisdictionis. Prima quidem potestas est aequaliter in omnibus sacerdotibus, non autem secunda. Et ideo ubi Dominus, Joan. xx, 22, dedit omnibus Apostolis communiter potestatem remittendi peccata, intelligitur de potestate quae consequitur ordinem. Unde et sacerdotibus, quando ordinantur, illa verba dicuntur. Sed Petro dedit singulariter potestatem remittendi peccata, Mat., xvi, 19, ut intelligatur quod ipse prae aliis habet potestatem jurisdictionis. Potestas autem ordinis, quantum est de se, se extendit ad omnes absolvendos. Et ideo indeterminate Dominus dixit: 'Quorum remiseritis peccata,' intelligens tamen quod usus illius potestatis esse deberet praesupposita potestate Petro collata secundum ipsius ordinationem." It is, of course, clear from the context that for Aquinas here (as elsewhere) what was said by Christ of Peter is to be understood as applying to the pope.

Here, certainly, the text is narrower in scope, in that it touches only the sacrament of penance proper; and the language is not so overtly that of derivation. It is, however, certainly derivational by implication: Peter's precedence over the other apostles cannot be taken to refer simply to chronological priority; it suggests rather that Peter has the right to control the exercise of the keys by others. This interpretation is confirmed by the concluding words where it is said that the use or exercise of the keys ought to take place according to the disposition of Peter, granted the power of jurisdiction given to him — or perhaps better "in dependence on the power given to Peter" ("praesupposita potestate Petro collata").

The passage has a further importance. It is the first in which Aquinas explicitly correlates the two biblical passages Matthew 16:19 and John 20:22. Furthermore, he does so at greater length here than anywhere else. I would maintain, therefore, that the passage ought to be accorded a paradigmatic status; failing indications to the contrary, Aquinas' shorter and less clear treatment elsewhere of the relationship between these two biblical texts should be interpreted in the light of this fuller statement, where John 20 is said to refer to orders and Matthew 16 to both orders and jurisdiction, with Peter possessing the latter preeminently and the apostles holding it in dependence on him. Thus it is a serious omission when Congar ignores this passage. (I may add, in anticipation, that it is also misleading when Zuckerman treats it as eccentric, and draws his basic theory from shorter passages where the interpretation of Aquinas' mind is more heavily dependent on the interpreter's reconstruction.)

The final text of importance in the *Commentary on the Sentences* which is not considered by Congar is IV, d. 24, q. 3, a. 2, q.ª 3, particularly the *ad primum*. The question addressed is whether there can be a ruling power in the Church above that of a bishop. Aquinas replies that, in accordance with the Aristotelian principle that "wherever there are many directed to a single end, there has to be a universal ruling power above particular ruling powers," the power of the pope is that by which the whole church is ruled.[40] The first argument to the contrary had been: "It seems that there cannot be some superior in the church who is above the bishops. For all the bishops are

---

[40] *In IV Sent.*, d. 24, q. 3, a. 2, q.ª 3: "Ad tertiam quaestionem dicendum, quod ubicumque sunt multa ordinata in unum, oportet esse aliquod universale regimen supra particularia regimina: quia in omnibus virtutibus et artibus, ut dicitur in I *Ethic.*, cap. 1, est ordo secundum ordinem finium. ... et ideo cum tota Ecclesia sit unum corpus, oportet, si ista unitas debet conservari, quod sit aliqua potestas regativa respectu totius Ecclesiae supra potestatem episcopalem, qua unaquaeque specialis Ecclesia regitur; et haec est potestas Papae; et ideo qui hanc potestatem negant, schismatici dicuntur, quasi divisores ecclesiasticae unitatis" (ed. Vivès, vol. 11).

successors of the apostles. But the power which is given to one apostle, namely Peter, at Matthew 16:19, is given also to all the apostles at John 20:23. So all the bishops are equal, and one is not above the other." [41] Aquinas comments: "In reply to the first argument, therefore, it must be said that although the power to bind and loose is given in common to all the apostles, nonetheless in order to indicate that a certain order obtains within this power, it is first given only to Peter, to show that this power ought to descend from him to the others. For this reason it is also said individually to him, at Luke 22:32: 'Strengthen your brothers'; and at John 21:17: 'Feed my sheep,' that is, in my place. Chrysostom comments on this: 'Be the leader and head of the brothers, so that they, acknowledging you in my place, may everywhere on earth preach you and confirm you seated on your throne'." [42]

Four features of this text are noteworthy. First, the power of Peter with respect to that of the apostles (which Aquinas here as elsewhere takes to be the same as the power of the pope with respect to that of the bishops) is presented as the source of the other apostles' power: the order which Christ wills within this power is a descending one, from Peter to the others. Second, the power of binding and loosing is properly interpreted in the context of the body of the *quaestiuncula*, where the subject is the power of ruling *as such*;[43] the power which is said to descend, then, is of the broadest extension, and may be understood to mean all that is required for ruling a diocese, that is, spiritual power in the widest sense. Third, Aquinas says that this power "ought to descend from Peter to the others," and suggests thereby that what he is speaking of is a proper order that may not be observed in practice. This indicates, therefore, that Aquinas has in mind a point made earlier in the passage in distinction 19 discussed above: orders are given equally to the apostles (and bishops), jurisdiction derives from Peter (and the pope). This interpretation is confirmed by the third response in the present text where Aquinas writes that "as regards what pertains to the episcopal order, all

---

[41] Ibid., arg. 1: "Videtur quod supra episcopos non possit aliquis esse superior in ecclesia. Quia omnes episcopi sunt apostolorum successores. Sed potestas quae est data uni apostolorum, scilicet Petro, Matth. xvi, 19, est etiam data omnibus apostolis, Joan. xx, 23. Ergo omnes episcopi sunt pares, et unus non est supra alterum."

[42] Ibid.: "Ad primum ergo dicendum, quod quamvis omnibus apostolis data sit communiter potestas ligandi et solvendi; tamen ut in hac potestate ordo aliquis significaretur, primo soli Petro data est, ut ostendatur quod ab eo in alios debeat ista potestas descendere, propter quod etiam ei dixit singulariter, Luc. xxii, 32: 'Confirma fratres tuos'; et Joan. xxi, 17: 'Pasce oves meas,' id est, loco mei; ubi Chrysostomus dicit: 'Praepositus et caput esto fratrum ut ipsi te in loco meo assumentes ubique terrarum te in throno tuo sedentem praedicent, et confirment'."

[43] Ibid.: see n. 40 above.

bishops are equal." [44] Finally, we should note the tenor of the words attributed to Chrysostom which, though they do not say that the power of the bishops derives from the pope, readily lend themselves to this view, as Aquinas intimates in quoting them here: Peter is the leader and head, he is in the place of Christ, and exercises that role as one seated on a throne.

It is a curious fact that when Aquinas replies, in the *Contra impugnantes*, to William of St. Amour's objections to the mendicants' ministry, he gives relatively little attention to the power of the pope, [45] choosing instead to argue at length the view that the power of the bishop is the source of the power of all priests who have the care of souls in his diocese. But he does not entirely ignore the question of papal power, and one passage in particular is worthy of attention. Responding to the objection that any priest has control by right over who exercises a ministry in his parish, because he is the spouse of the parish, Aquinas says that only Christ properly speaking is the spouse of the church, and others act in his stead, cooperating in an exterior way. The pope is spouse of the whole church, the bishop of the diocese, and the priest of the parish. But each of the superiors is also spouse at the lower level: the pope is spouse of the diocese and the bishop spouse of the parish. Concluding what is inevitably a cumbersome application of imagery, Aquinas writes: "Nor does it follow from this that there are several spouses of the one church, for priests by their ministry cooperate with the bishop *tamquam principali*, and similarly the bishops with the pope, and the pope with Christ. So Christ, the pope, the bishop and the priest are to be reckoned nothing other than one spouse of the church." [46]

---

[44] Ibid.: "... et ideo quantum ad ea quae sunt episcopalis ordinis, omnes episcopi sunt aequales...."

[45] This is curious because one of the major objections put forward by William of St. Amour was that the mendicants were in error when they argued that papal authority superseded that of the bishops, and that, therefore, the pope's grant of permission to exercise the priestly ministry sufficed, without need of further authorization from the bishop: see J. T. Marrone, "The Ecclesiology of the Parisian Secular Masters 1250-1320," unpublished Ph.D. thesis, Cornell University, 1972 (University Microfilms, Ann Arbor, Michigan, 1984), pp. 62-63, 68-69 and 76. On the novelty of William's views regarding the immediate divine origin of the governmental powers of bishops and parish priests see ibid., pp. 71 and 84, and J. D. Dawson, "William of Saint-Amour and the Apostolic Tradition," *MedS* 40 (1978) 223-238, at p. 235. For a recent study of Aquinas' views in the *Contra impugnantes* see M. R. Schmitz, "Die Beziehung Papst-Bischof-Priester im Opusculum 'Contra Impugnantes' des hl. Thomas von Aquin," *Theologie und Glaube* 74 (1984) 204-221. A detailed chronological account of the mendicant-secular dispute is given by M. M. Dufeil, *Guillaume de Saint-Amour et la polémique universitaire parisienne, 1250-1259* (Paris, 1972).

[46] *Contra impugnantes* 4 (#14, ll. 1340-1346): "Nec tamen propter hoc sequitur quod sint plures sponsi unius Ecclesiae, quia sacerdos suo ministerio cooperatur episcopo tamquam principali, et similiter episcopi papae, et papa ipso Christo; unde Christus et papa et episcopus et sacerdos non computantur nisi unus sponsus Ecclesiae."

I have left *tamquam principali* untranslated, for these words may have two significantly different meanings. They may simply mean that the one cooperates with the other "as with a superior." I would suggest, however, that a stronger meaning is intended: "as with a source." This interpretation would fit better with the application of the words to Christ, of whom the others are said to be merely instruments or ministers.[47] Furthermore, one of the major themes of the *Contra impugnantes* is that the priest holds his authority from the bishop, and has no independent power vis-à-vis the church.[48] It is, therefore, likely that when Aquinas says in this context that bishops cooperate with the pope *tamquam principali* he understands episcopal authority as being exercised in dependence on that of the pope, from whom the bishops' power derives. Understood thus, the linking together of priest, bishop, pope and Christ makes ready sense, while a weaker interpretation in terms merely of superiority would put the most important figure, Christ, in the implausible position of being, so to speak, the odd man out.[49]

To return now to the texts presented by Congar. He moves from Aquinas' *Commentary on the Sentences* to the *Summa contra Gentiles*, IV.76, which he dates "vers 1260."[50] I think it preferable to follow the dating adopted by James Weisheipl, who writes with respect to the *Summa contra Gentiles*: "It

---

[47] See, for example, ibid. 4 (#14, ll. 1289-1299).

[48] See, for example, ibid. 4 (#7, ll. 603-610).

[49] A thorough study of the meaning of *principalis* and its cognates, particularly in Aquinas' discussions of the exercise of spiritual power, would, of course, either confirm or weaken the case for the interpretation of *principalis* given here. I have not undertaken such a study, but an examination of some of the texts indicates that the use of *principalis* in the present text to mean "as a source" would by no means be unique in the context of Aquinas' discussions of spiritual power: see *Quaest. Quodl.* II, q. 8, a. 2: "... Papa enim potest principaliter, alii vero in quantum potestatem ab eo accipiunt vel ordinariam, vel commissam, vel delegatam" (ed. R. Spiazzi, revd. ed., Turin, 1949); *De forma absolutionis poenitentiae sacramentalis* 3 (ll. 45-49): "... potestas autem clavium non computatur inter gratias gratis datas, sed est virtus sacramentalis quae principaliter resident in Christo, instrumentaliter autem sive ministerialiter in sacerdotibus habentibus claves"; *S.T.* II-II, q. 184, a. 6 ad 3um: "Ad tertium dicendum quod sicut plebani et archidiaconi non habent principaliter curam, sed administrationem quandam secundum quod eis ab episcopo committitur; ita etiam ad eos non pertinet principaliter pastorale officium, nec obligatio ponendi animam pro ovibus, sed in quantum participant de cura"; cf. also *In II Ad Cor.*, ad I, 1; *S.T.* III, q. 63, a. 3 ad 2um and q. 71, a. 4 ad 1um. The difficulty of knowing whether Aquinas by *principaliter* means simply "mainly" or also "as a source" is acutely met in *S.T.* II-II, q. 11, a. 2 ad 3um. Speaking there of the authority in the church to determine what is or is not a doctrine of faith, Aquinas says: "Quae quidem auctoritas principaliter resident in Summo Pontifice. Dicitur enim XXIV^a, q. 1 cn. [12]: 'Quoties fidei ratio ventilatur, arbitror omnes fratres nostros et coepiscopos non nisi ad Petrum, idest sui nominis auctoritatem, referre debere.'" (Cf. "principaliter resident in Christo" in the passage from *De forma absolutionis* above; for the citation from the *Decretum*, see Friedberg 1: 970).

[50] Congar, p. 94.

seems that IV, c. 69, was completed after his treatise *Contra errores Graeco-rum* ... since Thomas summarizes the same arguments concerning the consecration of unleavened bread in this *Summa* that he had used in the *Contra errores Graecorum* in the summer of 1263." [51]

The third text discussed by Congar according to the latter chronology is the *Commentary on Matthew*. From Aquinas' discussion of 16:19 Congar cites the concluding words: "But another question arises, because elsewhere the following is found: 'Whose sins you shall remit they are remitted'; here however this is said only to Peter. It must be said that [Christ] directly gives to Peter; others, however, receive from Peter; so lest these words be thought to be spoken only to Peter, he says: 'Whose sins you shall remit.' For this reason the pope, who holds the place of Peter, has full power; others, however, from him." [52] As is apparent, I have translated this text fairly literally, declining to supply objects where none appears in the original. In quoting this text, Congar prefaces his quotation of Aquinas with the brief remark: "Vers la même date [1260] ou un peu avant, S. Thomas, dans son commentaire si discret sur le texte de Mt., 16, 19, *Quodcumque ligaveris super terram...*, s'objecte le texte de Jn, 20, 23, où Jésus dit à tous les Apôtres, *Quorum remiseritis....*" [53]

Si discret is a disconcertingly incomplete comment. [54] The passage is certainly short and free of emotion, but it contains strong assertions, the more notable for the absence of qualifications. That for Aquinas Peter is the source of the other apostles' power given at John 20 is patent: "others, however, receive from Peter ... [the pope] has full power; others, however, from him." What it is they receive may be deduced from Aquinas' imme-diately preceding words, where he discusses the power to bind and loose in terms both of the sacramental power of penance and of the power to withdraw a priest's power to administer the sacraments by excommunicating him. Since, as has been shown, Aquinas regarded possession of the sacra-mental power as such as originating in orders, the least we must understand him to mean in the context is that what derives from the pope is the right to exercise the power to forgive sins and the right to excommunicate. It seems plausible, however, granted the absence of specific objects for the

---

[51] James Weisheipl, *Friar Thomas d'Aquino* (Oxford, 1974), p. 360.

[52] *In Ev. Matth.*, ad XVI, 16: "Sed est alia quaestio, quia alibi habetur, Io. XX, 23: 'Quorum remiseritis peccata remittentur eis'; hic vero solum hoc dicit Petro. Dicendum quod immediate dedit Petro; alii vero a Petro recipiunt; ideo ne credantur ista solum dici Petro, dicit: 'Quorum remiseritis' etc. Et hac ratione papa, qui est loco sancti Petri, habet plenariam potestatem, alii vero ab ipso" (ed. R. Cai, Turin, 1951).

[53] Congar, p. 94.

[54] Contrast the comment of K. Froehlich above, p. 18.

verbs, and the attribution of an unqualified *plenaria potestas* to the pope, to understand him to mean that it is anything falling within the scope of binding and loosing, i.e., the general *regimen* of the church's life, that derives from the pope. The text cannot be overpressed, but neither can the bold and unqualified nature of its claim be ignored.

The fourth of Aquinas' discussions of the papacy on which Congar comments is that of the "textes fameux" in the *Contra errores Graecorum.*[55] Simply referring to these texts, Congar notes: "Ils attribuent au pape une autorité suprême"; but he goes on immediately to give two indications that this supreme authority is to be understood in a restricted sense. He asserts first: "Nulle part cependant S. Thomas n'en déduit la thèse d'une origine de tous les pouvoirs ecclésiastiques dans le 'primus et maximus omnium episcoporum'."[56] Congar is perfectly correct that Aquinas makes no explicit claim for such an origin here, but it must be said that *nulle part* fails to do justice to the force of Aquinas' language in these passages. Some of the texts cited by Aquinas from his putative patristic sources are either equivalent to, or fall little short of, describing the pope as the source of all authority in the Church. In particular, Cyril of Alexandria is reported by Aquinas (on the basis of the source on which he is commenting) as follows: " 'Just as Christ coming forth from Israel as the leader and ruler of the Church of the gentiles received from the Father the complete fulness of power over every principality and power, and over absolutely everything that exists, so that every knee should bend to him, so he in turn committed this in its complete fulness to Peter and to his successors' ";[57] " 'To no one other than to Peter did Christ give what was his in its fulness' ";[58] " 'they affirmed in the gospels and epistles that in all matters of doctrine Peter and his church served in the place of the Lord, by giving to that very one a place in every assembly and gathering, in

---

[55] Congar, p. 94. It is now known, of course, that many of the texts purporting to be patristic in the *Liber de fide Trinitatis* (on which Aquinas was asked to comment by Urban IV) are spurious; the notes to the Leonine edition (vol. 40, ed. H. F. Dondaine, Rome, 1969) deal with this in detail. For the nature and authorship of the *Liber* see ibid., pp. A 6-7 and 18-19. As was noted above, Cyril of Alexandria is the Father to whom are attributed the statements making the strongest claims regarding papal powers. The two other Fathers quoted in the chapters dealing with the papacy (*Contra errores Graecorum* II, 32-38), are John Chrysostom and Maximus the Confessor. Unlike the supposed quotations from Cyril, the ideas attributed to these latter have some foundation in their writings.

[56] Congar, p. 94.

[57] *Contra errores Graecorum* II, 34 (ll. 7-12): " 'Sicut Christus accepit a Patre dux et sceptrum Ecclesiae gentium ex Israel egrediens super omnem principatum et potestatem et super omne quodcumque est ut ei genu cuncta curventur plenissimam potestatem, sic et Petro et eius successoribus plenissime commisit.' "

[58] Ibid. II, 34 (ll. 13-14): " 'Nulli alii quam Petro Christus quod suum est plenum, sed ipsi soli dedit.' "

every decision and declaration. ... To him, that is, to Peter, all bow their heads by divine law, and the leaders of the world obey him as if he were the Lord Jesus himself";[59] "'to it alone', that is, to the apostolic throne of the Roman Pontiffs, 'does it belong to reprehend, correct, make decrees, settle affairs, and loose and bind in place of him who established it'."[60]

The second qualification which Congar enters is that Aquinas does not after this work cite the texts attributed to Cyril (whose texts make the strongest claims for Peter and the pope); Congar deduces from this that Aquinas must subsequently have doubted the authenticity of what was, in fact, a spurious source. Let us grant that this is the reason for the subsequent absence of these texts from Aquinas' writings. To do so does not call in question that Aquinas agreed with the substance of the texts cited, as Congar might well be taken to mean. In the first place, Aquinas would scarcely have quoted this putative source if he had believed that the degree of power attributed to the popes in the texts given there were excessive. Further, he explicitly states that the passages quoted can be verified from scripture: he remarks after citing the texts in favour of the universal prelacy of Peter over the whole church: "This also is drawn from the authority of sacred Scripture," and quotes John 21:17 and John 10:16;[61] he makes the same remark after the texts in favour of the pope's plenitude of power, this time quoting Matthew 16:19;[62] after the texts in favour of the view that it belongs to the pope to determine what pertains to faith, he remarks: "Not unjustly, for we read that Peter first confessed the perfect faith, through the revelation of the Lord," citing Matthew 16:16 and Luke 22:32a;[63] and, most notably perhaps, he comments after the words of Pseudo-Cyril and of Chrysostom, which he cites in support of the view that the pope is prelate even over the other patriarchs: "And this, too, is clear from the authority of the Lord," this time quoting Luke 22:32b.[64]

The chronologically fifth passage in Aquinas writings which Congar discusses is the final section of Book IV, chapter 76 of the *Summa contra*

---

[59] Ibid. II, 35 (ll. 21-27): "'in evangeliis et epistolis affirmaverunt in omni doctrina Petrum esse loco Domini et eius ecclesiam, eidem dantes locum in omni capitulo et synagoga, in omni electione et affirmatione. ... Cui, scilicet Petro, omnes iure divino caput inclinant et primates mundi tamquam ipsi Domino Iesu obediunt.'"

[60] Ibid. II, 37 (ll. 2-6): "Cyrillus dicit quod 'ipsius,' scilicet apostolici throni Romanorum pontificum, 'solius est reprehendere, corrigere, statuere, disponere, solvere et loco illius ligare qui ipsum aedificavit.'"

[61] Ibid. II, 33 (ll. 22-26): "Hoc etiam trahitur ex auctoritate sacrae Scripturae...."

[62] Ibid. II, 34 (ll. 29-32).

[63] Ibid. II, 36 (ll. 14-18): "Nec immerito, nam Petrus legitur primo perfectam fidem esse confessus Domino revelante...."

[64] Ibid. II, 37 (ll. 11-13): "Et hoc etiam patet ex auctoritate Domini...."

Gentiles.[65] A methodological point should be made before considering Congar's interpretation of this passage. Neither Congar nor Zuckerman gives this passage the importance it deserves: both quote only a short extract from it, and neither discusses it at length.[66] I would maintain that this chapter, together with the passage from *In IV Sent.* d. 19, where Aquinas distinguishes between the derivation of orders and the derivation of jurisdiction, ought to be given pride of place in considering Aquinas' treatment of our topic. Despite its relative brevity (it runs to no more than three printed pages), *S.C.G.* IV, 76 contains the longest single discussion by Aquinas of the relationship between bishops and the pope, and was written when Aquinas had attained full theological maturity. The discussion there acquires greater significance from the fact that it is Aquinas' last major statement on our subject; the sections of the *Summa theologiae* in which the papacy and its powers would have been treated at length, such as those on the sacrament of orders or on the minister of the sacrament of penance, were never written.

It is the more noteworthy, then, that it is in this discussion that Aquinas asserts most directly what I have termed "a universal derivational theory of spiritual power." The word *derivare* is a key term in the final, most relevant section of the chapter. Granted the importance of this chapter, it is likewise the more regrettable that Congar proposes a reading of the most crucial words which cannot be accepted. He quotes the following: "'To you I give the keys of the kingdom of heaven,' that it may be clear that the power of the keys is to be derived through [Peter] to others, in order to preserve the unity of the church."[67] On these words Congar comments: "La suite du texte suggère que cette 'derivatio ad alios' viserait, non la communication de la *potestas clavium* aux autres évêques ou prélats, mais la transmission de ce pouvoir pétrinien des clefs aux successeurs de Pierre ('derivatio ad posteros'): en ce cas, l'*unitas conservanda* serait l'unité dans le temps, la continuité, l'apostolicité romaine."[68] Such an interpretation is, I shall now argue, definitively excluded by the structure of Aquinas' argument.

---

[65] This passage is fifth according to the chronology adopted here (see above, p. 208); it comes third in Congar's discussion.

[66] Congar, p. 94; he refers to this chapter also at pp. 95 and 104-105; Zuckerman discusses it at pp. 122-123.

[67] *S.C.G.* IV, 76: "'Tibi davo claves regni caelorum'; ut ostenderetur potestas clavium per eum ad alios derivanda ad conservandam Ecclesiae unitatem."

[68] Congar, p. 94. Zuckerman also disputes Congar's reading of this final section: see his brief discussion at pp. 122-123, n. 48, where he justly remarks: "If Congar's interpretation of this passage were accepted, then Aquinas' proof of papal primacy would have consisted of a demonstration of the papal succession to the position of Peter without a prior demonstration of a petrine primacy among the first disciples of Christ."

Since the final section of this chapter is so important, and will require detailed analysis, it merits being quoted in full:

> And so in the church militant, too, there is one who presides over all. That is why it is said at Hosea 1:11: "Both the children of Juda and the children of Israel will be gathered together, and they will appoint one head over themselves." And the Lord says, at John 10:16: "There shall be one flock and one shepherd."
>
> If anyone should say that the one head and one shepherd is Christ, who is the one bridegroom of the one church, his reply is inadequate. It is clear, certainly, that it is Christ himself who is at work in all the sacraments of the church, for it is he himself who baptizes, he himself who remits sins, he himself is the true priest, who offered himself on the altar of the cross and by whose power his own body is daily consecrated on the altar. Nevertheless, because he would not in the future be bodily present to all the faithful, he chose ministers through whom he would dispense the sacraments to the faithful, as was said above [ch. 74]. For the same reason, then, namely, that he would be withdrawn in his bodily presence from the church, it was necessary that he should appoint someone who would have care of the universal church in his place. That is why he said to Peter before his ascension: "Feed my sheep" (in the final chapter of John); and before his passion: "When you have returned to me once more, confirm your brothers," Luke 22:32; and to him alone he promised: "To you I shall give the keys of the kingdom of heaven," that it might be clear that the power of the keys should derive from him to others, in order to preserve the unity of the church.
>
> It cannot be said, however, that although he gave this dignity to Peter it nonetheless does not derive to others. For it is clear that Christ so instituted the church that it would endure to the end of the world, in accordance with what is said at Isaiah 9:7: "He will sit on the throne of David ruling over his kingdom, that he might confirm it and strengthen it in justice and right-eousness thenceforth and for evermore." It is clear, therefore, that he so instituted those who at that time were in the ministry that their power would derive to those who were to come after them, for the good of the church, until the end of the world. This is particularly clear since he himself says in the final chapter of Matthew: "Behold, I am with you all days, until the consummation of the world."
>
> By this, then, is excluded the presumptuous error of some people who seek to withdraw themselves from obedience and subjection to Peter, by refusing to acknowledge his successor the Roman Pontiff as pastor of the universal church.[69]

---

[69] *S.C.G.* IV, 76: "Ergo et in Ecclesia militante unus est qui praesidet universis. Hinc est quod Os 1, 11, dicitur: 'Congregabuntur filii Iuda et filii Israel pariter, et ponent sibi caput unum.' Et Dominus dicit, Io 10, 16: 'Fiet unum ovile et unus pastor.' Si quis autem dicat quod

Aquinas begins his concluding comment, then, by proposing that it is insufficient to say that the words "one head" and "one shepherd" refer only to Christ. He substantiates this by saying that Christ instituted the sacraments and appointed ministers to dispense these when he would no longer be bodily with the faithful, and that Christ for the same reason (i.e., his absence in the body) appointed one to have universal care of the whole church in his stead. At this point Aquinas cites the three famous Petrine texts, and glosses Matthew 16 in the words quoted by Congar. Aquinas continues immediately after these words: "It cannot be said, however, that although he gave this dignity to Peter, it nonetheless does not derive to others. For it is clear that Christ so instituted the church that it would endure to the end of the world...." [70] The words just quoted mark, therefore, a transition point in the argument: having spoken of the relationship that obtained between Peter and the apostles, Aquinas then goes on to argue that this same relationship obtains between the successors of Peter and the successors of the apostles. While, therefore, the power of the keys is said to "derive" in the passage cited by Congar, and the dignity of Peter is said to "derive" in the immediately following words, the referent is different: in the first case what is referred to is the derivation of the power of the keys to the other apostles from Peter; in the second, to the derivation of the Petrine dignity to his successors in the papacy.

---

unum caput et unus pastor est Christus, qui est unus unius Ecclesiae sponsus: non sufficienter respondet. Manifestum est enim quod omnia ecclesiastica sacramenta ipse Christus perficit: ipse enim est qui baptizat; ipse qui peccata remittit; ipse est verus sacerdos, qui se obtulit in ara crucis, et cuius virtute corpus eius in altari quotidie consecratur: et tamen, quia corporaliter non cum omnibus fidelibus praesentialiter erat futurus, elegit ministros, per quos praedicta fidelibus dispensaret, ut supra (c. 74) dictum est. Eadem igitur ratione, quia praesentiam corporalem erat Ecclesiae subtracturus, oportuit ut alicui committeret qui loco sui universalis Ecclesiae gereret curam. Hinc est quod Petro dixit ante ascensionem: 'pasce oves meas,' Io ult.; et ante passionem: 'Tu iterum conversus, confirma fratres tuos,' Lc 22, 32; et ei soli promisit: 'Tibi dabo claves regni caelorum'; ut ostenderetur potestas clavium per eum ad alios derivanda ad conservandam Ecclesiae unitatem. Non potest autem dici quod, etsi Petro hanc dignitatem dederit, tamen ad alios non derivatur. Manifestum est enim quod Christus Ecclesiam sic instituit ut esset usque ad finem saeculi duratura: secundum illud Is 9, 7: 'Super solium David, et super regnum eius sedebit, ut confirmet illud et corroboret in iudicio et iustitia, amodo et usque in sempiternum.' Manifestum est igitur quod ita illos qui tunc erant in ministerio constituit, ut eorum potestas derivaretur ad posteros, pro utilitate Ecclesiae, usque ad finem saeculi: praesertim cum ipse dicat, Mt ult.: 'Ecce, ego vobiscum sum usque ad consummationem saeculi.' Per hoc autem excluditur quorumdam praesumptuosus error, qui se subducere nituntur ab obedientia et subiectione Petri, successorem eius Romanum Pontificem universalis Ecclesiae pastorem non recognoscentes."

[70] Ibid.: "Non potest autem dici quod, etsi Petro hanc dignitatem dederit, tamen ad alios non derivatur. Manifestum est enim quod Christus Ecclesiam sic instituit ut esset usque ad finem saeculi duratura...."

It is only thus that we can see a smooth sequence in the passage. If the two sentences which speak of derivation from Peter referred to the same derivation, as Congar suggests — that of Peter's power to his successors after his death — Aquinas in the second sentence would merely be reasserting what he had just previously stated, and be doing so in a distinctly odd way. Having put forward a proof for the derivation of the keys to Peter's successors based on Christ's words to Peter recorded at Matthew 16:19, he would immediately go on to speak as if his point had not been made, and to offer a different, independent proof, namely, that the derivation of Peter's power to his successors is to be deduced from the broader commission to the apostles recorded at Matthew 28, this commission (in Aquinas' eyes) being a proof that Christ wished the church he had already founded to continue to the end of time. Further, the text cited at Matthew 16:19 in fact refers only to Peter, and in itself does not indicate that it is applicable to Peter's successors. It is not until reference is made to Christ's words expressing his will that the church's work extend to the whole world and continue until the end of time, that another point, the application of Matthew 16:19 to Peter's successors, becomes readily comprehensible and is supported by some argument; this extension is introduced only in the second passage.

Moreover, the change in periods being spoken of in the two parts of the passage is plainly signalled by the word *tunc*: "those who *at that time* were in the ministry" in the second passage refers back to those spoken of as ministers in the previous passage, i.e., to the apostles, who in the second passage only are linked to, and distinguished from, their successors. In this second passage, too, the word *derivare* is used with reference to the derivation of the apostles' powers to their successors, and it is, therefore, in this sense that it is to be interpreted in the second passage with reference to the dignity of Peter. Aquinas is, then, arguing as follows in the second passage: what Christ did in instituting the apostles as ministers is to continue throughout the church's history, for we have the explicit words of Christ indicating that this is his will; from this (Aquinas believes) we ought to draw the further conclusion that the relation between the apostles and Peter is also to obtain in this continuation, that is, just as the apostles first derived their power from Peter, so the successors of the apostles are to derive their power from the successor of Peter — a point which would be redundant had Aquinas' words quoted by Congar already applied to derivation throughout time and not just to the period of the apostles. The derivation of the power of the keys from Peter spoken of in the first part of the passage must, then, *pace* Congar, be understood to refer simply to the derivation of that power from Peter to the other apostles. It is the second part of the passage that deals with the derivation of the power of the keys from Peter to his successors, i.e., with the transmission of the supreme authority through the line of the popes, who stand in the same relation to the bishops as that of Peter to the apostles.

This chapter is also illuminating with respect to the scope of the power of the keys which is said to derive from Peter to the apostles, and subsequently from the pope to the bishops. The immediate context of the discussion of the power of the keys (the concluding section of the chapter, quoted above) itself indicates that what is to be understood as falling within the scope of this power is the care of souls in the widest sense, including the administration of the sacraments. As I have noted, Matthew 16:19, which speaks of the power of the keys, is one of the three major Petrine texts which are quoted by Aquinas in that section, all of which are cited by him to show that Christ appointed Peter to exercise "universalis Ecclesiae ... curam." This indicates that what Aquinas saw as deriving from Peter was likewise a share in this *cura*. The statement about Peter's *cura* in turn follows Aquinas' saying that Christ instituted the sacraments so that he, Christ, might act through them, this being made possible through his appointing apostles to administer the sacraments. The *cura* spoken of, then, appears to be in the first place a sacramental one, referring to the perfection of people made possible through the entire sacramental life of the Church.

The accuracy of giving this broad interpretation to *cura* in this section is confirmed by the opening argument of the same chapter. This chapter, which follows two chapters dealing with (respectively) the sacrament of orders and distinctions within that sacrament, is designed to show both that there is a supreme dignity within the sacrament of orders, that of bishop, and that there is one who is supreme within the episcopacy, the pope. As regards the first point, Aquinas notes that the power of the bishop does not exceed that of a priest with respect to the consecration of the (eucharistic) body of Christ, but does exceed it in what pertains to the faithful. Explaining this, he writes: "For the sacerdotal power itself derives from the episcopal; and anything difficult that is required to be done with regard to the faithful is reserved to the bishop, by whose authority it is that priests can do what is committed to them to be done." [71] Where one might expect that Aquinas would then go on to speak of some matter requiring jurisdiction as explaining what priests can do in virtue of episcopal power, he says in fact: "So it is that in what priests do they use things consecrated by the bishop: for example, in consecrating the Eucharist they use a chalice, altar and pall consecrated by

---

[71] Ibid. (arg. 1): "Nam et ipsa sacerdotalis potestas ab episcopali derivatur; et quicquid arduum circa populum fidelem est agendum episcopis reservatur; quorum auctoritate etiam sacerdotes possunt hoc quod eis agendum committitur."

the bishop." [72] He draws the conclusion: "It is clear, therefore, that the highest rank in ruling the faithful ("summa regiminis fidelis populi") pertains to the episcopal dignity." [73] Aquinas continues by describing the bishop as head of the diocese and the pope as head of the whole church.

This opening argument indicates, therefore, that when in the remaining arguments of this chapter Aquinas describes the pope as "leading" the whole church, [74] as "ruling" it, [75] as "presiding over all in the church," [76] or, in the final section just discussed, as having "the power of the keys" from which the bishop's power derives, what he has in mind is not ruling in any narrow juridical sense, nor binding and loosing in any strict penitential sense, but governance of the entire life of the church, including (and supremely so) its sacramental life. This corresponds, as we have seen, to what is implied in the final section of this chapter, which is the immediate context of his assertion that the power of the keys derives from Peter.

The view that the power of the keys in chapter 76 has a broad extension is further confirmed by a remark Aquinas makes a little earlier. In chapter 72, which is concerned with the more limited question of the necessity of the sacrament of penance, Aquinas considers the question of whether prelates might dispense someone from the need to use this sacrament. In his answer he makes a striking comment which suggests that for him the entire range of episcopal power is encompassed by the power of the keys. He gives the following as the ground for denying that prelates can give this dispensation: "Prelates of the church cannot so act that 'they render useless the keys of the church,' in which [keys] the whole of their power consists." [77]

We also find in chapter 72 confirmation of the view that the power of the keys derives from the pope to the bishops. Having described the two keys of the church as "the authority to discern regarding sin, and the power to absolve or condemn," Aquinas goes on to say that Christ committed these to Peter according to Matthew 16. He continues: "Their having been committed to Peter is not so to be understood that he alone would hold

---

[72] Ibid.: "Unde et in his quae sacerdotes agunt, utuntur rebus per episcopum consecratis: ut in Eucharistiae consecratione utuntur consecratis per episcopum calice, altari et pallis."

[73] Ibid.: "Sic igitur manifestum est quod summa regiminis fidelis populi ad episcopalem pertinet dignitatem."

[74] Ibid. (arg. 2): "Non est igitur dubitandum quin ex ordinatione Christi unus toti Ecclesiae praesit."

[75] Ibid. (arg. 3): "Optimum autem regimen multitudinis est ut regatur per unum. ... Manifestum est igitur regimen Ecclesiae sic esse dispositum ut unus toti Ecclesiae praesit."

[76] Ibid. (arg. 4): "Ergo et in Ecclesia militante unus est qui praesidet universis."

[77] Ibid., 72: "Non enim hoc possunt praelati Ecclesiae, ut 'claves frustrentur Ecclesiae,' in quibus tota eorum potestas consistit...." The words quoted are from the Decretum II, causa 33 (Friedberg 1: 1186).

them, but that they would derive from him to others; otherwise there would not be sufficient provision for the salvation of the faithful." [78] There could scarcely be a stronger statement: the apostles are cast in the role of helping Peter by a power derived from him, and this power is handed on to them because Peter alone would not be able to exercise adequately the power he had been given. This text takes on added significance when we recall that Aquinas shortly thereafter says, as we have noted, that the entire power of prelates consists in those keys. In chapter 74 likewise, the notion of derivation is suggested where Aquinas writes in support of the view that the power to forgive sins is part of the sacrament of orders: "This power is signified by 'keys,' concerning which the Lord said to Peter at Matthew 16:19: 'To you I shall give the keys of the kingdom.'" [79] Aquinas apparently felt no need to refer to John 20, with its account of the bestowal of this power on all the apostles, to make a general point regarding the sacrament of orders. [80]

The final text to which Congar refers is *S.T.* II-II, q. 39. Of this he says simply: "*Sum. theol.*, IIa IIae, q. 39, a. 3 mis en rapport avec l'art. 1 ne donne qu'une indication implicite." [81] With this I would agree. I have already considered article 3 in discussing at the opening of this essay what Aquinas means by "spiritual power." In article 1, which is concerned with whether schism is a specific kind of sin, he says that the unity of the church is described in two things, the connection of the members to each other and the relationship of all members to one head. [82] This head, he says, is Christ himself, and adds "in whose place (*vicem*) the Supreme Pontiff acts in the church." [83]

---

[78] Ibid.: "Non autem sic intelligitur Petro commisisse ut ipse solus haberet, sed ut per eum derivarentur ad alios, alias non esset sufficienter fidelium saluti provisum."

[79] Ibid., 74: "Quae quidem potestas per 'claves' intelligitur, de quibus Dominus Petro, Mt. 16, 19 dixit: 'Tibi dabo claves regni caelorum.'"

[80] The language of derivation, shortly to be applied in chapter 76 to the broad power of governing the church, appears in this chapter with reference to *spiritualis potestas* in the narrow sense, the sacramental power of orders as such: "Non est autem dicendum quod potestas huiusmodi sic data sit Christi discipulis quod per eos ad alios derivanda non esset: data est enim eis 'ad Ecclesiae aedificationem,' secundum Apostoli dictum. ... Sic igitur data fuit discipulis Christi spiritualis potestas ut per eos deveniret ad alios." Aquinas here also goes on to justify his view regarding Christ's willing of such a derivation by quoting Matth. 28:20. He continues by speaking of Christ as the ultimate source of the derivation of this power: "Quia igitur haec spiritualis potestas a Christo in ministros Ecclesiae derivatur...."

[81] Congar, p. 94.

[82] *S.T.* II-II, q. 39, a. 1: "Ecclesiae autem unitas in duobus attenditur: scilicet in connexione membrorum Ecclesiae ad invicem, seu communicatione; et iterum in ordine omnium membrorum Ecclesiae ad unum caput...."

[83] Ibid.: "Hoc autem caput est ipse Christus: cuius vicem in Ecclesia gerit Summus Pontifex." It is perhaps worth noting that the head is described in the Colossians text quoted

Before turning to Zuckerman's analysis, I must briefly consider particular claims made by Congar after his review of the major texts, which purport to lend weight to his view that for Aquinas the pope is not the source of all spiritual power. Two claims merit attention: that the bishop has immediate jurisdiction, and that papal plenitude of power is concerned with particular acts or faculties.[84] It is true that Aquinas occasionally describes the bishop as having immediate jurisdiction in his diocese, but one may not infer that this means for Aquinas that the bishop has some power not deriving from the pope. This is clear from *In IV Sent.* d. 17, q. 3, a. 3, q.ª 5. There, in both the *solutio* and the *ad tertium*, Aquinas states that priest, bishop and pope have immediate jurisdiction over the same people. It is a constant theme of Aquinas' writings that the priest has no jurisdiction independent of the bishop, a point brought out here in the third argument of the *Sed contra*, where the following is said: "The power which a priest has with respect to people he has from the bishop."[85] Thus the phrase "in this way" (*secundum hoc*) which introduces the assertion of immediate jurisdiction must be given full weight, though it is omitted by Congar when he cites this text:[86] "And in this way the parish priest and the bishop and the pope have immediate authority over the same people." "In this way" refers to the fact that in each of these cases "one has a higher authority than the other over the same people."[87] What this means is simply that to ascribe immediate authority to the bishop is to say that there is no one in his diocese of lower authority through whom he must relate to his people; he has direct authority over every member of his diocese. Immediacy refers to a direct relationship from above to below, not to the possession of a power which is held independently of any superior. However, a further point is probably also intended, for if one takes each rank to be related to the higher in the same way, and one knows from the *Sed contra*, argument 3 (quoted above) that the relationship of the priest's power to that of the bishop is one of dependence, then Aquinas may

---

here by Aquinas (*Col.* II, 18-19) as that from which the whole body grows: " '... caput, ex quo totum corpus, per nexus et coniunctiones subministratum et constructum, crescit in augmentum Dei.' "

[84] See above, p. 198.

[85] *In IV Sent.*, d. 17, q. 3, a. 3, q.ª 5: "Potestatem quam habet sacerdos in populo, habet ab episcopo."

[86] Congar, p. 104, n. 215. His quotation reads: "Super eamdem plebem immediate sunt et sacerdos parochialis, et episcopus et papa." Cp. passage cited in next note.

[87] *In IV Sent.*, d. 17, q. 3, a. 3, q.ª 5: "Ad tertium dicendum quod inconveniens esset si duo aequaliter super eamdem plebem constituerentur. Sed quod duo quorum unus alio principalior est super eamdem plebem constituantur, non est inconveniens. Et secundum hoc super eamdem plebem immediate sunt et sacerdos parochialis et episcopus et papa....' "

readily be understood to imply that the pope is the source of the bishop's power.

Again, it is true as Congar notes that Aquinas frequently uses the phrase *plenitudo potestatis* or cognate terms to justify papal activity in some specific matter, such as dispensation from vows. However, Congar is being unduly restrictive when he says: "Chaque fois, *plenitudo potestatis* désigne une *potestas* ... supérieure à celle des simples évêques, mais rendant compte de facultés et d'actes précis." [88] In the first place, when the fulness of power is given by Aquinas as the justification for specific types of act by the pope, the principle enuntiated indicates that the fulness of power is universal in scope, and not confined to a limited range of activities. This can be illustrated from two of the texts given by Congar supposedly in support of his position.[89] Discussing the power to grant indulgences, Aquinas declares that such a power "resides fully in the pope ... but is limited in bishops according to the directive of the pope," and he justifies this by saying: "The pope has the fulness of pontifical power, like a king in a kingdom." [90] Similarly in discussing whether a pope can dispense from certain marriage laws, Aquinas states that "the pope has fulness of power in the church such that he can dispense from whatever has been instituted by the church or by prelates in the church; he is bound only to remain within the law of nature, the articles of faith and the sacraments of the new law." [91] Elsewhere Aquinas justifies the pope's ability to dispense from any vow subject to dispensation on the ground that the supreme pontiff "holds fully the place of Christ with respect to the whole church." [92]

Furthermore, it is not the case that when *plenitudo potestatis* or its cognates are spoken of by Aquinas this is always in the context of discussing specific acts or types of act. As we have seen, Aquinas in his commentary on Matthew 16:19 draws the conclusion from the fact that Peter alone was given the keys that the pope "who is in the place of Saint Peter has full power;

---

[88] Congar, p. 95.

[89] Ibid., p. 95, n. 171.

[90] *In IV Sent.*, d. 20, a. 4, q.ᵃ 3: "Papa habet plenitudinem pontificalis potestatis, quasi Rex in regno. ... Et ideo potestas faciendi indulgentias plene residet in Papa ... sed in Episcopis est taxata secundum ordinationem Papae."

[91] *Quodl.* ɪᴠ, q. 8, a. 2: "Dicendum, quod Papa habet plenitudinem potestatis in Ecclesia, ita scilicet quod quaecumque sunt instituta per Ecclesiam vel Ecclesiae praelatos, sunt dispensibilia a Papa. ... In solis vero his quae sunt de lege naturae, et in articulis fidei et sacramentis novae legis, dispensare non potest: hoc enim non esset posse pro veritate, sed contra veritatem."

[92] *S.T* ɪɪ-ɪɪ, q. 88, a. 12 ad 3ᵘᵐ:"Ad tertium, dicendum quod quia Summus Pontifex gerit plenarie vicem Christi in tota Ecclesia, ipse habet plenitudinem potestatis dispensandi in omnibus dispensabilibus votis."

others, however, have [their power] from him." [93] Likewise Aquinas cites the almost unlimited claims made in texts from Pseudo-Cyril and from Chrysostom in the *Contra errores Graecorum* in support of the view that "the Roman Pontiff has the fulness of power in the church." [94] It might well be argued to the contrary that, granted always the pope's being subject to divine law, natural or revealed, the unrestricted amplitude of his spiritual power is the counterpart in terms of the spiritual life of the geographically unrestricted *universalis cura.*

What, then, are we to make of the fact that Zuckerman comes to a radically different conclusion from Congar, namely, that for Aquinas the power of orders as well as that of jurisdiction derived from Peter? Since all the major relevant passages have been discussed in detail, I shall confine myself to summarizing Zuckerman's position, [95] and to stating the main objections to his case.

Zuckerman first quotes at length *In II Sent.*, d. 44, *expos. textus.* [96] He then cites *In IV Sent.* d. 19, q. 1, a. 3, q.ª 1 ad 1um, where Aquinas treats in some detail of the manner of the derivation of power from Peter to the apostles: the apostles receive the power of orders from Christ, but the power of jurisdiction from Peter. [97] He goes on to quote the short passage from *In IV Sent.* d. 24, q. 3, a. 2, q.ª 3 and the commentary on Matthew 16:19 in which Aquinas refers both to that text and to John 20:23 when stating that the apostles receive their power from Peter. Since Aquinas stated in the passage noted from *In IV Sent.*, d. 19 that John 20 deals with the sacrament of orders, he must in these last two passages (so Zuckerman argues) mean that the apostles received the power of orders as well as that of jurisdiction from the pope. In his view, the same conclusion can be drawn from Aquinas' referring to Matthew 16:19 in *S.C.G.* IV, 76 where Aquinas states that the power of the apostles derived from Peter, for elsewhere in Aquinas' writings the power of the keys spoken of in Matthew 16:19 "included orders as well as jurisdiction." [98] For Zuckerman, therefore, Aquinas' view in the long

---

[93] *In Ev. Matth.*, ad XVI, 19: "... qui est loco sancti Petri, habet plenariam potestatem, alii vero ab ipso."

[94] *Contra errores Graecorum* II, 34 (ll. 3-5): "Habetur enim ex praedictorum doctorum auctoritatibus quod Romanus Pontifex habeat in Ecclesia plenitudinem potestatis." Congar cites this work also at p. 95, n. 171.

[95] See Zuckerman, pp. 116-128. The essence of his argument is found at pp. 123-124.

[96] Zuckerman also cites briefly, as clarifying the meaning of this text, *In IV Sent.*, d. 19, q. 1, a. 3, q.ª 2, and *S.T.* II-II, q. 39, a. 3.

[97] The reference given to this text by Zuckerman at p. 120, n. 45 should read "a. 3" not "a. 1."

[98] Ibid., p. 123.

passage on obedience in *In II Sent.* that jurisdiction but not orders derived from Peter is anomalous.

It seems to me that there are three insurmountable objections to Zuckerman's case. The first is the methodological point which I raised earlier. All things being equal, the most reasonable procedure in interpreting an author is to understand his briefer treatment of a subject in the light of the longer, and only to conclude to their incompatibility if there is no other seriously plausible course. Since with Aquinas as with others *inter homines sumus*, it would clearly be ridiculous to think that he simply cannot contradict himself; but his characteristic lucidity of mind would make one more than usually hesitant to ascribe this fault to him. More importantly, there is, in fact, as the argument of this essay has sought to show, a straightforward way in which the texts can be read as a coherent whole and the charge of contradiction avoided, namely, by taking the view stated in the longer passage with reference to the keys as the power to forgive sins as applying generally in Aquinas' writings to the entire exercise of the episcopal office: all sacramental power as such comes from orders, while all right to the exercise of sacramental power and all jurisdictional power derive from the pope. We are justified in adopting this reading not only because it yields the best interpretation of the various individual passages discussed above, but also by the very fact that it allows Aquinas' discussions to form a coherent whole. In this view, full weight is given to his nonspecific statements about derivation of power from the papacy, without violence being done to any of his detailed discussions. Zuckerman has, in a sense, precluded his adoption of this view by his earlier, and in my opinion mistaken, argument, that for Aquinas government in the church is to be equated with a single, non-sacramental power of jurisdiction.[99] But whatever terms one uses, if one distinguishes between the power of orders conferred by the sacrament, and the right to exercise that power, with the latter only deriving from the pope, then Aquinas may be understood to present a single, coherent view of the relationship of bishops to the pope: the right to exercise sacramental power, and all jurisdiction in the strict sense, derive from the pope to the bishops.

Failure to take adequate account of the crucial distinction between sacramental power as such and the right to exercise it becomes evident in Zuckerman's improperly equating sacramental power, or the power of orders as such, and sacramental authority. In drawing his conclusions from Aquinas' discussions of the biblical texts noted above, Zuckerman states that these discussions imply that Aquinas held a "conception of Peter as the source, not only of the other apostles' jurisdiction, but of their sacramental authority as

---

[99] See n. 21 above.

well." He goes on to say: "None of Aquinas' mendicant contemporaries appears to have regarded the papacy as the source of sacramental authority. This is not surprising. Such a view would have contradicted the universal medieval belief in the direct divine origin of sacramental power...." [100] If, however, one regards sacramental authority as requiring not only the sacramental power of orders itself but the right to exercise that sacramental power, then to hold a belief in the direct divine origin of sacramental power does not contradict belief in the papacy as the source of sacramental authority. Similarly, if one holds that jurisdiction broadly understood is necessary for the licit exercise of sacramental power, then the complete distinction implied in Zuckerman's former statement between the derivation of jurisdiction and the derivation of sacramental authority does not hold. In short, to state that sacramental authority derived from Peter to the apostles is not to state that sacramental power or the power of orders *tout court* derived from him, as Zuckerman appears to believe. Thus to write "How then, it may well be asked, could Aquinas have repeatedly written of Peter as the source of the other apostles' authority ... in ways which implied that the authority derived from Peter to the other apostles had included orders as well?" [101] is to pose the wrong question by failing to distinguish between the possession of sacramental authority which involves the right to exercise the sacrament of orders, and the simple possession of sacramental power bestowed in ordination. Such a failure, I believe, reveals and invites confusion.

Two further objections to Zuckerman's position are that it conflicts with two central elements of Aquinas' theology of the sacrament of orders. Aquinas holds that this sacrament, and the sacramental or spiritual power which that sacrament gives through the character imparted to the soul, are conferred by the rite of ordination (or, more precisely, by Christ through that rite). I may recall here the brief statement of Aquinas with which this paper began: "Sacramental power ... is that power which is conferred by some form of consecration...." [102] Moreover, Aquinas, as has been noted, consistently portrays the derivation of power from the pope to the bishops in terms of a relationship of superior to inferiors; by contrast, for him pope and bishops are *equal* precisely in terms of their order of episcopacy. In the *ad primum* of *In IV Sent.* d. 24, q. 3, a. 2, q.ª 3, Aquinas explicitly rejects the idea that all bishops are equal with respect to the power to bind and loose. [103] He goes

---

[100] Zuckerman, p. 124.

[101] Ibid., p. 124.

[102] II-II, q. 39, a. 3, quoted above, n. 1. See also: *In IV Sent.*, d. 18, q. 1, a. 1, q.ª 2 ad 2ᵘᵐ; ibid., d. 18, q. 2, a. 2, q.ª 3 ad 2ᵘᵐ; ibid., d. 19, q. 2, a. 1, q.ª 3; ibid., d. 25, q. 1, a. 1; *S.C.G.* IV, 74.

[103] See above, n. 42.

on, however, in the *ad tertium* to accept equality with respect to the episcopal order: "... every hierarchical act which the pope can do in administering the sacraments can be done by a bishop; ... as regards what belongs to the episcopal order all bishops are equal...." [104] It seems impossible to make the derivation of orders which Zuckerman ascribes to Aquinas cohere with these two major aspects of Aquinas' sacramental theology; likewise, it is scarcely credible that Aquinas should have been so evidently at odds with himself in that theology.

It should be said, finally, that it also tells strongly against Zuckerman's position that if one attributes to Aquinas the view that the sacrament of orders itself derives from the pope one has to maintain that Aquinas in this differs from all his theological contemporaries (as Zuckerman himself accepts), and does so merely by implication, without drawing attention to a completely novel and highly significant point.

What broader conclusions might be drawn from this detailed analysis? I would note two. The secular-mendicant dispute had its more strictly practical aspects, [105] and was marked by a high degree of verbal violence. However, this ought not to blind us to the fact that a matter of principle also separated the groups regarding the extent of papal, or conversely local, power. No secular master held that all spiritual power derived from the pope, for at the heart of the secular masters' case was the view that the constitution of the church

---

[104] *In IV Sent.*, d. 24, q. 3, a. 2, q.ᵃ 3 ad 3ᵘᵐ. The full text reads: "Ad tertium dicendum, quod potestas sacerdotis exceditur a potestate Episcopi quasi a potestate alterius generis; sed potestas Episcopi exceditur a potestate Papae quasi a potestate ejusdem generis; et ideo omnem actum hierarchicum quem potest facere Papa in ministratione sacramentorum, potest facere Episcopus; non autem omnem actum quem potest facere Episcopus, potest facere sacerdos in sacramentorum collatione; et ideo quantum ad ea quae sunt episcopalis ordinis, omnes Episcopi sunt aequales; et propter hoc quilibet alium potest consecrare."

[105] Perhaps the most evident practical aspect of the dispute was the fact that the mendicants' activities depressed the income of the secular priests: see, for example, Marrone, *The Ecclesiology*, pp. 96-97 and 256-257. But, as Decima Douie remarks: "It was not merely a rather sordid matter of fees" ("St Bonaventure's Part in the Conflict between Seculars and Mendicants at Paris," in *S. Bonaventura 1274-1974*, vol. 2 [Grottaferrata, 1973], p. 76). Quite apart from the question of principle, this comment holds true in the realm of practice, for in fairness to the secular masters at Paris it ought to be remembered that in opposing papal policy with respect to the mendicants they courted the danger of dismissal from their teaching posts – a fate which actually befell William of Saint-Amour and Henry of Ghent. The latter is recorded, on the occasion of his deprivation of office when the papal legate Cardinal Gaetani (the future pope Boniface VIII) forbade further discussion of the position accorded the mendicants by the papacy, as having addressed to his fellow masters the ringing question: "Cum liceat nobis de evangeliis disputare, cur non de privilegio?" The report of the Paris National Council of 1290 in which this incident is described is contained in a fifteenth-century chronicle which has been published by A. Callebaut, "Les provinciaux de France au XIIIᵉ siècle," *Archivium Franciscanum Historicum* 10 (1917) 289-356 at pp. 347-349. See Marrone (cited above, n. 45), pp. 175-182.

gave local prelates an independence of power which could not be overruled even by the pope without imperilling the church as willed by Christ. The substantial point of this essay is that for Aquinas Christ did will that all power in the church should derive from the pope. To group Aquinas with the seculars, as Congar does, is to blur this difference in fundamental principle.

A second conclusion, implicit in the first, is that this was a difference of *religious* principle, and one dearly held. With the theological arguments and the sensibilities of the secular masters I have not been concerned in this essay. It would, however, be misleading to end this consideration of Aquinas without recognizing the deep religious conviction on this topic which pulses under the legendary coolness of style in his strictly theological works, and which shows itself more clearly in his polemical writings. It is signalled in the former in, for instance, the significant adjective at the conclusion of his longest treatment of the relation between the pope and the bishops, that of *S.C.G.* IV, 76: "By this, then, is excluded the *presumptuous* error of some people who seek to withdraw themselves from obedience and subjection to Peter, by refusing to acknowledge his successor the Roman Pontiff as the pastor of the universal church." [106] In the polemical *Contra impugnantes* we find Aquinas explicitly linking obedience to the see of Rome and obedience to Christ. Regarding those who would take away from the privilege of the Roman see as this is described in the *Decretum*, d. 22, he comments: "Christ gave this privilege to the Roman church, that all should obey it as they would Christ." [107] *Sicut Christo*: the words reflect both the ultimate source and the depth of Aquinas' convictions about the spiritual power attaching to the papacy. They also, of course, embody what is, to put it mildly, a religious claim of some gravity. Little wonder that, on both sides, passions were engaged.

---

[106] *S.C.G.* IV, 76, quoted at n. 69 above.

[107] *Contra impugnantes* 3 (#7, ll. 456-458): "Hoc autem privilegium Christus romanae ecclesiae contulit ut omnes ei sicut Christo obediant...." (Aquinas is commenting on the *Decretum*, d. 22, "Omnes": see Friedberg, 1: 73). In *De regno* Aquinas uses much the same language specifically of the relationship of kings to the pope; it is noteworthy that he here casts the pope personally in the role which is assigned to the Roman church in the text of the *Decretum* cited in the *Contra impugnantes* (and in his comment on it): "Huiusmodi ergo regni ministerium, ut a terrenis spiritualia essent discreta, non terrenis regibus sed sacerdotibus est commissum, et praecipue summo sacerdoti successori Petri, Christi uicario Romano pontifici, cui omnes reges populi Christiani oportet esse subiectos sicut ipso Domino Ihesu Christo" (*De regno* II, 3 [ll. 110-116]). It might be argued from the latter text, and from Aquinas' exalted view of the pope's role as vicar of Christ (the pope "acts fully in the place of Christ") that his very conception of the pope under this title implies that all are bound to obey the pope as they would Christ: see nn. 11 and 92 above. In any case, Aquinas goes on in the passage just cited from the *Contra impugnantes* to draw a conclusion which refers to the pope personally: "Unde patet quod quicumque dicit non esse obediendum his quae per papam statuuntur in haeresim labitur" (ll. 469-471).

Part Two

Sources from Local Churches

6

La Papauté et le droit liturgique
aux XIIᵉ et XIIIᵉ siècles

Pierre-Marie Gy

Les XIIᵉ et XIIIᵉ siècles sont à mi-chemin entre les deux unifications liturgiques de l'Occident, celle de Charlemagne adoptant pour sa chapelle et son empire les livres liturgiques romains, et celle d'après Trente, qui remplacera les livres liturgiques romano-diocésains par les livres romains de la Curie, et réservera tout le droit liturgique à la Papauté.

Cette période est marquée par quatre phénomènes liturgiques qui inté-ressent l'histoire de la Papauté. Pour la clarté de l'exposé je les énumère selon un ordre logique, mais en réalité leur developpement est interdépendant. Ce sont:

1. le retournement du rapport entre la liturgie de la basilique du Latran et celle de la chapelle papale;
2. l'unification de la liturgie à Rome;
3. le commencement de la diffusion de la liturgie de la chapelle papale hors de Rome;
4. le développement des interventions liturgiques du Pape hors de Rome ou, si l'on préfère, un commencement de réservation papale du droit liturgi-que.

Un passage d'Abélard au sujet des diversités liturgiques locales me donnera l'occasion de situer brièvement celles-ci dans le deuxième quart du XIIᵉ siècle. S. Bernard a visité le monastère du Paraclet et y a constaté des

The Religious Roles of the Papacy: Ideals and Realities, 1150-1300, ed. Christopher Ryan, Papers in Mediaeval Studies 8 (Toronto: Pontifical Institute of Mediaeval Studies, 1989), pp. 229-245. © P.I.M.S., 1989.

innovations liturgiques d'Abélard qui ne lui ont pas plu. Abélard lui écrit pour justifier ces innovations, et au passage il critique celles de Cîteaux et fait état de la diversité liturgique dans l'Église:

> Enfin, pour ce qui est de la liturgie, qui ignore les innombrables différences de coutumes, même parmi les clercs? L'ancienne coutume du Siège Romain n'est même pas observée par la ville de Rome, mais seule l'église du Latran, qui est la mère de toutes les églises, conserve l'Office ancien, alors qu'aucune de ses filles ne la suit en cela, pas même la basilique du palais romain. En cette manière la métropole de Milan s'éloigne à tel point de tous qu'aucune même des Églises qui sont ses suffragantes n'imite la règle liturgique de leur mère. Ainsi le siège de Lyon, le premier des Gaules, persiste seul dans sa liturgie. Et alors qu'il s'est produit tant de variété en ces choses, nonobstant les innovations d'une Église après l'autre, aucun reproche d'innovation n'a été exprimé, parce que rien n'a été contraire à la foi. De fait cette variété dans le culte divin a quelque chose d'agréable car, comme le rappelle Cicéron, l'uniformité complète engendre l'ennui. Celui qui a voulu être prêché en toutes les langues a aussi établi que le culte lui serait rendu dans une diversité de liturgies.[1]

En parlant du Latran, de Lyon et de Milan, ce texte touche la liturgie à Rome, les liturgies de type romain hors de Rome, les liturgies non romaines.

Pour ce qui est des liturgies non romaines, Grégoire VII, reprenant à son compte l'idéologie liturgique unitaire de Charlemagne, a supprimé l'ancienne liturgie hispanique, et le mouvement de la réforme grégorienne a supprimé ce qui pouvait rester, en Écosse et en Irlande, des anciennes liturgies celtiques. À ce propos S. Bernard loue S. Malachie d'Armagh d'avoir agi en faveur du "rite de l'Église universelle."[2] L'expression, dont on retrouvera plus tard l'analogue dans les canonisations,[3] est intéressante en ce qu'elle

---

[1] *Ep.* 10 (*PL* 178: 540BC): "Denique in divinis officiis quis ignoret diversas et innumeras Ecclesiae consuetudines inter ipsos etiam clericos? Antiquam certe Romanae Sedis consuetudinem nec ipsa civitas tenet, sed sola Ecclesia Lateranensis, quae mater est omnium, antiquum tenet officium, nulla filiarum suarum in hoc eam sequente, nec ipsa etiam Romani palatii basilica. Mediolanensis metropolis ita in talibus ab omnibus dissidet, ut nulla etiam suffraganearum suarum matris institutionem imitetur. Sic et Lugdunensis prima sedes Galliarum sola in suo persistit officio. Et cum tanta in istis facta sit varietas, quidquid una post aliam noviter instituit, nulla reprehensio novitatis incidit, quia nulla fidei contrarietas fuit. Nonnullam enim oblectationem haec divini cultus varietas habet, quia, ut Tullius meminit, identitas in omnibus mater est satietatis. Qui ergo omnium linguarum generibus praedicari voluit, ipse diversis officiorum modis venerari decrevit."
Cf. Cicéron, *De Inventione* I, 41, 76: "Variare autem orationem magnopere oportebit, nam omnibus in rebus similitudo mater est satietatis."

[2] *Vita S. Malachiae* III, 7 - IV, 8 (*Opera*, ed. Leclercq et Rochais [Rome, 1963], 3: 316).

[3] Cf. *Cérémonial de Jacques Stefaneschi*, III, 15 et 30 (Dykmans, *Le cérémonial papal de la fin du moyen âge à la Renaissance* [Bruxelles-Rome, 1981], 2: 459 et 465).

révèle ce qu'on pourrait appeler l'horizon romain de l'universalité, dans lequel les limites du rite romain sont confondues avec celles de l'Église même. De ce point de vue il a fallu du temps pour prendre conscience de la spécificité des liturgies orientales.[4]

Milan est un cas intermédiaire entre la liturgie romaine et les liturgies occidentales non romaines, du double fait que, vraisemblablement depuis S. Ambroise, elle emploie le canon romain et que son euchologie est exactement de type romain et a beaucoup reçu des sacramentaires romains à l'époque carolingienne. À l'époque grégorienne les tenants du rite ambrosien ont certainement eu peur d'une décision papale de romanisation, et leur crainte transparaît dans la légende d'un jugement de Dieu, d'où le sacramentaire ambrosien serait sorti indemne.[5] Innocent IV semble y faire allusion lorsqu'il autorise les Pauvres Catholiques de Milan à adopter le rite romain:

> De votre part nous a été présentée l'humble supplique que, étant donné que vous êtes réunis, en provenance de diverses parties du monde, pour servir Dieu et que vous ne savez pas psalmodier au Seigneur dans l'Office divin selon la manière et la règle du Bienheureux Ambroise qu'observe le clergé milanais, nous vous accordions, de par la bienveillance du Siège Apostolique, de psalmodier selon la manière de l'ordre du Bienheureux Grégoire. Nous donc ... vous accordons l'autorisation demandée.[6]

Par cette disposition les Pauvres Catholiques échappent à la règle de droit selon laquelle une fondation selon la Règle de S. Augustin, si elle est ce que nous appellerions aujourd'hui une maison-mère, doit adopter la liturgie du diocèse dans lequel elle est fondée.

Le cas de Lyon est différent, et prend place dans la diversité des liturgies de type romain qui s'est établie en terre franque à l'époque carolingienne. Toutes les Églises ont alors adopté la liturgie romaine, mais avec des grandes souplesses locales dans l'organisation du répertoire. À Lyon Agobard se caractérise par ce que j'ai appelé son monobiblisme, éliminant les pièces

---

[4] Benoît XIV, *De servorum Dei beatificatione et beatorum canonizatione* I, 38-8-15.

[5] Landolphe l'Ancien, *Historia Mediolanensis* II, 11-12 (MGH *Scriptores* 8: 49-50). Cf. Durand de Mende, *Rationale* V, 2, 5.

[6] Innocent IV, *Registres* (éd. E. Berger [Paris, 1884-1921]), n. 2539 (10 avril 1247): "Ex parte siquidem vestra fuit nobis humiliter supplicatum ut, cum de diversis mundi partibus in unum ad Dei obsequium congregati, psallere Domino in divinis officiis secundum modum et institutionem beati Ambrosii, prout Mediolanensis clerus utitur, nesciatis, psallendi secundum modum et ordinationem beati Gregorii, quibus utitur Ecclesia generalis, vobis de benignitate Sedis Apostolicae licentiam largiremur." Cf. également *Registres*, n. 4293 (23 décembre 1248) et, en ce qui concerne une concession de Grégoire IX aux Dominicaines de S. Maria Veterum à Milan, le 28 avril 1235: *Analecta Sacri Ordinis Fratrum Praedicatorum* 8 (1900) 498.

liturgiques non empruntées à l'Écriture.[7] Dans sa propre région il sera à peine suivi, sauf plus tard dans la liturgie cartusienne.[8]

À Rome même règne une certaine diversité, qui durera jusqu'au XIIIe siècle. D'où la remarque étonnée d'Abélard sur la position isolée de l'église du Latran qui seule "garde l'Office ancien." Ce qu'il dit de son isolement est exact, mais il faut ici expliquer son rapport à l'"Office ancien." La communauté canoniale du Latran, à la thèse de laquelle Abélard fait écho, justifie par l'argument de l'Église du Latran "tête de toutes les églises et la première d'entre elles," qui vient de la donation de Constantin, une liturgie que les chanoines ont en réalité apportée avec eux de Saint-Frigdien de Lucques.[9] Les chanoines de Lucques, et déjà Grégoire VII, lorsqu'ils veulent restaurer la tradition romaine authentique, vont la chercher dans ce qu'ils appellent l'*Ordo Romanus*, c'est-à-dire en fait dans le pontifical ottonien mayençais qu'Andrieu a découvert et appelé le pontifical romano-germanique. Les chanoines du Latran sont des non-romains qui font la leçon aux romains du cru, ceux de Saint-Pierre et d'ailleurs, mais pour les grandes fêtes ils sont obligés de faire appel à des chantres indigènes:

> Étant donné que, par la faveur de Dieu, la vie des chanoines réguliers est observée dans cette église et que des clercs venus des différentes régions de la terre y sont réunis pour y servir Dieu, ils ne savent pas chanter à la manière des Romains. Et comme c'est l'ancienne coutume que les chanoines fassent l'Office d'un côté du chœur tant à la vigile (nocturne) qu'aux Laudes, il est necessaire que, quelques jours auparavant, deux frères capables soient chargés par le prieur de recruter cinq ou six chantres choisis et vigoureux pour remplir cette tâche.[10]

Du point de vue des chanoines du Latran, la "basilique du palais romain" est une des filles de l'église du Latran, mais elle ne suit pas l'Office de sa mère. Ceci pose la question de l'origine de la liturgie de la chapelle papale, liturgie qui nous est seulement connue de façon concrète à partir d'Inno-

---

[7] "Les tropes dans l'histoire de la liturgie et de la théologie," dans G. Iversen, éd., *Research on Tropes* (Stockholm, 1983), pp. 7-16.

[8] Cf. H. Becker, *Die Responsorien des Kartäuserbreviers* (Munich, 1971); R.-J. Hesbert, *Corpus Antiphonalium Officii*, 5 (Rome, 1975), surtout pp. 308-310.

[9] Cf. mon étude "L'influence des chanoines de Lucques sur la liturgie du Latran," *Revue des Sciences Religieuses* 58 (1984) (Mélanges Chavasse) 31-41.

[10] L. Fischer, *Bernhardi Ordo Officiorum Ecclesiae Lateranensis* (Munich, 1916), p. 140: "Quia enim Deo propitio in hac ecclesia regularium canonicorum vita servatur et ex diversis terrarum partibus clerici ad serviendum Deo ibidem conveniunt, Romanorum more cantare nesciunt. Et cum de antiqua consuetudine sit ut canonici tam in vigilia quam etiam in matutinis ex una parte chori officium peragere debeant, necessario ante aliquos dies duobus ex fratribus, qui providi sint, a priore iniungitur ut electos et strenuos v vel vi cantores invitent, qui hoc officium peragere valeant...."

cent III. Pour ce qu'on appellera plus tard les fonctions papales, celles pour lesquelles le Pape va célébrer dans l'église du Latran ou les autres grandes basiliques, la tradition romaine ancienne s'est en gros bien conservée. Qu'en est-il de la liturgie de la chapelle papale proprement dite? Celle-ci comporte des éléments périphériques qui proviennent de Lucques: ainsi certainement l'Office des morts, probablement le rituel de l'extrême-onction.[11] Pour l'Office divin en général on ne sait pas encore. Ce n'est pas ici le lieu, je pense, d'indiquer les conditions, assez techniques, requises pour une telle recherche.

En revanche il faut essayer de préciser comment on en est venu à considérer la chapelle papale comme la réalisation liturgique la plus authentique de l'Église Romaine, à tel point que, dans ses statuts pour le Latran, Pierre Roger de Beaufort, le futur Grégoire XI, dira:

> Pour que les membres se conforment à la tête, nous décrétons par la règle présente que l'Office tant nocturne que diurne sera chanté dans l'église du Latran selon la rubrique, l'ordre ou coutume de la sainte Église Romaine, c'est-à-dire de la chapelle de notre seigneur le Pape.[12]

De ce texte on peut rapprocher, quelques années plus tôt, en 1337, la décision du synode d'Avignon adoptant pour ce diocèse la liturgie de la chapelle papale:

> En effet la Sainte Église Romaine est reconnue pour être mère et maîtresse de toutes les Églises en lesquelles est répandue la propagation de la foi chrétienne, et l'Église et par conséquent la curie Romaine habitent notre ville d'Avignon et son diocèse avec l'affection particulière d'une tendre mère, en sorte qu'elles ont de manière salutaire, par la grâce de Dieu, communiqué aux cœurs de notre clergé leurs louables mœurs, en sorte que les clercs surtout, en ce qui concerne l'ordre de l'Office divin, se conforment comme des fils dévots et comme des membres à leur tête, afin que, de même que l'arbre ne se sépare pas de sa racine, ni le rameau de l'arbre, pareillement les enfants ne dégénèrent pas de celle qui les a engendrés. Nous ordonnons donc et décidons que tous et chacun des clercs et personnes ecclésiastiques de la susdite ville et du diocèse soient désormais libres de leur Office habituel et que, omettant les anciens rudiments des vieux manuscrits, et comme revêtant pour cette part l'esprit de l'homme nouveau, ils puissent à partir de mainte-

---

[11] Pour l'Office des morts cf. "L'influence," p. 41. La question du nouveau rituel romain de l'extrême-onction n'est pas encore claire, du fait notamment que le pontifical d'Apamée doit être situé dans l'histoire liturgique autrement que ne l'avait pensé Andrieu.

[12] *Constitutiones Lateranenses*, 1 (*PL* 78: 1394): "Ut membra capiti se conforment, praesenti institutione decernimus quod tam nocturnum quam diurnum [officium] in Lateranensi ecclesia cum nota dicatur, iuxta rubricam, ordinem et morem sanctae Romanae ecclesiae, seu capellae domini nostri papae."

nant dire l'Office tant diurne que nocturne selon l'ordre, la coutume et le statut
qu'emploie la susdite Église et curie Romaine....[13]

Par delà sa rhétorique ce texte révèle une intention ecclésiologique précise:
puisque l'Église Romaine notre mère séjourne auprès de nous, il convient que
la fille — l'Église d'Avignon — se conforme à la mère. En Avignon ce rapport
entre la fille et la mère apparaît visuellement lorsqu'on regarde ensemble la
petite cathédrale et à côté d'elle, la dominant, le palais des Papes.

Ainsi, entre le milieu du XIIe siècle et le XIVe, le rapport entre l'église du
Latran et la chapelle papale s'est inversé: la fille est devenue la mère, et non
seulement la mère de toutes les églises romaines, mais même la mère de
toutes les Églises diocésaines. Deux éléments sont ici à considérer, dont le
premier concerne le fonctionnement de l'institution curiale, et le deuxième
le statut ecclésiologique de sa liturgie. Du point de vue institutionnel
Reinhard Elze a étudié le fait que les chapelains du Pape sont inséparable-
ment ceux qui célèbrent la liturgie dans la chapelle et les agents de l'administration papale en constant développement.[14] De cette conjonction il y a
lieu de souligner un aspect pratique qui a des incidences liturgiques importantes: la subsistance des chapelains est assurée par des bénéfices qu'ils possè-
dent à travers l'Occident et qu'ils accumulent ou échangent selon leur
avantage personnel. Ils sont donc habitués à dissocier leur bénéfice de la
liturgie locale à laquelle celui-ci est attaché dans son principe, et au contraire
à valoriser au maximum la liturgie de la chapelle papale, qui est leur liturgie
réelle.

L'équivalence entre Curie Romaine et Église Romaine se forme à cette
époque. Elle a été étudiée en histoire de la liturgie par S. J. P. Van Dijk et

---

[13] E. Martène et U. Durand, *Thesaurus novus anecdotorum* (Paris, 1717), 4:
col. 557e-558b: "Sacrosancta namque Romana Ecclesia, Ecclesiarum omnium in quas christianae fidei propagatio diffunditur, mater esse dignoscitur et magistra, et quia iam dudum ipsa
Ecclesia et Romana curia consequenter civitatem nostram Avenionensem eiusque dioecesim
ex peculiaris affectionis instinctu conversationis piae matris incolunt communiter, sic quod
suos mores digna reputatione laudabiles merito et creditur in cleri nostri pectoribus, Domino
auctore, salubriter indidisse; ut ipsi maxime clerici quantum ad divini officii ordinem sibi
tanquam devotionis filii et membra capiti se conforment, cum sicut arbor a radice non
discrepat, nec differt ramus ab arbore, ita nec geniti a sua degenerent genitrice. Ordinamus
ergo atque statuimus quod amodo universi et singuli clerici ac personae ecclesiasticae
praedictae civitatis et dioecesis a consuetis officiis liberi et immunes existant et, pristinis
veterum codicum rudimentis omissis, tanquam spiritum in hac parte novi hominis induentes,
dummodo [amodo?] officium diurnum pariter et nocturnum dicere valeant iuxta ordinem,
morem seu statutum quo Ecclesia utitur et Romana curia supradicta...."
[14] "Die päpstliche Kapelle im 12. und 13. Jahrhundert," *Zeitschrift der Savigny-Stiftung
für Rechtsgeschichte, Kan. Abt.*, 36, pp. 145-204, reproduit dans *Päpste-Kaiser-Könige und die
mittelalterliche Herrschaftssymbolik* (London, 1982).

J. Hazelden Walker.[15] Les deux textes essentiels sont ici la règle franciscaine de 1223 et l'incipit de l'Ordinaire de la Curie. La règle de 1223 prescrit: "Que les clercs fassent l'Office divin selon l'ordre de la sainte Église Romaine, sauf le psautier."[16] Je suis d'accord avec Van Dijk qu'il s'agit là du rite de la chapelle papale, identifiée à l'Église Romaine.[17]

Une question plus complexe se pose au sujet de l'incipit de l'Ordinaire de la Curie, tel que nous le lisons dans l'unique manuscrit, qui date du XIVe siècle: "Commencement de l'Ordinaire de l'Église Curie Romaine, comme nous avons coutume de l'observer depuis le temps du Pape Innocent III et des autres pontifes."[18] Nous ne savons pas à quelle époque cet incipit a été placé en tête de l'Ordinaire; les deux mots Église Curie sont à la fois un doublet et le signe d'une identification dont Van Dijk a montré qu'elle était courante depuis le XIIe siècle. Par ailleurs je me demande si l'Ordinaire lui-même a été rédigé principalement pour l'usage interne des chapelains, ou aussi en vue d'une diffusion liturgique au dehors.

L'UNIFICATION DE LA LITURGIE À ROME

Nous disposons à ce sujet de la description de Pierre Roger de Beaufort pour le Latran et d'un texte de Raoul de Rivo au sujet de Nicolas III. La prescription de Pierre Roger de Beaufort paraît claire: "nous décrétons par la règle présente." Je la comprends comme imposant la liturgie de la chapelle papale au Latran qui ne la pratiquait pas encore. Ce pourrait être le point final de l'unification liturgique à Rome. Toutefois le doyen de Tongres Raoul de Rivo (Van der Beke), dans la deuxième moitié du XIVe siècle, rapporte de la manière suivante l'action de Nicolas III pour unifier la liturgie urbaine:

> Nicolas III, romain de la famille Orsini, qui commença à être Pape en 1277 et construisit le palais auprès de Saint-Pierre, fit enlever des églises de la ville cinquante antiphonaires, graduels, missels et autres vieux livres liturgiques, et prescrivit que désormais les églises de la ville se serviraient des livres et des

---

[15] S. J. P. Van Dijk et J. Hazelden Walker, *The Origins of the Modern Roman Liturgy: The Liturgy of the Papal Court and the Franciscan Order in the Thirteenth Century* (London, 1960), pp. 84-85.

[16] *Première Règle*, 3, 4, dans S. François, *Écrits*, éd. Th. Desbonnets, Th. Matura, J.-F. Godet et D. Vorreux, Sources chrétiennes 285 (Paris, 1981), p. 184: "Clerici faciant divinum officium secundum ordinem sanctae Romanae Ecclesiae excepto psalterio...."

[17] *The Origins*, p. 188.

[18] S. J. P. Van Dijk, *The Ordinal of the Papal Court from Innocent III to Boniface VIII and Related Documents*, Spicilegium Friburgense 22 (Fribourg, 1975), p. 90: "Incipit Ordo Romane Ecclesie Curie, quem consuevimus observare tempore Innocentii Tertii Pape et aliorum pontificum."

bréviaires des Frères Mineurs, dont il confirma également la Règle. C'est pourquoi aujourd'hui à Rome tous les livres sont nouveaux et franciscains.[19]

Van Dijk a prouvé que Raoul s'était trompé en parlant ici des livres franciscains, mais il estime que Nicolas III a effectivement fait quelque chose dans le sens d'une unification liturgique.[20] Je pense qu'il a raison sur ce point. À cela Van Dijk ajoute une hypothèse: le Cardinal Jean Cajetan Orsini, le futur Nicolas III, aurait développé auparavant, dans les églises romaines de sa juridiction, une sorte de mouvement liturgique particulier caractérisé principalement par un sanctoral plus abondant que celui de la chapelle papale et comportant les fêtes de tous les saints nouvellement canonisés. Son argumentation repose sur l'analyse d'un groupe de manuscrits liturgiques, deux sacramentaires et un lectionnaire de l'Office en deux volumes. Cette question a été si débattue entre Andrieu[21] et Van Dijk,[22] et elle est si complexe que je ne voudrais pas m'y engager complètement. Je dirai seulement que deux données de détail me paraissent orienter vers l'attribution de ces livres à la chapelle papale même. Tout d'abord un des deux sacramentaires, le manuscrit Avignon 100, contient comme addition les oraisons de la messe liégeoise du Corpus Christi, ensuite rayées et remplacées par celles de la messe instituée par Urbain IV. On peut toujours supposer que Jean Cajetan Orsini s'est procuré d'une manière ou d'une autre le texte de ces oraisons, mais l'hypothèse de beaucoup la plus simple est que c'est Urbain IV lui-même, ancien archidiacre de Liège et ami des béguines zélatrices de la fête, qui a mis ou fait mettre ces oraisons sur un sacramentaire de sa chapelle, avant même de donner à cette fête l'institution papale et une liturgie nouvelle.

Une deuxième donnée concerne également la fête du Corpus Christi, mais cette fois dans le lectionnaire de l'Office Paris, Bibl. Nat., Latin 755. Celui-ci contient deux états successifs de l'Office qui, selon l'hypothèse de Dom Cyrille Lambot reprise par moi-même[23] et par le P. Zawilla dans sa thèse

---

[19] *De canonum observantia*, Prop. XXII, éd. L. C. Mohlberg (Münster, 1915), p. 126: "Nicolaus papa tertius, natione Romanus de genere Ursinorum, qui coepit anno Domini millesimo ducentesimo septuagesimo septimo et palatium apud sanctum Petrum construxit, fecit in ecclesiis urbis amoveri antiphonarios, gradualia, missalia et alios libros officii antiquos quinquaginta et mandavit ut de cetero ecclesiae urbis uterentur libris et breviariis Fratrum Minorum, quorum regulam etiam confirmavit. Unde hodie in Roma omnes libri sunt novi et franciscani...."

[20] "The Legend of 'the Missal of the Papal Chapel' and the Fact of Cardinal Orsini's Reform," *Sacris Erudiri* 8 (1956) 76-142; *The Origins*, p. 411.

[21] Cf. en dernier lieu M. Andrieu, "L'authenticité du 'missel de la chapelle papale'," *Scriptorium* 9 (1955) 17-34.

[22] Cf. ci-dessus, note 20.

[23] "L'Office du Corpus Christi et S. Thomas d'Aquin. État d'une recherche," *Revue des Sciences Philosophiques et Théologiques* 64 (1980) 491-507, surtout pp. 496-498.

inédite sur les sources de l'Office du Corpus Christi, ont été composés à la Curie, en 1264, à quelques mois de distance, le premier pour une première célébration improvisée de la nouvelle fête, le deuxième pour être mis en circulation avec la bulle *Transiturus*, dont je reparlerai plus loin. Aucune difficulté à ce que les deux Offices successifs figurent dans le lectionnaire de la chapelle papale. Mais on comprendrait mal qu'un des cardinaux, assurément informé de la préparation de l'Office définitif, ait voulu placer l'Office provisoire dans le lectionnaire d'une église de sa juridiction.

Je me hasarderai à une autre hypothèse, sans être encore sûr qu'elle permette de tenir compte de tous les aspects du problème. Elle consisterait à mettre le calendrier très abondant des quatre manuscrits isolés par Van Dijk en rapport avec les canonisations, du fait que le Pape avait à célébrer non seulement les fêtes des saints dont il prescrivait la célébration à toutes les Églises, mais même, du moins lors de la canonisation, les fêtes instituées seulement pour des Églises particulières. J'aurai à revenir sur la question des canonisations dans la quatrième partie de cet exposé.

COMMENCEMENT DE LA DIFFUSION DE LA LITURGIE PAPALE HORS DE ROME

Considérons d'abord la diffusion du pontifical papal, puis celle de la liturgie de la chapelle papale au sens propre. On connaît assez bien, grâce à Andrieu et Leroquais, des exemplaires du pontifical romain utilisés hors de Rome. Toutefois la frontière tracée par Andrieu entre le pontifical romain du XIIe siècle et le pontifical de la Curie romaine au XIIIe siècle — peut-être serait-il plus clair de dire: le pontifical d'Innocent III — est à corriger du fait de la redécouverte par Sir Francis Wormald du manuscrit du pontifical d'Apamée:[24] il apparaît maintenant que celui-ci a été copié au Saint-Sépulcre entre 1229 et 1244 et que ce pontifical, au lieu d'être, comme le pensait Andrieu, le témoin de la dernière modernisation du pontifical romain avant Innocent III, préparant en quelque sorte Innocent III, est en réalité le résultat de la double influence du pontifical du XIIe siècle et de celui d'Innocent III. De façon générale il faudrait compléter l'œuvre d'Andrieu et de Leroquais en cherchant à établir une géographie des pontificaux romains ou non-romains. Une telle enquête nous serait instructive au sujet des modalités réelles de la diffusion des livres liturgiques au XIIe et au XIIIe siècles. De cela je vais donner un double exemple qui concerne Guillaume Durand de Mende l'Ancien (je l'appelle ainsi pour le distinguer de son neveu et successeur à Mende).

---

[24] F. Wormald, "The Pontifical of Apamea," *Nederlands Kunsthistorisch Jaarboek 5* (1951) 271 sq.

Vers la fin du XIIIe siècle Durand compile un pontifical romain avec quelques éléments languedociens.[25] Son pontifical sera souvent copié dans la suite parce qu'il représente la modernité cérémonielle. Le cas de Durand est représentatif d'abord parce qu'il appartient à un type d'évêque relativement nouveau: il est le premier évêque de Mende qui vienne d'ailleurs et n'appartienne pas aux familles baroniales qui se partagent le chapitre. De plus, ce languedocien a passé sa carrière avant l'épiscopat à la Curie et, après quelques années à Mende, il est retourné au service du Pape tout en gardant le siège épiscopal de Mende. Au moment où il devient évêque, il achève au moins la première rédaction de son "Rational," [26] où il apparaît qu'il n'a pas encore connaissance du pontifical romain de la Curie.[27] Je ne pense pas qu'il ait emporté un exemplaire du pontifical de la Curie lorsqu'il est parti en 1286 pour son nouveau diocèse, ce qui aurait dû être le cas si, comme le supposait Andrieu, il a composé son propre pontifical à Mende; le plus probable est au contraire qu'il n'a pris connaissance du pontifical de la Curie qu'au cours de son dernier séjour en Italie. En revanche le P. Dykmans a solidement établi que Durand a introduit à Mende un *Ordo Missae* dépendant du cérémonial de Latino Malabranca.[28] Pour le reste la liturgie de Mende n'a rien de romain.[29]

Intéressante par ailleurs est la première diffusion du pontifical de Durand. À la mort de Durand le neveu, arrive à Mende comme évêque le bourguignon Jean d'Arcy. Celui-ci ne reste à Mende qu'un an (1330-1331), et se fait bientôt transférer dans sa région d'origine, à Autun puis à Langres. Il emporte le pontifical des Durand, que le chapitre de Mende lui réclame en vain en 1334. La veille de sa mort, en 1344, il fait son testament, dans lequel il prescrit entre autres que son pontifical soit restitué à l'Église de Mende et qu'une messe y soit fondée pour le repos de son âme. Comme cette messe ne figure pas au livre des obits et fondations de la cathédrale, je doute que le pontifical ait été restitué. En tout cas le manuscrit emporté par Jean d'Arcy est à l'origine de la meilleure branche de la tradition manuscrite du pontifical de Durand.

---

[25] Cf. R. Cabié, "Le pontifical de Guillaume Durand l'Ancien et les livres liturgiques languedociens," dans *Liturgie et musique (IXe-XIVe s.)*, Cahiers de Fanjeaux 17 (Toulouse-Fanjeaux, 1982), pp. 225-237.

[26] Sur les différentes rédactions du *Rational* cf. mon "Bulletin de Liturgie," *Revue des Sciences Philosophiques et Théologiques* 69 (1985) 312.

[27] Cf. mon étude "L'Ordinaire de Mende, une œuvre inédite de Guillaume Durand l'Ancien," dans *Liturgie et musique*, pp. 239-249, spécialement p. 246.

[28] Cf. M. Dykmans, *Le cérémonial papal de la fin du moyen âge à la Renaissance. I. Le cérémonial papal du XIIIe s.* (Bruxelles-Rome, 1977).

[29] Cf. mon étude sur "Les livres liturgiques de l'Église de Mende," dans *Mens concordet voci*, Mélanges Martimort (Tournai, 1983), pp. 497-507.

En ce qui concerne la liturgie de la chapelle papale Van Dijk a clarifié deux questions. Tout d'abord, comme je l'ai déjà signalé, il a montré que la thèse de Raoul de Rivo selon laquelle l'Église Romaine avait adopté les livres liturgiques franciscains était sans fondement. En second lieu il a non seulement établi que la Règle franciscaine de 1223 déterminait l'emploi par les clercs franciscains des livres de la chapelle papale, mais mis le doigt sur un passage important d'Angelus de Chiarino dans son Exposition de la Règle franciscaine (1321-1323). Aux Frères Mineurs qui demandaient à Grégoire IX certains allègements par rapport à l'Office de la Curie, le Pape répond:

> Frères, si vous voulez faire l'Office de l'église sans rien en enlever, je prescrirai à tous les religieux qui sont dans l'Église, sauf aux chanoines réguliers et aux moines, qu'ils adoptent votre Office.[30]

Bien que le témoignage d'Angelus soit tardif, il correspond bien à la fois à l'histoire de la liturgie franciscaine, qui ne nous intéresse pas ici, et à la ligne de conduite des Papes du XIIIᵉ siècle envers les nouveaux Ordres religieux non canoniaux, ou plus précisément qui ne sont pas liés dans leur origine à une communauté canoniale insérée dans une Église diocésaine déterminée, mais ont un caractère universel. Ces Ordres ont tous adopté ou reçu la liturgie de la Curie, à l'exception des Frères Prêcheurs, qui n'ont formellement renoncé à la qualité de chanoines qu'en 1241,[31] et, à leur suite, au moins des Croisiers et des Carmes.[32] La situation particulière de la liturgie des Prêcheurs doit-elle être mise en rapport avec le fait que leur bulle de fondation les considère comme un *Ordo canonicus*?

Ceci définit les limites de la diffusion de la liturgie de la chapelle papale au XIIIᵉ siècle. Les exceptions qui viennent s'y ajouter sont alors très peu nombreuses.[33] C'est seulement au XIVᵉ siècle que l'Office de la chapelle papale sera concédé à un certain nombre de clercs de Curie nommés à des sièges épiscopaux.[34] Leur motivation est clairement exprimée par Durand de

[30] Angelus Clarenus, *Expositio Regulae Fratrum Minorum*, 3 (éd. Oliger [Quaracchi, 1912], p. 88): "Fratres, si vultis absque detruncatione officium ecclesie facere, omnibus religiosis qui sunt in Ecclesia exceptis canonicis regularibus et monachis sancti Benedicti, mandabo quod vestrum officium faciant."
[31] Cf. R. Creytens, "Les constitutions des Frères Prêcheurs dans la rédaction de S. Raymond de Peñafort (1241)," *Archivum Fratrum Praedicatorum* 18 (1948) 5-68, spécialement pp. 22-23.
[32] Cf. W. R. Bonniwell, *A History of the Dominican Liturgy 1215-1945*, 2ᵉ éd. (New York, 1945), pp. 197-199. Je n'examinerai pas ici les autres influences liturgiques dont le P. Bonniwell a signalé des cas sans que la preuve en soit établie.
[33] Cf. Van Dijk, *The Origins*, pp. 398 sq.
[34] Cf. l'index de G. Mollat aux *Lettres communes de Jean XXII* (Paris, 1935), sous la rubrique "Indulta horas dicendi et divina officia celebrandi secundum ritum liturgicum,"

Mende le neveu dans un passage de son traité-programme pour le concile de Vienne où il critique la diversité des liturgies particulières:

> De la diversité susdite s'ensuit une grand incommodité pour les personnes ecclésiastiques: lorsque celles-ci se sont appliquées pendant très longtemps à savoir l'Office de leur Église ou diocèse, et qu'elles sont transférées à une autre, elles se trouvent comme ignorantes de l'Office, alors qu'il est difficile que des inexpérimentés soient attachés au culte divin. À cause de cette diversité beaucoup de pauvres clercs et prêtres perdent leur subsistance, et beaucoup de prélats ne parviennent pas à trouver des serviteurs convenables et idoines pour les divins Offices....[35]

Dans la suite certains diocèses adopteront la liturgie de la Curie mais, au moins en France, de tels cas seront rares avant l'invention de l'imprimerie.

DÉVELOPPEMENT DES INTERVENTIONS LITURGIQUES DU PAPE HORS DE ROME

Je considérerai ici quatre cas:

1. la prescription de célébrer de nouvelles fêtes;
2. la prescription de l'Office du Corpus Christi;
3. la concession de la liturgie de la Sainte-Chapelle de Paris aux autres chapelles de la famille de S. Louis;
4. la confirmation de la liturgie des Prêcheurs par Clément IV.

La réservation papale du pouvoir de canoniser est bien connue, et il n'est pas utile de revenir ici sur le débat entre Stephan Kuttner[36] et Eric Kemp[37] au sujet de la date à laquelle cette réservation a effectivement été considérée comme le droit général. Par contre on n'a guère étudié, à ma connaissance, l'aspect liturgique de la canonisation, à savoir l'obligation faite à toute l'Église, ou à une partie de l'Église, de célébrer la fête d'un saint nouvellement canonisé, et le choix des textes liturgiques pour une fête donnée. Sur

---

c. 167; M. Tangl, *Die päpstlichen Kanzlei-Ordnungen von 1200-1500* (Innsbruck, 1894), n. 149, p. 338.

[35] *Tractatus de modo generalis Concilii celebrandi* II, 68 ([Paris, 1671], pp. 206-207): "Ex praedicta etiam diversitate sequitur magna incommoditas ecclesiasticis personis quia, cum longissimis temporibus laboraverint ad sciendum officium unius ecclesiae vel dioecesis, translati ad aliam quasi officii reperiuntur ignari. Difficile namque est inexpertos divinis officiis mancipari, C. 19, q. 3, c. 6 *Monasteriis* [Friedberg, 1: 841]. Unde ex praedicta diversitate perdunt multi pauperes clerici et presbyteri victum suum, et multi praelati convenientes et idoneos non inveniunt in divino officio servitores."

[36] S. Kuttner, "La réservation papale du droit de canonisation," *Revue historique du droit français et étranger*, 4e série, 17 (1938) 172-228.

[37] E. Kemp, *Canonisation and Authority in the Western Church* (Oxford, 1948).

le premier point j'ai examiné les bulles de canonisation pour la période qui va du début du pontificat de Grégoire IX jusqu'à la fin de celui de Clément IV, grâce au recueil publié en 1729 par Fontanini.[38] Sur onze saints canonisés il y en a quatre ou cinq dont le culte est commandé pour une province ecclésiastique (Edmond de Canterbury, Guillaume de Saint-Brieuc, Stanislas, Hedwige, peut-être aussi Richard de Chichester), le culte des autres étant à célébrer partout. Dans toutes les bulles la célébration de la fête est introduite par la formule "vous commandant par cet écrit apostolique,"[39] mais dans certaines le commandement est renforcé par une clause préceptive: "vous commandant et vous prescrivant"[40] (Edmond de Canterbury, Guillaume de Saint-Brieuc) ou "vous prescrivant strictement"[41] (Élisabeth de Thuringe, Pierre de Vérone, Stanislas). De même la bulle instituant l'Office du Corpus Christi disait dans sa première rédaction "vous commandant par cet écrit apostolique,"[42] puis a été corrigée dans un sens beaucoup plus précis: "par cet écrit apostolique vous commandant et vous prescrivant strictement en vertu de la sainte obéissance, et vous enjoignant en rémission de vos péchés."[43] Il est clair que parmi ces formules certaines insistent plus que d'autres, mais j'ignore s'il y a une distinction précise entre commandement et précepte. Quoiqu'il en soit à cet égard, on peut constater que, parmi toutes les fêtes dont la célébration a été commandée par les Papes, deux seulement ont été reçues partout, celles de S. Thomas Becket et de S. François d'Assise, auxquelles on peut joindre la fête du Corpus Christi, mais seulement après la republication de la bulle d'Urbain IV par Clément V et sa diffusion dans les Clémentines.

À ces prescriptions concernant la célébration des fêtes on peut joindre une décrétale de Boniface VIII déterminant que les fêtes des quatre grands docteurs seraient célébrées avec un office double: "Nous donc ... avec le conseil et l'assentiment de nos frères (les Cardinaux), voulons, décidons et prescrivons que les fêtes principales des apôtres, des évangélistes et des

---

[38] Giusto Fontanini, *Codex constitutionum quas Summi Pontifices ediderunt in solemni canonizatione sanctorum, a Johanne XV ad Benedictum XIII...* (Rome, 1729).

[39] "Per apostolica scripta vobis mandantes."

[40] "Praecipiendo mandantes."

[41] "Districte praecipiendo."

[42] "Per apostolica vobis scripta mandantes." La première rédaction et la troisième (celle de Clément V) sont publiées ensemble par E. Franceschini, "Origine e stile della bolla 'Transiturus'," *Aevum* 39 (1965) 235-240 (article reproduit dans E. Franceschini, *Scritti di filologia medievale*, Medioevo e Umanesimo 26 (Padova, 1981), 1: 332-365. La deuxième rédaction, postérieure de quelques semaines à la première, a été publiée par T. Bertamini, "La bolla 'Transiturus' di papa Urbano IV e l'uffizio del 'Corpus Christi' secondo il codice di S. Lorenzo di Bognanco," *Aevum* 42 (1968) 42-49.

[43] "Per apostolica scripta in virtute sanctae obedientiae districte praecipiendo mandamus, in remissione peccaminum iniungentes."

docteurs soient célébrées dans toutes les églises du monde avec un Office double....."[44]

Ici encore c'est le droit canonique qui assurera la diffusion de la détermination liturgique, dans le cas de la publication du Sexte. Il est à noter que cette décision sur un point particulier aura indirectement pour effet, dans un certain nombre de liturgies, de modifier toute la hiérarchie des fêtes.

Au fond toute cette première catégorie de cas ne faisait que mettre en œuvre le principe de Grégoire VII selon lequel le Pape avait le droit de prescrire la célébration de nouvelles fêtes, principe qu'il ne semble pas avoir affirmé pour lui-même, mais qui est impliqué dans la décision que les Papes martyrs seraient fêtés partout au même titre que le patron de chaque Église locale.[45]

Les bulles de canonisation du XIIIe siècle ne disent rien des textes liturgiques à employer, même si, de fait, la collecte composée pour être utilisée une première fois par le Pape en l'honneur du nouveau saint recevait une large diffusion. À cet égard la bulle *Transiturus* instituant la fête du Corpus Christi comporte une innovation importante:

> commandant (enjoignant) que vous célébriez dévotement et solennellement cette fête si haute et si glorieuse chaque année le jeudi qui a été indiqué, avec les neuf leçons, avec les répons, versets, antiennes, psaumes, hymnes et oraisons convenant spécialement à la fête, que nous vous envoyons ci-inclus dans notre bulle avec le propre de la Messe; et nous vous commandons également de veiller à faire célébrer la fête dans toutes les églises de vos villes et diocèses.[46]

Le document papal plié et scellé contient inclus un deuxième document, à savoir l'Office que le Pape enjoint d'utiliser pour la fête. Cette clause sur l'Office inclus sera omise par Clément V lorsque celui-ci republiera *Transiturus* dans la bulle *Si Dominum*, mais elle se trouve dans tous les témoins antérieurs, assez nombreux, de *Transiturus*. Je ne connais pas de précédent à une prescription de ce genre portant sur un texte liturgique dans les

---

[44] *Sexte* III, 22 (Friedberg 2: 1060): "Nos itaque ... eorundem Apostolorum, Evangelistarum et Confessorum [=les docteurs] festivitates praecipuas, de fratrum nostrorum consilio et assensu, sub officio duplici per universas orbis ecclesias volumus, statuimus et praecipimus...."

[45] Cf. Bernold de Constance, *Micrologus*, 45 (*PL* 151: 1010), et P. Jounel, *Le culte des saints dans les basiliques du Latran et du Vatican au XIIe s.* (Rome, 1977), pp. 180-181.

[46] "... Mandantes (iniungentes) quatenus tam excelsum et tam gloriosum festum predicta quinta feria singulis annis cum novem lectionibus, cum responsoriis, versiculis, antiphonis, psalmis, ymnis et orationibus ipsi festo specialiter congruentibus, que cum proprio misse officio vobis sub bulla nostra mittimus interclusa, devote ac sollempniter celebretis et faciatis studiose per universas ecclesias vestrarum civitatum et dioecesium celebrari...."

documents émanant des prédécesseurs d'Urbain IV. S'il fallait chercher quelque chose de comparable, ce serait plutôt dans la décision des chapitres généraux des Prêcheurs donnant force de constitution à la liturgie de l'Ordre. Ainsi au chapitre de Bude en 1254:

> Dans le chapitre sur l'Office de l'église, là où il est dit: "tout l'Office tant diurne que nocturne," on ajoutera: "selon l'organisation et l'exemplaire du vénérable Père Humbert, maître de l'Ordre." [47]

Quant aux prescriptions papales sur des textes liturgiques, je ne sais s'il y en a eu avant la Renaissance. De toute façon, aussi bien l'établissement de nouvelles fêtes par l'autorité papale que la prescription de l'Office du Corpus Christi sont des modifications relativement mineures si on les compare à l'ensemble des liturgies médiévales qui, dans leur espace, sont enracinées localement et procèdent de la coutume, y compris à la chapelle papale, comme le souligne l'intitulé même de l'Ordinaire de la Curie "que nous avons coutume d'observer."

La confirmation de la liturgie des Prêcheurs par Clément IV[48] a un caractère très particulier dû à ce que leur liturgie n'a, semble-t-il, qu'un enracinement local relativement faible; qu'elle a d'abord été élaborée et approuvée par un chapitre général; enfin que, dix ans après son approbation définitive à l'intérieur de l'Ordre, celui-ci a jugé qu'il fallait recourir à la confirmation du Pape.

Dans l'état actuel les recherches sur les origines et les sources de la liturgie dominicaine posent un problème compliqué. Je crois voir dans cette liturgie quelques indices des fondations canoniales originelles à Toulouse; peut-être la trace d'une première adaptation canoniale dans les différents lieux où l'Ordre fondait des couvents; enfin le travail d'une commission de quatre frères venus respectivement de France (ou de Provence, le texte est douteux), d'Angleterre, de Lombardie et d'Allemagne. Les sondages effectués par Dom Le Roux semblent indiquer que, suivant les temps liturgiques de l'année, la liturgie des Prêcheurs puise dans des sources différentes, comme sous l'effet de l'éclectisme des quatre frères. Quoiqu'il en soit à cet égard, se manifeste ici le caractère de l'ordre même, d'abord enraciné localement comme tout *Ordo canonicus*, puis en quelque sorte déraciné par sa vocation universelle.

---

[47] *Acta Capitulorum Generalium Ordinis Praedicatorum*, éd. B. M. Reichert (Rome, 1898), 1: 68: "In capitulo de officio ecclesie, ubi dicitur: 'totum officium tam diurnum quam nocturnum,' addatur: 'secundum ordinacionem et exemplar venerabilis patris Humberti, magistri ordinis' ('confirmamus')."

[48] Th. Ripoll et A. Bremond, *Bullarium Ordinis Fr. Praedicatorum* (Rome, 1729), 1: 486 (7 juillet 1267).

Pour ce qui est de l'intervention de Clément ɪv, dont nous ignorons les
tenants et aboutissants, je suis tenté d'y voir, non la résultante de conflits
internes à l'Ordre, mais un signe de la conscience croissante qu'on a à
l'époque de l'autorité papale dans les choses de la liturgie.

En dernier lieu je mentionnerai l'extension de la liturgie de la Sainte-
Chapelle de Paris (elle-même une variante de la liturgie de la cathédrale
Notre-Dame) soit aux clercs accompagnant le roi ou la reine de France en
voyage, soit à des églises comme Saint-Nicolas de Bari ou la Sainte-Chapelle
de Bourges. À mon avis le cas le plus intéressant est celui de Saint-Nicolas
de Bari, église bénédictine transformée par Charles ɪɪ de Naples en une
chapelle royale dont l'organisation et la liturgie sont calquées sur celles de
Paris: "Du reste, comme on vit de manière louable lorsqu'en vivant on prend
exemple sur les meilleurs, nous ordonnons et voulons que désormais l'Office
divin soit célébré en cette église selon les livres de l'Église de Paris que nous
lui avons donnés...." [49] Lorsque le roi angevin organise en 1304 le clergé et
la liturgie de la chapelle de Bari, il a déjà obtenu de Boniface vɪɪɪ que celle-ci
soit exempte de l'évêque et soumise directement au Saint-Siège.[50] Je signale
en passant que les documents d'exemption sont une des voies par lesquelles
s'affirme de façon de plus en plus accentuée la juridiction papale universelle.
En exemptant de la juridiction épiscopale les chapelles royales de Bari ou de
Paris, Boniface vɪɪɪ pour Charles ɪɪ d'Anjou, Benoît xɪ pour Philippe le Bel
profitent de l'occasion pour souligner leur propre primauté.[51] Pour ce qui est
des livres liturgiques, en 1304 Charles ɪɪ signale qu'il a doté Saint-Nicolas de
Bari de livres parisiens qui effectivement s'y trouvent encore et dont Robert
Branner a signalé l'intérêt pour l'histoire de la peinture à Paris sous
S. Louis.[52] Aux yeux de l'autorité papale un tel changement de liturgie
présupposait certainement une concession spéciale, dont nous n'avons pas
la trace. Un document de ce genre a-t-il existé, ou le roi s'en est-il délibé-
rément dispensé, par exemple en invoquant son droit légatin? Tout en
hésitant à trancher, j'inclinerais plutôt vers la première hypothèse. Même du
temps des démêlés de Philippe le Bel avec Boniface vɪɪɪ nous sommes loin

[49] F. Ughelli, *Italia Sacra*, 2ᵉ éd. (Venise, 1721), 7: c. 635: "Caeterum quia laudabiliter
vivitur cum in vivendo exemplum et instar assumitur meliorum, ordinamus et volumus quod
in ipsa deinceps ecclesia secundum ordinem Parisiorum Ecclesiae per libros quos eidem
ecclesiae dedimus, divinum officium celebretur...."

[50] *Registres de Boniface VIII*, éd. R. Fawtier (Paris, 1939), 4: n. 5592, c. 82.

[51] *Registre de Benoît XI*, éd. Ch. Grandjean (Paris, 1905), n. 1251 (18 avril 1304), c. 778:
"Licet omnes ecclesie per universalem orbem diffuse Sedi Apostolice, que super illas obtinet
principatum, disponente Domino sint subjecte, Sedes tamen eadem nonnulla ex ipsis aliquando specialiter sibi subdit...."

[52] Robert Branner, *Manuscript Painting in Paris during the Reign of Saint Louis* (Berke-
ley-Los Angeles-London, 1977), surtout pp. 102 et 229.

de l'époque où la chapelle impériale jouait un rôle liturgique prédominant dans l'Occident carolingien et ottonien.

Au terme de cette enquête une double conclusion apparaît. D'une part, au cours de la période étudiée, l'influence liturgique du Pape et de sa chapelle est relativement peu étendue. D'autre part le principe sur lequel cette influence repose contient déjà d'avance les développements qui se réaliseront après Trente, à savoir l'extension du rite de la chapelle papale à tout l'Occident et la réservation au Pape de tout le droit liturgique. Cela est bien dit, et même mis dans une sorte de perspective historique, par Jean Beleth:

> Nous disons donc que de façon générale dans l'Église rien ne doit être chanté, psalmodié ou lu qui ne soit canonisé par le Souverain Pontife. ... Dans l'Église primitive on chantait des choses diverses, chacun comme il voulait, à la condition cependant que ce qui était chanté fût en rapport avec la louange de Dieu.[53]

Dans son *Rational*, Durand de Mende reprend la phrase de Jean Beleth à peu près telle quelle. Il ajoute néanmoins une précision significative: "rien ne doit être chanté ou lu qui ne soit canonisé par la Sainte Église Romaine, approuvé expressément ou par tolérance (*per patientiam*)."[54] Durand savait bien que de son temps les cas d'approbation expresse n'étaient que l'exception.

---

[53] Jean Beleth, *Summa de ecclesiasticis officiis*, 19bc (CCCM 41 A: 41): "Dicimus ergo generaliter in ecclesia nihil esse cantandum uel psallendum uel legendum, quod a summo pontifice non sit canonizatum. ... In primitiua ecclesia diuersi diuersa cantabant in ecclesia quisque ad uoluntatem suam, ita tamen quod illud quod cantabant ad laudem diuinam pertineret."

[54] *Rationale divinorum officiorum* v, 2, 2: "Caeterum in ecclesia generaliter nil canendum aut legendum est quod a Sancta Romana Ecclesia canonizatum et approbatum expresse aut per patientiam non sit."

7

La Papauté dans les sermons médiévaux français et italiens

Jacques Guy Bougerol

On a longtemps négligé de présenter l'étude des sermons médiévaux comme un élément important de notre connaissance des hommes et des idées. A. Lecoy de la Marche avait donné en son temps une vision d'ensemble de la prédication médiévale propre à exciter l'intérêt des historiens,[1] mais la tâche est ingrate de repérer les sources manuscrites, d'en authentifier les auteurs, d'en transcrire le contenu et de dépasser l'appareil technique de la composition pour en dégager la pensée.

La recherche entreprise ici voudrait apporter une contribution à l'histoire des mentalités et en même temps présenter ce qu'ont dit de la papauté les prédicateurs médiévaux.

Il se produisit au début du treizième siècle un événement historique d'une portée considérable. Jusqu'alors la prédication était considérée par les théologiens et les canonistes comme le ministère privilégié du pape, des évêques et des prêtres, selon la conception de l'*Ordo ecclesiasticus* dont les appuis traditionnels, selon le mot du P. Y. M. Congar, n'étaient "nullement négligeables."[2]

---

[1] Cf. A. Lecoy de la Marche, *La chaire française au moyen âge*, 2ᵉ éd. (Paris, 1886); J. B. Schneyer, *Geschichte der katholischen Predigt* (Freiburg, 1969). Plus récemment: A. Longère, *Œuvres oratoires de maîtres parisiens au XIIᵉ siècle*, 2 vol., I. Texte, II. Notes (Paris, 1975); idem, *La prédication médiévale* (Paris, 1983).

[2] Y. M. Congar, "Aspects ecclésiologiques de la querelle entre mendiants et séculiers dans la seconde moitié du XIIIᵉ siècle et le début du XIVᵉ," *Archives d'Histoire doctrinale et littéraire du Moyen Âge* 28 (1961) 54 [="Aspects"].

The Religious Roles of the Papacy: Ideals and Realities, 1150-1300, ed. Christopher Ryan, Papers in Mediaeval Studies 8 (Toronto: Pontifical Institute of Mediaeval Studies, 1989), pp. 247-275. © P.I.M.S., 1989.

Les papes du treizième siècle ont sans nul doute prêché, mais nous en avons bien peu d'échos dans les collections manuscrites; les évêques ont rempli leur mission apostolique avec plus ou moins de zèle. À Paris, l'influence de maîtres comme Pierre le Chantre et Maurice de Sully a suscité un vaste mouvement pastoral parmi les nombreux disciples formés à leur école. Étienne Langton, qui prêchait déjà beaucoup étant maître à Paris, continua de le faire lorsqu'il devint cardinal archevêque de Canterbury.[3] Un ancien étudiant de Paris dans les années 1180 reçut de ses maîtres, dont Pierre de Corbeil, une connaissance étonnante de l'Écriture et un sens profond de l'ouverture pastorale. C'est lui, Lotario dei Conti di Segni, devenu le pape Innocent III, qui étendit à l'Église universelle le programme de réforme dont il avait vérifié les effets à Paris. Non seulement il suggéra l'institution dans chaque diocèse de groupes de prêtres voués à la prédication, non seulement il approuva et regroupa les nombreuses initiatives apostoliques dont celle de saint Dominique, mais il rompit le programme rigoureux de réforme des ordres religieux en bénissant l'initiative de François d'Assise au lendemain du Concile. L'impulsion était donnée de sorte que l'arrivée des mendiants, prêcheurs et mineurs, va universaliser les mouvements pastoraux issus des milieux universitaires parisiens.[4] Il s'agit là d'une véritable révolution, non seulement dans la théorie et la pratique de la fonction ministérielle, mais aussi dans la technique même du sermon. Entre 1220 et 1237, la mission de prêcher est officiellement confiée et institutionnalisée chez les mendiants par Grégoire IX.[5] Il fallait désormais que les frères apprennent à prêcher, d'où la nécessité de nouveaux instruments de travail.[6]

LA PAPAUTÉ DANS LES SERMONS

Qu'allons-nous trouver dans les sermons qui puisse intéresser notre sujet? Les recherches entreprises à travers l'immense littérature des sermons médiévaux m'ont permis de retenir un certain nombre de textes significatifs

[3] Cf. P. B. Roberts, "Master Stephen Langton Preaches to the People and Clergy; Sermon Texts from Twelfth-Century Paris," *Traditio* 36 (1980) 237-268.

[4] Cf. Y. M. Congar, "Innocent III," *Catholicisme* 5: 1650-1658; M. Maccarrone, "Innocent III," *Dictionnaire de Spiritualité* 7: 1767-1773.

[5] Cf. J. G. Bougerol, "Le origine e la finalità dello studio nell'Ordine francescano," *Antonianum* 53 (1978) 406-407.

[6] Cf. L. Bataillon, "Les instruments de travail des prédicateurs au XIIIᵉ siècle," dans *Aspects culturels et méthodes de travail au moyen âge* (Paris, 1981), pp. 197-209; idem, "Intermédiaires entre les traités de morale pratique et les sermons: les Distinctions bibliques alphabétiques," dans *Les genres littéraires dans les sources théologiques médiévales*. Définition, critique et exploitation (Louvain-la-Neuve, 1982), pp. 213-226.

dont la plupart sont encore enfouis dans les documents manuscrits. La difficulté sera plutôt de construire une conclusion valable à partir de ces quelques éléments en évitant de majorer leur valeur de témoignage. D'Innocent III à Matthieu d'Aquasparta, disons de 1200 à 1300, la récolte ne sera pas tellement abondante. La plupart des recueils de sermons ne nous livrent que bien rarement une conception théologique de la papauté et de sa place dans l'univers mental des auditeurs et dans leur vie chrétienne de tous les jours.

La célébration où apparaît quelque allusion au pape et à la papauté est la fête du 22 février, la Chaire de saint Pierre.[7] Sur 70 textes étudiés, j'en ai trouvé sept, soit 10%, à y donner au moins le titre du successeur de Pierre. Mais beaucoup de prédicateurs et non des moindres paraissent plus désireux de mettre en lumière les défauts du pape et des évêques, compris sous le vocable générique de "prelati," que de souligner la continuité de la tradition apostolique sous l'impulsion puissante de l'Esprit au travers des siècles. Il semble bien que la tranquille possession de la vérité catholique se soit manifestée par l'acceptation pure et simple de l'organisation présente de l'Église. La seule requête présentée par les prédicateurs qui répondent ainsi à l'attente des fidèles, concerne la manière dont les "prelati" remplissent leur ministère. Un frère mineur anonyme, dans un sermon pour la fête des apôtres Philippe et Jacques, le 2 mai 1231, parla aux étudiants des prélats qui désirent sans honte les honneurs en faisant leur les paroles de l'Apôtre: "Si quelqu'un aspire à l'épiscopat, c'est une belle tâche qu'il désire." Une tâche, non pas un honneur. C'est l'ambition plus que le zèle apostolique qui les pousse. Quand ils croient pouvoir bénéficier d'un bon 'temporel,' alors ils se lèvent dès matines et disent avec Isaïe: "Me voici, Seigneur, envoie-moi!" Mais si la charge ne leur paraît pas bien payée, ils envoient leurs vicaires et disent avec Jérémie: "A, a, a, Seigneur, je ne sais pas parler, je suis trop jeune."[8]

---

[7] Voici les sermons *in cathedra sancti Petri* que j'ai utilisés. Ils sont cités ici dans leur ordre chronologique: MS Paris, BN nouv. acq. lat. 338, f. 133v-136r; MS Arras 691, f. 26va-27va; MS Nijmegen, UB 61, f. 1; MS Paris, BN lat. 14595, f. 106v-107r et f. 107v; MS Troyes 1778, f. 105va; MS Troyes 951, f. 66r; MS Troyes 1464, f. 38ra-rb; MS Troyes 2052, f. 34vb-37rb.

[8] MS Paris, BN nouv. acq. lat. 338, f. 197v-198r, "sermo cuiusdam fratris minoris de festo philippi et iacobi factus in crastino ascensionis" (2 mai 1231), ed. M. M. Davy, *Les sermons universitaires parisiens de 1230-1231* (Paris, 1931), pp. 400-401. Texte vérifié sur le manuscrit: "Item dicunt quod bene possunt appetere honores, inducentes pro se illud apostoli: Qui episcopatum desiderat, bonum opus desiderat. Verum est, sed non dicit bonum honorem, sed hoc non desiderant ex zelo animarum sed potius ex ambitione quod patet in ecclesiis. Quando enim emolumentum temporale aliquid credunt habere in ecclesia sua, tunc surgunt ad matutinas, dicentes cum Isaia: Ecce ego mitte me, etc. Sed quanto nihil putant habere, tunc ad Ecclesiam suos mittunt uicarios et nolunt surgere ad matutinas dicentes cum Ieremia: A, a, a, Domine, nescio loqui quia puer ego sum."

Le Cardinal Jacques de Vitry, prélat et prédicateur de grande classe, a composé une collection de sermons destinés aux différentes conditions de vie. Je retiens un passage du sermon v aux prélats et autres prêtres. Le texte scripturaire donne déjà le ton: "Qu'est-ce que j'entends dire de toi? Rends compte de ta gestion."

> Parole menaçante et terrible, parole de colère et d'indignation. ... Les clefs ont été enlevées à Simon Pierre et données à Simon le magicien. Plus encore, les clefs ont été changées en massues. Leur usage est devenu un abus car ce n'est pas durant le sommeil des pasteurs, mais avec leur complicité que l'ennemi a semé la zizanie au milieu du blé. ... Ils étalent sur les colonnes leurs vêtements luxueux alors que les pauvres du Christ meurent de faim et de froid devant leur porte. ... Pourquoi donc recherchent-ils les vêtements précieux, eux qui ont fait profession de suivre la pauvreté du Christ, de la prêcher et de l'imiter. C'est à eux que le Seigneur s'adresse en la personne de Pierre: "Pais mes agneaux, pais mes brebis." Eux, ils paissent par eux-mêmes et pour eux-mêmes. Ils vivent sur la substance de leur troupeau, ils se vautrent dans le concubinage et possèdent une progéniture ignominieuse.[9]

Le népotisme apparaît comme une plaie redoutable dont Jean de la Rochelle accuse les prélats. Leurs rejetons sont introduits comme des inutiles dans l'Église et les racines impures, charnelles et viles de la luxure sont plantées sur la montagne, c'est-à-dire sur les dignités de l'Église.[10]

Saint Bonaventure lui-même apostrophe sèchement quelque prélat ou quelque pape, on ne sait, car le sermon pour le deuxième dimanche de Carême du Corpus des "Sermons Dominicaux" a été recomposé sans doute

---

[9] Iacobus de Vitriaco, "Sermo v ad prelatos et alios sacerdotes," MS Paris, BN lat. 17509, f. 9rb-vb; un extrait en a été édité par J. B. Pitra, *Analecta Novissima* (Frascati, 1888), 2: 357: "Verbum comminationis et terroris, uerbum ire et indignationis. ... Ablate sunt claues symoni petro et date sunt symoni mago. Immo claues in clauas mutauerunt. Iam enim pene in usum uenit omnis abusio, quia non dormientibus pastoribus, sed collaborantibus, in medio tritici superseminauit inimicus homo zizania. ... Multa uestium mutatoria ad ostentationem iactantie in porticis extenduntur, et Christi pauperes ad ianuas fame et frigore cruciantur. ... Sed isti quare uel cuius gratiam ex preciosa ueste perquirunt, qui christi paupertatem, et predicare et imitari professi sunt, et cum eis in persona petri a domino ter dicatur: pasce oues seu agnos. Ipsi pascunt se, pascunt semet, pascunt semetipsos. Pascunt se in sua substantia, pascunt semet in turpi concubina, pascunt semetipsos in prole ignominiosa."

[10] Ioannes de Rupella, MS Troyes 816, f. 129va-vb, "dom. 16 p. pent.," *In caritate radicati.* Dans J. B. Schneyer, *Repert. der latein. Serm. des Mittelalters* (Münster, 1971), t. 3, Johannes de Rupella, p. 710, n. 95 (=Schn.): "Quidam uero radicantur radice concupiscencie uoluptatis. Unde ecc. 40, nepotes impiorum non multiplicabuntur ramos, et radices immunde super cacumen petre sonant. Quia proh dolor, hodie impletur in ecclesia, nam nepotes impiorum prelatorum inutiles in ecclesia introducuntur et radices immunde, hoc est carnales et uiles, per luxurias super cacumen petre sonant, id est super dignitatem ecclesie. Unde et carnali anime prelati sub typo adultere dicitur, ecc. 23, non dabit filii eius radices et rami eius non dabunt fructum, relinquuntur in maledictum memoria illius et dedecus illius non delebitur."

après avoir été prêché, si même il l'a été. Il s'agit du thème de la Transfiguration et Bonaventure montre comment le Seigneur prit avec lui Pierre et en lui tous les prélats appelés à gouverner l'Église. Il eût été tellement meilleur pour eux de rester dans la plaine, car plus haut on est élevé, plus dure est la chute.[11]

J'ai voulu attirer l'attention sur cet aspect que présentent un grand nombre de sermons médiévaux. Je m'abstiens de citer d'autres exemples, ce serait hors de notre propos. Je pense qu'alors, la robustesse de la foi et le désir de vivre dans une Église pure et sainte incitaient les chrétiens à montrer du doigt ceux qui trahissaient l'Évangile.

L'analyse des textes retenus m'a conduit à les grouper sous certains thèmes significatifs qui répondent à l'intention générale de ces études. La conclusion de ces recherches montrera comment le peuple chrétien ressentait la réalité de l'Église.

1. LES TITRES DONNÉS AU PAPE DANS LES SERMONS

Il est intéressant de noter les différents titres donnés au pape dans les sermons médiévaux; il est plus intéressant encore de livrer ces titres dans l'ordre de fréquence décroissante.

1. *Summus pontifex* avec toutes ses variantes: *supremus pontifex, pontifex romanus, summus sacerdos,* etc.

Ce titre apparaît dans le sermon prêché par Innocent III pour la fête de saint Grégoire le Grand,[12] tandis que dans un sermon pour l'anniversaire de sa consécration, il emploie *romanus pontifex*.[13] Le Chancelier Philippe nomme le pape *summus pontifex* dans un sermon prêché aux écoliers de Paris exilés à Orléans durant la grève scolaire de 1229-1231, le samedi-saint 6 avril 1230.[14] Le sermon anonyme que nous livre la collection du manuscrit

---

[11] S. Bonaventura, "Serm. dom. 2 Quadr.," éd. J. G. Bougerol, *S. Bonaventurae Sermones Dominicales* (Grottaferrata, 1977), p. 248. Ce sermon ne paraît ni dans le MS Milano, Ambros. 11 A sup., ni dans Paris, BN lat. 14595, ni dans aucun autre MS en dehors des manuscrits du *Corpus*. Cf. ibid., Introduction, pp. 20-30 et 31-42: "Primo assumpsit Petrum et in Petro ceteros de statu prelationis ad praesidentiam virtualis protectionis in regimine Ecclesiae. ... Quibus longe melius fuisset, si toto tempore vitae suae stetissent in plano, quia quanto status altior, tanto casus graviter."

[12] Innocens III, "In festo D. Gregorii I pape" (*PL* 217: 517): "supremus pontifex assumptus est in plenitudine potestatis."

[13] Innocens III, "Sermo III in consecr. Pont. Max." (*PL* 217: 664D-665A): "Propter causam vero fornicationis Ecclesia Romana posset dimittere Romanum Pontificem."

[14] Philippus Cancellarius, "Sermo Cancellarii parisiensis quod fecit aurielanis ad scholares de recessu scholarium a parisii quem fecit in uigilia pasche," MS Avranches 132, f. 340r: "Suspirantes nichilominus ad loca dimissa, quia spes est quod bonus et prudens paterfamilias,

Paris, BN lat. 14595, pour la chaire de saint Pierre, parle du *supremus pontifex*.[15] Eudes de Châteauroux, ancien Chancelier de l'Université de Paris devenu cardinal-archevêque de Tusculum, grand prélat et prédicateur de renom, va souvent apparaître dans cette étude; dès maintenant il faut souligner son habitude d'appeler le pape *summus pontifex*.[16] Un frère prêcheur, frère Daniel de Paris, a prêché aux béguines de Saint-Antoine pour la chaire de saint Pierre; lui aussi emploie le titre *summus pontifex*.[17] Servasanctus de Faenza, franciscain toscan, use une fois du mot *pontifex* dans un sermon sur saint Pierre.[18] Le pape Nicolas III désigne de ce mot le pape dans un sermon prêché le 22 février 1279.[19] Matthieu d'Aquasparta, cardinal

---

scilicet summus pontifex, purget amaritudinem origani." Sur le Chancelier Philippe, cf. N. Bériou, "Philippe le Chancelier," *Dict. de Spiritualité*, 12: 1289-1297.

[15] MS Paris, BN lat. 14595, f. 107v: "Et quantum pertinet ad presentem sollempnitatem in qua prelatus fuit beatus petrus a fidelibus in supremum pontificem; cathedram enim appellatur hodie sumpsisse fertur." Il faut remarquer le détail très important: Pierre a été porté à la chaire suprême par les fidèles, c'est-à-dire par l'Église.

[16] Voici les sermons d'Eudes de Châteauroux avec la fréquence du titre: "Sermo in obitu domini clementis pape quarti," MS Pisa, Cateriniana 21, f. 92rb-94rb (8: "summus pontifex"); "Responsio facta nunciis paleologi imperatoris grecorum," ibid., f. 128ra-129vb (5); "Sermo in cathedra sancti petri," MS Paris, BN lat. 15497, f. 119rb-122va (1); "Sermo in electione summi pontificis," Pisa, MS cit., f. 125va-126rb (15); "Responsio ad legatum grecorum," ibid., f. 122vb-123rb (4); "Exhortatio ne quis murmuret uel indignetur si aliquando minus sufficiens in summum pontificem assumatur," ibid., f. 135ra-136va (1); "Sermo in electione summi pontificis," ibid., f. 154ra-155va (6); "Sermo apostolorum petri et pauli," Paris, MS cit., f. 223va-225va (1). Sur Eudes de Châteauroux, cf. A. Paravicini-Bagliani, *Cardinali di Curia e "Familiae" cardinalizie dal 1227 al 1254* (Padova, 1972), 1: 198-212.

[17] "Sermo fratris danielis de parisius ad sanctum antonium in cathedra sancti petri," MS Paris, BN lat. 16481, f. 130va: "antequam beatus petrus eligeretur in summum pontificem."

[18] Servasanctus de Faenza, "Sermo secundus de eodem apostolo," MS Padova, Anton. 490, f. 97ra; éd. Basel, 1502, f. 221ra: "Primo igitur ostendit pontificium eius esse altum. ... Secundo uero ostendit pontificium esse latum et ubique diffusum." Cf. L. Oliger, "Servasanctus de Faenza OFM," dans *Miscell. Fr. Ehrle* (Roma, 1924), 1: 148-149; V. Gamboso, "I sermoni festivi di Servasanctus de Faenza nel codice 490 dell'Antoniana," *Il Santo* 13 (1973) 3-88.

[19] Nicolaus III, "Sermo pro cathedra sancti petri. xxxj. (predicatus set non in urbe in ipsius basilica secundo anno pontificatus domini...))," MS Vatic., Arch. S. Petri F.36, f. 155r: "predicatores enim a deo mittuntur, a quo habere debent auctoritatem predicandi, quia nullus presumere debet predicare nisi auctoritatem habeat ab eo qui dare potest, qualis est summus pontifex qui tenet locum dei in terris." Il est intéressant de rapprocher de ce texte, écrit en 1279, ce passage de l'*In Lucam* de saint Bonaventure, composé quelque 20 ans plus tôt, c. 9, n. 3 (7: 217b): "predicator a Deo mittatur ad Evangelium praedicandum. Primum est auctoritatis mittentis, cuiusmodi est pontificis, et maxime pontificis eius qui est loco Petri, immo loco Iesu Christi; unde qui ab eo mittitur a Christo mittitur." Le MS Vatic., Arch. S. Petri F.36 contient les sermons du pape Nicolas III ou faits par lui, selon leur ordre chronologique. Nicolas III a régné du 25 novembre 1277 au 22 août 1280. Les rubriques indiquées entre parenthèses ont été grattées. Il résulte de leur lecture à la lampe Wood, faite par le P. L. J. Bataillon, que certains sermons ont été prêchés, d'autres ont été rédigés une année et prêchés une autre; d'autres enfin n'ont jamais été prêchés. Certains mêmes portent l'indication que le prothème n'a pas été copié. Ce manuscrit mériterait une étude minutieuse.

franciscain, use du mot *pontifex* sans adjectif dans le sermon pour la chaire de saint Pierre.[20]

Nous pouvons inférer de cette fréquence majeure de *summus pontifex* une conclusion provisoire: l'expression est comprise par tous, elle est devenue un vocable générique du pape.

2. *Papa, pater patrum, pater pascens*

Le nom familier de *papa* se trouve employé aussi bien dans les sermons universitaires que dans les sermons au peuple. Jean de la Rochelle, dans un sermon prêché le 16e dimanche après la Pentecôte, le 28 septembre 1242, durant la vacance du siège apostolique, déclare que l'Église est veuve, elle n'a plus de pape. ... Si nous avions la moindre étincelle de piété, le Seigneur serait ému de miséricorde par les pleurs de son Église et il nous donnerait un bon pape.[21]

Humbert de Romans, du temps qu'il était prieur provincial des dominicains, employa, lui aussi, l'expression *pater* dans une collation pour la chaire de saint Pierre.[22] Saint Bonaventure nomme ainsi le pape dans le *Breviloquium*[23] et il s'attache à en expliquer l'étymologie dans les collations *In Hexaemeron*, d'après la triple parole du Seigneur à Pierre: "*Pasce ... pasce ... pasce*," ce qui conduit au mot *papa*: *pa*(ter) *pa*(trum), ou *pa*(sce) *pa*(sce). À ce propos d'ailleurs, la seconde réportation de ces collations rapporte les menaces de l'empereur Frédéric au pape Innocent iv et la réponse de celui-ci.[24]

---

[20] Matthaeus ab Aquasparta, "Sermo in cathedra beati petri," ms Assisi 460, f. 156v-157v; ms Assisi 682, f. 82v-84r: "reuoluens euuangelium uolumen et actuum apostolorum librum, inuenio in petro duodecim uirtutum prerogatiuas quibus tanquam duodecim lapidibus preciosis debet ornari corona pontificis."

[21] Joannes de Rupella, "Dom. xvj. fratris iohannis de rupella," ms Bruxelles II 1142 (1886), f. 43rb-44ra: "Iam ecclesia uidua est, non habet papam. ... Credo quod si nos haberemus aliquantulum scintillam pietatis, dominus moueretur misericordia ad fletum ecclesie et daret nobis bonum papam."

[22] Humbertus de Romans, "Eodem die collacio prioris prouincialis," ms Arras 691 (759), f. 232ra-rb: "sacrosancta ecclesia intendens exhibere ad condignam reuerenciam patri suo beato petro qui est pater eius, quasi summus post deum."

[23] S. Bonaventura, *Brevil.*, p. 6, c. 12 (5: 278b): "Et quia excellentia, quanto magis descendit, tanto magis dilatatur, et quanto magis ascendit, tanto magis unitur: hinc est, quod plures sunt episcopi, pauciores archiepiscopi, paucissimi patriarchae et unus pater patrum, quia Papa merito appellatur, tanquam unus, primus et summus pater spiritualis omnium patrum, immo omnium fidelium et hierarcha praecipuus, sponsus unicus, caput indivisum, pontifex summus, Christi vicarius, fons, origo et regula cunctorum principatum ecclesiasticorum; a quo tanquam a summo derivatur ordinata potestas usque ad infima Ecclesiae membra, secundum quod exigit praecellens dignitas in ecclesiastica hierarchia."

[24] S. Bonaventura, *Hexaem.*, reportatio Delorme, visio 1, coll. 2 (*Coll. in Hexaem.* [Quaracchi, 1934], pp. 73-74): "Et specialiter istud statum praelationis respicit, ut praelatus sit perfectus in consuetudine, in speculatione, in operatione, exemplo, verbo, subsidio,

Humbert de Romans emploie trois fois le mot *papa* dans un sermon modèle.[25] Eudes de Châteauroux dont nous avons vu combien il affectionnait l'expression *summus pontifex*, n'y est pas attaché exclusivement; il emploie parfois le mot *papa*, notamment dans le sermon qu'il prêcha à la mort de Clément iv,[26] de même que dans l'exhortation qu'il prononça devant on ne sait quel auditoire pour excuser les défauts possibles des papes.[27]

Les prières qu'on lisait au prône mentionnaient pour la plupart le *papa* dans leurs intentions de prière.[28] Un sermon anonyme enfin explique à sa

---

exponendo se et sua pro ovibus; unde dictum est Petro: Pasce, pasce, pasce, et inde dicitur 'Papa' quasi 'pater patrum' vel quasi 'pasce, pasce'." Idem, rep. Delorme, visio 3, coll. 4, n. 30 ([Quaracchi, 1934], pp. 192-193): "Septimo, tempore scilicet quietis mediae, fuerunt tria facta: aedificatio templi, restauratio civitatis, dilatatio pacis. − Sic in Novo Testamento, tempore pacis postremae, aedificatio Ecclesiae romanae et multiplicatio ecclesiarum. Item restauratio: quotiens enim tribulatur Ecclesia romana, totiens restauratur. Nam cum scriberet Fredericus ultimus papae Innocentio quarto: 'Fata docent et stella monet seu praedicat ales / quod Fredericus ego malleus orbis ero,' / papa sibi rescripsit: / Fata tacent nec stella docet, nec praedicat ales / quod navis Petri desinat esse caput." − Le même texte se trouve chez Salimbene, *Chronica*, éd. O. Holder-Egger, p. 362. Cf. O. Holder-Egger, "Italiänische Prophetien des 13. Jahrhunderts. iii," *Neues Archiv der Gesellschaft für ältere deutsche Geschichtskunde* 33 (1907) 106, d'après le ms London L.B., Harleian 3724, f. 49v; ms Vaticana, Chigi N.A.XXX, f. 341. Il s'agit d'un extrait des *Futura praesagia Lombardie, Tuscie, Romagnole et aliarum partium per magistrum Michaelem Scotum*.

[25] Humbertus de Romans, *Maxima Bibliotheca Patrum* xxv (Lugduni, 1677), p. 550c: "Praeterea Papa, qui est super omnes potest deponi ab Ecclesia, quae tota subest ei, in casu; ergo multo fortius quicumque rex deponi potest a Papa cui omnes subsunt. Praeterea si rex aliquis qui nil tenet nisi a Deo non posset deponi a Papa, cum interdum expediat eum deponi, ut ostensum est, ergo non relinquisset Deus sufficientem potestatem in Ecclesia ad regimen mundi, quod est inconveniens. Propter hoc tenendum est indubitanter quod Ecclesia habet huiusmodi potestatem."

[26] Odo de Castro Radulpho, "Sermo in obitu domini clementis pape quarti," ms Pisa, Caterin. 21, f. 92vb: "Quartus datur nobis spes quod ei bonus papa substituetur, immo plures boni ei succedent unus post alterum."

[27] Odo de Castro Radulpho, "Exhortacio ne quis murmuret uel indignetur si aliquando minus sufficiens in summum pontificem assumatur," ms Pisa, Caterin. 21, f. 135ra: "ut non discordia inter papam et cardinales."

[28] N. Bériou, "La prédication au béguinage de Paris pendant l'année liturgique 1272-1273," *Études Augustiniennes* 13 (1978) 105-229, selon le ms Paris, bn lat. 16841, p. 132 15 (f. 59rb), "Sermo magistri Humberti de Sorboniensibus ad beginas in festo beati Iohannis in mane" (mardi 27 décembre 1272), "Non coronabitur nisi qui legitime certauerit" (2 Tm 2:5): "Oretis pro tota sancta ecclesia, hec est tota quia non est rex nec papa qui in hac habeat auantagium. Tanta habet unus cauetarius in precibus ecclesie quantum rex uel papa, si tantum meruit ex bona fide." P. 140 25 (f. 165rb), "Sermo fratris Egidii de Aurelianis (ad beginas) dominica in passione seu dominica ramis palmarum" (26 mars 1273), "Repromissam accipiant qui uocati sunt eterne hereditatis" (He 9:15): "Faciamus orationem pro papa, qui est loco Dei positus in terra, et pro cardinalibus et aliis qui habent regere animas, ut possint ita, etc. quod possint ad 'aysias' paradisi peruenire." P. 146 34 (f. 244rb), "Sermo fratris Ebrardi Sancti Quintini predicatorum ad beginas dominica quinta post pascha" (14 mai 1273), "Usque modo non petistis quicquam in nomine meo: petite et accipietis, ut gaudium uestrum sit plenum" (In 16:24): "Oremus pro papa, cardinalibus, prelatis et omnibus curatis."

manière le sens du mot *papa*: qu'est-ce que le pape sinon le Christ sur terre?[29]

3. *Vicarius, vicarius Christi, vicarius generalis, vicaria substitucio*

Le titre que d'aucuns aujourd'hui considèrent comme la plus heureuse expression de la primauté papale,[30] ne vient qu'en troisième lieu dans l'ordre des fréquences; il semble bien qu'il soit plutôt réservé aux développements théologiques et qu'il contienne un soubassement politique. Il faut cependant noter que d'après l'*Index Busa*, le mot *papa* apparaît 211 fois dans les œuvres authentiques de saint Thomas, alors que *vicarius Christi* n'obtient que la fréquence 14. Il en est de même pour saint Bonaventure qui ne l'emploie guère.[31] Eudes de Châteauroux, dans un sermon prononcé avant l'un des nombreux scrutins du conclave de Viterbe, précise qu'à proprement parler, le pape n'est ni la tête, ni le pasteur, ni le recteur, mais bien plutôt le vicaire de la tête, le vicaire du pasteur, le vicaire du recteur. De même il est le vicaire de l'époux de l'Église et non l'époux.[32]

Un sermon anonyme que nous livre le manuscrit Troyes 2052 trahit son origine universitaire par un langage très spéculatif. Parlant de l'honneur rendu par Dieu à Pierre en lui confiant la *vicaria substitucio*, il entend par cette expression la plénitude de la puissance spirituelle et temporelle. La *vicaria substitucio* établit Pierre à la tête du corps du Christ qui est l'Église, car si le Christ s'est soustrait à notre regard, nous pouvons le rejoindre par la médiation de son vicaire. Par Pierre toute l'Église participe de la tête. Le vicaire du Christ est donc celui en qui réside le sommet et la plénitude du pouvoir.[33] Il faut mentionner enfin l'emploi significatif par Eudes de Château-

---

[29] Anonymus, "Sermo in cathedra petri," MS Troyes 2052, f. 34vb-37rb: "In medio fratrum rector in honore. Summus apostolorum petrus hodie legitur cathedraticus, ... hodie ipsum discipuli christiani apud antiochiam in pontificali cathedra collocarunt, ut quod erat per diuinam institucionem, appareret per rei manifestacionem et exteriorem in signis exaltacionem." Pierre est porté par les disciples dans la chaire suprême. En réalité, ils manifestent l'élection divine.

[30] Cf. M. Maccarrone, *Vicarius Christi* (Roma, 1952), p. 305; Y. M. Congar, "Titres donnés au pape," *Concilium* 108 (1975) 55-64. L'ordre de fréquence décroissante n'est pas celui dans lequel Y. Congar cite les différents titres, mais il y a au fond concordance entre les témoignages des œuvres théologiques et les sermons.

[31] S. Bonaventura, *IV Sent.*, d. 20, p. 2, a. 5, ad 4 (4: 539b): "Quidquid loquamur disputantes vel etiam praedicantes, hoc sana fide tenendum est, quod Dominus suo vicario plenitudinem potestatis contulit, et tantam utique suscepit potestatem quantam decebat homini puro dari; et hoc ad aedificationem corporis sui quod est ecclesia."

[32] Odo de Castro Radulpho, "Sermo in electione summi pontificis," MS Pisa, Caterin. 21, f. 155va: "Si proprie loqui uolumus caput non est, nec pastor, nec rector, sed potius uicarius capitis, pastoris et rectoris. Similiter uicarius est sponsi ecclesie et non sponsus."

[33] Anonymus, "Sermo in cathedra petri," MS Troyes 2052, f. 36rb: "Transeamus ad honorem petri propter quod dicit: regor *in honore*. O quantus honor a deo, honor ab homine. Honorauit autem deus petrum uicaria substitucione, tocius mundi imperiis et regnis subtrac-

roux de l'expression *vicarius generalis* de Dieu pour désigner le souverain pontife.[34] De même Guerric de Saint-Quentin emploie l'expression *vicarius ecclesie.*

4. *Princeps ecclesie, princeps apostolorum, principatus*

Ce titre est peu fréquent et se trouve plutôt dans les sermons du milieu du siècle, disons entre 1250 et 1275, chez Nicolas d'Acqueville: *princeps tocius ecclesie;*[35] chez Eudes de Châteauroux on ne le rencontre qu'une seule fois.[36] Deux prédicateurs anonymes l'emploient aux environ de 1270.[37] Servasanctus de Faenza préfère *principatus.*[38]

5. *Caput apostolorum, caput omnium ecclesiarum, caput tocius ecclesie*

Ce titre n'est employé que par Eudes de Châteauroux et Nicolas III. Eudes emploie le terme dans la réponse qu'il adressa aux envoyés de l'empereur

---

tione, prolis siue familie quasi gregis dominici multiplicacione, officii sibi commissi et fideliter administrati finali premiacione. Primus ergo honor est uicaria substitucio qua uice sui pretulit cum omnibus tanquam caput et commisit ei ecclesiam tanquam corpus suum et totum thesaurum suum, scilicet totam uirtutem passionis posuit in pectore eius de quo thesaurus plenissime posset succrescere animabus. Unde quid est papa nisi Christus in terris. ... Christo enim subtracto ab oculis nostris recessum habemus ad ipsum suo uicario mediante, et per eum participat tota ecclesia capitis, Ps (132:2): *Sicut unguentum in capite,* est plenitudo gratiarum in christo, *quod descendit in barbam,* scilicet uirilem et proximum sibi ordinem sacerdotalem, et per ipsum *in hora uestimenti* usque, scilicet ad infimos et extremos in ecclesia. Erit ergo aliquis intus primus et summus gradus, immo iam non gradus, sed terminus in quo resideat culmen et plenitudo potestatis [36vb] et istum dico christi uicarium."

[34] Odo de Castro Radulpho, "Responsio facta nunciis paleologis imperatoris grecorum," MS Pisa, Caterin. 21, f. 128ra: "verumptamen quia deus constituerat petrum caput apostolorum et suum uicarium generalem."

[35] Nicolas de Aqueville, "De eodem in cathedra sancti petri," MS Paris, BN lat. 15957, f. 232rb; MS Troyes 1594, f. 109va: "Primam dignitatem habuit in die ista, quia die ista primo constitutus fuit a discipulis in antyochia princeps tocius ecclesie sancte. ... Ipse hodie natus fuit et constitutus princeps fratrum, id est, apostolorum et aliorum christianorum."

[36] Odo de Castro Radulpho, "In festo beati petris in uinculis," MS Paris, BN lat. 15947, f. 260ra: "Tunc enim constitutus est rex et princeps super syon montem sanctum, id est, super totam ecclesiam."

[37] Anonymus, "In cathedra sancti petri," MS Troyes 1464, f. 38ra-rb: "sed notandum quod dominus tanquam sapiens et bonus rex beatum petrum principem ecclesie constituit triplicibus de causis, quia scilicet, sciuit eum fidelissimum ad dispensandum ecclesiasticum thesaurum; iustissimum ad subditorum causas iudicandum, constantissimum ad dimicandum contra inimicum uel aduersarium. Hec enim tres in bono baliuo exiguntur, scilicet ut sit fidelis ad dominum, iustus ad populum, constans contra inimicum." MS Paris, BN lat. 14595, f. 106v: "cathedra petri principis. Amice ascende superius. ... Intronizatio beati petri apostolorum principis describitur hic quantum ad quatuor...."

[38] Servasanctus de Faenza, "Sermo secundus de eodem apostolo," MS Padova, Anton. 490, f. 96va; éd. Basel, 1502, f. 220vb: "Apostolus petrus apud antiochiam ad cathedram sublimatus fuit, et principatum quem a Christo acceperat, hodie per ascensum cathedre publicauit."

Paléologue,[39] ainsi que dans deux autres sermons.[40] Dans un sermon rédigé mais non prêché pour le 22 février 1280, Nicolas III emploie le mot en précisant que le Christ quitta ce monde quant à sa présence humaine et monta au ciel en laissant à son successeur le bienheureux Pierre le gouvernement de l'Église universelle. Comme de la tête tous les fidèles ont reçu l'"influence"; en lui fut la plénitude de la puissance et de l'autorité. Et cette même plénitude fut et demeure dans ses successeurs.[41]

6. *Hierarcha*

Je n'ai trouvé ce terme d'origine dyonisienne que chez Bonaventure[42] et Barthélemy de Bologne. Mais il me paraît nécessaire de noter que jamais Bonaventure n'a employé ce mot pour désigner le pape dans les collations *In Hexaemeron.* Quant à Barthélemy de Bologne, il use de ce mot dans un sermon pour la chaire de saint Pierre, sans doute prêché le 22 février 1277 à Paris, en affirmant que rien n'est plus haut que la Trinité et, dans le genre des promotions ecclésiastiques, rien n'est plus éminent que le souverain

---

[39] Odo de Castro Radulpho, "Responsio facta nunciis paleologi imperatoris grecorum," MS Pisa, Caterin. 21, cf. note 34.

[40] Odo de Castro Radulpho, "In cathedra beati petri," MS Paris, BN lat. 15947, f. 119rb: "constitutus est super uniuerso factus caput omnium ecclesiarum. Unde et hic dicitur princeps inter tres, princeps quasi primum caput. Ipse enim factus est caput omnium et ecclesia romana in qua resedit sancta est, caput omnium ecclesiarum.... Sine enim omni contradictione minor confirmatur a maiori et petri successor caput et princeps est eorum qui apostolis successerunt, unde et hic dicitur princeps inter tres: preest enim episcopis, archiepiscopis et patriarchis, ut quia corpus ecclesie distinctum est et ordinatur et habetur membra diuersa, sicut dicit apostolus."

[41] Nicolaus III, "Sermo in cathedra sancti petri. 1. (factus set non predicatus)," MS Vatic., Arch. S. Petri F.36, f. 324v: "Sed quia christus quantum ad presentiam sue humanitatis recessit a mundo et ascendit in celum suum successorem reliquid beatum petrum committens sibi regimen uniuersalis ecclesie a quo tanquam a capite omnes fideles receperunt influentiam in quo fuit plenitudo potestatis et auctoritatis. Et hec eadem fuit et est in suis successoribus."

[42] S. Bonaventura, *De perf. evang.*, q. 4, a. 3, resp. (5: 194b): "Cum ipsa Ecclesia una sit hierachia, unum corpus et una sponsa, necesse est quod unum habeat hierarcham praecipuum, unum caput et unum sponsum; et quoniam huiusmodi unitas non tantum est in Ecclesia secundum interiorem influentiam charismatum, verum etiam secundum exteriorem dispensationem ministeriorum: hinc est quod ipsius Ecclesiae non tantum est hierarcha praecipuus, caput et sponsus ipse Iesus Christus, qui interius ipsam Ecclesiam regit, vivificat et fecundat, verum etiam exterius unus debet esse minister praecipuus tenens locum hierarchae primi, capitis et sponsi, ut Ecclesia non tantum interius, verum etiam exterius in unitate habeat conservari." Bonaventure a prêché à Orvieto le 4e dimanche de l'Avent devant le pape Urbain IV et à Pérouse le 20 décembre 1265 devant le pape Clément IV. Le thème et la structure des sermons est la même: "Sic vos existimet homo" (1 Cor. 4:1). Pour Bonaventure, le ministère du pape et des "prelati" les conforme à la hiérarchie angélique. Ces deux sermons se trouvent dans le MS Milano, Ambros. A.11 sup., f. 45v-46v et f. 46v.

sacerdoce. Le bienheureux Pierre a été constitué par la Hiérarchie incréée elle-même souverain Hiérarque de la Hiérarchie ecclésiastique.[43]

2. LA PRÉSENCE DU PAPE ET LA VACANCE DU SIÈGE

L'unité de l'Église, dans un monde dispersé comme l'était la chrétienté médiévale, était ressentie tout autrement qu'elle peut l'être de nos jours. Les événements étaient connus et vécus là où ils se produisaient. On trouvait sur les routes les marchands, les clercs, les paysans à la recherche d'une terre à cultiver. Ils colportaient les nouvelles et le temps se vivait en dehors du présent. Tous ces éléments concourraient à donner plus de valeur aux réalités accessibles par la foi. Le pape était loin et voyageait fort peu en dehors des terres pontificales, mais dans la chrétienté chacun savait qu'il était le Christ sur la terre.

Dans le sermon "Propheta magnus surrexit in nobis," prononcé le 28 septembre 1242, Jean de la Rochelle commente l'évangile de la veuve de Naïm. Tout dans le récit est fait pour mettre en lumière la figure de la mère dont la douleur est d'autant plus grande qu'elle n'a que cet enfant et qu'elle est veuve.[44] Jean de la Rochelle applique alors à l'Église la figure de la veuve et en transpose un à un les éléments dans une vision étonnante. L'Église est notre mère. Elle a de nombreux fils, mais le clergé forme comme un seul fils, son unique. L'idée de l'unité de tous les clercs sera reprise sous une toute autre forme par Henri de Gand dans son *Quodlibet* VII de Noël 1282.[45] Le discours de Jean de la Rochelle est fort séduisant et suggestif, mais la transposition allégorique du récit évangélique présente de grandes faiblesses. La mère Église est veuve parce que le pape est mort, mais le pape ne peut être à la fois l'époux et le fils.

[43] Bartholomaeus de Bononia, "Sermo fratris bartholomei de bononia in cathedra sancti petri," 22 février 1277, dans le MS Troyes 951, f. 66r: "Nil trinitate alcius et in genere promocionum ecclesiasticarum nil summo sacerdocio est eminencius, et beatus petrus ab ipsa ierarchia increata super ecclesiasticam ierarchiam constitutus est summus ierarchus."

[44] Ioannes de Rupella, "Dom. XVI. fratris iohannis de rupella," MS Bruxelles II: 1142 (1886), f. 43rb: "Propheta magnus surrexit in nobis et quia Deus uisitauit plebem suam" (Lc 7:16). Sermon prêché *sede vacante* le 28 septembre 1242: "Mater nostra ecclesia est, Is 54: plures filii deserte magis quam etc. Plures filios habet ecclesia, sed unicus filius eius clericus, uel omnes sunt unus filius; unde in hoc exprimitur caritas ecclesie, uel fidelis anime. Ita totum se dat pater misericordiarum cuilibet, ac si de aliis non curaret; similiter ecclesia et sancta anima: amor concipit in corde. Clerus autem est unicus ecclesie filius qui mortuus est modo: iam ecclesia uidua est, non habet papam."

[45] Henricus de Gandavo, *Quodlibet VII*, q. 24, cité par Congar, "Aspects," p. 77 et note 118: "Omnes habentes jurisdictionem ordinariam per ordinem secundum sub et supra una persona reputantur et unus sacerdos."

Il n'empêche que la durée des vacances du siège apostolique a été particulièrement dommageable pour l'Église médiévale. Quatre vacances ont dépassé les limites normales des conclaves entre 1241 et 1292: entre Célestin IV et Innocent IV, 18 mois et 15 jours (10.11.1241-25.6.1243); entre Urbain IV et Clément IV, 4 mois et 3 jours (2.10.1264-5.2.1265); entre Clément IV et Grégoire X, 36 mois et 2 jours (29.11.1268-1.12.1271); entre Nicolas IV et Célestin V, 27 mois et 1 jour (4.4.1292-5.7.1294). Jean de la Rochelle avait raison de parler du veuvage de l'Église.

L'expression moderne *sede vacante* est absente des sermons médiévaux. Eudes de Châteauroux lui préfère une formule beaucoup plus parlante et qui rejoint le sentiment exprimé par Jean de la Rochelle: *tempore vacantis ecclesie* ou *vacante ecclesia*.[46] Il faudrait d'ailleurs préciser le sens exact de cette expression.

Le document où se trouvent ces mots d'Eudes de Châteauroux est une sorte de bilan de ses prédications. Il est de la plus haute importance et n'a pas encore reçu des historiens le traitement qu'il mérite, car à sa lumière on se rend compte qu'au sein du Conclave de Viterbe, il a rempli un rôle particulier assez proche de la fonction exercée aujourd'hui par le Cardinal Camerlingue, sans qu'on puisse en déterminer la consistance et la durée.

La collection des sermons qui suivent ce document dans le manuscrit de Pise se révèle intéressante à plus d'un égard pour notre propos. Elle est ainsi rubriquée:

> Sermons du vénérable père Eudes évêque de Tusculum qu'il composa à Viterbe en l'année 1267, la troisième et quatrième année du pontificat du Seigneur pape Clément IV, et durant le temps de la vacance de l'Église.[47]

Eudes de Châteauroux s'avère un collaborateur très proche de Clément IV. Les sermons que je veux analyser ensemble sont les suivants, avec le numéro d'ordre et la rubrique qu'ils portent dans le manuscrit: 48. "Sermo in obitu domini clementis pape quarti";[48] 51. "Sermo ad inuitandum ad pacem et ad concordiam maxime in eligendo summum pontificem";[49] 52. "Prooemium in

---

[46] Odo de Castro Radulpho, MS Pisa, Caterin. 21, f. 2v: "Ego Odo episcopus tusculanus habens pre oculis.... Item apud uiterbium anno domini 1269, tempore uacantis ecclesie composui sermones 85, quorum primus incipit: Sobrii estote et uigilate, ultimus uero: Hunc humiliat, hunc exaltat. ... Item apud uiterbium, uacante ecclesia, anno domini 1270, composui sermones quorum primus incipit: Restituetur ut lutum signaculum, sed nondum perfeci."

[47] Ibid., f. 3ra: "Sermones uenerabilis patris odo episcopi tusculani quod composuit apud uiterbium, anno domini millesimo ducentesimo sexagesimo septimo pontificatus domini clementis pape quarti, anno tercio et quarto et tempore uacantis ecclesie."

[48] Ibid., f. 92rb-94rb.

[49] Ibid., f. 108vb-110rb.

confirmacione electionis";[50] 63. "Sermo in electione summi pontificis";[51] 72. "Exhortacio ne quis murmuret uel indignetur si aliquando minus sufficiens in summum pontificem assumatur";[52] 82. "Sermo in electione summi pontificis." [53]

On voit d'après cette liste qu'Eudes de Châteauroux a pris ses responsabilités durant le conclave de trente-huit mois et qu'il n'a sans doute pas dépendu de lui que les choses aient ainsi traîné au grand dommage de l'Église universelle.

Le thème scripturaire du sermon pour la mort du pape Clément IV est choisi avec beaucoup d'à propos: "Oritur sol et occidit et ad locum suum reuertitur, ibique renascens girat per meridiem et flectitur ad aquilonem." Eudes commente ce texte en soulignant la valeur du pape défunt:

> Il fut un soleil surpassant tous les autres en lumière, en science et en ferveur de charité. Comme un phénix il se consumait lui-même, brûlé par les scandales des autres et ses os, c'est-à-dire son intérieur brûlait comme du bois sec, lorsqu'il voyait abonder le mal et qu'il ne pouvait le corriger à cause de la malice des hommes. Dans la ferveur de sa dilection, par les macérations de la chair, les veilles assidues, les oraisons continues, les larmes et les sanglots, il se consumait lui-même, languissant d'amour pour son bien-aimé et, à le voir ainsi, il brillait et illuminait plus que les autres comme le soleil brille plus que les autres astres. Nous pouvons donc lui appliquer la parole: "Le soleil se lève et le soleil se couche." Il a ainsi vécu très brièvement dans la charge pontificale. ... Nous n'étions pas dignes d'un si grand pasteur.[54]

Même en faisant la part de la rhétorique, les termes employés par Eudes témoignent de sa sincérité. Il est intéressant de noter l'espoir exprimé qu'un très prochain pape aussi capable pourra envoyer des légats aux sarrasins et aux tartares; Eudes conclut:

---

[50] Ibid., f. 110rb-va.

[51] Ibid., f. 125va-126rb.

[52] Ibid., f. 135ra-136va.

[53] Ibid., f. 154ra-156vb.

[54] Ibid., f. 93ra-rb: "Ipse enim fuit sol preeminens aliis in luce scientie et calore seu feruore dilectionis qua dominum diligebat, et quasi fenix se ipsum cremabat, adustus scandalis aliorum et ossa eius, id est, interiora ipsius sicut cremium arruerunt, dum mala uidebat exuberare et ea propter maliciam hominum corrigere non ualebat et feruore dilectionis maceratione carnis, uigiliis assiduis orationibus continuis non sine lacrimis et singultibus se ipsum incinerabat amore dilecti languens et ad uidendum eum festinans, et quia pre aliis lucebat et feruebat sicut sol pre aliis syderibus, ideo recte nomine solis eum possumus intelligere cum dicit: Oritur sol et occidit, et in hoc ostenditur breuis uita ipsius in papatu.... Non eramus digni tali et tanto pastore." Sur le thème du soleil et du phénix, cf. E. H. Kantorowicz, *The King's Two Bodies. A Study in Mediaeval Political Theology* (Princeton, 1957), pp. 388-401 et 414, note 332.

En ceci une certaine espérance nous est donnée que, par les futurs souverains pontifes, visite soit rendue aux sarrazins qui habitent la partie méridionale du monde ... et aux tartares qui habitent à l'Est et s'avancent vers nous. Les souverains pontifes les visiteront en leur envoyant des hommes instruits dans la foi catholique qui les convertiront à notre religion, comme au commencement les pontifes romains envoyèrent des prédicateurs à ceux qui habitaient à l'Ouest et les convertirent à la foi.[55]

Est-ce en préambule au premier scrutin que fut prononcé le sermon suivant? Cela est possible car il suit de peu le sermon de la mort de Clément IV. Le thème choisi ferait penser à un jour très proche de Noël 1268: "Gloire à Dieu au plus haut des cieux et sur la terre, paix aux hommes objets de son amour." Comme la naissance du Sauveur a donné aux anges de glorifier Dieu et de promettre la paix aux hommes de bonne volonté, de même le Sauveur naît à nouveau quand un pape est élu dans l'Église. Eudes invite ses frères cardinaux à élire un père, un pasteur et à faire taire tout sentiment de discorde:

Qu'ils soient donc unis dans la concorde ceux dont la charge est d'élire le pape afin qu'on n'entende pas entre eux le son du marteau ou de la scie, c'est-à-dire de la discorde, car où est la paix, là est le Seigneur.[56]

Le sermon suivant est très significatif. La rubrique laisserait entendre que l'élection a eu lieu. En réalité, il s'agit d'une allocution précédant l'examen par le collège des cardinaux des conclusions de la commission qui examina l'élection de l'évêque de Besançon, Eudes de Rougemont. L'élection doit avoir lieu selon les *canonicas sanctiones*, c'est-à-dire selon les règles promulguées par les apôtres et les saints pères en qui a parlé l'Esprit Saint. Cette élection est examinée par trois membres du collège qui doivent juger sur la forme de l'élection et sur la personne de l'élu. Cette coutume est suivie par le *collegium romane ecclesie siue ipsa romana ecclesia penes quam uacante ecclesia residet potestas talia faciendi*. La forme de l'élection a été reconnue canonique, la culture de l'élu a été jugée suffisante selon la fragilité des hommes d'aujourd'hui. La personne de l'élu a été jugée valable. Cette élection a donc été faite par Dieu:

---

[55] Odo de Castro Radulpho, ibid., f. 94ra: "In hoc datur nobis certa spes quod per futuros summos pontifices, uisitabuntur sarraceni qui meridionem plagam inhabitant ... et tartari qui ad aquilonem habitant et ab aquilone prodierunt; uisitabunt summi pontifices mittendo eis uiros in fide catholica eruditos, qui eos conuertent ad fidem sicut a principio pontifices romani miserunt predicatores ad eos qui occidentalem plagam inhabitant et eos conuerterunt ad fidem."

[56] Ibid., f. 110ra: "Concordent ergo qui habent eligere ut non audiatur inter eos sonitus mallei uel securis, id est, discordie, quia ubi pax ibi dominus."

Et nous au nom du Collège, nous confirmons l'élection et s'il s'y rencontre quelque défaut, nous y suppléons au nom du collège.[57]

Un autre scrutin a été précédé d'un sermon d'Eudes de Châteauroux, "Ad uesperam demorabitur fletus et ad matutinum letitia." La vieille image des deux luminaires revient ici pour souligner la primauté du pouvoir spirituel sur le pouvoir temporel. À la tombée de la nuit, les bêtes sauvages sortent de leurs repaires pour se répandre dans la campagne et y rapiner avant de retourner à l'aurore dans leurs tanières. Ainsi à la mort du pape, les pillards et les bandits que la puissance pontificale tenait en respect dans leurs fosses, se risquent à sortir et menacent ceux qui se sentaient protégés. Si la vacance dure par trop, alors c'est un désastre. À la mort de Clément IV, la nuit est venue et nous attendons l'aube pour laisser éclater notre joie. Eudes ne mâche pas ses mots:

Mais le Seigneur dit ce qu'il nous faut faire en ces moments-là: si vous cherchez, cherchez, c'est-à-dire persévérez dans la recherche d'un souverain pontife et si vous voulez trouver, convertissez-vous au Seigneur et venez à lui et il vous donnera de trouver celui que vous cherchez. Mais si vous vous éloignez de lui et vous vous tournez vers les astuces et les malices que l'on rencontre dans les élections, Dieu vous retirera son secours et vous laissera à vous-mêmes, et vous errerez en vain et travaillerez sans succès.[58]

Plus loin dans la même collection de Pise, nous trouvons une exhortation très suggestive. L'incarnation du Messie annoncée par le prophète est suivie de manifestations merveilleuses dont celle-ci: un petit enfant conduira les bêtes sauvages à la pâture et elles lui obéiront. Eudes traduit: les nobles obéissent à un vilain, les puissants à un faible, les riches à un pauvre, les savants à un ignorant, etc. Le Seigneur a fréquemment choisi pour le siège apostolique des hommes du peuple sans puissance, des pauvres sans expérience, des hommes peu cultivés:

Le Seigneur a souvent permis que des hommes moins capables prennent possession du siège apostolique pour qu'ils aient conscience de leurs imperfections et de leurs défauts, qu'ils se sachent des hommes et qu'ils éprouvent le besoin de demander conseil et aide aux autres plutôt que de les dédaigner et de les fouler aux pieds. Qu'il les aime et les honore. Le Seigneur a permis cela pour éviter tout schisme dans le corps de l'Église romaine et des autres églises et qu'il n'y ait aucune discorde entre le pape et les cardinaux, entre l'église romaine et les autres églises.[59]

---

[57] Ibid., f. 110va: "Et nos auctoritate collegii eam confirmamus, et si quid ibi defectus fuit, auctoritate collegii supplemus."

[58] Ibid., f. 126ra-rb.

[59] Ibid., f. 135ra.

À l'instar de Paul, Eudes de Châteauroux indique que le pape a besoin de pieds et des autres membres et il conclut ainsi son exhortation:

> En prenant possession du siège apostolique le pape doit s'humilier sous la main puissante de Dieu et mettre sa confiance dans le Seigneur et non se fier à soi-même ou à sa propre puissance ou à sa propre prudence, ni se fier en l'homme, ni faire de la chair son appui. Il doit se sentir un homme et avoir devant les yeux ses défauts, prévenir d'honneur ses frères, ses fils et ses sujets, accueillir leurs conseils. Alors il sera dirigé par le Seigneur sur le chemin et aimé de ses sujets en même temps qu'il sera craint. Il pourra ainsi ramener la concorde entre ceux qui s'opposent entre eux et unir ceux qui se sont séparés. Que le Seigneur daigne pourvoir son Église sainte d'un tel souverain pontife. Amen.[60]

Un dernier sermon enfin annonce un nouveau scrutin. Il prend pour thème une parole du Lévitique (21:13-14) sur le choix que les prêtres doivent faire de leur épouse: ni veuve, ce qui exclut les Juifs, ni répudiée, ce qui exclut les schismatiques, ni sordide, ce qui exclut les hérétiques, ni courtisane, ce qui exclut les païens. L'Église romaine est l'épouse du Christ à un titre spécial, car les autres églises sont ses filles, et Eudes ajoute:

> À proprement parler Pierre n'est ni la tête, ni le pasteur, ni le recteur, mais bien plutôt le vicaire de la tête, le vicaire du pasteur, le vicaire du recteur. De même, il est le vicaire de l'époux de l'Église et non l'époux.[61]

Les sermons et allocutions d'Eudes de Châteauroux nous apportent ainsi beaucoup d'informations sur la manière dont s'est vécu le conclave de Viterbe, où finalement les quinze cardinaux restant ont choisi six d'entre eux et leur ont confié le choix d'un candidat de compromis dans la personne de Teobaldo Visconti.[62]

---

[60] Ibid., f. 136rb.

[61] Ibid., f. 155va.

[62] Cf. A. Franchi, "Analisi storiografica del ruolo di Bonaventura al Conclave di Viterbo (1268-1271)," *Bollettino d'Informazioni del Centro di studi bonaventuriani. Doctor Seraphicus* 28 (1981) 65-77. Cet article complète et corrige certaines des conclusions d'A. Molien, art. "Conclave," dans *Dict. Droit canon.* (Paris, 1942), 3: 1319-1342. Il faudrait aussi analyser la page de journal du Conclave qui se trouve dans le manuscrit de Pise, Caterin. 21, f. 156va-157r, et qui relate l'intervention devant le collège des cardinaux de l'archevêque de Tours Vincent de Pilmil (Gams, 640), qui adressa cinq paroles à l'assemblée: "infidelitas, scandalum, malum exemplum, dampnum multiplex, rancor siue odium. ... Hiis dictis flexis genibus et cum lacrimis dictus archiepiscopus adiurauit cardinales et rogauit eos humiliter et deuote ut essent intenti et solliciti ecclesie prouidere, et quod amplius non expectarent." Eudes de Châteauroux répondit en avouant que cinq paroles ne suffisent pas pour rendre compte de tout ce que les cardinaux ont entendu et entendent. Avec un ton désabusé, Eudes conclut: "prouidebit ecclesie sue prout voluerit et quando voluerit. Verba tamen uestra ut uerba sapientis que sunt quasi stimuli excitabunt nos iuxta illud (Ovide, *Pontiques*, 2, 6, 38): Nil

3. Le Pape pontife romain et universel

Nous retrouvons ici le cardinal Eudes de Châteauroux dont la prédication, pratiquement ignorée à part quelques extraits édités par le cardinal J. B. Pitra,[63] demeure une source très féconde pour la connaissance des mentalités. Certes Innocent III, prêchant pour la fête des saints Pierre et Paul, avait souligné que leur venue à Rome avait été une promotion à l'universalité. Écoutons plutôt:

> Le large dont parle le Christ quand il dit à Pierre: "Va au large," c'est Rome qui avait acquis et acquiert le primat et le principat sur le siècle universel. C'est Rome que la divine providence a voulu exalter; si, au temps du paganisme, Rome seule possédait la seigneurie sur toutes les nations, au temps de la chrétienté, elle possède seule le magistère sur l'universalité des fidèles. Dieu a donc dignement et justement prévu que celui qui était le prince de l'Église aurait son siège dans cette ville qui possédait déjà le principat séculier et donc le Seigneur dit à Pierre: "Va au large," comme s'il disait: "Va à Rome, toi et avec les tiens transfère-toi là et jetez les filets." [64]

Quant à Eudes de Châteauroux, le manuscrit de Pise nous livre le texte admirable de la réponse qu'au nom du collège des cardinaux, il fit aux envoyés de l'empereur Paléologue. Très habilement à l'aller ou au retour de leur voyage vers le roi saint Louis au début de 1269, Eudes leur présente et commente un texte d'Isaïe dont le sens ne peut tromper personne: "Locum pedum meorum glorificabo, et uenient ad te curui filii eorum qui humiliauerunt te, et adorabunt uestigia pedum tuorum omnes qui detrahebant tibi" (Is. 60:13-14). Après la très riche étude du Professeur Jannis Spiteris, ce sermon semble comme la réponse des Latins aux prétentions des Grecs et souligne l'incompatibilité des positions. La démonstration va être conduite avec une habileté consommée. Les pieds du Seigneur, ce sont Pierre et Paul. Les autres apôtres ont reçu chacun des provinces bien limitées. Pierre, au

---

nocet amisso subdere calcaria equo." Suit encore le récit de l'assassinat du cuisinier de Guy de Montfort qui se trouvait avec son frère Simon de Montfort à Viterbe en ce jeudi 14 août 1270.

[63] J. B. Pitra, *Analecta Novissima*, vol. 2 (Frascati, 1888), Notice, xxiii-xxxv; extraits 188-343.

[64] Innocens III, "In festo SS. Petri et Pauli" (*PL* 217: 556): "Altitudo maris istius, de qua Christus inquit ad petrum: Duc in altum, est Roma, quae primatum et principatum super uniuersum saeculum obtinebat et obtinet; quam in tantum divina dignatio voluit exaltare, ut cum tempore paganitatis sola dominium super omnes gentiles habuerit, christianitatis tempore sola magisterium super fideles habeat universos. Dignum ergo Deus providit et congruum, ut ille qui erat princeps Ecclesiae, sedem constitueret apud urbem, quae tenebat saeculi principatum; et ideo Dominus inquit ad petrum: Duc in altum. Quasi diceret: Vade Romam, te et cum tuis transfer ad urbem, et laxate ibi retia in capturam."

contraire, fut envoyé aux Juifs et Paul aux gentils. Mais Dieu constitua Pierre tête des apôtres, *caput apostolorum*, et son vicaire général, lui disant: "Tu es Pierre et sur cette pierre, je bâtirai mon église," montrant ainsi que la foi professée par Pierre, prêchée et enseignée par lui était le fondement de l'Église. Il ne dit pas cela de la foi de Jean ou de Jacques, bien que leur foi était celle de Pierre, car ils crurent avec la foi de Pierre et prêchèrent ce que prêchait Pierre. S'il y avait contestation on recourait à la foi de Pierre et de ses successeurs, car le Seigneur lui donna autorité à lui et à ses successeurs pour définir la foi et à personne d'autre. Ainsi le premier Concile et tous les autres qui furent célébrés par la suite et qui ont édifié la foi et défini ce que nous devons croire, ont été célébrés par l'autorité de Pierre et de ses successeurs.

Eudes continue en montrant que si Pierre est le pied droit du Seigneur et Paul le pied gauche, le socle de ces pieds a été Rome, car l'un et l'autre désirèrent y venir et y prêcher. Ils y demeurèrent comme en leur lieu propre, ne cherchant pas à se rendre autre part. Le Seigneur le voulut ainsi pour enlever à l'Église tout risque de division et de schisme et pour démontrer que Rome est le siège apostolique principal. Car si Pierre était demeuré à Rome et Paul s'était rendu à Constantinople ou à Nicée, alors on pourrait dire que Constantinople ou Nicée sont égaux au siège romain et ne lui sont pas soumis. Ainsi parce que Dieu a fait du siège romain le premier et le plus grand de tous les autres, le socle des pieds du Seigneur, c'est-à-dire Pierre et Paul, ont choisi ce lieu que Dieu a glorifié et glorifiera.

Arrivé à ce point Eudes se prend à espérer que viendra le temps où Juifs, hérétiques et sarrasins viendront s'agenouiller à Rome et professeront la foi catholique. Bienheureux ceux qui verront ce jour. Pourrait-il arriver maintenant! Le souverain pontife le désirerait tellement qu'il est prêt à recevoir les fils prodigues et à leur offrir le banquet de l'unité retrouvée. Il en confère souvent avec ses frères les cardinaux, cherchant avec eux les chemins d'une possible réconciliation.[65]

La présence de ce sermon dans le manuscrit de Pise indique que ce sermon a été prononcé à Viterbe. On en retrouve un texte plus ramassé dans le manuscrit Paris, BN lat. 15947, rubriqué: "Sermo de iisdem SS. Petro et Paulo." [66]

Ce même manuscrit contient un autre sermon qui fait, lui aussi, allusion aux prétentions des Grecs. S'il n'y a qu'une seule colombe du Christ, une

---

[65] Odo de Castro Radulpho, "Responsio facta nunciis...," MS Pisa, Caterin. 21, f. 128ra-129vb; éd. partielle dans Pitra, *Anal. Noviss.*, 2: 334-337. Le Cardinal Pitra fait remarquer qu'Eudes se montre dans ce sermon comme un précurseur de Vatican I. Il faudrait nuancer quelque peu ce jugement par trop sommaire.

[66] MS Paris, BN lat. 14595, f. 223va-225va.

seule épouse du Christ, l'Église ne doit avoir qu'une seule tête. Car si la tête était fragmentée, si l'Église avait plusieurs têtes comme le prétendent en mentant les Grecs, elle serait un monstre.[67]

Dans un autre sermon du même manuscrit pour la fête de saint Pierre aux Liens, Eudes de Châteauroux parle de la statue équestre de Marc-Aurèle qui, au XIIIe siècle, se trouvait près du Latran et que l'on identifiait alors comme étant celle de l'empereur Constantin, libérateur de Rome lorsqu'il battit l'empereur Maxence au Ponte Milvio en 312.[68]

4. LA CHAIRE DE PIERRE PLÉNITUDE DU POUVOIR

Innocent III a déjà souligné dans plusieurs sermons les prérogatives du pape. Ainsi dans le sermon pour la fête de saint Grégoire le Grand:

> Comme dans le corps humain seule la tête possède la plénitude des sens de sorte que les autres membres participent de sa plénitude, ainsi dans le corps ecclésiastique les autres évêques sont appelés à la "pars sollicitudinis," alors que le souverain pontife assume la plénitude de la puissance.[69]

Les prédicateurs médiévaux vont broder sur ce thème en développant l'un ou l'autre aspect. C'est ce que Jean de la Rochelle souligne dans un sermon prêché après l'élection d'Innocent IV, c'est-à-dire le 22 février 1244. On connaissait à Paris les qualités intellectuelles du pape, commentateur renommé des documents canoniques, les frères n'ignoraient pas non plus l'amitié qu'il leur témoignait, au moins jusqu'à la fameuse bulle du 21 noveembre 1254, "Etsi animarum."[70]

Dans ce sermon, "Exaltent eum in ecclesia plebis," Jean de la Rochelle observe que les paroles adressées à Pierre sont entendues dans l'Église universelle comme une leçon profonde. La chaire de Pierre est à la fois une chaire royale, une chaire magistrale et une chaire sacerdotale. La première est la chaire de l'équité, la seconde de la vérité, la troisième de la sainteté. Les rois, en effet, occupent leur chaire en signe d'autorité dans les jugements, les maîtres dans leur chaire enseignent avec autorité la vérité, les prêtres témoignent dans leur chaire de l'excellence de leur sainteté. Ainsi Pierre se

---

[67] MS Paris, BN lat. 15947, f. 119rb: "Si enim capite truncus esset, si diuersa capita haberet ut menciuntur greci monstruum esset." La même expression se retrouve dans un autre sermon, f. 125va: "Iustum autem fuit ut unus esset uicarius ihesu christi ne ecclesia sine capite remaneret uelut truncus, uel monstruum esset si multa capita haberet sicut ydra."

[68] MS Paris, BN lat. 15947, f. 264ra.

[69] Innocens III, "In festo D. Gregorii I Papae" (*PL* 217: 517).

[70] Cf. P. Pisanu, *Innocenzo IV e i Francescani* (Roma, 1968), pp. 270-277. La bulle *Etsi animarum*, promulguée grâce aux intrigues de Guillaume de Saint-Amour, supprimait tous les privilèges concédés aux mendiants, leur enlevant du même coup toute existence canonique.

recommande comme roi, comme maître, comme prêtre. Il possède la puissance royale de juger de toutes choses; il possède l'autorité magistrale d'enseigner la vérité; il possède enfin l'autorité et la puissance sacerdotale et il manifeste cette triple puissance de lier et de délier.[71]

Un sermon anonyme, "In cathedra Petri," dont un fragment se lit sur la page de garde du manuscrit Nijmegen, UB 61, va plus loin et célèbre la dignité sacerdotale et épiscopale en Pierre et dans tous les prélats, dignité qui se concrétise dans le pouvoir des clefs. C'est pourquoi d'ailleurs le pouvoir des clefs est conféré dans l'ordination sacerdotale.[72] Or les clefs sont au nombre de deux, la science du discernement entre vices et vertus, entre lèpre et lèpre, entre dignes et indignes.[73] La seconde clef est le pouvoir de juger, de lier et de délier. Et le prédicateur de prendre en exemple la clef matérielle comme l'avait fait jadis Étienne Langton.[74]

---

[71] Joannes de Rupella, "In cathedra Petri," MS Troyes 816, f. 173rb-174va; MS München, CLM 7776, f. 63va-64ra: "propter hec omnia ad honorem meruit promoueri qui merito cathedre designatur. Cathedra enim triplex inuenitur in sacra scriptura, sed differencias sedencium in cathedris; reperitur enim cathedra regalis, magistralis et sacerdotalis. Prima est equitatis, secunda ueritatis, tercia sanctitatis. Reges enim solent sedere in cathedris in signum auctoritatis iudiciorum. ... Magistri similiter ad ostendendam auctoritatem docende ueritatis. ... Sacerdotes solent sedere in cathedris in signum excellencie sanctitatis. ... Secundum hec petrus commendabilis est tripliciter, sicut rex, sicut magister, sicut sacerdos. ... Habet ergo petrus potestatem regiam, scilicet omnia iudicandi; habet eciam auctoritatem magistralem, scilicet docendi ueritatem; habet eciam auctoritatem et potestatem sacerdotalem et hoc secundum triplicem potestatem ligandi et soluendi confitentem; potestas ligandi et soluendi est in auctoritate regali, sentencia iudicandi que est alia clauis est in auctoritate magistrali."

[72] Anonymus, "Sermo in cathedra Petri," MS Nijmegen, UB 61, f. I: "*Tibi dabo claues regni celorum*, Mt xvj. In verbis istis tria possumus uidere. ... Notatur primo quare istud festum appellatur cathedra petri secundum legendam, quia ista die petrum uenientem in antiochiam, fecerunt illi cathedram in qua predicaret populo et sederet sicut episcopus et sacerdos. Unde festum cathedre respicit dignitatem sacerdotalem et episcopalem in petro et in omnibus prelatis et ad cathedram et dignitatem sacerdotalem pertinet potestas clauium; unde in ordine sacerdotali conferuntur."

[73] Ibid.: "Notandum ergo quod claues ecclesie sunt due, scilicet scientia discernendi uel auctoritatem in discernendo inter uicia et uirtutes, inter lepram et lepram, dignos et indignos." L'expression "inter lepram et lepram" (Deut. 17:8) semble être utilisée dans ce contexte à partir de Richard de Saint-Victor. Cf. Richardus de Sancto-Victore, *Opuscules théologiques*, éd. J. Ribaillier (Paris, 1967), *De potestate ligandi et solvendi*, c. 12, p. 93: "Ecce concedimus quod isti et illi idem habent officii, illi discernendi inter lepram et lepram, isti dijudicandi inter culpam et culpam." On trouve aussi l'expression dans la *Summa Lipsiensis*, ad c. 6, C.xxxiv, q. 1 (S. Kuttner, *Repertorium der Kanonist*, Prodromus Corporis Glossarum, Studi e Testi 71, 1: 196-198). L'expression "inter dignos et indignos," vient de P. Lombard, *IV Sent.*, d. 18, c. 2 (2: 356), ex *Glossa ordin.* in Matth. 16:19, ex Beda, *In Evang.*, II, hom. 16 (*PL* 92: 222D; *CCL* 122: 145).

[74] Anon., MS Nijmegen, UB 61, f. I: "Secunda clauis est potestas iudicandi, id est, ligandi et soluendi. Unde Mt xvj, quecumque ligaueritis etc. Glose hoc dicunt. Sciendum quod claues dicuntur per quamdam similitudinem ad claues materiales, quia sicut per claues materiales clauditur ostium indignis et aperitur dignis, ita per huiusmodi claues regnum celorum clauditur

Guibert de Tournai, à son tour, souligne la dignité de Pierre et de ses successeurs dans l'Église qui leur est confiée. Il reprend les mots mêmes du pape Innocent III pour distinguer les autres évêques chargés seulement d'une part de la "sollicitudo," alors que Pierre et ses successeurs ont la plénitude des pouvoirs.[75]

Barthélemy de Bologne, dans le sermon déjà cité, poursuit son discours extrêmement dense où il montre comment le pape, constitué hiérarque suprême par la hiérarchie incréée, s'élève dans le ciel de l'Église pour gouverner le peuple de Dieu par une influence spirituelle aux sept aspects parallèles à l'influence des sept planètes du ciel. Et de développer les sept influences des planètes en commençant par Saturne. Au passage d'ailleurs, il ne manque pas de vilipender ceux qui, promus à l'épiscopat, font de leur neveu un archidiacre et d'un ami font un doyen. Sont-ils donc constitués pour les hommes? Oui, mais pour les conduire à Dieu et non pour remplir leurs bourses.[76]

Eudes de Châteauroux va plus loin dans l'explication de la puissance pontificale:

> Les prélats sont comme les yeux de l'Église pour l'instruction des autres, les simples laïcs sont les pieds de l'Église et par leurs œuvres ils soutiennent les autres. Au-dessus de tous, quelles que soient leurs conditions, quelle que soit leur dignité ou leur nation, la chaire de Pierre, c'est-à-dire le siège apostolique, occupe la place primordiale. Car autant l'âme est plus que le corps, autant la

---

indignis et aperitur dignis. Quod patet sic: ecclesia dei est sicut quedam domus cuius ostium est christus, Ion x, ego sum ostium, si quis introierit per me saluabitur, et dicitur ostium christus, id est, fides christi siue sacramentum fidei christi sicut baptismus, et sicut extra archam nullus." Cf. *Glossa ordin.* in Matth. 16:19 (v, 52v), ex Hieron., *Comment. in Matth.*, III (*PL* 26: 118; *CCL* 77: 142). L'exemple de la clef matérielle vient d'Étienne Langton, MS Paris, BN lat. 14556, f. 7vb-9ra: "Et ideo dicitur clauis sicut in quibusdam hostiis uel seris cum prima et secunda sera, secunda que principalis est, quia claudit et firmet principaliter, potest reserari et aperiri sine prima, sed longe melius et facilius si prius aperitur prima, que secundaria est et preambula principalis." Cf. Anciaux, *La théologie du sacrement de pénitence* (Louvain, 1949), p. 566; L. Hödl, *Die Geschichte der scholastischen Literatur und der Theologie der Schlüsselgewalt* (Münster, 1960), p. 370.

[75] Guibertus de Tornaco, "In cathedra Petri," MS Troyes 1778, f. 105va: "Post sanctitatem meriti sequitur dignitas officii cum dicitur propterea unxit te deus, deus tuus, oleo letitie, de qua unctione, i.R.xvj. Surge unge eum et pertinet ad singularem dignitatem quam habuit et habet petrus et successores eius in ecclesia sibi commissa. Alii enim uocati sunt in partem sollicitudinis, ipse uero assumptus in plenitudinem potestatis et hoc est quod dicitur pre consortibus tuis."

[76] Bartholomaeus de Bononia, "Sermo Bartholomei de Bononia in cathedra sancti Petri," MS Troyes 951, f. 66r: "Intelligencia est quod a spiritu sancto prelati constituuntur esse in celo ecclesie [66v] id est, in altitudine prelacionis ecclesie ad gubernandum populum subditum per septemplicem influenciam spiritualem, sicut in celo sunt septem planete constitute ad regimen inferiorum per septemplicem influenciam naturalem."

dignité du souverain pontife surpasse la dignité impériale; celle-ci est le luminaire qui préside à la nuit, car le souverain pontife a deux glaives dont il est dit: "Cela suffit." Le glaive spirituel lui permet d'user du glaive matériel pour combattre et briller lorsqu'il invoque le bras séculier pour la défense de l'Église. Ainsi l'empereur reçoit du souverain pontife le glaive de la dignité, de sorte que Pierre et son successeur est "prince entre trois" (2 Rois 23:8).[77]

Cette plénitude de pouvoir, seul la possède le souverain pontife. Eudes n'entre évidemment pas dans les développements théologiques des écoles pour expliquer que le pape a reçu du Christ cette plénitude et le pouvoir d'en conférer une partie à d'autres, c'est-à-dire son exercice même. Et il donne un exemple assez singulier:

> En outre si une femme a accompli des œuvres bonnes et si elle a reçu l'Esprit, il est certain que c'est elle à qui il a été dit: "Salut pleine de grâce, l'Esprit saint viendra sur toi." Jamais cependant nous avons lu que le Seigneur lui ait dit: "À qui tu remettras les péchés, ils lui seront remis," ou qu'elle ait reçu le pouvoir de consacrer l'Eucharistie ou qu'il lui ait été dit: "Fais ceci en mémoire de moi."[78]

On retrouve dans de nombreux autres sermons d'Eudes de Châteauroux le même souci d'exalter la plénitude du pouvoir pontifical et son pourquoi. Ainsi dans un des sermons prononcés avant les scrutins du conclave de Viterbe, revient-il sur la comparaison qui remonte, semble-t-il, à Nicolas I,[79] repris plus tard par Grégoire VII.[80] Il en profite pour supplier ses frères

---

[77] Odo de Castro Radulpho, "In cathedra beati Petri," MS Paris, BN lat. 15947, f. 122va: "Sunt enim in ecclesia prelati ut oculi ecclesie per aliorum instructionem, sunt laici simplices tanquam pedes ecclesie per manuum suarum laborem alios sustendendo. Super hos omnes cuiuscumque condicionis sint, cuiuscumque dignitatis seu nationis petri cathedra sedes, scilicet apostolica, optinet principatum. Quantum enim plus est anima quam corpus, tanto dignitas summi pontificis imperiali preminet dignitati; his ille uero luminare quod preest nocti; cum enim summus pontifex duos habet gladios de cuius dictum est, sufficit, Luc 22. Gladium spiritualem habet ad exercendum materialem, ad conferendum et uibrandum, dum brachium seculare inuocat ad defensionem ecclesie. Unde imperator a summo pontifice recipit gladium et dignitatem. Sic tam petrus quam eius successor princeps est inter tres (cf. 2 Rg 23:8)."

[78] Odo de Castro Radulpho, "In festo beati Petri," MS Paris, BN lat. 15947, f. 125ra: "Preterea si aliqua mulier bona fecit et habuerit spiritum constat quod illa cui dictum est: Aue gracia plena, spiritus sanctus superueniet in te; nunquam tamen legimus quod dominus ei dixit: Cui dimiseris peccata remittuntur uel quod ipsa confecerit, uel quod ei dictum sit aliquando: Hoc fac in meam commemoracionem."

[79] Nicolaus I, *Epist. I* (*PL* 119: 769B): "Contra illos nimirum, qui beatissimi apostolorum principis Petri eiusque successorum luculentissimam doctrinam sedemque spernentes, quem Dei Filius in sancta Ecclesia sua, tanquam luminare maius in caelo constituit, veluti quidam scorpiones palantes incedunt in meridie, et cum adhuc dies, occidit eis sol."

[80] Gregorius VII, *Epist. VII*, 25 "ad Guilelmum regem Anglorum" (*PL* 148: 569): "Credimus prudentiam non latere omnibus aliis excellentiores apostolicam et regiam dignitates huic mundo ad eius regimina omnipotentem Deum distribuisse. Sicut enim ad mundi pulcritudi-

cardinaux d'aboutir enfin. Dans un autre discours, il rappelle devant les Grecs l'espoir que nourrit toujours l'Église romaine de voir revenir à elle tous ceux qui se sont éloignés.[81]

Le dominicain Daniel de Paris comme le franciscain Servasanctus de Faenza font appel à une source historique, connue au moyen âge sous le nom des *Itineraria Clementis*, pour montrer la puissance de Pierre comme prédicateur. Daniel attribue à Pierre la triple chaire de docteur, de martyr et de prélat.[82] Il le fait dans un style très simple et dans un latin bardé de français que je ne traduis pas:

> In uia peccatorum non stetit et in cathedra pestilencie non sedit. Hoc uerbum dauid prophete et si est souent recordee en seinte eglise, et uult tantum dicere: beatus uir qui ne sa resta pas in uia peccatorum, ne ne sit pas en la cheere de pestilence.[83]

Servasanctus emploie une langue plus savante pour montrer que la puissance temporelle doit être soumis à la puissance spirituelle: Pierre domine tous les hommes. Servasanctus reprend la traditionnelle formule "ratione culpe," pour montrer que le pape peut juger de tout et peut juger tous les hommes et déposer les dignités terrestres. Sa puissance pontificale est glorieuse en dignité et universelle en pouvoir.

---

nem, oculis carnis diversas temporibus repraesentandam, solem et lunam omnibus aliis eminentiora disposuit luminaria, sic, ne creatura, quam sui benignitas ad imaginem suam in hoc mundo creaverat, in erronea et mortifera traheretur pericula, providit in apostolica et regia dignitate per diversa regeretur officia."

[81] Odo de Castro Radulpho, "Responsio ad idem," MS Pisa, Caterin. 21, f. 123ra-rb: "Nichilominus adhuc aspirat ecclesia romana grecos reuocare ad se eis sinum misericordie aperiendo et tartaros et sarracenos ecclesie catholice aggregare, eis sacramenta fidei offerendo, et ecclesia romana sicut pia mater suspirat ad reditum eorum et ad aduentum eorum considerat uias et modos per quos possit eos trahere ad se, et circonspicit si forte uelint uenire, sicut mater thobie faciebat."

[82] Daniel de Parisius, "Sermo fratris Danielis de Parisius ad sanctum Antonium in cathedra sancti Petri," MS Paris, BN lat. 16481, f. 129va: "uocatur istud festum, festum cathedre, scilicet, sancti petri, quia ad la jornee due secundum quod narratur in itinerario clementis, in quo gesta romanorum pontificum narrantur, quod antequam beatus petrus eligeretur in summum pontificem, scilicet, quo ad cathedram et intronizationem, erat rome. Vere pulcre nobis signatus in libri machabeorum per dauid, de quo dicitur ibi quod dauid sedebat in cathedra sapientissimus inter tres. Per istum dauid intelligimus beatum petrum, per cathedram in qua sedebat intelligimus cathedram in qua sedebat beatus petrus quando populo predicabat, quando personis religiosis predicatur. Sapientissimus inter tres, sicut beatus petrus, scilicet, inter confessores, martires et apostolos." Il s'agit ici de ce que le moyen âge appelle les "Itineraria Clementis," c'est-à-dire le roman du Pseudo-Clément qui raconte les voyages de Pierre et ses luttes avec Simon le Magicien. Cf. B. Altaner, *Précis de Patrologie* (Mulhouse, 1961), pp. 148-151.

[83] Daniel de Parisius, ibid., f. 129va.

C'est donc à bon droit que le Christ dit à Pierre: "Voici que je te constitue sur la terre entière." Dans cette parole le Seigneur décrit à Pierre le principat quant à deux choses: d'abord quant à la hauteur à laquelle il a mérité d'être élevé; ensuite quant à l'étendue à laquelle il a étendu son empire. Ces deux réalités dans l'état de la vie présente, où n'existe pas l'éternité, portent à son achèvement le principat, mais si la gloire de la dignité l'élève à une belle hauteur, la grandeur de la puissance la dilate à une étendue étonnante.[84]

Cette plénitude de pouvoir a son origine dans la foi de Pierre qui est le fondement même de l'Église.

Si l'on trouve dans les sermons d'Innocent III certaines formules qui ont fait école, personne après lui, sinon Humbert de Romans, n'osera dire ce que nous lisons dans le sermon de son sacre. À peine élu et sacré, le pape pèse chacun des mots qui sont la parole du Verbe Jésus-Christ. Il sait que la foi lui est nécessaire et il supplie toute l'Église de prier pour que sa foi ne défaille jamais. Et il ajoute:

La foi m'est nécessaire dans la mesure où, parmi tous les péchés, du seul péché commis contre la foi, je puisse être jugé par l'Église. Car celui qui ne croit pas est déjà jugé.[85]

Le pape est encore plus explicite dans l'un des sermons pour l'anniversaire de son sacre en concluant ainsi son apologue des noces spirituelles:

Pour cause de fornication, l'Église romaine pourrait démettre le pontife romain; fornication, je ne dis pas charnelle mais spirituelle, car le mariage n'est pas charnel mais spirituel, c'est-à-dire pour l'erreur d'infidélité.[86]

Mais il ajoute aussitôt qu'il ne croit pas que Dieu puisse abandonner le pape: "J'ai prié pour toi, Pierre."[87]

Un frère mineur anonyme, prêchant pour la chaire de saint Pierre, demande à ses auditeurs de prier Dieu pour le pape et les prélats afin qu'ils

---

[84] Servasanctus de Faenza, "Sermo secundus de eodem apostolo," MS Padova, Anton. 490, f. 96va; éd. Basel, 1502, f. 220vb: "Bene igitur a christo dicitur petro: Ecce constitui te super uniuersam terram. In quo uerbo describit dominus petri principatum quantum ad duo. Primum quantum ad altitudinem qua sublimari promeruit. Secundo uero quo ad latitudinem qua se eius imperium dilatauit. Ista enim duo quantum ad statum uite presentis ubi eternitatis esse non potest, perficiunt principatum, sed misit altum gloria dignitatis, et sit latum altitudine potestatis."

[85] Innocens III, "Serm. 2 in consecr. Pont." (*PL* 217: 656): "In tantum enim fides mihi necessaria est, ut cum de caeteris peccatis solum peccatum quod in fide committitur possem ab Ecclesia iudicari. Nam qui non credit, iam iudicatus est." Cf. Congar, "Aspects," p. 53.

[86] Innocens III, "In consecr. Pont. max." (*PL* 217: 664D-665A): "Propter causam vero fornicationis Ecclesia Romana posset dimittere Romanum pontificem. Fornicationem non dico carnalem, sed spiritualem: quia non est carnale, sed spirituale coniugium, id est, propter infidelitatis errorem."

[87] Innocens III, "Serm. IV in consecr. Pont." (*PL* 217: 670A-671A).

soient absous de leurs péchés et qu'ils se convertissent comme le dit à Pierre le Seigneur lui-même: "J'ai prié pour toi pour que ta foi ne défaille pas. Lorsque tu seras revenu, confirme tes frères." [88] Ce dernier texte tiré de l'évangile de Luc (22:32) réapparaît chez Eudes de Châteauroux dans un texte très typique de sa prédication.[89] La foi de Pierre est donc l'origine de la *sollicitudo*, comme Eudes le souligne:

> Le Seigneur l'a consacré comme roi sur Israel en le constituant prince des apôtres et chef de toute l'Église et en lui confiant la charge de toute l'Église et la sollicitude pastorale quand il lui dit, Luc 22: "Et toi quand tu seras revenu, confirme tes frères." [90]

Sans citer la parole évangélique, Bonaventure dit la même chose dans le sermon sur la Transfiguration:

> En premier lieu le Christ a été transfiguré devant Pierre afin d'illuminer en lui tous les prélats de la splendeur de la vérité et de l'intelligence et que, par eux, les autres soient illuminés dans la foi.[91]

De même un prédicateur anonyme énumère, parmi les qualités que doit posséder le pape, la fidélité.[92] Daniel de Paris cite le texte de Luc,[93] ainsi que Servasanctus de Faenza.[94]

---

[88] Anonymus, "Sermo cuiusdam fratris minoris in cathedra sancti Petri," MS Paris, BN nouv. acq. lat. 338, f. 136r: "Hoc eciam est quia subditi prelatos persequuntur qui penis pro ipsis orare deberent quod insinuat dominus dicens petro, ego rogaui pro te ne deficeret fides tua."

[89] Odo de Castro Radulpho, "In cathedra sancti Petri," MS Paris, BN lat. 15947, f. 122va-123rb. Cf. Anonymus, "In cathedra sancti Petri," MS Innsbruck, UB 340, f. 15r-16r.

[90] Odo de Castro Radulpho, "In Festo sancti Petri in uincula," MS Paris, BN lat. 15947, f. 260ra: "Unxitque eum dominus in regem super israel, eum principem apostolorum et caput totius ecclesie constituendo, committendo ei curam totius ecclesie, et sollicitudinem pastoralem quando ei dictum est, luc 22: Et tu aliquando conuersus, confirma fratres tuos."

[91] S. Bonaventure, "Dom. 2 Quadr." (éd. J. G. Bougerol, pp. 249-250): "Primo transfiguratus est ante Petrum, ut in Petro illuminaret praelatos splendore veritatis et intelligentiae, ut per ipsos ceteri in fide illuminarentur."

[92] Anonymus, "In cathedra sancti Petri," MS Troyes 1464, f. 38rb: "Sed notandum quod dominus tanquam sapiens et bonus rex beatum petrum principem ecclesie constituit triplicibus de causis, quia, scilicet sciuit eum fidelissimum ad dispensandum ecclesiasticum thesaurum. ... Hec enim tres in bono baiulo exiguntur, scilicet ut sit fidelis ad dominum, iustus ad populum, constans contra inimicum." Pour le sens et l'histoire du mot "baiulus," cf. P. J. Olivi, "Quaestio quid ponat ius uel dominum," dans *Miscell. historica Oliger*, éd. F. Delorme (Roma, 1945), pp. 309-310: "Potestas regis dicitur esse alia a potestate dei et potestas baiuli a potestate regis, quia sicut aliud est esse deum uel regem et aliud tenere locum dei uel regis, sic inter se differunt huiusmodi potestates."

[93] Daniel de Parisius, "In cathedra Petri," MS Paris, BN lat. 16481, f. 130va-vb.

[94] Servasanctus de Faenza, f. 221vb, ps.: "Constituit eum super excelsam terram ut comederet fructus agrorum. Excelsa terra est ipsa ecclesia que omnibus terris aliis iam dictis est prelata. Cui petrus prefuit et fructus agrorum comedit quando sibi per fidem infideles incorporauit, uel quando premicias et decimas agrorum accepit, ex quibus ecclesia uitam ducit. Dicit autem: Constituit eum de petra, quia ipse quodammodo singulariter pre ceteris audire

Nicolas III témoigne de l'évolution des mentalités non seulement parmi les théologiens et les canonistes, mais aussi parmi le peuple de Dieu qui est l'Église. Alors que l'on admettait couramment au début du XIIIᵉ siècle une rigoureuse égalité entre le pape, les évêques et les prêtres qui tenaient les uns et les autres directement de Dieu le pouvoir des clefs, Nicolas III en 1280 spécifie:

> Ces clefs le bienheureux Pierre les a reçues en plénitude et immédiatement du Christ et ses successeurs les ont reçues de la même manière. Quant aux autres prélats, il est nécessaire qu'ils les aient reçues et les reçoivent de Pierre et de ses successeurs.[95]

CONCLUSION

Pouvons-nous, à partir des textes analysés au long de cette recherche, construire une conclusion valable? Les prédicateurs ont été très divers, des papes Innocent III et Nicolas III, des cardinaux Eudes de Châteauroux et Matthieu d'Aquasparta, des maîtres dominicains et franciscains, des prédicateurs anonymes. Ils ont témoigné et il est possible de synthétiser leur témoignage.

Certes, je l'ai déjà souligné au début, nombre de prédicateurs avaient plus envie de stigmatiser les défauts du pape ou des évêques que d'expliquer à leur auditoire la place du pape dans la communauté des chrétiens qui est l'Église. Je ne dis pas à dessein 'la chrétienté,' car cette expression semble avoir été employée dans les sermons dans un sens politique, quand elle y apparaît.

1. Il me semble, en premier lieu, que les sermons ne reflètent pas les mêmes préoccupations que les œuvres proprement théologiques ou canoniques. En ce sens, le témoignage apporté par la prédication devient extrêmement précieux pour la connaissance de la réalité vécue par les chrétiens du moyen âge. Les titres donnés par les prédicateurs ne sont pas seulement conçus par eux comme la traduction de leurs préoccupations théologiques, ils correspondent au besoin profond des fidèles. Le 'souverain pontife' est le

---

meruit: Tu es petrus et super hanc petram edificabo ecclesiam meam et tibi dabo claues regni celorum. Ipse enim solus audiuit: Tu uocaberis cephas quod interpretatur caput. Ipse etiam solus audiuit: Ego pro te rogaui petre ut non deficiat fides tua, et tu aliquando conuersus confirma fratres tuos. Ipse etiam solus audiuit: Symon iohannis diligis me plus his. Pasce oues meas. Unde potest de eo accipi illud Matthei .xxiiij.: Quis putas est fidelis seruus et prudens quam constituit dominus super familiam suam. Optime in petro et in quolibet prelato coniunguntur hec duo prudentia et fidelitas, quia prudentia sine fidelitate transit in maliciam sed fidelitas sine prudentia declinat in stultitiam."

[95] Nicolas III, "Sermo in cathedra sancti Petri," MS Vatic., Arch. S. Petri F.36, f. 326r: "Istas claues recepit beatus petrus in plenitudine immediate a christo et recipiunt sui successores. Ceteri uero prelati necesse est quod has claues receperint et recipiant a petro et suis successoribus."

titre le plus employé parce qu'il est le plus apte à rendre compte de la continuité du dessein de Dieu. L'Ancien Testament avait un souverain prêtre; dans le Nouveau Testament, le pape continue la fonction sacerdotale de Jésus-Christ dont Melchisedech était la figure. Les textes scripturaires cités dans les sermons confirment d'ailleurs cette interprétation. Le mot 'papa' est plus simple, plus familier, comme un rayon de lumière venu du Père des cieux sur ses enfants pélerins de la terre. Et la modeste place du 'vicaire du Christ' dans la liste de fréquence décroissante souligne son caractère intellectuel qui relève plus de l'enseignement universitaire que de la langue courante. On peut le dire encore mieux des deux derniers titres: 'prince' et 'hiérarque.'

2. Les chrétiens ressentaient profondément comme une peine partagée les longues vacances du siège apostolique. L'Église est veuve, elle est vide, comme si l'on disait qu'elle est sans le Christ. Le *sensus fidelium* est présent chez les prédicateurs comme Jean de la Rochelle ou Eudes de Châteauroux. Le pape Clément IV est mort, ses qualités humaines et spirituelles sont mises en relief, mais l'essentiel est que l'Église ait très rapidement un nouveau pape. Le témoignage d'Eudes de Châteauroux est, à cet égard, de grande valeur. Une étude minutieuse des textes viendra jeter des lumières nouvelles sur certains aspects du conclave de Viterbe.

J'ai souligné une phrase significative qui précise un fait canonique loin d'être évident: d'après Eudes de Châteauroux, le collège des cardinaux est le collège de l'Église romaine en cas de vacance du siège apostolique. Il a donc le pouvoir de confirmer les élections épiscopales, de recevoir les envoyés de Paléologue en engageant la politique pontificale, de consacrer un évêque, tous actes qui semblent interdits durant le conclave.

L'ambiance qui régna durant ce trop long conclave est mieux connue grâce aux détails et aux petites phrases lâchées par Eudes de Châteauroux. La discorde est évidente entre les cardinaux. Les uns veulent un pape parfait tel qu'il n'en a jamais existé, d'autres défendent la continuité de la politique pontificale. Ce sont des hommes limités et empêtrés dans des problèmes temporels et auxquels échappe l'essentiel de leur devoir.

3. Innocent III et Eudes de Châteauroux ont mis en valeur la primauté de l'Église romaine. Les affirmations de leur discours rejoignent les conclusions des théologiens et des canonistes, mais les développements s'appuient principalement sur l'Écriture. Nous sommes loin alors d'Innocent IV ou de l'*Hostiensis*. Les sermons célébrant les apôtres Pierre et Paul ou la chaire de Pierre sont pour les prédicateurs l'occasion de rappeler à l'Église universelle que Rome est son centre voulu par le Christ.

4. Et cette primauté est concrétisée par la chaire dont les éléments peuvent varier d'un prédicateur à l'autre, mais sous les mots différents se

cache la même réalité: Pierre est roi, docteur et prêtre. La puissance pontificale est une nécessité historique pour les chrétiens du moyen âge, car tout pouvoir se manifeste par une seigneurie territoriale. On ne conçoit pas que le pape soit investi d'une puissance uniquement spirituelle. La clausule *ratione peccati* a été reprise par Servasanctus de Faenza; elle signifie que, dans ce monde pécheur, le pape s'élève au-dessus des puissances temporelles. Il peut juger de tout et juger tous les hommes et déposer les empereurs, comme ne manqua pas de le faire Innocent IV.

Cette puissance prend son origine dans la personne de Pierre. Eudes de Châteauroux a mis en lumière l'enchaînement du dialogue entre le Christ et Pierre. La foi de Pierre, illuminé par le Père, lui a valu d'être le fondement de l'Église et de recevoir le pouvoir de lier et de délier. L'évolution des théologiens et des canonistes est évidente. Nous en avons la preuve dans le texte du manuscrit de Nimègue comme témoin du début du siècle, alors que le dernier texte cité de Nicolas III signifie que le pouvoir des clefs est en plénitude immédiate en Pierre et en ses successeurs, plénitude à laquelle ne font que participer les autres prêtres dans l'Église.

En guise de conclusion, je citerai un texte du sermon de saint Bonaventure pour la fête des apôtres Pierre et Paul. Parlant de Pierre, Bonaventure a devant les yeux le pape de Rome. Le langage biblique lui convient parfaitement pour exposer la doctrine commune des médiévaux:

> L'Église fondée sur la foi de Pierre dans le Christ, même si elle semble chanceler, ne sera cependant jamais submergée; c'est pourquoi il est dit dans l'Évangile: "J'ai prié pour toi, Pierre, afin que ta foi ne défaille point." En figure de cette assurance, Élie avait dit à la femme, c'est-à-dire le Christ à l'Église: "Tu ne manqueras jamais de farine," c'est-à-dire du sacrement de l'Eucharistie; "ni l'huile ne diminuera pas dans le vase," c'est-à-dire la grâce de l'Esprit saint par laquelle s'accomplit dans l'Église la rémission des péchés. Cette huile de la grâce sanctifiante, par l'onction sacerdotale, a été infusée en Pierre et dans les apôtres et, par eux, dans les prêtres qui ont suivi. D'où le Psaume: "Comme l'huile coule de la tête," c'est-à-dire la grâce dans le Christ "descend sur la barbe, la barbe d'Aaron," dans les apôtres; "qui descend sur le col du vêtement," c'est-à-dire sur les prélats mineurs de l'Église.[96]

---

[96] S. Bonaventura, "In festo beatorum Petri et Pauli bone auenture," MS Troyes 1464, f. 18va-20ra (éd. 9: 548a-b): "In fide etiam Christi Petrus, Ecclesia solidata, etsi periclitetur, non tamen submergetur; unde in Evangelio: "Ego pro te rogavi, petre, ut non deficiat fides tua." In huius enim figuram dixit Elias mulieri, id est Christus Ecclesiae: "Hydriae farinae non deficiet," id est sacramentum eucharistiae; 'nec lecythus olei minuetur,' id est gratiae sancti Spiritus per quam fit in Ecclesia remissio peccati. Hoc oleum gratiae sanctificantis sacerdotali auctoritate fusum est in petrum et in apostolos et per eos in reliquos sacerdotes; Psalmus: 'Sicut unguentum in capite,' id est gratia in Christo, 'quod descendit in barbam, barbam Aaron,' in Apostolos, 'quod descendit in oram vestimenti,' id est in minores Ecclesiae praelatos." Cf. B. Tierney, "Modèles historiques de la papauté," *Concilium* 108 (1975) 65-74.

8

The Pope and the Preachers

Perceptions of the Religious Role of the Papacy in the Preaching Tradition of the Thirteenth-Century English Church

Phyllis B. Roberts

The twelfth-century master Peter the Chanter tells an illuminating story in his *Verbum abbreviatum*. When someone told Alexander III that he was a good pope, saying: "What you do is papal," Alexander replied in the vernacular: "If I knew how to judge well, to preach well, and to give Penance, I would be a good pope." In these three qualities, concluded the Chanter, is expressed the tripartite office of a prelate.[1] Thus did this twelfth-century pope, Alexander III, sum up the essence of the papal role: the pope as judge, as priest, and as preacher.

The juxtaposition of preaching alongside the judicial and spiritual roles of the pope underscores the increasing importance attached to the preaching

[1] *Verbum abbreviatum*, c. 75 (*PL* 205: 199): "Nec hoc est praetermittendum quod quidam, nescio quo animo, dixit Alexandro tertio: 'Domine, bonus papa es. Quidquid facis papale est.' Et respondit Alexander in vulgari suo dicens: 'Si scirem, Bien jujar, et bien predicar, et penitense donar, je seroie boene pape'. Et ita his tribus expressit totum officium praelati." ibid., c. 76: "Tripartitum officium praelati, scilicet judicare, poenitentiam dare, praedicare...."

I should like to extend my appreciation to Dr. J. Robert Wright and to Dr. Patrick Horner for their advice on certain aspects of this paper; and to the Librarian and staff of the General Theological Seminary, a warm thanks for their generous hospitality.

The Religious Roles of the Papacy: Ideals and Realities, 1150-1300, ed. Christopher Ryan, Papers in Mediaeval Studies 8 (Toronto: Pontifical Institute of Mediaeval Studies, 1989), pp. 277-297. © P.I.M.S., 1989.

office in the high middle ages. Popes were not only preachers, they also encouraged those who themselves went out to preach. In an age when heresy was a perceived danger and internal reform a necessity for the Church, popular preaching played an important role in the intensification of Christian piety. Emphasis on the preaching art led both to the incorporation of a preaching requirement for masters of theology in the university and to the development of the *artes predicandi* and of a wide variety of devotional literature which afforded the opportunity for the clergy to reach the higher standards of preaching which contemporary society required. The formation and recognition of the mendicant orders in the thirteenth century emphasized the importance of sermons and preaching which was, furthermore, specifically articulated in the program of the Fourth Lateran Council in 1215.

My purpose in this paper is to examine what the preaching tradition in the English church in the era of Lateran IV can tell us about the perception of the religious role of the papacy. The Fourth Lateran Council, convened under the leadership of Pope Innocent III, initiated a wave of reforms in the western church that included an emphasis on preaching and raising the general level of the clergy. My focus will be on Stephen Langton who, as the controversial archbishop of Canterbury caught in the struggle between King John and his barons and in his own conflict with the pope, was a leader in this reform movement and a preacher whose sermon-making won him the sobriquet, "Stephanus de Lingua-Tonante."

Conclusions regarding the nature of the papacy may be drawn either directly or indirectly from the sources. While we shall have occasion later in this paper to consider some of Langton's remarks about the pope and/or the papacy, we are left for the most part with indirect evidence that is not, however, without significance. There are a variety of sources that indicate a positive stance and cooperative effort in the reformist aims of the papacy. This is evident in Langton's synodical statutes concerning preaching and the precedent these set in the law of the English church and is apparent as well in his sermons where he commented on preachers, on preaching, and on bishops and their role in the reform movement of the Church. We can, therefore, arrive at some understanding about the nature of the papacy from what was said and done regarding matters connected with the papacy, such as the initiatives made by Pope Innocent III in the era of the Fourth Lateran Council.

The great council that was called by Pope Innocent III in 1213 enacted a broad program of disciplinary reform that was to guide the leadership of the Church for many years to come. The canons that were decreed at the council represent the effort of a papacy that was intent on reform of the Church and the implementation of a religious renewal that had been gaining ground in the Church since the Gregorian era of the mid-eleventh century. This theme of renewal and reform is immediately apparent in the papal letter of convocation wherein Innocent wrote:

> We would summon a general council according to the ancient custom of the Holy Fathers—this council to be held at a convenient time and to be concerned only with the spiritual good of souls.[2]

The theme of reform is also echoed in his sermon to the council in which the pope saw in the restoration of the Temple in the eighteenth year of King Josiah (described in the Book of Kings) "a parable of our own time, so that in the eighteenth year of our pontificate the temple of the Lord, that is the Church, might be restored."[3]

The council which was held in November 1215 was one of the most impressive in the history of the Church. Four hundred and twelve bishops, some 800 abbots and priors and the delegates of most of the rulers of Europe were in attendance. In less than a month, the council completed its work and at its final session promulgated seventy decrees which were directed at the renewal and reformation of the Church and expressed the aims of the papacy as formulated by Innocent III.[4]

To this great and celebrated council came Stephen Langton, an old school friend of Pope Innocent III who had raised him to the Cardinalate and had largely been responsible for his selection as archbishop of Canterbury. Those had been happier years for the notable Paris master of theology. By 1215 the conflict with both king and pope had accelerated. On 19 March 1215, Pope Innocent III wrote to Langton and his suffragans, urging the archbishop to restore agreement between King John and his barons. The pope was clearly

---

[2] For Innocent III's letter of convocation, see *PL* 216: 823-827: "... generale concilium juxta priscam sanctorum Patrum consuetudinem convocemus propter lucra solummodo animarum opportuno tempore celebrandum..." (col. 824). See Christopher R. Cheney and William H. Semple, eds, *Selected Letters of Pope Innocent III concerning England (1198-1216)* (London, 1953), pp. 144-147. See also the references in Christopher Cheney and Mary G. Cheney, eds, *The Letters of Pope Innocent III (1198-1216) concerning England and Wales: A Calendar with an Appendix of Texts* (Oxford, 1967), nos. 915, 916 and 1019.

[3] For Innocent III's sermons at the Fourth Lateran Council, see *PL* 217: 673-680 and 679-688: "Legitur quippe in libro Regum, et in Paralipomenon apertissime continetur, quod XVIII anno regni Josiae regis restauratum est templum, et celebratum est Phase, quale non fuit in Israel a diebus judicum atque regum (IV Reg. xxiv; II Paral. xxxv). Utinam haec historia, instantis temporis sit parabola, ut in hoc nostri pontificatus anno XVIII templum Domini, quod est Ecclesia restauretur..." (col. 675).

[4] Henry J. Schroeder, *Disciplinary Decrees of the Great Councils: Text, Translation and Commentary* (London, 1937), p. 237. See also C. J. Hefele and H. Leclercq, *Histoire des conciles* 5[2] (Paris, 1913), pp. 1316-1398. The standard text for the decrees is *Conciliorum Oecumenicorum Decreta* (Freiburg-Rome-Vienna, 1962).

becoming more impatient, for his tone was sterner in a letter of 7 July wherein he wrote that Langton and some of his fellow-bishops "have afforded him (i.e., John) neither help nor favour against the disturbers of the kingdom which admittedly now belongs, by right of feudal lordship, to the Roman Church: they thus appear as accomplices, if not partners, in a wicked conspiracy." Several weeks earlier, in a letter of 18 June, Langton and his suffragans had been directed to excommunicate the barons unless they came to terms with the king within eight days of the receipt of the papal letter. Archbishop Langton refused to act until he had talked with the pope himself. He was subsequently denounced as disobedient and suspended from his office by Pandulf, the papal legate, and by Peter, bishop of Winchester. In September 1215, an exile once again, a discouraged Langton left for Rome to attend the Fourth Lateran Council. Despite Langton's opposition to the pope, the deliberations in Rome had a marked effect on the latter part of the archbishop's career, from his return to England in 1218 until his death in 1228.[5]

The Fourth Lateran Council of 1215, under the leadership of Pope Innocent III, recognized the importance of preaching and the significance of the preaching office in its broad program of Church reform. The tenth canon adopted by the Council stated:

> Wherefore we decree that bishops provide suitable men, powerful in work and word, to exercise with fruitful result the office of preaching; who in place of the bishops, since these cannot do it, diligently visiting the people committed to them, may instruct them by word and example.[6]

---

[5] See Phyllis B. Roberts, *Stephanus de Lingua-Tonante: Studies in the Sermons of Stephen Langton* (Toronto, 1968), ch. 1, on the life of Stephen Langton, for all these references. The English delegation at IV Lateran included, besides Langton, Bishops Benedict of Sawston (Rochester), Hugh of Wells (Lincoln), William of Cornhill (Coventry), Simon of Apulia (Exeter), Richard Poore (Chichester), Walter Gray (Worcester), Robert of York (elect of Ely) and Pandulf (elect of Norwich). Others attended including proctors who represented the king's interests and a number of abbots, priors and monks. Frederick M. Powicke and Christopher R. Cheney, eds, *Councils and Synods with other Documents relating to the English Church*, 2. *A.D. 1205-1313* (Oxford, 1964), p. 48. See also the article by Stephan Kuttner and Antonio Garcia y Garcia, "A New Eyewitness Account of the Fourth Lateran Council," *Traditio* (1964) 115-178.

[6] *Conciliorum Oecumenicorum Decreta*, pp. 215-216: "... ut episcopi viros idoneos ad sanctae praedicationis officium salubriter exequendum assumant, potentes in opere et sermone, qui plebes sibi commissas vice ipsorum, cum per se idem nequiverint, sollicite visitantes, eas verbo aedificent et exemplo. ... Unde praecipimus tam in cathedralibus quam in aliis conventualibus ecclesiis viros idoneos ordinari, quos episcopi possint coadiutores et cooperatores habere, non solum in praedicationis officio verum etiam in audiendis confessionibus et poenitentiis iniungendis ac caeteris, quae ad salutem pertinent animarum." Translated in Schroeder, *Disciplinary Decrees*, pp. 251-252.

This canon also stressed the importance of hearing confessions and enjoining penance.

Preaching was also seen as important to the effort to combat heresy, but preachers were to be carefully regulated, as we note in canon 3:

> ... all those prohibited or not sent, who without the authority of the Apostolic See or of the Catholic bishop of the locality, shall presume to usurp the office of preaching either publicly or privately, shall be excommunicated.[7]

These canons of the Fourth Lateran Council emphasized the central importance of preaching and the need to exercise some control or licensing constraints over preachers. As such they became a part of the law of the Church that reflected the concerns of the reforming papacy and were to be taken up in the various churches in western Christendom. Pope Innocent III, who was himself a renowned preacher, expressly encouraged the development of preaching in an age when the sermon was coming into its own not only in fighting the enemies of the Church, but also in winning popular support for Church reform.

In his study on the circle of Peter the Chanter, John Baldwin has argued quite persuasively, I think, for the important influence exerted by the Paris masters surrounding Peter the Chanter on many of the reforms articulated in the canons of the Fourth Lateran Council.[8] These Paris masters, including Stephen Langton, were dedicated to the reinvigoration of Christian teaching in line with the reform efforts of the papacy. To that end, they enthusiastically championed the development of popular preaching. Recent research has revised the older view of such authors as Lecoy de la Marche that popular preaching was generally neglected at the end of the twelfth century, and that preaching in that period was largely restricted to clerics and monks. Instead we find a revival of popular preaching in the twelfth century which was rapidly extended in the first decades of the thirteenth century under the leadership of the reforming papacy.[9]

How, then, were the canons concerning preaching and other decrees affecting the reform of the clergy incorporated in the law and practice of the

---

[7] *Conciliorum Oecumenicorum Decreta*, p. 211: "... omnes qui prohibiti vel non missi, praeter auctoritatem ab apostolica sede vel catholico episcopo loci susceptam, publice vel privatim praedicationis officium usurpare praesumpserint, excommunicationis vinculo innodentur...." Translated in Schroeder, p. 244.

[8] John W. Baldwin, *Masters, Princes and Merchants: The Social Views of Peter the Chanter and his Circle*, 2 vols (Princeton, 1970), 1: 342-343.

[9] On the revival of popular preaching in the twelfth century, see Beryl Smalley, *The Study of the Bible in the Middle Ages*, 2nd ed. (Oxford, 1952), p. 244. The older view is represented by A. Lecoy de la Marche, *La chaire française au moyen âge, spécialement au XIIIᵉ siècle*, 2nd ed. (Paris, 1886), p. 11.

English church, and what does this say about the attitude of the English church to the spiritual concerns of the reforming papacy? If we turn now to Langton's role in this transmission process, we see him at the beginning of a movement that made the years 1214 to 1283, in Professor Cheney's view, a most fruitful period of local legislation in the English church.[10] The implementation of the reform decrees, at least on the highest level of the English church, reflects a very positive attitude of the episcopate in conforming to the aims of the papacy. We can also see in these moves a remarkable zeal and enthusiasm for the carrying out of papal directives.

Even before the meeting of IV Lateran, in the interval between his return from exile (June-July 1213) and the lifting of the Interdict (2 July 1214), Archbishop Langton anticipated many of the Lateran reforms in his statutes for the diocese of Canterbury which included a provision emphasizing the need for a license for preaching and the requirement that two reputable men be associated with each preacher who collected contributions.[11]

The positive response to the actions of the papacy under Langton's leadership can be seen again in the first provincial council to legislate in England since the Lateran assembly. The council of the province of Canterbury, held at Oxford 17 April 1222, was notable for the promulgation of the Lateran decrees and, with its own supplementary canons, came to form the basis of the local law of the English church in the later Middle Ages.[12] In these canons as well, there is an emphasis on preaching, i.e., providing the people with the food of the word of God.[13]

---

[10] Christopher R. Cheney, "Statute-Making in the English Church in the Thirteenth Century," in *Proceedings of the Second International Congress of Medieval Canon Law, Boston College, 12-16 August 1963*, ed. Stephan Kuttner and J. Joseph Ryan (Vatican, 1965), p. 399. Of Professor Cheney's many important studies on this subject, I should like to cite several that were most helpful in illuminating aspects of this complex topic: "Legislation of the Medieval English Church," *English Historical Review* 50 (1935) 193-224, 385-417; *English Synodalia of the Thirteenth Century* (Oxford, 1941; repr. 1968); *From Becket to Langton: English Church Government 1170-1213* (Manchester, 1956; repr. 1965); "The Earliest English Diocesan Statutes," *English Historical Review* 75 (1960) 1-29.

[11] Powicke and Cheney, *Councils and Synods*, 2. *A.D. 1205-1313*, pp. 33-34: "Ad hec prohibemus ne sine litteris nostris ad fidelium elemosinas postulandas aliquis admittatur predicator. Nec si litteris nostris aliquis munitus adveniat ad predicandum admittatur, nisi littere nostre nomen eius exprimant et expresse contineant quod ei dederimus licentiam predicandi. Negotium vero vel necessitatem tantummodo pro qua advenerit bene poterit populo demonstrare, licet predicandi licentiam non habeat, dumtamen litteris nostris, ut diximus, sit munitus. Volumus autem ut sacerdos ecclesie in qua predicatur pecuniam collectam accipiat, et salvo custodiat sub duorum virorum testimonio fidedignorum, quousque de mandato nostro vel officialis nostri illi loco ad quem facta est collectio conferatur."

[12] Ibid., p. 100.

[13] Ibid., p. 110.

There is a remarkable thread throughout the statutes of the era of IV Lateran: in those of Langton (1213-1214) and those of Richard Poore (1217-1219); in the second group of statutes from 1224-1230 which owed much to the stimulus given by Langton's provincial council of Oxford in 1222; and in those statutes in a third group from 1239-1247 which followed the legatine council of London held in 1237 and from 1239 on, when Robert Grosseteste was most influential in statute-making, borrowing and collecting from earlier texts.[14] Whether transcribed or publicly recited, these various statutes reflected "what sort of instruction thirteenth-century prelates thought necessary and desirable for their clergy and people."[15] The texts of these statutes show constant borrowing and repetition of materials, especially from one diocese to another.[16] They also demonstrate over and over again a responsiveness to the ideals and aims of the reforming papacy in the area of promoting preaching to the people and encouraging religious instruction among the lower clergy. The statutes require preaching by bishops, by friars, and by parish priests, and mirror the overall reformist aims of the thirteenth-century papacy set out in the Lateran program.[17]

---

[14] Cheney, "Statute-Making," pp. 403-405.

[15] Ibid., p. 414.

[16] Ibid., p. 401.

[17] The synodal statutes of Bishop Richard Poore for the diocese of Salisbury, 1217 × 1219, with additions, 1219 × 1228, and as reissued for the diocese of Durham, 1228 × 1236, are "some of the most important diocesan legislation of medieval England" appearing as they did shortly after IV Lateran (Powicke and Cheney, *Councils and Synods*, p. 57). Langton's earlier language is echoed here in the call for licensing preachers: "Prohibemus ne sine literis nostris ad fidelium elemosinas postulandas aliquis admittatur predicator, nisi litere nostre nomen eius exprimant et expresse contineant quod ei damus licentiam predicandi" (ibid., p. 85). The wording of the Lateran decree is also reflected here: "Quoniam propter occupationes multiplices vel invalitudines corporales seu alias causas non sufficiunt episcopi per se ministrare populo verbum dei, in concilio statutum est ut ipsi viros ydoneos ad sancte predicationis officium exequendum assumant..." (ibid., p. 94). In succeeding synodal statutes, there are repeated provisions for enforcing the preaching decree of IV Lateran. See the synodal statutes of Bishop Peter des Roches for the diocese of Winchester 1224? (ibid., pp. 128, 130) and the "Constitutiones cuiusdam episcopi" 1225 × 1230? (ibid., p. 194). Records connected with visitations by Robert Grosseteste in 1238-1239 mention the importance of preaching (ibid., p. 263) and in the Annals of Dunstable, s.a. 1238, there is a reference to Grosseteste's having preached a sermon himself (ibid., p. 264). In Bishop Grosseteste's Statutes for the diocese of Lincoln, 1239? (which at least one MS identifies with the rubric, *Sermo in sinodo*), Grosseteste is quite specific about enforcing the reforming mandate: "Quia igitur sine decalogi observatione salus animarum non consistit, exhortamur in domino, firmiter iniungentes ut unusquisque pastor animarum et quilibet sacerdos parochialis sciat decalogum, id est, decem mandata legis mosaice, eademque populo sibi subiecto frequenter predicet et exponat..." (ibid., p. 268). Notice these additional references to preaching in thirteenth-century synodal statutes: 26 July 1240, Synodal statutes of Bishop Walter de Cantilupe for the diocese of Winchester, with later additions (ibid., pp. 304, 306); 1240 × 1243, Synodal statutes of Bishop William Raleigh for the diocese of Norwich, with

If we turn from the language of the statutes on preaching and the preaching office to the language of Langton's sermons, we shall likewise notice a positive affirmation of the ideals of the reforming papacy. Langton often commented on the importance of preaching and the essentials of the preacher:

> Every preacher ought to have three things: he ought to think in advance about what he should say, he ought to pray to God that what he says is useful for himself and his listeners; he ought also to live a good life, so that what he says by word is fulfilled by the example of good deeds.

Drawing frequently and vividly on a variety of scriptural similes, Langton likened the preacher to a creditor, a messenger, a legate, a soldier, and to the champion of the Lord.[18]

There is also evidence in Langton's sermons of the importance he attached to bishops as instruments of reform which had been emphasized in the Lateran decrees on preaching. In his explanation of the meaning of *episcopus*, Langton commented on the prelate's supervisory powers: "*Episcopus* in Greek is *speculator* in Latin, and as the word indicates, it refers to one with supervisory powers." The welfare of the Church as a whole especially

---

additions of various dates (ibid., pp. 345, 352); 1238 × 1244, Synodal statutes of Bishop Robert Bingham for the diocese of Salisbury (ibid., p. 386); 1247?, Synodal statutes of Bishop William Raleigh for the diocese of Winchester (ibid., p. 403); 1241 × 1249?, Statutes for peculiars of the church of Durham in the diocese of York (ibid., p. 443); 1258?, Synodal statutes of Bishop William of Bitton I for the diocese of Bath and Wells (ibid., pp. 595-596); 1245 × 1259, Synodal statutes of Bishop Fulk Basset for the diocese of London, with later additions (ibid., p. 648); 7-10 October 1281, Council of the province of Canterbury at Lambeth, summoned by Archbishop Pecham—there is a lengthy chapter here which furnished parish priests with the basis of religious instruction which they needed for themselves and for the teaching of their congregations: ch. 9, "De informatione simplicium sacerdotum," calls for preaching at least four times a year in the language of the people (ibid., pp. 900-905); 16 April 1287, Synodal statutes of Bishop Peter Quinel (or Quivel) for the diocese of Exeter (ibid., pp. 995, 1016-1017); 8 July 1287, Injunctions for the parish clergy of the diocese of Canterbury (ibid., p. 1079); 6 October 1289, Synodal statutes of Bishop Gilbert of St. Leofard for the diocese of Chichester (ibid., p. 1088).

[18] MS Arras 222, fol. 135va: "Omnis predicator debet habere tria. Debet precogitare quid dicat; debet orare Deum ut illud quod dicit prosit sibi et auditoribus; debet etiam esse bone vite, ut quod predicat ore, impleat bone operationis exemplo." MS Troyes 1100, fol. 246rb: "Nomine creditoris predicator intelligitur. Credit enim censum verbi divini auditoribus..."; ibid., fol. 277vb: "Omnis predicator nuncius est Domini eius mandata nuntians populo." MS Leipzig 443, fol. 52vb: "Ille qui verbum predicationis aliis elucidat est quasi nuncius missus ad predam tollendam de manibus inimici." MS Paris, BN lat. 12420, fol. 46ra: "Ecce ego quasi legatus, licet indignus vobis omnibus...." MS Paris, BN lat. 16463, fol. 92vb: "Qui dicit verbum Domini est quasi miles Domini ... sed miles Domini est predicans verbum eius...." Ibid., fol. 66rb: "Predicator pugil Domini est...." For descriptions of these MSS and for all MSS cited below, see the Appendices in Roberts, *Studies*, pp. 139-167.

concerned Langton and notably its wise administration by prelates. Langton drew on many comparisons to convey this message. The Church, said he, is signified by a ship whose helmsmen are the prelates. Noah, helmsman of the ark, represents the prelates of the Church. The Church he also compared to a vineyard whose vinetenders and cultivators were its prelates.[19]

Nor did Langton ignore the special responsibilities of the lower clergy. In several sermons delivered in synod, Langton cites a number of abuses that were detailed in the Lateran decrees as a cause of papal concern. To an audience of clerics assembled in synod, Langton said:

> The delight of the Lord ought to be the clerical order and especially the priesthood. ... You are the ones who are entrusted with dispensing the ineffable sacrament of the body and blood of the Lord. ... The root of all sins is cupidity, as the Apostle says (1 Tim. 6.10). Although it is reprehensible in anyone at all, it is detestable in a priest. There are, nevertheless, certain priests who turn the sacrament of the altar into a quest for worldly profit.

Other priests abuse the sacrament by performing it ineptly. Langton also denounced those prelates whose skill in giving advice about familial administration, about fund raising, and keeping in the good graces of the nobility exceeds their capacity to save souls.[20] These passages lend gloomy support

---

[19] MS Paris, BN lat. 16463, fol. 144vb: " 'Episcopus' Grece, Latine 'speculator', et ut alludat vocabulo, dicitur quasi superintendens...." MS Troyes 1100, fol. 241ra: "Navis ecclesiam significat. Rectores navis sunt prelati ecclesie ... Noah ... rector arche...." MS Leipzig 443, fol. 48rb: "Per hanc vineam intelligitur ecclesia, cuius vinitores et cultores sunt prelati...." For a further discussion of Langton's views on the Church, see Jean Longère, *Œuvres oratoires de maîtres parisiens au XIIe siècle: Étude historique et doctrinale*, 2 vols (Paris, 1975), 1: 157-158 and 2: 123-124.

[20] MS Paris, BN lat. 16463, fols. 142vb-143vb: "Dilectus Domini deberet ordo clericalis et precipue sacerdotalis. ... Vos estis quibus dispensatio ineffabilis sacramenti corporis et sanguinis Domini commissa. ... Radix omnium est cupiditas, ut ait Apostolus. Sed licet in quolibet sit reprehensibilis, in sacerdote detestabilis. Sunt enim quidam sacerdotes qui sacramentum altaris convertunt ad questum lucri temporalis..."; ibid., fol. 37rb: "... quod hodie faciunt prelati cupidi qui per cupiditatem male dispensant Christi corpus." MS Troyes 1100, fol. 259rb: "Plurimi [i.e., prelati] periti sunt in dandis consiliis de gubernatione familie, de colleccione opum, de conservando favore potentum, sed ad consulendum saluti anime hebetes sunt...." See the sermon addressed *Ad sacerdotes*, which is edited in Phyllis B. Roberts, "Master Stephen Langton Preaches to the People and the Clergy: Sermon Texts from Twelfth-Century Paris," *Traditio* (1980) 258-268. For another example of a synodal sermon, see Langton's *Sermo ad episcopos*, MS Brussels II.953, fols. 123vb-126vb, in which he urges the clergy to a higher standard of learning and decorum, emphasizing, as well, the need for preaching: "Valde enim dampnosa et dampnabilis est ignorantia sacerdotis et quasi res monstruosa est sacerdos ignorans et doctor indoctus. ... Notum est quare dictum sit ei tercio: Pasce oves (Ioh. 21.17), scil. quia prelatus debet pascere sibi commissum gregem—pabulo sancte conversationis, exemplo bone vite et predicationis. ... Caute etiam debet considerare sacerdos quibus predicet, aliter enim predicandum est prudentibus, aliter simplicibus; aliter divitibus, aliter pauperibus..." (ibid., fols. 124va-126ra).

to J. R. H. Moorman's description of the dismal condition of the thirteenth-century English church.[21]

Moorman's view, however, was not without substance. Pope Innocent III had denounced many of the evils of contemporary society in his sermon at the Fourth Lateran Council:

> Here also evils come forth in the Christian people. Faith perishes, religion is deformed, liberty is confounded, justice is trampled under foot, heretics burgeon, schismatics grow insolent, the perfidious rage, the Agarenes prevail....[22]

In this sermon which takes as its theme: "With desire I have desired to eat this passover with you before I suffer" (Luke 22.15), the pope, in a call for a crusade, explicates the commemoration of the bodily Passover, i.e., "a crossing to the place [the Holy Land] to liberate unhappy Jerusalem." He distinguishes this from the celebration of the spiritual Passover, i.e., "a crossing from one condition to another to reform the universal church." Of this spiritual crossing, he said:

> The supreme pontiff who is made watcher over the house of Israel ought to pass through the universal church, investigating and inquiring into the merits of all, lest they call the good evil and the evil good, lest they put darkness for light and light for darkness... (Isa. 5.20).[23]

---

[21] John R. H. Moorman, *Church Life in England in the Thirteenth Century* (Cambridge, 1945). The picture that Moorman gives us of the Church in this period is one in which lax discipline and widespread corruption prevailed despite the efforts of the reforming bishops. There was not much progress in reform, concludes Moorman, but not for lack of zeal of the reforming clergy. Sermons were a rare event, and in the early thirteenth century, there was no regular Sunday sermon in parish churches. Sermons were associated with the schools, and the average parish priest had no instruction in the art of preaching. Moorman attributes the revival of preaching to the influence of the Friars in the latter part of the thirteenth century (pp. 77-79). See the Bibliographical Note below for more recent references on preaching and devotional literature in thirteenth-century England.

[22] See *PL* 217: 673-680: "Hinc etiam mala provenerunt in populo Christiano. Perit fides, religio deformatur, libertas confunditur, justitia conculcatur, haeretici pullulant, insolescunt schismatici, perfidi saeviunt, praevalent Agareni..." (ibid., col. 678). Translated by Marshall W. Baldwin, ed., *Christianity Through the Thirteenth Century* (New York, 1970), p. 298.

[23] "*Desiderio desideravi hoc pascha manducare vobiscum, antequam patiar, idest antequam moriar* (Luke 22.15). ... Triplex autem Pascha sive Phase desidero vobiscum celebrare, corporale, spirituale, aeternale: corporale, ut fiat transitus ad locum, pro miserabili Jerusalem liberanda; spirituale, ut fiat transitus de statu ad statum, pro universali Ecclesia reformanda; aeternale, ut fiat transitus de vita in vitam, pro coelesti gloria obtinenda ... quoniam summus pontifex, qui super domum Israel constitutus est speculator, transire debet per universam Ecclesiam, quae est civitas regis magni, civitas posita supra montem, investigando et inquirendo merita singulorum: ne dicant bonum malum, vel malum bonum; ne ponant tenebras lucem et lucem tenebras (Isa. 5.20)." See *PL* 217: 673-677. Translated by Baldwin, pp. 295-298.

Pope Innocent's preaching, therefore, articulated a role for the papacy that was watchman, spiritual and religious leader, and active reformer. The agenda that he set forth at IV Lateran was in keeping with these goals, and the responses in the English church by Archbishop Stephen Langton in his statute-making, in his promulgation of the decrees of the Council, and in his own preaching reflect a positive response to these aims, and mirror the pope's role as he had defined it. In yet another sermon preached at the Council,[24] Pope Innocent commented on the role of preaching which he likened to a golden bell which adorns the priest.[25]

The relationship between Langton and the pope was more complex, however, than their agreement on reform of the Church and was not without its difficulties.[26] When King John took the Crusader's oath and became vassal to the pope, the previously harmonious relationship between Innocent and Langton became increasingly discordant. By and large, as we have seen, Langton was in agreement with the overall policy of reform that Innocent initiated and which formed the basis of discussion at IV Lateran which Langton attended, and which was effected in England by several provincial councils which Langton supported. So long as these policies did not interfere with Langton's independent line in the English church, there was no essential quarrel with the pope. Once, however, it became apparent that this position was threatened, then conflict with Rome became inevitable.

Langton challenged Rome on several issues. He refused to excommunicate the barons despite threats from Rome. He insisted on the restitution of church property, even though the Interdict was prolonged because of the delay in meeting this demand. His emphasis on canonical and valid elections, free of interference from papal legates and of intervention by the king, placed major emphasis on the suitability of the man for the office. The move obtains all the more significance if we apply it to the episcopate in his scheme of reform. On the question of papal taxation, increasing objections by local clergy and magnates indicate a growing resistance in the English church toward these papal policies.

The divergence became all the more pronounced and emphatic once the pope became suzerain of England, a move which Langton himself criticized. Chenu has called attention to the significant shift in Innocent's policy after the French defeat of the Empire at Bouvines in 1214, namely, that this event

---

[24] *PL* 217: 679-688.

[25] Ibid., col. 679: "Hinc est igitur, quod a veste pontificali dependebant mala granata, cum tintinnabulis aureis [cf. Exod. 28.34]. Per malum granatum accipitur operatio, per tintinnabulum aureum intelligitur praedicatio: quae duo debent in sacerdote conjungi, ne sine illis ingrediens sanctuarium moriatur."

[26] See the Conclusion, in Roberts, *Studies*, pp. 131-136.

marked a break from the theocratic era of the papacy to an increasing temporal role, which was not without its dangers for the Roman church.[27] So long as Innocent was the pope acting in the cause of reform and essentially having the qualities of the good prelate, Langton had no cause for argument. Once, however, papal policies threatened the freedom of the English church and its clergy and, furthermore, became temporally allied with the very secular power from which the church wanted its freedom of action, then the conflict between Langton and the pope becomes more comprehensible. In these events we can see the paradox of Langton's sympathy with the ideals of the papacy and the papal reform movement which expressed the religious role of the papacy, and his resistance and disobedience to a particular pope. There is no more striking example of the marked distinction between ideals and realities defining the papacy in this period.

This conflict between ideals and realities can be seen in other examples of the way the leadership in the English church perceived the medieval papacy. Robert Grosseteste, for example, who has been called one of the most thoroughgoing papalists of the age,[28] denounced the papacy and the Curia, calling it the source of many of the evils that beset the English church.[29] On another occasion, however, Grosseteste identified the pope with Moses who sat in judgment over the people of Israel. In the following simile which draws upon Aristotelean cosmology, Grosseteste gave expression to the doctrine of papal plenitude of power:

---

[27] M.-D. Chenu, *La théologie au douzième siècle* (Paris, 1957), p. 398.

[28] W. A. Pantin, "Grosseteste's Relations with the Papacy and the Crown," in *Robert Grossesteste: Scholar and Bishop: Essays in Commemoration of the Seventh Centenary of his Death*, ed. Daniel A. Callus (Oxford, 1955), p. 183.

[29] See Servus Gieben, "Robert Grosseteste at the Papal Curia, Lyons 1250: Edition of the Documents," *Collectanea Franciscana*, t. 41, fasc. 3-4 (1971), 340-393: "Sed quae est huius tanti mali prior et originalis causa, fons et origo? Dicere vehementissime tremesco et expavesco. Silere tamen non audeo, ne incidam in illud vae prophetae dicentis: 'Vae mihi, quia tacui, quia vir pollutus labiis ego sum' (Is. 6.5). Causa, fons et origo huius est haec curia. Non solum eo quod haec mala non dissipat et has abominationes non purgat, cum ea sola hoc maxime possit et ad hoc summe teneatur, sed et eo amplius quod ipsamet per suas provisiones, dispensationes et collationes curae pastoralis tales quales praetacti sunt pastores, immo mundi perditores, in oculis solis huius constituit" (ibid., 355). For Grosseteste's role in the preaching tradition of the English church, see idem, "Robert Grosseteste on Preaching: with the Edition of the Sermon 'Ex Rerum Initiatarum' on Redemption," *Collectanea Franciscana*, t. 37, fasc. 1-2 (1967), 100-141. For an updated bibliography on Grosseteste, see idem, "Bibliographia Universi Roberti Grosseteste ab an. 1473 ad an. 1969," *Collectanea Franciscana*, t. 39 (1969), 362-418. I am especially indebted for these references and for his lucid discussion of this subject to Fr Leonard E. Boyle, "Robert Grosseteste and the Pastoral Care," first published in 1979 and reprinted in *Pastoral Care, Clerical Education and Canon Law 1200-1400* (London: Variorum Reprints, 1981), I, orig. pag. 3-51. See also R. W. Southern, *Robert Grosseteste: The Growth of an English Mind in Medieval Europe* (Oxford, 1986).

... So is the Lord Pope, in respect of whom all other prelates are as the moon and stars, receiving from him whatever power they have to illumine and fertilise the Church.[30]

Papal control over the episcopate and the emphasis on the bishops in their pastoral role (which we have seen in the Lateran decrees and in various English synodical statutes) had implications for the English church. Bishops such as Walter de Gray of York, Richard Poore of Salisbury and Durham, William Blois of Worcester, and Alexander Stavensby of Coventry-Lichfield owed their advancement to acts of Innocent III and Honorius III.[31] Papal influence also continued to be strong in the succession to the see of Canterbury, as Professor C. H. Lawrence has observed:

> It is interesting to consider the character of these men who were regarded by the papacy as suitable instruments of its policy. All six (i.e., those who were in effect designated by the pope in the thirteenth century) were Schoolmen and five, Langton, Edmund, Kilwardby, Pecham and Winchelsey were theologians of eminence; all had incepted and taught in the schools of Paris; all were profoundly involved in the religious movements of their time and treated their pastoral responsibilities with the utmost seriousness ... they were men filled with the reforming zeal of which the papacy was still a source, and they were drawn from the newly fledged universities, which the popes assiduously nursed with their favour and protection. They mirrored the mind of a papacy which was still a creative, as well as a subduing force.[32]

The leader of this reform movement, as we have seen, was the pope, Vicar of Christ and supreme pontiff. It was largely Innocent III, as Maccarone tells us, who transformed the pope from Vicar of Peter into Vicar of Christ.[33] The canonists of this period defined the papal office in the light of ancient

---

[30] Quoted by C. H. Lawrence, "The Thirteenth Century," in *The English Church and the Papacy in the Middle Ages*, ed. C. H. Lawrence (London, 1965), p. 119. See *Roberti Grosseteste Episcopi quondam Lincolniensis Epistole*, ed. H. R. Luard, RS 25, pp. 357-431, *Epistola [cxxvii] Decano et capitulo Lincolniae 1239?*: "Propter haec, ad instar praedictae ordinationis in veteri Testamento factae, dominus Papa, qui est in omni domo Domini fidelissimus et in omni populo ejus velut Moyses, quem constituerat Dominus *servum suum in omni domo sua fidelissimum* [Num. 12.7] et principem super omnem populum suum Israeliticum. ... Ita dominus Papa, respectu cujus omnes alii praelati sunt sicut luna et stellae, suscipientes ab ipso quicquid habent potestatis ad illuminationem et vegetationem..." (ibid., pp. 364, 390).

[31] On Honorius III's interest in preaching, see James M. Powell, "Pastor Bonus: Some Evidence of Honorius III's Use of the Sermons of Pope Innocent III," *Speculum* 52 (1977) 522-537, and idem, "The Prefatory Letters to the Sermons of Pope Honorius III and the Reform of Preaching," *Rivista di storia della chiesa in Italia* 33, no. 1 (1979) 95-104.

[32] Lawrence, "The Thirteenth Century," pp. 146-147.

[33] See M. Maccarrone, *Vicarius Christi: Storia del titolo papale* (Rome, 1952), pp. 109-118.

tradition and contemporary circumstance. They described papal power to legislate and render judicial decisions. Gratian more than once affirmed the primacy of Peter and of the Roman church, reserving to the pope legislative power and the right to call councils. Hostiensis lent justification to the papal prerogative to oversee bishops and to establish canons.[34] Pope Innocent III, himself, in the decretal *Cum instantia*, wrote that the pope may never cease exercising his pastoral duties. Vincentius Hispanus, referring to Innocent's decretal, also emphasized the pope's duty to preserve and care for his Christian flock.[35] Brian Tierney summed up the view of the papacy in the following words:

> The Decretists' exegesis of Matthew xvi.16-18 thus led them to a doctrine of the Pope as head of the Church, supreme exponent of the power of juris-diction conferred on the Church, symbol of the Church's enduring faith.[36]

Archbishop Stephen Langton accepted the doctrine of papal plenitude of power but insisted that all questions had to be examined in the light of Scripture as an exposition of the moral law. The pope was "the mouthpiece of God" but there might be questions of interpretation of specific papal decrees. When Langton addressed questions of papal power, these were issues that, more often than not, were discussed in his *Questiones*. The various cases in which Langton commented on papal power were usually quite specific, e.g., a decree on fasting and an issue of tithes paid by laymen in a particular parish. Powicke pointed out long ago in his pioneering biography of Langton that the archbishop was not a subtle thinker. The Fourth Lateran Council which he attended with many other prelates had to face the problems of Christian society. Langton was very much at the center of this movement and was "one of those who exerted an influence upon the life and thought of the Church." [37]

This influence made itself felt in many sermons whose theme was the reinvigoration of Christian life by a rededicated clergy, devoted to the spread of popular piety. Pope Innocent III recognized the importance of this popular movement for the Church. In effect, the recognition given the mendicant orders in the first part of the thirteenth century followed through on a

---

[34] Brian Tierney, *Foundations of the Conciliar Theory: The Contribution of the Medieval Canonists from Gratian to the Great Schism* (Cambridge, 1955; repr. 1968), pp. 28-29. Also see his *Origins of Papal Infallibility 1150-1350: A Study on the Concepts of Infallibility, Sovereignty and Tradition in the Middle Ages* (Leiden, 1972).

[35] Kenneth Pennington, *Pope and Bishops: The Papal Monarchy in the Twelfth and Thirteenth Centuries* (Philadelphia, 1984), p. 25.

[36] Tierney, *Foundations*, pp. 35-36.

[37] See Frederick M. Powicke, *Stephen Langton: being the Ford Lectures delivered in the University of Oxford in Hilary Term 1927* (Oxford, 1928), pp. 138-142.

movement that appears to have had its beginnings in the late twelfth century in Paris. Stephen Langton, as a preacher who was interested in reform, was, insofar as we can judge by the evidence in his sermons, in accord with the overall aims of his former Paris friend, Innocent III. How then can we explain the paucity of actual references to the pope and the virtual absence of any discussion relating to the papal office?

References to the pope in contemporary sermons generally appeared in the prayers of the people, especially those recited at the end of the sermon.[38] This feature may be helpful in explaining the absence of any mention of the pope in most of Langton's sermons. The transmission of texts by *reportatio* and their subsequent collection in sermon manuals as model sermons may have led copyists to eliminate references of a topical or contemporary nature which could be added orally by the preacher who used the model sermon. Similarly, closing prayers were usually indicated in the manuscripts by standard formulae, and these were either abbreviated or omitted entirely. A special prayer for the pope may well have been pronounced, but it would not necessarily appear in the manuscripts. In short, given the condition of our texts, we cannot say with certainty that the pope was not mentioned in the prayers of the people. Since the practice during this period generally called for such a prayer, this may well have been the case in Langton's sermons.[39]

What is clear, however, is the absence of any theoretical discussion relating to the papal office. We have seen that Langton's preaching was consonant with the aims of the pope in carrying out the broad program of reform spelled out in the conciliar legislation of IV Lateran and the English decrees and statutes. It would be highly unlikely that a preacher addressing a popular audience would discuss the papal office. Nor would sermons addressed to the clergy in synod necessarily take up what the canonists of the period did so well: theoretical and legal discussions of the nature of the papacy. Langton and his colleagues were men intent on reform and bent on the overall purpose of cure of souls. Langton's preaching to the clergy and the people was not the place for the kind of cases that attracted his attention in the *Questiones*, which, as we described earlier, were specific in nature and related to particular issues of interpretation. In this instance too, we must be impressed by Langton as Powicke's "sensible Englishman" addressing particular issues in the life of the Church rather than given to theoretical and legal speculation.[40]

---

[38] See Lecoy de la Marche, p. 345.
[39] On the transmission of the sermons, see Roberts, *Studies*, pp. 56-62.
[40] Powicke, *Stephen Langton*, pp. 17 and 142.

Nowhere is this more striking than in the sermon delivered by Langton at St. Paul's, London on 25 August 1213 where a direct reference to the pope appears. The sermon, addressed *ad populum* to a great throng of ecclesiastical dignitaries and magnates, is an apology to raise the interdict which had been pronounced on England and Wales on 23 March 1208 and remained in effect until 2 July 1214. The interdict had been imposed by Innocent III in an effort to force King John's acceptance of Langton as archbishop. John, who had been excommunicated, was also threatened with deposition should he not submit to the pope by 1 June 1213. King John finally received Langton with four of his suffragan bishops at Winchester in July 1213 and was subsequently absolved from his excommunication. The king was fearful of domestic rebellion and the possibility of foreign invasion, and these were strong motivations for his eventual submission. In the course of the sermon, Langton insists that the king make full restitution to the Church of goods and property that had been unjustly seized. He reminds his lay listeners of their obligation to trust in the judgment and counsel of their prelates, and speaking of the pope, he says: "The Lord Pope is lord of Christendom and it is necessary to obey him." [41]

"Dominus papa Christianitatis dominus est et eidem oportet obedire." There is no more direct and telling reflection of this archbishop's attitude toward the papal office. The pope as mouthpiece of God must be obeyed, but there might very well be questions of interpretation of specific papal decrees and actions. In this instance, Langton called for obedience to the Lord Pope, but his inflexibility on the particular issue of John's restitution of property to the Church contributed to the prolongation of the interdict. Once King John had come to terms with respect to the surrender of England to the papacy, it was Langton who stood in the way of restoration of normal relations between England and Rome.

There remains in the Langton sermons another area which may be fruitful in our examination of the perception of the religious role of the papacy. In sermons for the feast day of St. Peter, Langton comments on relevant passages in Matthew.[42] For example, in the sermon on the theme *Beatus es Symon bar Jona* (Mt 16.17), notice Langton's explication of these names:

---

[41] "Uos enim cum sitis laici, uestros prelatos tales esse debetis credere ut omnia discrete agant et cum consilio. Dominus papa Christianitatis dominus est et eidem oportet obedire" (Sermon II.18-19), p. 47 in *Selected Sermons of Stephen Langton*, ed. Phyllis B. Roberts, Toronto Medieval Latin Texts (Toronto, 1980). For the complete sermon cited here, see pp. 37-51.

[42] On Langton's discussion of the power of the keys (Mt 16.19), see the relevant passages from his *Questiones* quoted in Paul Anciaux, *La théologie du Sacrement de Pénitence au XII⁰ siècle* (Louvain-Gembloux, 1949), pp. 564-569.

Symon is interpreted as one who is obedient; Bar-Yona, as son of a dove. Truly was Peter obedient since he obeyed the Lord and firmly trusted in Him. ... Obedience is threefold. There is obedience that is a consequence of fear, which one finds in the attitude of one of lower status. There is also the obedience that one finds as a motive for material gain as in the case of greedy men; and there is the obedience for the sake of God as in the case of just men. This was the obedience that Peter had because he obeyed the Lord.[43]

As Peter and his successors, the popes, owed obedience to God, so do all Christians owe obedience to the pope as the mouthpiece of God and the lord of Christendom. This is, in essence, a view of the religious role of the papacy as it was perceived by one of the great preachers of the medieval English church, Archbishop Stephen Langton. Finally, in a sermon on the theme *Ego sum pastor bonus* (John 10.11), Langton urges that he who would be *pastor animarum*, should look to the example of Christ. He should cultivate the characteristics of a prelate: *conversatio sancta, fama integra, auctoritas et scientia.*[44] With these words Langton echoes those characteristics which Pope Alexander III had earlier associated with the good pope.

Thus we come round full circle to a perception of the papacy that reflected its complex role as leader and as role model in the Church. My purpose has been to assess what the preaching tradition in the English church, especially during the archiepiscopate of Stephen Langton, tells us about how the religious role of the papacy was perceived. The sources in the statutes and decrees, as we have seen, argue for a positive attitude and cooperation with the aims of the reforming papacy of IV Lateran. Langton's statutes on preaching which informed the legislation of the English church on this subject thereafter, and the content of his sermons, as well, reflect a concern shared with the pope for the reform of Christian society.

Insofar as he commented on the pope and on papal power, Langton was practical and specific rather than theoretical and speculative. As we have seen, there is virtually no discussion of the papal office in the sermons, but there is clearly spelled out the need to obey the pope as the mouthpiece of God. This is not to say that all was harmonious in the relationship between this archbishop and the pope he knew so well. Questions of the relationship

---

[43] "Symon interpretatur obediens. Bariona filius columbe. Vere Petrus fuit obediens, quia obedivit Domino et firmiter credidit. ... Item Petrus fuit obediens, et nota quod triplex est obediencia. Est obediencia propter timorem, ut inferius; est obediencia propter lucrum ut in avaris; est obediencia propter Deum ut in iustis et hanc habuit Petrus quia obedivit Domino" (MS Leipzig 443, fols. 157ra-157rb). See also the Langton sermon in MS Brussels II.953, fols. 130rb-131rb *In natali sancti Petri et Pauli* and MS Arras 222, fols. 120ra-121vb *De sancto Petro* on the theme *Ecce ego mittam vobis piscatores* (Jer 16.16).

[44] MS Leipzig 443, fol. 85vb.

between Church and State drew Langton into the controversy that involved the king, the barons, and a pope who became feudal suzerain of England. This, however, was the pope acting in a political role which Langton understandably rejected. On the other hand, the pope acting in a religious role is what Langton's sermons and preaching reflected.

BIBLIOGRAPHICAL NOTE

The problem of the impact of the reform decrees on the English church as a whole is one that is very complex, for here we have to assess whether the reforming papacy in fact had an influence on parish life and how the religious role of the papacy was perceived by the Christian community as a whole. On the episcopal level, diocesan synods aimed to bring the conciliar canons to the attention of their clergy and to encourage instruction in the duties of their office. Yet, one of the principal works on the introduction of the IV Lateran decrees into England, Marion Gibbs and Jane Lang, *Bishops and Reform 1215-1272* (Oxford, 1934) concludes that although the Lateran decrees were received into England and many were enforced, "the reformation so ardently desired by Innocent was never brought about." The Church was permeated by a spirit of materialism that worked against any thorough-going reform (p. 179).

Much of more recent research has given attention to the areas of complaint and abuse, with particular emphasis on the improvement of clerical instruction and the promotion of preaching. Fr Boyle in several articles has touched on this problem as it applied to the thirteenth century. He has shown, for example, how Pecham's promulgation of the *Ignorantia Sacerdotum*, followed by the *Summula* of Bishop Quivil of Exeter in 1287, ultimately influenced the *Oculus Sacerdotis* by William of Pagula which, although written in 1320, is an elaboration of Pecham's Syllabus to assist parish clergy in carrying out the Lambeth program of 1281. See the article by Fr Leonard Boyle, "The *Oculus Sacerdotis* and some other works of William of Pagula," [first publ. London, 1955] in *Pastoral Care...* (London: Variorum Reprints, 1981), IV, pp. 81-83. Other examples of devotional literature of the period include Thomas de Chabham's *Summa de Casibus*, ca. 1220 and manuals of pastoral instruction like Grosseteste's *Templum Dei* and the anonymous *Manuel des péchés* written in Anglo-Norman verse.

For works that deal with the extent of preaching in thirteenth-century England, see Durant W. Robertson, Jr., "Frequency of Preaching in Thirteenth-Century England," *Speculum* 24 (1949) 378-388, reprinted in his *Essays in Medieval Culture* (Princeton, 1980), pp. 114-128; Jennifer Sweet, "Some Thirteenth-Century Sermons and their Authors," *Journal of Ecclesias-*

tical History 4 (1953) 27-36; and Kathleen Greenfield, "Literacy and Preaching in Medieval England: the Evidence of the Vernacular Homiletic Literature," an unpublished paper given at the Colloquium on Literacy and Society in the Middle Ages, University of Pennsylvania, 15 November 1980.

With the publication of Johannes Baptist Schneyer's *Repertorium der lateinischen Sermones des Mittelalters für die Zeit von 1150-1350*, 9 vols (Münster, 1969-1980), we can now survey the extent of Latin preaching in England in this period. I include in the following list all references in Schneyer to preachers (mainly Dominicans and Franciscans) associated with England in the thirteenth century.

Adamus de Hoveden OM: Oxford, 1290 [Schneyer, *Rep.* 1: 45-46]
Adamus de Lincolnia OM: dr theol. Oxford ca. 1293 [p. 46]
Alardus OP: Provincial prior, Engl. 1235-1236 [p. 84]

Bothale OM: preached Oxford 1290 [p. 694]
Broy OM (Johannes de Broya?): preached Oxford 1292 [p. 695]

Clemens Scotus OP: 1233 ep. Dunblanensis, d. 1258 [p. 716]

Edmundus, archbp. Canterbury, d. 1240 [*Rep.* 2: 32]
Eustachius de Normanville OM: 1251, chancellor Oxford [p. 45]

Gryffin (Griffin) de Wales OP: preached Oxford 1292/1293 [p. 247]
Guido de Marchia OM Anglicus: 1291 [p. 366]
Guilelmus de Altona (Southampton) OP: Winchester, d. 1265 [p. 372]
fr. Guilelmus de Bulwick, Anglus: n.d. [p. 453]
Guilelmus de Durham: 1229 docuit Oxford, archdeacon Durham, ep. Rouen, d. 1249 [p. 455]
Guilelmus de Gaynesburgh OM: 1292 lector Oxford, 1302 ep. Worcester [p. 459]
Guilelmus de Hecham OESA: 1293 mgr reg theol. Oxford, 1300 (1292/93?) prior provincialis Angliae [p. 459]
Guilelmus de Hothum (Houdaing) OP: Oxford 1245, 1290-1296 provincial, Engl., 1296 archbp Dublin, d. 1298 [p. 468]
Guilelmus Jaclyn OP: preached Oxford 1292 [p. 470]
Guilelmus de Lee: preached Oxford 1291/92 [p. 476]
Guilelmus de Leoministre OP: preached Oxford 1291-1293 [p. 476]
Guilelmus de Lincoln: ca. 1220-1230 canon of Lincoln, composed *Distinctiones*, London, BL MS 10.A.VII, f. 1-116 [p. 481]
Guilelmus de la Mare OM Anglicus: studied Oxford, d. ca. 1285 [p. 493]
Guilelmus de Melitona (Milton) OM: 1253-1256 taught theology at Cambridge, d. 1257 [p. 493]
Guilelmus de Notingham OP: preached Oxford 1290-1293 [p. 525]
Guilelmus de Notingham OM: 1240-1254, provincialis Angliae, d. 1254 [p. 525]
Guilelmus de Southamptoria (Trisconton, Wintoniensis) OP: 1277 provincialis Angliae, d. 1278 [p. 596]
Guilelmus de Ware OM (sic): studied Oxford, ca. 1295 [*Rep.*, 3: 793]

Henricus de Anglia op: n.d. [*Rep.* 2: 622]

Henricus de Brisingham om: 1266-1268 lector Oxford, 1278-1280 mgr Cambridge [p. 637]

Henricus de Esseburne op: studied Oxford, prior Chester [p. 639]

Henricus de Sutton om 1292/93 Oxford, d. 1327 (1328) [p. 680]

Hiclyng (Hyclink) om: preached Oxford 1292/93 [p. 706]

Hugo de Hertipol om: ca. 1288 lector Oxford, 1298-1302 provincialis Angliae, d. 1302 [p. 736]

Hugo de Sneyth op: 1282-1290 Oxford [p. 814]

Johannes Barwick om: ca. 1290 lector Oxford, d. 1340 [*Rep.*, 3: 349]

Johannes Bromyard op: mgr Oxon. fl. ca. 1271 [p. 374]

Johannes de Cesterlade op: 1291 Oxford, 1306 mgr reg [p. 432]

Johannes Derlyngton op: 1279 archbp Dublin, d. 1284 [p. 444]

Johannes de Dumbleton: ca. 1290 studied Oxford [p. 446]

Johannes Guallensis (De Waleys, Wales) om: ca. 1260 mgr reg Oxon., d. 1303 [p. 480]

Johannes de Monmouth op: 1290 mgr reg Oxon., cancell. univ. d. 1323 [p. 601]

Johannes Peckham om: ca. 1272 lector Oxford, 1275 provincialis Angliae, 1279 archbp Canterbury, d. 1292 [p. 666]

Johannes de S. Aegedio (de Saint Gilles) op: after 1235 mgr reg Oxford., d. p. 1258 [p. 720]

Johannes Westerfeld op: preached Oxford 1292/93 [p. 801]

Leulyn op: preached Oxford 1292 [*Rep.*, 4: 41]

Nicolaus de Dale (Tale) op: preached 1292/93 Oxford, 1303 mgr reg Cambridge [p. 253]

Nicolaus de Gatecumbe: 1284-1289 studied Oxford [p. 254]

Nicolaus de Ocham om: 1286 lector, preached Oxford 1290 [p. 375]

Odo de Cheriton ocist: b. 1180/90, d. 1247 [p. 483]

Radulphus Bocking op: Anglus, ca. 1264 (1270) [*Rep.*, 5: 16]

Richardus Fishacre op: p. 1227 lector Oxford, d. 1248 [p. 147]

Richardus (Rufus) Cornubiensis om: 1250-1253 docuit Oxford, p. 1256 lector et mgr Oxford, d. p. 1259 [p. 149]

Richardus Poore (Pauper): 1198 deacon Salisbury, 1215 ep. Chichester, 1217 Salisbury, 1228 Durham, d. 1237 [p. 161]

Richardus de Winton (Wincester): 1292 probably mgr reg theol., 1297 canon at Wells, Salisbury, d. 1304 [p. 170]

Robertus Bacon op: 1219-1227 praebendarius Oxford, ca. 1227 docuit Oxford, d. 1248 [p. 170]

Robertus Grosseteste: ca. 1205-1209 docuit Oxford, 1208-1214 Cambridge, ca. 1214-1235 Oxford, 1215-1221 chancellor Oxford, 1235 ep. Lincoln, d. 1253 [p. 176]

Robertus Kilwardby OP: 1254-1261 taught theology Oxford, 1272-1278 archbp Canterbury, d. 1279 [p. 195]

Robertus de Orford OM: 1293 preached Oxford [p. 219]

Robertus de Ware OM: ca. 1265/68 entered the Order, studied at Oxford [p. 330]

Rogerus Bacon OM: 1250-1256 docuit Oxford, d. 1292 [p. 340]

Rogerus Marston (de Anglia) OM: 1275-1279 lector Cambridge, 1282-1284 mgr reg Oxford, ca. 1292-1298 provincialis Angliae [p. 340]

Rogerus de Salesburia (Salisbury): 1223 canon Salisbury, 1242 ep. Wells, d. 1247 [p. 341]

Simon de Gandavo (Gent): ca. 1268 studied Oxford, 1291 mgr reg theol., chancellor, 1297 ep. Salisbury, d. 1315 [p. 459]

Simon de Hinton (Wintonia) OP: 1248-1254 taught theology Oxford, 1254-1261 provincialis Angliae [p. 459]

Stephanus Langton: 1207 archbp Canterbury, d. 1228 [p. 466]

Thomas Chabman: 1207/08-1237/38 subdeacon Salisbury [p. 627]

Thomas Jorz (York, Anglus) OP: 1295 prior Oxford, 1297 provincialis Angliae, d. 1310 [p. 630]

Thomas de Malmesbury OP: 1292 prior Oxford [p. 670]

Thomas de Sutton OP: ca. 1299-1302 mgr reg Oxford, d. 1315 [p. 672]

Thomas de Whapelade OM: 1292 Oxford, 1297 London, d. p. 1303 [p. 711]

9

Archbishop John Pecham's Perception
of the Papacy

Michael M. Sheehan, CSB

On 3 June 1279, John Pecham, recently consecrated archbishop of Canterbury, arrived at Dover. During the next three days he sent letters to John de Chishull, bishop of London, and to Pope Nicholas III, letters that suggest the qualities of the reign that was beginning. The letter to the bishop of London began with a brief but convincingly warm expression of Pecham's desire to meet his fellow bishops, then ordered ("vobis in virtute obedientiae firmiter injungendo mandamus") that they be summoned to meet at Reading on 29 July to discuss important matters touching the province of Canterbury.[1] Pecham chose not to wait until he had been formally enthroned before embarking on a headlong program of reform that was soon to be resented. The letter to the pope revealed his filial devotion to the Holy See and a warm personal relationship with Nicholas III, but it also showed his astonishment on meeting the hard facts of the network of administration into which he had come: he had learned that the prior and obedientiaries of his cathedral

---

[1] *Registrum epistolarum Johannis Peckham, archiepiscopi Cantuariensis*, ed. C. T. Martin, 3 vols, RS 77 (London, 1882-1885), 1: 9 (henceforth *Reg.*). The remaining part of the volume was edited in *The Register of John Pecham Archbishop of Canterbury 1279-1292*, vol. 1, ed. F. N. Davis, Canterbury and York Society 63 (1969) and vol. 2, ed. Decima Douie, Canterbury and York Society 65 (1968). On the Council of Reading see Decima Douie, *Archbishop Pecham* (Oxford, 1952), pp. 95-104 (henceforth *Pecham*), and *Councils and Synods*, 2. *A.D. 1205-1313*, ed. F. M. Powicke and C. R. Cheney (Oxford, 1964), 2: 828-857 (henceforth P-C).

The Religious Roles of the Papacy: Ideals and Realities, 1150-1300, ed. Christopher Ryan, Papers in Mediaeval Studies 8 (Toronto: Pontifical Institute of Mediaeval Studies, 1989), pp. 299-320. © P.I.M.S., 1989.

church at Canterbury had been excommunicated by collectors of the papal-tenth.[2] He would complain with bewilderment a few weeks later when he found himself threatened by a like fate because of his inability to repay the money he had borrowed to finance the initial expenses of his reign. His letter ended with the remark that he would never have accepted episcopal consecration if he had believed that such a curse would be visited on him for a trivial matter.[3] It is the attitude to the papacy of this volatile man as it was expressed during the fourteen difficult years of his reign at Canterbury that is to be examined here.

Pecham's background was not without influence on the formation and development of his attitude. He was one of a series of remarkable men appointed to the see of Canterbury largely under papal influence during the thirteenth century.[4] Until his postulation, like most of them, he had spent his adult life as a scholar. When he entered the Friars Minor about 1250, Pecham had already completed his training in arts at Paris and Oxford. The late Decima Douie describes his conversion to the Franciscan ideal, imitating the poverty of Christ.[5] The life of humility for which he strove was somewhat diminished by his inability to remain tranquil in the presence of the sinner, a virtue which St. Francis counselled and which he himself saw as a sign of perfection,[6] but he seems to have been a man of prayer with a sincere desire for holiness. When he reprimanded the king and others less powerful, and informed them that his conscience required that he do so, when he pointed out to members of the Roman Curia that his obligation to obey the law of the Church left no room for certain arguments, one is convinced that Pecham meant what he said, hackneyed though his expression may have been.[7] Perhaps the best indication of the depths on which he drew is found in a letter written during a bitter dispute with the Roman Curia over a pluralist whom he had deprived: he noted that the case brought disgrace to the "Holy Roman Church" and difficulties for him, but he at least could convert his

---

[2] *Reg.* 1: 10-11.

[3] "Nec unquam consecrationis gratiam suscepissem, si credidissem pro causa tam modica mihi maledictionis tam horrendam maculam irrogandam" (*Reg.* 1: 20).

[4] C. H. Lawrence, "The Thirteenth Century," in *The English Church and the Papacy in the Middle Ages*, ed. C. H. Lawrence (London, 1965), pp. 146-147.

[5] *Pecham*, pp. 5-6.

[6] See *Regula Non Bullata*, Cap. 5, "Et caveant omnes fratres tam ministri et servi quam alii, quod propter peccatum alterius vel malum non turbentur vel irascantur...": *Opuscula Sancti Patris Francisci Assisiensis*, ed. Caietanus Esser, Bibliotheca Franciscana Ascetica Medii Aevi 12 (Grottaferrata, 1978), p. 251, and *Tractatus Pauperis a Fratre Johanne de Pecham ... conscriptus*, ed. A. van den Wyngaert (Paris, 1925), p. 13.

[7] See *Reg.* 1: 239, 243; 2: 560, 603, 629 et passim.

sorrow to spiritual good.[8] After the completion of the novitiate, Pecham returned to Paris, probably between 1257 and 1259, to study theology. There, having completed his training, he became lector at the Franciscan friary and, eventually, regent master.[9] In those years he played an important role in the defence of the mendicants when the secular masters launched their second attack on them. It was probably at the end of this stage of the dispute, in 1272, that he returned to England where he served for three years as lector in theology at Oxford and two years as provincial of his order. The experience of men and affairs afforded by this interlude was much enhanced by the two years that he was to spend at the Curia as lector in theology. Pecham came to know the four popes who reigned during his years at Canterbury and it is clear not only that he knew many of the cardinals and other members of the Curia, but that some of them were his trusted friends.[10]

Pecham came to Canterbury at a rather difficult moment. When the opposition of the English clergy to the crusading tithe imposed on the Church at the Council of Lyons was at its height, his predecessor, the Dominican Robert Kilwardby, had been made cardinal bishop of Porto in April 1278, resigning his see two months later.[11] The monks of Canterbury, responding to royal pressure, chose Robert Burnell, bishop of Bath and Wells, to succeed. Burnell, royal chancellor and an able civil servant, one of the lesser charges against whom was his pluralism, was not accepted by the pope. Pecham was postulated instead. Though this choice, a surprise to Pecham as to most others, did not lead to conflict with Edward I nor with Burnell, the new archbishop found himself at the head of a church under serious pressure from the royal administration. The king saw in the Church not only a source of direct income through taxation but also a supply of the benefices needed to support the needs of many royal administrators. This usage, accepted by all levels of West European society, was confronted by the growing opposition to pluralism and absentee rectors that had been given rather precocious statement in English provincial councils and, most recently, at the Second Council of Lyons (1274).[12] There was also the question

---

[8] "... lamentantes plus dedecentiam sanctae Romanae curiae, quae solet omnibus se praebere speculum honestatis, quam nostra incommoda, quae speramus esse auctore Deo in spiritualia commoda convertenda" (*Reg.* 2: 693).

[9] The chronology of Douie, *Pecham*, pp. 8-34, is adopted here.

[10] Ibid., p. 35.

[11] On the reasons for Kilwardby's withdrawal to the *Curia* see Maurice Powicke, *The Thirteenth Century 1216-1307*, 2nd ed., The Oxford History of England 4 (Oxford, 1962), pp. 470-471 and *Pecham*, p. 97.

[12] See Pecham's account of legislation against pluralism at the Council of Reading (1279): c. 4, P-C 2: 837-838.

of the ecclesiastical courts and the steady pressure from royal jurisdictions that tended to limit their effectiveness.[13] In the disputes that were to develop about these matters, Pecham attached fundamental importance to papal support and, in more general terms, to the position of the papacy within the Church.

Reflection on *sacerdotium* and *imperium* does not seem to have occupied an important place in Pecham's activity during his years in the schools. In a *Quaestio* of the Roman period he remarked in passing that the king was bound to accept the guidance of Church law, but the position was not developed, the purpose of his argument being to show that theology rather than law was most necessary for bishops.[14] It was the role of the papacy within ecclesiastical structures that interested him. Thus, in the arguments that he developed during the poverty dispute, Pecham found his place within that Franciscan vision of the Church that looked beyond the diocese and the locally exclusive authority of the bishop, concluding that matters pertaining to belief, the instruction and pastoral care of the faithful and the defence of christendom, must be decided in terms of the good of the whole Church, a task that fell especially to the papacy. In his defence of Franciscan poverty he had to meet the argument of Gerard of Abbeville that the mendicant position involved a condemnation of the bishops who were wealthy, though they claimed to be the successors of the Apostles.[15] Thus in the *Tractatus pauperis* he distinguished within the apostle's role that of prelates, who govern the Church, and that of teachers by word and example, tasks that fall especially to the friars. The prelate, as such, is most perfect because of his responsibility for souls and the pope excels all.[16] This doctrine was further developed a few years later, probably while Pecham was English provincial, in his commentary on the Franciscan *Rule*. Discussing *Solet annuere*, the bull of Honorius III that promulgated the *Rule* of 1223, he remarks that the pope called himself "episcopus." It must be understood, Pecham notes, that the pope is "episcopus" not only of part but of all (*totius universitatis*). Referring to the account of Christ's appearance after his resurrection in John 21:7-8, he suggests that Peter leaped into the sea, the quicker to approach Christ on

---

[13] *Pecham*, pp. 113-120 and Powicke, *The Thirteenth Century*, pp. 445-485.

[14] "Utrum theologia sit prae ceteris scientiis necessaria prelatis ecclesie," Paris, BN lat. 3183, fols. 175r-v, 177v: pointing out that civil laws are made by the laity and often contradict "legem ierarchicam," he adds: "potius rex quicumque habet accipere quod regatur a sacerdotibus leviticis ut dicitur *Deut.* 17" (fol. 175r). Cf. *Pecham*, p. 45 and n. 2.

[15] See *Pecham*, pp. 26-33.

[16] "Quatre chapitres inédits de Jean de Pecham, O.F.M., sur la perfection religieuse et autres états de perfection," *Collectanea Franciscana* 14 (1944) 113: "In hoc enim Papa debet praecellere omnes homines qui omnes habet benedicere...."

the shore. The sea, he says, represents the world which Christ gave Peter to govern, whereas the boat in which the other disciples came to land represents the local episcopacy in various parts of the world, which other prelates exercise.[17] Christ gave Peter ordinary power over the other apostles. Peter was to confirm his brethren (Luke 22:31-32). There must be a head; otherwise their would be confusion in the Church.[18] As to the Franciscans themselves, Pecham noted that Brother Francis had promised obedience and reverence to Pope Honorius and his canonically appointed successors and to the Roman Church and that all the community was bound by that promise.[19] This reflection on the position of the pope within the Church was applied to a specific problem in a *Quodlibet* of the Roman period where in Article 7 he asked whether it were permitted to hear a parishioner's confession without the permission of his priest or against his wishes by license of a higher prelate or by privilege. Pecham replied that such permission can be given by the Apostolic See and that it would be heretical to say otherwise.[20]

But it is the papacy as understood and experienced by John Pecham the archbishop that is of special interest here. The questions that he had examined during his years as master took on an immediacy and piquancy that even the most vigorous opposition in the schools could not know. In the rough and tumble of jurisdictional conflict and the frustration and disappointment of seemingly unnecessary compromise on the matters of principle, and in the carelessness of some papal decisions that he found scandalous and redolent of personal betrayal, his understanding of the role of the Apostolic See took on nuances that might well have surprised him a few years before when he was writing the *Expositio super regulam Fratrum Minorum*. The principal indications of this understanding are to be found in Pecham's register. This volume is incomplete, containing as it does only a few items from the second half of his reign. Fortunately this lack can be supplied in part by documents that have survived in the registers of his contemporaries and in other collections of records.[21] Even were this source complete, one would

---

[17] *Expositio super regulam Fratrum Minorum*, in *Sancti Bonaventurae opera omnia*, vol. 8 (Quarrachi, 1898), p. 391. On Pecham's authorship see pp. lxxi-lxxii.

[18] Ibid., p. 392.

[19] Ibid., p. 396.

[20] *Johannis de Pecham archiepiscopi Cantuariensis quodlibet Romanum*, ed. F. M. Delorme, *Spicilegium Pontifici Athenaei Antoniani* (Rome, 1938), p. 111.

[21] On the edition of the register see above n. 1. Several of Pecham's letters survive in the registers of his fellow bishops and are published in *The Register of John Pecham*, 2: 241-247. See Decima Douie, "Archbishop Pecham's Register," *Studies in Church History* 1 (1964), 173-175. Others not yet published are in Vat. Cod. Lat. 4016, a manuscript incorporating material on the excommunication of St. Thomas de Cantilupe, bishop of Hereford; see R. C. Finucane, "The Cantilupe-Pecham Controversy," in *St. Thomas Cantilupe Bishop of Hereford: Essays in His Honour*, ed. Meryl Jancey (Hereford, 1982), pp. 103-123.

be excused for thinking that a collection of administrative papers, drawn up according to established formulae, would reveal little of the archbishop's more intimate reflection. While this judgment would be true of most episcopal registers, Pecham's is remarkably different. Needless to say, there are hundreds of documents — letters of appointment, commissions, dispensations etc. — that are formulaic; some letters that seem at first glance to be personal are found to be similar.[22] But there are many documents, especially letters asking for assistance in times of crisis, that are entirely different in the quality of their contents. Pecham's hopes, affection, disappointment, resentment and judgments of men and their motives are expressed with astonishing candor to correspondents who extend from the pope and king to minor members of the archbishop's administration. As will be seen, the register reveals much of Pecham's vision of the papacy, of his understanding of his role with regard to it and the anguish he bore as one frequently enmeshed in the great net of administration of which the Curia was the centre.

*
* *

In the prologue to Canon 4 of that Council of Reading held only eight weeks after his arrival in England, Pecham gave a brief account of previous legislation on residence and pluralism by general councils of the Church and by English provincial councils, then described the astonishment and repugnance of Pope Nicholas III on learning of the situation with regard to these matters in England and how he was ordered to proceed immediately to impose the law of the Church in England, compelling obedience if necessary.[23] This position, that he had been chosen as the pope's instrument of reform, occurs again and again in Pecham's correspondence. Thus in the letter of 11 July 1279 in which he complained of the appalling threat of excommunication for an unpaid debt, he reminded the pope that he had created him pastor of the church of Canterbury that he might reform it.[24] A

---

[22] Compare Pecham's letters excusing his inability to make an *ad limina* visit to the Apostolic See (*The Register of John Pecham*, 2: 38-39, *Reg.* 1: 273 and 3: 868) with his remarks about withdrawal to the Curia in *Reg.* 1: 310. The group of letters in which Pecham's more personal statements were made is the core of Oxford, All Souls College, MS 182, fols. 1-190, a collection of epistolary formulae.

[23] "Que omnia sepe et sepius ad aures summi pontificis devenerunt, qui hec omnia vehementer abhorrens, necnon admirans vehementius quod nec per constitutiones aut canones nec per cautelas aut penas hucusque tante presumptionis enormitas poterat coherceri nec eidem remedium adhiberi, nobisque etiam vive vocis iniunxit oraculo quod tanto incommodo celeri reformatione faceremus occurri, et huiusmodi presumptores a tante temeritatis audacia quacunque possemus cohercione compesci" (P-C 2: 838).

[24] "Confido nempe quod, sicuti deliberato consilio pastorem seu ministrum Cantuariensis ecclesiae me creastis, ut in illa meo ministerio reformarem..." (*Reg.* 1: 17).

few months later, in a happier mood as he reported progress in his campaign against pluralists, he spoke of the papal guidance under which he acted.[25] Under different circumstances, three years later when the hard consequences of a system of patronage to which Pecham refused to be reconciled were becoming apparent and when members of the Roman Curia had begun to suggest that he proceed more cautiously, he reminded Cardinal Benedetto Gaetani that, unlike the pluralist under discussion, he had entered his pastoral office through the door of the sheepfold by the uninfluenced choice of the pope and was instructed by him to impose the canons of the Second Council of Lyons. He went on to tell how he swore on the tomb of the Apostle with tears in his eyes that he would obey the law of the Church.[26] A further letter, dealing with the same vexing case, recalled that he accepted office at the pope's order, but that he would not have done so had he known what it would involve.[27]

Some notion of Pecham's attitude to the person of the pope can be observed in the few letters to Nicholas III and Martin IV that survive. All begin with customary statements of the pope's name and title and end the salutation with the statement that the author kisses or embraces the sacred feet.[28] What is of greater interest is the way these letters described the archbishop and suggest the quality of his relationship to the pope. The first letter to Nicholas III reads: "... frater Johannes permissione Divina Cantuariensis ecclesiae servus inutilis...." [29] (This reminder that Pecham was a friar and that, therefore, he should be considered to be a brother was used in all his correspondence.) Two weeks later, by the insertion of the possessive pronoun and the addition of "pauperculus," it is stated that Pecham is the pope's brother and a very special brother at that: "... suus pauperculus frater

---

[25] "Praeclarae considerationis vestrae, pater sanctissime, oculus non ignorat, qualiter sancta informatione vestra edoctus processerim, ad extirpandam effraenatam quorundam, quin potius multorum, audaciam, spreta apostolica dispensatione occupantium beneficia plurima curam habentia animarum" (*Reg.* 1: 137).

[26] *Reg.* 2: 558-560. On the case of Tedisius de Camilla, see below, pp. 308; 312-313, 318.

[27] A letter of 29 March 1284 (?) to Cardinal Jerome of Ascoli: "In primis veritate conscientiae protestantes, quod si praesensissemus amaritudinis aculeos, quos quotidie experimur, nunquam apostolicis jussionibus in hac parte fragilitatis nostrae humeros curvassemus" (*Reg.* 2: 693).

[28] In the salutation of the first three letters to Nicholas III (*Reg.* 1: 4, 10, 17) the pope is addressed: "Sanctissimo patri ac domino Nicholao, Dei gratia sacrosanctae Romanae ecclesiae summo pontifici." In the letter of the following year (*Reg.* 1: 137) the address is expanded to recognize the pope's universal authority explicitly: "Sanctissimo patri ... sacrosanctae Romanae ac universalis ecclesiae summo pontifici." This form would be used henceforth in the letters for which the full address survives: *Reg.* 1: 190, 213, 275, 293; 2: 591, 627, 628, 635, 638.

[29] "Brother John, by divine providence the useless servant of the church of Canterbury" (*Reg.* 1: 4).

Johannes, permissione Divina Cantuariensis ecclesiae servus inutilis...." The
archbishop of Canterbury becomes the poor little brother of the pope.[30] The
case of Martin IV was somewhat different. Pecham had known him when he
was *magister sacri palatii* and must surely have appreciated his protection of
the Franciscans, but the pope had a more understanding attitude to pluralism
than Pecham could countenance. Furthermore, he seems to have had serious
doubts about the wisdom of some of the archbishop's actions. Yet even here,
the salutation of Pecham's letters indicate a relationship that was both
humble and affectionate. He calls himself the pope's brother or the least of
his brothers and on only two occasions does he allow his self description to
include "totius Angliae primas." [31]

A similar tone of affection coupled with humility and respect for those in
authority is to be found in Pecham's extensive correspondence with members
of the Curia, especially those who had become his friends during the years
that he lived among them.[32] In a letter to his proctors in Rome, a letter in
which there was probably no temptation to flattery, he could write of their
delivering information to "amicis nostris et dominis." [33] It is clear that he
counted on their advice and support and that these were forthcoming.[34]
Pecham was careful to justify himself before members of the Curia when he
saw any threat to his reputation or his causes.[35] He also saw fit to contribute
to the support of his correspondents, and did so under conditions that make
his expression of disappointment at the suggestion that Pope Martin IV had
accepted a bribe seem excessive.[36] Finally it is important to note that he

---

[30] *Reg.* 1: 10. Pecham outdid himself in this letter, ending his self-description with a
parody of the traditional statement of primacy: "totius Angliae peripsema" (the offscouring of
all England). Cf. *Reg.* 1: 3, n. 2.

[31] *Reg.* 1: 190; 2: 627, 628. The phrase stating Pecham's primacy occurs in two rather
special letters, one a letter of credence for proctors (June 1282) and the other on behalf of
himself and several other bishops regarding the forgery of papal letters (Feb. 1282): see *Reg.*
1: 275, 293. As to Pecham's relationship with Martin IV, it should be noted that in the
instruction to his proctors who were expected to act against the archbishop, Bishop Cantilupe
remarked: "... Papam, cui est familiaris Archiepiscopus a quo appellatur...": *Registrum Thome
de Cantilupo, episcopi Herefordensis, A.D.MCCLXXV-MCCLXXXII*, ed. R. G. Griffiths, Canterbury
and York Society 2 (1907) 274.

[32] E.g., a letter to Cardinal Gerard Blancus of June 1282 (?): "Non posset temporis
diuturnitas vel intervallum spatii localis a nostra delere memoria, quam pio, quam praedulci
nos foveritis solatio, etiam ante assumptionem vestram ad cardinalatus honorem, cum essemus
in Curia laborantes" (*Reg.* 1: 369).

[33] *Reg.* 1: 310.

[34] See *Reg.*, Index s.v. 'Cardinals, letters to' 3: 1100. *Pecham*, p. 35 et passim.

[35] Among many examples see *Reg.* 1: 143; 2: 697, 711. Cardinals were often asked to
ensure that the pope was properly informed about Pecham's actions, motives etc.: e.g., *Reg.*
1: 143-144.

[36] See the instructions sent to his Roman proctors during the appeals touching his disputes
with the elect of Winchester and Bishop Cantilupe (*Reg.* 1: 277). As the dispute with the

frequently referred to the Curia as partaking of the holiness of the papal office, using the formal title "sacra Romana curia" even in letters where he found it necessary to criticize its activity severely.[37]

Devotion to the person of the pope and to the *ecclesia Romana* was expressed in the practical order in a variety of ways. On several occasions Pecham stated that the motive for his actions was reverence for God and for the Roman Church, and he was to suggest rather often that he had its good more in mind than did those who might have been expected to be its defenders.[38] He worked, he said, to bring his clergy to obey the pope.[39] From time to time he sought advice of pope or cardinal when dealing with a difficult problem. Thus, shortly after his arrival in England, he instructed his proctors to ask the pope what should be done with several English bishops who were incapacitated. A week after the Council of Reading he sent a copy of its proceedings to the Curia for ratification or correction and said that he would gladly accept the latter if it were necessary. Later, when charges were laid against him at Rome by several renegade monks he submitted the rulings to which they objected to Martin IV for his perusal.[40]

Pecham often reflected on the difficulties, the fears and the isolation of a person in his position and, in a letter to the Franciscan chapter at Cambridge in September 1279, complained of his lack of support: "defectus auxilii in praeliis Salvatoris."[41] It is clear that he considered the pope, the successor of him who, having been converted, was to confirm his brothers, to have a special obligation to support bishops in their lonely task.[42] This notion appeared in that early letter to Nicholas III asking for assistance against his creditors. There Pecham states that all bishops turn to Rome in times of trial for nourishment and protection.[43] Two years later he wrote Cardinal

---

Oxford Dominicans developed late in 1284, he wrote a series of explanatory letters, including several to cardinals on 1 January 1285. The same day he granted pensions to them and others in the Curia (*Reg.* 3: 870-873). Douie notes the connection in *Pecham*, p. 292.

[37] E.g., *Reg.* 1: 239; 2: 511, 693.

[38] "Quid mali facimus si ministerium nostrum honorificare nitimur, quod non cessant adversarii in Romana curia falso ut credimus per omnia depravare" (*Reg.* 1: 229). Also *Reg.* 1: 48, 49, 206, 227 et passim.

[39] *Reg.* 1: 50-51.

[40] On the bishops: *Reg.* 1: 34-35, 47-48 and the sequel 1: 92, 94-95, 167-168, 310; on the report on the Council of Reading: 1: 35; on the monastic rulings: 2: 628. Among many letters requesting advice from cardinals, see *Reg.* 1: 40, 47-48, 310.

[41] *Reg.* 1: 66. Similarly, in a letter of September 1281 (?) to Cardinal Matthew Orsini: "... reverentiae vestrae significamus quod die ac nocte circa reformationem ecclesiae Anglicanae, quae tot habet hiis temporibus oppressores, ut rarus sit qui eam consoletur ex omnibus caris ejus, laboramus ut possumus ad hoc habentes paucissimos adjutores" (*Reg.* 1: 227).

[42] Letter to Pope Martin IV, October 1283 (?): *Reg.* 2: 628-629.

[43] *Reg.* 1: 17.

Matthew Orsini that he would have no victory in his efforts for reform without the merciful assistance of the Roman Church.[44] A similar statement is made in the spring of 1282 when he wrote his Roman proctors that in the confrontation with the king over the liberties of the Church, it would be impossible to proceed without the assistance, counsel and protection of the papacy.[45] These notions received a more nuanced statement during the reign of Martin IV when Pecham faced serious opposition within his archdiocese and at Rome. A notable example was the appeal of Tedisius de Camilla, nephew of Cardinal Ottobono and a notorious pluralist, whom the archbishop had deprived of benefices and who had received support from several members of the Curia. Reminding the pope that, just as in his struggles against the gates of hell, the successor of Peter was consoled and supported by the Lord, so a bishop, in turn, hoped for papal protection.[46] It was with regard to the same case that he wrote Cardinal Ordonio that, though steering the ship of the Church was beyond his strength, it was consoling to know that the hand of Peter was at the helm. He noted, however, that in this case Peter had been replaced by another and that bribery was said to have played a role in the intrusion.[47] At the same time, in a letter to Cardinal Gervase de Clinchamps, he remarked that all his troubles would be bearable if the support of the Roman Church, which was his right, were forthcoming.[48]

*
* *

It is difficult to measure the extent to which Archbishop Pecham's understanding of the papacy was given formal statement during his reign. It is known that he attached much importance to preaching, that he held, in fact, that teaching the word of God was the bishop's principal duty.[49] It will be recalled that, at the Council of Reading, he spoke to his fellow bishops of the pope's role in the movement against pluralism; whether he developed his

---

[44] *Reg.* 1: 206.
[45] "... nec procedere valemus sine adjutorio, concilio et patrocinio sanctae Romanae ecclesiae..." (*Reg.* 1: 310).
[46] Matt. 16:18. *Reg.* 2: 629. See below, pp. 311-312.
[47] *Reg.* 2: 681-682.
[48] "Sed omnia quae nos tangunt essent nobis facilia, si dignaretur nos sancta Romana ecclesia juxta maternorum jura viscerum consolari" (*Reg.* 2: 698). See *Pecham*, p. 292.
[49] "Cum enim juxta doctrinam sanctorum officium pontificis consistat in doctrina praecipue verbi Dei, unde et ordo pontificum dicitur a sanctis patribus ordo praedicatorum..." (*Reg.* 2: 696). This position had received more developed treatment in the *Quaestio* discussed in n. 14 above: "Contra: ordo prelatorum a sanctis vocatur ordo predicatorum. ... Item: Cor. primo [1 Cor. 1:17] 'Non misit me Deus baptizare sed evangelizare.' Ex quibus patet quod predicare est principale officium prelati. ... certum est quod fides genita est in cordibus hominum a principio per sacra eloquentia" (fol. 175r).

broader ideas on the papacy in other instructions or in sermons is unknown at present. The pastoral side of Pecham's archiepiscopal activity has not yet been studied to the depth that is possible. One of its most important aspects, namely his preaching, suffers from that neglect; though his sermons seem to have been numerous, very little is yet known of their contents.[50]

If the matter of instruction is examined in more strategic terms, it becomes clear that Pecham was intent on providing at least some assistance to his lower clergy so that they could teach their people, especially at Sunday mass and in confession. Thus the first nine canons of the Provincial Council of Lambeth (1281) are essentially intended for that purpose. Canon 9, entitled "De informatione simplicium sacerdotum," is a brief compendium of doctrine and moral guidance. Usually called *Ignorantia sacerdotum*, from its initial phrase, it was to prove remarkably successful and in its various forms would be used well into the sixteenth century.[51] There is a brief reference to the papacy: within the exposition of the commandments of the Old Law, the fourth is explained to mean that the Christian's honouring of father and mother must be understood in both a carnal and a spiritual sense. In the latter meaning, the father signifies the prelates of the Church, the mother the Church itself. The prelates may be mediate or immediate. That the pope was to be included in this understanding seems indicated by the use of the same image in a letter to Cardinal Gervais Giancolet of March 1284. Complaining of the failure of the Roman Church to protect him as it should, Pecham points out that while it is proper for the child to honour its most holy father and most pious mother, it is also fitting that they care for their children.[52] Thus it seems proper to conclude that the brief reference in *Ignorantia sacerdotum* provided for instruction on the role of prelates, including the pope, and the Christian obligation to them. Once again, we are still ignorant of the ways in which this text was exploited, so the extent to which its potential regarding the papacy was realized is unknown.

---

[50] See J. B. Schneyer, *Repertorium der lateinische Sermones des Mittelalters für die Zeit von 1150-1350*, Beiträge zur Geschichte der Philosophie und Theologie des Mittelalters: Texte und Untersuchungen Band 43, Heft 3 (Munster, 1971), pp. 666-673, where the sets of *collationes* on the epistles and gospels for Sundays in Oxford, Bodl. Laud. misc. 85, fols. 1-31 and Rawlinson C116 are described. Other sermons by Pecham are indicated on p. 673; essential bibliography is on p. 666. Note especially, Decima Douie, "Archbishop Pecham's Sermons and Collations," in *Studies in Medieval History Presented to Frederick Maurice Powicke*, ed. R. W. Hunt, W. A. Pantin and R. W. Southern (Oxford, 1948), pp. 268-282.

[51] P-C 2: 900-905. See *Pecham*, pp. 138-142.

[52] *Reg.* 2: 698. See Lyndwood, *Provinciale*, 1.11.1, *gl. ad* 'mediatus': "Sicut Papa, Archiepiscopus, et hujusmodi, sub quibus sunt alii medii tanquam patres" (Oxford, 1679), p. 57b.

It was not in the tensions between the different levels of the hierarchy and the discussions they engendered, but in the conflict between civil and religious jurisdictions that Archbishop Pecham made his most developed statement of his understanding of the pope's position within the Church. Ten days before the bishops of the southern province gathered for the Council of Lambeth (October 1281), they received two writs from Edward I reminding them of their oaths to protect the dignity of the crown and warning them that, if they acted against the crown, or the king's person or state, or the state of the royal council, their baronies would be forfeit.[53] Warning of this kind was not unusual, though, given the forced withdrawal of Pecham from some of the positions of the Council of Reading and the strenuous discussion of royal encroachments at the Westminster parliament of November 1280, it would probably be an error to see these writs merely as pro forma precautions. The bishops did not entirely comply with the royal wishes, and three weeks later Archbishop Pecham wrote to the king and the Latin-reading members of his council ("ac ejus consiliariis literatis") to explain the cause of the conflict and to suggest the remedy. Here the role of the papacy assumed major proportions.[54]

Pecham begins his letter with a graceful acknowledgment of his obligations to the king, then, probably referring to the reminder of the bishops' oath to preserve royal rights in the second of the writs mentioned above, states that one must obey God rather than man, a principle before which a human constitution or even an oath must yield.[55] He then points out that for many years there has been a bitter dispute between the king and the magnates on one hand and the bishops and clergy on the other, a situation that has led to the oppression of the Church in spite of the decrees of popes, conciliar statutes and the authority of the Fathers. This state of affairs, Pecham says, should be corrected by the king. Of the three sanctions mentioned, it is that exercised by the pope that is especially developed. His authority is related to Matt. 16:19: "Whatever you shall bind on earth will also be bound in heaven." The bindings of papal authority, Pecham says, are spiritual, namely the sacred laws, and all must obey them; the king, because of his office, is under special obligation.[56] Pecham admits that some enemy of the Church might object that it is not for the pope to impose the yoke of the canons on

---

[53] P-C 2: 891-892.

[54] *Reg.* 1: 239-244. See *Pecham*, pp. 129-131; Powicke, *The Thirteenth Century*, p. 478.

[55] "Quia tamen oportet Deo magis quam hominibus obedire, ad praevaricationem legum illarum quae divina auctoritate absque omni dubio subsistunt, nulla possumus humana constitutione ligari, nec etiam juramento" (*Reg.* 1: 239).

[56] "Ab hac autem obedientia non est altitudo regis absoluta, sed plusquam ceteri laici ea inferiores eidem obnoxia" (*Reg.* 1: 240-241).

secular rulers in this way, but meets the argument with the simple statement that he, with the whole Church and all the holy and wise men of the world, maintains the opposite. He concludes that the resolution of all conflict that cannot be settled by inferior judges pertains to the pope.[57] In a brief history of the relationship between secular leaders and the Church from Constantine to Henry II, Pecham argues that an originally satisfactory arrangement deteriorated after the Conquest, resulting eventually in the martyrdom of St. Thomas Becket.[58] The situation, he insists, has not changed. Finally, the archbishop reminds the king that he is bound in conscience to speak in this manner and suggests that the royal oath of office requires that evil customs be removed. Should the king think that some aspect of the oath requires that he act against the Church, then the archbishop — who must surely have smiled at this point — would absolve him from his obligation. No precise point of conflict is identified within the letter, nor is there threat of excommunication or other ecclesiastical penalty, but Pecham reminds the king that it is the good of Edward's soul that is at stake and he suggests three times that, in the end, it is the prosperity of the kingdom and a peaceful succession that would be in jeopardy.[59]

Thus in the context of a serious dispute between the courts Christian and those of the king, Pecham claimed that the final judgment on the matter lay with the pope because, as the successor of Peter, he had been given that authority by Christ. Pecham made it clear that inferior jurisdictions are to be respected; it is only when they fail to resolve the problems put before them that the superior is to be invoked. This principle was applicable not only to conflicts between the two jurisdictions under discussion in the letter to the king, but also to the various levels of courts within the Church. Resolution of problems was provided by the canons, and it was the pope's responsibility to see to their application. Pecham's understanding of the papacy can thus be seen to involve a high concept of its role within European society: it was the ultimate authority, though it did not interfere with the activity of lower jurisdictions so long as they functioned properly. Furthermore, his attitude was not based uniquely on an understanding of the position of the papacy

---

[57] "Ergo ad summum pontificem pertinet omnis controversiae determinatio, quae non potest per inferiores quoscumque judices terminari" (*Reg.* 1: 242).

[58] From the beginning of his reign Pecham saw himself as sharing Becket's martyrdom. See *Reg.* 1: 22, 214, 230; 2: 693 et passim. See *Pecham*, p. 130, n. 2.

[59] "... pro honore Dei, ac animae suae suorumque salute, ac prosperitate stabili successionis suae..."; "Tenetur igitur rex ipse ex precepto legis expresso summo pontifice obedire, quod si non fecerit, timere potest ex legis insinuatione ne regni sui prolongatio minuatur." "... quod vos nec animae vestrae potestis salubriter prospicere, nec stabilitati regni vestri in posterum providere...." See *Reg.* 1: 240, 241, 244.

within a divinely constituted hierarchy, ultimately on his faith, but was also coloured by personal friendship or at least rather close acquaintance with those who held the office — facts of some importance to one of Pecham's make-up.

*
* *

The principle stated in Pecham's letter to the king implied that the authority of the pope did not limit that of inferiors so long as the latter was properly exercised. As archbishop he demonstrated his understanding of the difficult balance of authority and mutual respect that was required. For all the humility and affection expressed in his correspondence he was not subservient. Pecham discussed matters with pope and Curia and could resist them on occasion. Early in his reign, in his introduction to the canons of the Council of Lambeth, he noted that some of the regulations of the Second Council of Lyons did not accord with English usage and that the pope should adjust them as needed, tribute at once to his understanding of papal authority and of the legitimacy of claims by local churches.[60] At about the same time, after his quashing of the election of Richard de la More to the see of Winchester had been referred to Rome, Cardinal Hugh of Evesham wrote, suggesting that, since the case was under appeal, Pecham should discontinue his opposition. The archbishop replied with respect, but informed the cardinal that he intended to continue. He pointed out that it would be disgraceful if support for an unworthy candidate were allowed, while there was no place for one who, following his conscience and defending the rights of the Roman Church, resisted the choice of an unsuitable prelate.[61] A few months later, Cardinal Jerome of Ascoli suggested that Pecham's opposition was excessive, but the archbishop replied that the appeal in question was based on false information and was frivolous. He went on to criticize the general abuse of the system of appeals to the papacy.[62]

The development of an even stronger attitude of resistance can be observed in Pecham's long campaign to enforce the deprivation of Tedisius de Camilla. After this worthy had received letters overruling the archbishop's decision, the latter launched a counter appeal.[63] His register shows that he was advised

---

[60] "... si quid in ipso videatur intollerabile istius consuetudini regionis, que in multis ab omnibus aliis est distincta, circa illud temperamentum apostolice clementie humiliter imploretur..." (P-C 2: 893).

[61] Pecham had written Cardinal Hugh in August 1281, expressing his surprise at the report that he supported de la More's candidacy (Reg. 1: 219-220). The letter discussed here implies a very severe criticism of the cardinal's action; Hugh apparently replied and the archbishop stated his reasons for continued opposition once more: Reg. 1: 228-230, 281-282.

[62] Reg. 1: 377-378. This letter is discussed in detail below, pp. 320-322.

[63] On this dispute see Pecham, pp. 148-149. See Reg. 1: 419-420.

to withdraw.[64] Pecham not only refused to do so but proceeded to apply as much pressure as possible in Rome to vindicate his position. At first he used an indirect approach to the pope: a few months after his appeal, he heard a rumour that Pope Martin had received an opinion from Paris that would undermine his opposition to pluralism. Remarking that it was not for him to instruct Minerva, Pecham asked Cardinal Geffroi de Barbeau to do what he could to stiffen papal resistance to this evil.[65] A few months later, when it appeared that an unsympathetic judge delegate had been appointed, he wrote Pope Martin directly, explaining why he had deprived Camilla, emphasizing the scandal that would result in England were he reinstated and stating that the judge was incapable.[66] During the next year letter after letter came from his pen as he sought to bring pressure on the pope through members of the Curia and, incidentally, to justify his position before them as well. Often his expression was of the plainest; thus in a letter to Cardinal Ordonio, written the same day as that to the pope, he commented on the choice of judge delegate; a wolf had been made judge to bring in a decision on sheep![67] In this discussion Pecham attached much emphasis to the consequences of a reversal of his deprivation of Camilla: his campaign against pluralism would be undermined and grave scandal to the Church in England would follow. In the middle of this dispute, when it appeared that the agents of Camilla, in virtue of the papal decision that led to Pecham's counter appeal, would reoccupy his benefices, the archbishop forbade the parishioners to cooperate, threatening them with excommunication if they paid tithe to them.[68]

*
* *

John Pecham's activity as archbishop was exercised within a system of administration, judgment and recourse to appeal that embraced all of Western Europe and beyond. In the comparative effectiveness of this system lay one of the reasons for his successes; he exploited it knowingly and continually. But the system also limited him, standing in the way of his

---

[64] Notably by Cardinal Benedetto Gaetani, the future Pope Boniface VIII: *Reg.* 2: 512, 559, 602, 629.

[65] *Reg.* 2: 540-541.

[66] *Reg.* 2: 598-599. The judge, Geoffrey Vezzano, is described thus: "personae meae adversario manifesto, et impari tanto negotio, delegastis, qui in ipso procedens, sua contra leges quas nescit, utens pro legibus voluntate...."

[67] "... lupus judex efficitur sententiae pastoralis" (*Reg.* 2: 600). Other letters in support of his appeal: *Reg.* 2: 601-604, 628-630, 639-640, 692-694; 3: 822. The letter to Cardinal Ordonio about the seven evils in the Church is probably of the same period; see below, pp. 322-324.

[68] *Reg.* 2: 588-589. For his resistance to the letter of summons obtained by the abbot of Fécamp from the pope, see *Reg.* 3: 821-822, 882-886, 890.

reforming zeal. He came to England aware of the needs of the Church and, sustained from above as he knew himself to be, responded to those needs with energy, courage and remarkable tenacity. With regard to the intrusion of the royal courts on ecclesiastical jurisdiction, he was able to count on the steady support of his fellow bishops and the pope and, ultimately, on the essentially sympathetic attitude of the king. Whatever his expressions of doubt and fear may have been, his reign saw considerable progress in resolving the problem.[69] Applying the canons on pluralism and residence proved to be a more difficult matter. Pecham probably considered reform in this area to have been the principal reason for his appointment to Canterbury by Nicholas III. Here his efforts collided with vested interests that touched every level of society. The older need for clerical reform faced by the twelfth-century Church was stated in different terms as the ecclesiastical benefice was used more and more to support the bureaucracies of king, pope and bishop, masters and students in the schools and the younger sons of powerful families. Where regulations regarding dispensation and residence or the provision of adequate replacement were observed, Pecham would likely have accepted the pluralist, though probably with some reluctance.[70] But canon law was all too frequently ignored by those who used the advocacy of friends in the Curia or in the royal administration coupled with appeal to Rome to frustrate the efforts of those who would bring about reform. Finally, there were those potential reforms that involved the risk of conflict between different levels of jurisdiction. Pecham sought to exploit his rights as archbishop and primate to revitalize the whole southern province. In his visitations he examined the diocesan administrations of his suffragans and parish life as well; religious houses came under similar scrutiny. He was not

---

[69] See *Pecham*, pp. 119-128, 302-321 and Powicke, *The Thirteenth Century*, pp. 477-484.

[70] One of Pecham's most bitter disputes was with his former student and friend, Thomas de Cantilupe, bishop of Hereford. Cantilupe had been a pluralist since his youth but he seems always to have proceeded in a lawful manner: he had proper dispensations and was scrupulous in providing for the care of his flock in those benefices that required it. In a confrontation where little was left unsaid by the archbishop, pluralism does not seem to have been raised; on this dispute, see Finucane, "The Cantilupe-Pecham Controversy" (above, n. 21). It is clear, however, that Pecham would have preferred to avoid all plurality of benefices: see the letter to Cardinal Geffroi de Barbeau (April 1283?) where the practice is presented as opposing the command of the Gospel: "quo cavetur ut qui habet duas tunicas unam tribuat non habenti" (Luke 3:11): *Reg.* 2: 540-541. See W. T. Waugh, "Archbishop Peckham and Pluralities," *English Historical Review* 28 (1913) 625-635 and, for the broader question of the use of the benefice as a means of providing for the salaries of the officers of the Curia, Jane Sayers, "Centre and Locality: Aspects of Papal Administration in England in the Later Middle Ages," in *Authority and Power: Studies in Medieval Law and Government Presented to Walter Ullmann on his Seventieth Birthday*, ed. Brian Tierney and Peter Linehan (Cambridge, 1980), pp. 115-126.

slow to suggest and enforce remedies. The archiepiscopal court not only received appeals and provided protection for appellants who brought their cases to Rome, but proved to be willing to intervene *ex officio* where diocesan administration or jurisdiction seemed to fail in their responsibility. Further-more, and here Pecham probably shared a papal awareness of the limitations of a diocesan structure that could not always respond to the true needs of the faithful, he sought to develop some supradiocesan jurisdictions that would provide more effective as well as more consistent supervision. (His attempt to impose the prerogative probate of wills dealing with property in several dioceses was the most obvious example of his inventiveness in this regard.[71]) Proceeding in a manner that was often intemperate and clumsy, Pecham aroused the opposition of many, especially that of his fellow bishops, who like most medieval authorities were determined to maintain their rights of jurisdiction. Thus it was that they, too, for reasons that were variously justified, limited their archbishop's efforts by concerted opposition and, eventually, by appeal to the Apostolic See. Hence the papacy, in so many ways the model and source of Pecham's zeal, by its acceptance of appeals, became his greatest trial.

It would be a mistake to conclude that Archbishop Pecham opposed the proper appeal to Rome. He consistently honoured that jurisdiction and saw to it that his courts assisted it. Thus when discussing the complaints of his suffragans at the London Council of 1282, he met their objection to the procedure then in use, whereby a tuitorial appeal was received by the court of Canterbury without examining the legitimacy of the recourse to the Apostolic See, arguing that to do so would obtrude on the Roman court.[72] He also reminded correspondents of the loyal assistance provided by his court for many years and not without expense.[73] At the height of the dispute over the appointment to the see of Winchester, in the letter to Cardinal Jerome of Ascoli mentioned above, a letter that included severe criticism of the abuse of appeals and of the manner in which such cases were heard, Pecham was still able to state that anyone who objected to a legitimate appeal to the Apostolic See should not be considered a Christian.[74] Yet there were

---

[71] See the article by Finucane cited in the previous note, and Michael M. Sheehan, *The Will in Medieval England,* Studies and Texts 6 (Toronto, 1963), pp. 200-205. That the archbishops should supervise the execution of the testaments of suffragans and intervene in the doctrinal disputes of the University of Oxford seems to have been accepted by the other bishops without demur.

[72] See "Responsiones domini ad articulos" viii; Pecham's motives are set out more fully in the version preserved in the register of Thomas de Cantilupe; see P-C 2: 926, 928.

[73] "... in eo praecipue quo curia nostra Cantuariensis sacrosanctae sedis apostolicae, tanquam devota filia continue famulatur..." (*Reg.* 2: 521); also 2: 550.

[74] *Reg.* 1: 378.

difficulties that were intrinsic to the system of appeals: it had to be inefficient and expensive. As C. H. Lawrence has expressed it so well: "The effective working of the pope's plenitude of power in the Church represented an extraordinary triumph of doctrine over the facts of medieval geography." [75] As would be anyone of his experience, Pecham was well aware of the problem. Shortly after his arrival in England he suggested how the prior and obedientiaries of his cathedral priory might have their excommunication lifted, then went on to say that, if they chose to pursue their case at the Curia, he would support them there. He added, however, that they could expect delay, discord and, in the end, weariness or despair.[76] Yet, at this stage of his career, he showed an even-handed approach to an appeal that affected him indirectly, an attitude that implied at least a modicum of confidence. Writing to Cardinal Matthew Orsini and several other members of the Curia about a case involving the *sede vacante* jurisdiction of his see, he expressed affection for both sides but asked that he might be allowed to express a preference for the church where he took his repose.[77] As the years passed, however, Pecham seemed less able to accept that the right of appeal to Rome involved the possibility that his opponents would prevail and that their success need not mean a failure of justice or even a failure of that confirmation of the brethren that was expected of the successor of Peter. Beginning in 1282, when the disputes resulting from the appeals of Richard de la More, Tedisius de Camilla and Thomas Cantilupe weighed heavily, he wrote a series of letters to friends in the Curia, notably Cardinals Jerome of Ascoli, Ordonio and Matthew Orsini in which he complained even more bitterly of abuses in the Apostolic See. Of these, the most remarkable is a letter to Cardinal Ordonio, probably written in 1284, modelled on Apocalypse 15:5-16:21, the account of angels pouring out the seven vials of divine wrath. Contemplating the Roman Church with sorrow, he describes the seven abuses for which it must suffer.[78] The threat of excommunication for debt during the first months of his reign, for which he blamed the Curia, still rankled; abuses of this kind, so humiliating to members of the hierarchy, were set out as the first evil.[79] The misuse of the Church's income to provide for the absentee and the pluralist is presented as an area in which there has been some improvement, but he mourns the fact that the Apostolic See has

---

[75] "The Thirteenth Century," p. 129 (above, n. 4).

[76] "... credite nobis quod tanta erit dilatio, tanta mora, tanta discissio, quod nunquam ex illa parte nisi languor veniet, vel finalis desperatio successura" (*Reg.* 1: 29).

[77] "... aequali statera dilectionis amplectar in visceribus caritatis, quia tamen specialiter agitur de utilitate ecclesiae in cujus quiete et pace quiesco..." (*Reg.* 1: 32).

[78] *Reg.* 2: 694-697.

[79] *Reg.* 2: 695; see *Reg.* 1: 22, 50.

sometimes defended this abuse.[80] But it is the appeal to Rome, the subject of most of these letters of complaint that is central to his argument.

It will be recalled that Pecham admitted the value of the legitimate appeal in his correspondence with Cardinal Jerome of Ascoli. He insisted, however, that this procedure must be used with moderation, reminding him that such is the teaching not only of Roman law but also of Christ who, although he gave the power of the keys to Peter alone after the profession of faith by the Sea of Galilee (Matt. 16:19), gave it to all the apostles when he appeared to them the night of his resurrection (John 21:23).[81] (The principle that the pope should act when lower jurisdictions had failed, stated in the letter to Edward I, discussed above, is implied here.) This moderation had not been observed, and the resulting abuse of "apostolic solicitude" he saw as a plague that affected the whole Church. Furthermore, as Pecham remarked more than once and with a certainty that is worrisome to the modern reader, appeals were often based on false claims and were frivolous.[82] They were expensive, sometimes involved bribery and caused endless delay.[83] To make matters worse, judges appointed to hear appeals were often unworthy and incompetent. Cases that were referred to the papacy ran the risk of passing from the care of a judge with a truly pastoral interest in the matter in dispute to those sheep-judging wolves of whom Pecham wrote so often.[84] In a letter of August 1283 (?) to Cardinal Ordonio, he insisted that the abuse involved in these appointments was intolerable, that it was probably the greatest danger to the Church and the root cause of the separation of the oriental Church from Rome.[85] And there were other consequences. Appeals hindered reform. They robbed bishops of their determination. Often, like the true mother in Solomon's judgment, they withdrew from a case rather than see their flock destroyed in a lawsuit.[86] Pecham remarked several times that the Roman appeal dissolved the sinews of the Church, a complaint that he was to repeat in one of the last entries in his register, a letter to the Minister General of his order a year before he died.[87] In the longer term, he said, the

---

[80] "... dolendum est tamen si per sedem apostolicam hujusmodi defensentur" (*Reg.* 2: 695).

[81] *Reg.* 1: 378.

[82] *Reg.* 1: 378; cf. p. 229.

[83] *Reg.* 1: 377; 2: 681.

[84] *Reg.* 1: 377; 2: 600.

[85] "Nec credimus quod majus periculum in ecclesia valeat inveniri. Ex hiis enim radicibus discessit orientalis ecclesia a matris suae uberibus imprudenter" (*Reg.* 2: 600).

[86] *Reg.* 2: 696.

[87] *Reg.* 1: 378; 3: 982.

position of the bishop was weakened, for much of his power passed to the judge-delegate. The confirmation that Peter should have given was denied.[88]

These abuses had another effect, perhaps the most serious of all — scandal. Pecham returned to this theme again and again. In the development of his arguments against it, something can be learned of how his very strong ideal of the papacy weathered years of disappointment and the occasional betrayal. The preoccupation with scandal becomes evident in Pecham's exchange with Cardinal Hugh of Evesham regarding the choice of Richard de la More for the see of Winchester. Pecham refused to withdraw his opposition because, as he said, such an action would weaken the whole clergy of England. It would symbolize the defeat of his opposition to pluralism and would cause the clergy to fall back into that complacent attitude in its regard from which their archbishop has begun to extricate them.[89] Recalling the injunction of Matt. 5:29 to pluck out the eye that gives scandal, he informed the cardinal that he would not dare to sacrifice a public good for the apparent advantage of an individual.[90] When he returned to the subject a few months later, it was again the clergy who were in jeopardy, for they would be edified or scandalized depending on the decision taken.[91] What was at stake was an attitude to pluralism, not an attitude to the papacy. But, as the dispute over the deprivation of Tedisius de Camilla developed, the discussion of scandal took on a deeper meaning. Thus in a letter of January 1283 to Cardinal John Cholet, Pecham warned that to side with Camilla would dishonour the Church and would scandalize not only the simple but the learned as well.[92] Similarly, in the letter of April to Martin IV he noted that a decision favouring the pluralist would scandalize not only a multitude in England but anyone who knew him.[93] Later in 1283 in a letter to Cardinal Orsini, it becomes clear that the scandal of which he wrote was a threat to the Roman Church. It would not only affect England but those everywhere who scrutinized the Church, a group among whom Pecham included himself.[94] His plea that the "sancta Romana ecclesia" be spared dishonour implies that the christian's

---

[88] *Reg.* 1: 378.

[89] "... non potuimus nisi totum clerum Angliae infirmando" (*Reg.* 1: 229).

[90] "... nec audemus verum bonum rei publicae extinguere pro bono unius hominis apparente" (ibid.).

[91] "... ipsum vel in maximam aedificationem vel in maximum scandalum cleri Angliae terminandum" (*Reg.* 1: 282).

[92] "... scandalo quod inde sequetur, non solum pusillorum sed etiam illorum qui scientes qualiter Christus docuerit carnales affectus curae postponere animarum, cernunt eum ibi reperire favorem quo debuerat captivari" (*Reg.* 2: 511).

[93] *Reg.* 2: 599.

[94] "... non solum totam scandalizabit Angliam, verum etiam alios per orbem speculatores ecclesiae cum quibus nos didicimus speculari" (*Reg.* 2: 640).

attitude to that Church was under threat. He had prefaced his observations with the remark that he would accept any apostolic decree no matter how strange, implying that such might not be the case with others.[95] It is in this letter that Pecham approached what seems to have been his final position: he admitted that actions of the Roman Church were sometimes scandalous while insisting that, in his eyes, this grave limitation did not detract from its essential authority.

Thus it does not come as a surprise that, in that apocalyptic letter to Cardinal Ordonio in which Archbishop Pecham described the abuses in the Church, he should have come to a position that approached the serene. He began with a description of his vision of God and the celestial hierarchy, then told how his feeble glance fell on the Church in the world.[96] He admired the position of the Roman Church at its head, then recalled the divine punishment that could be expected should it be diminished. Having set out the evils from which the contemporary Church suffered, he asked Cardinal Ordonio whether they were the seven vials of wrath of the Apocalypse. Remarking that since they had been foreseen by God they must indeed come to pass, he left the question unanswered and argued that, if everything possible were done to avoid the scandal of little ones, the divine wrath would be diminished.[97] These little ones, not having the fuller vision of which Pecham wrote in the introduction to the letter, were especially prone to scandal for it was a vision of the Church in the world that came to them. Pecham ended the letter with a profession of faith and a warning:

> Although those things that proceed from the holy Roman Church are beyond doubt holy and honourable — indeed it is guided by the Spirit of Christ the Lord and hence it is impossible for it to err in that which is of right — as I profess with a pure heart, yet weak eyes are frequently hurt by light and, when a mother carelessly exposes the eyes of a little one to a ray of light from the side, all of a sudden the child develops a squint.[98]

[95] "Et licet nos simus omni tempore decreta apostolica, quantumcumque extranea videantur, cum reverentia suscepturi..." (ibid.).

[96] "... et demum in subcoelestis hierarchiae speciem imbecilles radios inclino" (*Reg.* 2: 694).

[97] *Reg.* 2: 697.

[98] "Licet enim quae procedunt a sancta Romana ecclesia sint sancta procul dubio et honesta, quippe quae a Spiritu Christi Domini gubernatur, pro quo impossibile est ipsam errare in jure, ut ore profiteor puro corde, tamen oculi infirmi a lumine pluries vulnerantur, et dum mater incaute parvuli oculos exponit radio laterali, strabo efficitur improvise" (ibid.). Pecham presents his vision (n. 96, above) in terms of extramission theory: rays reach from his eyes to the objects contemplated, whereas in the case of the scandalized child vision is considered in terms of intromission theory: the damaging ray comes from outside the subject; thus the fact that the scandalized person is the victim of what he sees is emphasized. On the extramission-intromission question Pecham's position is that of the Arab optical writer,

Having weathered the conflicts that resulted from the practical compromises he found in the papal exercise of its role in the Church and in society, and in spite of all the disappointment, frustration and anger that they caused him, Pecham remained convinced of the authority of the Roman Church and of its divine guidance. But he realized that many believers did not have the capacity to resolve the tensions between those two positions and that the offensive aspect of the exercise of papal authority was a scandal to them, a scandal that not only caused error of understanding of one or other facet of the life of the Church, but that threatened their faith in the papacy and in the Church itself. One of his tasks, as he saw it, was to convince the papacy of this fact.

Alhazen (d. 1039), as taken over also by his contemporaries, Witelo and Roger Bacon: an immaterial visual power goes out from the eye while material light rays enter it. See D. C. Lindberg, *Theories of Vision from Al-Kindi to Kepler* (Chicago, 1976), pp. 58-121. I am much indebted to Dr. Heather Phillips for assistance in understanding this text.

10

Popular Religious Roots
of the Byzantine Reaction
to the Second Council of Lyons

D. M. Nicol

In 1054 Cardinal Humbert, representing Rome, and the Patriarch Michael Kerullarios, representing Constantinople, excommunicated each other to their mutual satisfaction. It used to be supposed that this marked the date of the final schism between the Greek and Latin churches. It was indeed a moment of high drama and bad temper. But the bad temper shown by both parties was a symptom and not a cause of schism, a symptom of a much deeper conflict between two incompatible ideologies; and the drama was enacted at the highest level, above the simpler minds of the common people. It was the crusades which involved the ordinary Christians of both persuasions in the schism and so made it a reality. In his summing up at the end of his *History of the Crusades* Sir Steven Runciman observes that "throughout the ages there have always been hopeful politicians who believe that if only the peoples of the world could come together they would love and understand each other. It is a tragic delusion." [1] Fifty years after 1054 ordinary Christians of east and west were for the first time thrown together in large numbers as the crusaders passed through Constantinople and the Byzantine empire. The experience nourished the roots of mutual antipathy and intolerance at a popular level in the course of the twelfth century. Byzantine

[1] S. Runciman, *A History of the Crusades* (Cambridge, 1954), 3: 475.

The Religious Roles of the Papacy: Ideals and Realities, 1150-1300, ed. Christopher Ryan, Papers in Mediaeval Studies 8 (Toronto: Pontifical Institute of Mediaeval Studies, 1989), pp. 321-339. © P.I.M.S., 1989.

hostility to the Latins mounted as more and more of them, especially Venetians, arrived in the empire as merchants and bankers. The Emperor Manuel I earned himself the unflattering title of "Latinophrone" for encouraging Italians to settle in Constantinople. They were heartily disliked for their arrogance, greed and boorishness. They were also rather sharper at business and so able to undersell the natives by exploiting the trade privileges showered on them by previous emperors. They lived in their own quarter along the Golden Horn. They had their own Catholic priests and monks and their own churches of the Latin rite. The Venetians, perhaps as many as 20,000, were the most unruly, for ever plundering the quarters of their commercial rivals, the Pisans and the Genoese. The Emperor Manuel finally decided to show them the door. In 1171 he had them all arrested and their goods impounded.[2] A few years laters, in 1182, the people of Constantinople took the law into their own hands in a dreadful massacre of the remaining Latins in their city. The victims were mainly from Pisa and Genoa. But the mob were particularly vicious towards the Catholic clergy and monks. The cardinal legate to Constantinople sent by Pope Alexander III was decapitated and his severed head was dragged through the streets tied to the tail of a dog.[3] The scene of carnage in 1182 is vividly described by William of Tyre, who got his facts from refugees. It is described with equal horror by the Byzantine writers Eustathios of Thessalonica and Niketas Choniates. They were sophisticated and intelligent men who deplored the mindless fury of the mob. But they understood it. Eustathios also witnessed and recorded the brutal and bloody sack of Thessalonica by the Normans in 1185, when the western Christians plundered the Orthodox churches and violated the tomb of the city's patron saint. When ordered to cease the slaughter of citizens, some of the Normans had complained: "Why should heads be left on such bodies," they cried, "their blood can never blend with ours." [4] Choniates lived through an even more horrifying experience, the sack of Constantinople by the Fourth Crusade in 1204. He was echoing popular belief when he wrote: "Between us and the Latins is set the widest gulf. We have not a single thought in common. We are poles apart, even though we may happen to live together in the same house. They are arrogant ... and affect to look down on the smoothness and modesty of our manners as base and fawning. But we regard their arrogance and boasting and pride as a flux of the snivel which

[2] M. Angold, *The Byzantine Empire 1025-1204. A Political History* (London, 1984), pp. 196-203.

[3] C. M. Brand, *Byzantium Confronts the West 1180-1204* (Cambridge, Mass., 1968), pp. 41-42, 223.

[4] Brand, pp. 166-167.

keeps their noses in the air, and we tread them down by the might of Christ who giveth us power to trample unhurt upon the adder and the scorpion." [5]

There are those who say that the Byzantines brought the Fourth Crusade upon themselves. There may be some truth in this. But no one could have foreseen the barbarous behaviour of the western "soldiers of Christ" when they broke in to the city of Constantinople for the second time in April 1204. They directed a special hatred against the church, the clergy, the monks and nuns. They had been taught that the Greeks were in schism and in heresy. The desecration of their churches, the torture of their monks and the rape of their nuns could thus be excused. "Such," says a Greek observer at the time, "was the reverence for holy things of those who bore the Lord's Cross on their shoulders. Thus their own bishops taught them to act." [6] After 1204 it was hard for the Byzantines to believe that the Latins were Christians in any sense of the word. All the forebodings and prejudices of the most bigoted anti-western polemicists seemed to have been confirmed. The crimes against God and man that they committed were all that one would expect from people who believed in the double procession of the Holy Spirit and celebrated the Eucharist with unleavened bread.

Lists of the heresies and other aberrations of the Latins had fortified the simple faith or bigotry of the pious Orthodox people for many years before the Fourth Crusade. The compilation of such lists was of course an industry on both sides. The Dominicans were later to show an extraordinary lack of tact, publishing tracts *Contra errores Graecorum* from their house in the middle of Constantinople. On the Greek side the industry had begun with the great Patriarch Photios in the ninth century, though he had listed no more than five errors in the Roman creed and ritual. The Byzantine church was provoked into a more extensive campaign by the arrogance of Cardinal Humbert who, in 1054, issued his famous list of charges against the Orthodox. The no less arrogant Patriarch Michael Kerullarios replied with a list demonstrating twenty-three Latin heresies or malpractices, eighteen more than Photios had detected. A few years later the number had grown to thirty-six, in a Treatise against the Franks and other Latins (*Opusculum contra Francos*), which probably dates from the eleventh century despite its attribution to Photios. This document set the tone for the popularisation of such anti-Latin tracts, for it was not confined to rarefied points of theology.

---

[5] Niketas Choniates, *Historia*, ed. J. A. van Dieten, *Corpus Fontium Historiae Byzantinae* 11/1 (Berlin, 1975), pp. 301-302.

[6] Nicholas Mesarites, ed. A. Heisenberg, *Der Epitaphios des Nikolaos Mesarites auf seinen Bruder Johannes*, in Heisenberg, *Neue Quellen zur Geschichte des lateinischen Kaisertums und der Kirchenunion* (Munich, 1920), reprinted in A. Heisenberg, *Quellen und Studien zur spätbyzantinischen Geschichte*, ed. H.-G. Beck (London, 1973), p. 47, ll. 1-3.

The *Opusculum contra Francos* became a kind of standard textbook or reference work of what was wrong with the Roman church. The Latins themselves found it useful. It was translated from the Greek by Hugo Etherianus in 1178 and again in 1252 by the Dominican Bartholomew of Constantinople, who appended it to his *Tractatus contra Graecos.*[7]

The documents produced by Photios and Kerullarios had been phrased in the high rhetorical style of literary Greek. They were fired above the heads of the common people; though their fallout helped to poison minds on both sides. For them the two most serious charges against the Latins were the addition to the Creed of the *Filioque* and the use of unleavened bread in the sacrament. The man in the street in Constantinople could hardly comprehend the niceties of the theology involved in these questions. He was sure, however, that his church and its bishops must be right. His natural loyalty and his native prejudices were immeasurably reinforced by that greatest of all Latin crimes, the Fourth Crusade. For those who had lost their city, their emperor and their patriarch, it was comforting to their wounded feelings to be reassured that their conquerors were such misguided Christians. The list of Latin errors multiplied. Soon after 1204 a former Bishop of Kyzikos, Constantine Stilbes, compiled a new one.[8] Stilbes was a man of letters, a retired professor; but he tempered the style of his language to suit a popular audience. His work is especially interesting because it contains a section on the acts of sacrilege committed by the crusaders during the sack of Constantinople. These acts, he says, have not been condemned or punished by their own church, which leads one to the conclusion that their church has approved such wickedness and stands itself condemned on the same charge.[9] The *Opusculum contra Francos* had catalogued thirty-six Latin errors. The list compiled by Stilbes contains seventy-five. Most of them were already known. The matters of the Holy Spirit and the unleavened bread still take pride of place. But some of the accusations are elaborated and subdivided to make the list longer; and some are rather curious. The Latins, for example, are charged with rejecting the writings of John Chrysostom, Basil and Gregory; with despising the Epistles of St Paul; with letting dogs and bears into their churches; with eating bears, jackals, tortoises, crows, rats and other abominable beasts; with allowing their dogs to lick the plates they eat off at

---

[7] *Opusculum contra Francos,* ed. J. Hergenroether, *Monumenta graeca ad Photium ejusque historiam pertinentia* (Ratisbon, 1869), pp. 62-71; A. Argyriou, "Remarques sur quelques listes grecques énumérant les hérésies latines," *Byzantinische Forschungen* 4 (1972) 9-30, especially pp. 13-15.

[8] J. Darrouzès, "Le Mémoire de Constantin Stilbès contre les Latins," *Revue des Études Byzantines* 21 (1963) 50-100 (text with French translation, pp. 61-91).

[9] Stilbes, ed. Darrouzès, c. 98, p. 86.

table; and with washing in their own urine, and even drinking it, like the Armenians.[10]

Tracts such as this, enthusiastically circulated by the monks, provided chapter and verse for popular belief about the enormities of western Christians. In 1261 after fifty-seven years of exile the Byzantines recovered their capital city and their church. The emperors and patriarchs in exile during those years had from time to time tried to come to terms with the popes, to win back their city by proposing a union of the churches. The negotiations had been conducted at a high level and they had seldom shown any sign of success. The ordinary people were not concerned with high diplomacy. Most of the clergy and the monks condemned the idea of a rapprochement with Rome as base treachery. Yet they found to their horror that their Emperor, Michael VIII Palaiologos, who had restored Constantinople to them in 1261, believed that such a rapprochement was vital to the security of his empire. The emperor must have known that he stood very little chance of persuading his people of the advantages of union with Rome barely two generations after the Fourth Crusade. But he could see no other way of averting a repetition of that crusade. By 1267 the plans for an expedition to rescue Constantinople from the schismatic Greeks and restore it to the Holy Roman church had been blessed by Pope Clement IV. It was to be led by Charles of Anjou who had emerged as King of the Two Sicilies and the pope's acknowledged champion. As an emperor trying to rebuild the ruined resources of his empire, Michael VIII was doubtful whether he could fend off the invasion by force of arms alone. His weapon of defence must therefore be diplomacy. The only power that could authorise a crusade from the west was the papacy. The pope alone could declare such an expeditionary war to be unjust. The only way to make him do so was to persuade him that the Greeks had seen the error of their ways and accepted obedience to Rome. The emperor's diplomatic purpose was to see that the pope was so persuaded.[11]

---

[10] Stilbes, ed. Darrouzès, cc. 7, 8, p. 62; cc. 55, 58, pp. 75, 76; c. 66, p. 79; c. 72, p. 80; c. 75, p. 81.

[11] On the background to the Union of Lyons, see: S. Runciman, *The Sicilian Vespers. A History of the Mediterranean World in the Late Thirteenth Century* (Cambridge, 1958); D. J. Geanakoplos, *Emperor Michael Palaeologus and the West, 1258-1282. A Study in Byzantine-Latin Relations* (Cambridge, Mass., 1959): D. M. Nicol, "The Greeks and the Union of the Churches: the Preliminaries to the Second Council of Lyons, 1261-1274," in *Medieval Studies presented to A. Gwyn, S.J.*, ed. J. A. Watt et al. (Dublin, 1961), pp. 454-480 (repr. in Nicol, *Byzantium: its Ecclesiastical History and Relations with the Western World* [London, 1972], no. v); B. Roberg, *Die Union zwischen der griechischen und der lateinischen Kirche auf dem II. Konzil von Lyon (1274)* (Bonn, 1964); D. M. Nicol, *The Last Centuries of Byzantium, 1261-1453* (London, 1972).

Such was the diplomatic and political background to the Second Council of Lyons in 1274. The negotiations were long and arduous. Opposition to the emperor's proposals in Constantinople and elsewhere was even stronger than he had expected. The terms on which Pope Clement IV insisted were worse than he had feared. There was to be no compromise on the issues of papal sovereignty and Greek disobedience. The emperor and his church were presented with a detailed profession of the Roman faith to every letter of which they must subscribe if they wished to be assured of papal protection against their enemies. It is an interesting document, not least because it became the model for all subsequent popes in their dealings with Byzantine emperors right up to the Council of Florence in 1439.[12] But it did not make life any easier for the Emperor Michael VIII. In the end he was able to send a small delegation from Constantinople to Lyons. Their members were far from representative of the Byzantine church or people. They took with them the required profession of faith signed by the emperor. There was no discussion and no debate at the Council. The delegates merely swore an oath of obedience to the See of Rome and, on 6 July 1274, the reunion of the Greek church under Rome was declared to have occurred. When they got back to Constantinople the storm broke. They and the emperor who had sent them were denounced and reviled as traitors to the faith. The Patriarch Joseph, who had condemned the whole exercise, had to be removed from office. He became the symbol and the soul of the opposition. He was replaced by John Bekkos, a cleric who had convinced himself that the Roman creed and doctrine were not entirely unacceptable. In later years Bekkos was to be labelled as the arch-heretic who, along with his emperor, had sullied the purity of the Orthodox faith.

The emperor was driven to conducting a reign of terror, persecution, imprisonment and torture to stifle or dissuade the opponents of the Union of Lyons after 1274. The facts are well enough known from the Byzantine historians of the time and from the later hagiographies and eulogies of those who courted martyrdom in their defiance of the emperor. The popes were well informed of what was happening partly through their agents in Constantinople, and partly because the emperor wanted them to know, so that they would be impressed by his devotion to the cause of union. The ranks of the anti-unionists were by no means confined to the xenophobic rabble of the streets. Several members of the aristocracy, of the emperor's own family, were thrown into prison for their high principles and eloquent opposition.

---

[12] Letter of Clement IV (4 March 1267), in A. L. Taŭtu, *Acta Urbani IV, Clementis IV, Gregorii X (1261-1276)*, Pontificia Commissio ad redigendum CIC orientalis, Fontes, ser. 3, V, 1 (Vatican City, 1953), no. 23, pp. 61-69.

The monks, being those most violently opposed to the emperor's policy, were singled out for specially violent treatment. It became impossible, as one historian says, for people to speak their minds freely. A samizdat literature was born. Pamphlets were circulated in secret, condemning the emperor and his false patriarch. Their authors were anonymous and could not be identified or found. A decree therefore went out that anyone caught with such a document, whether reading it to himself or to others, would be put to death if he did not at once burn it.[13] These propaganda leaflets were probably more seditious than apologetic in tone, aimed at libelling the emperor and his patriarch as traitors to the cause of the true Orthodox faith. Certainly the emperor himself had identified anti-unionism with treason. The charge could be turned against him. But some of the pamphlets were also designed to rally the faithful to martyrdom if necessary by enumerating the frightful heresies and enormities of Latin Christians.

A fascinating example of this kind of propaganda has survived in a document written between 1274 and 1282. It is written in a demotic form of Greek, and its popularity in the Orthodox world is attested by the number of its manuscripts and by the fact that it was early rendered into Serbian and Slav versions. It takes the form of a Dialogue between a Roman Cardinal and an Orthodox monk called Constantine.[14] Both are fictitious characters. The cardinal is said to have been one of twelve who had come to Constantinople. He is designated as the "Azymite," the "unleavened breader," whereas the pious Constantine is called Panagiotes, or all holy. The Dialogue between Panagiotes and Azymites takes place in the presence of the Emperor Michael VIII and the Patriarch John Bekkos. The patriarch is said to be wearing the Latin mitre and a ring on one finger, "which is the sign of the pope." The emperor holds the bridle of a mule. The mule carries a casket holding an icon of the pope, which the emperor venerates before entering his palace. The twelve cardinals who accompany him then announce that they have been sent by the pope "so that all Christians may partake of the

---

[13] George Pachymeres, *De Michaele Palaeologo*, VI.24 (ed. I. Bekker [Bonn, 1835], 1: 491-492).

[14] Partial text in A. Vasiliev, *Anecdota graeco-byzantina* (Moscow, 1893), 1: 179-188; full text in N. Krasnoselčev, *Letopis istoriko-filologičeskago obŝŝestva pri novorossijskom Universitete*, Viz. otd. (Odessa, 1896), 3: 295-328. M. Concasty, "La fin d'un dialogue contre les Latins azymites d'après le Paris. Suppl. gr. 1191," in *Akten des XI. Internationalen Byzantinistenkongresses München 1958* (Munich, 1960), pp. 86-89. Cf. Argyriou, "Remarques," pp. 21-23; D. J. Geanakoplos, "A Greek Libellus against Religious Union with Rome after the Council of Lyons (1274)," in Geanakoplos, *Interaction of the "Sibling" Byzantine and Western Cultures in the Middle Ages and Italian Renaissance (330-1600)* (New Haven, 1976), pp. 156-170.

communion of the unleavened bread" — which is, says the anonymous author, a manifestly heretical practice. The first part of the Dialogue which then begins between Panagiotes and Azymites, the Greek and the Latin, is a truly remarkable mishmash of half popular, half learned superstitions and ideas on theology, on cosmology, on the Trinity, the Incarnation, the after-life and the shape and structure of the heavens and the earth. They seem to be drawn from many sources, from the Scriptures and the Fathers, from apocryphal versions of the former and misunderstandings of the latter, from the Pseudo-Dionysios, from the sixth-century Cosmography of Cosmas Indicopleustes, but above all from the Book of Revelation. There is much that is mystifying but little that is palpably anti-Latin in this part of the Dialogue; though there are moments when it seems that Panagiotes is deliberately mocking the scholastic method of argument, which most Byzantines felt to be inapplicable to theology. The Cardinal asks him, for example: "How many tips does my beard have?" To which Panagiotes replies: "Tell me how many roots there are and I will tell you how many they are at the tip."

The second part of the Dialogue, however, provides a further catalogue of what the Greeks popularly believed to be aberrations in the creed, ritual and customs of the Latins. There are about thirty, some of them new. The Latins are accused of belittling the status of the Virgin by calling her simply a saint instead of the Theotokos, the Mother of God; and of making the sign of the Cross with only two fingers and the wrong way round. The dialogue develops into a near monologue as Panagiotes warms to his theme. The Latins are charged, as they had been before, with eating strangled meat; with eating hedgehogs and other polluted creatures; and with all manner of irregularities in the matter of fasting during Lent. The question of the celibacy of the clergy drives Panagiotes to some particularly scurrilous accusations, to the general effect that it is better to marry than to burn, better to have married priests than priests who resort to concubines and make hypocritical confession of their sins. He also complains of the brutish behaviour of Latin priests with respect to the Liturgy. They are not above stuffing the host into their belts or trousers and then going to relieve themselves or meet a woman. They think it no sin to celebrate the Eucharist twice a day and five or ten times a night, popping off to the lavatory in between whiles and returning unwashed to the altar. The Byzantines never understood the western practice of saying numerous masses for the dead. But the grosser charges invented by Pana-giotes reflect a general Byzantine distaste for what was felt to be the base materialism and insensitivity of the Latins in religious affairs. The document concludes with the moral victory of the pious Greek over the Azymite. He anathematizes and lays his curse upon the emperor, the patriarch and the cardinals, upon all unleavened-breaders, all Latin heretics and all pro-unionist Greeks. He is thereupon sentenced to death; and at the end the unknown author of the text awards his hero the crown of martyrdom.

There were martyrs in plenty for the cause of Orthodoxy in the years after 1274. The fictitious Constantine Panagiotes, who so trounced the cardinal in his one-sided debate, claimed to have been a pupil of Manuel Holobolos, whom he praises as the "champion of the Christian people," that is of Orthodoxy. Holobolos, as we know from more reputable sources and from his own learned writings, was Rector of the Patriarchal Academy in Constantinople and court orator to the emperor. He was far too intelligent a man to believe half the nonsense allegedly retailed by his alleged pupil. He had indeed favoured the cause of union with Rome at the outset. It was he who drafted the first text of a letter from his emperor to Pope Clement IV in 1267, though he suggested that union would be better achieved by means of an oecumenical council than by the fiat of the pope. Yet when he declared himself opposed to the Union of Lyons in 1274 he was mercilessly punished for his sincerity. The emperor exiled him to a monastery in Nicaea and then had him brought back to Constantinople to be humiliated in public. Along with ten others Holobolos was festooned with sheep's entrails and flogged through the streets of the city and round the church of St. Sophia.[15] The historian of the time tells many other similarly grisly tales of how the emperor dealt with those who opposed him. His intention was to make examples of them. His achievement was to produce a new cloud of witnesses and confessors for the purest and most inflexible and uncompromising Orthodoxy. Some of the new martyrs who suffered under Michael VIII are commemorated as such in the Orthodox church to this day.

In 1872 a martyrs' memorial was erected in the courtyard of the monastery of Zographou on Mount Athos. It is still there. It commemorates the twenty-six monks who were burnt alive six centuries earlier for their refusal to accept the Union of Lyons in 1274. The story went, and still goes, that the Emperor Michael VIII took soldiers to the Holy Mountain to enforce the union with Rome. The monks who resisted were punished. The monks of Zographou had shut themselves up in the tower of their monastery. The soldiers set fire to it on 10 October 1276. The rebels were incinerated. High on the cliff face of the southernmost tip of Athos, above the monastery of the Great Lavra, there is a cave, known as the Cave of the Wicked Dead or the Excommunicated Ones. Again the story goes that when the emperor Michael gave orders that the Liturgy was to be celebrated according to the Latin rite on the Holy Mountain, the monks of the Great Lavra gave in; although a mist

---

[15] Pachymeres, *De Michaele Palaeologo*, v. 20 (1: 392-394).

rolled down from the mountain to envelop their church every time they took the unleavened bread and recited the *Filioque*. When the union was renounced in 1282 these "apostate" monks died and were buried; and when, as is the custom on Mount Athos, their remains were dug up three years later, it was found that their bodies were black and swollen, their skin stretched tight like drums. They had failed to disintegrate. Their hair, teeth and nails were still growing. So they were placed in this inaccessible cave; and there they still lie, wrapped in cocoons of hair, their nails growing through their flesh.[16]

Such incorruptibility of the flesh could indeed be a sign of sanctity; but combined with the drum-like tautness of the skin it was sure evidence that a man had died in heresy. The same fate befell the Emperor Michael himself. It was true that his diplomacy had helped to save his empire from its western enemies. But he was not given a hero's burial when he died. His church and his people could never forgive him having supped with the heretical Latin Christians. Once again the story goes that when the emperor died in his camp in Thrace on a cold December night in 1282, his son Andronikos ordered that the body be left unburied on the hillside, though covered with a mound of earth to protect it from wild animals. There it lay for some time, "a plaything and a laughing stock," as one writer puts it.[17] Later it was laid to rest in a tomb in the monastery of the Saviour at Selymbria; and there, a hundred years later, it was still to be seen, uncorrupted, bloated and blown up like a drum.[18] Michael VIII was never given a state funeral in Constantinople. Nor was his name ever added to the list of right-minded emperors commemorated in the Synodikon of Orthodoxy. Not even his son and heir Andronikos dared to suggest that his father might be forgiven. His widow Theodora was obliged to make a public recantation and profession of her Orthodox faith and to swear that she would never seek a proper burial for her husband's corpse.[19]

[16] S. Binon, *Les origines légendaires et l'histoire de Xéropotamou et de Saint-Paul de l'Athos*, Bibliothèque du Muséon 13 (Louvain, 1942), pp. 110-113; J. Anastasiou, Ὁ θρυλούμενος διωγμὸς τῶν ἁγιορειτῶν ὑπὸ τοῦ Μιχαὴλ Η' τοῦ Παλαιολόγου καὶ τοῦ Ἰωάννου Βέκκου (Thessalonike, 1963) ; R. M. Dawkins, *The Monks of Athos* (London, 1936), pp. 297-307.

[17] Theodore Agallianos, *Dialogue with a Monk against the Latins*, in Dositheos of Jerusalem, Τόμος Χαρᾶς (Jassy, 1705), p. 626; Pachymeres, *De Andronico Palaeologo*, I.37 (2: 107-108); Nikephoros Gregoras, *Byzantina Historia*, VI.1 (ed. L. Schopen [Bonn, 1829], 1: 159).

[18] Philotheos of Selymbria, *Oratio in Sanctum Agathonicum*, in *PG* 154: 1237-1238. Cf. P. Magdalino, "Byzantine Churches of Selymbria," *Dumbarton Oaks Papers* 32 (1978) 309-318, especially pp. 314-315.

[19] D. M. Nicol, "The Byzantine Reaction to the Second Council of Lyons, 1274," in *Studies in Church History* 7, ed. G. J. Cuming and D. Baker (Cambridge, 1971), pp. 137-138 (repr. in Nicol, *Byzantium: its Ecclesiastical History...* [London, 1972], no. VI); Ruth

How far can one believe these tales? A major difficulty in probing the roots of popular piety, sentiment, or superstition in Byzantine society is that nearly all the surviving literature is written in a highly artificial and sophisticated Greek. The historians who narrate the reign of Michael VIII, George Pachymeres and Nikephoros Gregoras, never stoop so low as to write the spoken Greek of their time or to record the opinions of the man in the street. Even the saints' lives are for the most part, and quite deliberately, expressed in a stylised Greek which the common man must have found more baffling than edifying, though he may have enjoyed listening to its beautiful cadences. The tales about the persecution of the monks on Athos and the Cave of the Wicked Dead may have grown wilder with the telling in oral tradition. Legends have their own momentum in the enclosed world of the Holy Mountain. The tales of the makeshift burial of the Emperor Michael and of the incorruptibility of his bloated corpse might also be dismissed as no more than popular superstition. Yet the story of his burial is recorded as sober fact by the erudite historians; and the drum-like quality of his corpse is attested as observable fact by a learned bishop in the fourteenth century and a pious scholar in the fifteenth century.[20]

Similarly, the tales about the persecution of the anti-unionist monks on Mount Athos have a basis of truth and fact which can now be disentangled from the overgrowth of legend. The legend has it that the emperor himself visited Athos accompanied by his Patriarch John Bekkos, on their way back from the west after the Council of Lyons. Some versions say that the pope was with them. They visited a number of the great monasteries, massacring those monks who refused to subscribe to the Latin heresies and burning and pillaging their monasteries. We have seen what happened at Zographou and at the Great Lavra. At Xeropotamou the monks were so terrified that they agreed to celebrate the Eucharist with unleavened bread, whereupon God arranged an earthquake which buried them all under the ruins of their monastery.[21] These tales were repeated and elaborated in later years by generations of pious Orthodox monks in praise of those before them who had

---

Macrides, "Saints and Sainthood in the Early Palaiologan Period," in *The Byzantine Saint*, ed. S. Hackel, Studies Supplementary to Sobornost 5 (London, 1981), p. 78; J. Gouillard, "Le Synodikon de l'Orthodoxie: édition et commentaire," *Travaux et Mémoires* 2 (1967) 97.

[20] Pachymeres, loc. cit.; Gregoras, v.7 (1: 153); Philotheos of Selymbria, loc. cit.; Theodore Agallianos, loc. cit. Only the pro-unionist monk Manuel Kalekas is on record as having refuted the story, in his tract *Adversus Graecos*, in *PG* 152: 211.

[21] Sp. Lambros, "Τὰ Πάτρια τοῦ Ἁγίου Ὄρους," *Neos Hellenomnenon* 9 (1912) 157-161; J. Koder, "Patres Athonenses a Latinophilis occisi sub Michaele VIII," *Jahrbuch der österreichischen Byzantinistik* 18 (1969) 79-88. Cf. Binon, *Les origines*; Anastasiou, *Ὁ θρυλούμενος*.

won crowns of martyrdom in defence of the true faith. Yet there is an element of fact at the root of them.

It is known that the Emperor Michael VIII issued a decree to the monks of Athos ordering them to conform to the terms of the Union of Lyons. The text of their reply is also known and has been published. It is a letter to the emperor from all the Hagiorites as a profession of faith "when he was urging them by main force and contrary to reason to unite with the Italians, who remain incorrigibly and irremediably in heresy." It is a verbose document, outlining and refuting the well-known aberrations of the Latins. Some of the monks followed it with a second letter addressed to the synod of bishops in Constantinople. The content is similar, though the conclusion is still more emphatic. The "Italians" are described as being "completely atheist." Both of these documents were clearly written before the persecution began.[22] The earliest and the most factual account of the emperor's punishment of recalcitrant monks on Athos is contained in a third document which can be dated to the year 1276. It was written by a monk called Nikephoros and it tells of the emperor's decree that the union with Rome was to be universally accepted under pain of imprisonment. The monks refused to obey. When he heard that they had gone so far as to cease commemorating his name in their prayers, the emperor sent in the troops. There were mass arrests, abbots were rounded up and sent in chains to Constantinople; monks were stripped and driven into exile. Nikephoros and his fellow monk Clement were among those taken on a sixteen-day trek to the capital to stand trial before the emperor. For five and a half months they were subjected to threats and torture. They refused to give in, and the emperor finally handed them over to the discretion of the pope's legate. A Venetian ship, on which they suffered still further ill treatment, took them to Acre where the papal legate threatened them with death and damnation if they would not retract their errors. He arranged for them to discuss their differences with some Latin priests, who tried to enlighten them on the subject of Purgatory. After forty-eight days it was clear that they were beyond redemption and the legate sentenced them to exile in the French Kingdom of Cyprus. There the story abruptly ends with a brief statement that both monks were eventually set at liberty by the Emperor Michael, a conclusion that deprived Nikephoros of his cherished hope of martyrdom.[23]

[22] M. Živojinović, "Sveta Gora i Lionska Unija (Mount Athos and the Union of Lyons)," *Zbornik Radova Vizantološkog Instituta* 18 (1978) 141-154; *Actes de Lavra*, IV, ed. P. Lemerle, A. Guillou, N. Svoronos, Denis Papachryssanthou, Archives de l'Athos 11 (Paris, 1982), pp. 11-14. The texts are published in V. Laurent and J. Darrouzès, *Dossier grec de l'Union de Lyon (1273-1277)*, Archives de l'Orient chrétien 16 (Paris, 1976), pp. 376-403 and 404-423.

[23] *Actes de Lavra*, IV, p. 13; text in Laurent-Darrouzès, *Dossier grec*, pp. 486-507.

Mount Athos was not the only breeding-ground of martyrs for the cause. The monastery on Mount Galesion near Ephesos also produced its anti-unionist heroes. Prominent among them was the Patriarch of Constantinople, Joseph, a man of mild and gentle character who had personal friends among the Franciscans in the city. Joseph objected to the fact that union with Rome was being forced upon his flock without proper consultation and without the correct procedure of an oecumenical council. In his position as patriarch he felt it his duty to protest. But his public protestations were drafted for him by a monk of less serene temperament called Job Iasites, a notorious anti-unionist and demagogue. Joseph was relieved of his office and replaced as patriarch by the more amenable John Bekkos. In 1282, when the union was over, he was brought back to his patriarchate in triumph. By then he was old and sick and he died a few months later. Unlike the emperor who had dismissed him, however, Joseph was acclaimed as a hero and honoured as a Confessor. As such he is commemorated to this day in the Orthodox calendar.[24]

Another leading hero of the Orthodox cause from the same monastic stable near Ephesos was Meletios, still commemorated as a Confessor every 19 January. Meletios was a much travelled and exemplary ascetic and his life is well documented. The historian Pachymeres records his sufferings; there is a hagiography of him which narrates some of his miracles as well as his martyrdom; and there are his own writings.[25] The longest of these, written during his imprisonment, is described as a Florilegium of the Old and the New Testaments. It is divided into seven books and is all in verse, of a kind. The third book, as yet unpublished, enumerates yet again the errors and malpractices of the Latins in forty chapters. It is the longest such list since that compiled by Stilbes, but it contains little that is new. Its general conclusion is that, since the Latins are heretics, communion with them must be forbidden, and those who opt for union with them are endangering their own souls. The Epilogue to the whole work represents a call to arms and an invitation to martyrdom.[26] It was to fight on the side of truth, as his biographer says, that Meletios left the spiritual comforts of his ascetic life to

---

[24] Joseph is now commemorated on 30 October, though the date does not accord with the date of his death (23 March 1283). See Laurent-Darrouzès, *Dossier grec*, p. 525 and n. 2; Macrides, "Saints," pp. 79-81.

[25] On Meletios the Confessor, see Pachymeres, *De Michaele Palaeologo*, VI.17-18 (1: 462-463); *De Andronico Palaeologo*, I.3 (2: 17-18). His *Life* was edited by Sp. Lavriotes in Γρηγόριος ὁ Παλαμᾶς 5 (1921) 582-584, 609-624, and Ὁ Ἄθως 2 (1928) 9-11. Cf. Macrides, "Saints," pp. 81-82.

[26] On the *Florilegium* (*Apanthismos*) of Meletios, see Argyriou, "Remarques," pp. 23-24; Nicol, "Byzantine Reaction," pp. 132-133; Laurent-Darrouzès, *Dossier grec*, pp. 104-112 (part of the text of the third book is printed there, pp. 554-563).

go to Constantinople about 1275. He went with a fellow monk from Mount Galesion called Galaktion. Their outspoken opposition to the union quickly brought them to the notice of the emperor. They accused him to his face of heresy. They were thrown into prison and then shipped to exile on the island of Skyros. Such brazen confrontations between monks and emperors had been a stock in trade of hagiographers since the iconoclast persecutions. It was the kind of saintly bravado that the pious public loved to hear. The emperor, however, then decided to send Meletios to Rome along with some papal legates who were going home, so that the pope could see a real live anti-unionist and take appropriate measures. The pope, Gregory X, kept Meletios in Rome for over a year before sending him back more in pity than in anger. He rejoined his friend Galaktion in exile on Skyros. Later they were both transferred to prison in Constantinople where, after hideous tortures bravely born, Meletios had his tongue cut out to silence his outspokenness and Galaktion was blinded. Both survived, however; and when the union with the heretics was solemnly renounced in 1282, both were set free to be hailed as heroes and to assist in the ritual purification of the cathedral of St. Sophia.

Contemporary observers on both sides were aware that popular feeling against the union and against the Latins was deliberately whipped up by the monks. Humbertus de Romanis, General of the Dominican Order at the time of the Council of Lyons, remarks that "the errors and heresies of the Greeks are nurtured and inspired particularly by those whom they call their calogeri (monks)." [27] The historian Gregoras, while commending those whose brave opposition to their emperor was based on reason and principle, writes scathingly of the much greater rabble of hair-shirted ignoramuses who travelled around stirring up trouble and pretending to be prophets in districts where they were safe from the emperor's agents. [28] Nonetheless, the common people of Byzantium felt closer to their monks than to their secular clergy. The monk was thought to be a living icon, a medium through which humble people could acquire a measure of grace. He was by the nature of his higher calling in constant touch with the divine; he might be blessed with supernatural gifts; and as a rule he presented the most conservative and so the most stable element in an unstable world.

Many of the monks and clergy were bitterly opposed to the Emperor Michael VIII before the question of union with Rome was ever raised; for they thought him to be a usurper and deplored the crime by which he had reached

---

[27] Humbertus de Romanis, *Opus Tripartitum*, in J. D. Mansi, *Sacrorum Conciliorum nova et amplissima collectio* 24 (Venice, 1780), col. 126.

[28] Gregoras, v.2 (1: 127-128).

his throne. There was a strong faction in the Byzantine church known as the Arsenites in memory of the Patriarch Arsenios who had had the courage to excommunicate the emperor in punishment for that crime. The Arsenites refused to recognise the appointment and the authority of subsequent patriarchs, including the anti-unionist Patriarch Joseph; and church and society were deeply divided by the Arsenite schism. Yet in the circumstances after the union of Lyons these differences were temporarily forgotten. The Arsenites joined forces with the anti-unionists in the greater cause of defending the purity of Orthodoxy against its adulterers. The monastic party was also of course defending the principle that the emperor had no right to dictate to the church in matters of faith and doctrine. It was a principle which the monks had always strenuously upheld since the days of the iconoclast emperors who had likewise tried to impose their will upon the church, and since most Byzantine bishops were former monks the hierarchy shared their view. Here lay one of the areas of misunderstanding between the leaders of eastern and western Christians. The popes, from their scant knowledge of the history of the Byzantine church, vainly believed that the emperors in Constantinople were authoritarian caesaropapists who could bend their bishops to their will; and that if the emperor saw the light in the matter of union with Rome so would his submissive clergy and people. The emperor for his part vainly hoped that the popes would be content with a declaration and a show of union. As he pointed out to his bishops, Rome was a long way away from Constantinople. It was most unlikely that the popes would ever make the long and hazardous journey to come and assert their primacy and the authority that they claimed. The commemoration of their names in the Liturgy was a mere formality. It would be better to accept some superficial compromises than to unleash another Fourth Crusade upon Byzantium. The emperor protested that he would never force anyone to add "one accent or one iota" to the Orthodox creed.[29] Yet in the end, as his bishops were well aware, he was required to subscribe to every letter of the Roman creed and to commit the gravest of all doctrinal sins by professing the double procession of the Holy Spirit.

This was the hardest pill for the Byzantines to swallow. It headed the list of most of their catalogues of Latin heresies. The primacy of the See of Rome, even the papal claim to universal jurisdiction over the church, were arguable points. But there could be no possible argument and no compromise over the illegal and heretical addition to the creed of the *Filioque*. As a theological issue it may have been above the heads of most ordinary Christians. But the

---

[29] Pachymeres, *De Michaele Palaeologo*, v.18 (1: 387).

monks, pamphleteers and propagandists made sure that the message was understood in general terms. In later years, when the union was no more, the former Patriarch John Bekkos, then in exile, admitted that it had brought not peace but a sword. He recalled the famous remark of Gregory of Nyssa, that one could not go to the baker or the barber without hearing arguments about the relationship of the Son to the Father. So it had been in the years after 1274. "Children in school," says Bekkos, "women chatting over their distaffs and spindles, farmers and labourers, all of them are obsessed with but one subject in their minds and conversations, the Procession of the Holy Spirit from the Son." "What can one say," he writes, "when women and children still in the nursery, ignorant farmers and untutored navvies all cry criminal to anyone who so much as whispers about the union of the churches." His words are echoed by the historian Pachymeres: "Apart from the emperor and the patriarch and some of their close associates, everyone loathed the union, the more so as the emperor tried to enforce it with outrageous penalties." [30]

One could conclude that the fanatically anti-unionist monks did their work well and spread their propaganda to good effect. Yet the fanaticism of the monks alone is not enough to explain the Byzantine hostility. Many of those who suffered for their opposition were far from being simple farmers and labourers. They were well-bred members of the aristocracy, educated men and women who could make up their own minds on theological as well as political issues. One example may suffice. The emperor's niece Theodora Raoulaina was a woman of great culture and learning. She possessed a fine library in Constantinople and copied manuscripts with her own hand. Yet she was a confessed Arsenite and a vigorous opponent of the union of Lyons, for which she was harried and imprisoned. Later in her life she wrote a hagiography of the two celebrated martyrs of the iconoclast period, Theodore and Theophanes. She must surely have had in mind the fate of her two brothers-in-law, Manuel and Isaac Raoul, who suffered and died for the cause of Orthodoxy in similar circumstances at the hands of the Emperor Michael VIII.[31] The unionist Patriarch John Bekkos sadly acknowledged that the anti-unionists came from all walks of life, from the emperor's own family, from the senate, the bishops, the leaders of the church, the priests, the monks and the laity. But he was particularly grieved and shocked that there were so

---

[30] John Bekkos (Beccus), *De Injustitia qua affectus est, a proprio throno ejectus*, in *PG* 143: 984; cf. cols. 952-953. Pachymeres, *De Michaele Palaeologo*, VI.30 (1: 505).

[31] On Theodora Raoulaina, see D. M. Nicol, *The Byzantine Family of Kantakouzenos (Cantacuzenus) ca. 1100-1460*, Dumbarton Oaks Studies 11 (Washington, DC, 1968), no. 14, pp. 16-18; Alice-Mary M. Talbot, "Bluestocking Nuns: Intellectual Life in the Convents of Late Byzantium," *Harvard Ukrainian Studies* 7 (1983) 604-618 (=*Okeanos. Essays presented to Ihor Ševčenko on his Sixtieth Birthday*, ed. C. Mango and O. Pritsak).

many women among them. This, he said, must surely be the work of the Devil.[32]

Nothing illustrates more vividly the depth of Byzantine popular feeling against the Latins than the ceremony enacted to purify and fumigate the cathedral of St. Sophia after the death of the Emperor Michael. As early as 1215 Pope Innocent III had complained that the Greeks had come to hate the Latins to such an extent that if Latin priests had celebrated mass on their altars the Greeks would not use them for their own sacrament until they had been washed clean of this pollution.[33] In 1261, when Constantinople was recovered from the Latins, the Emperor Michael had made a great show of refurbishing the sanctuary of St. Sophia and installing at his own expense an entirely new altar.[34] After his death, when Orthodoxy was again restored, the procedure was even more elaborate. The prayers prescribed for the dedication of a new church were recited in the cathedral. The naves, narthex, walls, columns and icons were sprinkled with holy water; and the pollution of the Latins was washed away. The monk Galaktion who had been blinded for his obstinate faith was led into the church to take his part in the purification; and the congregation also sought to be cleansed.[35] The Byzantines had always lived in a world which made no clearly defined distinction between things spiritual and things temporal. Heresy was popularly believed to be a contamination. It could be caught like a disease. It must be guarded against like a psychosomatic infection. The consequences for those who succumbed to it were to be seen in their bloated corpses after death.

The Byzantines disliked the Latins for a variety of obvious reasons. But they were also afraid of them. They were afraid of losing their own identity through the influence of what they called *latinismos* or westernisation. Niketas Choniates had said, "Their hatred for us is so extreme and our antipathy to them is so excessive that there are no feelings of humanity between us." [36] To believe as the Franks or Latins believed was to imperil one's immortal soul by being latinised. One of the imperial envoys returning from Lyons in 1274 was taunted with the words, "You have become a Frank." [37] The biographer of the monk and martyr Meletios opens his

---

[32] John Bekkos, in Laurent-Darrouzès, *Dossier grec*, pp. 464-465.

[33] Fourth Lateran Council (1215), cap. 4 (*De Superbia Graecorum contra Latinos*), in Mansi, *Sacrorum Conciliorum ... collectio*, 22: 989-990. Odo of Deuil had indignantly commented on this practice in the twelfth century. Eudes de Deuil, *La Croisade de Louis VII Roi de France*, ed. H. Waquet, Documents relatifs à l'histoire des Croisades (Paris, 1949), p. 42.

[34] Pachymeres, *De Michaele Palaeologo*, VII.2 (1: 172-173).

[35] Pachymeres, *De Andronico Palaeologo*, I.4 (2: 19-20).

[36] Niketas Choniates, ed. van Dieten, p. 568.

[37] Cited by Geanakoplos, *Emperor Michael*, p. 271.

account of the union by saying, "There looms over our church a deadly and destructive storm cloud, Latinism ... Latinism was our emperor's obsession." [38] Those who had lived through the aftermath of the Fourth Crusade knew that the westerners were out to latinise them, to take them over spiritually as well as physically. Even by 1274 there were those who felt and said that the Sultan's turban would be preferable to the Latin mitre. A Dialogue between a patriarch and an emperor which was invented at the time has the patriarch say, "I care nothing for those who do harm to my body, but I repulse those who damage my soul. As human beings we are living temples of the Lord. If we are ruled by infidels we come to no harm. But if we take communion with the Italians then we pay the extreme penalty, for we court the danger that threatens belief itself. Let the Saracen be my master in material things, but let no Italian walk with me in spirit. With the former I have no thought in common, though I be his subject; with the latter, if I accept agreement on the faith, I shall separate myself from my God, embracing that which God repels." [39] The monk Meletios put this passage or this sentiment into verse in his chapter against the Latins: "The infidel I can serve in the flesh without having to agree with him. But if I agree with the Latin in the faith then I shall suffer a mortal sickness of the soul." [40]

It was with the germ of these feelings in their minds that the Greek clergy and people of Constantinople had written to Pope Innocent III in 1206, just after the Fourth Crusade and the establishment of the Latin Empire. [41] They accepted that they were now a conquered race, politically and materially subject to a Latin, western emperor, whom they were prepared to serve. But they saw no reason why they should also be spiritually subjected to a Latin patriarch. They wrote not querulously or bitterly but politely and with due reverence to the great pope. All they asked was his permission for them to elect a Patriarch of Constantinople who would be of their own race, speech and faith. Under his spiritual leadership they would feel secure; and they would then ask the pope to convene a council of the church at which Greeks and Latins could discuss and resolve the differences that divided them. "Why," they asked, "do you choose to order us around like brute beasts, compelling us unquestioningly to change our ways without giving us a chance

---

[38] *Life of Meletios*, ed. Lavriotes, pp. 617, 620.

[39] This Dialogue was formerly attributed (as its title proposes) to the Patriarch Michael III of Anchialos and the Emperor Manuel I Komnenos in the twelfth century. But see now Laurent-Darrouzès, *Dossier grec*, pp. 45-52, and text pp. 346-375, especially cap. 28, pp. 365-367.

[40] Meletios, *Florilegium*, in Laurent-Darrouzès, *Dossier grec*, p. 56, ll. 234-236.

[41] Letter of the Greek clergy to Innocent III, in Nicholas Mesarites, ed. Heisenberg [see above, note 6], pp. 63-66.

to speak and to exchange reasoned argument with you so that the truth in divine matters may be revealed?"[42] It appears that the pope made no response to these letters. It has been said that he thus lost a great opportunity for "a grand conciliatory gesture" towards the church and people of Constantinople.[43] Yet such a gesture would have run counter to Innocent's firm belief in his own authority and his own ideals. It was really not necessary for him to reply to such tiresome requests. The Greeks must surely know that, in an ideal world, only the pope had the right to appoint a Patriarch of Constantinople; and, as Pope Clement IV was later to put it to the Emperor Michael VIII, there was no need to call a council for discussion of the faith, confirmed as it was by the authority of so much holy writ, by the judgement of so many saints, and by the clear definition of so many Roman Pontiffs.[44] The Byzantines may perhaps be forgiven for not appreciating the lofty motives of Pope Innocent III and for not sharing his persistent delusion that the end had justified the means, that through the establishment of the Latin Empire the Lord's work had been accomplished by the return of the Greek church to the Apostolic See.[45] They were after all the victims of the practical application of the high ideal of universal papal sovereignty.

---

[42] Letter of the Greek people to Innocent III, in *PG* 140: 293-298, especially col. 296. Cf. D. M. Nicol, "The Papal Scandal," in *Studies in Church History*, 13. *The Orthodox Churches and the West*, ed. D. Baker (Oxford, 1976), pp. 141-168, especially pp. 148-149.

[43] S. Runciman, *The Eastern Schism* (Oxford, 1955), pp. 154-155.

[44] Letter of Clement IV (4 March 1267), ed. A. L. Tăutu, *Acta* (see above, note 12), no. 23, pp. 61-69. Cf. J. Gill, SJ, "Innocent III and the Greeks: Aggressor or Apostle?" in *Relations between East and West in the Middle Ages*, ed. D. Baker (Edinburgh, 1973), pp. 95-108 (repr. in Gill, *Church Union: Rome and Byzantium (1204-1453)* [London, 1979], no. II).

[45] Gill, pp. 100-101.

Part Three

Papal Sources

11

Of Sleep and Sleeplessness:
The Papacy and Law, 1150-1300

Giulio Silano

Toward the middle of the twelfth century, Bernard of Clairvaux, in the apparent belief that his former subject needed instruction about the nature of his office, wrote the *De consideratione* for the benefit of Pope Eugenius.[1] In this treatise, while giving expression to his high view of the papacy, Bernard also identified the tendencies which he found worrisome in that institution. Bernard's worries might be said to find their focus in the increased "juridicization" of activity at the papal Curia, in the fact that the ever increasing amount of legal business to be transacted before the Pope allowed him no time for consideration, or even for sleep.[2] Eugenius is invited to wake up and

---

[1] Bernard of Clairvaux, *De consideratione*, ed. J. Leclercq and H. Rochais, *Sancti Bernardi Opera* (Roma, 1963), 3: 381-493. On St. Bernard and the papacy still instructive is B. Jacqueline, *Papauté et épiscopat selon S. Bernard de Clairvaux* (Saint-Lô, 1963); see also: S. Chodorow, *Christian Political Theory and Church Politics in the Mid-Thirteenth Century* (Berkeley, 1972), passim, but especially, for our topic, Appendix 2, pp. 260-265, on St. Bernard and law.

[2] *De consideratione*, I.3.4 (p. 397): "Quaeso te, quale est istud, de mane usque ad vesperam litigare aut litigantes audire? Et utinam sufficeret diei malitia sua! Non sunt liberae noctes. Vix relinquitur necessitati naturae, quod corpusculi pausationi sufficiat, et rursum ad iurgia surgitur. Dies diei eructat lites, et nox nocti indicat malitiam: usque adeo non est respirare in bonis, non est alternam capessere requiem, non vel rara interseri otia."

The Religious Roles of the Papacy: Ideals and Realities, 1150-1300, ed. Christopher Ryan, Papers in Mediaeval Studies 8 (Toronto: Pontifical Institute of Mediaeval Studies, 1989), pp. 343-361. © P.I.M.S., 1989.

shake off this yoke of misunderstood service which binds him to the decision of causes too petty for papal attention.[3]

That St. Bernard had a sublime view of the papacy cannot be doubted; for him, the Apostolic See is the refuge of the poor,[4] and is responsible for the unity, defense, and liberty of the Church;[5] the Pope is called *vicarius Petri* and, after Eugenius is made Pope, Bernard addresses him as *vicarius Christi*;[6] the power entrusted by Christ to Peter is what the Pope has at his own disposal,[7] and this same power, without reservation, is defined as *plenitudo potestatis*;[8] the holder of such plenitude of power is the highest judge from whom no further appeal may be made;[9] the Pope is the guardian of law and the Apostolic See is the seat of sovereign justice whose decisions are definitive.[10]

Bernard can define the Pope's functions in transported poetical and juridical language;[11] the Saint, nevertheless, remains profoundly aware of the

---

[3] Ibid., I.3.4 (pp. 397-398), 4.5 (pp. 398-399), and, especially, 6.7 (pp. 401-402), which, in part, states: "Audi tamen Apostolum, quid de huiusmodi sentiat: 'Sic non est inter vos sapiens,' ait ille, 'qui iudicet inter fratrem et fratrem?' Et infert: 'Ad ignominiam vobis dico: contemptibiliores qui sunt in ecclesia, illos constituite ad iudicandum.' (1 Cor. 6.5) Itaque, secundum Apostolum, indigne tibi usurpas tu, Apostolice, officium vile, gradum contemptibilium. Unde et dicebat Episcopus, Episcopum instruens: 'Nemo, militans Deo, implicat se negotiis saecularibus.' (2 Tim. 2.4)."

[4] Letter 351 (*PL* 182: 554); Jacqueline, *Papauté et épiscopat*, p. 8.

[5] Letter 358, to Callixtus II (*PL* 182: 560); Jacqueline, p. 7.

[6] For *vicarius Petri* see Letter 183 (*PL* 182: 345) and Letter 346 (*PL* 182: 551); for *vicarius Christi*, Letter 251 (*PL* 182: 451); Jacqueline, pp. 39-41.

[7] *Serm. in Cant., Sermo 69*, 4.5 (*PL* 183: 1114).

[8] Letter 131, 2 (*PL* 182: 286-287); Letter 239 (*PL* 182: 431).

[9] Cf. Letter 213 (*PL* 182: 378); Jacqueline, pp. 50-54.

[10] Letter 158, 1 (*PL* 182: 316); Jacqueline, pp. 56-58.

[11] Cf. Jacqueline, p. 61. The following address to Pope Eugenius, from *De cons.*, IV.7.23 (pp. 465-466), perhaps best illustrates the tension and sense of the beautiful which Bernard could bring to his description of the papal office: "Consideres ante omnia sanctam Romanam ecclesiam, cui Deo auctore praees, ecclesiarum matrem esse, non dominam; te vero non dominum episcoporum, sed unum ex ipsis, porro fratrem diligentium Deum et participem timentium eum. De cetero oportere te esse considera formam iustitiae, sanctimoniae speculum, pietatis exemplar, assertorem veritatis, fidei defensorem, doctorem gentium, christianorum ducem, amicum sponsi, sponsae paranymphum, cleri ordinatorem, pastorem plebium, magistrum insipientium, refugium oppressorum, pauperum advocatum, miserorum spem, tutorem pupillorum, iudicem viduarum, oculum caecorum, linguam mutorum, baculum senum, ultorem scelerum, malorum metum, bonorum gloriam, virgam potentium, malleum tyrannorum, regum patrem, legum moderatorem, canonum dispensatorem, sal terrae, orbis lumen, sacerdotem Altissimi, vicarium Christi, christum Domini, postremo deum Pharaonis. Intellige quae dico: dabit tibi Dominus intellectum. Ubi malitiae iuncta potentia est, aliquid tibi supra hominem praesumendum. Vultus tuus super facientes mala. Timeat spiritum irae tuae, qui hominem non veretur, gladium non formidat. Timeat orationem, qui admonitionem contempsit. Cui irasceris tu, Deum sibi iratum, non hominem putet. Qui te non audierit, auditurum Deum, et contra se, paveat."

danger that all the charisms which have been granted to Peter and his successors may be perverted by temptation. Chief among the temptations which Bernard thinks may beset Eugenius is that of confusing spiritual and earthly power, of exercising spiritual power as if it were earthly, and of not leaving to the earthly power that which properly belongs to it.[12] The chief safeguard which Eugenius may exercise against such a temptation is the clear recollection that his power is given to him for the sake of ministry, not of dominion (*ministerium*, not *dominium*).[13] This distinction can be usefully applied to the way in which some of the practices adopted by the papacy are working, or failing to do so: the Pope must hear cases, but they must not be heard in a worldly fashion, nor indiscriminately;[14] appeals belong to the Pope by his own unique primacy, but they may easily be abused if they are not regulated and limited, and heard merely because of the fruits they bring.[15] Especially virulent is Bernard's attack on papal grants of exemption, by which the natural relationship of ecclesial bodies is subverted for the sake of the exercise of mere power; although the Pope has the necessary power, its exercise by the interested grants of exemption is not suitable and, especially

[12] *De cons.*, 1.6.7, on the division of estates pertaining more properly to secular judges; some of the numerous passages, especially from *De cons.*, which treat of the proper mode of exercise of spiritual authority will be cited below.

[13] This distinction constitutes a continuous thread in the *De cons.*: II.6.9 (pp. 416-417): Eugenius has been elected Sovereign Pontiff for the sake of labour like a peasant's, not to rule, and has been given a hoe, not a scepter; II.6.10 (pp. 417-418): dominion is forbidden to the Apostles and to their successors; II.6.11 (pp. 418-419): if the Pope enjoys dominion, he does so by usurpation; III.1.2 (p. 432): the Pope is to preside, not rule, to administer, not own; IV.7.23 (pp. 465-466): the Roman Church is the mother of Churches, not their mistress (*domina*), and the Pope is not the lord of bishops, but one of them (see the complete text in n. 11 above).

[14] *De cons.*, 1.10.13 (pp. 408-409): "Agitentur causae, sed sicut oportet. Nam is modus, qui frequentatur, exsecrabilis plane, et qui, non dico Ecclesiam, sed nec forum deceret. Miror namque quemadmodum religiosae aures tuae audire sustinent huiusmodi disputationes advocatorum et pugnas verborum, quae magis ad subversionem quam ad inventionem proficiunt veritatis. Corrige pravum morem et praecide linguas vaniloquas, et labia dolosa claude. Hi sunt qui docuerunt linguas suas loqui mendacium, diserti adversus iustitiam, eruditi pro falsitate. Sapientes sunt ut faciant malum, eloquentes ut impugnent verum. Hi sunt qui instruunt a quibus fuerant instruendi, adstruunt non comperta, sed sua; struunt de proprio calumnias innocentiae, destruunt simplicitatem veritatis, obstruunt iudicii vias. Nihil ita absque labore manifestam facit veritatem, ut brevis et pura narratio. Ergo illas quas ad te necesse erit intrare causas — neque enim necesse erit omnes — diligenter, velim, sed breviter, decidere assuescas, frustratoriasque et venatorias praecide dilationes. Causa viduae intret ad te, causa pauperis et eius qui non habet quod det. Aliis alias multas poteris committere terminandas, quam plures nec dignas audientia iudicare. Quid enim opus est admittere illos, quorum peccata manifesta sunt praecedentia ad iudicium?"

[15] *De cons.*, III.2.6-10 (pp. 435-438); in the same place, Bernard has praise for the new figure of the judge delegate, who can hear appeals better and more easily than they may be heard in the Curia.

because there is no one to whom such grants may be appealed, Eugenius ought not to make them. Indeed, Bernard even doubts whether the Pope has the power to make these grants because by them justice is seen unjustly to take away rights which ought not to be violated; in contrast to what the Roman lawyers seemed to think of the will of the prince, Bernard thinks that the exercise of the Pope's will does not make the unlawful lawful.[16] In Bernard's view, Eugenius will be able to indulge in necessary consideration, and even to sleep at night, if both in his life and in his laws he remembers that he succeeds to the Apostles and not to Constantine or Justinian.[17]

On 3 March 1298, Pope Boniface VIII promulgated the *Liber sextus.* The letter of promulgation, *Sacrosanctae Romanae Ecclesiae*, begins with the assertion of the divine election of the Roman Church as head of all the Churches and as the foremost magistracy in the whole world.[18] Boniface,

[16] *De cons.*, III.4.14-18 (pp. 441-446) in which Eugenius is told that the intermediate powers in the Church also come from God and, therefore, have their own inalienable rights; the Pope may dispense, not dissipate. Bernard cites the Pope's own canons to remind Eugenius that bishops are also called to share in the responsibility for souls: ibid., II.8.16 (p. 424).

[17] *De cons.*, IV.2.3-4 (pp. 450-452): life at the Curia is criticized as being fitter for inheritors of Constantine than of Peter; I.4.5 (pp. 398-399): the Pope is harassed every day and finds no rest as the laws of Justinian, not the Lord's, resound throughout his palace.

[18] E. Friedberg, ed., *Corpus iuris canonici* (Leipzig, 1879; repr. Graz, 1959), 2: 934-935: "Bonifacius, episcopus servus servorum Dei, dilectis filiis doctoribus et scholaribus universis Bononiae commorantibus salutem et apostolicam benedictionem. Sacrosanctae Romanae ecclesiae, quam imperscrutabilis divinae providentiae altitudo universis dispositione incommutabili praetulit ecclesiis, et totius orbis praecipuum obtinere voluit magistratum, regimini praesidentes, curis sollicitamur continuis, et assidua meditatione urgemur, ut iuxta creditae nobis dispensationis officium subditorum commodis, in quorum prosperitate utique prosperamur, iugi, quantum nobis ex alto concessum fuerit, sollicitudinis studio intendamus. Amplectimur quippe voluntarios pro ipsorum quiete labores, et noctes quandoque transimus insomnes, ut scandala removeamus ab ipsis, et, quas humana natura, novas semper deproperans edere formas, lites quotidie invenire conatur, nunc antiquorum declaratione, nunc vero novorum editione iurium, prout nobis est possibile, reprimamus. Sane, quum post volumen decretalium, a felicis recordationis Gregorio Papa IX. praedecessore nostro tam provide quam utiliter compilatum, nonnullae ab eo et ab aliis Romanis Pontificibus successive super diversis dicerentur articulis editae decretales, de quarum aliquibus, an decretales existerent, earumque auctoribus dubitabatur sollicite in iudiciis et in scholis: nos ad, apicem summi pontificatus superna dispositione vocati, super hoc cum instantia requisiti a multis, ambiguitatem et incertitudinem huiusmodi, dispendium pluribus afferentem, omnino tollere, ac elucidare, quae de decretalibus ipsis teneri, quaeve deberent in posterum refutari, gratia suffragante divina pro utilitate publica desiderabiliter affectantes, per venerabiles fratres nostros Guillielmum archiepiscopum Ebrudunensem, Berengarium episcopum Biterensem, ac dilectum filium magistrum Richardum de Senis, sanctae Romanae ecclesiae vicecancellarium, iuris utriusque doctorem, decretales huiusmodi diligentius fecimus recenseri, et tandem, pluribus ex ipsis, quum vel temporales, aut sibi ipsis vel aliis iuribus contrariae, seu omnino superfluae viderentur, penitus resecatis, reliquas, quibusdam ex eis abbreviatis, et aliquibus in toto vel in parte mutatis, multisque correctionibus, detractionibus et additionibus, prout expedire vidimus, factis in ipsis, in unum librum cum nonnullis nostris constitutionibus, in quibus ad

called to the rule of this Church, is perpetually beset by the incessant preoccupation to bring about the prosperity of his subjects. For the sake of their rest, he willingly takes upon himself many cares and sometimes spends sleepless nights in order to remove scandals from their midst and to repress those disputes which human nature is ever prone to bring forth anew; the remedy for this ill will be the declaration of old laws and the making of new ones, insofar as it is granted to him from above. Because many decretals have been published since the compilation of Gregory IX's volume and the authenticity of many other decretals has been questioned, Boniface had entrusted to a commission of experienced jurists the examination of such decretals so that, after excision of the superfluous, the temporary, and the contradictory, and the correction of the rest, these might be collected together with some constitutions which he himself had published for the correction of customs and the peace of his subjects. These, published as the sixth book, are to be added to the five of Gregory's compilation and to be used in schools and judgements as the exclusive and authentic constitutions of all Popes since Gregory IX, except for those decretals and constitutions which have been specially reserved.

The ordinary gloss on the *Sext* was written at Bologna by Johannes Andreae, undoubtedly the foremost canon law commentator of the first half of the fourteenth century; his commentary on the constitution just described yields some interesting elements.[19] At the beginning of his commentary, the

---

correctionem morum subditorumque quietem multa statuuntur salubria, fructus uberes Deo propitio in domo Domini allatura, et plurima in iudiciis et extra frequentata dubia deciduntur, redigi mandavimus, et sub debitis titulis collocari. Quem librum, quinque libris aliis dicti voluminis decretalium anectendum, sextum censuimus nuncupari, ut idem volumen senarium, qui numerus est perfectus, librorum illo adiuncto numerum comprehendens, perfectam in rebus agendis formam tribuat et in moribus disciplinam. Nec sine causa morem praedecessorem nostrorum, qui, quum constitutiones aliquas promulgabant noviter, eas mandabant sub antiquarum serie situari, omisimus in hac parte servare. Haec enim fecimus, ne infinitos libros destrui, et alios non sine maximis dispendiis, laboribus et expensis de novo fieri oporteret. Universitati vestrae igitur per apostolica scripta mandamus, quatenus librum huiusmodi cum multa maturitate digestum, quem sub bulla nostra vobis transmittimus, prompto suscipientes affectu, eo utamini de cetero in iudiciis et in scholis, nullas alias praeter illas, quae inseruntur aut specialiter reservantur in eo, decretales aut constitutiones, a quibuscumque nostris praedecessoribus Romanis Pontificibus post editionem dicti voluminis promulgatas, recepturi ulterius aut pro decretalibus habituri." On the *Sext*'s composition and its place in the history of canonical codification, see G. Le Bras, Ch. Lefebvre, J. Rambaud, *L'âge classique 1140-1378. Sources et théories du droit*, Histoire du droit et des institutions de l'Église en Occident 7 (Paris, 1965), pp. 247-251.

[19] Citations of Johannes Andreae's gloss are from *Sextus Decretalium a Bonifacio octavo in concilio Lugdunensi editus, cum Epitomis, Divisionibus, et Glossa ordinaria Io. Andreae...* (Venetiis, 1572); punctuation, capitalization, and style of reference to the legal sources have been normalized. On Johannes Andreae, şee *L'âge classique*, pp. 327-328 and passim.

glossator implicitly notes that the production of decretals seems to have increased vastly in recent times since, in the entire compilation of decretals, he can find only one such letter published by any other Pope called Boniface.[20] In glossing the labours of the Pope, Johannes refers the reader to one of Justinian's Novels; in that text, the Emperor had stated that the solicitude of his serenity was ever on the look out for remedies which would make the lives of his subjects easier and, to this end, Justinian willingly took on labours so that others might have rest.[21] The Pope's sleeplessness evokes the stark mention of another Novel in which Justinian confesses that, with God-pleasing utility, he devotes both days and nights to pondering ways in which he may remove some of the cares his subjects bear so that in his sleeplessness they may find rest.[22] Boniface's mention of new forms of quarrels ever brought forth by nature causes Johannes to refer to Justinian's *Codex*, where the Emperor had also confessed that he did not think the laws would ever be able to comprehend all the causes which nature is capable of bringing forth.[23] The provident nature of Boniface's provisions is paralleled

---

[20] Gloss *ad v.* "Bonifacius": "Ex praedecessoribus suis eiusdem nominis, licet ipse fuerit octauus, credo quod unicam decretalem habuimus, scilicet supra, de praesump. Nullus (x 2.23.4)."

[21] Gloss *ad v.* "Labores": "Idem dicit imperator in authen. ut diui. ius. subsc. hab. ... (=Nov. 114.pr.)." The text in question, from the Novel, reads: "Nostrae serenitatis sollicitudo remediis invigilat subiectorum, nec cessamus inquirere, si quid sit in nostra republica corrigendum, ideo namque voluntarios labores appetimus, ut quietem aliis praeparemus. Unde ad universorum utilitatem pertinere perspeximus, si sacras etiam iussiones cum competente iubeamus cautela procedere, ne aliquibus liceat eas pro sua voluntate profiteri." Citations of the Novels are from *Corpus iuris civilis*, 3. *Novellae*, ed. R. Schoell and G. Kroll, 6th ed. (Berlin, 1954).

[22] Gloss *ad v.* "Insomnes": "in authenti. ut iudi sine quoquo suffrag., in princ. (=Nov. 8.pr.)." The prologue of the Novel, in part, states: "Omnes nobis dies ac noctes contingit cum omni lucubratione et cogitatione degere, semper volentibus, ut aliquid utile et placens Deo a nobis collatoribus praebeatur; et non in vano vigilias ducimus, sed in huiusmodi eas expendimus consilia, pernoctantes et noctibus sub aequalitate dierum, utentes, ut nostri subiecti sub omni quiete consistant sollicitudine liberati, nobis in nosmet ipsos pro omnibus cogitationem suscipientibus. Per omnem namque curiositatem et inquisitionem subtilem discurrimus, illa agere querentes, quae utilitatem nostris subiectis introducendo, omni eos onere liberent et omni damno extrinsecus illato...."

[23] Gloss *ad v.* "Formas": "C. de vete. iure enuc. 1. ii. Sed quia divinae (=C. 1.17.2.18.)" The text to which reference is made states: "Sed quia divinae quidem res perfectissimae sunt, humani vero iuris conditio semper in infinitum decurrit, et nihil est in ea, quod stare perpetuo possit (multas etenim formas edere natura novas deproperat), non desperamus, quaedam postea emergi negotia, quae adhuc legum laqueis non sunt innodata. Si quid igitur tale contigerit, augustum imploretur remedium, quia ideo imperialem fortunam rebus humanis Deus praeposuit, ut possit omnia, quae noviter contingunt, et emendare, et componere, et modis et regulis competentibus tradere." Citations of the *Codex* are from *Corpus iuris civilis*, vol. 2, ed. P. Krueger, 5th ed. (Berlin, 1892).

with Justinian's program for the composition of the *Codex*.[24] One of the authorities for the statement that the correction of customs is the end of law is again Justinian.[25] Even the mention of the apposition of a bull to Boniface's letter as proof of its authenticity evokes a reference to a *Codex* provision requiring that, when imperial letters are presented, they be carefully examined for their authenticity before they are obeyed.[26]

It seems that Bernard's invitation to sleep had not found a favourable reception with the Pope, nor can this be said to have happened because the Popes were unfamiliar with the arguments of the *De consideratione*.[27] The non-reception of Bernard's invitation must instead be ascribed to its extender's misjudgement (or, perhaps, painfully correct judgement) of the direction of canonistic thought about the nature of Church discipline and the relationship of the Pope to canon law. If he was familiar with the work, Bernard did not guess the effects of Gratian's *Decretum*. With the Gregorian reformers, Bernard saw submission of the entire Church to the Roman discipline as necessary for the right conduct of Christian life; even as he condemned the recrudescent *imitatio imperii* on the part of the papacy, he could not see that an even more complete imitation of imperial models of government was the only avenue which would seem respectable to those whose task it was to reflect on the social nature of the Church and on the function of the papacy within it.

---

[24] Gloss *ad v.* "Provide": "C. de no. codi. compo., in prima constitutione." The constitution *Haec, quae*, commissioning the composition of the first *Codex*, contains wording which is extremely similar to Boniface's instructions to his own commission, as is noted by Johannes in the gloss *ad v.* "Successive": "Et sicut successive, sic ordinate poni debuerunt, ut ex ordinatione ipsarum quae prior fuerit pateat, ut in prima constitutione C. de novo codice compo., quod in huius libri compilatione bene servatur...." The same point is made again by Johannes in regard to the kind of persons the commissioners were to be, *ad v.* "Doctorem": "Hii erant gloriosi, non solum doctrina legum, sed etiam experientia rerum, et tales debent esse iuris compositores, C. de novo codi. compo., in prima constitutione."

[25] Gloss *ad v.* "Correctionem morum": "Quia hoc solum bene agitur, ut uita hominum corrigatur, uigesima tertia, quaestione quinta, Prodest, circa finem (=C. 23 q. 5 c. 4), et Imperator dicit: 'Legibus nostris mores intendimus corrigere,' C. de secun. nupt. 1. i. (=C. 5.9.1). Ad idem xlvi. dist. c. i, ibi: 'Ne eum eleuatis moribus, etc.,' et supra, de vita et honest. cler. Vt clericorum (=x 3.1.13)."

[26] Gloss *ad v.* "Bulla": "Alias non creditur esse mandatum principis, ut xcvii. dist. Nobilissimus (=D. 97 c. 3), ubi de hoc, et C. de man. princ. 1. Vna (=C. 1.15.1)." In this last authority, however, no bull is mentioned; Justinian simply requires that, when imperial letters are presented, they are to be examined carefully before they are brought to execution.

[27] The influence of the *De consideratione* on Innocent iii's sermons and Boniface viii's *Unam sanctam* was noted by J. D. Anderson and E. T. Kennan, trans., *Five Books on Consideration: Advice to a Pope*, The Works of Bernard of Clairvaux 13 (Kalamazoo, 1976), p. 187.

In his work, Gratian had gathered together a millenary heritage which, when subjected to scrutiny, proved to be disparate, partial, and ultimately unable to satisfy the scientific requirements of the new class of academic canonists.[28] In the new intellectual climate, which owed not a little to the impulses issuing from the efforts of the Gregorian reformers, the elementary systematization of Church law which Gratian had attempted could not but be unfavourably compared with the well-proportioned edifice of Roman law and evoke the desire for the coherence and completeness which Justinian had brought about in the imperial laws. The frequently still unsettled discordance of canons and the clear need for development in the canon law, in line with the theoretical and practical requirements of the age, invited reflection on, and imitation of, the development of Roman law enshrined in Justinian's *Corpus*. From one point of view, the internal history of the Church in the period with which we are concerned consists in the passage, by means of the example of Roman law, from the Pope as supreme judge in Christendom to the Pope as supreme legislator. As supreme judge, the Pope had long been acknowledged to be the declarer, in the context of specific cases brought before him, of the *ius vetus*, the presumedly immutable and immemorial, if haphazard, discipline of the Church; as supreme legislator, the Pope would become the maker of *leges generales* meant to settle cases which no one had brought before him, and these laws would be framed in a technical language which would rival the precision and comprehensiveness of the imperial constitutions they would imitate.

In the history of Roman law, the dichotomy between *ius vetus* and *leges* has been traced back at least to Constantine.[29] In the usage of the Chanceries of that Emperor and of his successors, the dichotomy served as a quick summary of the historical development of Roman law: the *iura* were the result of the participation in the making of law by disparate organs, the *leges* issued entirely from imperial authority.[30] The same dichotomy served to emphasize that the creation of *iura* had come to an end, that their part in legislative activity belonged to history, and that henceforth *leges* were to be the sole means of creative developments in law: this was the view which constituted the background and reason for the fifth-century Theodosian codification.[31] Subsidiary to this dichotomy, if fundamental for the achievement of certainty in law, is the further distinction between *leges generales* and *rescripta*, between emanations of the imperial will which bind all subjects,

---

[28] Cf. *L'âge classique*, pp. 3-5.
[29] G. G. Archi, *Giustiniano legislatore* (Bologna, 1970), pp. 53-58.
[30] Ibid., p. 58.
[31] Ibid., pp. 71-81, esp. pp. 80-81.

unless the same imperial will dispense any of them from their observance, and particular acts of interpretation which may or may not extend to other cases, in accordance with the mandates of the same imperial will.[32]

Justinian begins his legislative activity with the same concern for certainty in law which had characterized the work of Theodosius. In the constitution *Haec, quae*, on the making of the first *Codex*, he gave as his purpose and desire in the commissioning of the great work the curbing of causes;[33] the texts included in the *Codex* were to be alleged by advocates in their *recitatio* before the judge so that the latter might speedily and surely cull the principle to be applied to the case before him. The constitution *Summa reipublicae* adds that, by the imperial constitutions in the *Codex* and the labours of the old jurisconsults, judges will be able to decide all causes coming before them.[34] These several constitutions insist that, by the work of the imperial commissioners, the multitude of constitutions is reduced to manageable size and coherence; by this means, too, the *caligo*, or obscurity, which might impede the meet decision of causes is removed.[35] So long as it remains clear that all law emanates from the Emperor and that he is the sole *conditor et interpres legum*,[36] a more exalted role can again be found for the *iura*; these, codified in the *Digest* and *Institutions*, may point out the essential consonance of Roman law, both ancient and modern, and serve as the tools for the formation of jurists for all time to come.[37]

Justinian's *Corpus* is pervaded by the conviction that the science of law can be reduced to a coherent and finite system now that it has become clear that the Emperor may resolve all contradictions and fill all *lacunae* which might be identified; although legal activity must always be open-ended because of the inventiveness of human nature, imperial interpretation will preserve the *consonantia iuris* which has been brought about by the amazing compilation of the *Corpus*. The organizing principles of the system having been clarified, the law will no longer vacillate and be uncertain.[38] The *Corpus iuris* will be

---

[32] Ibid., pp. 85-86.

[33] Ibid., pp. 124-125; the relevant section of the constitution states: "... censuimus ... prolixitatem litium amputare, multitudo quidem constitutionum ... resecanda, uno autem codice ... componendo, in quem colligi tam memoratorum trium codicum quam novellas post eos positas constitutiones oportet."

[34] Archi, p. 127; *Summa reipublicae*, par. 3: "... adiectis etiam ueterum iuris interpretatorum laboribus...."

[35] Archi, p. 133: *Haec, quae*, pr.; *Summa rei publicae*, par. 1; *Cordi*, pr.; *Imperatoriam*.

[36] *Deo auctore*, par. 7; C. 1.14.12.5.

[37] Archi, pp. 142-144; at p. 144, Archi cites the ever instructive c. *Tanta*, par. 18, for the text of which see note 23, above. This text will need to be called to mind in considering Honorius III's contribution to the development of papal codification.

[38] Archi, p. 144; *Tanta*, pr. and par. 11.

able to respond to the two-fold needs of law, legal education and the certain and speedy administration of justice, even as it manages to preserve within its covers the far from pacific records of a millenary debate about the theoretical and practical aspects of law.[39]

By 1150, canon law had a teaching book which attempted to reconcile the canonical analogue to the opinions of the Roman jurists (*proelia auctorum*) and to identify *lacunae* in the disciplinary system of the Church, without possessing, at the same time, a clear definition of the organizing principles of the system as a whole, which would in turn allow for the resolution of the identified difficulties. Although canonists were duly appreciative of Gratian's achievement, they would reach the inescapable conclusion that, if their system were to be as perfectly complete as the Roman one, its development would have to move beyond the confines of the teaching book which the Master had given them. That the paedagogical function of Gratian's work was the element which most distinguished it from previous compilations of the canonical tradition is perhaps an aspect of it which has not been sufficiently stressed. It is not the nature of the material which it contains that sets the *Decretum* apart from older compilations, but the fact that its author, familiar with the work of the Bolognese teachers of Roman law, could aim to satisfy more than the needs of ecclesiastical administrators for works which made the disciplinary tradition of the Church more easily accessible to them; familiarity with *Institutions* and *Digest* led *magister Gratianus* to the choice of an arrangement of the old material which was highly original because, for the first time in the history of canon law, it addressed the problem of the formation of adepts, an aim which Justinian's *Corpus* clearly identified as the other necessary end and purpose of a legal system.

The astounding success of Gratian's endeavour, as is the case with seminal works, was placed in the clearest evidence by the speed and acuteness with which numberless commentators who had been enabled to achieve a juridical formation through it felt the need for canon law to move beyond it. Already by the 1160s, decretists had begun to treat papal decretals as "precedents" by means of which problems emerging from the study of Gratian's compilation could be solved.[40] These papal decisions, at times together with other authorities from pre-Gratian canon law which were thought to have been wrongly omitted by Gratian, soon began to be collected by canonists on their own authority. Apparently because these texts "wandered outside" the *Decre-*

---

[39] Archi, p. 195; pp. 208-209.

[40] Cf. S. Kuttner, "The Revival of Jurisprudence," in *Renaissance and Renewal in the Twelfth Century*, ed. R. L. Benson, G. Constable, with C. D. Lanham (Cambridge, Mass., 1982), pp. 299-323, at p. 317.

tum, they were called *extravagantes*. By this process of compilation of collections of *extravagantes* and the "good fortune" of recourse to Roman law and its definition of what a legal system and a legislator ought to be, the canonists embarked on the process of definition of the "classical" Romano-canonical law of the Church, which has been called a fascinating process of fusion of law and theology.[41]

Mindful of the lesson contained in Justinian's *Corpus*, the decretists immediately turned to the definition of the sources of ecclesial law. Although Gratian had proclaimed the existence of conciliar canons and papal decretals as concurrent sources of law,[42] the commentators quickly reached the conclusion that decretals were more important than conciliar canons.[43] The sweeping law-making powers which the decretists and decretalists, on the lines of the Roman model and by the refinement of the concept of *plenitudo potestatis*, ascribed to the Pope have formed the subject of exhaustive study in the last few decades;[44] what may still bear pointing out is the slowness with which the concepts of *lex generalis* and codification, readily accepted as possibilities for canon law by the commentators, make their way into the *Quinque compilationes antiquae* and find their fulfilment in the *Decretales* of Gregory IX and in the *Liber sextus*. These two concepts are singled out because they furnish exemplary evidence of the official reception of Roman law in the canonical system and of the gradual passage of the Popes themselves from a sort of sleep on the highest judicial bench of all to the imperial sleeplessness which has been their burden ever since the classical age of canon law.

The *Quinque compilationes antiquae* stand out among the many compilations of *extravagantes* compiled between the end of the twelfth century and the third decade of the thirteenth not merely because of their relative technical perfection, but also because they became authoritative text-books of the *ius novum* at Bologna and, therefore, were of particular authority everywhere. Two of these compilations, the *Tertia* and the *Quinta*, had an official character because they were approved, respectively, by Innocent III, in 1210, and by Honorius III, in 1226.[45]

---

[41] *L'âge classique*, pp. 8-10, 34-35, 39.

[42] D. 15 *et segg.*; *dictum Gratiani ante* D. 21 c. 1.

[43] Cf. *L'âge classique*, p. 133; K. Pennington, *Pope and Bishops: The Papal Monarchy in the Twelfth and Thirteenth Centuries* (Philadelphia, 1984), pp. 3, 22-23, 53; J. A. Watt, *The Theory of Papal Monarchy in the Thirteenth Century* (London, 1965), pp. 1-2, 77-79, 87-88.

[44] The works cited in the note immediately above will provide an ample introduction to this topic.

[45] The five ancient compilations were edited by E. Friedberg, *Quinque compilationes antiquae* (Leipzig, 1882). On the *Compilatio III*, see *L'âge classique*, pp. 230-231; K. Pen-

The *Compilatio prima* was composed by Bernard of Pavia and published in 1191; it was the most influential of the five compilations because it produced the principles of organization and arrangement of the material which would become normative for all subsequent compilations until the *Liber sextus* of Boniface VIII.[46] Johannes Galensis composed the *Compilatio secunda*, which had appeared by 1212, in order to collect material which had been produced between the publication of the *Prima* and the beginning of the pontificate of Innocent III and so to fill the gap which had been created by the fact that the *Tertia* included only Innocentian material.[47] The *Quarta* was composed by Johannes Teutonicus on his own initiative; it appeared in 1216 and contained most of the canons of Lateran IV and decretals from the years of the pontificate of Innocent III following the publication of the *Tertia*. Because of Innocent III's refusal to promulgate the *Quarta* officially, it took some years for the unaided reputation of its author to ensure its reception; the compiler never seems to have forgotten Innocent's slight to his labours.[48] In the same way that Innocent III had commissioned Petrus Beneventanus to compile the *Tertia*, Honorius III commissioned Tancred of Bologna to compile a collection of his own decretals; this collection was constituted by decretals of Honorius and a constitution of Frederick II (*Hac edictali lege*) which he had issued at his coronation by Honorius to deal with several problems in ways that pleased the Pope.

The crowning glory of this mighty labour of compilation was the publication of the *Extravagantes* of Gregory IX, published in 1234, which pruned and gathered together the material contained in the *Quinque compilationes antiquae*. This work of editing had been entrusted to Raymond of Peñafort who had actually been given authority to change the texts he found in the old compilations and to add new ones, if he should think it necessary, in order

nington, "The French Recension of *Compilatio Tertia*," *Bulletin of Medieval Canon Law*, n.s. 5 (1975) 53-71. On the *Compilatio V*, see *L'âge classique*, p. 232; L. E. Boyle, OP, "The *Compilatio quinta* and the Registers of Honorius III," *Bulletin of Medieval Canon Law*, n.s. 8 (1978) 9-19 (repr. in *Pastoral Care, Clerical Education and Canon Law, 1200-1400* [London, 1981], XI). On the constitution of Frederick II included in the *Compilatio V*, to which reference is made below, and on the fact that it had probably emanated from the Curia, which would explain its inclusion in the *Quinta* and the papal intention to have it observed as general law throughout Christendom, see G. De Vergottini, *Studi sulla legislazione imperiale di Federico II in Italia (Le leggi del 1220)* (Milan, 1952), esp. p. 171.

[46] *L'âge classique*, pp. 277-228.

[47] Ibid., p. 231.

[48] Ibid., pp. 231-232; see also S. Kuttner, "Johannes Teutonicus, das Vierte Laterankonzil und die Compilatio Quarta," in *Miscellanea Giovanni Mercati*, Studi e Testi 125 (Città del Vaticano, 1946), 5: 608-634; repr. in *Medieval Councils, Decretals, and Collections of Canon Law* (London, 1980), X. In this latter work (p. 633), one can find a vivid description of Johannes Teutonicus's reaction to Innocent's refusal to grant his blessing to the *Quarta*.

to clear up doubts in the law. Raymond carried out his splendid work on the basis of editorial criteria which he developed by reference to the scholastic (Bolognese) commentaries on the *Quinque compilationes.* By his editorial work and the addition of 195 new decisions, Raymond strove to achieve that *Concordia* (dare one say that *consonantia iuris?*) which had been the object of Gratian's work and the ardent wish of his successors.[49]

In view of the quickness with which decretists and early decretalists had applied attributes of the Emperors as sole legislators to the Popes, it is surprising to note how gradually the notion that the Popes might produce

---

[49] S. Kuttner, "Raymond of Peñafort as Editor: the 'Decretales' and 'Constitutiones' of Gregory IX," *Bulletin of Medieval Canon Law,* n.s. 12 (1982) 65-80, esp. p. 66. The terms of Raymond's commission, the principles which were to guide his work, and the extent to which the example of Justinian was being imitated by Gregory IX will readily appear from the tenor of the constitution promulgating the work; it reads as follows (Friedberg, *Corpus iuris canonici,* 2: 2-3): "Gregorius, Episcopus servus servorum Dei, dilectis filiis doctoribus et scholaribus universis Bononiae commorantibus salutem et apostolicam benedictionem. Rex pacificus pia miseratione disposuit sibi subditos fore pudicos, pacificos et honestos. Sed effrenata cupiditas, sui prodiga, pacis aemula, mater litium, materia iurgiorum, tot quotidie nova litigia generat, ut, nisi iustitia conatus eius sua virtute reprimeret, et quaestiones ipsius implicitas explicaret, ius humani foederis litigatorum abusus exstingueret, et dato libello repudii concordia extra mundi terminos exsularet. Ideoque lex proditur, ut appetitus noxius sub iuris regula limitetur, per quam genus humanum, ut honeste vivat, alterum non laedat, ius suum unicuique tribuat, informatur. Sane diversas constitutiones et decretales epistolas praedecessorum nostrorum, in diversa dispersas volumina, quarum aliquae propter nimiam similitudinem, et quaedam propter contrarietatem, nonnullae etiam propter sui prolixitatem, confusionem inducere videbantur, aliquae vero vagabantur extra volumina supradicta, quae tamquam incertae frequenter in iudiciis vacillabant, ad communem, et maxime studentium, utilitatem per dilectum filium fratrem Raymundum, capellanum et poenitentiarium nostrum, illas in unum volumen resecatis superfluis providimus redigendas, adiicientes constitutiones nostras et decretales epistolas, per quas nonnulla, quae in prioribus erant dubia, declarantur. Volentes igitur, ut hac tantum compilatione universi utantur in iudiciis et in scholis, districtius prohibemus, ne quis praesumat aliam facere absque auctoritate sedis apostolicae speciali." The *glossa ordinaria* does a very good job of identifying the references, both explicit and implicit, which this letter makes to various parts of Justinian's compilation; the texts referred to are usually the ones with which we have already dealt in discussing the relationship between the letter publishing the *Sext* and Justinian's laws. Some of the more interesting examples of this correlation between Gregory's views and those of Justinian will be found in the glosses on the following *lemmata*: "Seruus," in which it is pointed out that Justinian had also called himself a servant and the unselfish sleeplessness of Pope and Emperor is pointed out; "Noua litigia," where imperial statements about the prodigality with which new causes are produced are indicated; "Honeste uiuat, etc.," and "Ius suum unicuique tribuat," where the sources for Gregory's definition of the ends of law are found in Justinian's *Corpus;* "Similitudinem," "Contrarietatem" and "Per dilectum filium fratrem Raymundum," in which it is pointed out that the editorial criteria for the handling of the legal texts and the qualifications of the editor(s) to whom the job had been entrusted were the same as the ones which Justinian had outlined. The edition of the *glossa ordinaria* which has been consulted is the following: *Decretales Gregorii Noni Pont. Max. Cum Glossis ordinariis, Argumentis, Casibus litteralibus, et Adnotationibus tam veterum quam recentium Iurisconsultorum illustratae...* (Venetiis, 1572).

constitutions, or general laws framed without reference to specific cases, became acceptable at official levels and made its way into the compilations of *extravagantes*. The delay is more noteworthy still if we remember that even Bolognese civilians such as Azo thought that what was said of imperial constitutions could be applied to papal decretals.[50] Nevertheless, when Bernard of Pavia compiled the *Compilatio I,* although he was open to the notion of the Pope legislating in the same way as the Emperor and included a title on constitutions in his work, he had no example of a papal general law to offer for discussion.[51] His seven chapters on constitutions, of which five were to be accepted in Gregory IX's compilation, all address general principles for the interpretation of written law of whatever kind. In his *Casus* on the same title, the only example of a constitution made by a Pope which Bernard can offer is one of the constitutions of Lateran III.[52] Although the *Compilationes II, III, V* contain titles on constitutions, none of the chapters contained in these titles is concerned with papal constitutions. The relevant title in the *Extravagantes* of Gregory IX, receiving as it does many of the provisions contained in these *Compilationes,* would be equally disappointing, were it not for the addition of a last chapter by Gregory IX in which the generally binding nature of a papal constitution is defined and a tag from the *Codex* on the non-retroactivity of constitutions is tacitly received.[53] Nevertheless, the letter of promulgation of Gregory's *Extravagantes* did take the significant step of referring to that Pope's own general decrees included in the compilation as *constitutiones.*[54]

[50] *Azonis Lectura super Codicem* (Paris, 1577; repr. Torino, 1966). Glossing the term *leges,* which is the incipit of the text at C. 1.14.3, Azo writes (p. 40): "Supra dixit quando lex erat specialis, modo de generali. Nec intellige de legibus quae sunt in corpore iuris, licet enim quaedam ad speciales personas mittantur, omnes tamen generales sunt ... nisi in eadem legem uel per aliam prohibeatur. ... Praeterea quod hic dicit, potes et ducere ad extravagantes decretales Papae."

[51] *Compilatio I,* 1.1.

[52] E. A. D. Laspeyeres, ed., *Bernardi Papiensis Faventini Episcopi Summa decretalium* (Regensburg, 1860; repr. Graz, 1956), p. 255.

[53] X 1.2.13; the tag is from C. 1.14.7. Despite the paucity of relevant examples in the title in question, the ordinary gloss here goes on to define once more the powers of the Pope as legislator: gloss *ad v.* "Omnes astringit": "Cum sit iudex ordinarius omnium christianorum et mater omnium ecclesiarum, ut ix. q. iii. Cuncta per mundum (=C. 9 q. 3 cc. 17, 18), et si etiam aliquid grave precipiat, faciendum est. xix. di. In memoriam (=D. 19 c. 3) ... idem est in sententia papae, quia sicut ipse iudicat alii iudicare debent, infra, de re iudi. cap. In causis (=X 2.27.19)." Similar views are expressed in the gloss *ad v.* "Declaramus": "Bene dicit 'declaramus,' quia nullus alius posset eam declarare sive interpretari, quia ad eum pertinet constituere, infra, de sent. excom. Inter alia, par. Vt igitur (=X 5.39.31), et xi. q. i. cap. Clericum, par. Ex his omnibus (=d.G. post C. 11 q. 1 c. 47), et C. de leg. l. i. et ulti. (=C. 1.14.1, 12)...."

[54] S. Kuttner, "Raymond of Peñafort," pp. 68-69; Dr. Kuttner there suggests that the imitation of Justinian may have motivated this change; he also notes (p. 71) that, in

In the *Sext*, under the appropriate title, we find a fuller reception of the analogy between Pope and Emperor as constitution makers. In the first chapter of the title, Boniface, borrowing imperial words, defines the papal heart as the repository in which all laws are deemed to reside; he then proceeds to define the limits which the Pope's possible ignorance of matters of fact imposes on the formal generality of papal constitutions.[55] The commentators' definition of the papal power to make general law, modelled on the imperial one, has now achieved a full and technical reception in the official sources.

On the question of the acceptance at canon law of Roman law notions of codification, Stephan Kuttner, in a now classic paper, while considering the nature of decretal letters, warned of the dangers of exaggerating the distinction between the relative binding force of the *Decretum* and of the official compilations of decretals, at least before that of Gregory IX.[56] While the universal legislative power of the Popes had been clarified during the Investiture Contest, the notion that papal compilations of decretals could dislodge the old law was late in coming.[57] Professor Kuttner suggested that the very distinction between official and private collections of decretals was not present to twelfth-century canonists and could not be so present until the Papacy had claimed the right to produce official collections. Moreover, the official authorizations of the *Compilatio III* and *Compilatio V* did not, according to the argument, confer on these greater authority than the private collections had previously enjoyed. It was carefully acknowledged, nevertheless, that Innocent III's approval of the *Compilatio III* constituted the first step in the direction of an official determination and codification of binding canonical *auctoritates*.[58]

Gregory IX's contribution to his own compilation, the proportion of more traditional decretal letters to more general laws "is approximately two to one, which means a major shift toward 'legislation' by statute, even if the compilation as a whole still retained the character of the collections from which most of its contents came." Dr. Kuttner further concludes that, if it is correct to assume that many of these general laws had never seen the light of day before their publication in the *Extravagantes*, an assumption about which there seems to be substantial agreement among scholars, then, "the Gregorian compilation indeed marks an important step towards what nowadays we call a Code" (p. 72).

[55] VI 1.2.1; cf. C. 6.23.19. A gloss on this chapter, *ad v.* "Habere," notes an apparent conflict between this statement and an *auctoritas* in the *Decretum*, but claims it is soluble.

[56] S. Kuttner, "Quelques observations sur l'autorité des collections canoniques dans le droit classique de l'Église," in *Actes du Congrès de droit canonique, Paris 22-26 Avril 1947* (Paris, 1950), pp. 305-312; repr. in *Medieval Councils, Decretals and Collections of Canon Law* (London, 1980), I.

[57] Ibid., pp. 307-308.

[58] Ibid., p. 308.

Professor Kuttner's carefully nuanced argument had been offered in order to provide a *locus poenitentiae*, as it were, to the many scholars who had drawn facile and anachronistic analogies between medieval legislative realities and positivist analyses of legislation. That the distinction between private and official collections could not have been present until it had been formulated and the rights ensuing from the definition had been exercised by the Papacy can now seem to us peacefully accepted as an important insight in the scholarly discourse about the evolution of canonical legislative forms. That the authorization of the two official compilations made no difference to their authority, on the other hand, seems a more problematic statement, especially in the more radical forms in which the position has been presented by more recent writers.

A foremost student of the *Compilatio III*, upon discovering a French recension of the work which added other decretals to the official version and tampered with some of the texts included in it, has concluded that papal approval of the collection did not increase its authority.[59] In this view, decretal compilations, whether official or not, are to be seen essentially as reports of cases or as responses to queries, not as collections of legislative decrees.[60] The view is imputed to canonists that papal sanction of a decretal collection did not add authority to the material contained within it.[61] The latter conclusion is bolstered, in its proponent's opinion, by the fact that Johannes Teutonicus and Tancred thought that Innocent's official compilation did not preclude references to other decretals not included in them.[62]

---

[59] K. Pennington, "The French Recension of *Compilatio Tertia*," pp. 64-67; Dr. Pennington has restated similar views in "The Making of a Decretal Collection: the Genesis of *Compilatio Tertia*," in *Proceedings of the Fifth International Congress of Medieval Canon Law, Salamanca 21-25 September 1976*, MIC ser. C (Città del Vaticano, 1980), 6: 67-92.

[60] Pennington, "The French Recension," p. 64.

[61] Ibid., p. 65. The text of Innocent's letter promulgating the *Tertia* is the following (Friedberg, *Quinque compilationes*, p. 105): "Innocentius episcopus servus servorum Dei universis magistris et scolaribus Bononiae commorantibus salutem et apostolicam benedictionem. Deuotioni uestrae insinuatione presentium innotescat, decretales epistolas a dilecto filio magistro P. subdiacono et notario nostro compilatas fideliter, et sub competentibus titulis collocatas, in nostris usque ad XII. annum contineri registris, quas ad cautelam uobis sub bulla nostra duximus transmittendas, ut eisdem absque quolibet dubitationis scrupulo uti possitis, cum opus fuerit, tam in iudiciis quam in scholis." It will be noticed that all Innocent seems to be asserting in this letter is the reliability of the texts to be found in the compilation because they are contained in the papal registers. Decretalists, in commenting on this compilation, might have avoided, if they had wished and had they not found it natural to import into the canon law the Roman lawyer's approach to and respect for his own compilations, any discussion of whether the publication of the *Tertia* left them free to refer to other papal decretals not included in it.

[62] Tancred's gloss on Innocent's letter, *ad v.* "uti possitis," is transcribed by Dr. Pennington and published at p. 65, n. 18, of his article; it reads as follows: "Set si extra

A student of Honorius III's pontificate has, in like manner, concluded that, in view of the fact that some decretals were added by canonists to the *Compilatio V* after its official promulgation, contemporaries must have viewed the official collections as little different from the unofficial ones and has adduced the same canonistic authorities to justify this view.[63]

Beguiling as these conclusions are, they seem to the present writer to be unacceptable in their radical simplicity. The answer which Johannes Teutonicus and Tancred give to the question of whether decretals not included in Innocent's compilation may be cited is indeed interesting, but perhaps not quite as interesting as the posing of the question itself. It is difficult to believe that such a question would ever have been raised about a private collection, or about one which had no more authority than a private one, and, indeed, no glosses have yet been found which ask similar questions about such collections. In view of the fact that neither Innocent nor Honorius had seemed to claim any exclusiveness for their authorized compilation, why should the question have been asked at all? If official authorization made no difference to the authority of a collection, why should Johannes Teutonicus's own *Compilatio quarta* have found such resistance in the schools and why should its author have nursed his well-known resentment at Innocent's failure to grant his seal of approval to it? Indeed, why did the critics of the official versions of the *Tertia* and *Quinta* merely add to, or tamper with, the texts of these rather than produce their own integral and equally authoritative compilations?

---

compilationes istas inueniatur decretalis et allegetur, numquid secundum eam iudicandum erit? Respondeo si constat illam esse decretalem per bullam siue quia publice insinuata est, uel etiam si consonat iuri communi, tunc secundum eam iudicandum erit. Alioquin consulendus est dominus papa super illa, ut infra de fide instrum. Pastoralis (3 Comp. 2.13.3; X 2.22.8). t." Johannes Teutonicus's very similar gloss on the same letter, *ad v.* "ad cautelam," is to be found in his *Apparatus glossarum in Compilationem tertiam*, ed. K. Pennington, MIC, ser. A: Corpus glossatorum 3 (Città del Vaticano, 1981), 1: 1, and reads as follows: "Tamen, licet non sit in hac compilatione, si tamen apparet bulla uel si est insinuata publice, recipitur, ut infra de fide instrum. Pastoralis (3 Comp. 2.13.3; X 2.22.8), uel etiam si inter alias decretales pro decretali est habita, arg. xx. q. i. Quem progenitores (C. 20 q. 1 c. 6) et arg. infra de paroch. Coram, ibi, 'Sic agebat' et cetera (3 Comp. 3.22.1; X 1.29.34). jo."

It does not seem to us that these two glosses unequivocally support the contention that, in the view of the canonists, the official character of a compilation made little or no difference to its authority. These glosses, by another reading, seem to make clear that, as a rule, no reference is to be made to decretals not included in the compilation. The exceptions which they would allow rely on the legislator's own explicit or implicit desire that such should be the case. Justinian himself, after publishing the authentic and exclusive *Codex*, had seen fit to publish many more constitutions; could canonists grant the Pope any less?

[63] J. E. Sayers, *Papal Government and England during the Pontificate of Honorius III (1216-1227)* (Cambridge, 1984), esp. pp. 135-137.

Bernard of Pavia had defined the purpose of his collection as the provision of more abundant matter, taken from the old and the new law, for the more copious allegation, or citation, in judgements and for the utility of students;[64] these concerns fit well with Justinian's concern for the provision of material for the *recitatio* by advocates and for the legal education of the young, concerns which we have examined earlier. Bernard's expression of these same concerns makes clear that a consensus had begun to build among canonists about the form and purpose of a compilation of laws and about the similarities which such compilations were to bear to the ideal represented by Justinian's *Corpus*.

Even a compilation such as Innocent's, which, it is true, merely attests to the authenticity of the texts contained in it, is approached by the canonists with questions more proper to an exclusive and authentic compilation. These questions make clear that the canonists foresaw and desired no more fitting development in the science of canonical codification than the imitation by the popes of the work of Justinian, with the resultant production of exclusive and authentic collections of the laws. It seems now unarguable that, as Professor Kuttner had seen, this development was a gradual one and that its first results are not to be compared or confused with its later and more perfect ones. The *Tertia* and the *Quinta* are not as strikingly similar to Justinian's enviable compilation, nor as technically perfect, as later canonical compilations were to be. Nevertheless, both of these, implicitly or explicitly, as their contemporaries saw, were imitating Justinian and ought not to be misleadingly characterized as of equal authority with the private compilations which had preceded them.

It may be that the extent to which Honorius III's compilation attempts to imitate Justinian has not been fully pointed out. Honorius's letter of promulgation of the compilation, in justifying the appearance of yet another collection of papal decretals, borrows heavily from the *Corpus iuris civilis* and its definitions of the roles of law and legislator.[65] Thus, the view that causes,

---

[64] The prologue of *Compilatio I* reads as follows (Friedberg, *Quinque compilationes*, p. 1): "Iuste iudicate filii hominum et nolite iudicare secundum faciem, sed iustum iudicium iudicate, ut ostendatis uos diligere iustitiam, qui iudicatis terram, illum pre oculis cordis habentes, qui reddet unicuique secundum opera sua. Qua enim mensura mensi fueritis remetietur uobis, cum et de talento credito teneamur reddere rationem. Sit itaque iurisperitus in consilio cautus, in patrocinio fidelis, in iudicio iustus. Ut autem uberior allegationum uel iudiciorum copia preparetur ad honorem Dei sanctaeque Romanae ecclesiae ac studentium utilitatem, ego B. Papiensis praepositus extrauagantia de ueteri nouoque iure sub titulis compilaui super operis imperfectione ueniam postulans a lectore."

[65] The prologue of the *Compilatio V* (Friedberg, *Quinque compilationes*, p. 151) reads as follows: "Honorius episcopus, seruus seruorum Dei, dilecto filio magistro Tancredo, archidiacono bononiensi salutem et apostolicam benedictionem. Nouae causarum emergentium

like illnesses, are forever arising anew and need new remedies by new legislation echoes a Novel of Justinian in which it is stated that laws stand to human transactions in the same relationship as medicines to illnesses and the physician-legislator is to be ever on the look out so that his remedies may be fit for the ever new turns which illness is likely to take.[66] The definition of giving to each his due as an end and purpose of the duly healed social order follows from the *Digest*'s opening definition of justice.[67] The assertion that it is nature itself which is forever creating new situations that render the legislator's intervention necessary is another truth which Justinian had expressed.[68] That it pertains to the prince, by divine election, to see to it that the ravages of an overly creative nature find a corrective in adequate laws which provide the appropriate forms for human transactions is again borrowed from Justinian.[69]

The appropriation by Popes of Justinian's law-making powers was not a sudden development, nor one which can, in its completeness, be ascribed to any one Pope. Innocent III, Honorius III, Gregory IX, each took more and more deliberate steps in this appropriation. Honorius III's contribution to this process is not the least important. If the *Compilatio V* itself fails to include more than decretals of Honorius, thus discouraging comparison with the immense Roman law *Corpus* or, for that matter, with the much more comprehensive compilations of Gregory IX and Boniface VIII, nevertheless the program expressed in its prologue is a necessary, original, and considerate step in the definition of papal legislative sleeplessness.

---

questiones nouis exigunt decisionibus terminari, ut singulis morbis, competentibus remediis deputatis, ius suum cuique salubriter tribuatur. Licet igitur a quibusdam predecessoribus nostris per ea, que suis temporibus sunt decisa, forma futuris negotiis prouide sit relicta, quia tamen prodiga rerum natura secundum uarietates multiplicium casuum parit cottidie nouas causas, nos quasdam epistolas decretales super his, que nostris suborta temporibus, per nos uel fratres nostros decidimus, uel etiam aliis de ipsorum consilio commisimus decidenda, compilari fecimus, et tibi sub bulla nostra duximus destinandas. Quocirca discretioni tuae per apostolica scripta mandamus, quatinus eis solempniter publicatis absque ullo scrupulo dubitationis utaris et ab aliis recipi facias tam in iudiciis quam in scholis."

[66] Nov. 111.pr.

[67] Dig. 1.1.pr.

[68] Nov. 85.pr.; Cod. 1.17.2.18.

[69] Cod. 1.17.2.18. This text is the famous constitution *Tanta*. The fact that Honorius should have thought it fitting to make at least implicit reference to this constitution seems significant because this is the document in which Justinian glories in the fact that, by imperial efforts and divine favour, the much desired *consonantia iuris* has been achieved. Perhaps Honorius meant his readers to understand that papal law was also on the verge of reaching the same promised land.

12

Papal Ideals
and the University of Paris
1170-1303

P. Osmund Lewry, OP †

In the thirteenth century the popes' concern for sound learning as a service to faith became an insistent theme of their letters to the University of Paris. But even earlier, in the late twelfth century, the increasing importance of its schools had begun to make Paris an object of their special concern. Thus, in 1170, when the schools were coalescing into the corporate life of a university and the centralizing power of the papacy was in the ascendant, Alexander III, although probably not, as once was thought, a former student of Paris, showed his interest in what was taught there by urging the metropolitan to work for the rejection of what he regarded as the unsound Christological teaching of Peter Lombard and for the maintenance of the sound doctrine of Christ, perfect God as well as perfect man.[1]

If orthodox teaching was their primary concern, immunity from exactions by the local church was also enjoined as a condition for academic integrity and freedom. Alexander soberly warned the bishops of France against greed

---

[1] See H. Denifle and É. Chatelain, eds., *Chartularium Universitatis Parisiensis* [=*CUP*], 4 vols (Paris, 1899-1897), 1: 4, 8-9, nos. 3, 9 (28 May 1170, 18 Feb. 1177). D. E. Luscombe, *The School of Abelard: The Influence of Abelard's Thought in the Early Scholastic Period*, Cambridge Studies in Medieval Life and Thought, New Series 14 (Cambridge, 1969), p. 16, questions the assumption that Roland Bandinelli, later Alexander III, studied under Abelard.

The Religious Roles of the Papacy: Ideals and Realities, 1150-1300, ed. Christopher Ryan, Papers in Mediaeval Studies 8 (Toronto: Pontifical Institute of Mediaeval Studies, 1989), pp. 363-388. © P.I.M.S., 1989.

in exacting fees for the licence to teach.[2] He also intervened to reprove a priest who had executed summary justice on troublesome students who had jeered at the priest one Sunday for leading a dance: breaking down school doors and shattering windows, he said, was an offence against the liberty of scholars; justice, as they claimed, rightly belonged to their own master.[3] This incident occurred at Saint-Rémy, but similar immunities were being defended at Paris, and its liberties and customs were confirmed in 1174.[4]

Material support was often given, or commended, in furtherance of the popes' ideals. In Peter Comestor's time as chancellor, Gerard Pucelle was guaranteed access to his English revenues and restitution from the Apostolic See for losses during the German schism, "since many by God's grace make progress in the knowledge of letters under his teaching."[5] While the popes wrangled with Barbarossa and his successors in the Empire, France was a favoured daughter until the rift with Philip the Fair, and Paris benefited from this favoured status. In higher education financial considerations are always pressing, and from this time much is heard of benefices as a means of support for needy scholars. Thus, in 1179 the Third Lateran Council presented the Church as a kindly mother providing for the needy both in regard to bodily sustenance and the progress of souls, when it decreed that each cathedral church should offer a benefice to a master who would teach its clergy and other poor scholars. At the same time the ban on charging for the licence was repeated, but now under pain of deprivation from their benefices for those who would obstruct the progress of the Church.[6] The Parisian schools were also to profit by the papal concern with similar provisions.

Papal interventions in regard to those schools are rare until the pontificate of Innocent III, but Urban III has a place in the cartulary of Paris—the principal source for this cursory reading—bestowing his patronage on a foundation, initially for canons but later for poor scholars, in 1186-1187.[7] Such endowed houses were intended to provide a stable environment for study and prayer, comparable with the religious *studia*. The aged Celestine III, a former student of Abelard, also appears in the 1190s, confirming the ancient rights of clerics to immunity from trial by the secular power,[8] another

[2] See *CUP* 1: 4-5, no. 4 (20 Oct. 1170-1172).

[3] See *CUP* 1: 5-6, no. 5 (8 Nov. 1170-1172).

[4] See *CUP* 1: 7-8, no. 7 (28 Oct. 1174).

[5] See *CUP* 1: 9-10, nos. 10-11 (7 Feb., 15 Mar. 1178).

[6] See *CUP* 1: 10, no. 12 (19 Mar. 1179), and the similar provisions of the Fourth Lateran Council, ibid., 1: 81-82, no. 22, § 11 (30 Nov. 1215).

[7] See *CUP* 1: 11, no. 14 (22 July 1186-1187). The original charter of Robert I, count of Droix, for this *domus S. Thomae de Lupara* is missing; the text of that of Robert II is given, ibid., 1: 15-16, no. 18 (1198).

[8] See *CUP* 1: 12, no. 15 (1191-1198), and Luscombe, *The School of Abelard*, p. 22.

shield for learning against the hostile elements of the world. Innocent himself, commending Peter of Corbeil for a prebend of York in 1198, dwelt on his reputation for learning and good character and became more expansive as he recalled that he had once profited by his Scripture teaching.[9] As with Celestine, the loyalties of an alumnus may have nourished the papal concern.

Between 1192 and 1203 Stephen of Tournai gives us a rare insight into a churchman's expectations of the papacy in the matter of sound learning. Confident that God had given the pope power to cut short errors and the knowledge to correct them before the sickness became incurable, he complains that students only applaud novelties and masters scribble away at new summae and commentaries. As if the Fathers were not enough for the exposition of Scripture, they are serving up strange new dishes. There is public dispute against conciliar decrees: the Incarnation of the Word is exposed to wordy argument; the undivided Trinity is dissected with trivialities. In canon law hucksters offer an impenetrable forest of fresh decretals. The liberal arts have been reduced to slavery by long-haired youths sitting beardless in the chairs of their elders, caught like flies in a web of sophistry. The torn garments of Boethius' Lady Philosophy scarcely cover her nakedness as Stephen looks to the pope to restore some order in this disarray, lest the divine word be cheapened while it is said, "See, here is Christ, or there."[10]

---

[9] See *CUP* 1: 14-15, no. 17 (17 Dec. 1198): "Sane licet dilectum filium magistrum P. de Corbolio, de cujus litteratura et scientia in longinquis et remotis partibus predicatur, sue tantum probitatis et honestatis intuitu habere debeamus in visceribus caritatis, cum tamen ad memoriam nostram reducimus, nos aliquando sub ipsius magisterio extitisse et ab eo divinarum audisse paginam scripturarum, quod ubique non pudet nos dicere immo reputare volumus gloriosum, ad dilectionem ipsius efficimur promptiores et ejus libentius augmento intendimus et honori" (p. 14).

[10] See *CUP* 1: 47-48, no. 48 (1192-1203): "Id tantum, quod dolet, significare volumus sancte paternitati vestre, cui Deus contulit et potestatem corripiendi errores, et scientiam corrigendi. Lapsa sunt apud nos in confusionis officinam sacrarum studia litterarum, dum et discipuli solis novitatibus applaudant, et magistri glorie potius invigilant quam doctrine, novas recentesque summulas et commentaria firmantia super theologia passim conscribunt, quibus auditores suos demulceant, detineant, decipiant, quasi nondum suffecerint sanctorum opuscula patrum, quos eodem spiritu sacram scripturam legimus exposuisse, quo eam composuisse credimus apostolos et prophetas. Ignota et peregrina convivis suis apponunt fercula.... Disputatur publice contra sacras constitutiones de incomprehensibili deitate, de incarnatione verbi verbosa caro et sanguis irreverenter litigat. Individua Trinitas et in triviis secatur et discrepitur, ut tot jam sint errores quot doctores, tot scandala quot auditoria, tot blasphemie quot platee. Rursus si ventum fuerit ad judicia que jure canonico sint tractanda, vel a vobis commissa vel ab ordinariis judicibus cognoscenda, profertur a venditoribus inextricabilis silva Decretalium epistolarum quasi sub nomine sancte recordationis Alexandri pape, et antiquiores sacri canones abjiciuntur, respuuntur, expuuntur. Hoc involucro prolato in medium ea que in Conciliis sanctorum patrum salubriter instituta sunt, nec formam conciliis, nec finem negociis

Complaint against worthless novelties was not new—one can find as much in the 1160s with Peter of Celle's lament to John of Salisbury over "that blessed school where Christ had taught their hearts the word of his power, where they had learnt, without study and reading, how one might live well for ever" [11]—but at the turn of the twelfth century it was appropriately directed to the papacy. A direct response has yet to be found. Innocent's first intervention, in 1205, was an inducement to scholars to leave Paris and support the emperor in Constantinople by building up schools there. The Greek Church, he says, is awaking from its sleep of death, and a return to obedience is to be hoped for with a revival of learning in the Orient.[12] In 1207, however, Innocent wrote to the bishop of Paris, recognizing the need for masters there who would nourish souls with God's word, though he limits their number to eight, so that the office may not be cheapened or carried out in a disorderly fashion.[13] In 1212 he threatened censure for exactions regarding the licence never seen in his days at Paris.[14] The compact reached the following year between the university and the chancellor was alluded to in 1215 when, as Stephen Ferruolo has suggested, the legatine ordinances may have endorsed the teaching practices already developed by the university itself.[15]

---

imponunt prevalentibus epistolis, quas forsitan advocati conductim sub nomine Romanorum Pontificum in apothecis sive cubiculis suis confingunt et conscribunt. Novum volumen ex eis compactum et in scolis solempniter legitur et in foro venaliter exponitur.... Ve duo predicta sunt, et ecce restat tertium ve: facultates quas liberales appellant amissa libertate pristina in tantam servitutem devocantur, ut comatuli adolescentes earum magisteria impudentes usurpent, et in cathedra seniorum sedeant imberbes.... Omissis regulis artius abjectisque libris autenticis artificum muscas innanium verbulorum sophismatibus suis tamquam aranearum tendiculis includunt. Clamat philosophia vestes suas conscindi et disrumpi, et quibusdam particulariter seminanciis nuditatem suam verecunde contegens, ne consulitur ab antiquo, nec antiquam consolatur. Hec omnia, pater, correptionis apostolice manum desiderant, ut informitas docendi, discendi, disputandi auctoritate vestra certam redigatur ad formam, ne sermo divinus attricione vulgari vilescat, ne in angulis dicatur: Ecce his Christus aut ecce illic, ne sanctum canibus et margarite porcis conculcande tradantur."

[11] See *CUP* 1: 24, no. 22 (1164): "O beata scola, ubi Christus docet corda nostra verbo virtutis sue, ubi sine studio et lectione apprehendimus, quomodo debeamus eternaliter beate vivere!"

[12] See *CUP* 1: 62-63, no. 3 (25 May 1205).

[13] See *CUP* 1: 65, no. 5 (14 Nov. 1207). Honorius III waives this restriction for Matthew of Scotland; ibid., 1: 85, no. 27 (16 Nov. 1218).

[14] See *CUP* 1: 73-74, no. 14 (20 Jan. 1212): "Cum igitur tempore, quo vacavimus Parisius studio litterarum, nunquam scolares viderimus sic tractari, eidem cancellario nostris litteris dedimus in preceptis, ut sic hujusmodi corrigat per seipsum, quod eum per alium ad id compelli minime faciamus" (p. 73).

[15] See *CUP* 1: 75-77, nos. 16-18 (1213), for the compact, and ibid., 1: 78-80, no. 20 (Aug. 1215), for the legatine ordinances of Robert de Courçon. Stephen C. Ferruolo in a paper to the annual meeting of the American Historical Association, San Francisco, 28 Dec. 1983 (see "The Paris Statutes of 1215 Reconsidered," *History of Universities*, 5 (1985), 1-14),

Honorius III, like Innocent, was initially concerned, in 1217, with the extension of learning from Paris, but he was looking only to the Albigensian territory around Toulouse. Through the ministry of God's servants there, navigable streams flow in the tractless waste once given over to the briar and the nettle; the people are converted and the heretics have fled. Lest this freshly ploughed field should revert to a worse state than before, Honorius urged that some of those trees long planted by the waters of the Seine should be transplanted to the banks of the Garonne, to lecture, preach and exhort, making a people acceptable to the Lord.[16]

Ernst Pitz, in his study of rescripts, has tried to relate this document to the response of a reforming circle around Cardinal Hugolino to the petition of St Dominic for a school to combat heresy.[17] Whatever the origin, without the petitions it is easy to read such papal documents as initiatives of the Apostolic See, but where, as here, they show an intimate knowledge of local situations, one may suspect that they are responses, echoing a petitioner's language in granting what is asked. Similarly, in 1219, when Honorius supported the claim that censures should not be bandied about without his sanction, Paris may have provided its own refreshing vision of its catholic mission, to catch the pope's imagination by the *arenga*: a flood that spreads to make fruitful the land of the universal church, dew and rain on the mountains of Gilboa to cause rejoicing in the City of God.[18]

Later that year Honorius surveyed the state of the universal church from that vantage-point on which he had been set, echoing Innocent's letters in *Super specula*. There is scarcely anyone, Honorius says, who will give drink to those thirsting for the water of saving wisdom; many draw water with the Samaritan woman's bucket from the well of unbelief. Tired of manna, they sigh for the garlic and melons of Egypt, more lucrative studies. The masters in theology are charmingly compared to the lovely girls sought throughout the provinces for King Ahasuerus. Being so scarce, suitable candidates may be excused from other offices so that they may shine in the theological firmament and teach many righteousness. Such workers in the Lord's

---

suggested that the statutes provided official papal recognition of the corporate right of the university; rather than being imposed upon the university, they were the product of cooperation between a legate, who had himself been educated at Paris, and the existing guild of masters.

[16] See *CUP* 1: 83-84, no. 25 (19 Jan. 1217).

[17] Ernst Pitz, *Papstreskript und Kaiserreskript im Mittelalter*, Bibliothek des Deutschen Historischen Instituts in Rom 36 (Tübingen, 1971), p. 172.

[18] See *CUP* 1: 88-90, no. 31 (11 May 1219): "... doctrine sue fluenta usquequaque diffundens universalis ecclesie terram irrigat et fecundat, in montes Gelboe, super quos nec ros cadit nec pluvia, commutare impetum fluminis, qui civitatem Dei letificat, cursum doctrine videlicet, sistere presumpserunt" (p. 88).

vineyard are not to be cheated of their penny, papal provision of prebends and benefices. The grace is deceptive and the beauty vain of studies in civil law and medicine, so Alexander III's ban is now extended to the diocesan clergy. Many innkeepers water the wine, mingling the false with the true, but—mixing the metaphors—Honorius looks for a band of hunters to catch the little foxes that maraud among the vines. Gold already has its place for smelting in Paris, where the tower of David has been constructed, with an armed guard around Solomon's bed: so that more attention may be given to Scripture, the teaching of civil law at Paris is forbidden under pain of excommunication.[19]

Here again Pitz would see the hand of St Dominic, with efforts to secure the place of theology following the establishment of Saint-Jacques, the Dominican house, in 1218, but other evidence may point to longer established stars in the theological firmament.[20] In 1220 Honorius thanked the university for accepting the Dominicans, perhaps anticipating the criticism, which was not slow in coming, with his stress on their apostolic task.[21] A letter of introduction for William, a member of his household who was to study at Saint-Jacques, pictures the friar as sitting like Mary at the feet of the Lord and resisting the importunity of Leah for the much desired embraces of Rachel.[22]

Honorius' last intervention, in 1225, related to a condemnation of Eriugena's *Periphyseon*. His pastoral concern was directed against those

[19] See *CUP* 1: 90-93, no. 32 (16 Nov. 1219).

[20] Pitz, *Papstreskript*, pp. 171-191, "Die Konstitution *super Speculam* von 1219." Stephan Kuttner, "Papst Honorius III. und das Studium des Zivilrechts," in *Festschrift für Martin Wolff*, ed. E. von Caemmerer et al. (Tübingen, 1952), pp. 79-101, reprinted in Kuttner, *Gratian and the Schools of Law, 1140-1234* (London, 1983), x.79-101, maintains that this letter is a *constitutio motu proprio* of the pope, although Roffredus Beneventanus (*Libelli in iure canonico*, 6.1) alludes to two advisers who were simply theologians: "... sed si audeo dicere, tam lator canonis illius quam et duo consiliarii, qui fuerunt pure theologi, fecerunt sicut vulpes quae, dum non posset gustare de cerasis, cepit illa publice vituperare" (cited by Kuttner, p. 90). In the reprint of his *Festschrift* paper Kuttner adds "Retractationes" (ibid., pp. 43-47). He takes issue there (pp. 43-44) with Pitz's characterization of this letter as a rescript and (p. 45) reports a personal communication from Leonard E. Boyle (who also drew my attention to the witness of Roffredus), suggesting that one of the pope's advisers may have been Master William of Auxerre, the university's proctor at the curia (cf. *CUP* 1: 162-163, no. 116, 8 Aug. 1237). Kuttner suggests that the other may have been Cardinal Peter of Capua, who features in Pitz's discussion of the document.

[21] See *CUP* 1: 95, no. 36 (27 Feb. 1220).

[22] See *CUP* 1: 97, no. 39 (30 Dec. 1220): "Cum Lie importunitas desiderabiles Rachelis amplexus fere continue nobis invideat, religionem vestram rogamus attentius et instantius postulamus, quatinus vos, qui sedetis ad pedes Domini cum Maria ipsum humiliter exoretis, ut gressus nostros dirigat in suorum semitas mandatorum, quatinus que sibi sunt placita facientes dignam sibi possimus de commissa nobis sollicitudine rederre rationem."

profane novelties that St Paul also warned us to shun.[23] Three years later his successor, Gregory IX, who as a cardinal had supported St Dominic, also warned against novelties. In his *Ab Egyptiis* of 1228 philosophy was firmly relegated to the service of heavenly teaching: that patristic theme of the despoiling of the Egyptians, the cropping of hair and paring of nails of captive brides, argues for the dominance of the theological mind. It is mental adultery to mix the teaching of the philosophers with the heavenly oracles in such a way as to compromise their purity. Silversmiths of natural eloquence ignore the path of heavenly instruction; tale-spinners from Theman cross the bounds set by patristic interpretation of the Scriptures. These theophants invert the true order of knowledge, making the sacred subservient to the elements of this world. When faith tries to build with natural reason more than is fit, it is rendered vain, for that faith has no value to which human reason supplies the justification. Teachers are exhorted to teach theology in its purity without the leaven of worldly knowledge, not adulterating the word of God with the constructions of philosophers.[24]

But the criticism was not of natural philosophy as such, anymore than it had been under Honorius. In 1224 Honorius had written to Stephen Langton, recognizing the outstanding reputation for learning of Michael Scot and directing that he be accorded a suitable benefice to support his studies.[25] In 1227 Gregory added his backing, referring explicitly to Michael's knowledge of Hebrew and Arabic.[26] At a time, then, when the skill of the translator and his collaborators was making available the *libri naturales*, banned at Paris, the popes were asking for financial support to keep this channel open, much as they might deplore its ill-judged incursions into the proper realm of theology.

By 1229 Gregory was regretting that while the church of Paris is a city set on a hill, William of Auvergne, his recent choice as bishop, had not proved to be its hoped-for morning star. He had failed to intervene effectively in the dispute that had led to the dispersal of the *studium*, so that that river by which the Paradise of the universal church is watered had dried up like a stream diverted into many rivulets. William was blamed for hiding the Parisian light under a bushel, for the laying waste of the Lord's vineyard, the triumph of the idol Bel, the reconsignment of Daniel to the lions' den, the closing of

---

[23] See *CUP* 1: 106-107, no. 50 (23 Jan. 1225): "... cum apostolus profanas novitates doceat evitare: nos juxta pastoralis sollicitudinis debitum corruptele quam posset ingerere liber hujusmodi occurrere satagentes vobis universis et singulis in virtute Spiritus Sancti districte precipiendo mandamus quatinus librum ipsum sollicite perquiratis..." (p. 107).

[24] See *CUP* 1: 114-116, no. 59 (7 July 1228).

[25] See *CUP* 1: 105, no. 48 (16 Jan. 1224).

[26] See *CUP* 1: 110, no. 54 (28 Apr. 1227).

heaven to Scripture, the darkening of sun, moon and stars.[27] Similar language coloured the letter appointing arbitrators.[28] Gregory then wrote to the young King Louis and his mother, urging that power be tempered with wisdom lest it degenerate into foolishness. Wisdom is nourished by learning, he said, so once more the complaint was rehearsed with the familiar images of dessication and darkness to impress the need for clemency.[29]

The threat of migration was not an empty one, and Toulouse profited by the occasion to send round a circular with language as fulsome as that of the popes. Their whole effort, they said, had been to lay a durable foundation for philosophical studies, on which the rest might build. Papal approval and the uninterrupted course of lectures and disputations had brought a flood of scholars there from Paris, seeing that the flowers had appeared in their land flowing with honey, or—in pagan terms—where Bacchus reigns. If Bordeaux wine was not inducement enough, there were theologians not only instructing from their professorial chairs but also—in what sounds like extension lectures—teaching the people at the crossroads. The books of natural philosophy, banned at Paris, could be heard there by those who wished to examine the heart of nature. They would be assured, too, the liberal support of the counts of Toulouse and the local courts, and it was hoped that the papal legate would augment their teachers of theology and canon law.[30]

Gregory's efforts to restore the studies at Paris continued. In 1230 he wrote comparing it to Jerusalem, the blissful city, a vision of peace from the Lord's watch-tower, whose flood of living water had now been diminished by discord affecting the study of theology and other branches of learning.[31] With the resumption in 1231 Gregory addressed it as *Parens scientiarum* and *Civitas litterarum*, using the etymology of "Cariath Sepher" from Joshua

---

[27] See *CUP* 1: 125-127, no. 69 (23 Nov. 1229): "... te machinante fluvius, studium videlicet litterarum, quo irrigatur et fecundatur post Spiritus Sancti gratiam generalis ecclesie paradisus, a suo alveo, civitate Parisiensi videlicet, in qua viguisse dinoscitur hactenus, est distortus..." (p. 126). Giles Constable, "Renewal and Reform in Religious Life: Concepts and Realities," in *Renaissance and Renewal in the Twelfth Century*, ed. Robert L. Benson and Giles Constable (Cambridge, Mass., 1982), pp. 48-51, describes a tendency in the eleventh and twelfth centuries to use paradisiacal imagery for the cloister rather than for the Church as a whole. Here it is used for the Church, but a privileged role is given to Paris, which Alexander Neckam had already described as "quidam paradisus deliciarum" in his *De laudibus divinae sapientiae*, ed. Thomas Wright, with *De naturis rerum libri duo*, RS 34 (London, 1863), p. 453; cf. *CUP* 1: 21, no. 20, n. 8. Later it will be increasingly used for the university.

[28] See *CUP* 1: 127-128, no. 70 (24 Nov. 1229).

[29] See *CUP* 1: 128-129, no. 71 (26 Nov. 1229).

[30] See *CUP* 1: 129-131, no. 72 (end of 1229).

[31] See *CUP* 1: 133-134, no. 75 (10 May 1230): "... Parisius par Syon videbatur effecta, et tanquam Jerusalem similis dici poterat urbs beata, quia speculatores ejus in specula Domini constituti pacis videre poterant et ostendere visionem" (p. 133).

15:15, applied to it by the twelfth-century Premonstratensian, Philip de Harvengt (1158-1181).[32] It was hailed as a workshop of wisdom, where priceless jewellery of mystical eloquence is fashioned to adorn Christ's bride; iron furnishes the armour of Christian warfare, the breastplate of faith and the sword of the Spirit; stony hearts are inflamed with the fervour of that Spirit in an academic forge resonant with the preaching of Christ. Certain statutory provisions were agreed for examination of licence candidates; detailed regulations on other matters were left to the university. The status of scholars was protected against the impositions of the chancellor. The *libri naturales* were not to be used until they had been purged. Theologians were not to put themselves forward as philosophers. They must strive to become "theodocti," only disputing those questions that can be settled from theological works and the patristic writings.[33] The same preamble was used in writing to the king to renew the privileges granted under Philip Augustus.[34] The hair-clipping, nail-paring and despoiling of the Egyptians were entrusted to William of Auxerre and two canons of Rheims, who were to extract what was of value from the Aristotelian texts.[35]

Writing to the king in 1233, Gregory briefly returned to his metallurgical imagery: the young men, beaten into shape in the forge of the liberal arts with the hammers of unwearied exercise, are being prepared as vessels in which the waters of saving wisdom may be drawn from the springs of the Saviour; with hearts trained in wisdom, they may utter the word of life amongst the people. The kingdom of France is made a very Paradise of the Lord by the vernal growth of religious communities, from which offshoots spread around the globe; its clergy are glittering jewels, ennobling it with their life, knowledge and teaching. However, a more sombre picture emerged from the resurgence of heresy and attacks on religious and scholars.[36] Philip the Chancellor had been attacked, and Gregory had a special concern to protect this "herald of the Lord, who had sat in the chair of the elders, disputing wisdom among the perfect and making the learned more learned." [37]

---

[32] See *CUP* 1: 50, nos. 51, 52; *PL* 203: 26, 34. Philip was abbot of Bonne-Espérance, 1158-1181, when he wrote these letters. He died in 1182.

[33] See *CUP* 1: 136-139, no. 79 (13 Apr. 1231). A copy of this letter was sent to the dean and chapter of Paris on the same day; ibid., 1: 139, no. 80. A garbled version from the Rheims chapter is found in Oct. 1256; ibid., 1: 341-342, no. 295.

[34] See *CUP* 1: 140-141, no. 82 (14 Apr. 1231).

[35] See *CUP* 1: 143-144, no. 87 (23 Apr. 1231). On 20 April Gregory had granted powers of absolution to the abbot of Saint-Victor and the prior of Saint-Jacques in regard to censures incurred because of the banning of the *libri naturales* in 1210 and 1215; ibid., 1: 143, no. 86.

[36] See *CUP* 1: 148-149, no. 96 (27 Feb. 1233).

[37] See *CUP* 1: 149-150, no. 97 (28 Feb. 1233): "Nuper siquidem inter alia quoddam horrendum nobis innotuit, super quo, si te ac alios clericos et laicos, ut deberet, zelus

After the brief pontificate of Celestine IV, Innocent IV in 1245 lent his authority to a proposal to send monks of Clairvaux for study at Paris: the light of knowledge and holiness will enhance the standing of the Cistercian Order as a light for the nations; monks, living together and engaged in the study of Scripture, will add to the comeliness of the Church at large.[38] In a letter to the Cistercian general chapter he favoured Paris as a city uniquely suitable for their *studium*, where the minds of monks might inhere in the firmament of Scripture, undarkened by the shadow of the world's sinfulness.[39] He looked to the Dominicans to provide a teacher for these monks.[40]

Again, the stress on Paris was not exclusive. The liberties of Toulouse were confirmed as those of another fountain of saving knowledge to bring about a fresh flowering of Catholic faith where it had been almost overthrown by Catharism. With Rachel, Innocent said, the thirsty may water their camels, burdened by a hump of sin, turning from what is transitory to the flood of theological learning. The bread of Scripture is broken in Toulouse for the little ones, and Peter trails his net, so that no one lacks rewards who approaches knowledge with a pure heart. The liberal arts play the subservient part of handmaids at the bulwarks of the heavenly city.[41] In 1246 Grosseteste was given Paris as a model for examination practice at Oxford.[42] In 1248 Piacenza was approved as yet another fountain of living water and well-defended tower of David.[43]

After extending the seizure of the Talmud to other parts of France in 1244,[44] in 1247 Innocent wrote to the king, decreeing that their books were

---

comederet domus Dei, prius ad nos vindicte fama perferri debuit, quam querela, quod videlicet ille preco Domini, qui valenter argentea tuba clamat ad opulos, qui sedens in cathedra seniorum, cum linguam habeat eruditam, de sapientia inter perfectos disputat, audientes doctos efficiens doctiores, dilectus videlicet filius Ph. cancellarius Parisiensis ... dum vellet ... abbatem Sancti Prejecti ... in sua sede juxta officii sui debitum installare, Egidius Fontis Somensis senescallus ... sic turpiter tractavit eundem, quod referre forsan non expedit..." (p. 150). Letters in these terms were addressed to the bishops of Noyon, Rheims and Sens.

[38] See *CUP* 1: 175-176, no. 133 (5 Jan. 1245).

[39] See *CUP* 1: 183-184, no. 146 (4 Sep. 1245). Further letters extend the Cistercian privileges: ibid., 1: 190-191, no. 157 (19 June 1246), 1: 219-220, no. 192 (26 Aug. 1250).

[40] See *CUP* 1: 187, no. 151 (8 Jan. 1246).

[41] See *CUP* 1: 184, no. 147 (11 Sep. 1245), 1: 185-186, no. 149 (22 Sep. 1245): "... nunc conversi ad fluenta theologice discipline in ipsius lumine vident lumen a quo tanquam a patre luminum omne datum optimum et omne donum perfectum emanat verius et descendit. Ibi lactentes ad ubera pendent matris. Ibi parvulis panis frangitur scripturarum. Ibi exercitatos habentibus sensus in altum retia ducit Petrus ita ut nullus expers munerum inveniatur ipsius qui ad eandem scientiam accesserit puro corde. Vocat hec siquidem ancillas artes videlicet liberales ad sui obsequium ad superne menia civitatis" (p. 185).

[42] See *CUP* 1: 189, no. 154 (20 May 1246).

[43] See *CUP* 1: 208-209, no. 177ª (6 Feb. 1248).

[44] See *CUP* 1: 173-174, no. 131 (9 May 1244).

not to be restored to the rabbis. He then compared the universal vigilance of the *summus pontifex* to that of the living creatures of the Apocalypse, with eyes before and behind.[45] Looking beyond the confines of Christendom, with a missionary concern, he told the chancellor that his heart was set on the accomplishment by study of whatever would advance the salvation of souls and extend the guy-ropes of the tent of Christian faith. Ten boys, sent to Paris to study Arabic and other oriental languages, were intended to be trained in God's commandments so that they might train others overseas for salvation through their teaching of Scripture.[46]

In 1253 the Apostolic See's special good will towards the friars as useful coadjutors for the Catholic faith led Innocent to press for the acceptance of their candidates by the secular masters;[47] in 1254 it was the Cistercians' candidate who was being promoted.[48] When the university complained against the consequent restriction of secular chairs in theology to three, it was they who now described this as a threat to the divinely planted Paradise of delights. Of the four streams of theology, law, medicine and philosophy, they urged the close connection of the first with the cure of souls.[49] Innocent

---

[45] See *CUP* 1: 201-202, no. 172 (12 Aug. 1247): "Ad instar animalium, que vidit in Apocalipsi Johannes plena oculis ante et retro, summus pontifex oculatus undique circumspiciens tanquam sapientibus et insipientibus debitor, nulli debet injuste nocere, sed juste quod justum exequendo tenetur reddere cuilibet jura sua" (p. 201). The legate reported unfavourably at some time after 12 Aug. 1247 (ibid., 1: 202-205, no. 173) and decreed on 15 May 1248 (ibid., 1: 209-211, no. 178) that the writings were not to be restored to the rabbis.

[46] See *CUP* 1: 212, no. 180 (before 22 June 1248): "Quia cordi nobis est illa debita meditatione perficere, per que salus animarum proveniat et fidei christiane religio dilatato tentorii sui loco funiculos suos faciat longiores, quosdam pueros tam in arabica quam in aliis linguis orientalium partium peritos Parisius mitti disposuimus ad studendum, ut in sacra pagina docente vias mandatorum Domini eruditi alios in ultramarinis partibus erudiant ad salutem." Pensions for these studies were to be paid for three years by the monastery of Saint-Pierre, Chartres; ibid., 1: 212-213, nos. 181-182 (22 June 1248). Cf. Honorius IV, ibid., 1: 638-639, no. 527 (23 Jan. 1286).

[47] See *CUP* 1: 247-248, nos. 222-223 (1 July 1253); 1: 249-251, nos. 225-226 (26 Aug. 1253): "... apostolica sedes jam dictos fratres velud coadjutores catholice fidei et cooperatores bonorum perutiles benivolentia speciali prosequitur..." (p. 250).

[48] See *CUP* 1: 251-252, nos. 227-229 (28 Jan. 1254).

[49] See *CUP* 1: 252-258, no. 230 (4 Feb. 1254): "Excelsi dextera paradisum voluptatis olym plantavit Parisius venerandum gignasium litterarum, unde sapientie fons ascendit, qui in quatuor facultates, videlicet theologiam, jurisperitiam, medicinam necnon rationalem, naturalem, moralem philosophiam quasi in iiij^{or} paradysi flumina distributus per quatuor mundi climata derivatus universam terram irrigat et infundit, ex quo quam multifarios, spirituales ac temporales profectus christiana professio experitur, luce clarius patet cunctis" (p. 252). In the late twelfth century, Guy de Bazoches had spoken of three streams of spiritual exegesis: "Hic fons doctrine salutaris exuberat, et, quasi tres rivos ex se limpidissimos ad prata mentium irriganda producens, dividit tripliciter intellectum sacre pagine spiritualem in hystoricum, allegoricum et moralem" (ibid., 1: 56, no. 54). In the 1250s the university has caught the significance for the universal church of its four faculties, extending the papal image.

supported theological study again in a letter to the prelates of France, the British Isles, Spain and Hungary, banning the teaching of law to curb clerical careerism and direct attention to studies directly showing the way to salvation, or even to philosophy which, though lacking a religious character, aims at knowledge and the banishment of cupidity.[50]

Whatever Innocent's dispositions towards the mendicants at the beginning of his pontificate may have been, it was clear by 1254 that he was acceding to the demands of the seculars, giving financial assistance to William of Saint-Amour and others and imposing restrictions where mendicants were judged to have encroached on their pastoral preserve.[51] The pope said that his universal care brooked such interference, but he wished that he, as much as the religious, should be beyond criticism; as he wrote to Saint-Quentin, he desired to be "governed by such a concern that a curious critic should find nothing worthy of note."[52] But one of the first acts of Alexander IV was to rescind Innocent's restrictions as decisions made without full discussion when otherwise preoccupied.[53] Alexander's *Quasi lignum vitae* of 1255 made detailed provision for teaching in theology and canon law so as not to exclude properly qualified religious. If Parisian learning is the tree of life, the Creator's providence has directed the work of teachers in Paris, leading the desire of rational creatures towards the fruit of life. The pope says this his care for the common good is expressed by maintaining peace and bestowing patronage. From the high-point of God's house, overseeing all mankind, he is aroused to special vigilance and his heart is inflamed by this special charge.[54] Four months later, however, the seculars were telling Alexander

---

[50] See *CUP* 1: 261-262, no. 235 (12 Oct. 1253 - 27 Apr. 1254).

[51] See *CUP* 1: 265-270, nos. 238-240 (15 July, 31 Aug., 21 Nov. 1254).

[52] See *CUP* 1: 263-264, no. 236 (10 May 1254): "Nos itaque, qui cunctos Christi fideles et presertim regularis ordinis professores eo providentie studio gubernari cupimus, ut in eis curiosus etiam scrutator nichil inveniat nota dignum..." (p. 264).

[53] See *CUP* 1: 276-277, no. 244 (22 Dec. 1254): "Nec insolitum est nec novum, ut ea que per occupationem vel festinantiam fiunt, pro eo quod congrue deliberationis limam pretereunt, in propensioris considerationis reducantur examen, ut rectiora et elimatiora per attentionem plenioris discussionis emaneant. Sane quedam ab apostolica sede tempore felicis recordationis Innocentii pape IV predecessoris nostri littere processerunt.... Verum, quia super premissis litteris cogitare attentius et studiosus deliberare proponimus, pacis commodum et quietis solatium ecclesiis et personis ecclesiasticis potissime cupientes, prefatas litteras ... ac mandata seu precepta facta in eis, vel earum auctoritate duximus penitus revocanda."

[54] See *CUP* 1: 279-285, no. 247 (14 Apr. 1255): "Ut igitur consortii vestri communicabile ac commune omnibus bonum omni pacis custodia servare curemus et favorabilibus patrociniis communire, ne in commune publice salutis exitium illud emula caritatis et unionis invida sathane labefactare possit astutia, instructa quippe modis innumerabilibus ad nocendum, in nobis, quos licet indignos cunctis mortalibus Dei dignatio superintendere voluit de supremo fastigio domus sue, precipua sollicitudinis vigilancia excitatur et cor nostrum urit cure stimulus specialis" (p. 280).

that the tree of life had become a tree of death; that they would rather leave their Paradise than eat the bitter fruit of the Dominicans. The universal desolation that they foresee might even, they add with a wry twist, bring to an end the rule of Peter, as had been foretold by Joachim in the Eternal Gospel.[55]

Efforts to enforce *Quasi lignum vitae* continued.[56] Alexander also continued to promote the Cistercians as shining lights in the household of faith, not hidden under a bushel.[57] In 1256 the pope was able to commend the chancellor for licensing Aquinas,[58] but the Dominicans were still living in a state of siege, as Humbert of Romans testifies.[59] Alexander complained to the bishop that the affair had been injurious to the Apostolic See, a handicap to the studies and a loss to souls.[60] The value he placed on mendicant teaching is seen in his directions for the completion of Alexander of Hales' *Summa*: the delicate reader may find it long-winded, but the pope appreciates its depth.[61]

By contrast, William of Saint-Amour's *De periculis novissimorum temporum* was condemned as a seed-bed for scandal, material for confusion, putting souls in jeopardy, withdrawing from devotion and impeding entry to religious life. The Roman pontiff looks out from the watchtower of his supreme apostolate to the city and world. Dutiful service preoccupies him with cares beyond number; he is taken up with limitless designs. A position above that of others brings more pressing concerns; greater authority increases the planning. The higher the place from which he presides, the more extensive the view and the more he can do by his office, the greater the burden of watchfulness that falls upon him; since the chief responsibility is attached to the greatest position, the heaviest burden goes with the highest honour and more extended care prods the mind with keener spurs. Since it

---

[55] See *CUP* 1: 292-297, no. 256 (2 Oct. 1255): "Tunc etiam, quod absit, finiendum Petri timeri posset imperium juxta heresiarche Joachimi prophetias in libro illo, qui perniciose et damnabiliter *Eternum Evangelium* appellatur" (p. 296). On 23 Oct. 1255 Alexander called for the destruction of Joachim's work: ibid., 1: 297, no. 257.

[56] See *CUP* 1: 298-300, 301-302, 304, nos. 259-261, 263-264, 267 (7 Dec. 1255, 28 Jan. 1256).

[57] See *CUP* 1: 289-290, 302-303, nos. 251-253, 265-266 (18, 22 June 1255, 31 Jan. 1256).

[58] See *CUP* 1: 307, no. 270 (3 Mar. 1256).

[59] See *CUP* 1: 312, no. 273 (beginning of April 1256).

[60] See *CUP* 1: 323-324, no. 281 (27 Jun. 1256): "Alias etiam non sine apostolice sedis injuria et impedimento dicti studii ac salutis animarum dispendio intentionem nostram circa effectum ordinationis ipsius evacuare multipliciter moliuntur" (p. 323). See, too, ibid., 1: 314-315, 319-323, 324-326, 327, nos. 275-276, 280-282, 284 (12 Apr., 5 May, 17, 27 Jun., 1 Jul. 1256).

[61] See *CUP* 1: 328-329, no. 286 (28 Jul. 1256).

is the business of other pastors to attend to their sheep, it is incumbent on the one who presides at Rome, to whom the flock as a whole is assigned, from the loftier summit, namely the Apostolic See, to look to it more broadly and perseveringly. As they preside over their limited peoples, this prelate is pontiff to everyone without distinctions, the general guardian and cultivator of the Lord's vineyard and supreme pastor of the entire Catholic sheepfold and of all the pastors.

With this general concern, since his mental gaze is bound to take in everything, at times his spirit is overwhelmed and trembles under the weight of such a heavy and difficult charge, so that the strength of failing nature scarcely has confidence in being able to support it. Business flows in to him from every side; disputes arrive; doubtful matters are referred and unpleasant and problematic cases are settled. Nor does the torrent flooding in ever cease; neither do the powerful and threatening tempests of this deep ocean grow still. Having dealt with those things that are now pressing, soon others follow. Nor can so many knots of complicated questions be resolved by apostolic decision, that others more tangled and knotty do not come on top, to be resolved by mature deliberation and skilled determination. Rather, from the fact that his declarative expressions have removed the fog of doubt from difficult and obscure issues, straightway new confusions assail, to be elucidated by the apostolic oracle and clarified for minds in doubt and uncertainty. The bishop of Rome has anxiety without leisure, work without rest, employment without vacation, enormous and exacting mental activity and wakefulness without sleep. Not for a little even does his daily pressure let up, going on all the time and taking all his time, continually pressing. For there is always matter for thought; nor does it end with the passage of time, but persists as long as time itself, since there is no lack of business as time goes by, and what passes is constantly renewed. Yet the enemy is not merely time but that ancient foe of mankind, on whose deceits the pope then expatiates and at whose door he finally lays the falsehood and malice of William's work.[62]

---

[62] See *CUP* 1: 331-333, no. 288 (5 Oct. 1256): "Romanus Pontifex de summi apostolatus specula Urbi et Orbi debita servitute prospiciens curis occupatus innumeris, et cogitationibus rapitur infinitis; quia eminentior ceteris sedes ejus sollicitudines sibi vehementiores accumulat, et ipsius auctoritas potior meditationes ei multiplicat ampliores: quo etiam altius presidet, eo longius latiusque circumspicit, et quanto plus potest officio, tanto majoris vigilantie sibi sarcina incumbente plus pensat, quoniam maxime dignitati potissima sollicitudo coheret, et altiorem honorem onus gravius comitatur, curaque profusior ardentioribus stimulis mentem urget. Unde cum aliis plebium fidelium pastoribus, quibus grex dominicus particulariter est commissus, immineat de suarum ecclesiarum eminentia vigilanter ad suas oves attendere incumbit utique Romano presuli, cui est grex ipse generaliter creditus, de sublimi ecclesiarum vertice, sede scilicet apostolica, propensius ad illum, et instantius intueri; quia cum hii suis limitatis

Alexander continued to praise the effective preaching of the friars, writing to the king.[63] To the bishops he stressed the apostolic authority he had invoked in imposing sanctions.[64] To the university he repeated the old blandishments, evoking a vision of Paris bringing the dawn of enlightenment. Its flood of writings and teaching nourish the Church with the sweet fruits of wisdom. A celebrated line of teachers enlightens Christian peoples and strengthens Christian faith. Theology has the highest place, presiding over the other disciplines as their superior, commanding others as their lady, governing others as their prelate. This life-giving vine in the Church's vineyard gives a wealth of vital refreshment to Catholic folk, so his concern is for its continuance, firm and unshaken, whole and undivided. This gathering of the nations is there to acquire the resources of knowledge and make progress in virtue. That is the reason for their sleepless nights and all those parental sacrifices to maintain them in this paradise of perfumes, reading with relish from the choice dishes of letters, increasing each day in goodness, so that labour and study may shine out to the praise of God, to their own honour and good estate and the joy of their neighbours. The pope praises the friars for their constant attachment to Scripture, defends them against their critics, and calls for the destruction of William's book, a challenge to papal and episcopal authority, and the acceptance of the friars.[65]

---

populis presint, singuli quidem singulis, hic sine distinctione prelatus est pontifex universis, dominice quidem vinee custos generalis et cultor, et totius ovilis catholici pastorumque omnium summus pastor. Incumbente itaque sibi generali sollicitudine super omnes, cum ex hoc sue mentis intuitum per cuncta diffundere teneatur, stupet nimirum ipsius animus, et sub tam gravis et difficilis cure pondere contremisit (sic), quod posset suffere, ut convenit, vis nature occidue vix confidit. Ad eum namque negotia undique confluunt, perveniunt lites, dubia deferuntur, et destinantur implacita et perplexa; nec unquam horum influens torrens cessat, nec hujus alti pelagi valide infesteque procelle quiescunt; sed hiis que imminent nunc expeditis, mox alia subsecuntur; nec tot implexarum questionum nodi decisione apostolica solvi possunt, quin et alie irretite et nodose superveniant, deliberatione matura et consulta diffinitione solvende. Immo ex quo de instantibus difficilibus, et obscuris dubietatis caliginem verbo sue declarationis amoverit, statim nova et recentia turbulenta ingruunt apostolico dilucidando oraculo et ambiguis ac incertis mentibus clare dissertionis lumine serenanda. Propter quod inest Romano antistiti sollicitudo sine otio, labor sine quiete, occupatio sine vacatione, exercitium sine tranquillo, ingens et sedula meditatio et vigilia sine sompno. Nec ad modicum etiam sua cotidiana intermissionem habet instantia, que nec omittitur aliquo tempore, nec aliquod ipsa tempus omittit, urget continue; quia cogitandi materia semper adest, nec successu temporis desinit, sed cum illius diuturnitate perdurat, quia nec decursu temporum deficiunt negotia, sed assidue illis succedentibus renascuntur" (p. 331). For the topos of the tireless ruler see Giulio Silano, "Of Sleep and Sleeplessness," above, pp. 343-361.

[63] See *CUP* 1: 333-337, nos. 289-290 (17, 19 Oct. 1256).

[64] See *CUP* 1: 337-338, no. 291 (21 Oct. 1256): "... ne quisquam predictum libellum ore apostolico jam dampnatum approbare vel quomodolibet defensare presumat, et si quis presumpserit, tanquam contumax, inobediens, et rebellis Romane ecclesie ab omnibus fidelibus habeatur..." (p. 337).

[65] See *CUP* 1: 342-346, no. 296 (10 Nov. 1256): "Libellum etiam quemdam valde

In 1257 Alexander says he is exhausted by a ministry of care that goes beyond his powers, with controversies assailing on all sides and remedies to be found, old affairs reviving with even greater din, stones of even greater scandal being strewn on the rough path he has cleared. He fears bad example may lead to decay of due obedience to God and his vicar (*in debita Deo ejusque vicario obedientia*), obstructing the faculty of theology and so endangering orthodox faith, which derives growth and vigour from the progress of scriptural studies. Rejecting as frivolous what has been alleged by the seculars, he calls for full observance of his ordinances and rescripts.[66]

The pope's commendation of the Order of Preachers as a fruitful tree in Paradise and his support in their vicissitudes won from Humbert of Romans recognition of a beneficence that could hardly be described.[67] Even after William's exile secular opposition went on until 1259, when the pope

---

perniciosum et detestabilem temere de novo compositum post plenam ipsius examinationem, quia in eo quedam contra auctoritatem Romani pontificis et coepiscoporum suorum ... tanquam iniquum, scelestum et execrabilem de fratrum nostrorum consilio auctoritate apostolica reprobandum duximus..." (p. 345).

[66] See *CUP* 1: 354-356, no. 309 (12 May 1257): "Circa frequens cotidiane sollicitudinis ministerium occupati supra vires nostras assiduis ingruentium undique disceptationum incursibus fatigamur, que nos inevitabili necessitate constringunt emergentibus litigiorum morbis varia remedia providere. Sed interdum pacem credimur dedisse negotiis, et eadem majori strepitu recidivant, dumque offensionis lapides, quibus vie vite hujus inhorret asperitas, ut rationalium afectuum pietas liberius procurrat in Deum, salutaribus studiis removemus, hominis inimici malignitas petras aliquando scandali superjacit gravioris. Hinc utique fit, quod operosior cura plerumque nobis imminet circa plurima, que salubri sategimus curasse medela et propensior nos labor repetit post labores, quibus altam aliis studuimus preparare quietem" (p. 354); "Aggravat autem culpam eorum exempli contagium, quo fideles tam principes quam populi facile possent in debita Deo ejusque vicario obedientia et devotione corrumpi, si qua ex dissimulationis nostre patientia illorum inobedientie proveniret auctoritas, quibus fidem prebet in plebe fideli scientia fidei, qua eminere creduntur per doctrine studium et exercitium discipline" (p. 355). Alexander's theme of the overwhelming cares of his office, here and in n. 62, may be related to the enormous growth of curial business in the thirteenth century. Jane E. Sayers, *Papal Government and England during the Pontificate of Honorius III (1216-1227)*, Cambridge Studies in Medieval Life and Thought, 3rd Series 21 (Cambridge, 1984), pp. 50-51, estimates an annual output of letters from the papal chancery of Honorius as 1930, multiplying by four the number actually registered, and refers to the upward curve under Innocent IV and Alexander IV. She regards as realistic Fawtier's estimate that at the end of the century Boniface VIII was issuing 50,000 letters a year. Few of these, she thinks (p. 59), "were not actively sought and petitioned for."

[67] See *CUP* 1: 356-358, no. 310 (23 May 1257) for Alexander's commendation. This follows on further attempts to impose the pope's will in letters to the bishops and the chancellor and eventually the episcopate throughout the world; ibid., 1: 346-349, 350-352, 352-353, nos. 297-301, 303-306, 307-308 (31 Dec. 1256, 7, 13 Jan., 2 Feb., 10, 11, 13, 30 Mar. 1257). Humbert's letter to the Order of Preachers was written at the end of May 1257; ibid., 1: 358-359, no. 311: "... tantis patrociniis non ingrati, pro eis orate devote, et specialissime pro domino papa beatissimo nostro, cujus benignatio ad Ordinem vix exprimi lingua posset" (p. 358).

instructed the chancellor of Sainte-Geneviève, to whom many arts students went for the licence, that it was only to be conferred on those who had sworn to uphold the papal ordinances.[68] The bishop was warned against interference in regard to inceptions in theology.[69] The Picard bedel was deprived for circulating opposition literature during a sermon by Aquinas.[70] The *studium*, the pope says, is a light from heaven for the Church militant, whence young men, clad in the scales of sensuality, are directed towards the hidden principles of higher learning by going through the rudiments of the liberal arts. In that gymnasium of sacred doctrine a spring of limpid clarity gushes forth to revive the thirst for righteousness in the reborn, so that those who look for the image of the divine may see the exemplar of the uncreated likeness, to reform the minds of rational creatures in the pure form of creation and gracious re-creation. The pope's predecessors have knit together the university with a covenant of association through privileges and other aids to give stability to its shared life, making it a place of peaceful retreat. Alexander has shown tireless care in providing against any disturbance with remedies, now harsh, now gentle. The Dominicans, who being religious are counted as members of the universal Church, ought not in their teaching to be excluded from the society of the university.[71]

[68] See *CUP* 1: 387-388, no. 337 (18 Jun. 1259). Earlier letters on the dispute are: ibid., 1: 359-370, 381-383, 387, nos. 312-316, 318-321, 331-332, 336 (14, 31 Jul., 9, 11, 23 Aug., 24, 27 Sep., 2, 13 Oct. 1257, 5 Apr., 13 Jun. 1259).

[69] See *CUP* 1: 388, no. 338 (19 Jun. 1259). The following day he is warned against communication between the university and William; ibid., 1: 388-389, no. 339 (20 Jun. 1259).

[70] See *CUP* 1: 390-392, no. 342 (26 Jun. 1259).

[71] See *CUP* 1: 392-395, no. 343 (11 July 1259): "... predecessores nostri Romani posthabuere pontifices ... universitatem vestram unanimitatis vinculo et societatis federe nexuerunt, sede apostolica privilegiis, indulgentiis aliisque roborum amminiculis communionis vestre stabiliente consortium et egregiis doctoribus cum disciplinatis sapientie filiis, quorum vos esse convenit sectatores, sibimet vobisque commendantibus pacis otium secessumque silentii, sine quibus vix prudentie studia convalescunt. Nos quoque, licet predictis predecessoribus impares merito et virtute, ad ipsorum tamen vestigia circa profectus Universitatis et studii predictorum affectu non impari gestientes, si quid temporibus nostris emersisse comperimus, quod in vobis turbaret pacem, caritatem lederet aut scinderet unitatem, contra id sincera intentione medendi pariter ac sanandi morbos noxios, quibus commune salutis vestre commodum tangebatur, remedia nunc aspera, nunc levia, prout res attentius considerata suasit, impigra sollicitudine priscorum exempla ammoniti curavimus providere. Ea utique cura illud consilium peperit, ut inter alia, que olim pro Universitatis et discipline vestre profectu salubriter ordinanda perspeximus, quod religiosi viri presertim fratres Predicatores et Minores degentes Parisius, qui sicut merito religionis et vite decora membra universalis ecclesie sunt censendi, sic eodem merito et participatione doctrine atque scientie Universitatis vestre debent pars non incongrua nec indigna videri, ejusdem Universitatis tam consortio quam beneficio gauderent in omnibus sub certa forma duximus statuendum. Sed licet non forsan in omnibus, in plurimis tamen animose voluntatis arbitrio rationabilis equitatis evertente judicium aliqui contra ordinationem nostram, cui voluntarie approbationis assensus et prompte obeditionis

But the dispute over the mendicants was not the pope's only concern. In 1259 he wrote to the chancellor of Sainte-Geneviève that the licence was to be granted only to those duly examined;[72] to the king he praised Robert de Sorbonne's college, where studies in theology would advance the cause of God and the salvation of souls;[73] to the hierarchy of France he encouraged support of needy students of theology for the good that might come out of that faculty.[74] Pleas for William's restoration were still rejected and, shortly before he died, Alexander's only concession was to grant a faculty for absolving those who handled the proscribed literature.[75]

In 1262 Urban IV, a Frenchman of humble origins who was to befriend Aquinas, wrote to the secular masters Gerard of Abbeville and Gerard of Goignelin that the apostolic protection must ensure that those who seek the pearl of knowledge are not impeded by vicious men.[76] A universal appeal for support for the Sorbonne also included the reminder that amidst all the fecundity of the rich field of Paris some are not escaping hardship to come by that pearl.[77] Repeating Gregory's decree on immunity from censure, Urban declared in 1263 that it would be unfitting for him to deny the apostolic favour to those who had given themselves up to wisdom, he too once sweated away at the tasks of the schools and is now called, although unworthy, to the supreme magisterium.[78] To the Sorbonne itself he said that he rejoiced to learn of their common life given over to the study of Scripture, from which the faculty of theology might hope for a fine growth. Their good grounding in arts gave promise that they would swiftly make others fruitful through teaching moistened with divine grace.[79] Palencia too was encouraged in similarly moist and fruity terms.[80] In 1264, in his last months, however,

---

obsequium debebatur, presumptuosum rebellionis levavere calcaneum, aliqui mandatorum nostrorum vim et potestatem ingeniosis adinventionibus vacuantes superficialiter sic nostris detulere sermonibus, quod verius illusisse probantur" (pp. 392-393).

[72] See *CUP* 1: 397, no. 346 (2 Aug. 1259).

[73] See *CUP* 1: 397-398, no. 347 (2 Aug. 1259).

[74] See *CUP* 1: 398-399, no. 348 (4 Aug. 1259).

[75] See *CUP* 1: 414, no. 366 (3 Dec. 1260). Other relevant documents of this period are: ibid., 1: 395-396, 401-405, nos. 344-345, 353-357 (25 Jul., 11 Aug., 24 Sep. 1259).

[76] See *CUP* 1: 423, no. 377 (3 Jun. 1262).

[77] See *CUP* 1: 423-424, no. 378 (22 Jun. 1262).

[78] See *CUP* 1: 427, no. 383 (19 Jan. 1263): "Non decet nos vobis apostolicum negare favorem, quem vobis vestris videmini meritis comparare, dum dantes operam sapientie, que plurimum nos delectat, nostre vos gratie coaptetis, qui aliquando disciplinis scolasticis insudantes ad summum licet immeriti magisterium evocati." Urban went on to confirm the Parisian statutes and offer protection against episcopal intervention in regard to the university's debts: ibid., 1: 427-429, nos. 384-385 (19, 27 Jan. 1263).

[79] See *CUP* 1: 430-431, no. 388 (4 May 1263).

[80] See *CUP* 1: 431, no. 389 (14 May 1263).

Urban's eyes were again on Paris, as he intervened to ensure that licensing in theology was not abused by the chancellor, Étienne Tempier, who had refused to take the statutory oath and had usurped the role of the dean of theology.[81]

There is a sharper note with Clement IV, another Frenchman, as he writes to the legate Simon de Brie in 1266 about undisciplined masters and scholars and those who pass themselves off as students. Error, wherever it occurs, he says, is displeasing to the one who loves in Christ all faithful peoples, but the pope is all the more concerned that abuses should be avoided in a city that makes special claims on his charity, shining with a diffused brilliance throughout the world because of the lustre of those educated there and the starry immortality of their educators.[82] In the same year Clement wrote to William of Saint-Amour in measured terms as he began to leaf through his latest book. First impressions are unfavourable, but he suspends judgement as he is ever under pressure of affairs from different parts of the world that keenly trouble him and he has no wish to detain the messenger.[83] In 1268 he acted to protect the holdings of the Sorbonne and promote a project of Ralph of Aubusson for a house for ten poor scholars, to be maintained by tithes.[84]

Towards the end of his pontificate Clement addressed his *Quasi flumen* to the bishops of Rheims and Auxerre. God's river in full stream, he writes, the Parisian *studium*, has proved most useful to the religion of the Catholic faith. This river that gives joy to the city of God has enlightened the universal Church, educating the uncultivated and enhancing the light of the learned; this river of living water, coming forth like brilliant crystal from the seat of God and the Lamb, with the teaching of life enlivens souls and makes them resplendent with virtues. The abundant fruit it has produced, like a rich field

---

[81] See *CUP* 1: 438, 441-442, 444-445, nos. 396, 400, 404 (26 May, 26 Jun., 18 July 1264).

[82] See *CUP* 1: 446-448, no. 407 (27 May 1266): "Licet igitur universa erronea nobis, quibus omnium fidelium populorum est in Christo dilectio generalis, ubique displiceant, in civitate tamen tam nobili, tam famosa, que propter scientie fontem in universum mundum diffusa claritate refulgens celestis gloriam firmamenti presentare dinoscitur, dum qui erudiuntur ibidem celebri fiunt splendore conspicui, et qui erudiunt in eternitatem cum stellis perpetuam assumuntur, abusiones hujusmodi eo magis nostris obviant desideriis, quo ad civitatem eandem propter tantam prerogativam ipsius specialiorem affectum gerimus caritatis" (p. 447).

[83] See *CUP* 1: 459, no. 412 (18 Oct. 1266): "Nos autem, cum nobis relegerimus hoc opusculum et aliis amatoribus veritatis et eandem intelligentibus id communicaverimus, tunc quod nobis videbitur tibi dabimus intimare. Sed quia res forsan abibit in longum propter negotiorum instantiam que de mundi diversis partibus nos solito acrius inquietant, dilectum filium magistrum Thomam supradicti presentatorem operis ultra nolumus detinere."

[84] See *CUP* 1: 474-475, nos. 420-421 (23 Jan., 23 Mar. 1268).

blessed by the Lord in the universal Church, arouses special feeling in the pope who, when he was young, was turned over to its tutelage, freely tasting its sweetness for several years as he sat through its courses. Now, however, he is saddened by clouds that overshadow its wonted splendour: scholars are not drawing the waters of Siloam in silence, but going with Rasin and the sons of Romeliah to draw muddy waters down in Egypt; there are battles in the streets; the unworthy are being admitted without examination; masters are being made through favour and influence, not to say bribery; studies are dispersed with frequent toing and froing; meetings are used as an escape from disputations; frequent breaks in teaching protract the studies of the serious-minded; debts daily increase, and the university is in deep water with its creditors. Clement urged consultation with men of learning to alleviate the situation.[85]

His sucessor, the Italian Gregory x, had also been a student at Paris, but his personal interest was expressed mainly in business-like letters on legal protection for the Sorbonne.[86] To his legate Simon was entrusted the resolution of the schism among the nations in the faculty of arts in 1275.[87] After the month-long pontificate of Adrian v, hopes may have been raised by the election of another alumnus, John xxi, the Portuguese logician and medical man, Petrus Hispanus, formerly physician to Gregory x, but his brief reign has often been remembered only for the anxious letter of January 1277 to Étienne Tempier. Tempier, by then bishop of Paris, was to report on errors prejudicial to faith, threatening to muddy the limpid streams that make the Catholic faith accessible to the ends of the earth.[88] The content of the bishop's peremptory condemnation in March is not our present concern;[89] what is relevant is the papal ideal for the university, which may have sparked the powder keg.

[85] See *CUP* 1: 479-481, no. 425. The editors hesitate over the attribution and date this letter only to 1261-1268, but E. Jordan, *Les registres de Clément IV (1265-1268)*, Bibliothèque des Écoles Françaises d'Athènes et de Rome, 2ᵉ série 11 (Paris, 1893-1945), p. 341, no. 864, assigns it to the period after 12 July 1266. The pope relates his own feelings for the place of his studies thus: "Ipsius itaque studii fructus uberes, quos velut ager plenus cui benedixit Dominus in ecclesia universali produxit, meditatione frequenti revolventes in animo ex eo etiam specialiori affectu ad ejus prosperitatem afficimur quod olim, dum nos minor status haberet, in ejus laribus obversati de illius dulcedine grata libavimus per plures annos secus decursus sedentes ipsius" (p. 479).

[86] See *CUP* 1: 519-521, nos. 457-459 (5 Jan. 1275).

[87] See *CUP* 1: 521-530, no. 460 (7 May 1275).

[88] See *CUP* 1: 541-542, no. 471 (18 Jan. 1277): "Relatio nimis implacida nostrum nuper turbavit auditum, amaricavit et animum, quod Parisius, ubi fons vivus sapientie salutaris habundanter huc usque scaturiit suos rivos limpidissimos fidem patefacientes catholicam usque ad terminos orbis terre diffundens, quidam errores in prejudicium ejusdem fidei de novo pullulasse dicuntur" (p. 541).

[89] See *CUP* 1: 543-558, no. 473 (7 Mar. 1277).

Under the Orsini pope Nicholas III the burden of dealing with university problems again fell largely upon the French legate.[90] Having been their cardinal protector, Nicholas continued to devote much attention to the Franciscans. Writing to the Franciscan bishop of Poitiers, he appealed to the bishop's own experience of friary education leading to a chair in theology, to secure support for the numerous friars studying in Paris at a *studium* on which the whole Order might draw as from a spring.[91]

In 1281 when the rector appealed against the chancellor's grant of the licence without examination to the king of Aragon's brother, it was to the former legate, Simon de Brie, now pope as Martin IV.[92] In 1284 Martin wrote in similar terms both to the university and to Sainte-Geneviève to ensure that appropriate contributions were made to the common fund.[93] In that or the preceding year their proctor at the curia, John of Maligny, made a lengthy defence of the faculty of arts against charges brought by the chancellor.[94] Its substance is of less account here than its development of the paradisal imagery familiar from the papal letters. The strongest statement of the university's allegiance to the pope is in John's denial of the chancellor's pretensions to being its head:

> The university, as everyone there acknowledges, belongs to the Roman Church without intermediary: to the extent that, Holy Father, the university does not believe it has, nor acknowledges above its rector, any head other than Your Holiness. From which it follows that the chancellor, in saying that he is the head of the university, has spoken against Your Holiness in a bigheaded and fatuous fashion.[95]

---

[90] See *CUP* 1: 569-570, 575-576, 576-579, nos. 484, 490, 492-493 (18 Sep. 1278, 5 Aug., 1, 19 Oct. 1279).

[91] See *CUP* 1: 582-584, no. 498 (13 June 1280): "Circa ea que summo patri sunt placita [placida *ed.*] sedulo cogitantes, et circumspicientes undique quid illi a quo cuncta proveniunt debeatur speciale debitum, inter alia pietatis opera reputamus pie manum auxilii aperire pauperibus illis potissime, qui mandatorum Christi humiles sectatores mundi spretis divitiis degunt in presenti vita sub exercitio paupertatis voluntarii non coacti, ut tandem militent habundantius in gloria supernorum. Tunc enim ipse Christus glorificatur et collaudatur in gentibus et illi condigna laus et honor impenditur, cum talibus saltem in oportunitatibus subvenitur qui ejus vestigia sunt secuti, ut clarius eluceat fides obsequentium creatori" (p. 582).

[92] See *CUP* 1: 588-589, no. 503 (23 May 1281).

[93] See *CUP* 1: 600-602, nos. 512-513 (7 Mar. 1284): "Nos itaque paterne sollicitudinis studio ad ipsius Universitatis statum tranquillum et pacificum intendentes ac volentes hujusmodi dispendiis obviare..." is the pope's language (p. 602; cf. p. 601).

[94] See *CUP* 1: 605-623, no. 515 (between 1283 and 24 Oct. 1284).

[95] "Item, Universitas, sicut ipsa tota confitetur, nullo medio pertinet ad Romanam ecclesiam; pro quanto, pater sancte, Parisiensis Universitas non credit nec confitetur supra suum rectorem habere capud aliud a vestra Sanctitate; ad quod sequitur quod cancellarius in dicendo se Universitatis capud esse, locutus est contra vestram Sanctitatem capitose et fatue" (ibid., p. 618).

The chancellor died at the curia, but there are indications that Martin instituted an inquiry by the bishop of Amiens and Périgueux along with Henry of Ghent.[96]

A response to the allegations was made by Honorius ix in 1286, opening with the customary fulsome tribute to an unfailing well spreading streams of saving doctrine, a defence work against onslaughts on the Church. Honorius echoed Clement's words, in recalling the sweetness he had tasted from the lofty fruit-laden trees of Paris, but the sour lesson for the faculty of arts was that more respect should be shown to the chancellor in future.[97] Later Honorius helped the Austin Friars to acquire land for a *studium*, promoting yet another religious and intellectual presence, whose progress was to owe much to the prestige of a distinguished master, Giles of Rome.[98]

The Franciscan's first pope, Nicholas iv, a former Minister General, cared for his own. He wrote three times to the chancellors in 1288, urging them to license a future Minister, John de Murro, "lest the treasure of erudition this friar has been adorned with, by the gift of heaven, should be hidden and without profit." The pope's eye was on a likely lector for the curia, but the chancellors were uncooperative.[99] In 1290 the rector complained about uncooperativeness in the same quarter and irregularities over licensing in arts.[100] Difficulties persisted, and in 1292 Nicholas set up a commission to examine the university's grievance, being concerned about the abundant fruit that might derive through the teaching of various branches of knowledge and wishing to see that, with disagreements removed, those intent on study might

---

[96] See *CUP* 1: 623-624, no. 516 (14 Oct. 1284).

[97] See *CUP* 1: 639-642, no. 528 (1 Feb. 1286): "Quasi ortus irriguus arboribus sublimibus et fructiferis consitus Parisiense studium viros producens scientia fructuosos, vita et moribus eminentes, et sicut fons cujus aque non deficiunt sed exhuberanter emanant doctrine salutaris undique fluenta diffundens, quanto ab olim talium productione utili et emanatione uberi orthodossam fidem roborans sanctam catholicam munivit ecclesiam contra insidias et impetus latenter obrepentium, vel patenter ascendentium ex adverso, tanto culture diligentioris est cura colendum, ut domesticis seditionibus quo familioribus eo procul dubio efficacioribus ad nocendum purgetur intrinsecus et velut extrinsecus apostolici favoris muro circumdatum ejusque directoria provisione munitum in statu pacifico et tranquillo ipsius remedio perseverabiliter statuatur. Ad quod illud etiam nos specialiter afficit quod olim, dum nos minor status haberet, in ejusdem studii laribus observati de illius dulcedine libamina grata libavimus per plures annos secus decursus sedentes ipsius" (p. 639). Cf. Clement iv in n. 85.

[98] See *CUP* 2: 4, 8, nos. 533, 538 (1 Apr., 15 Nov. 1286).

[99] See *CUP* 2: 20-21, 22-24, nos. 548, 550-551 (16 Jun., 1, 31 Dec. 1288): "Ne thesaurus litteralis quo dilectus filius frater Johannes de Murro, Ordinis Minorum, superni numinis munere decoratus agnoscitur inutiliter occultetur, quin immo eo utilius in publicum prodeat et uberiores fructus Domino favente producat ... discretionem tuam rogamus et hortamur attente per apostolica tibi scripta mandantes quatenus eidem fratri ... licentiam largiaris..." (pp. 20-21).

[100] See *CUP* 2: 43-46, no. 569 (6 Aug. 1290).

employ themselves more fervently and usefully with peace of mind.[101] Probably he did not see the outcome, but a week later, in granting the privilege to Parisian masters to exercise a regency anywhere without re-examination, the pope described the university as a place where men are educated by whom the truth of Scripture is expounded, the uncultivated are educated, the proficient grow together towards higher things and the Catholic faith becomes stronger. His desire is that those studying at Paris may be encouraged towards the prize of the *magisterium* so as to be able to educate everyone everywhere.[102]

After the brief episode of the pontificate of Celestine v, the thirteenth century ended in a rapid deterioration of papal relations with France. Boniface viii came from the legal tradition of Bologna, but in 1295 he was supporting the theological studies of the black monks and white canons in Paris.[103] Concerned that the university should suffer no harmful loss in his time, he reserved to himself the choice of a chancellor from names submitted by the canon theologians. His imagery was that of corn and wine and the pounding of aromatic spices; his purpose was that Christian kings and kingdoms might advance by the advice of the prudent as much as by the control of their rulers. Mother Church, he said, rejoices that young shoots planted in the field of faith are ever conveyed to the heavenly plantation; heretics are shamed; falsifiers of the gospel of truth are brought into despite; the catholic and apostolic witness grows stronger, so that pained lips become mute and impudent faces hang in confusion.[104] In 1296, in view of his desire

---

[101] See *CUP* 2: 53-54, no. 577 (15 Mar. 1292).

[102] See *CUP* 2: 54-55, no. 578 (23 Mar. 1292): "Dum attente considerationis indagine perscrutamur quod per litterarum studia cooperante illo a quo omne datum optimum omneque donum confluit et perfectum, viri efficiuntur scientiis eruditi, per quos scripturarum veritas explicatur, erudiuntur rudes, provecti ad altiora concrescunt et fides catholica invalescit, libenter loca ubi pollent hujusmodi studia et studentes in eis gratis munimus immunitatibus et libertatibus honoramus."

[103] See *CUP* 2: 63-64, nos. 587, 591 (8 Mar., 1 Aug. 1295): "Exultamus in Domino, quod in tue mentis archivo hoc precipuum desiderium habetur reconditum, ut canonici tui Ordinis splendore virtutum refulgeant, et maxime illius scientie dono prerutilent, que illuminat animam, et cibo reficit refectionis eterne" (p. 66).

[104] See *CUP* 2: 66-67, no. 592 (16 Nov. 1295): "Inter cetera desideria cordis nostri et hominis interioris affectus hoc preter divinam gratiam nimirum specialiter affectamus, ut temporibus nostris Parisiense studium nullum diminutionis detrimentum incurrat, set optatum de die in diem auctore Domino suscipiat incrementum, per hoc enim veluti granum frumenti procul dubio semen Dei cadens in terram et in fidelium compressum cordibus consurgit in spicam, per hoc veluti botrus in torculari calcatus liquoris redundat in copiam, per hoc triticum attritum in area in dominicum orreum excussa pallea deportatur, per hoc aromata pilo concussa odorem plenius circumfundunt, per hoc ipse regum et regnorum Dominus honoratur, et tam reges et regna quam populi Christianorum plurimi floridis et fructuosis proficiunt incrementis, cum non minus prudentum consilio quam strenuitate robustorum regnorum

for reform, the pope appointed a new chancellor[105] and, imposing a duty of residence, assured his addressee that Paris is still favoured among the churches, as he dwells on good memories of his time there as legate and looks for its increase.[106]

A year later two cardinals were trying to persuade the university that the pope was tyrannizing over the Church and that it should withdraw its obedience from one who had lost the authority of supreme pontiff.[107] Boniface, however, pursued his interests still, sanctioning the Montrouge *studium* and publishing his *Liber sextus*.[108] In 1301, when he summoned doctors to advise him on dealing with Philip IV, he showed concern that a number stay behind so that the studies should not suffer; when he allowed Philip to bestow prebends, he insisted that they be given only to persons worthy on account of their learning and not because of family connections or influence.[109] He supported a Cistercian candidate, Jean de la Chapelle, for

---

ipsorum moderamina disponantur. Exultat igitur et in hoc mater ecclesia que palmites, quos per hujusmodi studium in agro fidei plantat, in celeste plantarium sepe transfert. Erubescant fallaces heretici evangelici quidem falsarii veritatis, quod sua mendatia commenta vilescunt, et convalescunt catholica et apostolica documenta, obmutescunt dolosa ipsorum labia et eorum confuse frontes decidunt impudentes."

[105] See *CUP* 2: 69-71, no. 595 (17 Jun. 1296): "... nos siquidem diligenti indagine de persona ad cancellariam ipsam assumenda cum pluribus et pluries ad reformationem studii Parisiensis, quam optamus, habita, ac vite meritum et scientie donum aliaque quibus juvari dinosceris diligentius attendentes ... cancellariam ipsam ... conferimus et providemus..." (p. 70).

[106] See *CUP* 2: 73-75, no. 600 (18 Dec. 1296): "Digna nos provocat ac excitat ratio legitima et efficax animum causa movet, ut inter ceteras orbis ecclesias, quibus nos pretulit benigna clementia Salvatoris, Parisiensem ecclesiam favoribus prosequamur eximiis, et ad statum ejus votivum et prosperum vigilantibus studiis intendamus. Non enim de nostri sacrario pectoris oblivio dampnose subripuit, quin potius tenaci memoria retinemus, quod ejusdem ecclesie copiosa benignitas nos olim, dum in minoribus ageremus, de ipsius honorabili gremio existentes fovit et tractavit ut filium, maternis pavit et refecit uberibus, respexit gratiis, beneficiis honoravit. Ideoque non immerito illam infra caritatis viscera gerimus et specialis favoris affluentia confovemus apostolice sedis partes solertius adhibendo, ut ejusdem status ecclesie honoris multiplicis incrementa suscipiat, felicibus fulciatur eventibus, et successibus prosperis fecundetur, ut ipsa quasi per condigne retributionis officium in nobis gratiosum patris affectum per effectum inveniat, que anteactis temporibus mostro dulcia matris ubera gustui propinavit" (pp. 73-74).

[107] See *CUP* 2: 78, no. 604ᵃ (15 June 1297): "Intendite ... ut justiciam cause nostre, immo verius sponse Christi, et iniquitatem Benedicti Gaytani, generalis istius ecclesie non presulis, sed tyramni, qui per solum nephas Romanam tenet ecclesiam occupatam, tam vos quam reges, principes orbis et populi in considerationis recte statera, veritate verumptamen vestrum concomitante judicium appendatis. ... Et interim ei qui non habet auctoritatem summi pontificis, quamvis locum huc usque temere de facto detineat, nullus obediat quomodolibet vel intendat, in hiis maxime ubi periculum vertitur animarum."

[108] See *CUP* 2: 78-79, 81, nos. 605, 608 (18 July 1297, 3 Mar. 1298).

[109] See *CUP* 2: 93-94, 96-97, nos. 621-623, 627 (5 Dec. 1301, 24 June 1302).

a chair in theology.[110] All the same, in December 1302 the university agreed to the proposal for a general council to decide charges against Boniface. It submitted itself to the protection of such a council and a future true and legitimate pope.[111] In August 1303, two months before his death, Boniface sadly recalled the Apostolic See's goodwill towards the French crown, while suspending the right to confer the licence in theology and law until the king had submitted. University men had been drawn into the royal rebellion, and the pope was concerned that fear or favour might lead to bad choices.[112]

The new century opened with bitter attacks on the person of the pope but apparently without criticism of papal dealings with the university. From the twelfth century papal interventions had been accepted to maintain doctrinal orthodoxy in teaching at Paris. The local church was less willing to attend to the popes' appeals to preserve academic integrity and freedom in the face of exactions from the chancellor. Support for students from the diocesan clergy, collegial foundations and communities of monks was less controversial than the promotion of the friars. Their progress in the faculty of theology met with prolonged opposition despite repeated injunctions from the pope. Difficulties with the Empire may have favoured Paris in the period studied here. Although other *studia* were not neglected, the fond feelings of former students and agreeable memories of residence in France during their legations strengthened the popes' concern at times. However, their ideals were those of the universal pastoral care. They wrote their letters in the conviction that theology—and it is the study of Scripture that is primarily in

---

[110] See *CUP* 2: 98-99, no. 629 (18 Dec. 1302).

[111] See *CUP* 2: 101-102, no. 634 (21 June 1303): "Nos autem ... convocationem et congregationem ipsius Concilii reputantes utilem, necessariam et salubrem ac expedientem fidei negotio et ecclesie sancte Dei, ejusdem convocationi et congregationi Concilii assentimus, ac opem et operam libenter dabimus juxta posse, et provocationi et appellationi prefati domini regis adheremus, quantum de jure possumus et debemus secundum Deum et justitiam, et sancte permittunt canonice sanctiones, supponentes nos ac nobis adherentes et adherere volentes, statum nostrum et Universitatem nostram protectioni divine et predicti Concilii generalis ac futuri veri et legitimi summi pontificis" (p. 102).

[112] See *CUP* 2: 104, no. 636 (15 Aug. 1303): "Sedes apostolica ... regnum Francorum ejusque reges, tam antiquis, quam modernis temporibus, magnis dotavit largitionibus gratiarum, et amplis privilegiis communivit, que si Philippus rex Francie in examen debite considerationis adduceret, dictam sedem et nos, quos precipue habuit ad sua beneplacita promptos, liberales in gratiis, et in cunctis oportunitatibus gratiosos, contumeliis non conaretur afficere, nec injuriis provocare, sed ad nos et ipsam ex debito gereret affectum devotionis et reverentie specialis ... nos nolentes quod ob favorem vel timorem ipsius aliqui a nostra et ejusdem sedis reverentia deviantes ad alias minus ydonei cathedram possint ascendere magistralem, omnes de regno predicto potestatem habentes dandi licentiam regendi seu docendi ac approbandi volentes licentiam hujusmodi obtinere in theologica facultate ac jure canonico et civili, ab hujusmodi potestate, donec idem rex ad nostra et ejusdem sedis mandata cum satisfactione debita revertatur, apostolica auctoritate suspendimus...."

view there—will nourish the faith of the Church and, associated with appropriate linguistic studies, may even be a preparation for evangelizing non-Christians. Arts and canon law may serve theology; medicine and civil law are better left to those pursuing a secular career. The peace of this city of letters is the condition for sound learning; the untroubled pursuit of a life of study is also for individual scholars as well as for religious and collegial communities a seed-bed of virtue. The imagery of Paradise and the heavenly Jerusalem as sources of the water of salvation expresses an idealism that sees in the University of Paris a working model for the whole Church as an abundant spring of saving truth.

13

"The Popes' Other Sheep"

Edward A. Synan

Unsympathetic critics of the medieval Church have seen in her a neoplatonic procession of a many from a one, that "one," of course, not the Lord of Abraham, Isaac, and Jacob, of Jesus and of Mohammed, but the pope. Holding the apex of human authority in Christendom, the popes of our period are said to have aspired to the apex of human power as well. What follows will be an effort to nuance this perception.

A different view, to be sure, was expressed long ago. Oderico Rinaldi, for instance, who continued with indifferent success the *Annales ecclesiastici* from the point to which Cardinal Baronio had brought the work,[1] wrote of Pope Innocent III:

> This too I have thought something not to be passed over in silence, that this most even-handed Pontiff defended against violations of their rights, not only his own beloved sons, but outsiders as well, even those who were otherwise undeserving. For when distressed Jews implored his patronage, having given them an official certificate, these where his commands: "... no Christian can compel them, unwilling or refusing, to come to baptism through violence ...

---

[1] Edition cited here is: Caesaris Card. Baronii, Od. Raynaldi et Jac. Laderchii, *Annales Ecclesiastici*, denuo excusi ... ab Augusto Theiner (Barri-Ducis, 1864 sqq.); for judgment on Rinaldi by J. D. Mansi see ibid., vol. 20, p. IV: "... unus, quem eligerem, superat Raynaldus, non quod ab illo naevos omnes abesse recognoscerem, sed quod digniorem existimaverim ut adjungeretur Baronio, cujus vestigia caeteris pressius calcavit..."; Baronio had brought the *Annales* to the accession of Innocent III, 1198.

The Religious Roles of the Papacy: Ideals and Realities, 1150-1300, ed. Christopher Ryan, Papers in Mediaeval Studies 8 (Toronto: Pontifical Institute of Mediaeval Studies, 1989), pp. 389-411. © P.I.M.S., 1989.

still, if one of them should take flight spontaneously to the Christians, and for the sake of the faith, let him be made a Christian without any snide talk."[2]

Rinaldi went on to echo 1 Corinthians 9:22 in giving what he thought the reason for the pope's so acting:

... he used to burn with zeal for gaining souls for Christ; inflamed by the admonition of the Apostle, his talent bent everything to the purpose of leading all to Christ, whether Jews or gentiles or heretics or schismatics.[3]

In the period assigned for this consultation, 1150 to 1300, warfare and commerce were daily revealing to the popes' Latin Christendom an expanding wealth of human communities, all of them potential participants in salvation. Neither the challenge nor the opportunity were new in principle, but significantly changed conditions posed the old issues in new ways.

By the beginning of our period, Latin Christendom had been assaulting the Islamic east at the behest of popes for fifty years. For the first time in Christian history a current of attack ran from west to east; the invasion of western Europe by bellicose peoples had never truly ended. Visigoths and Ostrogoths, Franks and Vandals, had been succeeded by Saxons, Angles, Norsemen, and Moslems; despite crusades, human tides of Turks and Mongols rose and ebbed. How, one may ask, did the popes respond to what was at once a summons to their zeal and a threat to Christian security? Here it will be argued that the popes manifested not only crusading zeal, but also religious concern for those whose status, vis-à-vis Christendom, was that of "the other," "the outsider"—Moslems and Mongols (to say nothing of that all but unassimilable minority, the Jews).

A difficulty we shall do well to face from the beginning is inseparable from generalizing on those strong personalities who were chosen to be "Vicar of Peter" and, in our period, had begun to style themselves "Vicar of Christ."[4] In one direction, the imposing file of eminent popes might seduce us into a prosopography without intelligible pattern; in the opposite direction, the

---

[2] "Reticendum quoque non putavi, aequissimum Pontificem non solum dilectos filios, verum etiam exteros ipsos, caeteroqui immeritos, ab injuriis vindicasse; cum enim exagitati Judaei patrocinium ejus implorarent, dato pro ipsis Diplomate haec jussit: ... ut nullus Christianus invitos vel nolentes eos ad baptismum per violentiam venire compellat, sed si eorum quilibet sponte ad Christianos fidei causa confugerit, postquam voluntas ejus fuerit patefacta, sine qualibet efficiatur calumnia Christianus..." (*Annales*, 20: 56, n. 54).

[3] "Incendebat nimirum illum zelus lucrandarum Christo animarum, quo inflammatus ex Apostoli monito ingenium ad omnia flectebat, ut omnes, sive Judaeos, sive gentiles, sive haereticos, sive schismaticos ad Christum adduceret..." (ibid., n. 55).

[4] Michele Maccarone, *Vicarius Christi: storia del titolo papale* (Rome, 1952); Walter Ullman, *The Growth of Papal Government in the Middle Ages* (London, 1955); Innocent III first used this title habitually.

majesty and continuity of the papal office, hypostasized in imagination as "the papacy," might mask the existential diversity of those who held the office. In medieval philosophical terms, there is a danger of an individualism so radical as to parallel "nominalism"; against this is the peril of an analogue to extreme philosophical "realism": "the papacy" might seem to be more real than were the flesh-and-blood popes in whom that abstraction was incarnate. A procedure by which one may hope to avoid shipwreck on this passage between the Scylla of individualism and the Charybdis of abstraction is to begin with theory and to end with practice.

THEORY

A series of four sermons, preached by Pope Innocent III on anniversaries of his consecration as bishop of Rome, proffers an incontrovertibly authentic picture of the way this pope understood the papacy. A purple passage in one of these sermons, not easy to defend, has often been quoted (I have done so myself).[5] In those lines Innocent located popes "this side of God," but "beyond man," "less than God" yet "greater than man"; the pope is the one "who judges all and is judged by no one."[6] An eminent theologian once qualified this pericope in my hearing (while we were waiting for the present pope to arrive) as approximately the way in which Arius thought of Jesus. One is glad to note that this is not the only evidence of how Innocent understood the office he held.

Innocent likened the office of bishop and pope to marriage, an image he elaborated with considerable theological ingenuity. In the first of his four sermons on the pontifical office, to be sure, the marriage metaphor is present only by indirection:

> Let us live, not only chastely, dearest brothers, but also with caution—"chastely" lest we contaminate the unction of the order we have received ... "with caution" lest we corrupt others through example.[7]

These words he reinforced by citing Leviticus 4:3, according to the Vulgate, "making the people sin," but then (as it was his custom to lace his work with

---

[5] E. A. Synan, *The Popes and the Jews in the Middle Ages* (New York, 1965), p. 85.

[6] "... Jam ergo videtis quis iste servus, qui super familiam constituitur, profecto vicarius Jesu Christi, successor Petri, Christus Domini, Deus Pharaonis: inter Deum et hominem medius constitutus, citra Deum, sed ultra hominem: minor Deo, sed major homine: qui de omnibus judicat, et a nemine judicatur..." (*Sermo II in consecratione pontificis maximi*, in *PL* 217: 658A).

[7] "Vivamus ergo, fratres charissimi, non solum caste, sed etiam caute. Caste, ne contaminemus unctionem ordinis quem accepimus... . Caute, ne corrumpamus alios per exemplum..." (*Sermo I in consecratione pontificis maximi*, in *PL* 217: 654A).

learned allusions) "according to 'the Hebrew truth': If a priest, who is anointed, shall have sinned to the guilt of the people...." [8] Only the adverb "chastely," *caste*, intimates the virtuous marriage in which the Pope saw analogues to his own role. In his second pontifical sermon marriage symbolism does not occur at all.

Innocent's extensive use of marriage imagery in the third of his sermons in the series harks back to a short work, a *libellum*, of his own on the "four sorts," *quatuor species*, of marriage. [9] What here follows immediately is a doublet of the opening lines of that work (*PL* 217: 923A), there buttressed with an analysis designed to show that the four "species" of marriage correspond to the four "senses" of medieval scriptural exegesis. It would be tedious to note all the parallels between these two works by the same author who felt that a good thing cannot be repeated too often.

Not unexpectedly Innocent counted as the first of his four "sorts" of marriage that between a man and "a woman lawful" to wed, *legitima femina*. The second he designated as the union between Christ and Holy Church, the third as the union between God and "a justified soul," *anima justa*, and the fourth as that between the eternal Word and human nature.

Each sort of marriage has its characteristic consequence. For the first type this effect is that two be "in one flesh" (Matthew 19:5), the second that two be in one body, that is to say, the Pauline conception of the Church as a single body of which Jesus is the head and believers in their variety the various "members" of that body (1 Corinthians 12:12-31; cf. ibid., 10:17). The third union makes it come to pass that two be in one Spirit, and the fourth that two be in one Person, this last the theological position of the great Christological and Trinitarian Councils that two natures, divine and human, are united in the single Person of the Son, eternal Word of the Father. [10] Put another way, Innocent explained, the first sort of marriage is "carnal," the second "sacramental," the third "spiritual," and the fourth "personal." [11]

Echoing the text of John (3:29) with which he had begun this sermon, Innocent termed himself the "friend of the groom," the *paranymphus*; [12] he

---

[8] "... propter quod dicitur: *Faciens delinquere populum*.... Vel secundum Hebraicam veritatem: *Si sacerdos, qui est unctus, peccaverit ad culpam populi...*" (ibid.).

[9] *De quadripartita specie nuptiarum liber*, in *PL* 217: 921-968.

[10] "... Et primam, inter virum et legitimam feminam: secundam, inter Christum et sanctam Ecclesiam: tertiam, inter Deum et animam justam: quartam, inter Verbum et humanam naturam. ... Per primas efficitur, ut sint duo in carne una: per secundas efficitur, ut sint duo in uno corpore: per tertias efficitur, ut sint duo in uno spiritu: per quartas efficitur, ut sint duo in una persona..." (*Sermo III in consecratione pontificis maximi*, in *PL* 217: 661A-B).

[11] "... Primam ergo unionem recte carnalem, secundam sacramentalem, tertiam spiritualem, et quartam personalem..." (ibid.).

[12] "*Qui habet sponsam, sponsus est. Amicus autem sponsi, qui stat, et audit eum, gaudio*

hears with joy the voice of Christ, who is the groom. In the way of preachers, and not only of medieval ones, the pope added to this text another which he thought applicable to the papal dignity: "Friend, go up higher" (Luke 14:10), for had not Innocent become the successor of him who had thrice said to the Groom: "Lord, you know that I love you" (John 21:17)?[13]

True enough, the Groom had "piled up" in Innocent both "natural boons" and "gifts of grace." Having granted "spiritual boons," the divine Groom "had super-added temporal ones" and Innocent hoped that he would give at the last "eternal ones" as well.[14] As for the joy felt by a "friend of the Groom" when he heard the Groom's voice, Innocent wondered aloud: in which of the things he had "heard" ought he to rejoice? Was it in his having heard the words "I give you the keys" (Matthew 16:19), or in the pronouncement "I have set you over the nations" (Jeremiah 1:10)? To hold keys that have their effect in heaven, and to be above all earthly kings, are roles that entail no small responsibility; on reflection Innocent felt that he "ought to fear rather than to rejoice."[15]

What was truly reason for joy was the Lord's promise: "I shall be with you until the consummation of the world" (Matthew 28:20) and: "Simon, Simon, behold Satan has asked to sift you like wheat, but for you I have prayed that your faith may not fail" (Luke 22:31). Since the Lord had foretold conflict for Simon Peter, to whom he had promised victory, Innocent felt he could infer the general rule: "He who enjoins an office," a duty, here the papal throne, "is the one who proffers assistance."[16]

With all this in place, Innocent shifted the focus of his gospel image. He himself, rather than Jesus, became the "groom" and his hearers became the "friends of the groom." The pope thought he might be considered the "groom" because he could say with truth: "I possess the noble, rich, sublime, beautiful, chaste, pleasing, sacred Roman Church, under God's disposition,

---

gaudet propter vocem sponsi (Jo. 3:29). Paranymphus ait ista de sponso, vox de Verbo, lucerna de sole, Joannes de Christo..." (ibid., 659D-660D).

[13] "Ego factus sum amicus Sponsi, cui Sponsus amicaliter: 'Amice, ascende superius' (Lk. 14:10): illius successor effectus, qui terna responsione dixit Sponso: 'Domine, tu scis quia amo te'" (Jo. 21:17) (ibid., 661D).

[14] "Accumulavit enim in me bona naturae, multiplicavit in me munera gratiae, contulit mihi spiritualia beneficia, superaddidit temporalia, spero quidem quod donabit aeterna..." (ibid., 662A).

[15] "... gaudeo propter quam vocem? An propter illam ... 'Tibi dabo claves...' (Mtt. 16:19)? An propter illam quam mihi locutus est in propheta: 'Constitui te super gentes...' (Jer. 1:10)? Sed propter hanc vocem magis mihi timendum est, quam gaudendum..." (ibid.).

[16] "... sicut praedicit Simoni pugnam, qui promittit victoriam, sic injungit officium, qui impendit auxilium" (ibid., 662B).

Mother and Mistress of all the faithful." [17] We cannot miss the implication of the pope's series of adjectives; they are precisely such as would qualify the best of all conceivable brides in his "first sort" of marriage, the primary analogate (as logicians might have put it) of the term "marriage."

The marriage of any bishop with a local Church is a "spiritual" one. In canonical terminology, that wedding originates with the bishop's election, is "ratified" in his confirmation for that see, and "consummated" by his consecration. The papal marriage with the Roman Church is exceptional among the spiritual marriages of bishops with their Churches in that it is "originated" and "ratified" at once, *simul*, for "the Roman Pontiff is confirmed when elected, and when confirmed he is elected." [18]

Thanks to the spiritual nature of such marriages of bishops with their Churches there follows the paradox that, whereas from "carnal" marriages, those who are closely related to a spouse are excluded and outsiders admitted, in a "spiritual" marriage there is an exclusion "by rule" of outsiders and the closely related are admitted. [19] For indeed, only Christians, already by that fact intimately related owing to their "marriage" of the second (and, one may hope, of the third) sort are eligible for the episcopal office.

Innocent then adverted to the celebration of the anniversary of the day on which his own "spiritual marriage" to the Roman Church had been "consummated," that is, the day on which, having been elected and in that act confirmed, Innocent had been consecrated Bishop of the Roman Church—he had been in deacon's orders only when elected. This was also the very day on which, as he put it, the Blessed Apostle had been established in his "Chair." [20] Innocent had respectful words for his great predecessor:

> As the light of the sun does not suffer the light of the stars to be seen with it, so that solemnity [the Chair of Peter] does not tolerate this one [the

---

[17] "An non ego sponsus sum, et quilibet vestrum amicus sponsi? Utique. Sponsus, quia habeo nobilem, divitem, et sublimem, decoram, castam, gratiosam, sacrosanctam, Romanam Ecclesiam: quae disponente Deo, cunctorum fidelium mater est et magistra" (ibid.).

[18] "Sic et spirituale conjugium, quod est inter episcopum et Ecclesiam, initiatum dicitur in electione, ratum in confirmatione, consummatum in consecratione. Illud autem conjugium, quod ego Sponsus cum hac mea sponsa contraxi, simul fuit initiatum et ratum: quia Romanus pontifex cum eligitur, confirmatur, et cum confirmatur, eligitur..." (ibid., 663A).

[19] "Certe cum ego contraherem, filius ducebat matrem in conjugem: ubi vero contraxi, pater habuit filiam in uxorem. In carnali conjugio excluduntur propinqui, et admittuntur extranei; sed in spirituali conjugio prima facie regulariter excluduntur extranei, et admittuntur propinqui..." (ibid., 663B).

[20] "Anniversarium ergo diem, quo fuit hoc conjugium spirituale consummatum, hodie mecum primum celebratis, licet ipso die fuerim in sede apostolica consecratus, quo beatus Petrus apostolus in episcopali fuit cathedra constitutus" (ibid., 663C).

consecration of Innocent] to be celebrated with it. The lesser cedes to the greater because the lesser succeeds to the greater.[21]

The relationship of the Roman Church to the local Churches in communion with her and with her bishop, the Roman Pontiff, was seen by Innocent as an unexpected instantiation of the marriage metaphor. For the plurality of Churches to whom the pope is "wedded"—should he stay with the image of a wedding—raised the issue of polygamy. Innocent met this challenge with a scriptural warrant: Abram possessed, not only Sarai, but Hagar as well, not an adultery, but a duty for the patriarch.[22] So does the Roman Pontiff "possess" all the Churches in order that, from him, they may receive the "debt" he owes them, a term which evokes the Pauline insistence that married couples fulfill their marriage obligations, their "debt," to each other (1 Corinthians 7:3). In the case of the pope, the "debt" at stake he expressed as the duty to foresee and to supply the needs of all the Churches so that they all might receive from him the *debitum providentiae*. As will be clear shortly, this reference to the matrimonial debt accounts for the pope's conviction that the analogy with marriage clarifies the papacy as he saw it. In the measure that he had received, in that measure he was obligated to render what they might need to the Churches.[23]

This concern with legitimate "polygamy" in the spiritual marriage of bishops and Churches led Innocent to question whether one bishopric might be possessed by two bishops or one bishop possess two bishoprics. He found an instance of the second close to Rome: the two Churches of Ostia and Velletri[24] had but a single bishop, an arrangement Innocent must have known to exist from 1150 forward (it was to end only in 1914). As for the first, two bishops in possession of a single See, Innocent adduced the instance of Hippo, held not only by Bishop Valerius, but by Augustine as well; in Innocent's language, Augustine did not so much "succeed" Valerius as "accede" to him.[25] The pope omitted all reference to the scruples Augustine

---

[21] "Sed sicut lux solis, lucem stellae secum videri non patitur: sic illa solemnitas hanc secum non sustinet celebrari. Cedit ergo minor majori, quia minor majori succedit" (ibid.).

[22] "Nonne legistis quod Abraham Saram habebat uxorem, quae tamen Agar famulam suam introduxit ad ipsum: nec commisit propter hoc adulterium, sed officium adimplevit" (ibid., 664A-B).

[23] "Sic et Romanus pontifex sponsam habet Romanam Ecclesiam, quae tamen Ecclesias sibi subjectas introducit ad ipsum, ut ab eo recipiant debitum providentiae: quia quanto plus redditur, tanto magis debetur" (ibid.).

[24] The *PL* text proffers "Hostiensis et Vellucensis" with a variant reading for the second ascribed to "f.": "Vercellensis."

[25] "Rursus Hipponensis Ecclesia, quae conjuncta erat Valerio, ipso vivente etiam nupsit beato Augustino: qui non tam successit, quam accessit Valerio" (*Sermon III* cit., *PL* 217: 664B).

had felt and expressed when he asked the congregation of Hippo to authorize the succession to himself by Eraclius, but only after his own death, in contrast to his uncanonical "accession" to Valerius.[26] In any case, and this is the ultimate ground of the marriage metaphor, bishop and Church are "married" for the sake of "generating a religious progeny for Messiah." [27] In this passing reference Innocent put his finger on the fundamental similarity between the two. Both have communal growth for their goal: in marriage, the extension of the human race through fruitful love thanks to the fulfillment of the *debitum*; in episcopacy and papacy, a multiplication of believers in the Lord Jesus. The evangelization of the world is not one duty among many; it is the primary precept for bishops and especially for the bishop of Rome.

Another parallel between the union of bishop and Church and carnal marriage is the durability of both unions (Matthew 19:6). Both endure until the death of the bishop as spouse of the bride-Church, or to the death of a spouse in the paradigmatic marriage of the "first sort." [28] Furthermore, a Roman Pontiff could only be dismissed for "fornication" (Matthew 19:9), well understood, in the spiritual order, a dismissal legitimate in Innocent's view, for error in faith only.[29] "However," the pope added in a noteworthy anticipation of Vatican I on the role of papal teaching as one authentic voice of a Church guarded from error by the Holy Spirit: "I should not easily believe that God would permit a Roman Pontiff to err against the faith." [30] The ground of this confidence was the prayer by the Lord for Peter that his faith not fail (Luke 22:31, 32).[31]

---

[26] See formal report submitted to the Consuls from the Church at Hippo in which Augustine, seeking and receiving the consent of his congregation for naming Eraclius as his successor, recounted his own ordination as bishop while Valerius was still alive: "Adhuc in corpore posito beatae memoriae patre et episcopo meo sene Valerio, episcopus ordinatus sum, et sedi cum illo: quod concilio Nicaeno prohibitum fuisse nesciebam, nec ipse sciebat," a reference to the last phrase of that Council's canon 8: ἵνα μή ἐν τῇ πόλει δύο ἐπίσκοποι ὦσιν and followed immediately by Augustine's explicit provision with respect to Eraclius: "Erit presbyter ut est; quando Deus voluerit, futurus episcopus," i.e., on the death of Augustine (*Epistola 213, Acta ecclesiastica,* in *PL* 33: 967, nn. 4, 5).

[27] "Sed qua ratione possunt haec fieri salva lege conjugii, vos exquirite, quos delectat inquisitio quaestionum: me alia sollicitudo detinet occupatum. Contra hoc conjugium inter episcopum et Ecclesiam, ut religiosam prolem Christo generet..." (*Sermo III* cit., *PL* 217: 664c).

[28] "Sacramentum autem inter Romanum pontificem et Romanam ecclesiam tam firmum et stabile perseverat, ut non nisi per mortem unquam ab invicem separentur.... Vir autem iste alligatus uxori, solutionem non quaerit, non cedit, non deponitur..." (ibid., 664D).

[29] "Propter causam vero fornicationis Ecclesia Romana posset dimittere Romanum pontificem. Fornicationem non dico carnalem, sed spiritualem; quia non est carnale, sed spirituale conjugium, id est propter infidelitatis errorem..." (ibid., 664D-665A).

[30] "Ego tamen facile non crediderim, ut Deus permitteret Romanum pontificem contra fidem errare..." (ibid.).

[31] "... pro quo spiritualiter oravit in Petro," i.e., the prayer of Jesus, materially taken, for Peter was to be, in the spiritual order, for all the successors of Peter (ibid.).

A woman did not enter marriage in Innocent's world without a dowry. The Church had brought to Innocent a dowry beyond price, both spiritual plenitude and temporal breadth. Others, to be sure, were called to take "a part" of his solicitude, for each bishop was responsible for his own Church. Still, only "Peter," bishop of Rome, was called to the "plenitude of power," [32] with the implication that to this corresponded his plenitude of responsibility for all the Churches. Innocent had an interest in the symbolic value of priestly vestments, including those of the Levitical priesthood. [33] Here he remarked that the mitre of a pope is a sign of his pre-eminence in spiritual matters, the crown a symbol of his lordship in temporal ones. The situation, he conceded, called for a gift on his part to the Church, his bride. "Whether I shall make her some gift on account of our nuptials, you shall see: I am unwilling to make a boastful assertion." [34]

Both bishop and Church, as groom and bride, must give free assent to permanent collaboration, an assent first posed in "a mutual consent" of those who elect and of him who is elected. The election thus freely agreed upon must indeed be "confirmed" by appropriate authority, but before consecration the elected and confirmed candidate "will vindicate neither the name nor the function of pontiff." [35]

In the fourth of his sermons on the role of pontiffs Innocent addressed the pope's position as beyond all human judgment. He pointed out that, to the extent that a pope is less under human authority than are other dignitaries, to that degree he is the more under divine judgment. [36] Still, he had noted that a bishop, even a bishop of Rome, might be dismissed owing to a failure in faith. The pope thought it right to adduce a line from the Gospel according to John: one "who does not believe," that is, one whose faith is fallacious, "is already judged" (John 3:18), [37] but gave no indication as to the process by which this judgment against a putative heretic in the papacy might be implemented. He raised quite another consideration at this point, namely, the

---

[32] "Haec autem sponsa non nupsit vacua, sed dotem mihi tribuit absque pretio pretiosam, spiritualem videlicet plenitudinem et latitudinem temporalium, magnitudinem et multitudinem utrorumque. Nam caeteri vocati sunt in partem sollicitudinis, solus autem Petrus assumptus est in plenitudinem potestatis" (ibid., 665B).

[33] See Innocent's treatise De sacro altaris mysterio libri sex in PL 217: 773-916; for his remarks on the mitre, see liber 1, capp. 44 and 60 (cols 790 and 796).

[34] "Amplem mihi tribuit dotem, sed utrum ego donationem aliquam sibi fecerim propter nuptias, vos videritis. Ego nolo asseverare jactanter" (Sermo III cit., PL 217: 665B).

[35] "... antequam consecratur, nec nomen pontificis, officium vindicabit" (ibid., 666A).

[36] "Verum non frustra sibi blandiatur de potestate, neque de sublimitate vel honore temere glorietur; quia quanto minus judicatur ab homine, tanto magis judicatur a Deo" (Sermo IV in consecratione pontificis maximi, in PL 217: 670B).

[37] "Minus dico; quia potest ab hominibus judicari, vel potius judicatus ostendi, si videlicet evanescat in haeresim; quoniam 'qui non credit, jam judicatus est'" (Jo. 3:18) (ibid.).

divine intent that, in the words of Ezechiel (18:27, 28), the sinner turn from his iniquity and that, in consequence, "he will not die." [38] To reinforce his point Innocent appealed to a series of scriptural parables and episodes. First, that God welcomes and receives the lost sinner is the intent of the parables of the Good Shepherd who goes into the desert for the sake of a single stray (Matthew 18:12, 13; Luke 15:4-7) and of the woman who turns her house upside down to find a single lost coin (Luke 15:8-10). Second, David, despite his adultery and murder (2 Samuel 11:1-12:15), maintained his kingship and Peter's triple denial of the Lord (Matthew 26:69-75; Mark 14:66-72; Luke 22:54-62; John 18:15-27) not only did not entail loss of rank as apostle, but he was given first rank among the Eleven (John 21:15-17). [39] This situation persuaded the pope that to "lose savor" (Matthew 5:13) in the faith is worse than to "lose savor" in deeds. Both King David and Simon-Peter had failed, not in belief, but in what they did; thus it is one thing to fail in action, another to fail in belief. A failure in faith is heresy or apostasy; grace can surely be restored, even in such major disasters, but only with difficulty can a rank, the papacy for instance, be restored after a failure in faith. Peter denied the Lord "in word," *ore*, not "in heart," *corde*. Innocent concluded by asking the prayers of the people that in his own case "the salt not lose its savor" and that the Lord pray that he, "the undeserving and unworthy" successor to Peter, not fail in faith. [40] The "generating of a religious progeny for Messiah" was seen to be the papal reality symbolized by the shepherd searching out a lost sheep and by the distracted housewife looking for her lost coin. This will serve as the theoretical key to papal practice.

PRACTICE

Although proverbial enemies, Moslems and Mongols counted among the "other sheep"; thirteenth-century popes felt compelled to generate "progeny

---

[38] "... cum averterit se impius ab impietate sua ... vita vivet et non morietur" (Ex. 18:27, 28).

[39] "Nonne Petrus evanuit, qui tertio Christum negavit? et tamen non solum apostolatum non perdidit, sed etiam principatum accepit" (Mtt. 26:69-75) (*Sermo IV* cit., *PL* 217: 670c-d).

[40] "Verum aliud est evanescere in agendis, et aliud est evanescere in credendis ... qui autem evanescit in fide, ut fiat haereticus aut apostata, reparari quidem potest ad gratiam, sed difficile restauratur ad gradum; quia remanet cicatrix ex hujusmodi lepra contracta. Petrus enim non corde, sed ore negavit. Ne autem evanescat sal in me, quod damnosum nimis et periculosum existeret, vos fratres et filii, et apud misericordissimum Patrem piis precibus imploretis, ut ipse qui beato Petro praedixit: 'Ego pro te rogavi, Petre, ut non deficiat fides tua: et tu aliquando conversus, confirma fratres tuos' (Lk. 22:31, 32) in me successore suo immerito et indigno fidem illam confirmet" (ibid., 670d-672a).

for Messiah" by bringing those outsiders into the sheepfold of the Lord.
Correspondence between Moslem or Mongol rulers and a number of popes
from Innocent III forward, collected and edited by K. E. Lupprian,[41] reveal
their relationships.

In diplomatic correspondence such as this a courteous rhetoric must be
expected and this is most conspicuous in the formulae with which popes,
sultans, califs, and khans opened their letters. The Moslem authorities at
Morocco and Aleppo were addressed by Pope Innocent III with an expression of hope that they, and their subjects, might "arrive at a knowledge of the
Truth and in It perdure to salvation." [42] So patent a reference to conversion
must strike ears attuned to the ecumenical as tactless, if not discourteous, but
medieval popes could think of conversion to Christianity only as an invitation
to share their most precious possession. Pope Gregory IX proposed "the Way
of Truth" to the sultan of Damascus and to the sultan of Cairo ("Babylon").[43]
The same pope urged the Almohad Calif ar-Rasid "to acknowledge the way
of Truth and faithfully to perdure in It," an invitation to conversion which
he reinforced with a reference to a bishop and to Franciscan missionaries,
already dispatched to the calif. Gregory concluded with the observation that,
should the calif "prefer to be an enemy, rather than a friend," the pope would
no longer be able to allow Christians to serve the calif,[44] a provision which
seems to imply that Lateran IV legislation on service to Jewish masters by
Christians may have been extended to Moslem masters and that both
Moslem and Jewish masters could hope for the appropriate dispensation in
friendly circumstances.

The stream of courtesy was notably more excessive in the other direction,
and the Latin versions of Moslems' letters in the papal archives echo the
luxuriant oriental rhetoric of the original texts. Thus the sultan of Konya
(Iconium) addressed Pope Gregory IX as "equal to the angels," [45] and a letter
from the sultan of Cairo to Innocent IV called him, not only "noble, great,
spiritual, affectionate, and holy," but also "the thirteenth apostle, universal

---

[41] Karl-Ernst Lupprian, *Die Beziehungen der Papste zu islamischen und mongolischen Herrschern im 13. Jahrhundert anhand ihres Briefwechsels*, Studi e testi 291 (Vatican City, 1981).

[42] "... ad veritatis noticiam pervenire ac in ea salubriter permanere" (Lupprian, nn. 1, [with inversion of word order] 2, pp. 107, 108).

[43] "... viam agnoscere veritatis" (ibid., nn. 7, 14, pp. 120, 130).

[44] "... viam agnoscere veritatis et in ea fideliter permanere.... Et utinam fiducia quam concepimus non fallamur, de tua conversatione (*sic*) sperantes ... venerabili fratri nostro A. Fecensi episcopo et aliis fratribus de ordine Minorum te mansuetum exhibes et benignum.... Alioquin, si forte Christi hostis esse malueris quam amicus, nullatenus patiemur, sicut nec pati debemus, quod tibi a suis fidelibus serviatur" (ibid., n. 13, pp. 128, 129).

[45] "Sanctissime et angelis equalis..." (ibid., n. 15, p. 133).

spokesman of Christians, guide of all who venerate the cross, judge of the Christian people, leader of the sons of baptism, Supreme Pontiff of all Christians." The sultan rounded off these honorific titles for the pope with the hope that "God might strengthen him and grant him felicity." [46] The same pope was greated in a succeeding letter as "A Presence—lofty, holy, lordly, apostolic, venerable, honorable, lording it over the necks of the Franks, leading his people with the bridles of Christian Law, source of life for the Christian sect—May God lengthen and protect his life!" [47]

What issues occasioned these splendid inscriptions? Innocent III wanted the calif of Morocco to deliver prisoners to members of the Order of the Holy Trinity (Innocent had lately approved their rule), religious committed to expend a third of their resources to redeem prisoners or, as it was their right and duty to do, arrange the exchange of captured "pagans," Moslems, for captive Christians.[48] In the pope's own words, this barter would be of advantage to both sides and his conclusion expanded the conversionist sentiments of his opening lines: "May he who is the Way, the Truth, and the Life (John 14:6) inspire you in such wise that, having acknowledged the Truth that is Christ, you may hasten to arrive at that Truth as soon as may be." [49]

Innocent III was equally candid in his hope to gain a convert when he wrote to the sultan of Aleppo in behalf of the patriarch of Antioch, namely, that the patriarch and his Church, not only not be molested, but that they be given both "help and timely counsel." [50] Although, as the pope put it, the sultan had "not yet received the sacraments of the Christian religion, nonetheless, you venerate the Catholic faith, deferring in many matters to the faithful of Christ." [51] The pope did not think it too much to draw a conversionist conclusion:

---

[46] "Presentie pape nobilis, magni, spiritualis, affectuosi, sancti, tertii decimi apostolorum, universalis loquele Christianorum, manutenentis adoratores crucis, iudicis populi Christiani, ductoris filiorum baptismatis, summi pontificis Christianorum—confirmet eum deus et det sibi felicitatem" (ibid., n. 22, p. 151).

[47] "Presentie excelse, sancte, dominative, apostolice, venerabili, honorabili, dominanti cervicibus Francorum, ductori capistrorum legis Christiane, vivificatori secte Christianitatis—prolonget deus vitam eius et protegat" (ibid., n. 23, p. 155).

[48] Ibid., n. 1, p. 107.

[49] "Inspiret autem vobis ille, qui via, veritas est et vita, ut agnita veritate, que Christus est, ad eam venire quamtotius festinetis" (ibid.).

[50] "... ipsum et ecclesiam eius non permittas, quantum in te fuerit, ab aliquibus indebite molestari, quin immo eidem exhibeas auxilium et consilium oportunum..." (ibid., n. 2, p. 109).

[51] "... etsi nondum Christiane religionis susceperis sacramenta, fidem tamen catholicam veneraris in multis Christi fidelibus deferendo..." (ibid., pp. 108, 109).

Hence We are confident that, in his immense kindness, he will illuminate you with the rays of his visitation and the result will be, the grace of divine knowledge having been received, you will aspire devoutly to the worship of the eternal and true God who, for the salvation of men, was made a true man in the course of time.[52]

If papal chancery style diluted somewhat a courteous address with references to conversion, papal letters with a harsh substantive message carried intimations of their content in the formula of address. "Fear and love of the divine Name" was the ambiguous, indeed ominous, greeting from Innocent III to the sultan of Damascus and Cairo,[53] as it was the formula by which Honorius III greeted the Almohad Calif, al-Mustansir;[54] Gregory IX employed it in writing to Sultan al-Kamil of Cairo.[55] In every case this formula announces a letter with a hostile content.

Innocent III began such a letter to the sultan of Damascus and Cairo with that portentous greeting, "fear and love of the divine Name," and went on to say "We think you have heard" of an army mustering to recapture the Province of Jerusalem, an army powerfully equipped and "prepared to conquer or to die," an army relying "not so much on their own power as on divine strength."[56] Papal rhetoric disclaimed an intent to terrorize, but did suggest that it would be better all round for the sultan to relinquish what, after all, was "another's," *alienum*, especially since there could be no humiliation in responding to this plea to spare the shedding of human blood, a plea the pope made "humbly" and "as a suppliant." Holding the Province, in fact, apart from what Innocent termed "empty glory," was more difficult than useful for the Moslems. Citing Daniel 2:28, 29 and 4:14 on the divine power to transfer sovereignty, Innocent proffered an interpretation of the Islamic conquest of the Holy Land as having been permitted by God, not owing to Moslem virtue, but to Christian offenses which had provoked divine wrath. This, of course, is a standard explanation for failed crusades in imitation of Psalmist and Prophets. Now, the pope dared to hope, converted to the Lord,

---

[52] "Unde de illius immensa pietate confidimus, quod te sue visitationis radiis illustrabit, ut gratia divine cognicionis accepta ad cultum eterni et veri dei, qui pro salute hominum factus est temporaliter verus homo, devotus aspires" (ibid., p. 109).

[53] "... timorem divini nominis et amorem" (ibid., n. 3, p. 112).

[54] Ibid., n. 5, p. 116.

[55] "... divini nominis timorem pariter et amorem" (ibid., n. 6, p. 118); as above, note 42, only accidental differences separate the formulas.

[56] "Audisse te credimus, quod multi reges et principes Christiani cum innumeris pene populis devotionis et fidei zelo succensi ad recuperationem Ierosolimitane provincie se potenter accingunt, aut vincere aut mori parati, non tantum de sua presumentes potentia, quantum de divina virtute sperantes" (ibid., n. 3, p. 112).

Christians would be under divine mercy, for Psalm 76(77):10 assures us that divine wrath does not make the Holy One forgetful of his mercy. Hence, mindful of evangelical gentleness (Matthew 11:29), Pope Innocent proposed the restitution of The Land to Christians, the mutual release of captives, the cessation of all conflict to the end that "the condition of our people among you may not be worse than the condition of your people among us." [57] This letter was delivered by a group of significant notables: a papal scribe, one Roger, a Knight Templar, a Knight of the Jerusalem Hospital, along with "messengers" and miscellaneous members of the pontifical household. Should the pope's offer be rejected, the sultan was given due warning by the pope: "may the God who resists the proud and imparts favors to the humble judge between us and you." [58] The threat was hardly veiled and that threat was the crusade, along with the inner renewal of the Church herself, a major objective of Innocent's pontificate.[59] For all the threatening aspect of a letter announcing preparation for war, delivered by a commission that included two military monks, it is significant that this pope spoke of peace and of terms before alluding to a possible resort to arms.

Honorius III, the immediate successor of Innocent III, under the less than friendly allusion to "fear and love of the divine Name," summoned the Almohad Calif al-Mustansir to grant Christians under his rule full freedom to practice "their Law" as Moslems "beyond number" were given freedom to fulfill the precepts of Islam in Christian lands.[60] This request was buttressed by a series of biblical figures who either had granted freedom to the people of God (the prefect of eunuchs to Daniel and his three companions, Daniel 1:6-16; Holofernes to Judith, Judith 12:6-9; Cyrus to Esdras, Ezra 1:1-4 and 7:12-26) or denied them freedom, as pharaoh had done with the consequent plagues that went so far as the death of Egyptian eldest sons (Exodus 7:14-12; 30). The pope qualified his own intention as "not to seem mercenary" (John 10:12) and to be "meek and humble of heart" (Matthew 11:29). This second citation, as the editor noted, had been cited by Innocent III in letter number 3. A final point of interest is that the bearer of this letter was named as Gonsalvus, a Knight Hospitaler of Jerusalem.

---

[57] "... ita quod apud te non sit deterior conditio gentis nostre quam apud nos est conditio gentis tue" (ibid., p. 114).

[58] "... inter nos et vos iudicet ipse deus, qui superbis in terre (sic) resistit et humilibus gratiam impertitur" (ibid.).

[59] "... inter omnia desiderabilia cordis nostri duo in hoc saeculo principaliter affectamus, ut ad recuperationem videlicet terrae sanctae ac reformationem universalis Ecclesiae valeamus intendere cum effectu..." (Innocent III, *Epistola 30, PL* 216: 824A).

[60] "... patiamus innumeram legis tue hominum multitudinem ritus suos, ut in hoc nostre ac tue gentis non sit dispar conditio..." (Lupprian, n. 5, p. 117).

Once more with a variants of the threatening form of address, "fear of the divine Name, equally with its love," Gregory IX urged upon the sultan of Cairo the "rapid correction" of abuses suffered in Alexandria by Christian merchants from Ancona. Held under arrest, despoiled of their goods in violation of good "faith and peace," the merchants' plight was as damaging to the sultan's advantage as to his honor. Both the conscience and the reputation of the sultan were touched. To restore liberty and goods to the injured merchants would allow the sultan to avoid offense to God and to men; not least, this double restitution would have the result that the pope "would be obliged to listen in greater matters" to his correspondent.[61] Once more, under the diplomatic forms is the threat that in those "greater matters" the pope reserved his freedom of action.

Thus far the papal evidence has been largely inferential. With a 1233 letter from Gregory IX to the sultan of Damascus[62] we have explicit statements that reveal the pope's goal more clearly. In a heavily theological opening, Gregory set revelation in a detailed, progressive, program.

First, by a divine disposition, the rational creature alone, thanks to "the eye of wisdom," can acknowledge the Artisan through his work, the Creator through creation. Three orders of divinely chosen human agents broaden this perception; Patriarchs, Prophets, and Apostles dispel every shadow of ignorance as if they were candelabra.

The pope then proposed intimations of the Christian doctrine of a divine Trinity in Abraham's three guests (Genesis 18:1-15), in whom the Patriarch "saw a One" (vv. 13, 14), in the threefold "holy!" of Isaiah (6:3), and in David's Psalm (66(67):7, 8), and in two verses tailored to be a triple invocation: "May God bless us! our God!—May God bless us!—and may all the ends of the earth fear him!" Scripture, the pope assured the sultan, ascribes "power to the Father, wisdom to the Son, kindness to the Holy Spirit"—"One of Three, as They are One."

Having set out the biblical ground for the most fundamental doctrine of the Christian Church, and the one least compatible with Islam, Pope Gregory moved to an examination of Prophets and Apostles on the theme of Incarnation, hardly less compatible with Islam than is the Trinity. With this step the pope introduced his own role:

> We, therefore, are obliged to seek the salvation of all as servant of the servants of him who wishes no one to perish (2 Peter 3:9; cf. 1 Timothy 2:4), by no means wrongly moved with intimate compassion toward you and your

---

[61] "... et nos te debeamus in maioribus exaudire" (ibid., n. 6, p. 119).
[62] Ibid., n. 7, pp. 120-125.

subjects, we put on the affection of Paul, Teacher of the Nations, ... we seek you, not what you possess (2 Corinthians 12:14); with Jesus Messiah we thirst for the gain which is your souls.[63]

With this theological prelude in place, the pope came to the practical issue: Franciscan friars had been provided: "May they be received willingly, heard diligently!" In these last days the pope, by divine inspiration and by the advice of his brethren, as well as with the warrant of sacred Scripture, had made this provision: "They thirst for the illumination of all peoples." In short, Pope Gregory IX, for all his blunt proposal of Christian beliefs, was persuaded of a divine imperative to do what he could for the salvation of Moslems despite the fact that they had been the target of crusading armies for more than a century.

While the hesitations of modern Christians on the crusades against Moslems in the Holy Land, Africa, and Spain, arise from a conviction that those wars were wars of aggression, no one can fail to realize that Mongol incursions into Europe during our period put all Europe on the defensive and, in a special way, the popes who felt responsible for the common welfare. A striking letter of Innocent IV "to the Tartars," edited in Lupprian's collection,[64] spells out the woeful experience as seen from Rome.

Innocent began with a sweeping survey which may owe something to a passage in Augustine's *City of God* 19, 13. Not only humans, the pope wrote, but animals without reason, indeed the very elements of the cosmos in their conjoined union, thanks to an "inborn covenant" follow the troops of supernal spirits, set in their ranks by the creating God in the stability of a peaceful order. The pope expressed his astonishment at the reports he had heard of Mongol invaders (to whom papal documents regularly refer as "Tartars")[65] devastating not only Christian lands, but others as well, the still continuing depopulation of those lands, the sparing of neither sex nor age.

Following the example of "the peaceable King" in his desire that all men live in a union of peace and fear of God, the pope expressed himself in a phrase often encountered in papal letters: "We warn, we beseech, and we

---

[63] "Quia igitur debitores sumus omnium salutem querere, servus servorum illius, qui neminem vult perire <2 Peter 3:9>, non inmerito circa te et subditos tuos misericordie visceribus affluentes, affectum Pauli gentium doctoris induimus ... vos, non vestra requirimus <2 Corinthians 12:14>, animarum vestrarum cum Ihesu Christo lucra sitimus..." (ibid., p. 124).

[64] "... regi et populo Tartarorum, viam agnoscere veritatis" (ibid., n. 20, pp. 142-145).

[65] At least one papal correspondent thought this worthy of note: "Notum sit sanctissimo patri summo pontifici ... quod predecessores potentissimi regis Abaga gentis Mongalorum (*sic*), quos vocatis Tartaros..." (ibid., n. 44, p. 228).

energetically exhort"[66] the Mongol notables to desist from such attacks, particularly from the persecution of Christians, and to "do penance" for provocations which, without doubt, provoke the wrath of God. Although God had permitted various nations to be brought low before the Mongol terror, they ought not to take this as a sign that further savagery might be permissible. If Innocent read the signs of the time correctly, God sometimes delays for a time to seize upon the proud of this world with the result that, should they fail to abase themselves, he will not forever set aside their temporal punishment and in future he will take vengeance all the more grievously.

Into this unpromising field of Mongol strength and violence the pope dispatched John de Plano Carpini, the celebrated Franciscan, along with a number of companions as "bearers" of the papal letter. Innocent characterized the Franciscans as "men outstanding in religion, seemly in their respectability, and endowed with knowledge of sacred Scripture," terms which more than suggest that he had some hope that the Mongols might be open to conversion. The pope expressed the hope that these emissaries, or rather the pope through them, might be received kindly and honorably out of reverence for God. He asked the Mongol leaders to say what they intended to do in the future. Last, he requested that his Franciscans be sent back to make their report, safe-conducts and all else necessary for their return provided. For these religious brothers, "long tested under regular observance" and "fully instructed in the sacred Scriptures" had been chosen "because we believed they would be the more useful to you."

From this single text a number of themes have been raised and future documents will bear them out. First, there is the "savagery" of the Mongol—or "Tartar"—armies, and second, their devastating military expertise.[67] Against these two negative perceptions are convictions discreetly, but unmistakably, visible beneath the formal diplomatic language. Tartars, like all men, may be converted; strong armies make welcome allies; not even a legate's report can replace a written statement of intent by a foreign notable and this, not only in the case of Tartars. Papal insistence on documents harks

---

[66] "Ideoque universitatem vestram monemus, rogamus, et hortamur attente..." (ibid., n. 20, p. 144 and n. 21, p. 147).

[67] In his last report as Chief of Staff, United States Army, General Douglas MacArthur ascribed the "successes" of Genghis Khan, "beside which the triumphs of most other commanders in history pale into insignificance," to his "unerring instinct for the fundamental qualifications of an army..."; cited by D. Clayton James, *The Years of MacArthur*, 1. *1880-1941* (Boston, 1970), pp. 457, 458 and by William Manchester, *American Caesar. Douglas MacArthur. 1880-1964* (Boston, 1978), pp. 158, 159.

back to a 1227 letter directed to "all the Kings of Russia" by Honorius III.[68] Responding to a report from his legate *a latere*, Honorius requested evidence in writing that the Russian kings were in good faith. For the pope had heard that they were ready to abandon all their errors, errors that were, in fact, the result of an absence of preachers. The kings themselves were persuaded that those errors were the cause of their many tribulations. The pope said nothing to disabuse them of this conclusion; indeed, he confirmed their view and added the reflection, not quite a threat, that the longer they remained in error, the more grievous those tribulations would be. He offered to send them a legate of the Roman Church in order that they might embrace "the Catholic faith, without which no one can be saved," but first the pope wanted written testimony: "We ask, we warn, and we energetically exhort" that letters as to their intention be forthcoming. This demand is easy to understand on the part of popes who maintained, and now maintain, the most imposing of all archives. Meanwhile, the Russian rulers were to do nothing to impede the progress of the Christian faith and to keep the peace in Lithuania and Estonia lest they offend both God and the Apostolic See, an offense, the pope did not hesitate to remark, that could be avenged easily, *facile de vobis potest, quando vult, sumere ultionem.* Much better, Honorius suggested, through true obedience and the observance of true devotion, to merit "the grace and favor of both," of the Lord and of the Apostolic See.

Rinaldi was able to note under the entries for 1245 that the reigning pope, Innocent IV, was anxious in a particular way for the conversion of schismatics and "gentiles," those races outside the range of biblical faith. Chief among them were the Tartars, so worthy of note for

> ... their multitude, for the number of provinces they had subdued, for their wealth and power, for the ferocity of their manners, for the glory of the victories they had achieved, and for the darkness of the insane superstition in which they were wrapped. To them he sent ... some Franciscans to enlighten them with the light of the Gospel and drew up Apostolic letters as well.[69]

Those Franciscans were led by a Brother Laurence of Portugal and were men who rejoiced in the standard threefold qualification of the competent missionary: "outstanding in religion, seemly in respectability, endowed with

---

[68] Text not in Lupprian; see *Annales*, AD 1227, 20: 528, 529, n. 8.

[69] "Sacro illo et Apostolico zelo succensus Innocentius, quo schismaticos ab Ecclesia divulsos revocare nisus gentiles superstitionibus imbutos ad Christi ovile adducere conatus est. Insignes erant inter eos Tartari gentium multitudine, provinciarum quas subegerant numero, opum potentia, morum ferocitate, victoriarum partarum gloria, vesanaeque superstitionis tenebris involuti. Ad quos Evangelii luce collustrando nonnullos Minoritas ... misit; tum litteras Apostolicas exaravit" (ibid., AD 1245, 21: 293, 294, n. 15).

knowledge of the sacred Scripture."[70] Still according to Rinaldi, the *felix annus*, "the fortunate year," for the pope's efforts was 1254, a year which "glittered" with the conversions of Tartars, of many schismatics, and with a widening evangelization of the northern nations.[71]

A 1254 letter from Innocent IV to Sattach, "illustrious King of the Tartars," assured Sattach that "humanity and all the faithful of Christ" rejoiced that his own conversion, as well as that of his subjects, had increased the joy of the very angels, an echo of Luke 15:10.[72] The pope reflected that "the Savior of all had given to all humans the power to become children of God," the same Savior who desired that no one perish (2 Peter 3:9).

Alas, a new threat from the Tartars was such that in 1259 Pope Alexander IV was obliged to write an awkward letter to Frederick, the Christian king of Hungary.[73] In the time of his predecessor, Gregory IX, aid against the Tartars had been requested. The pope had died and the cardinals of the Roman Church had failed to provide the promised support, "affliction was added to the already afflicted, sorrows to the already mournful" in the pope's sympathetic words, and now the king's request was renewed.

Alexander pointed out, however, that the king ought not ignore "the circumstances and the times," *casus et tempora*, to the disadvantage of the Roman Church. Frederick, *quondam* Emperor, was savage in his tyranny against the Apostolic See. Furthermore, the king had felt compelled to strike a bargain for which he claimed to have had no stomach: either a daughter of the Tartar prince marry the king's son, or a daughter of the king marry a son of the Tartar prince, and this with the odious condition that a quarter of the king of Hungary's people, led by his son, go before the Tartars for the extermination of the Christian people.

---

[70] "... vicarium sibi reliquit in terris, cui animarum curam ... commisit.... Unde predicti vicarii disponente domino nos licet inmeriti successores effecti ... ad vestram aliorumque salutem nostre intentionis dirigimus aciem ... ut errantes in viam veritatis educere ... valeamus ... uno eodemque tempore diversis locis presentialiter adesse nequimus ... ad eos viros providos et discretos transmittimus vice nostra, ipsorum ministerio circa illos apostolice servitutis debitum exsolventes ... dilectum filium fratrem Laurentium de Portugallia et socios eius latores presentium ordinis fratrum Minorum viros religione conspicuos, honestate decoros et sacre scripture scientia preditos..." (Lupprian, n. 20, pp. 142-145).

[71] "Affulsit Ecclesia Orientalium Tartarorum ad Christum conversione, plurimum schismaticorum ad illius gremium redeuntium ... atque Evangelii apud Septentrionales nationes amplificatione felix annus..." (*Annales*, AD 1254, 21: 453, n. 1).

[72] "... Applaudans tibi exultat humanitas, et fidelium Christi universitas colletatur ... non modicum de tua et tuorum conversione crevisse gaudium angelorum <Luke 15:10> ... salvator omnium dedit omnibus hominibus potestatem filios dei fieri ... qui neminem vult perire" <2 Peter 3:9> (Lupprian, n. 39, pp. 210, 211).

[73] *Annales*, AD 1259, 22: 41-44, nn. 34-44.

The pope took seriously this opportunity to explain something of Church Law on marriage. No bond of marriage joins a pagan and a Christian; between two pagans there is no true marriage, but the bond is deficient owing to the "defect of faith." Such a "marriage" is neither ratified nor, in consequence, is it "inseparable" as is the Christian sacrament.

Having said so much about the former impossibility of aid from the court of Gregory IX, Alexander proceeded to his own situation. He had heard with "a benevolent ear" the petitions of the king and was disposed to fulfill them as time and place might permit. Still, he hoped the king would not take it amiss if in the matter of a thousand crossbowmen his request not be met; the Pope was convinced that what the Apostolic See was granting would be of much more importance. He particularly hoped that the king would understand that it was not possible to provide Templars and knights of other military orders; they were already in peril from the Tartars and from "other unbelievers," Moslems, in the overseas territories. The same was the case with the Cistercians who had been requested. If, however, the necessity that the king feared should come to pass, the Apostolic See would call to his aid the Christian princes and peoples, that is, the pope would proclaim a crusade. Nor would that See neglect to provide advice in the struggle against those who were "enemies of God, and your enemies." Finally, the king ought not to think that the aforesaid See had unduly burdened the Churches of Hungary in their time of trial with unwarranted taxes.

In 1263 Alexander wrote to Olaoni, king of the Tartars,[74] with generous praise of the king's intention to receive instruction in order to be baptized, news conveyed to the pope by messenger along with a request for "some suitable man"—marked by a knowledge of Christian doctrine and resplendent for the purity of his life. The pope went on to note that the Tartar king had not neglected to mention that much could be done to subdue the kingdoms of the "Saracens" should Christian armies assist the Tartars, thus bringing to the enterprise the blessing of heaven as well as temporal advantage.

Having thus summarized the king's letter, the pope ended on a less accepting note. Since the king had given "us no adequate letters, nor shown any other ground for full certitude," the pope urged that the king make a full disclosure of his intentions to the patriarch of Jerusalem in order that the patriarch might "explore the proposal of your Serenity" and, in turn, report his findings to the pope. Using the familiar formula, "We warn, we beseech, we energetically exhort," Alexander IV asked the king to "reveal his inmost

---

[74] Lupprian, n. 41, p. 216; this text dated erroneously by Rinaldi as AD 1260, *Annales*, 22: 59, nn. 29-31.

will in all security" to the patriarch so that the pope, with all due speed, might do whatever might be necessary to forward the affair.

Parallel reluctance on the part of Pope Urban IV is visible in his letter of 1264 to Bela, king of Hungary.[75] In this document the pope professed himself astounded that the king, after the universally known depredations by Tartars against the Christian religion, should have been deceived by Tartar messengers, *nuntii*, "or rather pestilential spies," *exploratores pestiferi*, to the point of committing his son, Stephen, to "bonds of family, or some other amicable covenant with them." Past experience with the Tartars, the pope asserted, had always meant the shedding of innocent blood.

Of peculiar interest in the interplay between Tartars and popes is a letter of 1285 from the Tartar, Argon, to the reigning pope,[76] Honorius IV, "in a Latin so barbarous that it has not seemed useless to me that I here attempt its translation"—thus the editor, Maurice Prou.[77] Beginning with the formula "In the Name of Christ. Amen!" the Tartar prince wrote "to our Holy Father the Pope" to recall that the greatest of Tartar rulers, "Ginghis Khan," had entertained the greatest affection for the king of the Franks; he had decided that Christians need pay no tribute; indeed, they were "free" in his lands. The current Great Khan had sent Argon with presents of clothing and perfumes, with ambassadors and interpreters, to remind the pope that "their first mother," their grandmother, had been a Christian, and that "You, Holy Father, ought to know that Christians retained their own lands under Tartar rulers." Now, at the order of the khan, the Tartars proposed to "deliver the lands of the Christians and to take them under protection."

Not all was well, however; during the year just past the Christian convert, Ahmed, had become a Moslem and, instead of guarding the lands of the Christians, had invaded them, an episode which had delayed Argon's embassy.

Here Argon reached the point of his letter. Since the land of Cham, Egypt, lay between Tartar and Christian forces, should each attack simultaneously, this would surely deliver a Moslem califate to the Christians and the Tartars in their alliance. Confident that the pope would see the wisdom of this pincer movement, Argon asked the pope to inform him by "a sure messenger" as to where the pope would wish the combat to take place. Thus the defeat of

---

[75] *Annales*, AD 1264, p. 137, n. 48.

[76] Edition and French version, *Les registres d'Honorius IV...*, ed. Maurice Prou, Bibliothèque des Écoles françaises d'Athènes et de Rome (Paris, 1886), fascicule 2, coll. 346, 347, n. 489; see also Lupprian, n. 49, pp. 244-246.

[77] Prou edition, fascicule 4, p. LXIX: "... Elle est rédigée dans un latin si barbare qu'il ne nous paraît pas inutile d'en essayer ici la traduction."

the Saracens would be effected with "the aid of the Lord, of the Pope, and of the Khan." The letter was dated according to the Tartar zodiac "in the year of the rooster (1285) and the 18th day of the moon of May."

Three years later Pope Nicholas IV was in correspondence with Argon over his baptism. In a courteous answer to Argon the pope expressed his pleasure that Argon was showing himself benevolent to those who hold the Christian faith and that "a multitude beyond number" might be expected to follow him into the Church.[78]

On the same day in another letter to Argon the pope took up a difficulty in Argon's plan, for the Tartar prince hoped to be baptized in Jerusalem, and the city was still in the hands of the Moslems. The pope suggested the reverse order: the liberation of the Kingdom of Jerusalem would, "God favoring," be easier were Argon already a Christian. The sooner and the more willingly Argon should proceed to the reception of the sacrament, the more numerous would be the people encouraged to follow the example of their prince.[79]

It is not easy to think that Argon's inclination toward baptism was innocent of political considerations. In 1291 the same pope was still urging him in the most courteous terms to hasten to receive the sacrament, this time in the context of yet another crusade against "the most unspeakable Saracens." Omitting the usual "We warn" from the formula and replacing those words with "we ask earnestly," "we seek confidently," Nicholas urged that Argon not only go forward to baptism, but that he "shape himself to the divine good pleasure" and, with his powerful resources, guarantee the rapid recuperation of The Land as well as "the crushing of the wickedness and pride of its enemies." [80]

THE SHEEPFOLD AND THE OTHER SHEEP

Thanks to papal concern to keep records and thanks to the expertise of scholars, from Cardinal Baronio forward, it is possible for our time to recover the raw material produced by medieval popes in their conduct of the affairs of the Roman Church.

Despite significant differences, twentieth-century observers will recognize in the enigmas that preoccupied those popes parallels to those which exercise us. Hostile military powers, Moslem or Tartar, varied active hostility with interludes of friendship. Local interests resisted initiatives conceived by the popes to be necessary for the common good, the well-being of Christian

---

[78] Lupprian, n. 50, pp. 247-250.
[79] Ibid., n. 53, pp. 253-254.
[80] Ibid., n. 62, pp. 274-276.

society as a whole. Their conception of religious truth and of its importance, a faith "without which no one can be saved," can be matched on another plane in our time by secular ideologies: democracy, the class struggle, science, and those now obsolete vagaries: fascism, nazism, "progress." Then, as now, transcendental goals provoked men to violence; defense suggested preparation for war, for the pre-emptive strike, alliance with the enemy of one's enemy.

Still, it would be unjust as well as unrealistic to diminish the religious dedication of our popes, and that of their principal collaborators in their mission to unbelievers, the begging friars, Franciscan and Dominican. Nothing in the life of Saint Francis of Assisi has so compelled admiration as did his efforts at dialogue with Moslem dignitaries. Even his charismatic offer to walk through fire in order to "prove" the validity of his Christian faith has been extolled.[81] On a more pedestrian plane we have seen popes and friars give institutional expression to the conviction that all men, however hostile, however ferocious, are open in principle to faith in Jesus.

How fundamental to our popes' horizon were the parables of recovery, the image of the lost sheep, the misplaced coin, the image of the "other sheep," not yet within the sheepfold.[82] No doubt we shall have reservations on the popes' choice of means as future generations will be stupified by our armaments, by our mal-distribution of the means of production, by our clumsiness and short-sightedness in our dealing with "the other," "the outsider." For the popes of the middle ages, despite tragic limitations in papal perspectives, those outsiders were held to be "the other sheep," destined for the sheepfold of the Lord.

---

[81] For accounts of this episode see Saint Bonaventure, *Opusculum XXIII*, "Legenda sancti Francisci," cap. ix, nn. 5-9 and *Opusculum XXIV*, "Legenda minor sancti Francisci," lectio 9, in *Opera omnia* (Quaracchi, 1882-1902), 8: 504-564 and 565-579; for an admiring interpretation of the event see: Guilio Basetti-Sani, OFM, "Muhammed and Saint Francis," in *The Francis Book*, ed. R. M. Gasnik, OFM (New York/London, 1980), pp. 186, 187.

[82] John 10:16.

14

The Cardinals' View of the Papacy, 1150-1300

Norman Zacour

If, for the moment, we take our stand at the end of the thirteenth century, when the college of cardinals had perhaps reached the apogee of its development, we shall find ourselves in the presence of an oligarchy of great dignity, influential in the distribution of a large amount of patronage, exerting wide political influence, and viewed at the time, whether with favour or not, as men of great wealth and power. We shall also be confronted with some well developed metaphors about the successors of the apostles;[1] pillars of the church of God; part of the pope's body; the *cardines*—the hinges—upon which the great door of the universal church swings;[2] senators of the church,[3] reminiscent of the senators of the Roman empire now absorbed into the Christian body politic; *patres conscripti*, as Francesco Petrarca would later call them, of the Christian church. There were other more material signs of their importance: the red hat that Innocent IV allowed them to wear to go with the many other symbols that marked them off from other churchmen;[4]

---

[1] Cf. Michael Wilks, *The Problem of Sovereignty in the Later Middle Ages* (Cambridge, 1963), p. 460, n. 2.

[2] So Leo IX in 1054; see Stephan Kuttner, "Cardinalis: The History of a Canonical Concept," *Traditio* 3 (1945) 176.

[3] Peter Damian, in *PL* 145: 540.

[4] F. Pagnotti, "Niccolò da Calvi e la sua Vita d'Innocenzo IV," *Archivio della R. Società Romana di Storia Patria* 21 (1898) 97: "Interim dictus pontifex, post concilium [Lyons,

The Religious Roles of the Papacy: Ideals and Realities, 1150-1300, ed. Christopher Ryan, Papers in Mediaeval Studies 8 (Toronto: Pontifical Institute of Mediaeval Studies, 1989), pp. 413-438. © P.I.M.S., 1989.

and their display of high rank in the large number of attendants who accompanied them in public, churchmen and laymen alike, who by the fourteenth century would dress in the livery of their masters. They enjoyed a special legal status given them by Pope Honorius III who defined an attack on the person of a cardinal as *lèse majesté*.[5] There were also institutional features that underlined their status, the most important being their very own *archa*,[6] or common treasury, into which went half the regular revenues of the Roman church to be shared equally by all the cardinals present in the papal court.

Whatever the definition of the papacy that the cardinals now entertained, it had been shaped by their relationship with the pope over a long period of time, from the eleventh century on. Originally marked out because they performed special liturgical services in certain Roman basilicas, the cardinals acquired great importance as a group after they were given sole control of papal elections. Beginning in the reform period of the eleventh century, they were continuously in the presence of the pope, assisting and advising him. As individuals they performed missions outside Rome on his behalf; some wrote treatises in support of the reform ideas being championed by the Roman church. Pope and cardinals were in constant consultation, and it would not be long before the cardinals began to take on administrative and judicial roles which gave to their title "cardinal" a new significance.

The cardinals had two functions that determined the way in which they came to view the papal office and their part in it: as papal advisers; and as papal electors. There was never any doctrine on the college of cardinals that was universally acceptable,[7] and opinions on the precise nature of both their electoral and advisory functions would tend to change during our period. It

---

1245], anno secundo, Cluniacum ivit cum rege Francie et ipsius fratribus locuturus; ubi domini cardinales primo capellos rubeos receperunt. In ipso concilio fuerat ordinatum." This MS was owned by Francesco Petrarca, who wrote in the margin at this point: "pillei rubei patrum conscriptorum." For Cardinal Luca Fieschi's white mule, see K. H. Schäfer, *Die Ausgaben der apostolischen Kammer unter Benedict XII, Klemens VI, und Innocenz VI (1334-1362)*, Vatikanische Quellen zur Geschichte der päpstlichen Hof- und Finanz-verwaltung, 1316-1378, 3 (Paderborn, 1914), p. 47.

    [5] C. Coquelines, *Bullarium ... Romanorum pontificum amplissima collectio* (Rome, 1740), 3: 239, no. 76.

    [6] "Sed et archam communem habent quo ad servitia communia, et camerarium specialem loco sindici qui et oblata equaliter dividit inter eos"; Hostiensis, *Comm. ad Decret.* 5.6.17. On the subject in general, see J. P. Kirsch, *Die Finanzverwaltung des Kardinalkollegiums im XIII. und XIV. Jahrhundert*, Kirchengeschichtliche Studien, II, 4 (Münster i. W., 1895); P. M. Baumgarten, *Untersuchungen und Urkunden über die Camera Collegii Cardinalium für die Zeit von 1295 bis 1434* (Leipzig, 1898).

    [7] But cf. Giuseppe Alberigo, *Cardinalato e collegialità: Studi sull'ecclesiologia tra l'XI e il XIV secolo* (Florence, 1969).

was assumed by the cardinals themselves, however, that the Roman church, the head of all other churches, comprised the pope and themselves.[8] They were therefore at one with the pope in encouraging the development of the authority of the Roman church, which could only enhance their own dignity and authority. It was their union with the pope, the product of two hundred years of intimate collaboration, that near the end of our period, in the second half of the thirteenth century, would allow the great canonist Hostiensis (Cardinal Henry of Susa) to say with an air of impressive authority: "today the Roman church holds that there is no greater dignity than that of the cardinalate, since the cardinals together with the pope judge all, but cannot themselves be judged by anyone other than the pope and their colleagues."[9]

ECCLESIA ROMANA

There is much evidence to indicate that the central direction of the church in the twelfth century was undertaken by the pope only in the closest cooperation with his advisers.[10] Increasingly, the papacy as such was referred to as "papa et cardinales."[11] While cardinals did not lack ideas about the papal office or their role as part of it, such ideas rarely received direct expression. Consequently we often have to search for them as they are reflected in events. We are fortunate, however, in one exception, an almost unanimous expression of the cardinals defining the Roman church, made at the very beginning of our period in the middle of the twelfth century. It was reported by Otto of Freising in his *Deeds of Frederick Barbarossa*, in the midst of his discussion of the synod of Rheims in 1148. This was the synod presided over by the Cistercian pope Eugenius III, in which Bernard of Clairvaux and others sought the condemnation of Gilbert, bishop of Poitiers. Bernard's activities disturbed and upset the cardinals, who complained to Eugenius "as though with one voice":

[8] Hostiensis, *Comm. ad Decret.* 2.24.4: "... papa et ipsi [cardinales] romanam ecclesiam consistunt...." The identification of pope and cardinals as the Roman church was already a commonplace when enunciated by the canonist Huguccio late in the twelfth century: "Romana ecclesia dicitur papa et cardinales," cited in B. Tierney, *Foundations of the Conciliar Theory* (Cambridge, 1955; repr. 1968), p. 42.

[9] *Comm. ad Decret.* 3.5.19.

[10] See Werner Maleczek, *Papst und Kardinalskolleg von 1191 bis 1216: Die Kardinäle unter Coelestin III. und Innocenz III*, Publikationen des Historischen Instituts beim österreichischen Kulturinstitut in Rom, ed. Otto Kresten and Adam Wandruszka, Abt. 1: Abhandlungen, Band 6 (Vienna, 1984), p. 255.

[11] From the beginning of the pontificate of Eugenius III it was a rare exception when references to the pope's taking advice implied prelates other than the cardinals (Maleczek, *Papst und Kardinalskolleg*, pp. 307-308).

You should know that, having been elevated to the rule of the entire church by us, around whom, like pivots [*cardines*], the axis of the church universal swings, and having been made by us from a private person into the father of the universal church, it is necessary from now on that you belong not just to yourself but to us; that you do not rank particular and recent friendships [an allusion to Bernard of Clairvaux] before those which are general and of ancient standing. You must look to the welfare of all and care for and watch over the dignity of the Roman court, as an obligation of your office. But what has this abbot of yours done, and the French church with him? With what insolence, what daring, has he raised his head against the primacy and the supremacy of the Roman see? For it is this see alone that shuts and no man opens, opens and no man shuts [Is 22:22; Apoc 3:7]. It alone has the right to judge matters of catholic faith and cannot, even when absent, tolerate anyone impinging on this unique privilege. But look—these Frenchmen, despising us to our very faces, have presumed to write down their profession of faith relative to the articles which we have been discussing these past few days as though they were putting the last touch to a final definition without consulting us. Surely, if this business were being treated in the east before all the patriarchs—in Alexandria, say, or Antioch—they could establish nothing firm and final without our authority. On the contrary, according to the decisions or precedents of the ancient fathers, it would be reserved to Rome for final decision. How then do these men dare in our presence to usurp what in our absence is not permitted to those more distant and more distinguished? We want you therefore to stand up against this rash novelty, and punish their insolence without delay.[12]

Eugenius was reminded that he owed his office to the cardinals, that he had become part of another body greater than himself—a body comprising himself and the cardinals, the Roman church. His obligation as pope, derived from what the cardinals viewed as the history of the office, was to exalt the Roman church over the rest of Christendom. Furthermore, it was not to the synod, not to some mere gathering of local churchmen, but to this Roman church, i.e., pope and cardinals, that the definition of faith belonged, than which there could be nothing more primatial. This had been so in the distant past, when the canons of the great eastern councils of antiquity received whatever validity they possessed only from their acceptance by the Roman see; and it was so now in Rheims.

John of Salisbury reported the same controversy, in terms somewhat more favourable to Bernard of Clairvaux. He records the preliminary meeting held

---

[12] B. de Simson, *Ottonis et Rahewini Gesta Friderici I imperatoris*, Scriptores rerum Germanicarum in usum scholarum (Hanover and Leipzig, 1912); *The Deeds of Frederick Barbarossa by Otto of Freising*, tr. C. C. Mierow, Records of Civilization (New York, 1953), p. 99.

by Bernard and others, including Suger of St. Denis, Theobald archbishop of Canterbury, and Henry of York, where certain doctrinal statements were agreed upon ahead of time, which so irritated the cardinals:

> As far as I recall there was not a single cardinal except Alberic bishop of Ostia of holy memory who was not wholeheartedly opposed to the abbot in spirit and deed; ... But as the abbot could not fail to hear of the cardinals' conspiracy, he forestalled them all, and going to the pope as a friend, urged him to put on zeal and manly courage in the Lord's cause, lest the weakness of the body of Christ and wounds of the faith should be found to be in the head. ... it was certain that some of the cardinals were filled with envy of him, and could not refrain from slander.[13]

What is inescapable is that the cardinals made a careful distinction between the person of the pope and the Roman church, the joint body of pope and cardinals. It was a distinction which threatened to limit the personal authority of the pope. It was not universally accepted, however, or rather, the consequences that the cardinals would seek to draw from it were not universally accepted. It was undoubtedly to counter their views that Bernard of Clairvaux spoke to the pope "familiariter" at Rheims, and would soon insist, in his *De consideratione*, that the cardinals enjoyed no authority except that bestowed by the pope. While at one time, when warning the cardinals about Peter Abelard's errors, he would acknowledge that they were men of great influence, and had written to them in conventional fashion that "there can be no doubt that it is for you especially to rid the kingdom of God of scandals, to cut down the thorns, to settle complaints,"[14] and would even refer to them as "iudices orbis,"[15] he would tell Eugenius that they had "no power except that which you grant them or permit them to exercise."[16] And he was particularly scathing when dealing with the pretensions of cardinal-deacons who, because of their proximity to the pope, claimed precedence over priests. "Non hoc ratio habet"—it makes no sense; "non antiquitas habuit"—it derived from no tradition; "non consentit auctoritas"—it had the support of no authority.[17]

---

[13] *John of Salisbury's Memoirs of the Papal Court*, tr. Marjorie Chibnall (London and Edinburgh, 1956), pp. 17-21.

[14] J. Leclercq and H. Rochais, *S. Bernardi opera*, 8: *Epistolae* (Rome, 1977), p. 10, ep. 188.

[15] *De consideratione*, 4.1.1 (Leclercq and Rochais, 3: *Tractatus et opuscula* [Rome, 1967], p. 449).

[16] Ibid., 4.4.9 (Leclercq and Rochais, 3: 455).

[17] Ibid., 4.5.16 (Leclercq and Rochais, 3: 461). At this time it was still held to be inappropriate for cardinal-deacons to take precedence over bishops. When Pope Eugenius III proposed to promote to the priesthood John Paparo, a cardinal-deacon, preparatory to his going to Ireland as a papal legate, John refused. Eugenius suspended him, whereupon John

N. ZACOUR

"Unus et idem"

Nevertheless, for the cardinals it was their union with the pope that defined for them the nature of the papacy. The language of this union was often cast in anthropomorphic terms, an echo of the apostle Paul's unity of all Christians in Christ (1 Cor 12:12), and as such was in common use. It was a language familiar to and frequently used by the canonist Hostiensis (d. 1271).[18] The cardinals were part of the pope's body; while the pope might be thought of as general head of the universal church and individual Christians his "members" in a general sense, he was the special head of the cardinals, who were then his "members" in a special sense. He and the cardinals together formed a single body. Cardinals did not have to take an oath to the pope like other ecclesiastics, because they were all one body; they were part of his very bowels, so to speak—"cardinales tanquam sibi [pape] inviscerati"; that is why cardinal-legates were said to come from the pope's side—"a latere"—as though from his very body. Hence the pope loves the cardinals as "himself." [19] Between pope and cardinals the union is so close that they consult together on all things; the cardinals are so united to the pope that together they are one and the same thing—"unum et idem est." [20]

The biological metaphor remained a popular one. Cardinal John Lemoine saw the cardinals not only as part of the pope's body, but, in somewhat more detail, members of his "head" whereas other prelates were only members of his "body"; the union of pope and cardinals was therefore even closer than the union of pope and bishops.[21]

---

threatened to lead a rebellion in Rome. Finally the other cardinals prevailed upon him to make his peace with the pope and accept the priesthood, "pointing out that it was not seemly for a deacon to bless archbishops, and that the lord pope would not give the Irish legation to anyone who was not a priest"; see *John of Salisbury's Memoirs*, tr. Chibnall, p. 71.

[18] "Inter cardinales quippe et papam tanta est unio ut sibi adinvicem omnia communicare deceat"; *Comm. ad Decret.* 4.17.13. Hostiensis' several comments on the college of cardinals have been conveniently brought together by John A. Watt, "The Constitutional Law of the College of Cardinals: Hostiensis to Joannes Andreae," *MedS* 33 (1971) 151-157. His opinions, together with those of cardinal John Lemoine after him, are of particular value for us as opinions not of distinguished canonists, but rather of cardinals reflecting on the ideas and practices of their order. See especially Brian Tierney, "Hostiensis and Collegiality," in *Proceedings of the Fourth International Congress of Medieval Canon Law*, ed. Stephan Kuttner (Vatican City, 1976), pp. 401-409.

[19] *Comm. ad Decret.* 5.33.23.

[20] Ibid., 5.6.17: "Cardinales ... sunt membra capitis: caeteri prelati sunt membra corporis"; cf. Martinus Laudunensis, *Tractatus de cardinalibus ad modum singularis digestus per centum quaestiones*, q. 5, in *Tractatus illustrium in utraque ... iuris facultate iurisconsultorum*, 13, pt. 2 (Venice, 1584), f. 60^b; Andreas de Barbatia, *Tractatus de praestantia card.*, ibid., f. 71^a.

[21] In his commentary on the *Extravagantes*, col. 328, on *Dudum* of Benedict XI. Pope John XXII, in a letter about the occupation by Roman noble families of houses and palaces in Rome belonging to the cardinals' churches, wrote: "cum ipsi qui fore noscuntur capitis nostri

A different though equally effective way of describing the union of pope and cardinals could also be made in legal terms. Corporation theory, developing swiftly in the thirteenth century, especially as it was applied to ecclesiastical bodies such as cathedral chapters, allowed the Roman church, i.e., pope and cardinals, to be described as a single legal body, a corporation of head and members, whose function it was to rule the universal church. The comparison to be made between bishop and chapter on the one hand, and pope and cardinals on the other, allowed one to apply the rights of chapters within their corporation to the college of cardinals within theirs.[22] Hostiensis insisted that the cardinals were not merely a collection of individuals, belonging to individual churches, their "tituli" in Rome; rather, they formed a college or corporation, "universitas," whose head was the pope and whose church was the church of Rome. They possessed the usual attributes of a corporation: they had their own treasury, one of the members serving as *camerarius*; their right of papal election was a right held in common—a corporate right, not the right of individuals; and finally, they were generally recognized as a corporate body, and a sacred one at that: "sacrum collegium vulgariter et communiter nominatur."[23]

COMMUNIS SOLLICITUDO

These various attempts to describe and define a unique relationship between pope and cardinals undoubtedly grew out of the challenges of the twelfth century: imperial hostility, Roman rebellion, the perverse disobedience of many ecclesiastics, and below the surface of all this the constant fear of papal schism, which must have brought pope and cardinals close together as though under siege. The popes of the twelfth century seem never to have been without the company of their cardinals, and never to have acted without consulting them. In the thirteenth century, with the rapid evolution of the idea of a papal plenitude of power connoting rulership over the entire church, it was almost inevitable that some would see the cardinals sharing in that plenitude. One way of expressing this was to contrast the relationship between pope and cardinals with the relationship between pope and other prelates: the pope had a general responsibility for the church; the bishops shared only in a part of that responsibility, within their particular dioceses ("vocati in partem sollicitudinis"). Where did the cardinals stand in such a

---

membra..."; A. Theiner, *Codex diplomaticus dominii temporalis s. sedis* (Rome, 1861), 1: 506, no. 669.

[22] B. Tierney, *Foundations of the Conciliar Theory*, pp. 68-84, 149-153, and passim.

[23] *Comm. ad Decret.* 5.6.17.

scheme? Hostiensis maintained that they shared the pope's general responsibility for the church at large: "Cardinales communem impendunt solicitudinem pro statu ecclesie generalis, sicut et papa."[24] Cardinal John Lemoine, early in the fourteenth century, would follow this lead, holding that it would be absurd if chapters of cathedral churches share in the responsibilities of their respective prelates while the cardinals, "in tota solicitudine," could not share in that of their prelate, the pope.[25]

The term "solicitude" to describe pastoral responsibility had a long history. Pope Leo I (440-461), oppressed by the burdens of his office, recognized the necessity of sharing his general responsibility for the church with others. It was on the occasion when one of these, a vicar in Illyricum, went beyond his mandate that Leo chastised him by reminding him that he had been "in partem ... vocatus sollicitudinis, non in plenitudinem potestatis." What began as an expression to put a papal subordinate in place would later, in the pseudo-Isidorean decretals, take on new dimensions of juridical, and ultimately theological, importance, by emphasizing the general jurisdiction of the pope over the church at large and the notion of Rome as the foundation of all churches. Rome exercised a plenitude of power; other churches were called to share in the pope's solicitude. In time, there emerged from all this two senses of the solicitude exercised by pope and prelates: the sense that each exercised the same kind of authority, that of the prelates limited in area, that of the pope universal, each derived directly from God—the sense reflected in Bernard of Clairvaux's *De consideratione*;[26] and the sense of an authority ordered hierarchically, whereby the power of a bishop could be explained as being derived from the pope, without, as Innocent III would have it, any diminution of the plenitude that the pope enjoyed.[27] In thirteenth-century usage the term increasingly bore this second sense,[28] in the growing awareness of the special significance now being given to the term "plenitudo potestatis"; for example, Innocent III explained why only the pope could use the pallium at all times, because he had a plenitude of power, while other prelates could do so only on special occasions,

---

[24] *Comm. ad Decret.* 5.6.17.

[25] Ad *Sext.*, 5.11.12: "absurdum enim esset quod capitula ecclesiarum cathedralium, quorum prelati in solicitudinis partem sunt vocati, haberent in illa parte solicitudinis ... et cetus cardinalium in tota solicitudine non haberet."

[26] 2.8.15 (Leclercq and Rochais, 3: 423-424).

[27] Jean Rivière, "*In partem sollicitudinis*: évolution d'une formule pontificale," *Revue des sciences religieuses* 5 (1925) 210-231.

[28] "[Apostolice sedis prelatus] ... vocatur ... summus pontifex quia caput est omnium pontificum, a quo illi tanquam a capite membra descendunt et de cuius plenitudine omnes accipiunt, quos ipse vocat in partem solicitudinis, non in plenitudinem potestatis"; William Durantis, bishop of Mende, *Rationale divinorum officiorum*, 3.1.17 (Venice, 1599), f. 31ʳ.

"quoniam vocati sint in partem sollicitudinis, non in plenitudinem potestatis." [29]

If, then, some cardinals now describe themselves as "vocati in *communem sollicitudinem*," it is because they see themselves as part of the papacy, partners in the government of the church, sharing fully in papal authority, participants in his plenitude of power.[30] It is true that this "common" solicitude of pope and cardinals was a conception with no real future, given the rapid growth of the pope's personal sovereignty. But its corollary, that the cardinals shared in some sense in the papal plenitude of power, would still be echoed in the fourteenth century by no less than pope Clement VI who, in his *collatio* marking the creation of his seventeen-year-old nephew and namesake, Pierre Roger, as a cardinal deacon, turned to the book of Job (9:13) to liken the cardinals to giants shouldering the world, bowing down only before the vicar of Christ, adding that cardinals were appointed not only to share in the papal solicitude for the church but, in a fashion, to share in the pope's plenitude of power.[31]

De fratrum nostrorum consilio...

In the Middle Ages there was an almost universal conviction that taking advice was important in government. "Do all things with counsel," Bernard

---

[29] So Innocent III, *Decretales*, 1.8.4; also in *PL* 215: 294D. Cf. ep. 320 (*PL* 214: 286c): "cuius [sc. Romanae ecclesiae] pastor ita suas aliis vices distribuit ut, caeteris vocatis in partem sollicitudinis, solus retineat plenitudinem potestatis, ut de ipso post Deum alii dicere possint: 'Et nos de plenitudine ipsius accepimus'."

[30] "Non solum papa sed et cardinales includerentur etiam in expressione plenitudinis potestatis"; "Participant ergo cardinales plenitudini potestatis"; Hostiensis, *Comm. ad Decret.* 4.17.13. The "universality" of the cardinals' solicitude was not unknown abroad; see the letter to the cardinals from the convent of Christ Church, Canterbury, in *Chronicles and Memorials of the Reign of Richard I*, vol. 2, *Epistolae Cantuariensis: the Letters of the Prior and Convent of Christ Church, Canterbury from A.D. 1187 to A.D. 1199*, ed. William Stubbs, RS 38, part 2 (London, 1865), p. 434, no. 469: "Ad vos omnium spectat sollicitudo ecclesiarum...," and to cardinal Gratian in 1159 (ibid., p. 503, no. 538): "Quia igitur amodo coram religionis vestrae praesentia jus nostrum prosequi compellimur, cui universalis sollicitudo incumbit ecclesiae, clementiam vestram affectuosa cordis devotione deposcimus, ut...."
  When discussing questions touching on the deposition or excommunication of cardinals, and marshalling arguments to limit arbitrary action by the pope ("papa per se non potest ipsum deponere, sed et plures testes requiruntur ad eum convincendum"; and again: "Papa non consuevit, nec etiam potest secundum quosdam, aliquem de cardinalibus excommunicare vel ei aliquod preceptum facere sine aliorum suorum fratrum consilio et consensu"), Hostiensis would still recognize that in the pope alone resides a plenitude of power: "Quicquid tamen dicitur, hoc de plano fateor, quod in solum papam plenitudo residet potestatis ... contra scribere non intendo..."; *Comm. ad Decret.* 3.4.2. Note that the power "resided" in the pope, not in the college of cardinals; but the cardinals shared it, i.e., they helped the pope to exercise it.

[31] Ste. Geneviève, MS 240, fol. 416^{v-a}: "Non solo assumuntur ad partem sollicitudinis set quodammodo in plenitudinem potestatis. Merito ergo celo comparentur."

of Clairvaux told Eugenius III; "afterwards you won't be sorry." [32] At the root of this conviction lay the idea that there was too much at stake to risk the independent decisions of one person no matter how venerable, how reliable, or how feared. It was a concern that was often expressed. When one discussed rulers and rulership one almost always had recourse to the notion that there was safety in numbers, frequently reinforced by a favourite text from Proverbs: "ubi multa consilia, ibi salus." [33] When dealing, for example, with the question whether a minor might be permitted to take up the reins of government while still under age, a fourteenth-century curial lawyer gave it as his opinion that the young ruler "non potest errare propter multos sibi astantes," [34] a pretty example of a bureaucrat's touching faith in advisory committees.

Of all the rulers of the Middle Ages, there was none whose authority was more often discussed than that of the pope, and just as often as secular princes were urged to consult their natural advisers, their great vassals, so too the pope was enjoined again and again to consult *his* natural advisers, the cardinals. Leaving aside the personal idiosyncracies of this pope or that, they needed little urging. Often they themselves bemoaned the immense practical difficulties of their position and described their pressing need for reliable advisers who would help them not only in the performance of their many liturgical, legal and administrative functions, but also in the wide range of ecclesiastical and political problems which constantly beset the papacy. "Since we cannot handle the entirety of ecclesiastical affairs ourselves," Eugenius III writes, "we entrust to our brethren [the cardinals], in whose discretion we have confidence, the completion of certain matters having respect to time and place." [35] John of Salisbury mentions the fact that although as a Cistercian Eugenius generally favoured his order, a request from it to restore to the priesthood a Cistercian who had once supported the anti-pope Anacletus II had no success: "although the pope seemed to lend a favourable ear to their appeals, he always referred the matter to the cardinals; and they maintained that no concession could be made on account of the constitution of Pope Innocent [II] condemning in perpetuity all who had received ordination from Peter Leonis [Anacletus II], and the decree of Eugenius himself just promulgated in the council of Rheims." [36] Alexander III

---

[32] *De consid.* 4.4.11 (Leclercq and Rochais, 3: 457), citing Eccles 32:24.

[33] Prov 11:14. See Innocent III in *PL* 215: 1128.

[34] *Oldradi de Ponte Laudensis ... Consilia seu Responsa* (Frankfurt am Main, 1576), con. 52.

[35] J. von Pflugk-Harttung, *Acta pontificum Romanorum inedita* (Tübingen and Stuttgart, 1881), 1: 187, no. 204.

[36] *John of Salisbury's Memoirs*, tr. Chibnall, p. 43.

would look upon the advisory role of the cardinals as so important that it could take the place of a church synod.[37] On one occasion, being approached by the ambassador of Frederick Barbarossa who asked for a private audience, Alexander replied that it was quite useless to speak to him privately since he would not reply without consulting his cardinals.[38] Popes frequently expressed themselves on the consultative role to be filled by the cardinals they appointed. Martin IV, when appointing a new cardinal, cited Jethro's advice to Moses who was trying to judge his people without any assistance: "provide from all the people able men who fear God, in whom there is truth, who hate avarice." [39]

One of the clearest expressions of a pope on the subject of the advisory role of cardinals comes from Nicholas III in the thirteenth century: "It is fitting," he said, "that the pope receive from his brethren, the cardinals of the holy Roman church, who assist him as coadjutors in the execution of his priestly office, counsel freely given. It is fitting that he not vacillate in his judgment in any way, so that the fear of no secular power frighten them, no momentary passion absorb them, no alarm threaten them, nothing restrain them from giving real, solid advice." [40]

This need to recruit reliable advisers was not in itself incompatible with the growing notion of a papal world monarchy and a sovereign pope of unlimited authority. Nevertheless, the pope's regular, systematic consultation with the body of cardinals in all important matters led many to believe that he could not, in fact, act legitimately in such matters without at least first asking for their advice. It was not only the cardinals who thought so. William Durantis, for example, who was no champion of cardinalatial prerogatives, said that the pope should make no important decisions or do anything of consequence without first taking the advice of the cardinals, and made the obvious comparison with the lay advisers of kings and princes: "for it is certain that those who rule in spiritual and temporal affairs are human, and

---

[37] Ep. 34 (*PL* 200: 107): "... quamvis negotium arduum et sublime non frequenter soleat nisi in solemnibus conciliis de more concedi, de communi tamen fratrum nostrorum consilio ... censuimus...." The matter had to do with the canonization of Edward the Confessor.

[38] *PL* 200: 36.

[39] E. Martène and U. Durand, *Veterum scriptorum ... collectio* (Paris, 1724), 2: 1283. The biblical text is from Ex 18:21. For a discussion of the formula *de fratrum nostrorum consilio* up to and including the pontificate of Innocent III, see Maleczek, *Papst und Kardinalskolleg*, chapter 7 (pp. 297-324).

[40] "Decet namque ipsi Romano Pontifici per fratres suos, sacrosancte Romane ecclesie cardinales, qui sibi in executione officii sacerdotalis coadiutores assistunt, libera provenire consilia. Decet ipsius nullo modo vacillare iudicia ut fratres ipsos nullus secularis potestatis metus exterreat, nullus temporalis furor absorbeat, nullus eis terror immineat, nihil eos a veri consilii soliditate removeat," in *Les Registres de Nicholas III*, ed. J. Gay and S. Vitte (Paris, 1898-1938), 1: 106, no. 296.

being human easily fail." [41] Pope Clement IV would himself testify to the hold that the practice had; when recommending to the king of Naples the value of consulting trusted advisers, he had this to say about what he himself did: "Believe me, my beloved son, I often find it the case, in this see over which I preside, unworthy as I am, that having sounded the opinions of the cardinals, I have followed their recommendations even when I thought the opposite course to be better, provided the matter was such that no sin was involved; and the reason is that I thought it rash to set my own opinion against the judgement of so many prudent men." [42]

At the very time, then, that theorists were erecting the structure of papal absolutism, the customary practices of the curia itself suggest a real limitation of the pope's personal authority by a "papacy" which still included the cardinals. In fact, by the end of our period there was no longer any question, if there had been before, that in important matters—in what were called *ardua negotia* or *cause ardue*—the pope had to consult the cardinals. Contemporaries cited as evidence the fact that Boniface VIII revoked some independent acts of his predecessor because they had been undertaken without such consultation, [43] and Boniface's successor, Benedict XI, in turn suspended some of Boniface's acts for the same reason. [44]

---

[41] "Certum namque est, quod presidentes spirituali et temporali potestati sunt homines. Et ideo tanquam homines de facili possunt labi." See his *Tractatus de modo generalis concilii celebrandi*, I, 3 (Paris, 1671), p. 17: "nec dominus papa sine consilio fratrum aliquid ageret notabile," ibid., III, 27 (p. 278). Ptolemy of Lucca, in his *Determinatio compendiosa*, while acknowledging the unlimited authority of the pope to make new law, urged him not to change old law without taking advice. Prelates had councils, he said, just as princes had parliaments. The ancient Romans had required their consuls to consult with the Senate. Now the place of the Senate was held by the cardinals, and the pope should consult with them. See Charles T. Davis, "Roman Patriotism and Republican Propaganda: Ptolemy of Lucca and Pope Nicholas III," *Speculum* 50 (1975) 422. The *Glossa palatina*, a compilation of glosses on the *Decretum*, probably written by Laurentius Hispanus (cf. Alfons M. Stickler, "Il decretista Laurentius Hispanus," *Studia Gratiana* 9 (1966) 461-549), had already insisted that the pope could not legislate for the whole church without the cardinals; see Tierney, *Foundations of the Conciliar Theory*, p. 81.

[42] E. Martène and U. Durand, *Thesaurus novus anecdotorum* (Paris, 1717), 2: 407 (no. 380); cf. O. Rinaldi, *Annales eɕclesiastici*, 14 (Rome, 1648), Clement IV, an. 1266, c. 21.

[43] "Scio quod Celestinus papa V, multos abbatias, episcopatus, et superiores dignitates, contulit sine fratrum consilio ... et scio quod dictae collationes fuerunt cassatae praesertim quia cetus cardinalium erat in hac possessione quod ardua negocia erant de eorum consilio tractanda..."; so cardinal John Lemoine, ad *Sext.* 5.2.4; cf. *Annales de Wigornia [Worcester]*, in *Annales Monastici*, 4, RS 36 (London, 1869), p. 518; *Annales de Dunstaplia*, ibid., 3 (London, 1866), p. 383; *Bartholomaei de Cotton Historia Anglicana*, ed. H. R. Luard, RS 16 (London, 1859), p. 268; and see Jacopo Stefaneschi's *Opus metricum*, 2, c. 10, in Franz Xaver Seppelt, *Monumenta Coelestiniana. Quellen zur Geschichte des Papstes Coelestin V.*, Quellen und Forschungen aus dem Gebiete der Geschichte, 19 (Paderborn, 1921), pp. 69-71.

[44] Theiner, *Codex diplomaticus*, 1: 393-394, no. 578; cf. Rinaldi, *Annales ecclesiastici*, ad an. 1304, para. 12.

The strength of these ideas may be measured by the fact that well into the fourteenth century popes would refer to the custom of consultation in terms such as to indicate that they were powerless to take action without it. We may prefer to think of these protestations of incapacity as convenient fictions whereby the pope could avoid some undesirable action without giving undue offence, but this is to ignore the force of their repetition and the authority they derive from their origin. Clement v told Philip iv of France that in the matter of conceding tithes to lay princes, the pope is not accustomed to act without the advice of the college of cardinals, and that in the present instance, in 1306, he could do nothing because most of his cardinals had not yet joined him.[45] Clement vi alleged the unanimous opinion of the college of cardinals in order to justify with the sovereigns of Europe his refusal to extend the benefits of the jubilee indulgence of 1350 to someone who did not actually go to Rome.[46] Innocent vi referred to the translation of a bishop from one see to another as *res ardua*,[47] adding that it therefore was *consistorialis*, meaning that it needed the formal approval of the college of cardinals.[48] Indeed, Innocent's reputation for acting only after discussion with the cardinals and other competent persons was sufficiently well known as to be commented on in one of the major chronicles of the Avignon popes in the fourteenth-fifteenth centuries.[49] Urban v told a papal legate who had been negotiating with Bernabò Visconti of Milan that he was personally willing to accept a candidate of Bernabò's for appointment to the see of Brescia, but that he could not deal with the matter without first consulting the consistory, i.e., the cardinals.[50] On another occasion, he told King John ii of France that it was an old custom ("ab antiquo") that a cardinal not be sent away from the curia on business "nisi de aliorum fratrum consilio," to explain why he had to turn down the king's request for having Cardinal Talleyrand of Périgord sent to France as a legate.[51]

---

[45] G. Lizerand, *Clément V et Philippe IV le Bel* (Paris, 1910), p. 427, doc. 4.

[46] E. Déprez and G. Mollat, *Clément VI: Lettres closes, patentes et curiales intéressant les pays autres que la France* (Paris, 1910-1961), no. 4426.

[47] Traditionally so, but by the fourteenth century a routine business.

[48] Jean Glénisson and Guillaume Mollat, *L'administration des états de l'Église au XIVᵉ siècle: correspondance des légats et vicaires-généraux*, I: *Gil Albornoz et Androin de la Roche (1353-1367)*, Bibliothèque des écoles françaises d'Athènes et de Rome, 203 (Paris, 1964), pp. 180-181, no. 497.

[49] E. Baluze, *Vitae paparum Avenionensium*, new ed. G. Mollat (Paris, 1914), 1: 329; cf. B. Guillemain, *La Cour pontificale d'Avignon (1309-1376): Étude d'une société* (Paris, 1962), p. 140.

[50] P. Lecacheux and G. Mollat, *Urbain V: Lettres secrètes et curiales se rapportant à la France* (Paris, 1954), pp. 121-122, no. 826.

[51] Ibid., p. 62, no. 475.

What was thought in the curia to fall within the category of *res ardua*, such that the cardinals had to be consulted? The list is long and impressive: the summoning of church councils; the granting of tithes to secular rulers; the canonization of saints; the suspension of bishops from office; the publication of papal decretal collections to be studied in the universities; the preaching of crusades; the appointment of papal legates and nuncios; the coronation of emperors; the appointment of senators of the city of Rome; all questions having to do with episcopal elections and translations; the authorization of new universities; all matters of political importance involving the princes of Europe; everything pertaining to possessions and incomes of the Roman church; the relations of the papacy with its feudal dependencies; and a wide range of matters of a domestic or administrative nature; in short, everything that expressed the primacy of the papacy. We have some idea of the mechanics of such consultation from Jacopo Stefaneschi, whom Boniface VIII appointed to the college. He had a great interest in liturgy and ceremonial, and spent much of his time revising and up-dating the protocol of the papal curia, describing the many rituals associated with the court and the person of the pope. He has pictured for us the manner in which the pope consulted the cardinals in consistory.[52] Unfortunately, his description is limited by his interest in the ceremonial, external aspects of the process: the placing of chairs, the order of speaking, the role of seniority in the college, and so on.

We know, however, from other sources that not only were many problems discussed in common and at length, and sometimes with a vigour bordering on violence,[53] but also that the pope would sometimes ask cardinals to put their opinions in writing. These *consilia*, so called, are rare indeed for our period; but we have a dossier of such *consilia* from the 1320s having to do with an abortive proposal for a crusade which throws a great deal of light on the mechanics of pope and cardinals working together. Preliminary negotiations between Pope John XXII and King Charles IV of France had led to a French crusading proposal which the pope and cardinals discussed off and on for some six weeks, during which time John asked the cardinals to write out their opinions. We have 18 of these *consilia*, 17 of which carry the names of their respective authors. Their contents are of no interest here, but one or two observations can be made: many of them show distinct similarities, both of ideas and language, such that we can assume that continued discussions

---

[52] When appointing a legate or nuncio, and when appointing new cardinals; see Marc Dykmans, SJ, *Le Cérémonial papal de la fin du moyen âge à la renaissance*, 2: *De Rome en Avignon ou Le Cérémonial de Jacques Stefaneschi* (Brussels and Rome, 1981), pp. 475 ff.

[53] Norman Zacour, *Talleyrand: The Cardinal of Périgord*, Transactions of the American Philosophical Society, 50, pt. 7 (Philadelphia, 1960), pp. 25-26.

went on amongst the cardinals even outside consistory; there is a high degree of concurrence among all of them, despite differences in length, argumentation, and style; some cardinals had much to say, while a few were quite willing to leave the discussion in the hands of others, merely indicating their general agreement; finally, the arguments, or many of them, determined the pope's response to the king, in which we often find points repeated that are to be found in one or other of the *consilia*.[54]

It might be objected that consultation of this kind was not technically obligatory on the pope, and that therefore it was not seen as an infringement of his authority. But the fact remains that by the end of the thirteenth century popes invariably consulted their cardinals on all important matters, all those matters that marked the Roman church as the mother of all churches. They did so from long and respected tradition, from the weight of venerable opinion, and out of a conviction that the practical advantages were undeniable. Consequently, the cardinals saw themselves as necessary for the validation of papal acts in all important matters as part of the papacy.

... ET CONSENSU

If the pope was in practice obliged to consult the cardinals, one might ask whether the unity of pope and cardinals was such that he was also obliged to follow their advice. The question is not merely of historic interest. It was current in the thirteenth century, and became increasingly uncomfortable for those cardinals who sought to maintain the prerogatives of their order. Cardinal John Lemoine asked whether the words "de fratrum nostrorum consilio"—the formula invariably found in papal letters dealing with *cause ardue*—meant that such consultation depended merely on whether the pope happened to ask for it or not, or was required by some standing agreement between pope and cardinals, or was thought to be the fitting or proper thing to do, or was a legal requirement.[55] That Nicholas III had already said "decet"[56] he seems to have overlooked, perhaps deliberately. He cited examples of papal acts being cancelled because they had not been made on the advice of the college (so implying that it might be a matter of "necessitas"), but then on the other hand he conditioned the Roman law maxim that the prince is not bound by the law by suggesting that it was fitting that he

---

[54] A. Coulon and S. Clemencet, *Lettres secrètes et curiales du pape Jean XXII relatives à la France* (Paris, 1900–), 2: 281 ff., nos. 1692 ff.

[55] Ad *Sext.* 5.2.4: "Quaero an haec sint verba voluntatis, congruentiae, decentiae, vel necessitatis."

[56] Above, n. 40.

should live according to the law (so implying instead that it was only a matter of "decentia"); finally he refrained from reaching any conclusion whatever!

John's question would continue to be asked by others.[57] On the surface it was merely whether the pope was required to consult the cardinals, not whether he was required to follow their advice once consulted. But the phrase "de fratrum nostrorum consilio," when it appeared in a papal act, did not refer merely to an act of consultation, did not mean that the cardinals had simply been consulted, but that in some general sense it was on their advice that the pope was acting, that the pope and cardinals were acting together. As we shall see,[58] Gregory x (1271-1276) consulted the cardinals about his proposed legislation on papal elections in 1274. The finished constitution, *Ubi periculum*, lacked the formula "de fratrum nostrorum consilio." The reason was not because the cardinals had not been consulted—they certainly had—but because they did not approve. The appearance of the formula implied acceptance.

There was one class of cases, however, that seems to have required the explicit consent of the cardinals. When it came to questions of finance, or the alienation of the property of the Roman church, we find that not only was the pope required to consult the cardinals, but that he sought their explicit consent before acting. The reason for this lies in the principle that "what touches all must be approved by all," and in the financial history of the college of cardinals whose corporate income was drawn in large part from the regular incomes and the patrimony of the Roman church. In 1234 Gregory ix allowed that there would be no further alienation from the patrimony without the advice and unanimous consent of the cardinals.[59] During much of the previous year some of the cardinals had remained separated from the pope.[60] This suggests that there may have been serious disagreements between Gregory and his cardinals, possibly respecting papal policy toward Frederick ii. The concession that he made, in effect allowing

---

[57] Guillaume de Montlauzun, ad *Sext.* 5.2.4, who said that consultation was certainly a necessity with lesser prelates and their canons, and then went on to follow John Lemoine on the pope and cardinals, likewise without any final resolution. Cf. Guido de Baysio, *App. ad Sext.* 1: 168 (cited by Watt in *MedS* 33 [1971] 144) on the continued debate in the college: "Saepius vidi in curia queri quod operentur ista verba de fratrum nostrorum consilio."

[58] Below, pp. 430-432.

[59] *Rex excelsus*, in L. Auvray, *Les Registres de Grégoire IX*, 1: 945, no. 1715; Theiner, *Codex diplomaticus*, 1: 102-103, no. 124: "... de patrimonialibus sine communi fratrum consilio et assensu alienatio nulla fiat, sitque uni facultas, quod ex causa legitima obstaculum libere contradictionis opponat."

[60] See *Ryccardi de Sancto Germano notarii Chronica*, ed. C. A. Garufi, Rerum italicarum scriptores, new ed., 7, pt. 2 (Bologna, n.d.), pp. 184, 186.

them a veto over the alienation of property belonging to the Roman church, seems to have been the price he had to pay for a united curia.

Nor was this his only concession. About the same time, he would acknowledge that the papal states had been mismanaged by the rectors whom he had previously appointed, and now provided for their future government by the cardinals themselves.[61] This provision may never have been put into full effect. The appointment of cardinals as rectors of the papal states, which was one of the provisions of the constitution, remained a hit-and-miss affair. However, throughout the rest of the thirteenth century the college seems always to have been consulted in all matters pertaining to the papal states, probably because their incomes were affected. There is one notable exception which proves the rule: shortly before his death, Boniface VIII promulgated a statute respecting the March of Ancona without consulting the cardinals, which a few months later was withdrawn by his successor for that very reason.[62]

Meanwhile the cardinals also received more papal concessions respecting their common income. Gregory IX set aside one-third of the income of the papal states for them.[63] In fact, his financial concessions seem to have gone even further than this, for although we lack other constitutions we know that the cardinals claimed to have been given half the annual tribute of 1000 marks that the kings of England owed the papacy ever since the time King John turned his kingdom over to Innocent III and received it back as a fief.[64] We know of still other concessions made to the cardinals later. For instance,

---

[61] "... ut semper deinceps aliqui ex fratribus nostris per tempora totius patrimonii regimini deputentur, qui gubernantes in equitate ac iustitia universa diligenti custodia servent, habita occupata defendant et alienata sollicite revocent et restaurare non negligant dissipata, papa qui pro tempore fuerit de fratrum suorum consilio ministrante...," in the constitution *Habet utilitas stimulo*, to be found only in the *Summa dictaminis* of Cardinal Thomas of Capua; it has been published by Karl Hampe, "Eine unbekannte Konstitution Gregors IX. zur Verwaltung und Finanzordnung des Kirchenstaates," *Zeitschrift für Kirchengeschichte* 45 (1926) 192; cf. Daniel Waley, *The Papal States in the Thirteenth Century* (London, 1961), pp. 122, 139, who feels that it may have been an unpromulgated draft, because the terms of the constitution seem not to have been observed.

[62] Theiner, *Codex diplomaticus*, 1: 391-395, no. 571; see also C. Grandjean, *Les Registres de Benoît XI* (Paris, 1883), pp. 694-695, no. 1147.

[63] Also in *Habet utilitas stimulo*.

[64] Henry III of England wrote to the cardinals (25 February 1235), rehearsing their complaint that he had not divided the latest payment of the tribute in half and sent them their share of 500 marks direct. He excused himself on the grounds that his father's original concession had said nothing of such a division. He suggested that if he was to make such a division in future the cardinals would have to get a written mandate from the pope on the subject. Obviously Henry was not going to get mixed up in an internal squabble of the curia. See Thomas Rymer, *Foedera*, 2nd ed. (London: J. Tonson, 1727), 1: 337.

in 1272 Gregory x gave them half the Sicilian tribute;[65] soon afterwards, Nicholas III (1277-1280) gave them half the common services.[66] There is evidence that even before this time the cardinals had some share in the common services paid by newly appointed prelates, whether half or not is not known.[67] The well known concession of Nicholas IV in 1289 giving the cardinals half the ordinary incomes of the Roman church was in large part a confirmation of concessions won by the college during the previous decades,[68] the material measure of the cardinals' share of the papacy.

PAPAL ELECTIONS AND PAPAL POWER

The constitution on papal elections promulgated by Alexander III (1159-1181) in 1179, *Licet de vitanda,* had finally settled two pressing problems, by ignoring distinctions of rank among the cardinals for purposes of the election, and by requiring a two-thirds majority. It had been a reform agreed to by the cardinals themselves, which is more than one can say about Gregory x's constitution *Ubi periculum* a century later. Gregory sought to fix the conclave as a permanent feature of papal elections. This "conclave" was the practice that had appeared in the thirteenth century, possibly under the influence of Italian communal elections, of locking up the cardinals and making life increasingly miserable for them until they produced a pope.[69] Gregory, who had not himself been a cardinal, shared the widespread indignation over the long vacancy that had preceded his election, and in his constitution, among other features designed to hasten the choice of a new pope, explicitly denied to the cardinals any exercise of papal authority during a vacancy. He not only sought to reduce their freedom of action and independence, but also subjected them to local lay authority, undoubtedly awakening fearful memories of past conclaves some of which had been brutal affairs.[70] No wonder that it lacks the formula "de fratrum nostrorum consi-

---

[65] J. B. Sägmüller, *Die Tätigkeit und Stellung der Cardinäle* (Freiburg im Breisgau, 1896), p. 190; Baumgarten, *Untersuchungen und Urkunden über die Camera Collegii cardinalium,* p. CXXVIII.

[66] See Kirsch, *Die Finanzverwaltung des Kardinalkollegiums,* p. 6.

[67] J. Guiraud, *Les Registres d'Urbain IV (1261-1264),* 1: 8-9, nos. 31-36; cf. E. Göller, *Die Einnahmen der apostolischen Kammer unter Johann XXII,* Vatikanische Quellen zur Geschichte der päpstlichen Hof- und Finanzverwaltung, 1316-1378 (Paderborn, 1910), 1: 30-31.

[68] *Celestis altitudo,* in Theiner, *Codex diplomaticus,* 1: 304-305, no. 468.

[69] See E. Ruffini-Avondo, "Le Origini del conclave papale," *Atti della reale Accademia delle scienze di Torino* 62 (1926-1927) 409-431.

[70] For example, see K. Hampe, *Ein ungedruckter Bericht über das Konklave von 1241 im römischen Septizonium,* Sitzungsberichte der Heidelberger Akademie der Wissenschaften, Phil.-hist. Klasse, 1 (Heidelberg, 1913). For papal elections in the thirteenth century, Olga

lio." He had shown it to the cardinals when he had first drawn it up, no doubt in the hope of winning their approval. He met instead with strong opposition. They quarrelled, and their disagreement could not be hushed up. In fact, both the cardinals and the pope canvassed the fathers of the council at Lyons (1274) for support, the cardinals claiming that they had been given no sufficient reason for consenting to such a measure, the pope demanding and getting from the prelates of the council the obedience that was his due.[71] There can be no doubt of the need for some such legislation to deal with the problem of long vacancies. In addition, however, for those who saw in the old claims of the college a threat to the personal authority of the pope,[72] that personal plenitude of power that excluded all others, here was an opportunity to get rid of the notion once and for all that the cardinals shared the papal plenitude of power or could exercise papal authority during a vacancy.

The idea that cardinals in some way inherited the papal authority during a vacancy had long held sway in the college, and would not be easily given up. Matthew Paris inserted a letter in his *Chronica majora* written by some eight cardinals in 1243 during the vacancy preceding the election of Innocent IV, not because of the subject matter itself, but because of what the letter revealed about the question of papal authority during a vacancy, which seems to have been a question of general interest at the time. The critical clause was "Nos autem penes quos potestas residet, apostolica sede vacante, volentes..." etc.[73] In this question, as in others, Hostiensis summarized the prevailing view of the college, giving it an air of legitimacy difficult to dispel. When the pope dies, he said, his power does not die with him. It remains within the Roman church which itself cannot die. Its exercise, however, ought normally to remain dormant until a new pope is elected. It was a power held in trust, so to speak, preserved intact to be passed on to the successor, and to be exercised by the cardinals only in emergencies or in matters of great moment. The argument that such exercise of authority by the cardinals might give rise to schism, scandal, or long vacancies might be valid, he agreed, if the concession were made without any limitation, but there was really nothing

---

Joelson, *Die Papstwahlen des 13. Jahrhunderts bis zur Einführung der Conclaveordnung Gregors X*, Historische Studien 178 (Berlin, 1928).

[71] Mansi, *Sacrorum conciliorum nova et amplissima collectio*, 24: 66-67.

[72] Whose criticisms were met head on by Hostiensis in his comments on the rights of the college: "Hec scribo ad confutandos illos qui potestatem cardinalium quasi omnino adnihilare videntur..."; *Comm. ad Decret.* 5.38.14: "Nota contra illos qui dicunt quod cardinales non habent ius capituli sive collegii, sed potius iure singulorum censentur tanquam homines a diversis mundi partibus singulariter vocati..." etc.; ibid., 5.6.17.

[73] *Matthaei Parisiensis monachi sancti Albani chronica majora*, ed. H. R. Luard, RS 57 (London, 1877), 4: 250-252.

to fear provided it were restricted, as he suggested, to cases of necessity and the ultimate good of the church. He was able, therefore, to preserve the sense of a college of cardinals sharing in and in some sense inheriting the papal plenitude of power, while turning aside criticism that saw an irresponsible college of cardinals doing whatever it wished, as long as it wished, during a vacancy.[74]

Gregory's constitution, which came only a few years later, incorporated this view that the cardinals could act during a vacancy in emergencies. But it also required that to do so they had to be unanimous, which in effect paralyzed the college, depriving it of any real independence of action. Not all the cardinals would accept this. They persuaded Gregory's successor but one, Hadrian v, pope for only a few weeks in 1276, to suspend the constitution and promulgate a substitute,[75] although three of their number—which three, we do not know—wanted it kept in force. Hadrian died before he could issue a new constitution,[76] and soon after his death a rumour spread that he had even cancelled his suspension. An enquiry by his successor John xxi failed, however, to confirm this, and John continued the suspension. He too promised a new constitution on papal elections,[77] but it was also prevented by his own early death when the ceiling of his library collapsed on

---

[74] *Comm. ad Decret.* 5.38.14. Cf. Augustinus Triumphus, *De potestate collegii mortuo papa* (in Richard Scholz, *Die Publizistik zur Zeit Philipps des Schönen und Bonifaz' VIII* [Stuttgart, 1903; repr. 1962], pp. 501-508), who also held that during a vacancy the papal authority rested with the college of cardinals, especially since papal power is perpetual and cannot die when a pope dies; but it rests with the college in a special way: "non in re sed tamquam in radice," a potential rather than an effective or active power. Just as a root, however, has a three-fold power of resisting opposition, of producing growth, and of sprouting, so the cardinals could (i) resist those who would injure the church, (ii) could elect a new pope, and (iii) so produce flower and fruit again. It was strongly to be doubted, however, that the cardinals could do with the pope dead what they could with him alive, else why elect a pope at all? Finally, "mortuo papa non videtur quod collegium possit tollere decreta et mandata facta per papam maxime illa que ligant eos." It is therefore impossible to credit Michael Wilks, *The Problem of Sovereignty in the Later Middle Ages* (Cambridge, 1963), p. 480: "... we find in his [Augustinus'] *De potestate collegii* an advocacy of the complete supremacy of the College over the pope."

[75] For the changes in the statute between the time of its presentation in the 5th session of the Council of Lyons on 16 July 1274 and the publication of the conciliar acts on 1 November, see S. Kuttner, "Conciliar Law in the Making: The Lyonese Constitutions (1274) of Gregory x in a Manuscript at Washington," in *Miscellanea Pio Paschini* (Rome, 1948), 2: 39-81, esp. pp. 43-44, 60-65; cf. Leonard E. Boyle, "The Date of the Commentary of William Duranti on the Constitutions of the Second Council of Lyons," *Bulletin of Medieval Canon Law* 4 (1974) 39-47.

[76] For Hadrian's intention of promulgating a substitute for or an amended version of *Ubi periculum*, see *Martini Oppaviensis Chronicon pontificum et imperatorum*, in MGH, SS 22: 443; also L. Duchesne, *Le Liber Pontificalis* (Paris, 1892), 2: 457.

[77] *Les registres de Grégoire X et de Jean XXI*, ed. J. Guiraud, E. Cadier, and G. Mollat (Paris, 1892-1960), p. 51, no. 159.

him. Gregory's constitution remained in limbo for another seventeen years until by a truly farsighted act in an otherwise sorry pontificate Celestine v revived it.[78] In all of this we can dimly discern a real difference of opinion within the college itself.

In the meantime, we have a good illustration of how the cardinals conducted themselves in conformity with cardinal Hostiensis' doctrine. In 1277, during the vacancy after John XXI's death, the cardinals wrote to Rudolf, king of Germany, to urge him to come to an agreement with the Roman church before undertaking an expedition into Italy. They were only too conscious that they were carrying on papal business without a pope. They were careful, therefore, to stress that what they were really doing was pursuing the policy of two popes, Innocent v and John XXI, originally undertaken on their own advice, and that they were doing so in pursuit of the public good and in what they called "fitting imitation" of the pope.[79] They clearly had Hostiensis' doctrine in mind.

Not even Celestine's revival of Gregory X's constitution, and its formal insertion into the corpus of canon law by Boniface VIII, would immediately unseat this doctrine. Cardinal John Lemoine, for example, would continue to hold the opinion that the cardinals inherited papal authority during a vacancy,[80] and other cardinals would do the same well into the fourteenth

---

[78] A. Potthast, *Regesta pontificum romanorum* (Berlin, 1875), 2: 1918, no. 23980; also John Lemoine (Johannes Monachus), *Glossa aurea super Sexto Decretalium Libro* (Paris, 1535; repr. 1968), fol. 63ᵛ.

[79] "Sed ne interim, que per eosdem pontifices, precipue Innocentium et Johannem, de nostro consilio processerunt, non sine verisimili grandis coniectura discriminis negligere videamur, eorundem pontificum provisionem laudabilem de nostro consilio inchoatam imitatione commodis publici status accomoda prosequentes, Serenitatem Regium affectuose rogamus et hortamur..." etc.; Theiner, *Codex diplomaticus*, 1: 201-202, no. 356. For another case of the cardinals acting *vice* the pope, in the consecration of and giving the pallium to the archbishop of Genoa (1292), shortly after Nicholas IV died, see G. Monleone, ed., *Iacobi da Varagine chronica civitatis ianuensis*, Fonti per la storia d'Italia 85 (Rome, 1941), 2: 404.

[80] Ad *Sext.* 5.11.2: "... penes quem [sc. cetum cardinalium] plenitudo potestatis sede vacante residet"; and again, ad *Sext.* 1.6.16: "... quia mortuo papa iurisdictio et iurisdictionis exercitium penes collegium cardinalium remanet." Cf. Johannes Andreae on the *Clementines*, *Ne Romani*, s.v. *Verum*, in the Lyons, 1584 ed., col. 32. Peter John Olivi also held that the cardinals had the power of acting "vicem pape defuncti saltem in casibus necessariis"; see Franz Ehrle, "Petrus Johannes Olivi, sein Leben und seine Schriften," *Archiv für Litteratur- und Kirchengeschichte des Mittelalters* 3 (1887) 526. Stephanus Hugoneti, long in the service of cardinal Bertrand du Poujet, held the same view in his *Apparatus super constitutionibus concilii Viennensis*. Commenting on *Ne Romani*, he followed John Lemoine's argument that since Boniface VIII restricted the cardinals during a vacancy from reinstating the deposed Colonna cardinals, the college must have general power or jurisdiction during a vacancy to have it so limited in this special case; if they had no such jurisdiction, then the limiation would make no sense. See Univ. of Pennsylvania, MS Lat. 95, fols 9ᵛ-10ʳ; cf. Norman Zacour, "Stephanus Hugoneti and his 'Apparatus' on the Clementines," *Traditio* 13 (1957) 456-462.

century. A gloss on Cardinal Jacopo Stefaneschi's metrical life of Celestine v, made by the author himself, is quite clear in this respect: during a vacancy the power of the pope resides in the college.[81] In Perugia, after Pope Benedict xi died, Cardinal Matteo Rosso showed Vidal de Villanova, the emissary of James ii of Aragon, a document drawn up by the cardinals in the conclave dealing, among other things, with the rights they thought they had during a vacancy. It included the claim that during a vacancy the college had all the rights of the pope, although there were many outside the college who disagreed. "E con la apostolical dingnitat vaga, lo collegii ha tot lo poder del papa. E, sejor, an aço a molt ben clergue en la cort, quin deneguen secretament, que non gosen parlar a paraules (?), que no lan lo poder, que els se donen."[82] So the quarrel was still going on in the curia.

The idea of a residual authority in the college during a vacancy continued to draw sustenance from the actual practice of the college, whose acts of "fitting imitation" during a vacancy could be confirmed by the newly elected pope. Upon his election, Boniface viii confirmed everything the college had done during the vacancy respecting excommunication, interdict, and a fine of 2000 marks levied on Orvieto,[83] all acts that he himself had participated in as a cardinal. Even further, however, some cardinals thought that they could take advantage of a vacancy to modify the terms of Gregory x's constitution on elections. This idea was so strongly held that Clement v had to legislate especially against it. In *Ne romani*, promulgated in the Council of Vienne and later published by his successor in the canonical collection called the *Clementines*, Clement reproved in unequivocal terms the notion that the cardinals could modify or cancel Gregory x's constitution during a vacancy before proceeding to an election, and declared invalid and inane the idea that the authority of the pope while alive could be exercised by the college after his death, except in those particular cases allowed for in papal legislation.[84]

[81] *Acta Sanctorum*, May vol. 4, pp. 448-449.
[82] Heinrich Finke, *Acta Aragonensia* (Berlin and Leipzig, 1908), 1: 178.
[83] Theiner, *Codex diplomaticus*, 1: 322-327, no. 494.
[84] *Clem.* 1.3.2: "Ne Romani electioni Pontificis indeterminata opinionum diversitas aliquod possit obstaculum vel dilationem afferre: nos, inter cetera praecipue attendentes, quod lex superioris per inferiorem tolli non potest, opinionem adstruere, sicut accepimus satagentem, quod constitutio felicis recordationis Gregorii Papae x, praedecessoris nostri, circa electionem praefatam edita in concilio Lugdunensi, per coetum cardinalium Romanae ecclesiae ipsa vacante modificari possit, corrigi vel immutari, aut quicquam ei detrahi sive addi, vel dispensari quomodolibet circa ipsam seu aliquam eius partem, aut eidem etiam renunciari per eum, tanquam veritati non consonam de fratrum nostrorum consilio reprobamus, irritum nihilominus et inane decernentes, quicquid potestatis aut iurisdictionis, ad Romanum, dum vivit, Pontificem pertinentis (nisi quatenus in constitutione praedicta permittitur), coetus ipse duxerit eadem vacante ecclesia exercendum."

BONIFACE VIII

With the pontificate of Clement V we have gone beyond our period. Already, however, in Boniface VIII's time, it would seem that the old view of the papacy as embracing pope and cardinals was losing ground even in the college itself. Boniface made it clear that he thought he could act without the cardinals if necessary. Berengar Fredoli, cardinal bishop of Tusculum, told the ambassador of the king of Aragon not to bother presenting his case in consistory, since Boniface never brought anything up in consistory except what he chose not to do.[85] He held weekly consistories for routine matters, but reserved all important affairs to himself and a small handful of trusted colleagues, and would brook no contradiction in consistory.[86] There was clearly a growing antipathy between him and some of his cardinals, in part the residue of rivalries which had sprung up during the pontificate of Celestine V.

This came to a head during the quarrel with the Colonnese cardinals, James (d. 1318) and Peter (d. 1326), which dramatized a sovereignty of the pope's person so great as to leave no room for the aspirations or ambitions of the cardinals. Much of the complaint that the Colonnesi made against Boniface was based on the assumption that the status or juridical character of the cardinals was perpetual.[87] But Boniface, we are told, would have none of this:

> Some might say that the cardinals do not have status. They do and they don't, since he who is established in plenitude of power over all and has the power to loose and to bind, as the vicar of Jesus Christ, is chosen by and proceeds from their canonical election. Indeed, there is no one, after the Roman pontiff himself, who has such an elevated status as this. It is well known that they are members of our head.
>
> However, they do not have the status of preeminence that the pope has. No one else has this kind of status except the pope alone, since he is not beneath that of anyone inferior to him. But the cardinals who have status are beneath

---

[85] "Si vos volets guardar la honor del rey Darago, vos no preposarets en consistory; que per certs sapiats, quel papa no met res en consistory, si no ço que no vel fer"; Finke, *Acta Aragonensia*, 2: 586.

[86] See Lorenzo Martini's diary in Heinrich Finke, *Aus den Tagen des Bonifaz VIII: Funde und Forschungen* (Münster i. W., 1902), Quellen: pp. XXXVIII-L; Richard Scholz, *Die Publizistik zur Zeit Philipps des Schönen und Bonifaz' VIII* (Stuttgart, 1903; repr. Amsterdam, 1962), pp. 190 ff.

[87] P. Dupuy, *Histoire du differend d'entre le pape Boniface VIII et Philippes le Bel roy de France* (Paris, 1655), p. 227: "Status cardinalis est perpetuus, figurantur enim in vectibus de lignis setim, qui inducuntur in lateribus arcae, id est Ecclesiae, ut portetur in eis, et subditur, quod in circulis semper erunt, et nunquam extrahentur ab ipsis, ut patet Exodi 21 [corr. 25:10]."

the status of the Roman pontiff, who has power to correct and to punish them.[88]

In the early stages of their struggle with Boniface, the Colonnese cardinals were not the only members of the college to oppose the pope. Several of their colleagues were in touch with King Philip IV of France, attacking Boniface behind his back. In April 1311, before an investigative commission set up by Clement V, the names of several of these emerged, the most prominent being John Lemoine, no friend of the pope. He admitted that he had told Philip IV that he thought Boniface was a heretic, presumably when he had been a legate in France, since he added that he could not remember having written to the king on the subject.[89] Rumours flew of a serious split in the college and a bitterness among those who were, for one reason or another, at odds with Boniface.[90] On the other hand there was a party of cardinals who stuck with the pope, one of whom, Matthew of Aquasparta, cardinal bishop of Porto, insisted that between pope and college there was no dissension, no differences, no division, but rather complete concord, peace and agreement, since whatever the pope wished the cardinals wished and vice versa.[91]

---

[88] "Poterint aliqui dicere, quod cardinales statum non habeant. Habent, et non habent; cum ex eorum electione canonica eligatur is et procedat, qui est super omnes in potestatis plenitudinem constitutus et qui habet solvere et ligare sicut vicarius Ihesu-Christi; et certe non est aliquis post Romanum pontificem tam nobilem statum habens. Constat, quod ipsi sunt membra capitis nostri. Etenim non habent statum ut summus pontifex eminentem, cum non sit nisi solus papa aliquis alius habens statum, quia ipse non est sub statu alicuius inferioris eo. Sed cardinales statum habentes sunt sub statu Romani pontificis, qui habet eos corrigere et punire." Finke, *Aus den Tagen*, p. 79, citing *Gesta Boemundi archiepiscopi Treverensis*, in MGH, SS 24: 479.

[89] Constantin Höfler, "Rückblick auf P. Bonifacius VIII, und die Literatur seiner Geschichte," *Abhandlungen der königliche Akademie der Wissenschaften, Historische Klasse* 3 (1841) 53; cf. pp. 48, 76.

[90] "Hiis diebus post mortem domini Sabinensis fuit dictum inter cardinales et tractatum, quod nominaret aliquas personas papa, et quilibet, ut credo, rogabat cardinales et amicos et instruebat pro dominis et amicis suis. Tandem venit rumor ad papam et dixit: Aliqui dicunt et credunt, quod nos debeamus creare cardinales. Nobis videtur magis tempus aliquos deponendi quam creandi"; from a letter of Laurentius Martinic, at the papal curia, March 1302, in Finke, *Aus den Tagen*, Quellen: pp. IL-L. Cardinal Landulf Brancacci said that it was better to be dead than to live with such a man as the pope, who was nothing but eyes and tongue in a putrefying body; ibid., pp. 106 and CXXIX.

[91] "Verum est etiam quod quaedam littera secreta fuit facta de communi consensu summi Pontificis et fratrum, quia volo quod sciatis et dicam veritatem, et non mentiar, quia in Collegio inter summum Pontificem qui est caput nostrum, et inter Fratres, nulla est dissensio, nulla diversitas, nulla divisio, sed est inter nos omnis concordia, omnis pax, omnis uniformitas, quia quicquid vult dominus noster nos volumus, et quicquid nos volumus sui gratia vult et ipse, ita est testimonium Spiritu sancto in conscientia, illa litera [!] sic facta non fuit subito missa, sed fuit ad consistorium pluries deportata, fuit lecta, relecta, diligenter examinata..." referring to a letter to Philip IV of France which Boniface VIII said was falsified by Pierre Flotte. See Dupuy, *Histoire du differend*, pp. 74-75.

After Boniface died, the king's demands that a general council be summoned to investigate the charges against him revealed a clear division in the college between those who favoured such a council, mainly those who had schemed with the king shortly after 1295, and those who opposed it, cardinals who had been appointed by Boniface after his election. There were a few, however, who sat on the fence, like Landulf Brancacci who, when he was called in 1311 to testify about the defection of cardinals, said not only that he had not himself communicated with Philip about Boniface, but that he had never even heard of any other cardinal doing so![92]

The emergence of a party of cardinals in opposition to the pope gives some colour to one of the claims of the Colonnesi, that Boniface had altered the status of the college of cardinals. The language they used was, by and large, the traditional language used in the past to describe the cardinals. They could not be deprived of their office at the whim of the pope. Their duty was to disagree with and stand up to the pope when necessary, as a kind of loyal opposition—a duty which would go by the board if they were to be dismissed "sine causa."[93]

The pontificate of Boniface VIII made manifest a view of the papacy within which the cardinals were ceasing to play a central role. As late as Celestine III (1191-1198) it was still the *sacrosancta Romana ecclesia* that was endowed with a plenitude of power.[94] With Innocent the term was coming to mean the full personal sovereignty of a ruler in his realm, albeit still the realm of the spirit.[95] It would be enlarged yet further by his successors. As expressed by Boniface VIII, the idea of the pope's personal sovereignty would have serious implications for the college of cardinals which suffered a sharp diminution of status. The following century, beyond the scope of this present study, saw two events which would reveal the role which the cardinals sought to reserve to themselves, given the limitations with which they now had to contend.

The first was the vacancy preceding the election of Innocent VI in 1352, during which the cardinals drew up a *capitulatio*, a written agreement to limit the future pope in the appointment of new cardinals, to restrict his discipli-

---

[92] Ibid., p. 68.

[93] Ibid., pp. 226-227; "Cardinales sunt coniudices Romani pontificis et sunt membra non tantum corporis Ecclesiae sed capitis" (p. 236).

[94] *PL* 206: 1075-1076.

[95] Gerhart B. Ladner, "The Concepts of 'Ecclesia' and 'Christianitas' and their Relationship to the Idea of Papal 'Plenitudo Potestatis,' from Gregory VII to Boniface VIII," in *Sacerdozio e regno da Gregorio VII a Bonifazio VIII*, Miscellanea historiae pontificiae 18 (Rome, 1954), pp. 64-68. The decline in the number of papal acts with the formula "de fratrum" during the pontificate of Innocent III is an indication of that pope's tendency to emancipate himself from the tutelage of the college as a whole; see Maleczek, *Papst und Kardinalskolleg*, pp. 315-316.

nary power over them, to guarantee their regular sources of income, to ensure their share in the supervision of the papal states, and in all such matters to require the concurrence of two-thirds of the college, or one-half, as the case might be. There was some doubt within the conclave that what they were doing was legal, for the oath that each swore, to uphold the capitulation if elected, was taken by some only with the stipulation: "scilicet, si et in quantum scriptura hujusmodi de jure procederet." [96] And indeed, upon election, Innocent VI declared their agreement void, not only because it was in contravention of papal constitutions which forbade dealing with any business other than the election itself during a vacancy, but also as redounding to the "diminution and prejudice of the plenitude of power granted from the lips of God to the Roman pontiff alone." [97]

The second was the double election of 1378, by which the college sought to exploit their one privilege, so firmly embedded in canon law as to be virtually untouchable—the election of the pope.

As dramatic as these events were, and as significant for an understanding of the oligarchical tendencies of the college of cardinals, neither marks any kind of return to the concept of the papacy as a union of pope and cardinals. The first had to do with personal privileges, incomes, and the cardinals' control of the membership of their college; the second was an attempt to enlarge their electoral function to include the power to depose. While there were large forces at work during the ensuing conciliar period that sought to locate ecclesiastical sovereignty elsewhere than in the person of the pope, it was to the church at large, represented by the universal council, not to the college of cardinals, that reformers would henceforth look.

[96] Pierre Gasnault and M. H. Laurents, eds., *Innocent VI: Lettres secrètes et curiales* (Paris, 1959–), 1: 137-138, no. 435.

[97] Ibid. They also refined some of the rules pertaining to the process of papal election; see M. Dykmans, *Le Cérémonial* (Brussels and Rome, 1983), 3: 57-58, n. 22.

15

Patterns of Papal Patronage
circa 1260–circa 1300

Julian Gardner

How far do the visual arts, either in representations of the papacy, or in works commissioned by individual pontiffs, cast light on the religious role of that office? Given the evident complexity of the problem, and the nature of the sources, I have restricted myself to the second half of the thirteenth century, a period relatively rich in recorded or surviving works, where at least there exists a relatively continuous body of material. Here too the distortions necessarily introduced by long intervals in the visual record are somewhat reduced. Further, I shall largely, but not exclusively, restrict myself to monuments in which the initiative of the papacy cannot seriously be doubted. The exceptions will be a small group of important monuments in which individual pontiffs are represented. Thus it will be on one hand intrinsic, insofar as it represents the self-perception of individual popes and of their religious role, or extrinsic in that it represents a viewpoint from outside the Curia. The pattern, if there be one, which may be yielded by the examination of the first group may then be compared with the control group of contemporary representations of the papacy. The monuments in the second group reflect a view from the periphery, England, one nearer at hand in Umbria, and that of the great ecclesiastical counterpoise, the Orthodox Church.

I am indebted to Father Leonard Boyle and Professor Robert Brentano for conversations which helped me to clarify my thoughts. It need hardly be added that the opacities which remain are mine alone.

The Religious Roles of the Papacy: Ideals and Realities, 1150-1300, ed. Christopher Ryan, Papers in Mediaeval Studies 8 (Toronto: Pontifical Institute of Mediaeval Studies, 1989), pp. 439-456. © P.I.M.S., 1989.

First there must be a measure of necessary ground-clearing. This task can
be illustrated by two "texts," one written and one visual, from the beginning
and from near the end of the period under consideration. The Sienese
emissaries to Urban IV in 1263 reported home in the following terms: "And
be aware that the pope does as he wishes: nobody dares to contradict him.
Assuredly, as I am convinced that you have heard from others, there has been
no pope, since the time of Alexander III, so constant in word and deed, and
who cares so little for his kin as this one does." [1] The man and his authority
are the main focus of the report, while physical description plays no part.
Even such a personal description, as for example that of Nicholas III in the
Continuatio Romana brevis, is a collage of conventional phrases. [2] The second
"text" is the tomb effigy by Arnolfo di Cambio of Honorius IV (d. 1287),
once in Old Saint Peters, and now set in the Savelli family chapel in the right
transept of the Franciscan church of Santa Maria in Aracoeli (Fig. 1). The
superbly executed head radiates serenity and a powerful physical presence.
It contrasts ill, however, with the story of the Bolognese Dominican
Francesco Pipino, that the octogenarian pontiff was so severely crippled by
gout that he required a small wooden engine to enable him to celebrate mass.
This anecdote is independently confirmed in Rishanger's Chronicle. [3] Para-
doxically, the most accurate physical description of a thirteenth century pope
may be that composed in 1605 by the papal notary Giacomo Grimaldi, on
the occasion of the opening of Boniface VIII's tomb. [4] His meticulous, almost
clinical record is far removed from the brutally worded caricature of Boniface
voiced by an exasperated Cardinal Landolfo Brancacci and diligently noted
and transmitted by Geraldus de Albalato in 1301: "He has nothing but eyes
and tongue, for the rest of his body putrefies." [5] As in the case of Honorius IV,

---

[1] "Et sciatis quod ipse facit id quod vult: non est aliquis ei contradicere ausus. Et certe,
sicut vos credo firmiter scire per alios non fuit aliquis papa, a tempore Alexandri iij, qui tantum
fuerit constans in factis et dictis suis, et qui minus curaret coniunctos sibi quam iste." Cf.
E. Casanova, "Urbano IV giudicato da un agente senese," *Miscellanea Storica Senese*, 5
(1898), 7-8, p. 171.
[2] "... genere nobilis, decorus facie, nobilitatem et pulchritudinem moribus et prospicuitate
decorans, statura procerus ... in vulgari pulcherrimus praedicator, cantorque sonorus, divinorum misteriorum amatissimus persecutor, elemosinarius largifluus publicus et occultus"
(MGH SS 30: 712). Cf. H. Schmiedinger, "Das Papstbild in der Geschichtsschreibung des
späteren Mittelalters," *Römische Historische Mitteilungen*, 1 (1956-1957) 114.
[3] "Chronicon Fratris Francisci Pipini Bononiensis Ordinis Praedicatorum," in *R.I.SS.*, 11:
727. *Willelmi Rishanger, quondam monachi S. Albani, et quorumdam anonymorum, Chronica
et Annales regnantibus Henrico Tertio et Edwardo Primo*, ed. H. T. Riley, RS 28.2 (London,
1865), p. 109. Cf. J. Gardner, "Arnolfo di Cambio and Roman Tomb Design," *Burlington
Magazine*, 115 (1973) 430.
[4] A. Starnd, "Giacomo Grimaldis Bericht über die Öffnung des Grabes Papst Bonifaz' VII.
(1605)," *Römische Quartalschrift*, 61 (1966) 191 quoting Vatican, MS Barb. Lat. 2733, f. 3r.
[5] H. Finke, *Acta Aragonensia* (Berlin, 1908-1922), 1: 104.

the image transmitted by the tomb effigy is of an idealized and serene authority. We should thus put out of our minds any concept of portraiture in terms of physical likeness. Even where direct contact between artist and pope can plausibly be postulated – let alone proved – it raises the highly problematic assumption that physical likeness was indeed the artist's aim.[6] The office and its occupant in certain specific roles is the sum of visual evidence. The sources, whether visual or written, have nothing of the specificity of Albertino Mussato's eye-witness descriptions of the Emperor Henry VII and his Empress Margaret of Brabant of circa 1310.[7] Certainly visual representations, like verbal critique, might well reflect a view of the papacy, and as much by omission as commission. Thus in the pyrotechnics of an Angevin broadside against a French cardinal regarded as a traitor to Charles I's interest at the Curia, Nicholas III is scathingly nicknamed *Veronica*, a jibe both at his piety and doubtless his interest in images of Christ.[8] There were, as we shall see, two differing views of Pope Liberius (352-366) during the late thirteenth century. Pipino also, in a well-known passage, describes a lampoon of Nicholas IV as a mitred head set upon a column, an all too evident sarcasm on his dependence on the aristocratic Roman family of Colonna.[9]

That the image of the pope could convey overtones of dominion can be shown by the erection of statues of Boniface VIII over the city gates of Orvieto, and other nuances of clientage were conveyed by other statues of the pope at Anagni, Florence and Bologna.[10] These images were made for a variety of reasons, gratification of a powerful patron and frequent visitor to Orvieto, at Bologna as at Florence acknowledgement of a political ally. It should be remembered that the statue of Boniface at Bologna was to have been accompanied by another of Charles d'Anjou, and that these statues, despite the French accusations of idolatry, were not erected by Boniface himself[11]

---

[6] E. Kitzinger, review of G. Ladner, *Die Papstbildnisse des Altertums und des Mittelalters,* Monumenti di Antichità Cristiana, 2, ser. 4, vol. 1 (Città del Vaticano, 1941), in *Speculum,* 23 (1948) 316.

[7] "Albertino Mussato Historia Augusta de Gestis Henrici VII Caesaris," in *R.I.SS.,* 10: 304 (Henry VII) and 340 (Margaret). Before his untimely death in 1986, Professor Kenneth Hyde of Manchester was preparing a book on personal descriptions in the Middle Ages. He generously talked to me about the subject on several occasions.

[8] F. Baethgen, "Ein Pamphlet Karls I. von Anjou zur Wahl Papst Nikolaus III," *Bayerische Akademie der Wissenschaften, Phil.-hist. Klasse, Sitzungsberichte,* Jhrg. 1960, Heft 7, p. 19.

[9] Pipino, col. 728.

[10] Ladner, *Die Papstbildnisse,* 2: 296ff. is the standard discussion. Cf. also J. Gardner, "Boniface VIII as a Patron of Sculpture," in *Roma Anno 1300, Atti del Congresso internazionale di Storia dell'Arte medievale, Roma 19-24 Maggio 1980* (Rome, 1983), pp. 513-527.

[11] M. Cremonini Beretta, "Il significato politico della statua offerta dai Bolognesi a Bonifacio VIII," in *Studi di Storia dedicati a P. C. Felletti* (Bologna, 1915), pp. 421-431. See

(Fig. 2). At Bologna, the choices of bronze as material, as well as the site, the Palazzo della Biada, had their own significance, but that was political. Although the recut statue of the pope at Florence, and the enigmatic figure at Anagni were set on cathedrals, their import may almost certainly be regarded as political also. In short we may very likely be justified in removing individual representations of popes from consideration. They yield little information on the pastoral or spiritual roles of the papacy in our period.

Yet the statues of Boniface VIII may also be regarded, in the main, as the statements of third parties. The silver statuette which he caused to be placed on the high altar of Amiens cathedral is difficult to comprehend, but it is exceptional in the group.[12] This point becomes clearer, if also more complicated, when we turn our attention to the painting of the Legend of Saint Francis in the Upper Church of San Francesco at Assisi. I do not wish here to become enmeshed in the intractable problems of precise dating and of attribution. Given the still prevailing view about the possession of property within the Order, I feel that one may with some safety assume that the Legend was painted either during the pontificate of Nicholas IV (1288-1292), or, more likely during that of Boniface VIII (1294-1303), and that the responsibility for the decision to decorate the nave was not taken at Assisi.[13] However, the direct responsibility for the commission of the fresco cycle is not a present concern. What is of importance in the present context is the prominence accorded to certain scenes. Three popes are represented: Innocent III appears twice – in the sixth fresco, where he dreams of Francis sustaining the tottering Lateran, and in Scene 7 where he approves the Franciscan Rule (Fig. 3). Honorius III (1216-1227) appears in Scene 17, where Francis is shown preaching to the Curia (Fig. 4). The canonization of the saint, which took place on 16 June 1228 forms the subject of the twenty-fourth scene. It, together with the subsequent scene, contains Gregory IX (1227-1241), the second fresco showing Gregory dreaming that Francis appears and shows the Stigmata. It is clear that both then, and later in the thirteenth century, dreams could condition papal actions. My immediate point is however rather different. What was the purpose of these scenes at the date of their painting?

---

now R. Grandi, *I monumenti dei dottori e la scultura a Bologna (1267-1348)* (Bologna, 1982), pp. 121ff., no. 8, figs. 11-15.

[12] Gardner, "Boniface VIII," p. 515. See now for the whole Amiens episode T. Schmidt, "Papst Bonifaz VIII und die Idolatrie," *Quellen und Forschungen*, 66 (1986) 75-107. I am very grateful to Dr. Schmidt for discussing the topic with me in advance of publication.

[13] The literature on Assisi is enormous. See recently H. Belting, *Die Oberkirche von San Francesco in Assisi* (Berlin, 1977). An early date, that is, during the pontificate of Nicholas IV, is suggested by L. Bellosi, *La Pecora di Giotto* (Turin, 1985), pp. 17ff.

The Legend of Saint Francis is not a simple narrative account of the main incidents of the Founder's life.[14] It conforms, in its broad outline, to the *Legenda maior* of Bonaventura, rather than to the *Vita prima* of Thomas of Celano, the account closest in date to the saint's own life. Equally it adheres more closely to the Bonaventuran *Legenda* than to the body of material which was brought together after the dissemination of the *Legenda maior* as the authorized version of the saint's life.[15] As the Legend of the Life of Saint Francis in the Upper Church was intended, at least in part, as a narrative of Francis' earthly existence and the development of his mission, the role of the papacy in supporting and encouraging the Franciscan Order was solicitously represented. It makes an illuminating comparison with the earlier, more elliptic cycle of Franciscan scenes in the Lower Church: there the emphases are different (Fig. 5). Specifically the comparison with Christ was made visually more explicit, Francis as *alter Christus*.[16] When the murals in the Lower Church were judged inadequate, very probably when they were damaged by the piercing of chapels in the nave bays of the Lower Church, a far more extensive cycle was painted in the nave of the church above. In the later cycle, the typological comparison with Christ was abandoned. The murals in the Lower Church, painted by the Maestro di San Francesco, are not securely dated. Whatever their precise dating may be, they were very probably painted during the generalate of Bonaventura (1257-1274).[17] The papacy occupies a more prominent role in the new cycle, and the crucial point of its oral approbation by Innocent III before the lateran Council of 1215 is clearly represented in Scene 7. In the fresco cycle in the Upper Church the role of the papacy in its approbation and encouragement of the Franciscan Order is as explicit as the role of the Order in supporting the papacy is implicit. Implicit too is the comparison between Christ and Francis.

It is almost certainly not coincidental that at Santa Maria in Aracoeli, which by the end of the thirteenth century was increasingly becoming the administrative centre of the Order, a scene of the Dream of Innocent III was

[14] J. Gardner, "The Louvre Stigmatization and the Problem of the Narrative Altarpiece," *Zeitschrift für Kunstgeschichte*, 45 (1982) 239ff.

[15] R. Brooke, *Scripta Leonis, Rufini et Angeli sociorum S. Francisci*, Oxford Mediaeval Texts (Oxford, 1970); R. Brooke, "Recent Work on St. Francis of Assisi," *Analecta Bollandiana*, 100 (1982) 653-670.

[16] J. Schulz, "Zur Kunst des 'Franziskusmeisters'," *Wallraf-Richartz Jahrbuch*, 25 (1963) 109-150; S. Romano, "Le storie parallele di Assisi. Il Maestro di S. Francesco," *Storia dell'Arte*, 44 (1982) 63-81; S. Esser, "Die Ausmalung der Unterkirche von San Francesco in Assisi durch den Franziskusmeister," Diss. Bonn 1983, Chapter v.

[17] For dating, B. Brenk, "Das Datum der Franzlegende der Unterkirche zu Assisi," in *Roma Anno 1300*, p. 231; J. Cannon, "Dating the Frescoes by the Maestro di S. Francesco," *Burlington Magazine*, 124 (1982) 65-69.

executed in the costly medium of mosaic on the side of the *cavetto* façade.[18] The mosaic has now deteriorated to a condition of near illegibility, but the choice of setting was not a casual one. Its viewpoint was from the Capitol immediately to the south. The purposeful choice of this particular episode in the Founder's life contained an element of admonition as well as representing an historical truth: the support of the papacy, duly illumined, for the emergence and affirmation of the mendicants.

This "secondment" of the papacy to a protective function, as it were *post factum*, had already been practised by the Dominicans. There is some point in regarding the elaborately carved *Arca di San Domenico* in the founder's burial church at Bologna as an emulatory response to the church at Assisi and its programme of decoration. Following the Minors, the Dominicans had engaged Giunta Pisano to paint a large Crucifix for their church at Bologna, in the manner of the monumental Crucifix he had made for the church of San Francesco at Assisi.[19] The Dominicans commissioned a series of marble reliefs illustrating the life of Dominic for his shrine at Bologna, "a precious casket of white marble supported on columns," into which his remains were translated in 1267.[20] It is in this series of reliefs that Dominic is first represented as supporting the Church (Fig. 6). What is significant here is that once again the presence of the papacy in the iconography of the Founder's life was felt to be desirable, and also that papal encouragement was contingent, in part at least, on divine revelation. But at Bologna the layers of meaning, present in the relative prominence of the papacy in the Assisi Legend of Saint Francis, are still absent.

Mendicant iconography which represented a divinely illumined papacy as sustaining their orders was obviously both aide-mémoire and shield. It was a point made partially, not in the interests of an historical objectivity. It is instructive to contrast it with the sparseness, the comparative lack of emphasis on curial involvement in Giotto's fresco of the Approval of the Franciscan Rule painted for a banker's private chapel in Santa Croce at Florence a generation after the Assisi cycle.

*
* *

[18] Gardner, "The Louvre Stigmatization," pp. 229ff. See M. Andaloro, "Il sogno di Innocenzo III all'Aracoeli, Nicolò IV e la basilica di S. Giovanni in Laterano," in *Studi in Onore di Giulio Carlo Argan* (Rome, 1984), 1: 29-37 for a different, but to my mind unconvincing interpretation. See also A. R. Vegonzones, "Escena musiva medieval en la fachada de Araceli (Roma) representando a Francisco en el sueno de Inocencio III," *Antonianum*, 57 (1982) 259-283.

[19] E. B. Garrison, *Italian Romanesque Panel Painting: An Illustrated Index* (Florence, 1949), no. 546, p. 208. The cross measures 3.16 × 2.85 m.

[20] "... capsam pretiosam candidi marmoris super columnas elevatam...." Cf. *Acta Sanctorum*, Aug. 1: 532.

The papacy's own artistic activity at the beginning of the period under discussion is traditional, and relatively mute about its religious role. Urban IV is known at Rome, a city in which he never set foot as pope, only by the church of Sant' Urbano ai Pantani: built near the Colosseum, it was razed to the ground in the 1930s[21] (Fig. 7). It was a modest, even pedestrian counterpart to the brilliantly adventurous church of Saint-Urbain which he began to build in his native town at Troyes[22] (Fig. 8). But despite the gulf in style and architectural ambition both commissions are essentially of a traditional type, intended to immortalize the name of their patron, particularly in his native territory. Little can be said of direct artistic patronage under his successor Clement IV, although he encouraged the rebuilding of his former cathedral at Narbonne; and the financial circumstances of a papacy committed to supporting Charles I d'Anjou scarcely permitted expenditure on the arts.[23] During his pontificate, however, Saint Hedwig was canonized, and her iconography may have gained stimulus from a possible representation of the saint on the pope's tomb.[24] It may be debated whether the canonization of the Duchess of Silesia represents the papacy acting wholly apolitically in its religious role, for there occurs a slowing down of canonizations in the later thirteenth century, and a persistent connexion of newly admitted saints with ruling houses with which the papacy was diplomatically involved. Nevertheless, the dissemination of the cults of new saints through visual images is a subject to which we must return.

The pontificate of Gregory X (1271-1276) has left little artistic record in either Rome or central Italy. It is emblematic however of the way in which the papacy's religious role was viewed from outside. For Gregory we have two astonishing documents, the first intended with some probability for him,

[21] C. Ceschi, "S. Urbano ai Pantani," *Capitolium*, 9 (1933) 380-391. It should be noted, however, that in Vasari's life of Margaritone there occurs the following passage: "... lavorò molte cose prima ch'è tornasse a Roma, dove già era stato molto grato a Papa Urbano Quarto, per fare alcune cose a fresco di commissione Sua nel portico di S. Piero, che di maniera greca, secondo qu' tempi, furono ragionevoli" (R. Bettarini, P. Barocchi, eds, *Giorgio Vasari: Le Vite de' più eccellenti Pittori Scultori e Architettori* [Florence, 1966ff.], 2: 91). For the surviving fragments from the *portico* of the basilica see I. Hueck, "Der Maler der Apostelszenen im Atrium von Alt-St. Peter," *Mitteilungen des Kunsthistorischen Institutes in Florenz*, 14 (1969) 115-144, who accepts this date, to my mind unpersuasively. For a later dating of the fragments cf. J. Wollesen, "Perduto e ritrovato: una riconsiderazione della pittura romana nell'ambiente di Niccolò III (1277-1280)," in *Roma Anno 1300*, pp. 343-353.

[22] Most recently cf. M. T. Davis, "On the Threshold of the Flamboyant: the Second Campaign of Construction of Saint-Urbain, Troyes," *Speculum*, 59 (1984) 847-884.

[23] I am preparing an extended study of papal patronage in the thirteenth century, in which this period is more fully discussed.

[24] D. Papenbroeck, *Conatus chronico-historicus ad catalogum Romanorum Pontificum* (Antwerp, 1685), p. 55*.

the other certainly designed as a personal gift. In 1288 Nicholas IV presented to his native Ascoli Piceno a cope of *Opus Anglicanum*.[25] The embroidery consists of a series of roundels, in which, together with a sequence of martyrdoms, appear four roundels representing recent popes, Innocent IV, Alexander IV, Urban IV and Clement IV. After an interval of three years Gregory X was elected as successor to Clement IV. Gregory himself is not shown, but Saint Gregory the Great appears in a roundel to the right of the central Crucifixion. The style of the embroidered scenes is generally dated towards the end of the thirteenth century, but the *terminus ante quem non* is likely the death of Clement IV in late November 1268, yet the gift — which obviously requires a reigning pontiff — may well be somewhat earlier than is commonly assumed. The design is unusual in its austerity, although materially very rich, particularly when it is recalled that it has lost the pearls with which it was once liberally seeded, and the composition is less intricate than the great copes of the end of the century. But essentially the Ascoli cope shows four recently deceased popes, fortified by their martyred predecessors and counselled by their fellow bishops, as supporters of the Virgin and Child. The English view of the religious role of a late thirteenth century pope as perceived in the Ascoli cope is traditional and timeless.

The Greek perspective differs. Our knowledge of a second great embroidery from the pontificate of Gregory X is provided by the inventory of the Holy See drawn up in 1295.[26] It is an altar-frontal dating from the period of the delicate negotiation concerning Byzantine participation in the Second Council of Lyons of 1274. The envoys of Gregory X, who had single-mindedly devoted his papacy to the achievement of union, were four Franciscans, led by the provincial of the Dalmatian province of the Order, the future Minister General and pope Jerome of Ascoli, another future Minister General Bonagrazia di San Giovanni in Persiceto and two companions.[27] The four were to spend a period of some eighteen months in Constantinople negotiating the articles of Union with the Emperor Michael

---

[25] *Reg. Nicolas IV*, ed. E. Langlois, no. 7101; A. G. I. Christie, *English Mediaeval Embroidery* (Oxford, 1938), pp. 91-95; Ladner, *Die Papstbildnisse*, 3: 131ff.

[26] A. Mölinier, "Inventaire du Trésor du Saint-Siège sous Boniface VIII (1295)," *BEC*, 43 (1882) 227-310, 626-646; 45 (1884) 31-57; 46 (1885) 16-44; 47 (1886) 646-667; 49 (1888) 226-237, no. 811.

[27] B. Roberg, *Die Union zwischen der griechischen und der lateinischen Kirche auf dem II. Konzil von Lyon (1274)*, Bonner Historische Forschungen 24 (Bonn, 1966), pp. 95ff.; D. J. Geanakoplos, *The Emperor Michael Palaeologus and the West* (Cambridge, Mass., 1959). For Jerome's Greek cf. Roberg, pp. 130ff. As pope he wrote to the archbishop of the Bulgars, reminding him that they had met in the imperial palace of the Blacherne when Jerome was at Constantinople. Cf. I. Dujčev, "Il Francescanesimo in Bulgaria," *Miscellanea Francescana*, 34 (1934) 258; Theiner, vol. 1, no. 609.

Palaeologus and his ecclesiastical supporters in the Byzantine hierarchy. On Jerome, who may perhaps have had some Greek, the experience was, as we shall later observe, to have an enduring influence. The return of the Franciscan ambassadors, together with the imperial plenipotentiaries was fateful. They travelled in two triremes of the imperial fleet, one with the majority of the ambassadors, the second with a freight of rich gifts, which included, the historian Georgios Pachymeres wrote with horror, the altar frontal of the Great Church. In a terrible tempest the trireme laden with gifts foundered off Malea in the southern Peloponnese.[28] The first galley struggled into harbour and the envoys travelled overland to Lyons to participate in the joyful celebration of the ephemeral Union. On the evidence of the 1295 Roman inventory, however, not all the gifts were lost at sea. A frontal is described as follows:[29]

> Item, a cloth for a dossal, entirely worked in silver thread, and in various places and figures with silver thread, ungilded, among which is the figure of Christ in gold thread, the folds of whose garments are picked out by pearls. He is within a mandorla of white silver from which run two vines with green leaves and grapes formed of seed pearls: the vines cover almost the whole

---

[28] I. Bekker, ed., *Georgii Pachymeris de Michaele et Andronico Palaeologis libri tredecim* (Bonn, 1835), 1: 384ff. The text reads as follows: "οἳ δὴ καὶ ἀνὰ μία τριήρη, ἐντεῦθεν μὲν οἱ τῆς ἐκκλησίας, ἐκεῖθεν δὲ πλὴν τοῦ μεγάλου λογοθέτου οἱ ἐκ τοῦ βασιλέως, λαβόντες ἀνήγοντο, ἐπιφερόμενοι καὶ πολλὰ τῶν ἱερῶν δώρων, στολὺς λέγω καὶ κατάχρυσα εἰκονίσματα καὶ σύνθετα πολύτιμα θυμιάματα, πρὸς δὲ καὶ τὴν τῆς ἐκκλησίας ἐνδυτὴν ἐκ χρυσοπάστου ὀξείας διὰ μαργάρων, ἣν ὁ βασιλεὺς προσενεγκὼν τῷ θείῳ τεμένει δῶρον ὄντως ἔπαξιον, συγχωρούμενος, ἐπεὶ οὐκ ἔφθασεν ἑτέρων εὐτρεπεσθῆναι τῷ μεγάλῳ τῶν κορυφαίων ναῷ, ἀνταλλαγὴν τοῦ γινομένου πρὸς τὸ ὂν οἷον ποιούμενος, λαβὼν ἀπέστελλε καὶ αὐτήν." Cf. D. Geanakoplos, "Bonaventura, the Two Mendicant Orders and the Greeks at the Council of Lyons," in *The Orthodox Churches and the West*, Studies in Church History 13 (Oxford, 1976), pp. 187ff.

[29] Cf. note 26 above. The Latin text reads: "Item, unum pannum pro dorsale, totum laboratum de argento tractitio, et in aliquibus partibus et figuris de argento tractitio non deaurato, in quo est imago Salvatoris deaurata cujus vestimenti plicature distincte sunt cum pernis et est in quodam circulo oblongo de argento albo et precedunt due vites cum foliis viridibus et uvis de pernis minutis; que vites quasi extendunt per totum dorsale; super imagine Salvatoris est quedam pars ad modum celi de argento albo tractitio in quo est quedam manus desuper benedicens, iiij. cherubini et in medio eorum quedam avis (!) et a quolibet latere dictorum cherubinorum sunt ij. angeli majores quasi extra celum; in pede Salvatoris est media imago Virginis in quodam throno habens quasdam imagines sanctorum a latere cum libris in manibus; et subtus dictas figuras est imago B. Petri, coram quo est imago domini Gregorii tenentis per manum Paleologum et presentat eum beato Petro reconciliatum, cum litteris grecis et latinis; et per pannum sunt multe historie apostolorum, prout predicaverunt et battizaverunt, cum litteris grecis et latinis, in provinciis eis decretis; in circuitu vero dicti panni sunt littere grece et latine, et perne per circuitum dicti panni; et per diademata sanctorum et imaginum et per plicaturas vestium sunt perne; et est dictus pannus foderatus de xamito rubeo et habet dictus pannus v. annulos argenti deauratos a quolibet latere."

dossal. Above Christ is an area representing Heaven embroidered with white silver in which appear a blessing hand above four cherubim and in the centre a certain bird (!) and on either side of the cherubim are two archangels almost outside the heaven. At Christ's feet is, in the centre, the Virgin enthroned, with saints holding books on either side. Beneath these figures appears the lord Gregory, holding the Palaeologus by the hand and presenting him to saint Peter in token of reconciliation with inscriptions in Greek and Latin. And there are many scenes of the apostles preaching and baptizing in their respective regions with Greek and Latin inscriptions. Greek and Latin inscriptions run around the border of the panel and pearls. For the haloes of the saints and the folds of the robes pearls are used. The frontal is lined with red samite and it has five silver gilt rings at each side.

In this amazing embroidery the imperial view of Gregory x is presented in a suitably flattering form. His realistic and patient diplomacy seemed to have borne glorious fruit at Lyons. Of course, the Union was to prove transient, despite Michael's ferocious attempts to coerce his clergy into acquiescence.[30] The frontal is of outstanding importance in that it necessarily involved an innovative iconography, and was also in some sense a record of an actual "historical" event, set once again within a frame of reference which arrogates divine approval for the action of the protagonist-patron.

The great imperial dossal celebrating Union is lost. In Rome rather more survives from the pontificate of a successor, Nicholas III, who rebuilt and redecorated the palace chapel of San Lorenzo at the Lateran, and who continued the building of the new papal palace on the Vatican hill.[31] Nicholas III was a more important patron of the arts than his immediate precursors, and as a member of the great Roman family of the Orsini, centred his endeavours on Rome. But even with Nicholas III's patronage, caution is necessary. For example, he completed the construction of the great Cistercian abbey of San Martino al Cimino near Viterbo (Fig. 9). At first glance this would appear to follow a practice observable earlier in the century, of the papacy encouraging the reformed monastic orders or the friars. Nicholas III in other words appears as a follower of Honorius III who rebuilt the great Cistercian abbey of Casamari in southern Latium, a church moreover with

---

[30] L. Gatto, *Il pontificato di Gregorio X (1271-1276)*, Istituto Storico Italiano per il Medio Evo, Studi Storici 28-30 (Rome, 1959), esp. Chapter IV; Roberg, pp. 79ff.; D. M. Nicol, "The Byzantine Reaction to the Second Council of Lyon," in *Councils and Assemblies*, Studies in Church History 7 (Cambridge, 1971), pp. 113-146; D. M. Nicol, above, pp. 321-339.

[31] J. Gardner, "Nicholas III's Oratory of the Sancta Sanctorum and its Decoration," *Burlington Magazine*, 115 (1973) 283-294; J. T. Wollesen, "Die Fresken in Sancta Sanctorum," *Römisches Jahrbuch für Kunstgeschichte*, 19 (1981) 36-83; K. B. Steinke, *Die mittelalterlichen Vatikanpaläste und ihre Kapellen*, Studi e Documenti per la Storia del Palazzo Apostolico Vaticano 5 (Città del Vaticano, 1984).

which San Martino has architectural links. The reality is otherwise. Nicholas III's part in completing the Cistercian abbey at San Martino derived largely from his earlier nomination as the testamentary executor of Cardinal Gil Torres, a Spaniard who had died in 1254.[32]

Nicholas III made Rome his centre. Martin IV who succeeded him never entered the city, and there is a falling away of artistic patronage until the accession of the first Franciscan pope Nicholas IV in 1288, when once again there occurs a major series of commissions in which a religious dynamic can be discerned. In a long mosaic inscription in the Lateran Nicholas explicitly connected his restoration of the basilica with the dream of Innocent III in which he saw Francis sustaining the Roman church.[33] In a second inscription bordering the apse mosaic itself, the pope describes himself as a son of Saint Francis.[34] Other historical circumstances obviously impinged. The thirteenth-century Lateran was closely linked with Nicholas IV's powerful allies the Colonna family, whereas the Vatican had been for almost a generation a fief of the Orsini, entrenched in its Chapter since the pontificate of their kinsman Nicholas III. On a more immediate level, Saint Peters had been relatively recently embellished with mosaics, its apse by Innocent III, who can scarcely have endeared himself to the Lateran canons by his use of the phrase *Mater Ecclesiarum* in the apse inscription, and by Gregory IX, who had commissioned the façade mosaic.[35] It should not be overlooked either, particularly within the ambit of this volume, that the papacy felt it continually incumbent upon itself to repair and redecorate the great Roman basilicas. Honorius III had commissioned the apse mosaic of San Paolo fuori le mura, and substantially restored San Lorenzo fuori le mura. It was the restoration

---

[32] P. Egidi, "L'abbazia di S. Martino al Cimino secondo documenti inediti," *Rivista Storica Benedettina*, 2 (1907), 193-194, note 3. A. Paravicini Bagliani, *I Testamenti dei Cardinali del Duecento*. Miscellanea della Società Romana di Storia Patria 25 (Rome, 1980), p. 14. For the architecture cf. R. Wagner-Rieger, *Die italienische Baukunst zu Beginn der Gotik*, Publikationen des Österreichischen Kulturinstituts in Rom, Abt. für historische Studien, Abh. 2 (Graz, Cologne, 1957), 2: 232 ff.

[33] V. Forcella, *Iscrizioni delle chiese e di altri edificii di Roma dal secolo XI fino ai giorni nostri* (Rome 1869-1884), 8: 15 no. 16. Cf. P. Murray, "Notes on some early Giotto Sources," *Journal of the Warburg and Courtauld Institutes*, 16 (1953), 70 ff.

[34] PARTEM.POSTERIOREM.ET ANTERIOREM RVINOSAS.HVIVS SANCTI TEMPLI A FVNDAMENTIS REEDIFICARI FECIT.ET ORNARI.OPERE MOSAYCO.NICOLAVS.PP.IIII.FILIVS.BEATI FRANCISCI SACRVM VVLTVM SALVATORIS INTEGRVM REPONI.FECIT.IN LOCO VBI PRIMO MIRACVLOSE.POPVLO ROMANO APPARVIT.QVANDO.FVIT.ISTA.ECCLESIA.CONSECRATA.ANNO DOMINI M.CC.NONAGESI I (sic).

For the original date of 1290, cf. C. Cecchelli, "A proposito del mosaico dell' abside Lateranense," *Miscellanea Hertziana = Römische Forschungen der Bibliotheca Hertziana*, 16 (1961), 14.

[35] R. Krautheimer, *Rome: Profile of a City 312-1308* (Princeton, 1980), p. 206. For the apse mosaic cf. W. N. Schumacher, "Eine römische Apsiskomposition," *RQ*, 54 (1959) 148ff.

of San Paolo, the Lateran and Saint Peters which, virtually alone, loosened the pursestrings of the Avignonese papacy.[36] Thus a repair and redecoration of the Lateran in the late thirteenth century could well have seemed overdue. But for Nicholas IV the restoration of that church was also an affirmation of his commitment to Rome, and in a deeply personal way a symbolic statement of his own role in the unfolding of the Franciscan design. His redecoration was in many ways conservative[37] (Fig. 10). The addition of an apse and transept to the Constantinian basilica must be seen in relation to Saint Peters, and in the new apse he took care, and recorded the fact in the inscription, to reinsert the head of Christ in mosaic which had miraculously appeared much earlier in the apse, in its original place. Unfortunately in the scandalous extension of the choir in 1876-1886 the apse mosaic was remade, and it is now impossible to make more than very limited comment. One significant detail must for the moment suffice. In the centre of the row of apostles between the windows, James the Less appears, and the scroll which he carries bears the following text from his Epistle: "Be ye doers of the word, and not hearers only, deceiving your own selves." For a Franciscan pope this choice is surely eloquent.

In his second great mosaic commission, the decoration of Santa Maria Maggiore, Nicholas once again rebuilt the apse and inserted a transept.[38] The apse, and also the façade were clad in mosaic. Once again there is a specific historical dimension. Santa Maria Maggiore was a Colonna church, where Cardinal Giacomo Colonna was archpriest. Both he and Cardinal Pietro Colonna were originally present in the façade mosaic[39] (Fig. 11). Whereas the basilica of the Lateran had been, like Saint Peters, an imperial foundation, the Esquiline basilica had been a papal foundation and also the first church dedicated to the Virgin.[40] Legend connected its miraculously inspired foundation with Pope Liberius, and it was this foundation legend which was splendidly displayed in the façade mosaics. There is a certain incongruousness in a pope from an Order whose guiding principle had been apostolic poverty decorating the great churches of Rome with mosaics, the most

---

[36] J. Gardner, "Copies of Roman Mosaics in Edinburgh," *Burlington Magazine*, 115 (1973) 587ff. Cf. I. Schuster, *La basilica e il monasterio di S. Paolo fuori le mura* (Turin, 1934), p. 153.

[37] R. Krautheimer, *Corpus Basilicarum Christianarum Romae*, Monumenti di Archeologia Cristiana 2, ser. 2 (Città del Vaticano, 1937-1977), 5: 91ff. (=*CBCR*); Cecchelli, "A proposito del mosaico," pp. 13-18.

[38] *CBCR*, 3: 31. Cf. J. Gardner, "Pope Nicholas IV and the Decoration of Santa Maria Maggiore," *Zeitschrift für Kunstgeschichte*, 36 (1973) 1-50.

[39] Gardner, ibid., pp. 22ff.

[40] *CBCR*, 3: 58. The dedication of Santa Maria in Trastevere to the Virgin is only documented from the late eighth century (ibid., p. 66).

expensive medium at his disposal. Certainly, after the disgrace of the Colonna, one of Boniface VIII's supporters, Cardinal Nicholas de Nonancour, made some sharp remarks about Liberius in a sermon directed against the schismatic cardinals.[41] It may have been his sojourn in Constantinople which prompted Nicholas IV to commission enormous mosaic programmes in the Lateran and Santa Maria Maggiore. But it could equally well have been the desire of his Colonna supporters, who, as Francesco Pipino reminds us, were popularly regarded as dominating the pope, to emulate or outshine "Orsini" Saint Peters.

Other aspects concern us here. There is the external consideration, which is made clear by the choice of the rather rare subject of the foundation legend on the façade. As Nicholas IV repaired the Lateran following the example of Saint Francis, so here he could be regarded as a second Liberius reconstituting the church of the Virgin. It is surely significant that, in the miraculous snowfall in which Liberius is shown in the façade mosaic tracing the groundplan of the new basilica, the transept is noticeably salient, a feature absent from the early Christian church. (That this is not merely an invention of a nineteenth century restorer is demonstrated by the prominent transept in Masolino's panel from the triptych painted in the early Quattrocento for the Capella Colonna in Santa Maria Maggiore, and now in Capodimonte [Fig. 12].)[42] A transept once again evokes Saint Peters, but, unlike the Vatican, Santa Maria Maggiore did not, indeed could not, possess a major relic of its dedicatee. The inserted transept is rather narrow, partly because of the difficulties presented by its sloping site, and its decoration was left incomplete after the fall of the Colonna.[43]

If, however, Nicholas IV was the partial rebuilder and decorator of two great early Christian churches, we must now enquire whether this activity sheds light on his own conception of his religious role. He was not free from constraints. At the Lateran, the dedication to the Saviour and the Baptist, together with the prominence of the Evangelist, added to the desire to preserve an earlier mosaic head of Christ, all conditioned the composition

---

[41] A. Maier, "Due documenti nuovi relativi alla lotta dei Cardinali Colonna contro Bonifazio VIII," *Rivista di Storia della Chiesa in Italia*, 3 (1949) 344-364; republished in Maier, *Ausgehendes Mittelalter* (Rome, 1967-1977), 2: 13-34: "Et ideo Liberius pingitur in Catalogo paparum primo cum dyademate quadrato, quia sanctitatem habuit in primo statu sed non perfectam et ideo non rotundam, quia figura rotunda est perfectissime. In secunda pictura ... pingitur sine aliquo dyademate, quia mortuus est hereticus" (p. 26). Cf. J. Gardner, "San Paolo fuori le mura, Nicholas III and Pietro Cavallini," *Zeitschrift für Kunstgeschichte*, 34 (1971) 242.

[42] M. Meiss, "The Altered Program of the Santa Maria Maggiore Altarpiece," in *Studien zur toskanischen Kunst, Festschrift L. H. Heydenreich* (Munich, 1964), pp. 169-190.

[43] Gardner, "Pope Nicholas IV," pp. 12ff.

of the apse mosaic. But the addition of the figures, albeit on a reduced scale, of Saints Francis and Anthony of Padua was unprecedented in a major Roman basilica. For the first time in such a context, "modern" saints from a mendicant order are set on a par with the Virgin, John the Baptist and the apostles. This innovation was to be developed further in the somewhat later apse mosaic of Santa Maria Maggiore, where a difference of scale no longer exists, and Francis and Anthony are informed with the same level of reality as the other figures. In the later apse, where the mosaic workshop was also directed by Jacopo Torriti, the kerygmatic aspect is more apparent.

There is a sense in which the façade mosaics of Santa Maria Maggiore address the outside world. Their narrative of divine illumination (which was originally more evident before the addition of Fuga's loggia) and subsequent papal foundation is displayed on a huge scale across the *cavetto* façade. The apse decoration is for the faithful within. Here Nicholas IV had a freer hand, for there were no older fragments awaiting inclusion, and apse and transept could be conceived in a concerted programme of decoration – as had already been done some years earlier in the Upper Church at Assisi.[44] As there, the Marian programme of the choir was to be accompanied by prophets in the transept. In Rome this combination suggested another continuity. At least from the pontificate of Honorius III onwards, liturgical changes indicate a growing concern that the dedication feast of the basilica of Santa Maria Maggiore should be on the same level as those of the Lateran and Vatican.[45] The feast of the Virgin of the Snow was accepted by the Franciscan General Chapter of 1269. All these elements came together in Nicholas IV's great decorative programme.

The central theme of the apse, the Coronation of the Virgin, set within an embracing ecclesiological programme, is novel (Fig. 13). The roundel in the apse semi-dome is borne up by nine orders of angels, and in it Christ and the Virgin are enthroned side by side. The subject had not heretofore been given so monumental a form in Italian art, although it had been recently used in panel painting and stained glass at Siena.[46] It may well be that the stimulus for the choice of imagery came from Franciscan circles. Adumbrated in the sermons of Bonaventura, it had been given greater relief in those of Cardinal

[44] J. White, *The Birth and Rebirth of Pictorial Space*, 2nd ed. (London, 1967), pp. 23ff.

[45] S. J. P. van Dijk, "Feasts of the Blessed Virgin Mary in the Thirteenth-Century Roman Liturgy," *AFH* 48 (1955) 454ff.

[46] G. Coor, "The Earliest Italian Representation of the Coronation of the Virgin," *Burlington Magazine* 99 (1957) 328-338; J. Stubblebine, *Guido da Siena* (Princeton, 1964), no. XIV, pp. 81-84 and figs. 44-47; E. Carli, *Vetrata Duccesca* (Florence, 1946), fig. III, and unnumbered folding plate. The window was commissioned and executed in 1287-1288. In general see P. Verdier, *Le couronnement de la Vierge* (Montreal-Paris, 1980), Chapter VII.

Matthew of Acquasparta, a fellow friar and one of the most influential of late thirteenth century cardinals.[47] Almost as significant for our understanding of the programme is the sequence of scenes below. Apart from two scenes of Saint Jerome addressing Paula and Eustochium, and Matthias preaching to the Jews at each end, a frieze of five scenes of the Life of the Virgin runs beneath the main mosaic. The Dormition has, however, been shifted out of chronological sequence and been set directly below the Coronation. In this way the bodily Assumption of Mary, a topic on which it was still possible, following Durandus, to entertain a pious doubt, was unequivocally implied, but not yet represented — as it had been a few years previously in the stained glass window of Siena cathedral.[48] Nicholas IV's role in giving visual currency to a doctrinal theme still in a delicate process of crystallization was of great importance. Its link with the Franciscan Order was to become ever more evident during the succeeding centuries, when the Coronation of the Virgin was to become the preferred subject of many Franciscan high altarpieces throughout Italy.[49] In the apse of Santa Maria Maggiore the bodily assumption is confirmed by the inscription, itself excerpted from an antiphon of the Office for the Feast of the Assumption, set above the mosaic of the Dormition and beneath the feet of the enthroned pair.[50]

A second element in Nicholas IV's apse decorations may more tentatively be identified in the prominence of Saint Andrew. In the Lateran there were no substantial relics of the apostle, and indeed in the aftermath of the fourth crusade the body of the apostle was brought from Constantinople to the Duomo at Amalfi where it was splendidly enshrined by the erstwhile Cardinal-legate Petrus Capuanus.[51] But the presence in the Roman apses of Andrew simply by virtue of his being the brother of Saint Peter is perhaps not wholly sufficient to explain the prominence he is accorded. As apostle of Constantinople, however, he had links with the pope's own earlier experience as a negotiator of Union with the Orthodox church, and his

---

[47] For Matthew cf. conveniently E. Longpré, *DTC*, 10: 375-389. Cf. F. Simoncioli, "La mariologia del Card. Matteo d'Acquasparta, OFM," *Divus Thomas*, 65 (1962) 321-352. Texts of his sermons are published in C. Piana, *Matthaei ab Aquasparta O.F.M.S.R.E. Cardinalis Sermones de Beata Virgine*, Bibliotheca Franciscana Ascetica Medii Aevi 9 (Quaracchi, 1962).

[48] Gardner, "Pope Nicholas IV," p. 10; G. Durandus, *Rationale Divinorum Officiorum*, Lib. VII, cap. xxiv; M. Jugie, *La Mort et l'Assomption de la Sainte Vierge: Étude historico-doctrinale*, Studi e Testi 114 (Città del Vaticano, 1944), pp. 389ff.; Carli, *Vetrata Duccesca*, folding plate.

[49] J. Gardner, review of K. Christiansen, *Gentile da Fabriano* (London, 1982), in *Burlington Magazine*, 125 (1983) 364.

[50] "Maria Virgo assumpta est ad aethereum thalamum quo Rex Regum stellato sedet solio †Exaltata est Sancta Dei Genetrix super choros angelorum ad celestia regna."

[51] P. Pirri, *Duomo di Amalfi e il chiostro del Paradiso* (Rome, 1941), pp. 141ff.

appearance in both apses may reflect Nicholas ɪᴠ's continuing hope for
oecumenacy. The same appears to have been true of Matthew of Acquasparta,
who freed John of Parma, the earlier Minister-General of the Franciscans
deposed for his Joachite leanings, intendedly to send him to convert
heretics.[52] Apostolicity was an ancient theme, and union was in Nicholas ɪᴠ's
bones. That this is a possible explanation may be confirmed by the prominent
mosaic figure of Saint Andrew, now lost, which was commissioned in these
years by the archbishop of Amalfi, Andrea de Alagno, for his own cathedral.[53] Whether or not this speculation proves correct, it remains nonetheless
clear that the apsidal programmes commissioned by Nicholas ɪᴠ yield
important evidence for his conception of the papacy's religious role. It is
further borne out by his interest in rebuilding the new cathedral at Orvieto.

The pope himself laid the foundation stone of the new building. The
cathedral was to be modelled on Santa Maria Maggiore in Rome, as a
contemporary document proves.[54] The extent to which the exemplar was
imitated may still be seen in the original groundplan, the columns and open
roof of the nave, and in the decision to have façade mosaics which, although
completed later, adhere to the original conception (Fig. 14). Orvieto gives
further substance to our understanding of Nicholas ɪᴠ's view of his religious
role, and also testifies to the influence of the Roman basilica which he was
in the process of redecorating.

*
* *

If a consistent conception of oecumenical and pastoral purpose is to be
discerned in the commissions of Nicholas ɪᴠ, the same may be suggested of
Boniface ᴠɪɪɪ. As was the case with Nicholas we have a monument in which
the pope was directly involved, the tomb chapel within Saint Peters.[55] This

---

[52] Longpré, col. 376. For Giovanni da Parma cf. A. Franchi, *La svolta politico-ecclesiastica
tra Roma e Bisanzio (1249-1254)*, Spicilegium Pontifici Athenaei Antoniani 21 (Rome,
1981), pp. 20ff.

[53] F. Dvornik, *The Idea of Apostolicity in Byzantium and the Legend of the Apostle Andrew*,
Dumbarton Oaks Studies 4 (Cambridge, Mass., 1958), pp. 149ff. For Andrea de Alagno cf.
M. Manfredi, *DBI*, 1: 552ff.; N. Kamp, *Kirche und Monarchie in staufischen Königreich
Sizilien* (Munich, 1973-1982), 1: 440. Cf. *Liber Pontif. Amalfitan.* quoted by Pirri, p. 182:
"In superiori Ecclesia tribunal de opere musayco picturis variis adornavit ... in pinnaculo
eiusdem Ecclesiae fieri fecit picturam ipsius Beati Andreae Apostoli de opere mosayco,
pulcherrimis aspectibus deauratam." He also decorated the crypt with the shrine of the apostle
in mosaic.

[54] L. Fumi, *Statuti e Regesti dell'Opera di Santa Maria Maggiore di Orvieto* (Rome, 1891),
p. 86: "... ad instar S. Marie maioris de Urbe...."

[55] Gardner, "Arnolfo di Cambio," pp. 437ff.; G. Poggi, "Arnolfo di Cambio e il sacello
di Bonifacio ɪᴠ," *Rivista d'Arte*, 3 (1905) 187-198.

project was, unusually, completed early in Boniface's pontificate, the chapel being consecrated on 6 May 1296.[56] It contained an effigy tomb surmounted by a mosaic depicting Boniface VIII being presented to the Virgin by Saints Peter and Paul. The papal tomb was not only associated with an altar containing the relics of an earlier pontiff, Boniface IV, but it predicated also a novel relationship between tomb and celebrant, which was later to prove influential.[57] Given this innovation, Boniface VIII himself must have played a significant, perhaps determining role in its conception. This conclusion is of weight when we consider one of the main events of Boniface's eventful pontificate, the Jubilee of 1300.

We shall not here concern ourselves with the problem of possible precedents for the Jubilee, nor the substantial change in papal policy over indulgences.[58] Of the works of art which were produced circa 1300, only one can be connected with the pope, the famous fresco, a fragment of which is preserved in the Lateran. The original composition is more extensively recorded in a water-colour copy now in the Biblioteca Ambrosiana[59] (Fig. 15). Whilst one may legitimately doubt the attribution of the painting to Giotto, no convincing reason has yet been brought forward to call in question a date of 1300, nor its connexion with the Jubilee.[60] Many unresolved questions remain about the other frescoes of the Bonifatian loggia at the Lateran with their apparently Constantinian overtones, or indeed about the form of the loggia itself.[61] The aspect I wish to consider here is not so much the "authenticity" of the fresco as the depiction of an actual historical event, but rather its subject, Boniface VIII promulgating the Jubilee indul-

---

[56] Poggi was the first to argue for an early date for the tomb chapel. For the consecration date cf. M. Maccarone, "Il sepolcro di Bonifacio VIII nella Basilica Vaticana," in *Roma Anno 1300*, p. 757.

[57] Gardner, "Arnolfo di Cambio," p. 437. Cf. R. Niggl, ed., *Giacomo Grimaldi, Descrizione della basilica antica di S. Pietro in Vaticano, codice Barberini Latino 2733* (Città del Vaticano, 1972), p. 37: "... dum sacerdos Missae sacrum perageret, tumulum ipsius Bonifacii conspicere." Maccarone, p. 757.

[58] N. Paulus, *Geschichte des Ablasses im Mittelalter vom Ursprung bis zum Mitte des 14. Jahrhunderts* (Paderborn, 1922-1923), 2: 17. For the Jubilee debate cf. A. Frugoni, "Il Giubileo di Bonifacio VIII," *BISIME*, 62 (1950) 1-122; R. Foreville, *Le Jubilé de Saint Thomas Becket. Du XIIIᵉ au XVᵉ siècle (1120-1470)* (Paris, 1958); A. Frugoni, "Il 'Giubileo' di Tommaso Becket," *Nova Historia*, 14 (1962) 29-37; M. Maccarone, "L'indulgenza del Giubileo del 1300 e la basilica di San Pietro," in *Roma Anno 1300*, pp. 731-752.

[59] C. Mitchell, "The Lateran Fresco of Boniface VIII," *JWCI*, 14 (1951), 1-6; C. Brandi, "Giotto recuperato a San Giovanni Laterano," in *Scritti di Storia dell'Arte in Onore di Lionello Venturi* (Rome, 1956), 1: 55-85.

[60] S. Maddalo, "Bonifacio VIII e Jacopo Stefaneschi. Ipotesi di lettura dell'affresco della loggia Lateranense," *Studi Romani*, 31 (1983) 129-150, has argued for a date of 1297 for the painting, but her arguments are unpersuasive.

[61] Mitchell, p. 1.

gence. It would thus have served as a representation, throughout the year of Jubilee, of the papal presence, and a reminder of the existence, under certain conditions, of plenary indulgence.[62] We know indeed that the pope was not uninterruptedly in Rome throughout 1300: he left for *villeggiatura* at Anagni on 7 May, and returned to the city only on 10 October. The representative function of the fresco has often been pointed out, and attention drawn also to the striking similarity which existed between the upper part of the composition and one of the reliefs on the base of the Theodosian obelisk in Constantinople.[63] The linkage between the crowd underneath the Lateran loggia and the pope may even have been anticipated in consular diptychs such as that of Probianus[64] (Fig. 16). This "vertical acclamation," as it has been termed, is clearly present in the Jubilee fresco.[65] Thus for "almost the whole world" who had hastened Rome-wards, to employ the phrase of the Heilbronn annalist, the painted pope may have been the only Boniface they saw.[66] The fresco stood in for the pope. Yet in this it reveals a significant pastoral aspect, and as such a significant innovation.

By way of conclusion I should like to amend the title of my paper, and add a question mark. There does seem to exist a group of works in painting and mosaic which can be connected with the papacy's religious role during the second half of the thirteenth century. My title spoke also of patterns. If they were present, they were shifting ones, refracted by copies, restorations, or damaged almost beyond recognition. But an important element of Roman art in this vital formative period has become clearer. A number of works reflect, in varying degrees, the specifically religious conceptions of several popes. They may suggest aspects of a consistent policy, such as seems to have been the case with Nicholas IV, or a more spontaneous decision, as seems to have been the Jubilee of 1300, but of their presence there can be little doubt.

---

[62] Maccarone, "L'indulgenza," p. 751.

[63] Mitchell, p. 5.

[64] R. Delbrueck, *Die Consulardiptychen und verwandte Denkmäler*, Studien zur spätantiken Kunstgeschichte 2 (Berlin-Leipzig, 1929), no. 65, pp. 250ff. Delbrueck suggests that the diptych was produced in Rome circa 400.

[65] J. Engemann, "Akklamationsrichtung, Sieger- und Besiegtenrichtung auf dem Galeriusbogen in Saloniki," *Jahrbuch für Antike und Christentum*, 22 (1979) 150-160.

[66] MGH SS 24: 46. Cf. L. Schmugge, "Die Anfänge des organisierten Pilgerverkehrs im Mittelalter," *Quellen und Forschungen*, 64 (1984) 74ff.

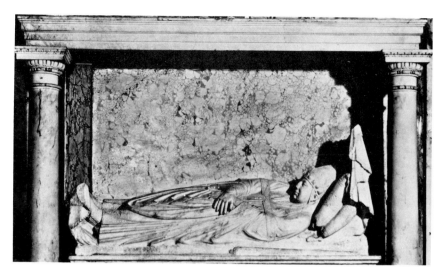

Fig. 1. Arnolfo di Cambio, Effigy of Pope Honorius IV († 1287); Detail of Head.
Rome, Santa Maria in Aracoeli. (GFN)

Fig. 2. Manno da Siena, Bronze Statue of Boniface VIII.
Bologna, Museo Civico Medievale. (Photo Museum)

Fig. 3. Approbation of the Franciscan Rule. Fresco, San Francesco, Assisi, Upper Church.

Fig. 4. Saint Francis Preaches before Pope Honorius III.
Fresco, San Francesco, Assisi, Upper Church.

Fig. 5. Maestro di San Francesco, The Dream of Pope Innocent III.
Mural, San Francesco, Assisi, Lower Church. (GFN)

Fig. 6. Nicola Pisano and Assistants, Arca di San Domenico,
Detail of The Dream of Pope Innocent III. Bologna, San Domenico.

Fig. 7. Sant' Urbano ai Pantani, Rome, Nave Wall of Church During Demolition.

Fig. 8. Saint-Urbain, Troyes (Aude).

Fig. 9. San Martino al Cimino, Latium, South elevation.

Fig. 10. San Giovanni in Laterano, Apse mosaic (restored).

Fig. 11. Seventeenth-Century Drawing of the Façade Mosaics of Santa Maria Maggiore.
Edinburgh, National Gallery of Scotland. (Photo Museum)

Fig. 12. Santa Maria Maggiore, Façade Mosaic, detail;
Pope Liberius Traces the Groundplan of the Basilica.

Fig. 13. Jacopo Torriti, Apse Mosaic. Santa Maria Maggiore.

Fig. 14. Orvieto Cathedral, Nave Looking towards the Façade.

Fig. 15. Pope Boniface VIII Proclaiming the Jubilee (1300);
Water-colour Copy of the Lost Fresco at San Giovanni in Laterano.
Milan, Biblioteca Ambrosiana.

Fig. 16. Diptych of Probianus; Ivory circa 400 AD.
Staatsbibliothek, Berlin. (Photo Museum)

Contributors

Jacques G. Bougerol OFM, Collegio S. Bonaventura, Grottaferrata

Karlfried Froehlich, Department of Church History, Princeton Theological Seminary

Julian Gardner, Department of the History of Art, University of Warwick

Pierre-Marie Gy OP, Institut Catholique, Paris

† P. Osmund Lewry OP

Donald M. Nicol, Department of Modern Greek and Byzantine Studies, King's College, University of London

Walter H. Principe CSB, Pontifical Institute of Mediaeval Studies, Toronto, and Centre for Medieval Studies, University of Toronto

Phyllis B. Roberts, College of Staten Island, and the Graduate Center, City University of New York

Christopher J. Ryan, St John's College, Cambridge, England

Michael M. Sheehan CSB, Pontifical Institute of Mediaeval Studies, Toronto, and Centre for Medieval Studies, University of Toronto

Giulio Silano, Pontifical Institute of Mediaeval Studies, Toronto, and Centre for Medieval Studies, University of Toronto

Jannis Spiteris OFMCap., Pontificio Ateneo Antoniano, Rome

Edward A. Synan, Pontifical Institute of Mediaeval Studies, Toronto, and Centre for Medieval Studies, University of Toronto

Norman P. Zacour, Department of History and Centre for Medieval Studies, University of Toronto

Index